# INTRODUCTION
## TO THE
# X WINDOW SYSTEM

# INTRODUCTION
## TO THE
# X WINDOW SYSTEM

Oliver Jones

Prentice Hall, Englewood Cliffs, New Jersey 07632

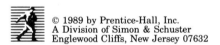
© 1989 by Prentice-Hall, Inc.
A Division of Simon & Schuster
Englewood Cliffs, New Jersey 07632

Printed in the United States of America

10  9  8  7  6  5  4  3  2

ISBN 0-13-499997-5

PRENTICE-HALL INTERNATIONAL (UK) LIMITED, *London*
PRENTICE-HALL OF AUSTRALIA PTY. LIMITED, *Sydney*
PRENTICE-HALL CANADA INC., *Toronto*
PRENTICE-HALL HISPANOAMERICANA, S.A., *Mexico*
PRENTICE-HALL OF INDIA PRIVATE LIMITED, *New Delhi*
PRENTICE-HALL OF JAPAN, INC., *Tokyo*
SIMON & SCHUSTER ASIA PTE. LTD., *Singapore*
EDITORA PRENTICE-HALL DO BRASIL, LTDA., *Rio de Janeiro*

# CONTENTS

## 1  Introduction                                    1

The X Environment                                       2
The X Window System's Goals                             4
Using X                                                 8
Programming X                                          10
Using this book                                        12

## 2  Hello, World!                                   17

What helloworld.c Does                                 18
An Outline of helloworld.c                             19
helloworld.c Dissected                                 20
Building and Running helloworld.c                      25
Structuring an X Window System Application             25

## 3     X Concepts                                           27

The X Network Protocol                            29
The Xlib Procedural Interface                    32
The Display Connection                           33
Resources                                        39
Events                                           46
Error Handling                                   57
Summary                                          62

## 4     Windows                                             65

Windows and the Desktop Model                    66
Windows Made Simple                              75
Window Configuration                             85
Attributes and Characteristics                   97
Advanced Window Manipulation                    108
Window Manager Interactions                     116
Window Sizing Strategies                        129
Notification Events                             131
Summary                                         142

## 5     Graphics                                           145

The Graphics Pipeline and Graphics Contexts     148
Manipulating GC Resources                       151
Drawing                                         160
Expose Events                                   179

Clearing Windows                                    184
Copying Areas                                       187
Advanced Drawing Techniques                         194
Workstation Performance                             205
Drawing size                                        208
Summary                                             209

## 6 Text                                           213

Fonts                                               214
Simple Font Selection                               217
Drawing Character Strings                           219
Font Structures                                     225
Searching for Fonts                                 235
16-bit Character Strings                            239
Summary                                             242

## 7 Color                                          243

Color Concepts                                      244
Workstation Capabilities                            254
Strategy:  Shared Color Cells                       261
Strategy:  Standard Color Maps                      265
Strategy:  Private Color Cells                      271
Service Functions                                   283
Mononchrome and Gray Scale                          287
Color Map Manipulation                              289
Summary                                             295

| 8 | **Pixmaps, Bitmaps, and Images** | 297 |
|---|---|---|
| | Pixmap Resources | 298 |
| | Bitmaps | 303 |
| | Images | 309 |
| | Summary | 326 |

| 9 | **The Mouse and Pointer** | 327 |
|---|---|---|
| | Mouse-Handling Strategies | 328 |
| | Pointer Control | 329 |
| | Cursors | 337 |
| | Mouse Events | 342 |
| | Summary | 359 |

| 10 | **The Keyboard** | 361 |
|---|---|---|
| | Keyboard Events | 362 |
| | Keycodes, Keymaps, Keysyms, and Text | 368 |
| | Keyboard Focus | 374 |
| | Controlling the Keyboard | 387 |
| | Summary | 392 |

| 11 | **Advanced Event Handling** | 395 |
|---|---|---|
| | Polling the Queue | 396 |
| | Event Compression | 401 |
| | Multiple Display Connections | 404 |

Putting Back and Sending Events                408
Grabbing the Pointer                           409
Grabbing Mouse Buttons                         416
Grabbing the Keyboard                          420
Grabbing Individual Keys                       423
Synchronous Delivery of Grabbed Events         425
Passive Grab Activation                        429
Summary                                        429

## 12   Communicating Between Applications   431

Cut Buffers                                    432
Properties                                     435
Selections                                     452
Summary                                        468

## Appendices   470

A   helloworld.c                               470
B   X Protocol Request Codes                   473
C   Latin-1 and Standard Keysyms               475
D   Fonts                                      480
E   Color Names                                489
F   Standard Cursor Shapes and Symbols         491
G   Predefined Atoms                           494

## Index   497

# PREFACE

The X Window System is a portable software standard developed at the Massachusetts Institute of Technology's Project Athena. It controls the displays of engineering workstations and provides a standard environment to application software such as page-layout editors and computer-aided-design packages. Applications which use X to operate a workstation display can easily be run on a variety of workstations from a variety of computer vendors.

The X Window System will stimulate the development of excellent application software for workstations. This book is for those who use version 11 of X to develop such software.

All users of X have the principal developers of the X Window System to thank. Robert W. Scheifler and Jim Gettys, the principal authors of the X software, patiently answered many questions. Ron Newman and David S. H. Rosenthal also made substantial intellectual contributions to the material I've written about.

A large number of people helped me with the writing of this book in one way or another. Vasudev Bhandarkar was a real instigator and agitator. He got me started and egged me on all the way through. Nancy Benovich gave me material assistance with the chapter on windows. Several people at Digital working in the X Testing Consortium, including Peter Vinsel, Erik Morse, and Jeff Ghannam gave early drafts a thorough going-over, and the book is substantially more accurate because of their work. Joe Bowbeer, Dany Guindi, Linda B. Merims, John Francis, Adrian Nye, Hugo Leiter, Paul Shearer, Al Tabayoyon, Glenn Widener, and Jeffrey Snover all made useful comments on early drafts.

Lots of people gave me encouragement when I needed it, including Axel Deininger, Al Mento, Tim O'Reilly, Jeff Graber, and Russ Sprunger. At Apollo, Tom Greene, Al Lopez, Anita Reiner, and Dave Gorgen were especially supportive. Jon Simonoff and Susan Keohan provided significant copy-editing help, and John Humphrys provided excellent no-hassle typesetting. The cover artwork was designed by John Humphrys and Paul Heurich based on the X Window System logo designed by Danny Chong.

The many participants in the xpert electronic mail list and later the comp.windows.x electronic news group have contributed substantially to this book, by asking good questions and by constantly challenging my assumptions about what is and isn't obvious. Likewise, the people who sat through my seminars and tutorials helped a great deal.

Thanks to my daughters Anna and Alice for putting up with my long hours and obsession. Thanks also to Loreen Santocki: good child-care is one of the most important and unsung underpinnings of the success of the computer industry.

None of this would have been possible without the help of my wife Carolyn, who not only kept me going but proofread the entire manuscript.

I've left people out, no doubt, but by mistake rather than intention. Of course, all the remaining errors in the text are my responsibility.

*Oliver Jones*

# INTRODUCTION
## TO THE
# X WINDOW SYSTEM

# CHAPTER 1
## INTRODUCTION

In the early days of interactive computing, users punched in commands on type-writer keyboards and the computer printed out results. As time went by, the proliferation of video display terminals allowed users to save paper, but everybody still communicated with computers using letters and numbers. It was not until the introduction of computer workstations that the technologies of computer graphics, bitmapped video display, keyboard entry, and pointer entry were integrated into a single package.

Integrated computer workstations proved very successful: users were demanding computers that were at once powerful and easy to use, and workstations met the demand. However, the advent of workstations increased the burdens on developers of application software. No longer is it sufficient to provide a simple text-based question-and-answer dialogue: users are demanding interactive software that exploits the graphical capabilities of workstations to their fullest.

The manufacturers of workstation hardware, in an effort to ease the transition to fully interactive programs, provided subroutine packages to expose their hardware's capabilities and features (such as, for example, subroutines for color graphics and mouse operations). This proved largely successful: sales of integrated workstations have grown, in the first seven years of their existence, from nothing to a total of well over $1.5 billion per year.

However, developers of workstation application software still are faced with the problem and expense of developing a different graphical interface for each workstation hardware vendor's product. Two large users of workstations from multiple vendors are Project Athena and the Laboratory for Computer Science, both at the Massachusetts Institute of Technology. Both organizations are responsible for developing and for using large quantities of workstation application programs. Out of their need to avoid reprogramming each application for each workstation grew the X Window System. The X Window System gave M. I. T. a way to program workstation applications using a common and portable interface to workstation hardware. Project Athena was sponsored by IBM and Digital Equipment Corporation. Both companies saw the value of X and had the foresight and generosity to donate substantial resources to X's development.

In January 1987, a dozen vendors announced a cooperative effort to standardize and promote X. Almost all workstation vendors have, by now, accepted the X Window System as a standard interface to their workstation hardware. Furthermore, most vendors are committed to the future of X: they are doing a great deal of work to ensure that their X products are fast and reliable.

## THE X ENVIRONMENT

The X Window System is a software environment for engineering workstations. It offers a rich and complex environment to the programmer and user of application software. The foundation of X is the *base window system*. As Figure 1-1 shows, the overall X environment consists of layers upon the base window system.

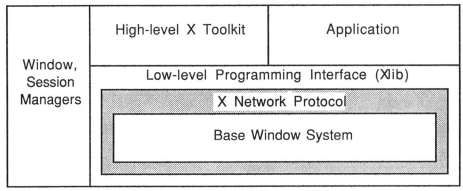

Figure 1-1. The structure of X.

The base window system interfaces with the outside world using the X network protocol. The network protocol interface is designed to work either within a single central processing unit (cpu) or between cpus. The existence of the network protocol confers device/vendor independence and network transparency upon X. As Figure 1-1 indicates, the network protocol is the *only* interface to the base window system. X does not provide any special "back-door" interfaces for privileged software. Rather, it uses the network protocol for all operations. This means that software such as session and window managers are treated by X as application software rather than as privileged system software.

X application programs ordinarily do not use the network protocol directly, but rather work through a programming interface. A C-language subroutine package known as *Xlib* is provided with the X Window System for the purpose of letting applications interface to the network protocol and thence to the base window system. Most application programs should use the high-level X toolkit to mask some of the complexity of the network protocol.

The user's interface to the workstation is the combination of the capabilities provided by the base window system, the X toolkit, window and session managers, and application software. The central dogma of X is that the base window system provides *mechanism, not policy*. The base window system provides mechanisms, such as output drawing capabilities. Human interface policy is left to the other components.

For example, X allows windows on the screen to overlap one another, and allows output to partially obscured windows: this is mechanism. Application programs and high-level toolkits may use popup menus (windows containing lists of options which pop up over and partially obscure other windows; see Figure 4-4 for example) as part of their human interface: this is policy.

Some users prefer a policy in which windows are *tiled* to abut one another precisely instead of overlapping. Tiling is possible in X: policy controlling the configuration of windows on the screen is enforced by a window manager application, so users wanting tiling should use a tiling window manager. If X's mechanism for displaying windows *required* that they be tiled, notice that it would be much harder to implement a popup menu policy. One of the beauties of X's base window system lies in the way it provides enough mechanism to support a wide variety of human interface policies, while leaving the implementation and enforcement of those policies to other software.

This book, like X's base window system, is about mechanism: it explains how to use X's base window system through the *Xlib* interface. *Xlib* has, as of this writing, been stable for several months, and is expected to have a useful lifetime of three to five years. As you read this book, you should keep in mind that high-level toolkit interfaces to X are actively being developed. Many applications will be able to use toolkits directly, almost never resorting to *Xlib*. However, many applications, especially those using techniques from interactive graphics, will have a need to use *Xlib* directly. The purpose of this book is to help workstation programmers understand the whys and wherefores of the X base window system as seen through the *Xlib* interface.

# THE X WINDOW SYSTEM'S GOALS

The purpose of the X Window System is to provide a *network-transparent* and *vendor-independent* operating environment for workstation software. The operating environment supports multiple overlapping windows on a variety of color and monochrome workstations.

## Network Transparency

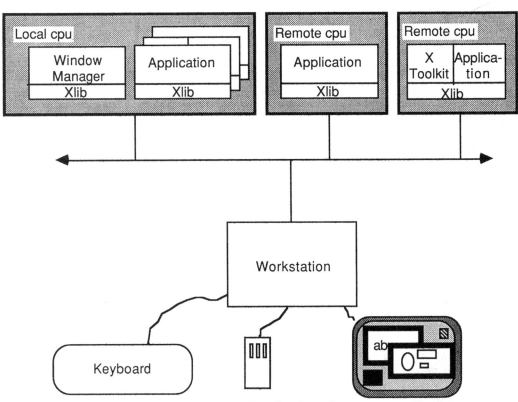

Figure 1-2. Workstation running local and remote applications.

Network transparency means that X applications running on one cpu can show their output using a display connected to either the same cpu, or some other cpu. Much of X's power derives from its integration into the local-area network environment: it allows a variety of computing styles ranging from stand-alone workstations running applications locally to time-shared mainframes using many different workstations as if they were terminals. All these styles can co-exist in the X environment. The network-transparency of X does not favor any one style over another, but rather synthesizes them all into a flexible networked computing environment suitable for use anywhere from a small office to a large campus. Experience with X has shown, in local-area-network environments, little or no performance penalty for networked X applications as compared to local (single-cpu) applications.

Network transparency implies that applications can run on whatever cpu is most convenient. For example, an application requiring a large shared data base can run on the cpu containing that data base, and connect to users' workstations over the network using X. Similarly, applications requiring extensive computations can run on a network-connected supercomputer. Of course, many applications (text-editors, terminal emulators, and window managers, for example) run locally on the same cpu as the workstation's display hardware. It is not necessary to alter an X program in any way to make it connect over the network to a remote workstation.

To the user, an X workstation looks like it is connected to many different host cpus at the same time. For example, Figure 1-2 shows a configuration in which applications on three different host cpus are running on the workstation. X workstations can connect to many different applications (at least a dozen), on any cpu in the network. Each of these applications can use as many windows as it needs to display output, and can receive input. Chapter 3 explains how an application program establishes a display connection (locally or across a network) to a workstation.

A single X application program, likewise, can display output windows on many different workstations at the same time. Chapter 11 describes how an application can work with multiple display connections.

## Vendor and Model Independence

X applications are portable. They deal with X, so they do not know the details of any particular workstation's display hardware. As long as an X application is able to establish a connection to a workstation, it can use all the capabilities of the base window system on that workstation. Because the workstation hardware is hidden by the protocol, an X application running on a cpu from one vendor can use any workstation model, either from that vendor or from another. It is not necessary to recompile or relink any application to give it access to all kinds of X workstations.

Like any other program, X applications must be compiled and linked for the particular combination of cpu and operating system environment it will run on. For example, it is necessary to recompile and relink applications when moving them from a Hewlett-Packard environment to an Apollo environment, or from a DEC VAX/Ultrix environment to a DEC VAX/VMS environment. X workstation vendors furnish precompiled versions of *Xlib* and other subroutine libraries which may be linked with applications.

One of the trickiest aspects of vendor-independence is the byte-ordering problem. Some vendors' computers (notably VAX computers from Digital Equipment Corporation) are *little-endian*: they store the least significant byte of multi-byte integers first. Others (notably the Motorola MC68000 series, used by several workstation vendors) are *big-endian*: they store the most significant byte first. X solves this problem neatly by having the workstation keep track of whether it must reorder the bytes in the protocol coming from and going to each application. The burden of changing byte-ordering is on the workstation, not the application. However, a little-endian workstation only needs to reorder bytes coming from a big-endian application, and vice versa.

## Output Capabilities

X's base window system offers a full-featured suite of bitmapped graphics operations. Applications and high-level toolkits use X's graphics operations to draw information on the workstations's screen for users to see. X offers the following graphics capabilities:

- X organizes display screens into a hierarchy of overlapping windows. Each application can use as many windows as it needs, resizing, moving, and stacking them on top of one another as needed. Chapter 4 of this book discusses the ways applications can exploit X's multiple window capability.

- X provides drawing capabilities. X's graphics operations are *immediate* rather than display-list-oriented: the workstation does not save series of graphics operations, but rather draws everything immediately.

  X's drawing operations are bitmap-oriented: applications specify all operations in terms of integer pixel addresses within windows. All X graphics operations are addressed to a particular window, so applications can draw things in their windows without regard to where their windows are positioned on-screen. Chapter 5 describes how to draw points, lines, rectangles, arcs, and polygons.

- X lets applications draw high-quality text. X's text supports many kinds of applications, ranging from video-display-terminal emulators to multilingual word processing programs. Chapter 6 discusses how to draw text.

- X is useful with a wide variety of color workstations, as well as black-and-white models. Chapter 7 describes how to use color in X, and how to write applications to work on both color and black-and-white workstations.

- X is useful for displaying, manipulating, and capturing images. Chapter 8 describes how to use X's image capabilities.

## Input Capabilities

X provides a comprehensive mechanism for distributing user input to application programs. The input-distributing part of X offers the following capabilities:

- Users generate input by pressing keys on the workstation's keyboard or manipulating the workstation's mouse. X's base window system distributes this input to applications in the form of *events*. Chapter 3 describes how the base window system puts events in a queue from which applications can read and process them.

- Many events allow applications to find out about changes to the window hierarchy. Chapters 4, 5, and 7 describe events relating to windows, graphics, and color, respectively.

- Input from the workstation's *pointer* or mouse arrives in the form of events. The base window system organizes pointer events so they are sent to the appropriate application, even when many applications are running simultaneously on the workstation. Chapters 9 describes how applications process pointer input events.

- X supports a large variety of typewriter keyboards. Chapter 10 describes the base window system's keyboard support and how to use it.

## Information-sharing Capabilities

When several application programs run on a single workstation, they often need to cooperate with each other (to permit cut-and-paste operations, for example). X provides ways for applications to communicate:

- Applications can use a simple *cut-and-paste* facility to share simple unstructured data, such as character strings.

- Applicatios can share structured data explicitly via X *properties*. Properties are data items which can be attached to windows. Each property has a name, a data type, and a data format.

- *Selections* provide a sophisticated (and complex) way for applications to interact with one another and pass data back and forth.

## Concurrency

The X Window System allows several applications at a time to be active on a workstation. Individual applications may start and stop at will during a user's session. Usually (but not always) each application uses a separate window or window sub-hierarchy to display its output. Using this capability, a user can, for example, edit several files simultaneously, run computations on several different computers, and read news in one window and mail in another.

Each application operates independently of others. This means that each application need not take any notice of other applications' windows before drawing to their own windows, nor do anything special to lock out other applications while drawing.

Each time a user generates input events, X's base window system delivers an input *event* to the right application's event queue. The base window system uses a variety of ways to control the distribution of events to applications. Chapters 9, 10, and 11 cover the things your application can do to exploit X's event-distribution control mechanisms.

## USING X

This section discusses the user's view of an X workstation and some of the standard application programs available to the user. However, this book is about how to create application programs for the X Window System, not how to run the existing ones.

In this book, when we refer to a *user* we mean *the human being sitting in front of the workstation*. The user sees an X workstation complete with a screen, mouse and keyboard. The screen displays one or more windows, each showing the output of some application program (also known as a client program) running on the workstation. Figure 4-1 shows a typical user's screen, with several application windows.

Each X application program has a specific purpose. A commonly used X application program is **xterm(1)**, which emulates traditional video display terminals (the DEC VT102 text terminal and the Tektronix 4014 graphics terminal). The purpose of **xterm** is to run traditional video display terminal software, including (but not limited to) all Unix system software. For example, **xterm** supports:

- Text-editors, including **vi(1)** and the various flavors of **emacs**.
- Shells (command-line-interpreters) such as **sh(1)** and **csh(1)**.
- Video-forms-entry software such as **curses(3X)**.
- Graphics terminal software such as **plot(5)**.

By using **xterm** alone, a user can pretend that an X window is an ordinary computer terminal. This compatibility is very important: it makes enormous quantities of existing software useful with X workstations. Notice that an X workstation can display several **xterm** sessions at a time. With this capability, a user can replace many computer terminals with a single X workstation.

**xterm** obviously exploits the workstation's keyboard: the user makes keystrokes and **xterm** passes them along to the application software running on the emulated terminal (just as keystrokes on an ordinary terminal are passed to the software running on it). Not so obvious is how the workstation's mouse and cursor interact with **xterm**. The user selects which window should receive keystrokes by *pointing to* that window: by manipulating the mouse so the cursor is inside the window (sometimes it may also be necessary to *click on* the window, or press a mouse button). Controlling the distribution of events from the keyboard (the keyboard's *focus*) is an important use of the mouse. **xterm** also provides mouse-controlled scrollbars and cut-and-paste, as well as a mouse-activated option menu (see **xterm**'s documentation).

Obviously, the capabilities of X workstations go far beyond those of video display terminals. A growing number of graphical application programs are provided with X, including:

- **bitmap(1)**, a bitmap editor.
- **xclock(1)**, a simulated clock.
- **xedit(1)**, a simple mouse-operated text editor.
- **xmh(1)**, a mouse-operated program for reading electronic mail.

Users interact with these programs by using the mouse to point to things such as simulated command-buttons on the screen and pressing the mouse buttons. As the user manipulates the mouse, the X workstation distributes input events to the appropriate applications, and the applications respond by altering their displays. For example, when a user points to a simulated command-button, **xedit** responds by highlighting the border of the button's area. When a user presses the simulated command button (by pressing a mouse button), **xedit** highlights the whole button. Only when the user releases the mouse button does **xedit** perform the command.

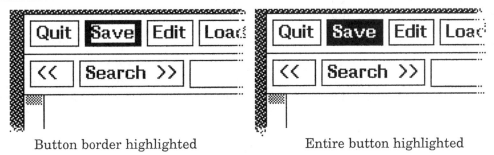

Button border highlighted          Entire button highlighted

Figure 1-3.  Simulated command button actions from **xedit**.

To the user, these interactive operations must appear smooth and natural. In a successful application, it should take very little time for a new user to become accustomed to using the simulated command buttons. Most interactive applications use a high-level X toolkit subroutine library to ease and standardize such interactive responses. The important thing to remember is that interactive responses (such as the highlighting of the button) are not provided by X's base window system alone, but are the responsibility of the application program or a subroutine library within it. To program an application successfully, you must understand how the base window system generates events to let you keep track of what the user is doing on the screen, and how your application must respond to those events.

## Window Managers

When a user has several different applications running, their windows may overlap one another. One application in particular, the *window manager application*, lets users organize and rearrange their application windows while providing a particular human interface policy. Users of the standard X Window System can choose between two window managers:

- **uwm(1)** is a customizable window manager based on popup menus.

- **wm(1)** puts *decorations*, including banners and buttons, around application program windows.

A window manager is just another X application (albeit a complex one). Most users prefer a particular window manager, and use a startup script to run it automatically every time they log in to a workstation session. For the details of starting and using a window manager, see the window manager's documentation.

# PROGRAMMING X

You are reading this book to learn what makes the X Window System tick from the point of view of an application program. In this book, the word *you* means *you the application programmer*, to distinguish *you* from the *user*. Of course, *you* can also be a user, when you operate your application or a standard application.

Most X applications are written in the C programming language. This book discusses how to use X's base window system by calling *Xlib* from C language programs. As the example in Chapter 2 shows, *Xlib* application programs interact with the workstation by

- Receiving events from the workstation, and
- Reacting appropriately to those events.

Almost everything that happens in an *Xlib* application happens in response to events. For example, the **xedit** application receives an event when the user points to the Save button, as shown in Figure 1-3. It responds to that event by highlighting the button's border.

Most *Xlib* applications are structured in such a way that they have a single main loop. At the top of the main loop, the application accepts an event from the workstation. The remainder of the loop decodes the event and figures out what to do with it.

## Protocol Specification

The formal definition of the X Window System is stated in terms of the communication protocol used for connecting application to workstation. The document *X Window System Protocol, Version 11,* by Robert W. Scheifler, specifies the protocol. This document is supplied in machine readable form as part of the X Window System distribution tape from the M.I.T. X Consortium. (On Unix and compatible systems the document is stored on the distribution directory tree in a file named **doc/Protocol/spec**; you may find the file under some other name on your system, however. In the same file directory as the specification is an index and a table of contents for the specification.) The protocol specification defines in detail the contents of each type of message that passes between applications and workstations, and what effects each message has.

*X Window System Protocol, Version 11* is difficult to read. Because it is the formal specification of the X Window System, however, most X application programmers will refer to it occasionally.

## Toolkits

A *toolkit* is a user-interface subroutine library. From the point of view of the user, a toolkit has the purpose of standardizing and modularizing the actions for such things as simulated buttons. Once a user becomes familiar with an application package, he develops intuition about how the human interface works. If applications use tookits, it is easy for the user's intuition about the human interface to transfer from one application to another. For example, the actions of **xedit**'s simulated buttons (see Figure 1-3) are actually provided by the X toolkit, not by **xedit** directly. Other applications (such as **xmh**) use the same style of interaction. Once a user is trained on one application, others seem natural.

From the point of view of you, the programmer, the purpose of a toolkit is to simplify the design and development of application user interfaces. For example, the keyboard operations provided by X's base window system are very primitive and low-level. If what you want to do is allow the user to type text, you will do well to use a toolkit: it will offer you a far more straightforward way of reading text than will the base window system.

Toolkits are libraries of programs. They are layered upon X's base window system via the *Xlib* subroutine interface. Three toolkits are provided on a standard X Window System workstation:

> The *X Toolkit*, developed primarily by Digital Equipment Corporation and M.I.T.'s Project Athena with the participation of other X vendors.

> *Xrlib*, developed and contributed by the Hewlett-Packard Company.

*ATK*, the Andrew Toolkit, developed and contributed by Carnegie-Mellon University and IBM.

Most application programs will use the X Toolkit. In fact, the final version of the Hewlett-Packard Company's Xrlib is integrated with the X Toolkit.

A typical X Toolkit application, when assembled from the various libraries, is made up of four layers:

The lowest layer is *Xlib*, just as it is for any X application. *Xlib* is, of course, supplied as part of standard X.

The next layer is the X Toolkit intrinsics library. Like *Xlib*, it is part of standard X.

The third layer consists of *widgets*. Widgets include such things as the simulated buttons shown in Figure 1-3 above. Included with standard X is a collection of standard widgets, for such things as buttons and text editing. Many X applications can simply use standard widgets. If you are writing a graphics application to run with the X Toolkit, however, you may have to create one or more custom widgets. To create a custom widget, you write several C subroutines which call *Xlib* and X Toolkit Intrinsics.

The top layer is the application code itself.

An X Toolkit application, like any other X application, has a main loop. However, it is buried in a Toolkit Intrinsics routine.

Detailed discussion of the X toolkits is beyond the scope of this book.

## USING THIS BOOK

The purpose of this book is to explain how to understand and use *Xlib*. *Xlib* is useful both for applications and for implementing custom X Toolkit widgets. After reading this book, you should be able to design, write and debug C language programs which use X's base window system via *Xlib*. You should also have an understanding of the motivations behind the design of X: *why* its components work the way they do.

This book augments, but does not replace, the reference documents provided as part of the standard X Window System. While we cover most of the capabilities of *Xlib* in detail, some features (especially those of interest only to window manager applications) are not covered here.

*Xlib* is described in *Xlib — C Language X Interface* by Jim Gettys, Ron Newman, and Robert W. Scheifler. Machine-readable source for this lengthy document is available on the X distribution from the M.I.T. X Consortium. On Unix and compatible systems it is in the directory **doc/Xlib**; it may be in a directory with some other name on your system.

## Prerequisites

This book assumes that the reader has a working knowledge of the C programming language and the Unix (or Unix-compatible) operating system. It also assumes a basic understanding of bitmapped computer graphics.

## Chapter Summary

It is hard to know where to start explaining the X Window System. Even the simplest X application program has many parts, all of which depend on the others. Chapter 2 ("Hello World!") jumps right into X by showing and superficially explaining an example of an *Xlib* application program.

Chapter 3, "X Concepts," discusses how application programs connect to and communicate with workstations. It covers the basics of the X protocol, the opening and closing of display connections, the processing of events, and the handling of errors.

Chapter 4 explains windows and how to create, manipulate, and destroy them. It also explains the rules applications must follow in order to coexist peacefully with other applications on the workstation.

Chapter 5 explains how to draw graphics (points, lines, arcs, shapes) with X.

Chapter 6 explains how to draw alphanumeric text with X.

Chapter 7 delves into the details of how X allows you to exploit the capabilities of color workstations.

Chapter 8 explains X's capabilities for drawing images.

Chapter 9 explains how X applications can use the workstation's mouse.

Chapter 10 explains how to use the workstation's keyboard.

Chapter 11 covers advanced techniques for event-handling.

Chapter 12 goes into X's information-sharing facilities, including cut-and-paste, property manipulation, and selections.

## Calls

*Xlib* contains a large number of subroutine and function calls. Most *Xlib* calls are covered in detail in this book. In each chapter, the calls are organized in a sequence which helps explain how X works. Generally, we use the following outline when discussing X features and calls:

- Conceptual discussion. From this section, you should be able to understand the purpose of the call and the circumstances under which you should use it. If there are alternatives to the call, or design decisions to be made, this section covers them.

- Call description. This presents the form of the call, including the types of all the parameters. It also cross-references the *Xlib—C Language X Interface* document's section number in which the call is described. The cross-references are parenthetical notes of the form (*Xlib* ¶1.1).

  Calls are shown in the form of *generic examples*. Each generic example contains all the declarations for call parameters, followed by an example of the call which uses the declared parameters.

- Discussion of parameters. This section gives the details of the call's input and output parameters.

- Examples. When appropriate, we present excerpts of code which do useful work with the call.

## Events

*Xlib* calls are only half the story. The other half are *events*, used by the workstation to notify applications of input or some other action. X provides a large number of types of events. The discussion of events is scattered throughout the book: each event type relates to certain *Xlib* calls, and is described in the same chapter as the related calls.

The fundamentals of event handling—ways to read the event queue—are explained in Chapter 3. The later chapters assume a knowledge of how to read the queue.

The discussion of each type of event adheres generally to this outline:

- How to solicit (arrange to receive) the events.

- A table showing the contents of the event's data structure. In X, events are stored in an **XEvent**: a C union of structures. Each event's table shows both the structure declaration for the particular event and the member names used to retrieve each data field from the **XEvent** union type.

- Detailed discussion of the meaning of each data field in the event's structure.

- Where appropriate, examples showing how to process the event types in question.

## Hazards

*Hazards* are pitfalls awaiting the unwary X programmer. Hazard warnings are shown in boxes. For example:

> Avoid trying to draw in a window before you create it.

X is robust: as long as you take reasonable precautions (such as avoiding debugging new code when logged in with elevated privileges), you cannot damage your workstation or cpu even if you make a serious error. Hazards do not, therefore, warn of physical damage: rather they point out mistakes commonly made by new X programmers.

## Terminology

An X *workstation* is a combination of a program, known as the *server*, along with hardware to run the server. The hardware consists of a bitmapped video display, a mouse and keyboard, and a computer to run it all. For the purposes of this book, it makes sense to discuss the workstation hardware and the server program running on it as if they were a single entity, called the *workstation*.

Likewise, client programs are called *applications* in this book.

Other discussions of X often use the word "server" for what we call the workstation, and the word "client" for what we call the application.

# CHAPTER 2
# HELLO, WORLD

The X Window System is made of many interlocking parts. A working X application program must put the parts together into a coherent whole. A minimal X application must

- Set up a connection to the workstation
- Create a window
- Inform a window manager of the window's properties
- Create X resources such as graphic contexts (GCs)
- Map the window to the screen (make it visible)
- Solicit the input events it is interested in
- Read and interpret these input events
- Generate graphical output
- Shut down when the application is complete

The whys and wherefores of these parts of an X Window System application are explained in detail in later chapters.

This chapter first presents, then dissects, the X program **helloworld.c**. The purpose of this chapter is to explain, by example, how to use the parts of X. You will leave this chapter with a mental road map, as well as code, for a working X application.

If possible, you should run this example on a workstation as you read this chapter. **helloworld.c** is short enough for you to type into your computer with a text editor in a few minutes, and will serve as a basis for examples and experimentation in later chapters.

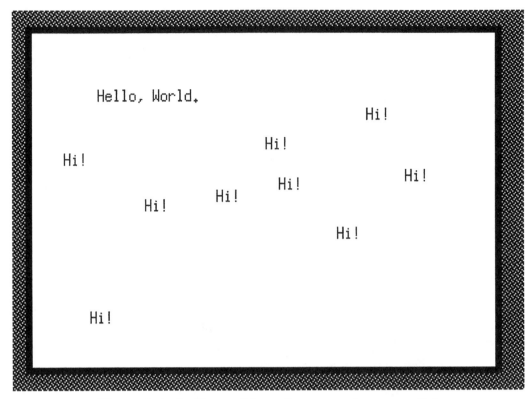

Figure 2-1. **helloworld.c** after several mouse clicks.

## What helloworld.c Does

**helloworld.c**, when compiled, loaded, and run on your workstation, creates a window and displays the text "Hello, World." in it. If you use the workstation's mouse to position the cursor inside the window and click any mouse button, it displays the text "Hi!" at the point of the mouse-click.

If you cover the window with some other window and then uncover or *expose* it, **helloworld.c** restores the original text display. It also restores the original text display if you move the window. This capability is an important part of an X Window System application; applications on an X workstation often do things to each other's windows, and each application is responsible for restoring the contents of its own windows on demand.

Finally, **helloworld.c** recognizes input from the workstation keyboard. It ignores all characters except lowercase "q," which causes **helloworld.c** to terminate.

**helloworld.c** is trivial, but it is a more-or-less complete skeleton X program. The complete source for **helloworld.c** is presented in Appendix A.

## An Outline of helloworld.c

In this section, we break apart the **helloworld.c** example. Taking a top-down approach, we start by looking at the example's overall structure. Finally, we describe each of the example's major components in more detail.

It is not necessary to understand everything the first time you read through the source and the dissection. We are asking you, at this point, to get the broad picture, and save the details for later.

**helloworld.c** has the following major sections, as do most X programs:

- **#include** directives to fetch pre-defined header files that declare X data types

- declarations, including the declaration of the main routine

- initialization, to open a connection to the display, create the window, and create a graphic context resource for use later in drawing

- input event selection, by which the program tells the workstation which types of X input events it requires

- window mapping, by which the program makes its window visible on the screen

- a main loop for reading events. Within the purview of the main loop is all the application code that generates output on the screen and recognizes input from the workstation keyboard and mouse. The main loop includes:

    —painting or repainting the window when it is exposed

    —processing keyboard mapping changes (notifications of keyboard reconfiguration)

    —processing mouse-button presses

    —processing keyboard input

- termination, in which the application destroys its X resources and closes its channel to the display

The main loop is the part of the structure that "does everything" in an X program. Initialization only sets things up; the main loop does all the displaying and processing in reaction to input events it receives from the workstation.

## helloworld.c  Dissected

## Header Files

```
#include <X11/Xlib.h>
#include <X11/Xutil.h>
```

This compiler directive fetches header files containing the declarations that are needed to define data for use with the various X Window System requests. The header file **<X11/Xlib.h>** is shown in Appendix B.  **<X11/Xlib.h>** itself includes <X11/X.h>, which is shown in Appendix C.

The header file **<X11/Xutil.h>** defines data for use with various utility operations.

## Declarations

```
char hello[ ]  = "Hello, World.";
char hi[ ]     = "Hi!";
```

These module-wide declarations set up strings containing the text that the example program will display on the screen.

```
main(argc,argv)
    int argc;
    char **argv;
{
  Display *mydisplay;
  Window  mywindow;
  GC mygc;
```

These are declarations of X Window System data items.  The item "mydisplay" is a pointer to an X data structure controlling the connection to the workstation. The "mywindow" and "mygc" items are X resource identifiers for the window and graphic context that the example creates.  The program must retain these data structures as long as it is using the workstation.

```
  XEvent myevent;
  KeySym mykey;
```

The "myevent" item is a data structure (actually, a union of several structures corresponding to the several types of events) into which X places information describing each input event the sample program receives from the workstation. The "mykey" item uniquely describes a keyboard key, regardless of whether it is an alphanumeric key or a function key.  When the sample program interprets a keyboard event, "mykey" identifies the key that was pressed.

```
  XSizeHints myhint;
```

The "myhint" item is a data structure which **helloworld** uses to inform other applications running on the same workstation about its window.

```
int myscreen;
unsigned long myforeground, mybackground;
int i;
char text[10];
int done;
```

These variables are used for setting the foreground and background colors for drawing, and for receiving keystrokes from the workstation and controlling the main loop.

## Initialization

```
mydisplay = XOpenDisplay("");
```

This is the first X Window System request carried out in any program. It initiates a display connection (network circuit) from the application to the workstation, creates and fills in a **Display** structure describing that connection, and returns a pointer to the **Display** structure. The argument, when it is not null, is a text string specifying the network node name and display number of the workstation, for example "expo:0". In the example, the argument is an empty text string, which, on Unix and compatible sytems, tells X to look at the DISPLAY environment variable for the display name.

Most X application programs check for **XOpenDisplay**'s failure by making sure that it returns a nonzero **Display** pointer. For simplicity, **helloworld.c** is more optimistic about **XOpenDisplay**'s success than a robust program would be.

```
myscreen = DefaultScreen (mydisplay);
mybackground = WhitePixel (mydisplay, myscreen);
myforeground = BlackPixel (mydisplay, myscreen);
```

These lines determine the pixel values (colors) to use for drawing the window's background area (black) and foreground text and border (white). The **Display** structure contains (among other things) the appropriate pixel values to use for drawing black and white. Because the pixel values to use vary from workstation to workstation, these lines allow your application to be device-independent.

```
myhint.x = 200; myhint.y = 300;
myhint.width=350;  myhint.height=250;
myhint.flags = PPosition | PSize;
```

These lines define the position and size of the window, by filling in part of the **XSizeHints** structure. The window's upper left corner will be at point (200,300) on the screen, and the window will be 350 pixels wide and 250 pixels high. The third line sets flags (PPosition and PSize) which indicate which fields in the **XSizeHints** structure are filled in. These flags mean that the program itself (not the user) chose the window position and size.

> mywindow = **XCreateSimpleWindow** (mydisplay,
>     DefaultRootWindow (mydisplay),
>     myhint.x, myhint.y, myhint.width, myhint.height,
>     5, myforeground, mybackground);

With this call, we request the workstation to create the sample application's window. The call returns, in *mywindow*, the window's resource identifier. The window is created in the default root window (the window covering the whole screen) with a 5-pixel-wide black (myforeground) border. The window's background is white (mybackground). The window is created, but is not yet made viewable—not yet mapped to the screen.

> **XSetStandardProperties** (mydisplay, mywindow, hello, hello,
>     None, argv, argc, &myhint);

This X Window System request describes the newly created window to other applications running on the workstation (such as a window-manager application). It lets other applications know the application's name and the size of the window.

> mygc = **XCreateGC** (mydisplay, mywindow, 0, 0);
> **XSetBackground** (mydisplay, mygc, mybackground);
> **XSetForeground** (mydisplay, mygc, myforeground);

This request creates a graphic context, then sets the foreground and background values into it. Besides color, a graphic context contains rendering attributes for graphical output such as line width and text font. This example creates a graphic context in which X sets the other attributes to default values.

## Input Event Solicitation

> **XSelectInput** (mydisplay, mywindow,
>     ButtonPressMask | KeyPressMask | ExposureMask );

This request tells the workstation that henceforth the example program wants to receive notification whenever the user presses a mouse button (ButtonPressMask) or keyboard key (KeyPressMask) in *mywindow*. It also tells the workstation to send Expose events (ExposureMask). Expose events are used by the workstation to ask the application program to redraw the graphical image in a window.

## Window Mapping

> **XMapRaised** (mydisplay, mywindow);

This request displays the window on the screen, on top of any other windows that may already be showing. The order in which we did the window creation, event selection, and mapping was quite deliberate. By the time we ask for the window to be mapped to the screen, we have already selected Expose events for the window (see above). As soon as the workstation maps the window, it sends our program an Expose event that asks our program to draw the contents of the window. So, the first time the main event loop asks for an event, it gets the Expose event and calls the routine that displays the initial "Hello, World" message.

## The Main Event-Reading Loop

```
done = 0;
while ( done == 0 ) {
    XNextEvent ( mydisplay, &myevent );
    switch (myevent.type) {
```

This code controls the main loop. **XNextEvent** reads the next event from the workstation, by filling in the *myevent* structure. The first field in *myevent* is the type of the event. The switch statement dispatches each event to the code cases that can handle its particular type (such as Expose, ButtonPress, and KeyPress).

### Repaint the Window on Expose Events

```
case Expose:
    if (myevent.xexpose.count == 0)
        XDrawImageString (
            myevent.xexpose.display, myevent.xexpose.window, mygc,
            50, 50,
            hello, strlen(hello) ) ;
    break;
```

This code draws the text for the "Hello, World." string in the window, once it has decided that it should honor this Expose event. Sometimes a workstation sends more than one Expose event for a single window; the **XEvent** field "myevent.xexpose.count" is zero in the last of a series of Expose events for a single window. The field is also zero if just one Expose event is sent. The sample program deals with the possibility of Expose event series by ignoring all but the last event in each series.

The **XDrawImageString** request (like all graphics output requests in X) requires the program to specify a display, window, and gc. We draw the text at point (50,50) relative to the upper left corner of the application's window.

Notice that we waited to draw the window's contents until the workstation mapped the window (which we requested earlier via **XMapRaised**) and sent an Expose event asking us to draw. Note also that this routine only draws "Hello, World." It does not redraw any "Hi!"s that might be displayed. In a real application, the code that handles Expose events must be capable of completely redrawing the window.

### Process Keyboard Mapping Changes

```
case MappingNotify:
    XRefreshKeyboardMapping ( &myevent );
    break;
```

All X Window System applications should have these three lines of code in their main loops. Just put them there and don't worry about them! (If the configuration of the keyboard changes, the workstation sends one of these MappingNotify events. **XRefreshKeyboardMapping** does what is needed.)

**Process Mouse-Button Presses**

```
case ButtonPress:
XDrawImageString (
        myevent.xbutton.display, myevent.xbutton.window, mygc,
        myevent.xbutton.x, myevent.xbutton.y,
        hi, strlen(hi)  ) ;
break;
```

This code handles the events generated when the user presses any mouse button. What it actually does is draw the string "Hi!" at the point in the window where the user pressed the button (this information is in the **XEvent** structure fields "myevent.xbutton.x" and "myevent.xbutton.y").

This drawing code does not play along with Expose events according to the rules. When an Expose event comes along, any "Hi!" strings that the user has drawn into the window with mouse clicks may disappear. If all the "Hi!" strings were to be redrawn at an Expose event, the program would have to store the (x,y) positions of the mouse clicks in an array or list, and go through that list redrawing all the "Hi!"s in the Expose event handler.

**Process Keyboard Input**

```
case KeyPress:
  i = XLookupString ( &myevent, text, 10, &mykey, 0 );
  if (i == 1 && text[0] == 'q') done = 1;
  break;
```

This code handles the events that result from the user pressing keys on the workstation's keyboard. The **XLookupString** function translates the information stored in the **XEvent** structure into a character string. This is a string rather than a single character because some keyboard keys can generate multi-character sequences such as escape sequences. This code also sets the data item "mykey" to the correct **Keysym**, or unique key identifier, for the actual key that was pressed. **XLookupString** is capable of returning multiple-character sequences (such as escape sequences) as well as single characters; hence the *text* array is ten characters long.

After it looks up the character string, this code sets the loop termination flag if the user pressed lower-case "q." We check both the length of the string (*i*), and the first character in the string.

## Termination

```
    }  /*  switch     (myevent.type)  */
}  /*  while (done  ==  0)  */

XFreeGC (mydisplay, mygc);
XDestroyWindow (mydisplay, mywindow);
XCloseDisplay (mydisplay);
```

```
    exit (0);
} /* main */
```

The remainder of the example program is concerned with tearing down what initialization set up on the workstation. Termination destroys the graphic context, destroys the window, closes the display and exits the example program. Many applications just use **XCloseDisplay** and allow the workstation to destroy the graphic context and window automatically.

## Building and Running helloworld.c

If you are running a Unix or compatible operating system, use a text editor to key in the **helloworld.c** source file. Then, compile and load **helloworld** using the following shell command:

```
% cc helloworld.c -lX11 -o helloworld
```

In order for you to use this command line, the following X files must be present on your Unix system:

| | |
|---|---|
| **/usr/lib/libX11.a** | The *Xlib* object library |
| **/usr/include/X11/Xlib.h** | The *Xlib* header file |
| **/usr/include/X11/X.h** | The *X* header file |

The result of compiling and loading is a program text file named **helloworld**. Log in to a Unix X workstation and issue the command

```
% helloworld
```

to run the program.

## Structuring an X Window System Application

How you structure your overall application in the X Window System is important to its quality and interactivity. A good X application is *modeless;* it is prepared to respond to all sorts of events in just about any order.

There are at least two good reasons for this. First, your application must deal with changes to your windows caused by other application programs running on the same workstation. After all, you (remember, in this book *you* are the application programmer) cannot control whether the user might pop another application window on top of yours, change your window's size, or expose your window. For that reason, the most important system-generated events are Expose events. They announce that all or part of your window needs redrawing because some other window has just stopped covering it. If your application does not process Expose events, you will find that other applications whose windows pop up over yours will leave holes in your pictures when they go away.

The second reason your application should be prepared to handle events in just about any order is because users will find the application easier to use if they are able to switch between mouse and keyboard input at will. Suppose your application was not modeless; suppose it alternated between two modes, one where it accepted mouse events and another where it read keyboard input. If your application worked this way, you would have to issue prompts to the user, saying "Now click the mouse" or "Now key in the text." Without such prompts, users might try typing when they were supposed to click the mouse or vice versa. In doing so, they will probably get the perception that the keyboard or the mouse "go dead" sometimes. Furthermore, you should remember that workstation screens are typically quite large, and the users may not see prompts. A much better alternative is to design your application so that either a keystroke or a mouse action is always valid.

The problem, then, is being able to handle input events in an order which your application cannot control. A is set up so there is no such thing as an unexpected event, or an unexpected order of events. One easy and effective way to make a modeless application is to build it, as we built **helloworld.c**, with a single main loop that reads an event from the queue and dispatches it, then loops back and reads the next event. For applications that have simple human interface rules and don't attempt complex operations such as simultaneous background processing, this simple "main loop" approach works nicely.

Real applications are, of course, much more complex than **helloworld.c**. They have multiple, interacting, hierarchical windows, non-trivial graphical output, and sophisticated user interfaces. However, they all can use some variant of the program structure described in this chapter.

# CHAPTER 3
# X CONCEPTS

Chapter 2 described a basic X application. This chapter presents the fundamentals of how an application interacts with an X Window System workstation. The concepts of this chapter are fundamental to the understanding of X graphic output and event input.

All application programs interact with an X Window System workstation through a *display connection*. A display connection is a logical network circuit between application and workstation. All application access to the workstation's screen, mouse, and keyboard hardware goes through the display connection. This network-transparent approach departs from tradition in the computer graphics industry; under X application programs often run on a cpu other than the one directly connected to the graphics hardware.

In X, the workstation hardware runs a piece of software called the X network *server* program. The server program accepts connection requests from *clients*, or application programs, and establishes a display connection to each application program. Through the display connection, the server program receives and responds to *requests* (for example, requests to create windows) from client application programs. The workstation also uses the display connection to send *events* (for example, notifications when the user presses mouse buttons) to applications.

The term *server* can be confusing. Many computer installations operate *file servers*, and call them, simply, "servers." Most file servers are networked computers lacking directly-connected video screens. An X workstation server, how-

*Kenneth B. Sall*

ever, must have a directly-connected screen.  This reverses the traditional idea that the server is "out there somewhere" and the client is "here."

The X Window System is formally defined in terms of the display connection's *network protocol*: the *wire format* (data structures) and the meaning of the messages sent back and forth over the display connection.  Every interaction between your application program and the workstation eventually reduces to one or more protocol messages passed over the network "wire."  The first part of this chapter discusses the elements of the protocol.

Fortunately, your application program does not have to generate protocol messages in wire format directly.  The *Xlib* subroutine package hides details of the wire format but gives application programs access to all of X's capabilities.  This book discusses interactions with the workstation in terms of *Xlib* calls rather than directly in terms of the X protocol.  Unfortunately, *Xlib* cannot hide the fact that application programs operate asynchronously with the workstation.  For example, many application requests to an X workstation are stored in buffers and carried out after some amount of delay.  For this reason, effective X application programming requires a general understanding of the elements of the X protocol.  The second part of this chapter covers the relationship between the *Xlib* procedural interface and the protocol.

Before your application can cause any output to appear on a workstation or receive any input from it, you must establish and maintain a display connection between the client application and the workstation server.  The third part of this chapter discusses the display connection in detail.  Your X application must set up a display connection during initialization.

As shown in Chapter 2, almost everything your application does on X workstations requires the use of X resources such as windows and graphic contexts.  The fourth part of this chapter discusses the fundamentals of X resources.  Many applications create at least some of their resources (windows, for example) during initialization.  However, resources can be created and destroyed dynamically throughout the lifetime of the application.

X Events are the means an X workstation uses to notify an application of user input actions, such as mouse manipulation or typing on the keyboard.  The functions of events extend well beyond user-input, however:  X provides a wide variety of types of events that permit multiple client applications to interact in sophisticated ways.  A well-designed X application has to have a way of soliciting, accepting and processing all sorts of events.  The next-to-last section of this chapter contains an outline of the types of X events and a general discussion of how your application may use them.

The concluding part of this chapter describes the error-handling facilities provided by X.

# THE X NETWORK PROTOCOL

The document *X Window System Protocol, Version 11,* by Robert W. Scheifler, formally defines the X Window System. Any software or hardware that correctly interprets the X Window System protocol is a true X implementation.

Note that the protocol specification does not specify the type of network communication to be used. While any reliable data communication method will support X, the first sample X Version 11 implementation distributed by M.I.T. contained support for Unix-Domain socket (UDS) circuits, TCP/IP circuits, and DECnet circuits. Workstation vendors will provide support for other types of networks as X implementations become more widespread.

The protocol specification is a useful reference document for everyone developing X software. Because the protocol specification is the "source of truth" about how the X Window System works, most application developers will consult it occasionally.

The remainder of this section discusses the fundamental elements of the X Window System protocol: *Requests* and *events*. Requests originate with the application, whereas events originate with the workstation.

## One-way protocol request messages

Your application uses *one-way protocol request messages* to instruct the workstation to do almost everything. For example, graphics operations such as line drawing are one-way requests: when you call the *Xlib* routine **XDrawLine** (see Chapter 5), *Xlib* formats (according to the X protocol specification) a protocol request message containing the information you supplied, then stores the message in a buffer. When the buffer fills up, *Xlib* sends it to the workstation. The workstation then draws the line you requested.

Because these one-way protocol requests can be buffered—transmitted in batches—and because your application does not have to wait for the workstation to carry them out and respond, you can achieve reasonably high performance even over slow network communication links. Once you have called *Xlib* to issue a one-way request, you forget about it and move on to other operations. There is, of course, a delay between the time you issue a request and the time the workstation performs it. The length of this delay depends on the amount of time the message waits in the buffer, and the network delay once the message is sent out over the display connection. However, your application does not wait during the delay time; it can proceed to generate more X requests or do other useful work.

The buffering of one-way requests is, ordinarily, transparent. If you structure your X application in a way equivalent to that shown in the example of Chapter 2, you should rarely need to be concerned with the mechanics of buffering. On the other hand, if your application delays for certain periods of time, or carries out long non-interactive computations, you may explicitly *flush* the buffer (force its

/ p.55

contents to be sent). You can also disable buffering completely for debugging purposes. See "Explicit Control of the Request Buffer" in this chapter.

Some request messages can be very long. For example, **XDrawLines** could specify hundreds of line segments in a single request. There is no limit on the size of a request message, other than the inherent addressing limits imposed by the computer system you are using.

## Round-trip protocol request messages

Not all application-originated requests fall into the "send-and-forget" one-way category. Some requests, primarily inquiries like **XQueryPointer** (Chapter 9), require a *round-trip protocol request message*. Your application issues a round-trip request by calling the appropriate *Xlib* function, just as it issues a one-way request. However, *Xlib* sends the round-trip request to the workstation immediately. While *Xlib blocks* (waits), the workstation responds by generating a reply message. When *Xlib* receives the reply, it makes the received information available to your application in the form appropriate to the particular *Xlib* call (as a function result, or as returned parameters). Finally, *Xlib* returns to your application. The length and content of the reply message vary depending on the type of request.

Request message buffering is impossible with round-trip requests. When your application program uses a round-trip request, *Xlib* must first flush any previously buffered requests, then transmit the round-trip request for you immediately, then wait for a reply. This means that your application cannot do useful work during the wait time. Design your application to use round-trip requests sparingly; they slow your application, especially over a slow display connection.

Each specific X request is either a one-way request or a round-trip request. Requests do not have one-way variants and round-trip variants.

Both the request message and the reply message in a round-trip request can be as long or short as necessary. Replies to some types of round-trip requests, for example **XGetMotionEvents** (Chapter 9), can be very long.

## Event Messages

Many things happen at the workstation outside of the direct control of your application program. For example, the user can move the mouse, press a mouse button, press a keyboard key, or use a window-manager application to change the layout of the screen. An *event message* informs your application that some such thing affecting your application has happened. Essentially, event messages let your application know what both the user and other applications have done at the workstation.

There are a variety of types of events, outlined under the heading "Summary of Event Types." Each application running on the workstation *solicits* event types of interest to it; it informs the workstation that, in the future, it wants to receive event messages notifying it of each occurrence of each solicited event type. The workstation sends an event message to the application whenever each solicited event type occurs.

When the workstation server sends such a message to the client application, it must use an event message rather than a request message—request messages cannot originate at the workstation, according to the rules of the X protocol. Events are more limited than requests in the information they can carry: an event message may contain a single eight-bit field declaring the type of the event (there may be up to 256 distinct event types). In addition to the event type, the event message may contain 248 additional bits (31 eight-bit bytes) of event-specific data. Most events are self-contained: the 248 bits are enough to specify the nature of the event. If 248 bits are not enough, an application can issue one or more round-trip inquiry requests; the workstation returns the rest of the information about the event in reply messages (which can be as long as they need to be).

The section entitled "Events" later in this chapter presents detailed information on how event messages are delivered and how your application reads them.

## Error event messages

The "send-and-forget" nature of one-way request messages presents a problem: what happens when the workstation server detects something wrong with such a request? For example, what happens if you ask the workstation to draw in a nonexistent window? After generating the bad request, the application moves on to other work, and there is no way to return an error-status code in response to the bad request. X solves this problem by using an *error event* message. An error event message is a special type of event message. It reports workstation-detected errors in requests. Error event messages are the same size as other event messages. Their 248 bits of information describe the error.

Most error events are caused by application programming errors. However, some errors can occur when the server is unable to honor a request because it has, for example, used up its memory.

The delay between when you generate the request that causes the error and when you get back an error event message is variable. It depends on how long

- the request waited in your application's *Xlib* buffer to be transmitted
- the buffer took to transmit to the workstation
- the workstation took to detect the error
- the error event message took to transmit back

The details of how *Xlib* and your application process error event messages are described in the "Error Handling" section of this chapter.

# THE XLIB PROCEDURAL INTERFACE

*Xlib* is the subroutine package you use within your application program to interact with an X workstation server. When you call *Xlib*, it generates X protocol requests on your behalf and sends them, over the display connection, to the workstation. An X application programmer is unlikely to be exposed to the X protocol directly; *Xlib* efficiently hides the protocol details.

*Xlib* is a complex and comprehensive package of subroutines. Many of the routines in *Xlib* interface directly to X protocol requests. Others are alternate (usually simplified) ways of generating protocol requests; these are called *convenience functions*. Still others are *service functions*. Service functions carry out local operations such as translating information from one form to another, rather than using the display connection to interact with the server. Informational *macros* let your application find out the connected workstation's capabilities.

All calls to *Xlib* have (with a very few exceptions) a pointer to a **Display** structure as their first argument. The **XOpenDisplay** function creates this **Display** structure as it sets up the display connection. See the section below entitled "The Display Connection" for details. When this book describes an *Xlib* function, the *display* argument is not discussed.

## Header files

All *Xlib* application programs must contain the following **#include** directive; it has necessary symbolic constants, data types, and data structure declarations.

        **#include   <X11/Xlib.h>**

The header file **<X11/Xlib.h>** contains an include directive to the header file **<X11/X.h>**. The latter header file contains further declarations.

You may need to use other header files (for example, **<X11/Xutil.h>**) to support other parts of the *Xlib* interface. They are described in this book along with the requests and functions that make use of them.

## Requests and Convenience Functions

A large number of *Xlib* calls serve as direct interfaces to protocol requests. Such calls accept parameters in formats natural for the CPU running the application (int, unsigned long, and so forth). When we discuss such *Xlib* request functions in this book, we will identify them as such.

Other *Xlib* calls are called convenience functions because, although they generate a protocol request, they support a subset of the entire protocol request using a simpler and more efficient call interface. For example, a foreground pixel value for drawing can be loaded into a graphics context either with **XChangeGC**, a request function, or with **XSetForeground**, a convenience function (see Chapter 5).

## Service Functions

*Xlib* contains a substantial number of calls that do not generate protocol requests at all. Among these are functions that read the event queue (such as **XNextEvent**; see below) and functions to manage data structures within the application (such as **XFree** and **XCreateImage**). *Xlib* calls falling into this category are identified as "functions" when they are discussed in this book.

## Informational Macros and Functions

*Xlib* provides a substantial number of macros and functions that return information describing the characteristics of the workstation. Two commonly used examples of informational macros are **RootWindow** and **DefaultScreen**. Use of these functions can be seen in the example program in Appendix A. Sections 2.2.1-2.2.3 of *Xlib — C Language X Interface* describe the entire set of informational macros and functions. Informational macros and functions are described in this book in conjunction with related requests and functions.

> The proper use of informational macros and functions is critical for developing portable applications. They let your application tailor itself to the characteristics of different workstations.

# THE DISPLAY CONNECTION

All X Window System application programs must establish a display connection on a network circuit between the application process and the workstation.

Most application programs establish a single display connection during initialization and use that connection for as long as they run. However, there is nothing keeping you from using multiple connections to multiple workstations from within a single application (see Chapter 11).

The discussion of display names, environment variables, and operating system commands in this section applies to Unix and compatible operating systems. If you are using some other operating system environment, consult your vendor's documentation.

## The Display Name

The first thing your application needs to know in order to establish a connection to a workstation server is the *display name*: the name identifying the workstation.

On Unix-based systems, the display name to use ordinarily comes from one of two places. First, applications ordinarily search their command-line argument vector for a display-name argument. By convention, a display-name argument is preceded by the string " display."

> Some early X applications used any command-line argument containing a colon as the display name. Avoid this.

If an application cannot find a suitable command-line argument, it specifies an empty string to *Xlib*. *Xlib* then uses the value of the DISPLAY environment variable for a display name. Note that the DISPLAY environment variable is set up automatically when a user logs in to an X workstation running Unix. The implication of this is that users do not ordinarily have to specify the display name when running X applications.

The **helloworld.c** example of Chapter 2, for simplicity, does not look for a display name in its command line argument vector. Rather, it depends on the DISPLAY environment variable.

Display names are text strings of the form "cpu:0", "cpu::0", "cpu:0.1", or "cpu::0.1" which identify the following aspects of the workstation:

a) The host (network node) name of the workstation's computer.

b) The number of the display on the cpu. This display number is usually ":0". However, some vendors supply workstation display hardware that permits multiple workstations per cpu.

c) Optionally, the screen number of the screen (".1") that will be used as the default for the display connection. This option is only useful for multiple-screen workstations. If the display name omits the screen number, screen zero is the default.

   Multiple-screen workstations have one keyboard and one mouse, and are designed to be operated by one user at a time.

d) The type of network to be used to establish the connection. A UDS connection is specified by a host name of *unix* or no host name. A TCP/IP connection is specified by a single colon, and a DECnet connection by a double colon, between the host name and the display number.

Items a, b, and c above select the workstation and screen from among the workstations available on a network. For example, Figure 3-1 shows an example local-area network. Four networked cpus, with node names *one*, *two*, *three*, and *four* are shown. *one* is a file and computation server; it does not have any workstations connected. *two* is an ordinary workstation cpu, such as an Apollo DN3000, a Digital Equipment Corporation VAXstation 2000, or a Sun 3/50. *three* is a cpu which hosts two separate workstation seats. Finally, the cpu named *four* hosts a three-screened workstation.

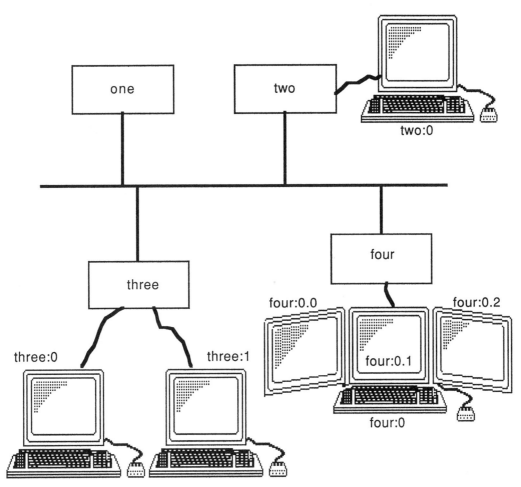

Figure 3-1. Local-area-network configuration.

Each workstation in this example network has a distinct name (*two:0, three:0, three:1,* and *four:0* ). Note that the term *workstation* in this context refers to a single seat; *four:0* only accommodates one interactive user even though it boasts three screens. An application can optionally specify via the display name which screen of a multiple-screen workstation it wants to use. *four:0.2* specifies the right-hand screen of the three-screened workstation in the example.

Users can run X applications on any cpu in this network. Each workstation has an X network server program running on its cpu. *two* and *four* each have a single network server program, while *three* has one for each workstation. Each cpu's job-control software is responsible for running the network server programs, and also for running one X application per workstation—usually a terminal emulator—to allow users to log in.

The form of the display name determines the type of network connection (UDS, TCP/IP, DECnet) as follows:

- If the name is *unix*, or if the name is omitted entirely, the network type is Unix-Domain sockets (UDS). This type of display connection must be local, because UDS only functions within a single cpu.

  For example, an application program running on *two* can access the local workstation using the display names *unix:0* or *:0*. Applications running on *one* cannot use *unix* in their display names; there is no display directly connected to *one*.

- If the workstation's cpu name (hostname or network node name) is followed by a single colon, followed by the workstation number, TCP/IP is used for the display connection.

  For example, an application running on any Unix cpu in the example could use TCP/IP to access the workstation on *two* using the display name *two:0*. An application running on *two* can use either *two:0* or *unix:0* for a display name.

- If the workstation name is followed by two colons, followed by the workstation number, DECnet is used for the connection.

  For example, an application running on *one* could access the second workstation running on *three* via DECnet by specifying *three::1* as the display name.

### Example: Running an application locally

Suppose a user wishes to log in to *three* (from the example above) and run the hypothetical X application **xcad**. The user walks up to the display *three:1* and finds that the cpu's job-control software (specifically, **init(8)** on a Unix-based system) had already run an X terminal emulator. The terminal emulator displays a prompt inviting the user to log in.

The user logs in, first by moving the mouse so the on-screen cursor lies inside the terminal emulator window, then by responding to the login prompts (presumably with a user name and password). During the login process, the terminal emulator creates the DISPLAY environment variable with the value *three:1*.

Upon completing the login process, the user responds to the shell prompt by issuing the command **xcad**. The user does not have to specify the display name on the **xcad** command line, because the display name stored in the DISPLAY variable is appropriate.

### Example: Running an application remotely

Suppose our user decides that the server cpu *one* is more suitable for running **xcad**, due to *one*'s faster computation speed. From his session on *three:1*, he logs in to *one*, possibly via a UNIX network login facility such as **rlogin(1)**. He then proceeds to issue the **xcad** command. This time, however he has to specify *"–display three:1"* on the **xcad** command line, because the display connection is remote. During initialization, **xcad** establishes an X display connection directly to the user's workstation.

An alternative approach for our remote user is explicitly to set the value of the DISPLAY environment variable to *"three:1"*. The method used for setting an environment variable depends on the command shell in use; from **csh(1)** our user issues this command:

    % setenv DISPLAY three:1

Thereafter, he can invoke **xcad** (or any other X application) without specifying the display name explicitly.

The X Window System takes no responsibility for starting applications. The host operating system's job-control software runs the first terminal emulator application on the workstation. Thereafter, the user must use standard techniques for process-creation and application-invocation. Some X applications—such as **uwm(1)**—provide ways of running applications; all such applications do this via standard operating-system services such as **execve(2)**, *not* via services provided by the X Window System.

## Opening the Display Connection

Use the **XOpenDisplay** request in the *Xlib* library to establish a connection to a workstation. **XOpenDisplay** (*Xlib* ¶2.1) has the form

```
Display *mydisplay;       /* current display */
char * display_name;      /* pointer to display name, or NULL */
 . . .
mydisplay = XOpenDisplay ( display_name );
if ( !mydisplay ) {
        fprintf (stderr, "Cannot establish display connection\n" );
     exit(1);
   }
```

**XOpenDisplay** takes a single argument: a pointer to the display name string (NULL-terminated). If *display_name* is a NULL (zero) pointer, or if it points to a character string with no characters in it, **XOpenDisplay** automatically uses (on Unix and compatible systems) the string stored in the DISPLAY environment variable.

**XOpenDisplay** establishes a network circuit connection to the workstation server using the network type specified in the display name. While the connection is being established, your application's *Xlib* software and the workstation exchange configuration data with each other. When the connection is completed, *Xlib* allocates a **Display** structure and fills it in with the configuration data sent by the workstation. Finally, **XOpenDisplay** returns, as its function result, a pointer to the newly filled-in **Display** structure. The section later in this chapter entitled "Display Configuration Information" discusses how to access and use the **Display** structure's contents.

Virtually all other *Xlib* calls require you to provide the display pointer returned by **XOpenDisplay** as the first argument.

Some applications may send output to several different workstations at a time. If you wish to do this, you may open multiple display connections from within a single application program. These connections can be to a single workstation or to multiple workstations. In subsequent *Xlib* calls, you issue requests to one workstation at a time, simply by specifying one display pointer. If you use several simultaneous display connections, there are some implications:

- Your application's event handling will have to be more sophisticated than Chapter 2's **helloworld.c** example; see the section entitled "Event Handling for Multiple Displays" in Chapter 11.

- Your application will have to take care not to confuse resources (such as windows; see below) that belong to different workstations.

On a multiple-screen workstation you may choose to specify a screen number as part of the display name (for example, *four:0.2* specifies screen 2). When you do this, the display connection you establish can still be used for all screens on the workstation. When you specify a screen number, it is treated as the default screen for the purposes of that connection.

If for some reason **XOpenDisplay** does not succeed, it returns a NULL pointer. When **XOpenDisplay** fails it is almost always for one of three reasons:

1) An incorrect or nonexistent display name. Make sure that the display name corresponds to an existing workstation.

2) A permission failure (on a remote connection attempt). See the documentation for the X utility program **xhost(1)**. **xhost** allows you to list which host cpus are authorized to connect to a workstation, and allows you to change the authorized list.

3) System or network problems. Ensure that all cpus involved in the connection are functioning properly and connected to the network.

## Closing the Display Connection

When your application no longer needs a display connection, it should close it using the **XCloseDisplay** request. **XCloseDisplay** (*Xlib* ¶2.5) has the form

```
Display*mydisplay;      /* display to close */
    . . .
XCloseDisplay ( mydisplay );
```

This request gracefully terminates your application's use of the workstation, and properly disposes of all the resources (windows, etc.; see below) your application has created while it was running. It closes the communication circuit to the workstation and releases all the memory (such as the **Display** structure) that *Xlib* was using to maintain the connection.

If your application terminates without calling **XCloseDisplay**, or terminates abnormally (due, for example, to a program bug or a network failure) then the actions of **XCloseDisplay** are carried out automatically.

> Avoid depending on the automatic execution of **XCloseDisplay**—call it explicitly in your application's termination code if possible. On some workstations and networks it can take a long time for the workstation to detect that a client application has "gone away."

If you wish, you may close one display connection and then open another without terminating your application.

# RESOURCES

X applications create, use, and destroy *resources* in the course of their operation. As will become obvious, resources are essential to the way applications interact with workstations. They allow applications to transmit state information, such as window positions and drawing colors, to the workstation just once, then use them repeatedly. Applications manipulate the following types of resources:

**Windows.** These resources are rectangular areas on a workstation's video screen. They let the user view output, and they give applications a rational way of managing the use of space on the screen. Whenever an X application generates visible graphical output, it must specify a particular window to receive that output. With a few exceptions, the workstation generates every input event with respect to some window.

Windows may overlap, and windows may nest inside other windows. X provides your application with many ways of controlling the visibility, nesting, overlapping, size, and color of windows. Chapter 4 describes the X requests for managing windows.

Each screen on a workstation always contains one window, the *root window*, which completely covers it. Root windows are special in that they cannot be created or destroyed. All other windows on a screen nest hierarchically inside the root window.

**Graphic Contexts.** These resources (known as **GC**s) are used to keep track of graphical rendering attributes such as foreground color, background color, line width, line style, text font, and stipple pattern. Every graphical output request must refer to a **GC**. X provides requests to create, alter, and destroy **GC**s. Also provided are a plethora of convenience functions such as **XSetForeground**. Applications can use convenience functions to set up **GC** contents while preparing to generate graphical output. Chapter 5 describes **GC**s and their use in detail.

Each root window has a default **GC** created for it. However, every application that generates graphical output should create one or more **GC**s of its own rather than trying to share **GC**s.

**Fonts**. These resources contain the information necessary to display text in a window. A font describes the size and shape of a collection of characters. X provides requests for creating font resources by loading information from a library of fonts. X also provides requests for displaying text. Chapter 6 describes fonts and textual output.

**Color Maps**. These resources (often known as color lookup tables), translate the graphical information that your application draws to windows into visible screen colors. Chapter 7 goes into detail about the use of color in X.

Each screen has a default color map associated with the root window.

**Pixmaps**. These resources, sometimes known as "hidden display memory," are similar to windows in that an application can generate graphical output to them. They differ from windows in that the user cannot see them directly. Pixmaps are made useful by the X requests for copying information back and forth between windows, Pixmaps, and your application: you can temporarily store complex graphical information in a Pixmap, and copy it into a visible window all at once. Pixmaps are also used to store patterns for use with tiles, hatches, backgrounds, and cursors. Pixmaps are described in Chapter 8.

**Cursors**. These resources describe the shape of the on-screen pointer (often an arrow or large X) which the user can move around by manipulating the mouse. Your application can create cursors with arbitrary shapes and colors, and can associate cursors with windows at will. The pointer is always "in" some window on the screen (the root window, if nothing else); the cursor shape showing at the pointer position depends on the cursor resource associated with that window. Chapter 9 describes cursors.

The default cursor (a large, hollow X) is associated with the root window on each screen. The default cursor cannot be destroyed; however, another cursor can be associated with the root window.

Despite their diverse purposes, all the types of X resources have a great deal in common:

- Resources are resident in the X workstation server. Client application programs create and destroy them, and alter their contents, by using requests to the workstation. The purpose of resources is to allow applications to control the state of the workstation explicitly.

- Resources are referred to in requests from client applications by means of resource identifiers (often called "ids"). All resource identifiers are 32-bit integers. *Xlib* functions for creating resources return the resource id of the created resource to the calling program.

- Resources are shareable among all applications running on a workstation. Each resource on a workstation has a unique resource identifier. Any application that knows the identifier of a particular resource can use, alter or destroy that resource. (However, applications should not share GCs because *Xlib* provides a GC cache that is private to each application.)

  If your application wants to create a resource, then share it with other applications, you must tell those applications the resource identifier explicitly. See "Window Manager Interactions" in Chapter 4 and "Properties" in Chapter 12 for further information.

  Conversely, resources are not shareable between workstations. A window identifier that is meaningful on one workstation will not be valid on any other.

- Resources are created via one-way X requests, not round-trip requests. *Xlib* actually generates a resource identifier based on a block of unused resource identifiers provided to *Xlib* by the workstation when the display connection was opened. *Xlib* inserts the resource id in the message to be sent to the server, and returns it to the application. This one-way creation greatly improves performance.

- Resources are ephemeral. As such, they are not suitable for storage of information between workstation sessions or overnight.

- Resources are cheap. Applications typically use dozens of windows and GCs, several fonts, several pixmaps, and several cursors.

## Controlling Resource Lifetime

Usually, all the resources created during the lifetime of a particular display connection are destroyed automatically when the display connection is closed. Most applications do not bother to destroy their resources explicitly, but merely call **XCloseDisplay** at the end of their session and rely on automatic resource destruction to clean things up.

It is possible, however, for an application to arrange for its resources to be preserved when the display connection is closed. The **XSetCloseDownMode** request may be used to arrange for the preservation of a client's resources when it closes its connection. All resources are destroyed when the user logs out of the workstation—that is, when the last connection closes (although there is a way to circumvent this; see *Xlib* ¶2.6). **XSetCloseDownMode** (*Xlib* ¶7.7.3) has the form

```
Display *mydisplay;      /* display */
int close_mode;          /* close-down mode */
    . . .
XSetCloseDownMode ( mydisplay, close_mode );
```

A subsequent closing of the display connection (via either **XCloseDisplay** or **XKillClient**) causes all the resources created by that client to be dealt with according to *close_mode*. *close_mode* can take the following values (defined in **<X11/X.h>**):

DestroyAll         This *close_mode* is the default case. All resources created by this display connection will be destroyed on a subsequent connection-close.

RetainTemporary    This *close_mode* causes all resources created by this display connection to be marked as temporary when the connection subsequently closes. Such resources are retained until either the last client connection to the workstation is closed (until the user logs out, in other words) or until some other client deletes all the temporary resources by executing a request (see below) of the form

**XKillClient** (*display*, AllTemporary );

RetainPermanent    This *close_mode* causes all resources created by this display connection to be marked as permanent when the connection subsequently closes. Such resources are retained until the user logs out.

Retained resources might be used in applications made up from suites of programs, in which some programs create resources for use by others.

Your application can close the display connection belonging to another application, or dispose of resources left by other applications, by using the **XKillClient** request. The **XKillClient** request is fairly destructive; most applications do not use it, except possibly to dispose of RetainTemporary resources. **XKillClient** (*Xlib* ¶7.7.3) has the form

```
Display *mydisplay;      /* display*/
XID resource;            /* any resource */
    . . .
XKillClient ( mydisplay, resource );
```

This request closes a display connection to any client application. The *resource* identifies the display connection to be closed; you may specify any X resource created by that connection. Ordinarily, you would specify the resource identifier of a window.

If the display connection identified by *resource* has already terminated with a *close_mode* of RetainPermanent or RetainTemporary, this request destroys all the resources the connection left when it terminated.

Instead of a resource identifier, you may specify the value AllTemporary. Specifying this *resource* parameter value causes the demise of all resources left by all previous connection closures with the *close_mode* of RetainTemporary.

## Display Configuration Information

When **XOpenDisplay** sets up a display connection, it fills in the **Display** structure with useful information about the workstation and some of the default resources (such as root windows) available on the workstation. This information is available to application programs via informational macros (for C language programs) and functions (which can be called from other languages than C). This information is useful to applications because it allows them to configure themselves for each make and model of workstation.

Most of the display configuration information applies to particular aspects of the X Window System, and is described in this book in the relevant chapter. For example, Chapter 7 covers X color resources and includes a discussion of the informational macros relating to color. However, a few universally useful informational macros are described here. Functions (for example, **XScreenCount**) corresponding to macros (**ScreenCount**) are provided for use with languages other than C.

## Screens

The **ScreenCount** macro and the **XScreenCount** function (*Xlib* ¶2.2.1) return the number of screens available on the workstation. This information is useful on multiple-screen workstations. If you have a single-screen workstation, the **ScreenCount** value will be zero. The macro and function have the form

```
Display * display;        /* pointer to current display structure */
int screens;
. . .
screens =  XScreenCount ( display ); /* callable function */
screens  =  ScreenCount ( display ); /* macro */
```

The **DefaultScreen** macro and the **XDefaultScreen** function (*Xlib* ¶2.2.1) return a workstation's default screen, given a **Display** pointer. This default screen comes from the default screen number in the display name, if any. The default screen comes in handy for use with other informational functions. The default screen functions have the form

```
Display * display;        /* pointer to current display structure */
int screen;
. . .
```

```
screen =  XDefaultScreen ( display ); /* callable function */
screen =  DefaultScreen ( display );  /* macro */
```

## Root Windows

The **DefaultRootWindow** macro and the **XDefaultRootWindow** function (*Xlib* ¶2.2.1) return the resource identifiers for the root window on the default screen on the specified display. They have the form

```
Display * display;        /* pointer to current display structure */
Window window;
. . .
window =  XDefaultRootWindow ( display ); /* callable function */
window =  DefaultRootWindow ( display ); /* macro */
```

The **RootWindow** macro and the **XRootWindow** function (*Xlib* ¶2.2.1) return the resource identifiers for the root window on the specified screen on the specified display. They have the form

```
int XRootWindow ( Display *, int );
Display * display;        /* pointer to current display structure */
int screen;               /* screen number */
Window window;
. . .
window =  XRootWindow ( display, screen ); /* callable function*/
window =  RootWindow ( display, screen ); /* macro */
```

## Pixel Values

In X, you specify colors on the screen as pixel values. The intricate details of how to use pixel values are described in Chapter 7. However, you must use pixel values to do some very basic things, such as create windows and draw. What the user perceives as different colors on screen are represented within application programs as different pixel values. *Xlib* provides macros and informational functions with which you can retrieve pixel values corresponding to the colors black and white: the **BlackPixel** and **WhitePixel** macros and the corresponding **XBlackPixel** and **XWhitePixel** functions (*Xlib* ¶2.2.1). They require *display* and *screen* parameters (use **DefaultScreen** to get a screen number) and have the form

```
Display * display;        /* pointer to current display structure */
int screen;               /* screen number */
unsigned long black;      /* pixel value for black */
unsigned long white;      /* pixel value for white */
. . .
black =  XBlackPixel ( display, screen ); /* callable function */
. . .
black =  BlackPixel ( display, screen ); /* macro */
```

```
white =   XWhitePixel ( display, screen ); /* callable function */
. . .
white =   WhitePixel ( display,  screen ); /* macro */
```

## Descriptive Information

The **DisplayString** macro and the **XDisplayString** function (*Xlib* ¶2.2.1) return a standard NULL-terminated text string containing the display name of the specified connection. This information is particularly useful for error reporting. The function and macro have the form

```
Display * display;        /* pointer to current display structure */
char * display_name;
. . .
display_name =   XDisplayString ( display ); /* callable function */
display_name =   DisplayString ( display ); /* macro */
```

The **ProtocolVersion**, **ProtocolRevision**, and **VendorRelease** macros return the major (11) and minor revision numbers of the X Window System Protocol being used on the connection, and the vendor release number of the workstation server. **XProtocolVersion**, **XProtocolRevision**, and **XVendorRelease** are the corresponding functions. They have the form

```
Display * display;        /* pointer to current display structure */
int major_version;
int minor_revision;
int release;
. . .
major_version   = XProtocolVersion  ( display );/* function */
major_version   = ProtocolVersion   ( display );/* macro  */
minor_revision  = XProtocolRevision ( display );/* function */
minor_revision  = ProtocolRevision  ( display );/* macro  */
release         = XVendorRelease    ( display );/* function */
release         = VendorRelease     ( display );/* macro  */
```

The **ServerVendor** macro and the **XServerVendor** function (*Xlib* ¶2.2.1) return a standard NULL-terminated text string identifying the vendor of the connected workstation. The function and macro have the form

```
Display * display;        /* pointer to current display structure */
char * vendor_name;
. . .
vendor_name =   XServerVendor ( display ); /* callable function */
vendor_name =   ServerVendor ( display ); /* macro */
```

> For portability, avoid making your application depend on the revision or the workstation vendor.

# EVENTS

While using an application program, a user moves the mouse, presses and releases mouse-buttons, and types on the keyboard. Each of these actions generates a time-stamped *event,* which is delivered via an *event queue* to the application that wants it. This section explains how an application reads and interprets events from the queue.

X encodes all user input as a series of events. An X application receives raw keystroke events, interspersed with events announcing mouse clicks, mouse motion, window visibility, and other things. This low-level processing means an application has to do a lot of work; the application could, if it solicited mouse button events, mouse button events, and keyboard events, have to explicitly process every mouse-button click, mouse movement, and keystroke (including backspaces, line deletes, and new-line characters). The application is entirely responsible for "understanding" these raw events and turning them into meaningful input. Notice that raw X events have a lot in common with a serial terminal in raw (uninterpreted) mode without automatic character echo: both offer great flexibility, but not without a cost in complexity.

For example, an application that uses a double-click of a mouse button to select some object must compare pairs of events as they are read and respond appropriately to two consecutive mouse clicks within a certain amount of time. The art of writing interactive X applications lies in soliciting appropriate events and processing them efficiently.

Your users will thank you if you take care in designing the human interface to your application. Fortunately, a good human interface is usually simple and modular. High-level toolkits are available to ease and standardize the human-interface design chore. These standard high-level facilities are similar in purpose to the Unix *scanf* or *curses* routines for formatted text.

> Even if you only use a toolkit, and never process a single event directly, you will be better off if you understand low level event handling. Your application will be easier to debug, will run faster, and will be a better "team player" when it shares a workstation with other applications. Conclusion: *learn how low-level event handling works!*

If you are used to high-level facilities, the X Window System's events will at first seem very inconvenient to you. Paradoxically, the availability of low level events is a major reason for X's success, because it does not mandate any specific human interface policy (such as double-clicking for object selection) but rather provides enough mechanism so applications have the flexibility to define their own conventions.

A general principle of X is that *an application never receives unsolicited input events.* Events are only delivered to clients that have explicitly solicited them *before* they occur. This is important, in that it lets applications control the number and type of events they receive, and the overhead of processing these events.

For example, most applications never want KeyRelease events, because their human interface does not call for anything to happen when the user lets go of a keyboard key (also because many vendors' keyboards do not reliably report KeyRelease events). Most applications use the **XSelectInput** request (described below) to solicit the events they want from each window they use.

There are a couple of exceptions to the general principle. First, the workstation generates a MappingNotify event and sends it to all programs running on the workstation when any application rearranges the mouse button numbers or keyboard key codes. The handling of MappingNotify events is straightforward when you use the appropriate *Xlib* service function. Second, one application program can send arbitrary events to another, regardless of what events have been solicited by the receiver. However, most applications don't do this.

## Events and Windows

Each event can be thought of as "coming from" a particular window on the display, called the *event window*.

At first glance, the way each direct input event is associated with a window seems simple. The mouse device drives a pointer on the screen, and the pointer always points to a single spot on the screen. Because every spot on the screen is unambiguously in a certain window (possibly the root window, which covers the whole screen) the pointer always points unambiguously to a certain source window. Mouse events "come from" that window, and go to whatever application knows about that window and wants events from it. Keyboard events "come from" a window known as the *focus window*, which is often the window the pointer is in. Given these rules, how does the user work with multiple windows on the screen at the same time? Easy—she points the cursor at the window she wants to work with, and presses the buttons she wants to press.

In real life the situation is not so simple, however. For one thing, applications often use nested groups of windows that appear, move around, and disappear as needed. Windows are a convenient way to draw output and receive input. For that reason, most applications use a large number of nested windows. Each item in a menu is, for example, usually a separate window.

Your application can modify event delivery. For example, you can specify that you want mouse events delivered to some window other than the source window; this makes input handling more complicated, but it also lets your application be modular. The various X toolkits make extensive use of subwindows.

## Summary of Event Types

The X Window System (without extensions) provides 33 distinct event types.

## Mouse and Keyboard Events

Five distinct event types can be generated when the user manipulates the mouse. See Chapter 9 for details on how to solicit these events and how to use them.

**ButtonPress**   The user pressed a mouse button
**ButtonRelease** The user released a mouse button
**MotionNotify**  The mouse moved (via user or request)
**EnterNotify**   The mouse entered a window (via user or request)
**LeaveNotify**   The mouse left a window (via user or request)

Six distinct event types are used for controlling and getting input from the workstation keyboard. These event types are described in detail in Chapter 10.

**KeyPress**       The user pressed a key
**KeyRelease**     The user released a key
**FocusIn**        A window gained the keyboard focus
**FocusOut**       A window lost the keyboard focus
**MappingNotify**  An application reconfigured the keyboard
**KeymapNotify**   State of keyboard after EnterNotify and FocusIn

All five mouse-related event types and the first four keyboard-related event types are direct input events. Each direct input event specifies

- What happened (the event type)
- The resource id of the event window
- The resource id of the root window of the event window
- The id of the child window of the event window containing the pointer
- When the event happened (the timestamp)
- The cursor x,y position at the time of the event
- The mouse button number or key number (if relevant)
- The up/down state of all mouse buttons and keyboard modifier (shift, shift lock, control, and meta) keys right before the event

For further details on the handling of mouse and keyboard events, see chapters 9, 10, and 11.

## Window and Graphics Events

Five different event types are used to inform your application when it has to take special action to draw or redraw the graphics in windows or portions of windows, or to inform it of configuration changes relating to graphics.

**VisibilityNotify** A window became newly visible or invisible (Ch. 4)
**Expose**           A window, or portion of window, became visible (Ch. 5)
**GraphicsExpose**   Source area unavailable during area copy (Ch. 5)
**NoExpose**         Source area available during area copy (Ch. 5)
**ColormapNotify**   Window's color map created, installed, uninstalled (Ch. 7)

VisibilityNotify, Expose, and ColormapNotify events are, like most events, so-licited using the **XSelectInput** request. GraphicsExpose and NoExpose events are solicited by setting a **GC** attribute. For further information see Chapter 5 un-der the "Copying Areas" heading.

## Client Communication Events

The following event types are used by facilities within X that permit applications to communicate, indirectly through the workstation server, with one another. ClientMessage events are described at the end of Chapter 4. The other types of client communication events are described in Chapter 12.

| | |
|---|---|
| **ClientMessage** | Result of **XSendEvent** requests |
| **PropertyNotify** | Signals property changes on a window |
| **SelectionClear** | Reported when a window loses selection ownership |
| **SelectionRequest** | Reports a selection conversion request |
| **SelectionNotify** | Reports completion of a selection conversion |

## Window Notification Events

These event types are used to keep track of changes to the layout of windows on the screen. These event types are described at the end of Chapter 4.

| | |
|---|---|
| **CirculateNotify** | A window was circulated (raised or lowered) |
| **ConfigureNotify** | A window was redimensioned, moved, restacked |
| **CreateNotify** | A (sub) window was created |
| **DestroyNotify** | A window was destroyed |
| **GravityNotify** | A window was moved because its parent was resized |
| **MapNotify** | A window became mapped |
| **ReparentNotify** | The parent of a window changed |
| **UnmapNotify** | A window became unmapped |

## Window Redirection Events

These event types are used by window-manager applications to intercept certain attempts to change the window layout. These event types are listed here for com-pleteness, but they are beyond the scope of this book.

| | |
|---|---|
| **CirculateRequest** | Attempt to circulate (raise, lower) a window |
| **ConfigureRequest** | Attempt to reconfigure a window |
| **MapRequest** | Attempt to map a window |
| **ResizeRequest** | Attempt to change a window's size |

## Soliciting Events

If your application wants to receive events of a particular type, you must solicit their delivery ahead of time. Events are delivered via windows (discussed in more detail in Chapter 4). You select the event types you want delivered to your application from each window by setting the *event_mask* attribute of that window (for a discussion of window attributes, see "Characteristics and Attributes" in Chapter 4). You can do one of several equivalent things to solicit events:

- Use the **XSelectInput** function to set the *event_mask* directly

- Set the *event_mask* while creating the window with the **XCreate-Window** request (see Chapter 4).

- Change the *event_mask* with the **XChangeWindowAttributes** request (see chapter 4).

You can also arrange to receive events by issuing a *grab* request (see Chapter 11).

You may want to change your event solicitation dynamically. For example, when the user is dragging an object around the screen, you will want detailed mouse motion events. At other times you may only care when the user moves the mouse-pointer out of the window. Thus, you might dynamically enable and disable MotionNotify events.

The easiest way of enabling and disabling solicitation for events is to use the **XSelectInput** convenience function. **XSelectInput** accepts a window identifier and an event selection mask. It has the form

```
Display        *display;     /* current display */
Window         eventwin;     /* input window */
long           *event_mask;  /* desired event mask */
. . .
XSelectInput ( display, eventwin, event_mask );
```

You may call **XSelectInput** for any window. You may call it repeatedly, whenever you want to change your event solicitation for a window, without degrading performance. *event_mask* is a 32-bit mask, where each bit specifies a particular event type and the circumstances under which it should be delivered. The bits for the event selection mask are named in the header file **<X11/X.h>**. There is no one-to-one relationship between the event selection mask bits and event types. Each mask bit has a specific meaning which is intimately related to the meaning of the related event types. For this reason, the event selection mask bits are not described here, but rather in the chapters which cover the specifics of each kind of event. See Table 3-I for a summary of *event_mask* bits.

In principle, you can request events for any window on the workstation. Each application has a separate *event_mask* selection for each window. If more than one application selects an event from a single window, they all get the event. However, you should probably refrain from selecting events from other applications' windows.

The presence of a bit in the *event_mask* argument of **XSelectInput** solicits event delivery, and the absence disables it. There is no direct way to solicit one new event type and keep the others as they were. Thus, if you are dynamically enabling and disabling certain events, you have to use a variable to keep track of the others, and make sure your *event_mask* parameter includes the logical OR of them all. If you don't do this, you may accidentally disable an event. The way this book is organized—with mouse and keyboard events described in separate chapters—may contribute to your making this error, so be careful.

The *event_mask* is actually a window attribute, and can also be set or changed with **XCreateWindow** and **XChangeWindowAttributes** requests (see under the heading "Characteristics and Attributes" in Chapter 5. As a matter of fact, **XSelectInput** is not a request, but rather is a convenience function. *Xlib* uses the **XChangeWindowAttributes** request to transmit **XSelectInput** operations to the workstation.

## Asynchronous Event Generation

As the user causes events, the events are sent asynchronously to the applications that have solicited them. Events are delivered *when and in the order they occur*. For example, if the user presses a key and then moves the mouse, the workstation delivers the KeyPress event before the MotionNotify event. This is true

regardless of what the application is doing at the moment the events actually occur. As they are delivered to the application, the events are placed in a queue.

## Accepting Events from the Event Queue

Even though events are *delivered* as they occur, your application usually *accepts* them synchronously (for example, at the top of the main loop of your program). Between delivery and acceptance, events wait in the queue. Each application has a single queue of its own (one queue per workstation connection if it uses several at the same time). Your application usually reads events from the queue in the same order they were delivered by using the **XNextEvent** function. Other X queue-management functions, such as **XWindowEvent** and **XPeekEvent**, allow you to read events from the queue out of order.

Event handling has a complication: all one-way X requests are accumulated in a buffer and sent to the workstation in batches. **XNextEvent** and related requests automatically flush the buffer—cause its contents to be transmitted to the workstation—before checking the display connection for input events.

There is a second complication: what should your application do if there are no input events waiting in your queue? Often, you want to simply "block execution," or just wait until an input event arrives. Sometimes, however, you will not want to block execution, but rather continue doing something else. Some requests, such as **XEventsQueued**, let you look at the queue and see how many events are waiting. Table 3-II summarizes the X requests for manipulating the event queue.

**XNextEvent** and **XEventsQueued** are the commonly-used functions for retrieving events from the queue, so they are discussed in this section. **XFlush**, **XSync** and **XSynchronize** are functions that control *Xlib*'s output queue; they

| *event_mask* Bit Name | Event Type | Description |
|---|---|---|
| StructureNotifyMask | CirculateNotify, ConfigureNotify, DestroyNotify, GravityNotify, MapNotify, ReparentNotify, UnmapNotify | StructureNotifyMask solicits all window notification event types except CreateEvent. See Chapter 4. |
| SubstructureNotifyMask | CirculateNotify, CreateNotify, ConfigureNotify, DestroyNotify, GravityNotify, MapNotify, ReparentNotify, UnmapNotify | StructureNotifyMask solicits all window notification event types, for all subwindows of the specified window. See Chapter 4. |
| VisibilityChangeMask | VisibilityNotify | Events when visiblity changes (Ch. 4) |
| ExposureMask | Expose | Events when windows need redrawing (Ch. 5) |
| ColormapChangeMask | ColormapNotify | Events when colormaps change (Ch. 7) |
| ButtonPressMask | ButtonPress | Events when mouse buttons pressed (Ch. 9) |
| OwnerGrabButtonMask | — | Modifier for ButtonPressMask |
| ButtonReleaseMask | ButtonRelease | Events when mouse buttons released (Ch. 9) |
| PointerMotionMask | MotionNotify | Events when pointer moves in window (Ch. 9) |
| ButtonMotionMask | MotionNotify | Events when pointer moves with any button pressed |
| Button1MotionMask | MotionNotify | Events when pointer moves with Button 1 pressed |
| Button2MotionMask | MotionNotify | Events when pointer moves with Button 2 pressed |
| Button3MotionMask | MotionNotify | Events when pointer moves with Button 3 pressed |
| Button4MotionMask | MotionNotify | Events when pointer moves with Button 4 pressed |
| Button5MotionMask | MotionNotify | Events when pointer moves with Button 5 pressed |
| PointerMotionHintMask | — | Modifier for all MotionNotify solicitations |
| EnterWindowMask | EnterNotify | Events when pointer enters window (Ch. 9) |
| LeaveWindowMask | LeaveNotify | Events when pointer leaves window |
| KeyPressMask | KeyPress | Events when keyboard keys pressed (Ch. 10) |
| KeyReleaseMask | KeyRelease | Events when keyboard keys released (Ch. 10) |
| FocusChangeMask | FocusIn, FocusOut | Events when keyboard focus changes (Ch. 10) |
| KeymapStateMask | KeymapNotify | Keymap events right after EnterNotify, FocusIn |
| PropertyChangeMask | PropertyNotify | Events when property data changes |

Table 3-I. *event_mask* bit names and event types.

are discussed in the next section. All the other queue-manipulation calls mentioned in Table 3-II are discussed in Chapter 11.

If you can structure your applications with a main loop, as shown in the **helloworld.c** example of Chapter 2, buffer flushing and execution blocking will be handled for you automatically and transparently. As Table 3-II shows, most of *Xlib*'s queue-management calls flush the output buffer on demand. That is, they flush only immediately before they use an operating system call to retrieve more events from the display connection, not necessarily before they return each event to the caller.

| Request | Flushes? | Blocks? | Description |
|---|---|---|---|
| **XNextEvent** | demand | yes | Reads first event in queue |
| **XEventsQueued** | (option) | no | Tells how many events are waiting |
| **XFlush** | yes | no | Flushes the output buffer |
| **XSync** | yes | yes | Flushes, waits for responses |
| **XSynchronize** | yes | no | Disables and enables request buffering |
| **XCheckWindowEvent** | demand | no | Get events from a certain window |
| **XCheckMaskEvent** | demand | no | Get certain event types |
| **XCheckTypedEvent** | demand | no | Get a certain event type |
| **XCheckTypedWindowEvent** | demand | no | Get a certain event type and window |
| **XWindowEvent** | demand | yes | Gets events from a certain window |
| **XMaskEvent** | demand | yes | Gets certain event types |
| **XCheckIfEvent** | demand | no | Gets event selected by a function |
| **XPeekIfEvent** | demand | yes | Copies event selected by a function |
| **XIfEvent** | demand | yes | Gets event selected by a function |
| **XPutBackEvent** | no | no | Puts an event back on the queue |
| **XSendEvent** | no | no | Sends an event for redelivery |

Table 3-II.   X Queue Management Functions

## XNextEvent

Use **XNextEvent** to read the event at the head of your display connection's queue (the oldest one waiting).  Whenever **XNextEvent** must read new events from the display connection, it first flushes out any remaining buffered output requests. This is convenient, because it means that simple applications structured with a main loop (such as **helloworld.c** from Chapter 2) need never concern themselves with buffer flushing.

If no events are waiting when you call **XNextEvent**, it does not return until the workstation delivers one.  **XNextEvent** (*Xlib* ¶8.8.1) has the form

```
Display*mydisplay;      /* current display */
XEvent myevent;         /* event storage */
    . . .
XNextEvent ( mydisplay, &myevent );
```

Chapter 2 shows an example of the use of **XNextEvent**.  Other chapters discuss the mouse, the keyboard, expose events, and other events.  The details of what to do with each type of event are discussed in the appropriate chapters.

## XEventsQueued

Use the function **XEventsQueued** to find out how many events are waiting to be read from the queue.  **XEventsQueued** has a *mode* parameter allowing you to control whether *Xlib* flushes the output buffer for you, and whether it performs a system call to get more events from the display connection.  **XEventsQueued** never blocks execution.  If no events are waiting, it returns a value of zero. **XEventsQueued** (*Xlib* ¶8.7) replaces **QLength** and **XPending** from earlier X versions.  It has the form

```
Display *mydisplay;
int mode;
int count;
    . . .
count = XEventsQueued ( mydisplay, mode );
```

Specify one of the following three symbolic values (defined in **<X11/Xlib.h>**) for the *mode* parameter:

QueuedAlready         If you specify this *mode* value, **XEventsQueued** does not perform any system calls, either to flush the output buffer or to get events that have been sent to your application's *Xlib* by the workstation, but not yet retrieved from the display connection. **XEventsQueued** is fastest when you use this mode, but it may falsely tell you that no events are waiting to be processed.

QueuedAfterReading    If you specify this *mode* value, **XEventsQueued** does not flush the output buffer. If any events already have been read from the display connection, it returns the count of those events. If no events remain, it performs a system call to read more events (if any) from the display connection.

QueuedAfterFlush      If you specify this *mode* value, **XEventsQueued** works as it does in QueuedAfterReading, but flushes the output buffer immediately before it reads events from the display connection.

Regardless of the *mode*, **XEventsQueued** does not perform any system calls when it finds previously-read events waiting in *Xlib*'s event queue.

---

**Example**: Background operations

One thing you might do with **XEventsQueued** is decide whether to carry out a low-priority background computation. You can put an **XEventsQueued** operation in your main loop. Then, when **XEventsQueued** returns zero (when there are no events from the workstation waiting to be processed) you can perform the background processing. Notice that we do an explicit **XFlush** call (see the next section) immediately before the background computation, rather than specifying an **XEventsQueued** *mode* of QueuedAfterFlush; this strategy improves performance because we avoid flushing *Xlib*'s buffers except when necessary.

```
Display * mydisplay;
XEvent myevent;
int done;

    . . .
/*  main loop  */
```

```
done = 0;
while ( done == 0 ) {
  if ( XEventsQueued (mydisplay, QueuedAfterReading)==0 )
    {
    XFlush ( mydisplay );
    /* do a background computation */
    . . .
  }
  XNextEvent ( mydisplay, &myevent );
  switch (myevent.type)  {
    /* event-handling */
    . . .
  }
}
```

## Explicit Control of the Request Buffer

All the X functions for reading queue elements automatically flush the request buffer immediately before they retrieve events from the display connection. This is important: the screen should be updated with the latest output before events are read, because the way events are delivered depends on the window configuration on the screen. Also, it is possible for one or more of the buffered output requests to cause events directly.

You often need to control the request buffer explicitly. **XFlush, XSync,** and **XSynchronize** are all service functions for controlling various aspects of *Xlib*'s buffering.

## XFlush—Force Buffer Transmission

Applications that start delays without looking at the event queue should use **XFlush. XFlush** causes all buffered one-way X request messages to be transmitted to the workstation server. Note that queue-reading operations such as **XNextEvent** automatically call **XFlush** before reading the queue. **XFlush** used by itself merely sends the buffered requests to the workstation, and does not wait for the workstation to finish processing them. If you call **XFlush** when the buffer is already empty, no harm is done. Excessive use of **XFlush** calls can reduce performance by preventing effective buffering of commands, however.

Forgetting to flush the output buffer before a programmed delay is the most common novice programming error in X, especially in quick-and-dirty programs that do not use event input. When you make this mistake, the workstation seems to "lose" the most recent graphics output requests. The automatic-flush action of **XNextEvent** can lull an unwary programmer into thinking that output buffering is completely transparent. It is not.

> Be sure to call **XFlush** before any long computation, standard input or output operation, timed wait (**sleep**), or program exit.

**XFlush** (*Xlib* ¶8.6) has the form

```
Display *mydisplay;      /* current display */
. . .
XFlush ( mydisplay );
```

## XSync—Wait for Buffer Execution to Complete

**XSync** flushes the request buffer and blocks execution until the workstation finishes processing everything in the buffer. Using **XSync**, you can optionally discard all events on the queue (note that this is a drastic and destructive action in a running application, and would only be used to implement an Abort function, or a function for changing some sort of major mode). Use **XSync** when you want to be sure one operation is finished before starting the next. For example, you might use **XSync** to give the appearance of blinking. First draw something in a window, next use **XSync** to make sure the user gets a chance to see it, then clear the window. Use **XSync** sparingly. It can hurt performance if you use it too much.

**XSync** (*Xlib* ¶8.6) takes a single *discard* argument which, if nonzero, causes all events on the queue to be discarded. The request has the form

```
Display *mydisplay; /* current display */
int discard;          /* 1=discard all events,  0 =don't discard */
. . .
XSync ( mydisplay,  discard );
```

## XSynchronize—Enable and Disable Buffering

To simplify debugging, you can choose to use X in synchronous mode, completely disabling output buffering. The **XSynchronize** function enables and disables synchronous mode: it makes *Xlib* flush the request buffer and wait for the workstation to respond to all requests. (**XSync**, on the other hand, causes a single syncronization.) **XSynchronize** (*Xlib* ¶8.12.1) has the form

```
Display *mydisplay;      /* current display */
int sync;                /* 1=disable all buffering,  0 = buffer normally*/
. . .
XSynchronize ( mydisplay,  sync );
```

If you use X in synchronous mode you will notice a drastic effect on performance: output-intensive X applications can run as much as *thirty times slower* without the benefit of buffering.

On Unix and compatible systems, *Xlib* provides a global symbol "_Xdebug". If you use a debugger to set this symbol to non-zero before starting your application, you can force synchronization without adding the **XSynchronize** call to your application program. If possible, use the "_Xdebug" symbol rather than the

**XSynchronize** call, to help you avoid leaving your application running in synchronous mode after you have finished debugging it.

# ERROR HANDLING

This section describes the *Xlib* facilities for handling error event messages. Error event messages are generated by the workstation and sent to your application when the workstation encounters a request with an error in it, or a request which cannot be processed for some other reason.

Error event messages are generated asynchronously by the workstation. They are sent to your application when they are generated. *Xlib* handles them, by calling an *error event handler*, immediately upon receipt. Error events are not placed in your application's event queue. If you want to receive error events you may establish your own error event handler.

See section 8.10.2 of *Xlib—C Language X Interface* for further details.

## Error Codes

Table 3-III shows the symbolic error codes (defined in **<X11/X.h>**). A glance at the table makes it clear that most of the possible errors (BadWindow, BadPixmap, BadAtom, BadCursor, BadFont, BadDrawable, BadColor, BadGC) have the purpose of announcing that your program specified some X resource identifier incorrectly. Other error codes (BadValue, BadMatch, BadAccess, BadIDChoice, and BadName) diagnose other problems with your program's use of *Xlib* calls. If your application receives any error events with these error codes, you should suspect a problem with your program.

The BadAlloc error code tells you that some resource in the workstation (probably memory) has been used up. If you receive an error event with the BadAlloc code, you should suspect that some application running on the workstation (possibly your application, but also possibly some other) has created an excessive number of resources (windows, GCs, cursors, fonts, or colormaps).

The remaining error codes (BadRequest, BadLength, and BadImplementation) are signs of system trouble with your *Xlib* software, your communication link, or your workstation server software.

```
X Error: parameter not a Window
   Request major code 2
   Request minor code
   Resource ID 0x1c900
   Error Serial #121
   Current Serial #127
```

Figure 3-2. Default Error Handler Message Example

## The Default Xlib Error Event Handler

The *Xlib* package provides, by default, a subroutine for handling error events. The default error handler formats the information in the event and displays it in ASCII on the standard error device — **stderr** on Unix and compatible systems. It then stops your application program. Figure 3-2 shows an example of the ASCII error message which the default error handler generates. The message contains the error code description and the major and minor request codes (each separate X request has a distinct major code; the minor code is used only in extensions).

Unfortunately it is difficult to translate the request's major code into the name of the offending request without recourse to the X protocol specification. The header file **<X11/Xproto.h>** (unused by X application programs for other purposes) contains the definitions of the major request codes. These definitions are also shown in Appendix B.

The error message also specifies the resource identifier of the resource involved (in hexadecimal). If the error code tells you that you specified an invalid resource identifier, the message displays the offending resource identifier.

The last two lines of the error message display the serial number of the erroneous request and the serial number of the current request. *Xlib* assigns a unique serial number to each request issued on a display connection (starting with one). You can use the difference between the error serial number and the current serial number to help you figure out which application request actually caused the error. Alternatively, you can use the **XSynchronize** function (or set the "_Xdebug" variable to nonzero with a debugger; see earlier in this chapter) to make sure that X reports every error event immediately after you issue the offending request.

## Application-Defined Error Event Handling

It is difficult for application programs to recover from error events and keep running. This is because most errors result either from bugs in application code or conditions outside the control of applications. Therefore, most applications will not be able to take advantage of *Xlib*'s ability to let you substitute your own error handler in place of the default. There are two situations in which you might want to define your own error handler:

- If you want to format the error event messages in your own way, or display them somewhere other than on the standard error device

- If you want to allow your application to continue execution after some or all error events, or if you must carry out application-specific shutdown procedures (such as saving files)

| Error  Code | Error   Description |
|---|---|
| BadWindow | parameter not a Window |
| BadPixmap | parameter not a Pixmap |
| BadAtom | parameter not an Atom |
| BadCursor | parameter not a Cursor |
| BadFont | parameter not a Font |
| BadDrawable | parameter not a Pixmap or Window |
| BadAlloc | insufficient  resources |
| BadColor | no such colormap |
| BadGC | parameter not a GC |
| BadValue | integer parameter out of range |
| BadMatch | parameter  mismatch |
| BadAccess | depending on context: |
| | - key/button already grabbed |
| | - invalid attempt to free a color map entry |
| | - attempt to store into a read-only color map entry |
| | - invalid attempt to modify the access control list |
| BadIDChoice | choice not in range or already used |
| BadName | font or color name doesn't exist |
| BadRequest | bad request code |
| BadLength | request length incorrect |
| BadImplementation | server is defective |
| Success | everything's okay (ignore this  error  event) |

Table 3-III.  X Error Code Symbols

## Error Event Handler Functions

If you do decide to define your own error event handler, you must write it as an integer function with two parameters, a **Display** pointer and an **XErrorEvent** structure pointer.  Figure 3-3 shows an example application-defined error handler coded in C.

This particular example error handler uses the **XGetErrorText** function to look up the text associated with the error code.  It then displays the error code on the standard error device.  Finally it returns, allowing the application to continue running.  Your error event handler should only return to its caller if you want your application to continue running after the error.

The function value returned by your error event handler should always be zero.

> Do not issue any requests to or perform any other actions on the display connection from within an error event handler.

```
int myhandler ( mydisplay, myerr )
Display * mydisplay;
XErrorEvent * myerr ;
{
    char msg [80];
    XGetErrorText ( mydisplay, myerr ->error_code, msg, 80 );
    fprintf ( stderr,"Error code %s\n", msg );
    return 0;
}
```

Figure 3-3.  Example Error Event Handler.

## XErrorEvent  Structure

The second parameter to the error-handler function is a pointer to an **XErrorEvent** structure. **<X11/Xlib.h>** defines this structure as follows:

```
typedef struct {
    int type;                      /* Event type (0=error event) */
    Display * display;             /* Display the event was read from */
    XID resourceid;                /* Resource id */
    int serial;                    /* Serial number of failed request */
    unsigned char error_code;      /* Error code of failed request */
    unsigned char request_code;    /* Major op-code of failed request */
    unsigned char minor_code;      /* Minor op-code of failed request */
} XErrorEvent;
```

See Appendix B, or the **<X11/Xproto.h>** header file, for the meanings of the values in the "request_code" field.

### Selecting an Error Event Handler

Most applications define just one error event handler and use **XSetErrorHandler** during initialization to select it.  You may define as many different error event handler functions as you wish, but only one may be in effect in your application program at any given time (even if you have several display connections).  Use the **XSetErrorHandler** function, as follows, to put one of your error event handlers into effect.  Each call to **XSetErrorHandler** overrides any setting made by any previous call.

```
XSetErrorHandler ( myhandler );
```

If you specify the value None to **XSetErrorHandler** in place of the pointer to the error handler procedure, the *Xlib* default error handler will be reestablished. Note that the first argument to **XSetErrorHandler** is *not* a **Display** pointer.

```
int myIOhandler ( mydisplay )
Display * mydisplay ;
{
    fprintf ( stderr,   "Fatal Error on X Display %s\n",
                    XDisplayName  ( mydisplay ) );
    exit  (1);
}
```

Figure 3-4.  Example I/O Error Handler

## Fatal I/O Error Handling

*Xlib* supplies a default handler for another category of error—input/output (I/O) or system call errors in *Xlib*. *Xlib* also gives you a way to substitute your own I/O error handler in place of the default.

An I/O error can result when *Xlib* software makes operating system calls to do things such as write buffers of data to a network communication circuit.  All I/O errors are fatal; your application program cannot continue if *Xlib* gets one of these errors.  There are several common things that cause I/O errors:

- An attempt to establish a connection to a nonexistent workstation

- A failure to establish a workstation connection due to insufficient access permission

- Computer system trouble or network trouble

The default I/O error handler uses standard system facilities (**perror(3)** on Unix and compatible systems) to display system error messages.

## I/O Error Handler Functions

If you do decide to define your own I/O error handler, you must write it as an integer function with a single parameter, a **Display** pointer.  Figure 3-4 shows an example application-defined I/O error handler coded in C.

This example error handler uses the **XDisplayName** function to look up the text name of the workstation display.  It prints a message containing the name of the display on the standard error device and exits.  Your I/O error event handler should not return to its caller.

## Selecting an I/O Error Handler

You may define as many I/O error handler functions as you wish.  However, only one may be in effect in your application program at any given time (even if you have several display connections).

Use the **XSetIOErrorHandler** function, as follows, to put one of your handlers into effect.  Each call to **XSetIOErrorHandler** overrides any setting made by any previous call.

**XSetIOErrorHandler  (**  *myIOhandler*  **);**

If you specify the value None to **XSetIOErrorHandler** in place of the pointer to the error handler procedure, the *Xlib* default error handler will be reestablished. Note that the first argument to **XSetIOErrorHandler** is *not* a **Display** pointer.

# SUMMARY

The X Window System is defined in terms of a *network protocol*. The network protocol specifies the format and meaning of messages passed over a *display connection* between application and workstation. Although applications may use any means to generate X protocol messages, C programs gain access to X workstations by calling the *Xlib* procedural interface (subroutine package). *Xlib* is the subject of this book.

The X protocol provides four kinds of messages for communications between application and workstation. The most common message type is the *one-way request*. Almost everything an application does (for example, drawing) on a workstation generates a one-way request. *Xlib* assembles consecutive one-way requests into *buffers* and transmits them in batches to improve performance. Applications send one-way requests, then forget about them and go on to other work. The workstation carries out one-way requests in order as it receives them.

*Round-trip requests* are used by applications for informational queries, such as finding out the size of a window. Applications originate round-trip requests. The workstation carries them out immediately and generates a reply. Round-trip requests can degrade performance, because *Xlib* cannot assemble them into buffered batches. Whereas applications originate requests, workstations originate *events* and *error events*, to inform applications of user actions and errors in requests.

All X applications begin execution by using *Xlib*'s **XOpenDisplay** call to establish a display connection. By specifying the appropriate *display name*, an application can establish a display connection, to a workstation on the same cpu, or to a workstation on a remote cpu. This capability for remote display connections provides X's *network transparency*. By using the appropriate form of display name, an application can specify the workstation's cpu, the type of communication *network* (Unix-Domain sockets, TCP/IP, or DECnet) to use, and the display and screen to use.

Once a display connection is established, applications interact with workstations by manipulating *resources*, including *windows, graphic contexts, fonts, color maps, pixmaps*, and *cursors*. These resources are resident in the workstation. They give a way for the application to load useful *state information*, such as window positions and drawing colors, into the workstation. The correct use of resources is central to the functioning of an X application. All resources are referred to by means of *resource identifers*:  32-bit integers containing unique identifying values.

Resources can be shared among applications running on a workstation. Ordinarily, resources continue to exist as long as their creating application keeps its display connection open. It is possible for applications to arrange for their resources to outlive them. Resources are ephemeral, however: in no event do they continue to exist after the end of a user's logged-in session on the workstation.

All workstations contain some pre-existing resources, such as root windows. Applications can use *informational macros* to find out the resource identifiers for the pre-existing resources. Informational macros are also useful for finding out other workstation-dependent display configuration parameters, such as the appropriate *pixel values* to use for drawing in black and white. If applications are to be portable, they must make proper use of this display configuration information.

X workstations let the application know about user-induced actions such as key presses and mouse motion by means of events. Events are also used to report application-induced changes to the workstation's display. Events report all kinds of actions, ranging from from mouse button presses to changes in window visibility to changes in color maps.

One of the most important types of events, the Expose event type, informs an application that it must redraw the contents of a window. A well-written X application processes events in a modeless way, in any order. Typically, a user uses many different application programs simultaneously. Expose events allow application programs to find out when their windows have been *damaged* (covered, then uncovered) by other windows. X applications must respond to Expose events by redrawing windows (see Chapter 5).

*Events come from windows.* With a very few exceptions, *applications only receive event types if they solicit them beforehand*, using the **XSelectInput** call or the equivalent. The workstation delivers events to applications *in the order they occur*.

Events wait in an application *event queue* between the time the workstation delivers them and the time the application accepts them. *Xlib* provides several ways of accepting events and removing them from the event queue. The most useful call for accepting events is **XNextEvent**. Often, applications contain a main loop with **XNextEvent** at the top of the loop. Applications can use **XEventsQueued** to determine how many events, if any, remain unprocessed in the event queue.

As described previously, *Xlib* saves one-way X requests in a buffer for transmission in batches. Applications using a main loop topped by **XNextEvent** do not have to do anything explicit to control *Xlib*'s request buffer, because **XNextEvent** automatically sends the buffer's contents when necessary. However, any application can explicitly *flush* its request buffer (send its contents to the workstation) by calling **XFlush**.

Applications can use **XSync** to *synchronize* the application and workstation: to flush the request buffer and wait for the workstation to complete all requests.

**XSync** synchronizes just once each time it is called. Applications can also use **XSynchronize** to put *Xlib* into *synchronous mode*, in which *Xlib* automatically waits for the completion of every request. (On Unix and compatible systems, setting the variable "_Xdebug" to a nonzero value has the same effect.) Synchronous mode severely degrades performance, but it makes debugging much simpler.

Because X allows applications to send requests to the workstation in batches, most *Xlib* calls do not return a success or failure status immediately. Instead, the workstation carries out the requests when it receives them. If the workstation detects an error in a request, it sends an error event message back to the application which generated the offending request. *Xlib* provides a default error event handler which prints the particulars of an error and stops the applcation. *Xlib* provides a way for application programs to define and use custom error event handlers. Custom error event handlers allow applications to recover from errors. *Xlib* also provides a way for application programs to define their own system (I/O) error handlers.

# CHAPTER 4
# WINDOWS

This chapter describes windows and how to create and manipulate them. In the X Window System, a window is a rectangular area on the screen of a workstation. Windows are the means by which X organizes a great many aspects of the workstation's operation, including graphical output as well as input from the workstation's mouse and keyboard.

The structure of the X Window System encourages applications to use many windows. In X, windows are plentiful and inexpensive. They make it easy for applications to organize the workstation screen into areas for particular purposes, such as text display, graphical display, and menus.

The first section of this chapter, "Windows and the Desktop Model," introduces some of the concepts behind windows. It introduces X's hierarchically organized windows, and discusses how a user perceives windows on the screen. The primary purpose of this section is to explain what your application is trying to accomplish when you use windows.

The second section, "Windows Made Simple," serves as a relatively painless introduction to programming an application to work with windows. It takes you through the various phases of a window's existence: creation, mapping, unmapping and destruction.

Once we understand the life cycle of windows, we can start manipulating them in interesting ways. "Window Configuration" explains how to change the sizes of windows and stack them on top of one another.

With "Attributes and Characteristics," we dive into the details of X's window capability. This section explains all the options an application can choose for each window.

"Advanced Window Manipulation" explains the X requests for allowing your application to take advantage of the full capabilities of windows.

Most users use a window-manager application to help them organize their workstation's screen. "Window Manager Interactions" explains what your application can do to cooperate with and make good use of the window manager.

Most X applications are made up of hierarchies of windows and subwindows. One of the most interesting parts of programming an application for X is dealing with the fact that users can, with the help of a window manager, arbitrarily change the size and shape of the windows at the top level of your application's window hierarchy. "Window Sizing Strategies" discusses some ways to deal with this problem.

Finally, "Notification Events" discusses how your application can find out about changes to windows. You can solicit events from the workstation to inform you of virtually any change to windows in your window hierarchy.

## WINDOWS AND THE DESKTOP MODEL

A workstation's video screen is large and can display a great deal of information. To make good use of the capabilities of an engineering workstation, a user must be able to organize all this information visually. X allows this by dividing up the screen into windows. Each window is used for a particular task or application. A typical user uses several windows at once. For example, Figure 4-1 shows a typical screen:

- Two **xterm(1)** terminal-emulator windows. One is running an interactive shell session and the other a **vi(1)** editing session.

- An **xclock(1)** clock window showing the time of day

- A window for the **bitmap(1)** editor

Of course, a user's screen layout is not static. In the course of a session on a workstation, users may use a variety of applications. They also move windows around on the screen, and change the order in which windows are stacked. In Figure 4-1, the bitmap editor's window is stacked on top of the terminal emulator windows.

This way of organizing the screen is known as the *desktop metaphor*. You can think of the entire screen as the surface of a desk, and of the individual application windows as pieces of paper lying on the surface. You can place pieces of real paper on your real desktop in arbitrary ways. Each piece of paper can be any size you choose, ranging from tiny scraps to sheets larger than the

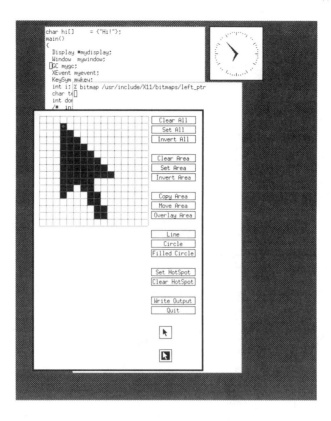

Figure 4-1.  A typical user's screen layout

whole desktop.  You can place each piece of paper anywhere on the desktop, and you can cover some, partly or completely, with others.  You can also remove pieces completely, and add new pieces any time you wish.

X's windows work much like paper on a desktop, with a few differences:

- All windows are rectangular.

- Window edges are aligned with desktop edges (windows cannot be tilted).

- The size of windows can change.

- While windows may extend beyond the desktop, those parts of windows not within the desktop are not visible.

- Most importantly, a window's contents can change.

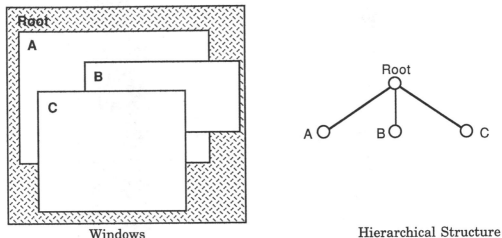

Windows                                                    Hierarchical Structure

Figure 4-2.  A two-level hierarchy of windows

## Window Hierarchy and Stacking

X's windows are arranged in a hierarchy.  In X, the function of the desktop is served by a a special window, known as the *root window*, which is at the top of the window hierarchy.  There is one root window per screen, covering the entire screen.  The root window, unlike other windows, cannot be moved around on or removed from the screen.  In the desktop metaphor, the root window corresponds to the desk itself, and other windows appear on it.

The root window is the only window on the screen that does not have a *parent window*.  Windows used for application programs are, in the window hierarchy, *children* of the root window.  All these windows are siblings of each other, and have a *stacking order*.  For example, the left side of Figure 4-2 shows a root window containing three overlapping *subwindows*: A, B, and C.  These three windows are *siblings*, because they share the same parent window, in this case the root window.  These overlapping siblings are stacked relative to each other: A is at the bottom of the stacking order, B is in the middle, and C is at the top.  The right side of Figure 4-2 is a tree diagram showing the window hierarchy (top-to-bottom) and the stacking order (left-to-right).

The capability of X's window hierarchy goes beyond what you can do with pieces of paper on a desktop: windows can be nested within other windows.  Figure 4-3 shows the same windows as Figure 4-2, but with subwindows of their own inside them.  Windows Q and R have window A for a parent, while Windows X, Y, and Z have window C for a parent.  Each group of sibling windows has its own stacking order.  Notice that the parent's stacking order takes precedence:  even

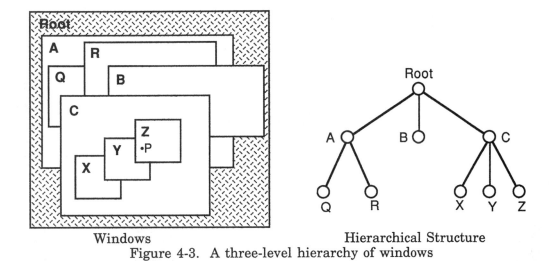

Windows                            Hierarchical Structure

Figure 4-3.  A three-level hierarchy of windows

though window R is stacked on top of window Q, window R is still not visible in the places where window B covers window A.

X uses special terminology to discuss the hierarchical relationship among windows.  Window N is called the *inferior* of window M if N lies anywhere below M in the hierarchy (not the stacking order).  In figure 4-3, Z is the inferior of C, and it is also the inferior of the root window.  Likewise, R is the inferior of both A and the root window.  However, Z is not the inferior of A; they lie on different branches of the hierarchy.

Similarly, window M is the *ancestor* of window N if M lies above N in the hierarchy.  The root window is, of course, the ancestor of all other windows on the screen. A is the ancestor of R, but R is not the ancestor of Z.  Each window's parent is specified by the application creating the window.

A point on the screen is *in* a window if it is within the boundaries of the visible part of that window , but is not within any inferior windows.  Similarly, a point is *contained in* a window if it is within the window's visible boundaries or any of its inferiors.  A point can only be *in* one window at a time.  However, each point is *contained in* the window it is *in*, and all of that window's ancestors.  For example, in Figure 4-3, point P is *in* window Z, and is *contained in* window C and the root window.  P is neither *in* nor *contained in* window Y, because it is not in the visible part of window Y.  If the stacking order between Y and Z were to be reversed, however, P would be *in* Y.

As Figure 4-3 suggests, application programs can nest windows within other windows.  Most application programs have one main window, or *top-level* window, and several other windows nested inside the top-level window.  The X Window System allows each application to create as many windows as it needs,

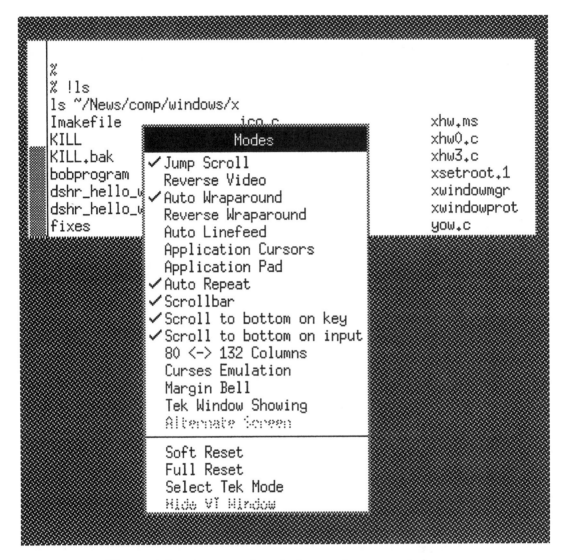

Figure 4-4. **xterm** main window and menu window.

and to control the hierarchical relationship between those windows. You, as an application programmer, may choose two things about your window hierarchy:

- the depth —the number of levels of window nesting
- the breadth—the number of sibling windows at each hierarchical level

X does not restrict applications to any given depth or breadth of window hierarchy. You may use as many windows as you wish, and organize them as you wish. For example, multiple-choice menus usually use one window for each menu item.

Nothing in X requires applications to use just one top-level window. That is, an application can create several different windows that are children of the root window. Many applications, such as **xterm(1)**, use one permanent top-level window for the application's regular display, and one or more *transient* top-level windows for menus. Figure 4-4 shows an example of an **xterm** main window with text displayed in it, overlapped by a transient menu window. Note that each item in the menu is drawn in its own subwindow of the menu's top-level window.

Applications may determine how windows overlap at each level of the hierarchy, by moving windows around and changing their stacking order. Applications may also draw pictures—text, graphics, and images—in windows, and solicit input events (such as mouse and keyboard operations) from individual windows. Thus, windows are X's way of letting your application organize the workstation's screen into useable areas for drawing output and receiving input.

## Window Geometry

In X, a window's *geometry* describes its size, shape, and placement within its parent window. As Figure 4-5 shows, each window has the following geometrical aspects:

width          The window's width in screen picture elements, or *pixels*, exclusive of the border

height         The window's height in pixels, exclusive of the border

border_width   The width, in pixels, of a border drawn around the outside of the window. A window may have a border_width of zero, which means that no surrounding line is drawn.

origin         The upper left corner of the window, just inside the border

x              The horizontal position of the window's upper left corner, outside the window's border, relative to the parent window's origin

y              The vertical position of the window's upper left corner, outside the the border, relative to the parent window's origin

Each window's origin always has the x,y coordinate position (0,0). X coordinates increase as you move to the right within the window, and Y coordinates increase as you move down. The important thing to understand about windows is that they provide frames of reference. Everything within a window—drawing, subwindow placement, and mouse actions—has a position relative to the window's origin.

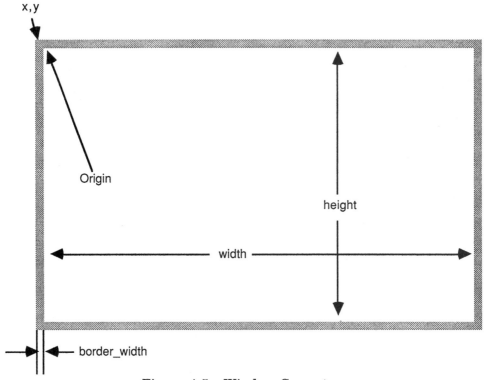

Figure 4-5.  Window Geometry

Items such as title bars and scroll bars are not provided by the X base window system, but must be drawn by application programs and toolkits.

The workstation automatically draws the border around each window (unless the border_width is zero).  Everything (drawings and subwindows) in a window is *clipped* so it does not appear anywhere except within the window's border.  A window's width and height are its inside dimensions, and do not include its border.

Unlike more traditional computer graphics software, the X Window System does not provide any absolute or device coordinate origin.  The closest thing to an absolute coordinate system in X is the coordinate system relative to the root window.

## Window State and Life Cycle

Windows are one of the types of resources in the X Window System (see "Resources" in Chapter 3).  They are created, manipulated, and destroyed by application programs, but they are workstation-resident, not application-resident. Applications refer to windows using resource identifiers; any application with a display connection to a workstation can (in principle) do things to any window. One application in particular, the *window manager application*, has the responsibility for organizing and rearranging other applications' windows under the user's control. As you design your application, remember that users routinely invoke the window manager to move your windows around, hide them, change their sizes, and stack them under or over other windows.

Window resources on a workstation can be in two different states: *unmapped* or *mapped*. Unmapped windows exist in limbo. Although unmapped windows retain their geometry and stacking order, and all their capabilities (drawing into an unmapped window is not wrong, even though it may be a waste of time) they cannot be seen. Each new window is created in an unmapped state. As **helloworld.c** in Chapter 2 showed, you must both create and map a window before the user can see it, and before there is any point in drawing into it.

However, in a complex window hierarchy, it is not enough just to map a window when you want to let the user look at it. For a window to be *viewable*, you must make sure it *and all its ancestors* are mapped. Furthermore, if a viewable window is to be *visible*, at least part of it must not be covered by other windows. A viewable window is said to be *invisible*, or *fully obscured*, if other windows completely cover it.

A visible window is *unobscured* if no other windows (except possibly its own inferior windows) cover it . In Figure 4-3, windows C and Z are both unobscured: Z is C's child, so it is not considered to obscure C. A *partially obscured* window is one with one or more (non-inferior) windows covering part of it. Window Y in Figure 4-3 is partially obscured by window Z.

Figure 4-6 shows the states a window can be in with respect to visibility. Fortunately, most applications do not have to care exactly what state each window is in at any given time. The workstation automatically handles each window's state, as long as your application (or the window manager application) correctly controls the following aspects of each window in the hierarchy:

- Mapping and unmapping
- Geometry
- Stacking order

To allow your application to make sure the window contents are redrawn correctly when the window's state changes, the workstation sends you Expose events. How you respond to these Expose events is another story, left to Chapter 5. Notice, though, that your application does not need to know whether a window is obscured before drawing into it: X allows you to use identical requests for drawing into unobscured or partially obscured windows. You may also issue requests for drawing into obscured windows; such requests do not cause errors, even though the user cannot see the results. This capability is one of the things

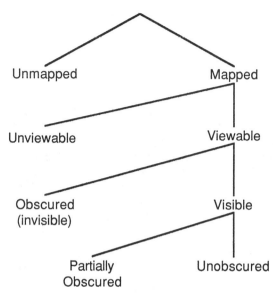

Figure 4-6.  Window State:  Mapping, Viewability, and Visibility

that makes X a true windowing system, in which several applications can operate independently without regard to the others' window configurations.

The first event in the life cycle of each window is its creation.  When your application creates a new window, it starts out unmapped: in limbo.  You can choose and alter its characteristics while it is still unmapped (for example, **helloworld.c** solicits input events from an unmapped window).

Applications commonly solicit events from windows before they are mapped for the first time.  The act of mapping a window can result in the generation of events.  If you want those events (or any events) you must solicit them before they occur.

The second major event for a window is making it viewable.  For top-level application windows, it is usually enough simply to map it.  However, in a deep window hierarchy, you may have to map several levels of windows.  Note that you may issue the X requests to map windows in hierarchies in any order:  subwindows can be mapped even when parent windows are not.  However, such windows will not be viewable.

A window manager may intervene as your application makes your window viewable.  A window manager will often issue prompts to the user asking exactly where your window should be placed on the screen.  It then moves and resizes your window if necessary, and finally maps it.  Some window managers move other windows out of the way, as well.  Keep in mind the fact that window managers can change the size of your windows; this means your application must be designed to handle changes in window sizes gracefully.

Design your application so that you allow the window manager to put your windows where it wants them. Avoid the temptation to fight with the window manager over window size, placement, or stacking. When the window manager alters one of your windows in some way, try to make the best of it instead of putting it back the way it was. The user is in charge. A well-designed application operates within the parameters set by the user. Your application should accept window changes from the window manager—users initiate almost all such changes directly. If your application cannot function properly with a chosen window size, you can always display some simple message, such as "Please make me larger!" in the window.

Once a window is viewable, it becomes worthwhile for your application to start drawing into it (Chapter 5) and to expect mouse (Chapter 9) and keyboard (Chapter 10) input events from it.

Windows can be unmapped, by the window manager or any other application running on the workstation, at any time. Most window managers offer the user a way of unmapping windows when they are not in use. Usually window managers do this by *iconifying* windows, which is to say they unmap them and represent them by drawing an *icon* object (a small window or some other meaningful symbol) somewhere on the screen.

Your application can also map and unmap windows at any time. For example, **xterm** keeps its menu available in the form of an unmapped main window containing several mapped subwindows. Figure 4-4 shows **xterm** displaying its menu. Because the menu's window extends beyond the application's main window, you can tell the windows are siblings rather than parent and child. **xterm** does not have to create the menu's windows anew each time the user requests it; positioning the menu's main window, then mapping it, is enough.

At any time during a window's life, your application (or the window manager) can change your window's background or border. Window managers often highlight window borders as a way of indicating which window works with the keyboard at any given time.

A window's life cycle ends with its destruction. Your application can destroy a window regardless of its state. Destroyed windows simply go away. The workstation destroys most application windows automatically when the application closes the display connection.

## WINDOWS MADE SIMPLE

This section describes the simplest and easiest ways for applications to create and manipulate windows throughout their life cycle. Many X applications, especially simple ones, will work using just the requests described in this

| Request/Function | Xlib ¶ | Description |
|---|---|---|
| **XCreateSimpleWindow** | 3.3 | Create a window the easy way |
| **XSelectInput** | 8.5 | Solicit events from windows |
| **XMapRaised** | 3.5 | Map a window and stack it on top |
| **XMapWindow** | 3.5 | Map a window |
| **XMapSubwindows** | 3.5 | Map all subwindows of specified window |
| **XSetBackground** | 3.5 | Change the window background |
| **XSetBorder** | 3.5 | Change the window border |
| **XUnmapWindow** | 3.6 | Unmap a window |
| **XUnmapSubwindows** | 3.6 | Unmap all subwindows of specified window |
| **XDestroyWindow** | 3.4 | Destroy a window |
| **XDestroySubwindows** | 3.4 | Destroy all subwindows of specified window |

Table 4-I. *Xlib* calls for simple window handling

section.  They are covered in the order your application will probably use them in the application's life cycle.  Table 4-I summarizes the requests.

These calls are quite effective for manipulating a simple hierarchy of windows.  However, sophisticated applications will want to do such things as scale their drawings and subwindows to the size of their windows.  Later sections of this chapter describe the requests for doing these things.

X allows application programs to create all their windows using just the requests in this section.  However, many applications (Chapter 2's **helloworld.c**, for example) inform the window manager of their presence.  The section entitled "Window Manager Interactions" later in this chapter describes some of the optional extra work your application can do to cooperate with the window manager when creating top-level windows.

## Creating Windows

Your application must establish a display connection (see "Opening the Display Connection" in Chapter 3) before creating any windows.  Once you have a display connection at your disposal, you may use the **XCreateSimpleWindow** request for each window you wish to create.  **XCreateSimpleWindow** creates windows useful both for drawing output and receiving events.

You can use **XCreateSimpleWindow** to create a new window anywhere in the window hierarchy you choose.  You control the placement of the new window in the hierarchy by specifying which already-existing window is to be the parent of the new window.  **XCreateSimpleWindow** also confers many of the attributes and characteristics of the parent window upon the new child window (see "Attributes and Characteristics" later in this chapter for further information).

The **XCreateSimpleWindow** call returns the *window id* (the X resource identifier) of the newly created, but as-yet unmapped, window to you.  Later on when you issue other requests to do other things to your window, you will refer to it using the window id.

The parent of your application's first, top-level, window is usually the root window. You could, in principle, use any window you want as the parent of your top-level window. However, the root window is the best parent to use at your top level for two reasons:

- It is easy to get the window id for the root window. *Xlib* lets you use the DefaultRootWindow macro to determine the root window id.

- Most window managers only manipulate first-level subwindows of the root window.

The **helloworld.c** example in Chapter 2 and the example at the end of this section both illustrate the creation of a top-level window.

One of the things you can do once you have created a new window is create subwindows for it. When you create a hierarchy of windows, you must start at the top of the hierarchy and work downwards.

**XCreateSimpleWindow** (*Xlib* ¶3.3) has the form

```
Display *display;          /* pointer to Display structure */
Window parent;             /* parent for new window */
int x,y;                   /* position of new window */
unsigned int width;        /* width of window*/
unsigned int height;       /* height of window*/
unsigned int border_width; /* border width*/
unsigned long border;      /* border "color" */
unsigned long background;  /* background "color" */
Window new;                /* newly created window*/
. . .
new  = XCreateSimpleWindow ( display, parent, x, y,
                             width, height, border_width,
                             border, background );
```

**XCreateSimpleWindow** creates a new, unmapped, window and returns its window resource identifier in *mywindow*.

Most of **XCreateSimpleWindow**'s parameters ($x, y, width, height, border\_width$) allow you to specify the window's geometry. You also specify colors for the window's *background* and *border*. For detailed information on how to specify color, see the example at the end of this section and see Chapter 7.

In the *parent* parameter, specify the X resource identifier of some existing window. The newly created window is created as a subwindow of the *parent* you specify. The *parent* window is very important, in some subtle and not-so-subtle ways:

- The new window is positioned (by $x$ and $y$) relative to the origin of the parent window. If a window manager or your application subsequently moves the parent window, the new window moves along with it.

- Each window is created for just one screen on a multiple-screen workstation. When you specify the parent window, you are implicitly specifying the screen for the new window as well.

- The new window inherits its attributes and characteristics from the parent window.

- The new window's siblings are the other subwindows of its parent. The new window is stacked on *top* of all its siblings when it is first created (although subsequent requests can change the stacking order). The new window is not mapped, so it cannot yet obscure any of its siblings.

- The new window is not viewable because it is not mapped. (it and all its ancestors must be mapped before it is viewable.)

**XCreateSimpleWindow** generates a one-way protocol request. Therefore, it is reasonably fast. *Xlib* synthesizes the new window's resource identifier and passes it both to the workstation and back to the caller.

### Example: Create a window and subwindows

In this example, we create a top-level application window with a wide black border around it. Inside that top-level window, we create two other windows:

> 1) a "message window" with a white background, across the top of the top-level window.

> 2) a "drawing window" just below the message window.

The two subwindows are arranged so they are adjacent to each other. This example illustrates the creation of a hierarchy of windows with varying background colors and border widths. Note that the window positions and sizes are hard-coded constants for the convenience of this example.

```
Display *display;
Window top;          /* top-level window */
Window message;      /* message window */
Window drawing;      /* drawing window */
unsigned long black; /* value for black */
unsigned long white; /* value for white */
int screen;

 . . .

screen = DefaultScreen (display);
```

```
white = WhitePixel (display, screen);
black = BlackPixel (display, screen);
top = XCreateSimpleWindow (display,
    DefaultRootWindow (display), 100, 100, 900, 700, 5, black, black);
message = XCreateSimpleWindow (display,
    top, 0, 0, 900, 60, 0, black, white);
drawing = XCreateSimpleWindow (display,
    top, 0, 60, 900, 640, 0, black, black);
```

## Soliciting Events from Windows

Ordinarily, after you create a new window, you next solicit events from it. *Xlib* provides the **XSelectInput** call for this purpose. **XSelectInput** (*Xlib* ¶8.5) is described in detail under "Soliciting Events" in Chapter 3. What **XSelectInput** actually does is set the *event_mask* attribute for the window.

Even if your application will only use the window for output and never use the workstation's mouse and keyboard, you probably have to solicit some types of events from the window. For example, **helloworld.c** solicits Expose events from its window, and uses these events to learn when to draw or redraw window contents. Almost all applications solicit Expose events from any window into which anything is drawn. The Expose events tell you which windows, and which areas within those windows, you must redraw.

The window manager, other applications, and your application can all do things to change the size, position, stacking order, state (viewable/ mapped/ unmapped), and visibility of your windows. The workstation generates several different kinds of events to notify your application of changes to your windows. If you solicit these notification events before the first time you map each new window, the workstation will inform your application of the state of your window as it is mapped. For example, you can tell from the notification events you get whether the window manager moved your window before mapping it, and whether it is totally visible, partially obscured, or completely obscured.

Window notification events are described at the end of this chapter. Expose events are described in Chapter 5.

## Mapping Windows

*Xlib* provides three mapping requests for three different purposes:

**XMapRaised**      maps a window after stacking it on top of its siblings
**XMapWindow**      maps a window, without changing its stacking order
**XMapSubwindows**  maps all the subwindows of a particular window

Windows cannot be seen until they and all their ancestors become mapped. Also, window managers ignore your application's newly created windows until you first map them. When you map a top-level application window, the window manager intercepts your mapping request and decides where to put the window and how big to make it. For example, the **uwm(1)** window manager, when you first map a window, prompts the user to hold down a mouse button while dragging out the corners of the screen rectangle to be used for the window. Once the user has selected the area, **uwm** resizes and moves the window using the user-specified parameters, then allows your mapping request to complete.

The **wm(1)** window manager creates title bars and window manipulation icons for your window when it intercepts your first window-mapping request. It, too, may move your window before actually mapping it.

Thus, when a window manager is running, a lot happens when you first map a window. Your application does not have to contain any code to deal with top-level window placement. As long as your application accepts the window's assigned size and position, this window manager intervention takes place automatically, without any need for special code.

## XMapRaised

Most applications use the **XMapRaised** request to map their top-level windows. The request *pops* the window: it both maps it (if it was unmapped) and puts it on top of of its siblings in the stacking order. This request will make a top-level (child of the root) window visible and unobscured (and cause a MapNotify event) as long as the window lies completely within the boundaries of the root window.

During creation, new windows are placed at the top of the stacking order, so it might appear that raising the window again with **XMapRaised** is redundant. However, several applications can be concurrently creating and mapping windows on the same workstation. This could result in a window no longer being at the top of the stack when mapped. Users usually expect new windows to appear on top, but users do not know windows exist until they are mapped. The use of **XMapRaised** preserves the user's illusion that windows are instantaneously created and mapped,with no time for something to push them down in the stacking order.

**XMapRaised** raises the window to the top of the stacking order even if the window is already mapped. It is useful for both mapping and stacking subwindows as well as top-level windows.

**XMapRaised** (*Xlib* ¶3.5) has the form

```
Display *display;          /* pointer to Display structure */
Window window;             /* window to map and raise*/
    . . .
XMapRaised ( display, window );
```

The *window* parameter specifies the X resource of the window to map and raise.

## XMapWindow

**XMapWindow** maps a window (and causes a MapNotify event) without altering its position in the stacking order. It (*Xlib* ¶3.5) has the form

```
Display *display;          /* pointer to Display structure */
Window window;             /* window to map */
    . . .
XMapWindow ( display, window );
```

The *window* parameter specifies the X resource identifier of the window to map.

## XMapSubwindows

**XMapSubwindows** maps all the subwindows of a specified window. It maps them one by one, starting with the top of the stacking order and working downward. If you are building a hierarchical structure of windows (like **xterm**'s menu; see Figure 4-4) it is far faster to map all subwindows at once rather than issuing a series of **XMapWindow** requests.

Of course, if you do not want to map *all* the subwindows of a particular window, but just some of them, **XMapSubwindows** will not work for you.

> Avoid issuing **XMapSubwindows** for the root window. You will confuse your window manager.

**XMapSubwindows** (*Xlib* ¶3.5) has the form

```
Display *display;          /* pointer to Display structure */
Window parent;             /* parent of windows to map */
    . . .
XMapSubwindows ( display, parent );
```

The *parent* parameter specifies the X resource identifier of the parent window of the windows to map. The request does not map the *parent* window itself.

## Backgrounds and Borders

During the lifetime of a window, you may alter its background or border color. It does not matter what state the window is in when you alter background or border color. You may also alter other window attributes at any time; see "Attributes and Characteristics" later in this chapter.

The example under "creating windows" above showed how to specify values for black and white pixels. See Chapter 7 for a full explanation of pixel values.

## XSetWindowBackground

You can use **XSetWindowBackground** to change the background pixel of a window. The new background is a solid color of the pixel you specify.

**XSetWindowBackground** does not cause the window to be repainted immediately, so you will probably want to clear and repaint the window after issuing it (see Chapter 5).

**XSetWindowBackground** (*Xlib* ¶3.9) has the form

    **Display** *\*display;*         */\* pointer to Display structure \*/*
    **Window** *window;*           */\* window to change \*/*
    unsigned long *pixel;*       */\* new background pixel \*/*
    . . .
    **XSetWindowBackground** ( *display, window, pixel* );

This request changes the background of the specified *window* to the specified *pixel*.

## XSetWindowBorder

You can use **XSetWindowBorder** to change the border pixel of a window. The new border is drawn immediately when you issue the request to make the change. It is a solid color of the pixel you specify. **XSetWindowBorder**, therefore, is useful for highlighting window borders, perhaps to draw a user's attention to a particular window.

**XSetWindowBorder** (*Xlib* ¶3.9) has the form

    **Display** *\*display;*         */\* pointer to Display structure \*/*
    **Window** *window;*           */\* window to change \*/*
    unsigned long *pixel;*       */\* new border pixel \*/*
    . . .
    **XSetWindowBorder** ( *display, window, pixel* );

This request changes the border of the specified *window* to the specified *pixel*.

## Unmapping Windows

*Xlib* provides two unmapping requests for two purposes:

    **XUnmapWindow**      unmaps a window
    **XUnmapSubwindows** unmaps all the subwindows of a particular window

By unmapping a window, an application puts it aside, hiding it from the user. Window managers do this to top-level application windows: they give the user a way to iconify some of the applications running on the workstation. The user is permitted to use the window manager to unmap your application's windows at any time.

Fortunately, this unpredictable unmapping of your windows does not present a very difficult programming problem to your application. You may issue drawing requests to unmapped windows without doing any harm, so you don't have to stop output when your window is unmapped. Furthermore, most mouse and keyboard events only go to mapped windows, so you do not have to do anything special to shut off input to unmapped windows. Thus, your application will work even if you pay no attention to whether your windows are mapped. If you do care when your windows are mapped and unmapped, you can use MapNotify and UnmapNotify events to keep track. See the last section of this chapter.

Your application can also unmap windows. This is commonly done with windows for various menus and dialogues when your application is not using them.

An unmapped window does not lose its place in the stacking order with respect to its siblings. A subsequent **XMapWindow** request for the window will restore it to the same visibility it had before it was unmapped (assuming that nothing else changed the stacking order in the meantime).

When you unmap a top-level window, the window manager may (or may not) intervene to reorganize other windows on the screen. Once you have mapped a top-level window, the window manager does not forget about it if it is unmapped: for example, **uwm** will not prompt the user for window placement the second time a window is mapped.

Unmapping a window may change the visibility of other windows in the hierarchy, and generate VisibilityNotify events (see the last section of this chapter) and Expose events (see Chapter 5).

It is not necessary to unmap windows before destroying them.

## XUnmapWindow

**XUnmapWindow** unmaps a single window. It (*Xlib* ¶3.6) has the form

```
Display *display;          /* pointer to Display structure */
Window window;             /* window to unmap */
    . . .
XUnmapWindow ( display, window );
```

The *window* parameter specifies the X resource identifier of the window to unmap. X ignores attempts to unmap root windows.

## XUnmapSubwindows

**XUnmapSubwindows** unmaps all the subwindows of a specified window. It unmaps them one by one, starting with the bottom of the stacking order and working upward. It is far faster to unmap all subwindows at once rather than issuing a series of **XUnmapWindow** requests.

**XUnmapSubwindows** (*Xlib* ¶3.6) has the form

```
Display *display;          /* pointer to Display structure */
Window parent;             /* parent of windows to unmap */
```

```
  . . .
  XUnmapSubwindows ( display, parent );
```

The *parent* parameter specifies the X resource identifier of the parent window of the windows to unmap. The request does not unmap the *parent* window itself.

## Destroying Windows

Most applications do not have to destroy windows explicitly, because the workstation destroys them automatically when the display connection closes. The rules for window lifetime are the same as for the lifetime of all other X resources; see "Controlling Resource Lifetime" in Chapter 3 for more information.

For applications that must destroy windows explicitly, *Xlib* provides two window-destruction requests, **XDestroyWindow and XDestroySubwindows**.

When a window is destroyed, the workstation (usually; window managers can arrange to work differently) destroys all its inferior windows first. There is no such thing as an orphan, or parentless, window in X.

The workstation generates DestroyNotify events (see the last section of this chapter) for each window destroyed. Destroying a window may change the visibility of other windows in the hierarchy, and generate VisibilityNotify events and Expose events (see Chapter 5).

### XDestroyWindow

**XDestroyWindow** destroys a window and all its inferiors in the window hierarchy. It (*Xlib* ¶3.4) has the form

```
  Display *display;          /* pointer to Display structure */
  Window window;             /* window to destroy */
  . . .
  XDestroyWindow ( display, window );
```

The *window* parameter specifies the X resource identifier of the window to destroy. X ignores attempts to destroy root windows.

### XDestroySubwindows

**XDestroySubwindows** destroys all the inferiors of a specified window. It (*Xlib* ¶3.4) has the form

```
  Display *display;          /* pointer to Display structure */
  Window parent;             /* ancestor of windows to destroy */
  . . .
  XDestroySubwindows ( display, parent );
```

The *parent* parameter specifies the X resource identifier of the ancestor window of the window hierarchy to destroy. The request does not destroy the *parent* window itself.

# WINDOW CONFIGURATION

A window's *configuration* is its geometry and its place in the stacking order relative to its siblings. X applications work with the window manager to control window configuration on top-level windows. Almost all applications explicitly control the configuration of their own hierarchies of subwindows.

The requests we described in the preceding section did not give us much control over window configuration: all your application could do with those requests is use **XCreateSimpleWindow** to create windows with appropriate sizes , and use **XMapRaised** to move them to the top of the stacking order. Using the requests described in this section, your application will be able to find out where windows are, as well as move them around, resize them, and change their stacking order in arbitrary ways.

## Manipulating Window Geometry

As shown in Figure 4-5, a window's geometry is its width, height, border width, and x,y position relative to its parent window's origin. This section details the requests, summarized in Table 4-II, by which you can operate on the window's geometry.

### Window Geometry Strings

There are two common ways, in X, to represent a window's geometry. One of them is with a handful of int and unsigned int variables. We have already used this representation in **XCreateSimpleWindow**. The other is the string representation. A window geometry string is a standard null-terminated text string formed like the examples on the next page.

| Request/Function | Xlib ¶ | Description |
|---|---|---|
| **XGeometry** | 10.3 | Apply defaults and parse a geometry string |
| **XGetGeometry** | 4.1 | Determine a window's current geometry |
| **XMoveWindow** | 3.5 | Move a window relative to its parent |
| **XResizeWindow** | 3.5 | Change a window's size |
| **XMoveResizeWindow** | 3.5 | Move and resize a window |
| **XSetWindowBorderWidth** | 3.5 | Change a window's border width |

Table 4-II. *Xlib* calls for window geometry handling

| | |
|---|---|
| 250x350+200+300 | A window 250 pixels wide and 350 pixels high positioned at (200,300) relative to the parent's upper left corner (this is **helloworld.c**'s geometry) |
| 250x350 | A 250x350 window, but with unspecified position |
| +200+300 | A window at (200, 300) relative to the parent's upper left corner, but with unspecified width and height |
| 250x350-200+300 | The same as the first example, but with the window's *right* edge positioned 200 pixels from the parent's *right* edge (note the minus sign before 200) |
| 250x350-200-300 | As above, but with the window's bottom edge 300 pixels above the parent's bottom edge as well |
| 250x350--20+-30 | As above, but with the window's right edge 20 pixels beyond the screen's right edge, and the window's top edge 30 pixels above the screen's top edge (note the double minus sign, and the plus followed by minus) |

Most X applications accept command-line arguments of the following form to specify the positioning of their default windows:

    -geometry   250x350-200-300

This representation is convenient for users, because it allows them to specify application window positions relative to any corner of the root window, not just the upper left.

*Xlib* provides the **XGeometry** call to convert the string representation to the handful of numbers required for a call to **XCreateSimpleWindow**. **XGeometry** accepts both a user-specified geometry string and a default specification. When the user's string is incomplete (=+200+300 specifies position but not size, for example), **XGeometry** completes the specification from the default string. **XGeometry** also uses *Xlib*'s knowledge of screen size to automatically convert all positions so they are relative to the screen's upper left corner.

**XGeometry** (*Xlib* ¶10.3) has the form

```
Display *display;              /* pointer to Display structure */
int screen;                    /* screen (to determine size)*/
char * position;               /* geometry specification string */
char * default;                /* default geometry specification */
unsigned int border_width;     /* desired border width */
unsigned int width_unit;       /* number of pixels in width unit */
unsigned int height_unit;      /* number of pixels in height unit */
int x_pad, y_pad;              /* extra padding just inside window border */
int x,y;                       /* returned window position */
unsigned int width, height;    /* returned window size */
```

```
int flag_mask;                    /* returned flag_mask */
. . .
flag_mask = XGeometry ( display, screen, position, default,
                        border_width, width_unit, height_unit,
                        x_pad, y_pad,
                        &x, &y, &width, &height );
```

As input, **XGeometry** accepts the following parameters describing a window.

*position*       A geometry specification string. This specification may be incomplete. It is usually the user-specified position for a window.

*default*        A second geometry specification string. This specification may be incomplete or you may specify a null string. It contains the default position and/or size for the window—the geometry to use if the user leaves it out of *position*.

*border_width*   The width of the desired window border.

*width_unit*     The number of pixels by which to multiply the user's width specification. For windows to be used for displaying text, this is often set to the width of characters in the font, so if the user specifies "=80x24", for example, a window wide enough for 80 characters, not 80 pixels, can be created. For graphics windows, use a *width_unit* value of one.

*height_unit*    The number of pixels by which to multiply the user's height specification, analagous to *width_unit*.

*x_pad*          Some applications require padding between the user-specified window size and the window's border. This parameter specifies the number of pixels of padding to add to the window's width.

*y_pad*          The number of pixels of padding to add to the window's height

**XGeometry** produces the window geometry in the $x$, $y$, *width*, and *height* output parameters. These numbers are suitable for use with **XCreateSimple-Window**.

**XGeometry** also returns a *flag_mask* as a function result. The bits in the *flag_mask* specify which of the output parameters were set. The *flag_mask* bits have the following symbolic names (defined in **<X11/Xutil.h>**):

XValue        The $x$ parameter was returned
YValue        The $y$ parameter was returned
WidthValue    The *width* parameter was returned
HeightValue   The *height* parameter was returned
XNegative     A negative horizontal position—a position relative to the screen's right edge—was specified (and the correct $x$ value was computed).

YNegative    A negative vertical position—a position relative to the screen's bottom edge—was specified (and the correct *y* value was computed).

## XGetGeometry

**XGetGeometry** (*Xlib* ¶4.1) is for finding out the geometry of any window (actually any drawable, window or Pixmap; see Chapter 8 as well). It is a round-trip request, so it can hurt your application's performance if you use it too much. It has the form

```
Display *display;          /* pointer to Display structure */
Drawable window;           /* window for which to retrieve geometry*/
Window root;               /* root window of window */
int x,y;                   /* origin of window relative to root */
unsigned int width, height;    /* size of window */
unsigned int border_width;     /* border_width of window */
unsigned int depth;        /* depth of window */
Status status;             /* status returned */
    . . .
status = XGetGeometry ( display, window,
                        &root, &x, &y, &width, &height,
                        &border_width, &depth );
```

This request retrieves the geometry and root window of the window (or Pixmap) you specify in the *window* parameter. The returned *root* window identifier specifies the root window of the screen for which the window (or Pixmap) was created. *x* and *y* return the origin of the *window* (they both return values of zero if the *window* is a Pixmap). *width* and *height* return the size of the window (or Pixmap). *border_width* returns the *window*'s border width (zero if the *window* is a Pixmap). Finally, *depth* returns the depth characteristic of the window (or Pixmap); see "Attributes and Characteristics" later in this Chapter.

> Be careful when interpreting the position of a top-level application window. Some window managers create other windows and use **XReparentWindow** (described later in this chapter) to change top-level windows so they are not children of the root window. The window's x,y position, as reported by **XGetGeometry** and **XGetWindowAttributes**, is relative to its parent. The parent may not be the root window, even if it was when you created the window.

The *status* value of zero is returned by **XGetGeometry** if it succeeds. The only reason it can fail is if you specify an invalid *window* parameter, in which case a nonzero *status* value is returned.

## Moving a Window

The **XMoveWindow** call changes the position of a window relative to its parent window. You may move any window, regardless of its state (unmapped, mapped, or viewable). When a window moves, its subwindows move along with it. If a window is not obscured, workstations can usually move it without losing its contents (but certain styles of window background may force repainting a window when it moves; see "Window Appearance Attributes" later in this chapter). If the workstation does lose part or all of the window's contents, for whatever reason, it sends Expose events to your application asking you to restore whatever was lost. If your application is set up to process Expose events properly, you do not have to worry about whether window contents are lost when windows move; you will be able to restore them.

If you issue an **XMoveWindow** request for a top-level application window, the window manager may intervene.

If your window is mapped when you move it, the workstation generates VisibilityNotify and Expose events for any other windows (belonging either to your application or other applications) uncovered when your window moves. In any case, the workstation generates a ConfigureNotify event for your window when it moves. See the last section of this chapter.

**XMoveWindow** (*Xlib* ¶3.7) causes the workstation to change the *x,y* position of the *window* you specify. The *x,y* position is specified relative to the origin of the *window*'s parent. **XMoveWindow** has the form

```
Display* display;        /* pointer to Display structure */
Window window;           /* window to move */
int x, y;                /* new window origin*/
   . . .
XMoveWindow ( display, window, x, y );
```

## Resizing a Window

The **XResizeWindow** call changes the width and height of a window, without changing its *x,y* position or its border width. You may resize any window regardless of its state (unmapped, mapped, or viewable).

You can exercise a great deal of control over what happens to a window's contents (drawn images and subwindows) when you resize it. See "Gravity: Resize Control Attributes" later in this chapter.

If you issue an **XResizeWindow** request for a top-level application window, the window manager may intervene.

If the window grows, or if the workstation loses part or all of the window's contents, it sends Expose events to your application asking you to draw whatever was lost. If your application is set up to process Expose events properly, you do not have to worry about whether window contents are lost when windows change size; you will be able to restore them.

If your window is mapped when you move it, the workstation generates VisibilityNotify and Expose events for any other windows (belonging either to your application or other applications) uncovered when your window moves. In any case, the workstation generates a ConfigureNotify event for your window when it moves. See the last section of this chapter.

**XResizeWindow** (*Xlib* ¶3.7) causes the workstation to change the *width* and *height* of the *window* you specify. **XResizeWindow** has the form

```
Display* display;              /* pointer to Display structure */
Window window;                 /* window to resize*/
unsigned int width, height;    /* new window size */
 . . .
XResizeWindow ( display, window, width, height );
```

## Moving and Resizing a Window

**XMoveResizeWindow** (*Xlib* ¶3.7) combines all the functions of **XMoveWindow** and **XResizeWindow** into a single request. It has the form

```
Display* display;              /* pointer to Display structure */
Window window;                 /* window to move and resize */
int x, y;                      /* new position*/
unsigned int width, height;    /* new size*/
 . . .
XMoveResizeWindow ( display, window, x, y, width, height );
```

## Changing Border Width

With **XSetWindowBorderWidth**, you may change the width of the border around a window. You may change the border width of any window regardless of its state (unmapped, mapped, or viewable).

If your window is mapped and you reduce its border width, the workstation generates VisibilityNotify and Expose events for any other windows (belonging either to your application or other applications) uncovered when your window's border shrinks. In any case, the workstation generates a ConfigureNotify event for your window. See the last section of this chapter.

**XSetWindowBorderWidth** (*Xlib* ¶3.7) changes the *border_width* of the *window* you specify. It has the form

```
Display* display;              /* pointer to Display structure */
Window window;                 /* window to change*/
unsigned int border_width;     /* new border width */
```

. . .

**XSetWindowBorderWidth** ( *display, window, border_width* );

## Manipulating Window Stacking Order

This section describes the X requests (summarized in Table 4-III) for altering window stacking order. Recall that each group of sibling windows (that is, all the windows sharing a single parent) have a stacking order among themselves. In the window hierarchy of Figure 4-3, for example, there are three separate stacking orders: (A,B,C), (Q,R), and (X,Y,Z). Recall also that sibling windows always have a stacking order relative to each other, even if they do not lie on top of one another geometrically. Unmapped windows as well as mapped windows are included in the stacking order.

Changing the stacking order of a group of windows can expose or hide all or part of the windows involved, but has no effect on their size or position.

When we speak of changing window stacking order, we use three different terms to describe the operations. *Raising* a window is a common and useful operation. It means moving the window to the top of the stack (from wherever it was). We have already discussed the **XMapRaised** request.

*Lowering* a window moves it to the bottom of the stack from wherever it was.

*Circulating* is an operation performed on a group of subwindows. *Circulating down* takes the topmost window and puts it at the bottom, and *circulating up* takes the bottom-most and puts it at the top. X's window-circulation requests, however, provide an additional feature: they ignore unviewable windows, and they do not change the stacking order of any windows positioned where they cannot obscure their siblings. A group of sibling windows always has a stacking order, even if they do not actually obscure one another. When they do not obscure one another, to the user it does not look as if they are stacked on one another. The window-circulation requests work with the same view of window-stacking as the user sees on the screen, not the internal stacking order. Thus, the requests are directly useful for implementing a "next-window" command in a user interface.

| Request/Function | Xlib ¶ | Description |
|---|---|---|
| **XCirculateSubwindows** | 3.8 | Circulate the children of a window |
| **XCirculateSubwindowsUp** | 3.8 | Raise the lowest child of a window |
| **XCirculateSubwindowsDown** | 3.8 | Lower the highest child of a window |
| **XRaiseWindow** | 3.8 | Raise a window |
| **XMapRaised** | 3.5 | Raise a window and map it |
| **XLowerWindow** | 3.8 | Lower a window |
| **XRestackWindows** | 3.8 | Stack a set of windows in order |

Table 4-III. *Xlib* calls for stacking-order handling

The window manager may intervene when you change the stacking order among top-level application windows. To learn exactly how your window manager responds when you change the top-level stacking order, see the manual for your window manager.

If your window is mapped when you change its stacking order, the workstation generates VisibilityNotify and Expose events for it and any other windows (belonging either to your application or other applications) which become uncovered. Stacking order changes may also cause the generation of CirculateNotify or ConfigureNotify events. See the last section of this chapter.

## Circulating Windows

*Xlib* provides three calls for circulating windows. **XCirculateSubwindowsUp** and **XCirculateSubwindowsDown** do what their names indicate. **XCirculateSubwindows** permits you to specify the direction of circulation as a parameter.

**XCirculateSubwindowsUp** (*Xlib* ¶3.8) performs a circulate-up operation (described in the preceding section) on the child windows of the specified *parent* window. It has the form

```
Display *display;      /* pointer to Display structure */
Window parent;         /* parent of windows to circulate*/
    . . .
XCirculateSubwindowsUp ( display, parent );
```

**XCirculateSubwindowsDown** (*Xlib* ¶3.8) performs a circulate-down operation (described in the preceding section) on the child windows of the specified *parent* window. It has the form

```
Display *display;      /* pointer to Display structure */
Window parent;         /* parent of windows to circulate*/
    . . .
XCirculateSubwindowsDown ( display, parent );
```

**XCirculateSubwindows** (*Xlib* ¶3.8) performs a circulate operation in the specified *direction* on the child windows of the specified *parent* window. It has the form

```
Display *display;      /* pointer to Display structure */
Window parent;         /* parent of windows to circulate*/
int direction;         /* RaiseLowest or LowerHighest */
    . . .
XCirculateSubwindows ( display, parent, direction );
```

Use the *direction* parameter to specify which direction you want the subwindows to circulate. The value RaiseLowest requests a circulate-up operation, and the value LowerHighest requests a circulate-down operation.

If a window-circulation request actually changes any subwindow's stacking order, it generates a CirculateNotify event.

## Raising a Window

**XRaiseWindow** (*Xlib* ¶3.8) raises the specified *window* so it lies above all its siblings in the stacking order. You may raise any window, regardless of its state (umapped, mapped, unviewable, or viewable). If the *window* has no siblings, or is already at the top of the stacking order, nothing happens. **XRaiseWindow** has the form

```
Display *display;    /* pointer to Display structure */
Window window;       /* window to raise */
   . . .
XRaiseWindow ( display, window );
```

The workstation generates a ConfigureNotify event when carrying out this request.

Note that you may use the **XMapRaised** request, described previously, for simultaneously mapping and raising a window.

## Lowering a Window

**XLowerWindow** (*Xlib* ¶3.8) lowers the specified *window* so it lies below all its siblings in the stacking order. You may lower any window, regardless of its state (umapped, mapped, unviewable, or viewable). If the *window* has no siblings, or is already at the bottom of the stacking order, nothing happens. **XLowerWindow** has the form

```
Display *display;    /* pointer to Display structure */
Window window;       /* window to lower */
   . . .
XLowerWindow ( display, window );
```

The workstation generates a ConfigureNotify event when carrying out this request.

## Restacking Windows

The **XRestackWindows** request permits your application explicitly to specify the stacking order for a list of sibling windows. **XRestackWindows** (*Xlib* ¶3.8) has the form

```
Display* display;     /* pointer to Display structure */
Window windows [ ];   /* list of windows to be restacked*/
int nwindows;         /* number of windows */
   . . .
XRestackWindows ( display, windows, nwindows );
```

The *windows* parameter is an array, *nwindows* in length, of window identifiers. The windows in this array must all be siblings. In the *windows* array, list the windows in the order you want them stacked. List the top window first.

You do not have to list all the children of a particular parent window. If you leave some of them out of the list, this is what happens:

- The first window in the list keeps its former position in the stacking order.

- Subsequent windows in the list are stacked immediately under the first window.

The workstation generates ConfigureNotify events on the affected windows when carrying out this request.

## XConfigureWindow

**XConfigureWindow** allows you, in a single request, to change both a window's geometry and stacking order. The request permits you to specify an arbitrary combination of window geometry and stacking information. In order to do this, you must declare an **XWindowChanges** structure and set the appropriate fields to the values you wish. Then, when you invoke the request, you must specify both the structure and a mask specifying which fields contain valid data.

The **XWindowChanges** structure is declared in the header file **<X11/Xlib.h>**, as shown in Table 4-IV. The table shows the structure declaration and the names of the mask bits used to declare which fields are valid.

The **XConfigureWindow** request (*Xlib* ¶3.7) has the form

```
Display* display;          /* pointer to Display structure */
Window window;             /* window to be changed */
unsigned int changemask;   /* mask for window changes */
XWindowChanges changes;    /* window changes */
   . . .
XConfigureWindow ( display, window, changemask, &changes );
```

If you wish to change a *window*'s geometry, fill in the appropriate fields of the **XWindowChanges** structure (*x, y, width, height,* or *border_width*) and set the corresponding *changemask* bits.

Use the *sibling* and *stack_mode* fields to specify a change in the *window*'s stacking order. If you do not specify a *sibling* (that is, if you do not set the CWSibling bit in the *changemask*) you are asking for your *window* to be restacked according to the value you specify for *stack_mode,* as follows:

Above    Put the *window* at the top of the stack.

Below    Put the *window* at the bottom of the stack.

TopIf     Put the *window* at the top of the stack, but only if some sibling window is occluding it.

BottomIf     Put the *window* at the bottom of the stack, but only if it is occluding some sibling.

Opposite     If some sibling is occluding the window, put it at the top of the stack. Otherwise, if it is occluding some sibling, put it at the bottom of the stack.

If you do specify a *sibling* (that is, if you set the CWSibling bit in the *changemask*) you are asking for your *window*'s stacking position to be exchanged with that sibling according to the value you specify for *stack_mode*, as follows:

Above     Put the *window* just above the *sibling*

Below     Put the *window* just below the *sibling*

TopIf     If the *sibling* occludes the *window*, put the *window* just above the sibling

BottomIf     If the *window* occludes the *sibling*, put the *window* just below the sibling

Opposite     If the *window* occludes the *sibling* or vice versa, exchange their order in the stack

This request generates a ConfigureNotify event for the affected *window*. If your window is mapped and you change its stacking order, the workstation generates VisibilityNotify and Expose events for any other windows (belonging either to your application or other applications) uncovered by the change. See the last section of this chapter.

| Structure Declaration | Mask Bit Name | Description |
|---|---|---|
| typedef struct { | | |
|    int x; | CWX | New window x position |
|    int y; | CWY | New window y position |
|    unsigned int width; | CWWidth | New window width |
|    unsigned int height; | CWHeight | New window height |
|    unsigned int border_width; | CWBorderWidth | New window border width |
|    **Window** sibling; | CWSibling | Sibling for stack operations |
|    int stack_mode; | CWStackMode | Above/Below/TopIf/ Bottomlf/Opposite |
| } **XWindowChanges**; | | |

Table 4-IV. **XWindowChanges** structure and mask bits

**Example**: Move a window ten pixels left and to the bottom of the stack

This example illustrates the use of the **XWindowChanges** structure and the **XConfigureWindow** request for simultaneously restacking and changing window geometry. It also shows how you can use **XConfigureWindow** to change just the X or Y dimensions of a window, but not both. It uses **XGetGeometry** to find out the original position of the window.

```
Display * display;
Window window;              /* window to reconfigure */
Window rw;                  /* root window id */
int x, y;                   /* window's x, y*/
unsigned int d, w, h, bw;   /* window's other geometry */
unsigned long changemask;   /* change mask to use */
XWindowChanges changes;     /* changes structure */
. . .
XGetGeometry ( display, window,
               &rw, &x, &y, &w, &h, &bw, &d );
changemask = 0;
changes.x = x - 10;
changemask |= CWX;
changes.stack_mode = Bottom;
changemask |= CWStackMode;
XConfigureWindow ( display, window, changemask, &changes );
```

# ATTRIBUTES AND CHARACTERISTICS

Each window is described and controlled by a number of attributes and characteristics. By *attributes*, we mean changeable things such as the background and border values. *Characteristics*, on the other hand, cannot change for the lifetime of the window.

Many applications ignore all but a few window attributes and characteristics. Windows created with **XCreateSimpleWindow** inherit most of their attributes from their parent window, which is a useful shortcut. Additionally, X provides a great many convenience functions, such as **XSetWindowBackground** and **XSetWindowBorder**, to give you easy ways to change window attributes your application does care about.

Another commonly-used convenience function is **XSelectInput** (described under "Soliciting Events" in Chapter 3). The workstation maintains each window's event selection mask in the form of a window attribute.

However, the simple approach to attributes and characteristics does not allow you to use the whole power of windows. To get enough control over windows some applications will have to set and change window attributes explicitly. You can achieve some subtle and useful effects by using window attributes, especially in window hierarchies. An understanding of window attributes allows you to exploit windows fully.

This section describes all window attributes and characteristics, and the next section, "Advanced Window Manipulation," describes the **XCreateWindow** request, for creating windows with any attributes and characteristics you want. It is worth emphasizing that all windows have equal status: **XCreateSimple-Window** does not create a simple window, but rather creates a full-fledged window in a simple way. Any window can have its attributes retrieved with **XGet-WindowAttributes** or changed with **XChangeWindowAttributes**; these requests are also described under "Advanced Window Manipulation."

## Window Characteristics

A window's characteristics are permanent for the lifetime of the window, and are chosen at the time you create the window. **XCreateSimpleWindow** automatically uses default values for window characteristics, whereas **XCreate-Window** (described later on) allows you to choose your own values.

### Class: InputOnly or InputOutput

A window's *class* is either InputOutput or InputOnly. Most windows are of the InputOutput class. All window capabilities are available to InputOutput windows.

*transparent / tracing*

(InputOnly windows,) on the other hand, are invisible, and do not have backgrounds or borders. Their sole purpose is to manage and divide up screen area for directing processing and delivery of events from the mouse and keyboard. For the purposes of output, the workstation acts as if InputOnly windows do not exist. If you issue a drawing request (see Chapter 5) to an InputOnly window, the workstation will send back an error event message. If you solicit Visibility-Notify or Expose events from InputOnly windows, you will never receive any.

InputOnly windows do not have the attributes which apply only to output operations (see the next section). You may not set any background, border, bit_gravity, backing-store, or color_map attributes in an InputOnly window (if you do, you will receive a BadMatch error event message from the workstation).

However, you may solicit events and specify a cursor for an InputOnly window. You may also create subwindows (either InputOutput or InputOnly) in an Input-Only window and control their placement with the win_gravity attribute.

Use the **XCreateWindow** request (described later on) to create a new InputOnly window. You must specify zero for an InputOnly window's *depth* and *border_width*. After creating an InputOnly window you must, of course, map it before you can use it.

## Depth

The *depth* of a window is defined as the number of bits per pixel in its pixel values. InputOnly windows must have a depth of zero. The allowable depth values for InputOutput windows depend on the make and model of workstation, so most portable applications specify their windows' depths using the symbol CopyFromParent. A detailed discussion of window depths and pixel values is beyond the scope of this chapter; see Chapter 7.

## Visual

On a few workstation models, it may be possible for your application to deal with depths and pixel values in more than one way. On such workstations, some windows may have a *depth* of eight, and an arbitrary mapping of pixel value to color (pseudo-color). Other windows may have a *depth* of 24, with subfields of eight bits each for red, green, and blue (direct color). This pixel-value format is called a *visual* in the X Window System.

Because most workstations only support a single visual, most applications specify their windows' visuals using the symbol CopyFromParent. See "Selecting Visual Structures" in Chapter 7 for information on how to specify a visual if your workstation supports more than one.

## Window Attributes

A window's attributes control various aspects of its operation, including:

- Appearance:  Border, background, color map, cursor
- How the window processes events
- What happens to images in the window when the window is resized
- What happens to the window when its parent window is resized
- Whether and how the contents of the window are saved when not visible

Each window attribute is assigned a value, either explicitly or by default, when the window is created.  You may change a window's attributes at any time using a variety of *Xlib* calls.

**XCreateSimpleWindow** automatically uses default values for window attributes, whereas **XCreateWindow** (described later on) allows you to choose your own attribute values.

## Window Appearance Attributes

The appearance of a window is, of course, largely determined by what you draw in it—the subject of Chapter 5.  However, using window attributes you can set a few things to control the overall appearance of the window:

- the pattern and color of the window's background area
- the pattern and color of the window's border
- the color map (for translating pixel values to screen colors)
- the shape, size, and color of the mouse cursor to be shown in the window

Your ability to control these aspects of window appearance gives your application subtle and powerful ways to communicate with the user.  For example, many applications use a bright border pattern or color to highlight a window that is currently receiving keyboard input.  Other applications change the shape of the mouse cursor to signal the user about what will happen when a mouse button is pressed.

## Background

A window's background pattern and color may be specified with one of two window attributes, either *background_pixel* or *background_pixmap*.  You may choose one of four kinds of window background:

- A solid color.  When you wish to specify a single color value (without a pattern) to use as a window background, you specify a *background_pixel* value.  Chapter 2's **helloworld.c** example used **XCreateWindow** to specify a white window background, for example.

- A repeating pattern.  When you want a patterned background, you may specify a *background_pixmap*.  A Pixmap is a rectangular array or tile of pixels (see Chapter 8).  To specify such a window background, you set the window's *background_pixmap* attribute value to the Pixmap's X resource identifier.  This background Pixmap can be of any size, but most workstations draw fastest when you specify an 8x8 or 16x16 pixel background Pixmap. You may find that large or odd-sized background Pixmaps slow down drawing substantially. Around the edges of **helloworld.c**'s window in Figure 2-1, you can see the background pattern used in the root window.

Note that the upper left corner of the first repetition of the pattern is aligned with the origin of the window.

- A transparent background, through which the contents of underlying windows are visible. To get a transparent background, set the value of the *background_pixmap* attribute to the symbolic value None.

- The same background as the window's parent window. To get this, set the value of the *background_pixmap* attribute to the symbolic value ParentRelative. The workstation draws ParentRelative background patterns so they align seamlessly with the parent window's background. This means that your application must redraw the window's contents whenever the window is moved relative to its parent; you will receive Expose events when this is the case.

When regions of your window become visible (because of the restacking or unmapping of some overlying window, for example) or are cleared, the workstation automatically draws the background pattern into those regions of the window. The workstation then generates Expose events so your application can redraw the affected window's contents. (Exception: some workstations have backing store and can sometimes restore window contents automatically).

If you have a workstation which supports more than one *depth* characteristic, you must make sure that your window's *depth* matches the depth of your *background_pixmap*. Chapter 8 shows examples of the creation of appropriate Pixmaps. If you are using a ParentRelative background, your window must have the same depth as its parent window. You should avoid a background of None when parent and child windows have different *visual* or *depth* characteristics; your background is unpredictable otherwise.

Setting a new background, whether by setting the *background_pixmap* or the *background_pixel* attribute, overrides any previous background setting. The workstation makes a copy of your Pixmap when you set the *background_pixmap* attribute, so you do not need to keep your Pixmap if you do not need it for anything else.

When you create a window with **XCreateSimpleWindow**, you must specify a *background_pixel* value, so there is no default background. When you use **XCreateWindow**, the default background is None. This default may give confusing results; avoid it unless you know you want it.

InputOnly windows do not have backgrounds.

## Border

A window's border pattern and color may be specified with one of two window attributes, either *border_pixel* or *border_pixmap*. You may choose one of three kinds of window border:

- A solid color. When you wish to specify a single color value (without a pattern) to use as a window border, you specify a *border_pixel* value. Chapter 2's **helloworld.c** example used **XCreateWindow** to specify a black window border, for example.

- A repeating pattern. To specify such a border, you set the window's *border_pixmap* attribute value to a Pixmap's X resource identifier. This border Pixmap can be of any size, but most workstations draw fastest when you specify a 4x4, 8x8 or 16x16 pixel border Pixmap.

  Border patterns and background patterns are aligned with one another.

- The same border as the window's parent window. To get this, set the value of the *border_pixmap* to the symbol CopyFromParent.

The workstation automatically draws your window's border whenever necessary. If you change a border, the workstation redraws it immediately. Of course, you may set a window's *border_width* to zero, in which case no border at all is drawn.

If you have a workstation which supports more than one *depth* characteristic, you must make sure that your window's *depth* matches the depth of your *border_pixmap*. Chapter 8 shows examples of the creation of appropriate Pixmaps. If you are using a CopyFromParent border, your window must have the same depth as its parent window.

Setting a new border, whether by setting the *border_pixmap* or the *border_pixel* attribute, overrides any previous border setting. The workstation makes a copy of your Pixmap when you set the *background_pixmap* attribute, so you do not need to keep your Pixmap if you do not need it for anything else.

When you create a window with **XCreateSimpleWindow**, you must specify a *border_pixel* value, so there is no default border. When you use **XCreateWindow**, the default border is CopyFromParent.

InputOnly windows do not have borders.

## Color Map

Each window has a color map. Color maps, described in detail in Chapter 7, are X resources with which you specify the relationship between pixel values drawn into your window and colors displayed on your workstation's screen.

To specify a color map, you set the window's *color_map* attribute value to the appropriate color map's X resource identifier. You may set the attribute to the symbolic value CopyFromParent if you want your window to use the same color map as its parent.

Most workstations only display one color map at a time. Therefore, portable applications should use CopyFromParent color map settings. CopyFromParent is the default for both **XCreateSimpleWindow** and **XCreateWindow**.

If you have a workstation which supports more than one *visual* characteristic, you must make sure that your window's *visual* matches the visual of your *color_map*. If you are using a CopyFromParent color map, your window must have the same *visual* as its parent window.

InputOnly windows do not have color maps.

## Cursor

The cursor shows where on the screen the mouse is pointing. Each window can have its own associated cursor resource, which allows your application to control the size, shape, and color of the cursor on a window-by-window basis. When the user manipulates the mouse and moves the cursor from one window to another, the workstation automatically changes the cursor's size, color, and shape. Chapter 9 discusses cursor resources in detail.

To specify a cursor, you set the window's *cursor* attribute value to the appropriate cursor's X resource identifier. You may set the attribute to the symbolic value None if you want your window to use the same cursor as its parent. None is the default for both **XCreateSimpleWindow** and **XCreateWindow**.

InputOnly windows can have their own cursors. In fact, an important use of InputOnly windows is for changing the cursor based on where the user is pointing with the mouse.

## Event-Processing Attributes

Each window has three attributes with which you can solicit and control event delivery and event propagation up the window hierarchy. Most applications just use the **XSelectInput** call to solicit event delivery to windows, but a few applications will need the additional control over event delivery afforded by direct manipulation of the event-processing attributes.

*event_mask*                    This is the attribute set by **XSelectInput** (which is actually a convenience function using **XChangeWindowAttributes**). *event_mask* contains a bit mask, each bit of which solicits certain events under certain circumstances. In this book, the bits in *event_mask* are described in the same section as the events they solicit. The bits all have symbolic names. For example, the bit called ButtonPressMask solicits ButtonPress events.

*do_not_propagate_mask*     This, too, is a bit mask.  Its bits have the same meaning as those in *event_mask*.  Certain types of events can propagate up the window hierarchy toward the root.  In Figure 4-3, for example, suppose the user clicked a mouse button with the cursor at point P in window Z, and window Z had not solicited ButtonPress events.  Ordinarily, the ButtonPress event would propagate up to window C.  If window C did not want the event either, it would propagate up to the root window.

The *do_not_propagate_mask* attribute prevents this propagation.  In our example, if the ButtonPressMask bit were set in Z's *do_not_propagate_mask* attribute, the ButtonPress event would be discarded and not sent up to window C.

No convenience function like **XSelectInput** is available to set the *do_not_propagate_mask*.  The rare application that uses this attribute must set it via **XCreateWindow** or **XChangeWindow-Attributes**.

*override_redirect*     This Boolean attribute is False by default.  If you set it to True, you are preventing the window manager from intervening when you map, configure, or change the stacking order of the window.  This is most often used for popup or transient windows like the **xterm** popup shown in Figure 4-4.

No convenience function like **XSelectInput** is available to set *override_redirect*.  If you use it, set it via **XCreateWindow** or **XChangeWindow-Attributes**.

Both window classes, InputOutput and InputOnly, have all three event-processing attributes.

## Gravity: Resize Control Attributes

What happens to the drawing in a window when the window is resized?  What happens to the position of a window relative to its parent when the parent is resized?  The *gravity* attributes in X allow your application a great deal of control over these actions.

One thing X cannot do automatically is scale a window's contents or subwindows so they stretch proportionally to fit a new window size.  Instead, the drawing—the *bits*—and the subwindows are treated as rigid objects, attracted by

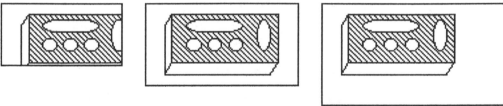

Figure 4-7.  NorthWestGravity example.

*gravity* to some side, some corner, or the center of the resized window. The gravity attribute values, named for the cardinal points of the compass, specify which side or corner attracts the bits.

Figure 4-8 shows the same situation, but illustrates the attraction to the southwest (lower left) corner of the window. Note that the image in the window maintains a constant relationship to the specified corner or edge, even if this requires part of the image to be clipped by other edges of the window after resizing.

This attraction is best explained by using two examples. In the center of Figure 4-7 an object is drawn in a window. On the right, the same object is shown in the window after the window grows larger, and on the left after it grows smaller. Figure 4-7 illustrates what happens when the attraction is to the northwest (upper left) corner of the window.

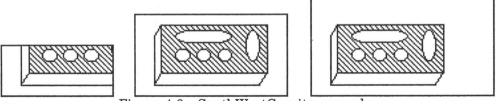

Figure 4-8.  SouthWestGravity example.

## Bit Gravity

A window's *bit_gravity* attribute specifies what happens to the image ( the bits) in the window when the size of the window changes. The *bit_gravity* attribute can have one of the compass cardinal-point values shown in Figure 4-9 and defined in the header file **<X11/X.h>**. When the window is resized, the workstation automatically moves its image bits as if they were attracted to the corresponding window edge or corner.

When the workstation moves your image bits, it saves your application the effort of redrawing the entire window contents. If your application must redraw part or all of a resized window (for example, if it was partially obscured before resizing) the workstation will generate Expose events telling your application what to redraw.

If the window grows, the workstation generates Expose events describing the new areas of the window. The location of the new areas depends on the *bit_gravity*. In Figure 4-7, the new areas are along the bottom and on the right. In Figure 4-8, the new areas are along the top and on the right. (Chapter 5 discusses Expose events.)

In addition to the cardinal points, you can also specify one of the following *bit_gravity* values:

CenterGravity    This value causes the workstation to center the image bits in the new window size.

StaticGravity    This value means that the image bits should not move relative to the root window. This only applies when a change in window size is coupled with a change in window position.

ForgetGravity    This value causes the workstation to discard all the image bits. When this value is in use, your application must redraw the entire contents of the window when the window changes size. The workstation generates Expose events to let you know you must redraw.

If your application scales your drawings by stretching them to fit your window, you should use a *bit_gravity* setting of ForgetGravity. ForgetGravity is the default *bit_gravity* setting. In addition, some workstations ignore the *bit_gravity* attribute and always take the ForgetGravity action when a window's size changes. If your application processes Expose events correctly, it will work regardless of the *bit_gravity* action, but it will have to process fewer Expose events if you set *bit_gravity* correctly.

No convenience function is available to set the *bit_gravity*. If you use this attribute you must set it via **XCreateWindow** or **XChangeWindowAttributes**. InputOnly windows do not have a *bit_gravity* attribute, because they do not have image bits.

In **helloworld.c** in Chapter 2, no *bit_gravity* setting was specified. As a result, the workstation uses the ForgetGravity action, and sends an Expose event to **helloworld** each time the user resizes the window (via the window manager). Notice that **helloworld.c** (and other "dumb" applications) would work well with a *bit_gravity* setting of NorthWestGravity, because all the drawing operations are specified relative to the upper left corner of the window.

## Window Gravity

With a window's *win_gravity* attribute, you tell the workstation how to reposition the window when its *parent's* size changes. When a particular window changes size, notice that the workstation applies:

- The *bit_gravity* attribute of the window that changed size

- The *win_gravity* attributes of the *children* of the window that changed size

Window gravity works analogously to bit gravity: it defines which edge or corner of the parent window attracts the current window. X treats windows as rigid (non-stretchable) objects. When a parent window changes size, the child windows maintain their position relative to the corner or side specified by the *win_gravity*. When a parent window's size changes, the workstation automatically moves each subwindow. Whenever the workstation moves a window as a result of window gravity, it generates a ConfigureNotify, then a GravityNotify event on the window (see the last section of this chapter).

*win_gravity* can be set to one of the cardinal compass-point values shown in Figure 4-9. It can also be set to one of the following values:

CenterGravity   This value causes the workstation to center the window in the new parent window size.

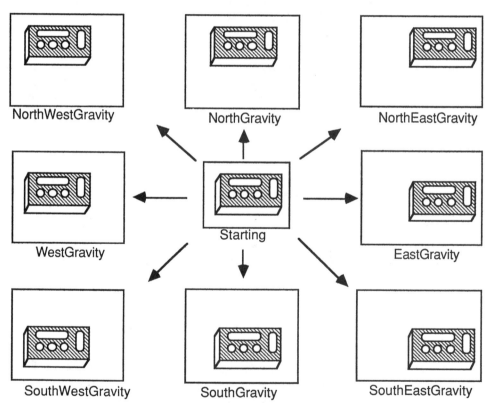

Figure 4-9. Gravity attribute values.

UnmapGravity    This value causes the workstation automatically to unmap a window when its parent is resized, but otherwise to act as if the *win_gravity* value were NorthWestGravity.    If your application scales subwindows to the main window, this is a good choice: it lets you recompute subwindow sizes and positions without showing the user an incorrectly sized hierarchy of windows.

When the workstation automatically unmaps a window as a result of a gravity operation, it generates an UnmapNotify event instead of ConfigureNotify and GravityNotify events (see the last section of this chapter).

NorthWestGravity is the default *win_gravity* setting.

No convenience function is available to set the *win_gravity*. If you use this attribute you must set it via **XCreateWindow** or **XChangeWindowAttributes**.

InputOnly and InputOutput windows both have *win_gravity* attributes.

## Backing Store

Some, but not all, X workstations are capable of maintaining the contents of windows when those windows are not viewable, not visible, or partially obscured. If the workstation does maintain window contents, it does so by storing the pixel values into off-screen memory known as *backing store*.   The net effect on your application of a backing-store workstation is a reduction in the number of Expose events you must handle:   the workstation appears automatically to redraw parts of windows uncovered when the stacking order changes, for example.

> Backing store does not eliminate your application's need to process Expose events.

Backing store, if your workstation has any at all, is usually in short supply. Therefore, X provides four window attributes to let your application give the workstation hints about when (and when not) to use backing store for each window.

*backing_store*              This attribute has one of these symbolic values:

NotUseful       tells the workstation that there is no point to maintaining backing store for the window.

WhenMapped      tells the workstation that your application can benefit from having obscured parts of the window maintained in backing store, but only when the window is mapped.   This value is suitable for applications that redraw windows completely whenever they are mapped.

| | |
|---|---|
| Always | tells the workstation that your application unmaps, then maps the window without changing its contents. |
| *save_under* | This Boolean attribute (it has a default value of False) should be set to True for popup windows. If it is true, the workstation attempts to save any areas of underlying windows that are covered by this window, and restore them when this window goes away. |
| *backing_planes* | This bit-mask attribute allows you to request backing storage for some of the bits in each pixel of your window. By default, it is set to all ones (meaning save all bits in each pixel). If you are using privately allocated color cells in a color application you may be able to save backing store by setting this attribute to some plane-mask value other than the default. See under the headings "Strategy: Private Color Cells" and "One Color, Several Planes" in Chapter 7. |
| *backing_pixel* | This pixel-value attribute works together with *backing_planes*. If you use private color cells, you may set this to an allocated pixel value. When the workstation restores on-screen pixels from backing store, it only can restore some of the bits in each pixel (those specified in *backing_planes*). The rest of the bits it gets from the *backing_pixel* attribute. |

These attributes are all hints, and the workstation is not required to honor them. Many workstations ignore them completely, and others can only honor them some of the time.

InputOnly windows do not have backing store attributes because they have nothing to save in the backing store.

## ADVANCED WINDOW MANIPULATION

This section describes the *Xlib* calls for setting, retrieving, and manipulating window characteristics and attributes. Table 4-V summarizes these calls.

All of these calls manipulate the window attributes and characteristics described in preceding sections.

| Request/Function | Xlib ¶ | Description |
|---|---|---|
| **XCreateWindow** | 3.3 | Create a window |
| **XChangeWindowAttributes** | 3.9 | Change a window's attributes |
| **XSetWindowBackgroundPixmap** | 3.9 | Change a window's background |
| **XSetWindowBorderPixmap** | 3.9 | Change a window's border |
| **XGetWindowAttributes** | 4.1 | Retrieve a window's attributes |
| **XQueryTree** | 4.1 | Retrieve a list of a window's children |
| **XReparentWindow** | 7.1 | Give a window a new parent |

Table 4-V.   Advanced Window Manipulation Calls.

## The XSetWindowAttributes Structure and Mask

The **XCreateWindow** and **XChangeWindowAttributes** requests both permit you to specify any combination of window attribute values. In order to do this, you must declare an **XSetWindowAttributes** structure and set the appropriate fields to the values you wish. Then, when you invoke the request, you must specify both the structure and a mask specifying which fields contain valid data.

The **XSetWindowAttributes** structure is declared in the header file **<X11/Xlib.h>**, as shown in Table 4-VI. The table shows the structure declaration, the names of the mask bits used to declare which fields are valid, and the default value for each attribute.

## XCreateWindow

To create a new, unmapped, window with arbitrary characteristics and attributes, use **XCreateWindow** (*Xlib* ¶3.3). It has the form

```
Display*display;                  /* pointer to Display structure */
Window parent;                    /* parent's window ID */
int x, y;                         /* window position*/
unsigned int width, height;       /* window dimensions */
unsigned int border_width;        /* window border width*/
int depth;                        /* window depth */
unsigned int class                /* class: InputOutput/InputOnly*/
Visual *visual                    /* window's visual */
unsigned long valuemask;          /* mask for window attributes*/
XSetWindowAttributes attributes;  /* window attributes*/
Window window;                    /* newly created window */

. . .
window = XCreateWindow ( display, parent, x, y,
                width, height, border_width, depth,
                class, visual, valuemask, &attributes );
```

| Structure   Declaration | Mask  Bit  Name | Default  Value |
|---|---|---|
| typedef struct { | | |
| **Pixmap** background_pixmap; | CWBackPixmap | None |
| unsigned long background_pixel; | CWBackPixel | (unpredictable) |
| **Pixmap** border_pixmap; | CWBorderPixmap | CopyFromParent |
| unsigned long border_pixel; | CWBorderPixel | (unpredictable) |
| int bit_gravity; | CWBitGravity | ForgetGravity |
| int win_gravity; | CWWinGravity | NorthWestGravity |
| int backing_store; | CWBackingStore | NotUseful |
| unsigned long backing_planes; | CWBackingPlanes | (all ones) |
| unsigned long backing_pixel; | CWBackingPixel | 0 (zero) |
| **Bool** save_under; | CWSaveUnder | False |
| long event_mask; | CWEventMask | (empty set) |
| long do_not_propagate_mask; | CWDontPropagate | (empty set) |
| **Bool** override_redirect; | CWOverrideRedirect | False |
| **Colormap** colormap; | CWColormap | CopyFromParent |
| **Cursor** cursor; | CWCursor | None |
| } **XSetWindowAttributes**; | | |

Table 4-VI. **XSetWindowAttributes** structure, mask bits, and defaults.

When you create a window this way, you must specify its

- Parent window

- Geometry (x, y, width, height, and border_width)

- Characteristics ( depth, class, and visual). You may specify explicit values, or you may substitute the symbolic value CopyFromParent for any characteristic. A window's characteristics cannot be changed during its lifetime.

- Attributes (via fields in attributes corresponding to bits in value-mask). The workstation will use default values (as shown in Table 4-VI) for any attributes you do not explicitly specify.

You may specify a zero valuemask. If you do, **XCreateWindow** ignores the attributes parameter completely and sets all attributes of the newly created windows to the defaults.

**XCreateWindow** is a function; its result is the resource identifier of the newly created window. Your program must store this resource identifier for later use.

**Example:** Create an InputOnly window covering the entire screen

This example creates an InputOnly window the same size as the root window. It uses **XGetGeometry** to find out the size of the root window, then uses **XCreateWindow** to create the InputOnly window. Note that the *depth* characteristic is specified as zero (as required for an Input-Only window), and the *visual* characteristic as CopyFromParent.

Note that we create a cursor resource (see Chapter 9) and set it as the window's cursor. We also solicit ButtonPress events by setting the *event_mask*, and set the *override_redirect* attribute to True.

```
Display * display;
int xr, yr;                   /* root window's x, y */
unsigned int dr,wr, hr, bwr;  /* root window's other geometry */
Window rr;                    /* root window id */
unsigned long valuemask;      /* value mask to use */
XSetWindowAttributes xswa;    /* attributes structure */
Window input_window;          /* newly created window id */
. . .
XGetGeometry ( display, DefaultRootWindow(display),
            &rr, &xr, &yr, &wr, &hr, &bwr, &dr );
valuemask = 0;
xswa.cursor = XCreateFontCursor (display, XC_left_ptr );
valuemask |= CWCursor;
xswa.override_redirect = True;
valuemask |= CWOverrideRedirect;
xswa.event_mask = ButtonPressMask;
valuemask |= CWEventMask;
input_window = XCreateWindow ( display, rr,
            xr, yr, wr, hr, 0, 0, InputOnly, CopyFromParent,
            valuemask, &xswa);
```

Such an InputOnly window might be created by a program for generating hard-copy screen dumps. When this InputOnly window is mapped, the application creating it can receive mouse events from anywhere on the screen, even from within other windows. The setting of the override_redirect attribute prevents the window-manager from intervening as the window is mapped; we do not want the window manager to try to change the window's size or shape, because it is transient.

## XChangeWindowAttributes

To change some or all of the attributes of an existing window, use the **XChangeWindowAttributes** request (*Xlib* ¶3.9). It has the form

```
Display *display;                 /* pointer to Display structure */
Window window;                    /* window to change */
unsigned long valuemask;          /* mask for window attributes*/
XSetWindowAttributes attributes;  /* window attributes*/
```

. . .

**XChangeWindowAttributes** ( *display, window , valuemask, &attributes* );

When using the **XChangeWindowAttributes** request you must, of course, specify the *window* resource identifier of the window you wish to change. You also specify an *attributes* structure, together with a *valuemask* indicating which values are set in *attributes*. For every bit set in *valuemask*, this request changes the corresponding window attribute to the value you specify in *attributes*.

**Example**: Change a window's *bit_gravity* to NorthWestGravity

In this code excerpt, we use the **XChangeWindowAttributes** request to change the *bit_gravity* attribute of a window.

```
Display * display;
Window window;         /* root window id */
unsigned long valuemask;  /* value mask to use
XSetWindowAttributes xswa; /* attributes structure */
. . .
xswa.bit_gravity = NorthWestGravity;
valuemask = CWBitGravity;
XChangeWindowAttributes (display, window, valuemask, &xswa );
```

Notice that all other window attributes are left unchanged; we only set one mask bit in the *valuemask*.

## XSetWindowBackgroundPixmap

**XSetWindowBackgroundPixmap** (*Xlib* ¶3.9) is a convenience function for setting a window's *background_pixmap* attribute. It has the form

```
Display *display;              /* pointer to Display structure */
Window window;                 /* window to change */
Pixmap background_pixmap;      /* Pixmap */
. . .
XSetWindowBackgroundPixmap (display, window, background_pixmap );
```

You specify the *background_pixmap* attribute you want for the *window* you want, and this convenience function uses the **XChangeWindowAttributes** request to carry out the operation.

## XSetWindowBorderPixmap

**XSetWindowBorderPixmap** (*Xlib* ¶3.9) is a convenience function for setting a window's *border_pixmap* and immediately redrawing the border. Its form is

```
Display *display;              /* pointer to Display structure */
Window window;                 /* window to change */
Pixmap border_pixmap;          /* Pixmap */
    . . .
XSetWindowBorderPixmap  (display, window, border_pixmap );
```

You specify the *border_pixmap* attribute you want for the *window* you want, and this convenience function uses the **XChangeWindowAttributes** request to carry out the operation.

## XGetWindowAttributes

**XGetWindowAttributes** is a round-trip request for retrieving the geometry, characteristics, and attributes of a window, as well as some other useful items of information. The **XGetWindowAttributes** request (*Xlib* ¶4.1) has the form

```
Display *display;              /* pointer to Display structure */
Window window;                 /* window for which to get attributes*/
XWindowAttributes attribs;     /*  window  attributes*/
    . . .
XGetWindowAttributes ( display, window, &attribs );
```

When you call **XGetWindowAttributes**, you specify the *window* you want information for, and the request fills in an **XWindowAttributes** structure for you. The **XWindowAttributes**  structure is defined (in the header file **<X11/Xlib.h>**) as shown in Table 4-VII.

Most of the fields in the **XWindowAttributes** structure correspond to parts of the window's geometry, characteristics, or attributes. It also contains a few fields with other useful information about the state of the window, including:

map_installed
: This Boolean field has the value True if the color map for this window is currently installed in the workstation's display hardware.

map_state
: This field can have one of the symbolic values IsUnmapped, IsUnviewable, or IsViewable. It tells you what state the window is in with respect to mapping. See Figure 4-6.

all_event_masks
: This field is the logical OR of the event masks specified for this window by all applications running on the workstation.

your_event_mask
: This field corresponds to the *event_mask* attribute set by your own application.

| typedef struct { | |
|---|---|
| int x, y; | position of window |
| int width, height; | width and height of window |
| int border_width; | border width of window |
| int depth; | depth of window |
| **Visual** *visual; | the associated visual structure |
| **Window** root; | root of screen containing window |
| int class; | InputOutput, InputOnly |
| int bit_gravity; | one of the bit gravity values |
| int win_gravity; | one of the window gravity values |
| int backing_store; | NotUseful, WhenMapped, Always |
| unsigned long backing_planes; | planes to be preserved if possible |
| unsigned long backing_pixel; | value to be used when restoring planes |
| Bool save_under; | Boolean, should bits under be saved? |
| **Colormap** colormap; | color map to be associated with window |
| Bool map_installed; | Boolean, is color map currently installed? |
| int map_state; | IsUnmapped, IsUnviewable, IsViewable |
| long all_event_masks; | set of events all applications have interest in |
| long your_event_mask; | my application's event mask |
| long do_not_propagate_mask; | set of events that should not propagate |
| Bool override_redirect; | Boolean value for override-redirect |
| **Screen** * screen; | back-pointer to correct screen |
| } **XWindowAttributes**; | |

Table 4-VII. **XWindowAttributes** structure.

screen           This is a pointer to a **Screen** structure within the **Display** structure describing the current screen. See the **<X11/Xlib.h>** header file for more information.

## XQueryTree

Use the **XQueryTree** request when you want to retrieve information about the structure of the window hierarchy. Each call to **XQueryTree** yields information about a single level of the hierarchy. **XQueryTree** (*Xlib* ¶4.1) has the form

| **Display*** display; | /* pointer to Display structure */ |
|---|---|
| **Window** window; | /* window to query */ |
| **Window** root; | /* returned root window*/ |
| **Window** parent; | /* returned parent window */ |
| **Window** *children; | /* returned list of children*/ |
| unsigned int nchildren; | /* returned number of children*/ |
| **Status** result; | /* call status*/ |

```
    . . .
status = XQueryTree ( display, window ,
                        &root, &parent, &children, &nchildren );
    . . .
if (status ) XFree ( children );
```

When you want to find out where a particular window (belonging to your application or to any other application) fits into the window hierarchy, you call **XQueryTree** and specify its resource identifier in the *window* parameter. **XQueryTree** returns the following information to you:

*root*      The root window of the hierarchy containing the specified *window*.

*parent*    The parent window of the specified *window*.

*children*  A pointer to a list of all the child windows of the specified *window*. The child windows are listed in the current stacking order, bottom window first.

*nchildren* The number of windows in the list pointed to by *children*. All subwindows of the specified window are included in the list, regardless of the application they belong to, and regardless of their state.

> **XQueryTree** can tell you resource identifiers for windows that do not belong to you. If you manipulate windows that do not belong to you, you may disrupt other applications running on the workstation.

*Xlib* allocates an array of **Window** identifiers for you and returns a pointer to that array. When you have finished using the *children* array, you should call **XFree** to release the associated memory.

**XQueryTree** is a function. It returns a *status* of zero if you ask for information about a nonexistent *window*, otherwise it returns a nonzero *status*.

## XReparentWindow

Use the **XReparentWindow** request if you want to alter the the window hierarchy. The request allows you to change a window's parent. **XReparentWindow** (*Xlib* ¶7.1) has the form

```
Display* display;          /* pointer to Display structure */
Window window;             /* window to reparent*/
Window parent;             /* new parent window */
int x, y;                  /* position of window in new parent*/
    . . .
XReparentWindow( display, window, parent, x, y);
```

**XReparentWindow** puts the specified *window* under the specified new *parent* window in the window hierarchy. The *window* is stacked on top of its new sibling windows and is placed at the specified *x, y* position with respect to the origin of its new *parent*.

**XReparentWindow** works by carrying out a series of actions:

1) If the *window* is mapped, the workstation does an automatic **XUnmapWindow** request for it.

2) The *window* is removed from its current position in the hierarchy and inserted as a child of the specified *parent*, on top of all siblings.

3) The workstation generates a ReparentNotify event for the *window*.

4) If the *window* started out mapped, the workstation performs an automatic **XMapWindow** request for it in its new position.

On a multiple-screen workstation, you cannot move a window from one screen to another (with **XReparentWindow** or any other way). If your window has a background_pixmap attribute value of ParentRelative, the new parent must have the same depth as the old one.

# WINDOW MANAGER INTERACTIONS

Up until now, we have been discussing how an application interacts with the X workstation to create and manipulate windows. In this section, we discuss the things your application can do to interact explicitly with an X window manager. Your application can run without using any of the techniques from this section. However, it will have a more polished look, and will coexist more smoothly with other applications, if you do use at least some of these techniques.

All of these techniques amount to giving *hints* to the window manager. Your application knows more about your windows than their geometry, characteristics, and attributes. These hints give your application a way to pass some of this additional information to the window manager. Once the window manager knows a little more about your windows, it can do sensible things when it changes window sizes, and it can show more information, such as window names in menus.

What the window manager actually does with the hints you give it is up to the window manager's developer. The hints described in this chapter are standardized in the X Window System, and all window managers honor at least some of them. You should consult the documentation for your window manager to determine whether it accepts any additional hints, and to learn what it does with each hint.

Window manager hints are stored in the workstation in the form of window properties. The *Xlib* calls in this section are convenience functions. They come in pairs; you can *set* and *get* the value of each hint (each of the predefined window manager properties).

## How the Window Manager Intervenes

Recall that the window manager is another application running on the workstation. In the preceding sections, we have referred to the window manager as "intervening" in certain requests. A detailed description of how to write a window manager is beyond the scope of this book. However, a brief discussion of what actually happens when a window manager intervenes is in order.

The window manager works by soliciting special window-manager events from root windows and from top-level application windows (actually from any windows it is managing). When the workstation detects that a window manager is soliciting these special events for a particular window, it refuses to execute any requests for circulating, configuring, mapping, or resizing the window, unless the request comes from the window manager (the application soliciting the special events). When such requests come from other applications, the workstation *redirects* them: it sends one of the special events to the window manager. These special event types are explained fully in *Xlib* ¶8.4.7. The window manager responds to these events by modifying the redirected request if necessary, then reissuing it.

This allows the window manager automatically (and transparently) to gain control over your windows whenever your application issues a request that changes the arrangement of windows on the screen. It may move other windows around to make room for your window when it gains control. It may also alter your request. For example, when you change the size of a window, the window manager may reissue your request with different sizes, so that your newly sized window will fit into the window manager's scheme for laying out the screen.

The window manager may also *decorate* your window: put another window containing a title and menu bar near it or surrounding it. Such window managers may use the **XReparentWindow** request to make your top-level window a child of the decoration window, rather than a child of the root window. Once the decoration window is created, the window manager intervenes in all your requests to move and resize your window, because it must move the decoration window as well. **wm(1)** is an example of a decorating window manager.

## Unmanaged (Transient) Windows

You can prevent window manager intervention entirely by setting a window's override_redirect attribute to True. This is useful for transient top-level windows like the **xterm** popup in Figure 4-4, both because it improves performance (by avoiding a round trip to the window manager) and because your application knows exactly where it wants the window and how big it wants it. The Input-

Only window created in the **XCreateWindow** example earlier in this chapter is such a transient window.

If you use a transient window, let the window manager know which application window it is for: use the **XSetTransientForHint** call after you create your windows but before you first map the transient window. **XSetTransient-ForHint** (*Xlib* ¶9.1.9) and **XGetTransientForHint** have the form

```
Display* display;              /* pointer to Display structure */
Window transient;              /* transient window */
Window application;            /* application window */
. . .
XSetTransientForHint ( display, transient, application );
. . .
XGetTransientForHint ( display, transient, &application );
```

## Managed Windows

Most windows are permanent for the life of the application rather than transient. All the top-level permanent windows of each application are *managed windows*, because they are the windows that the user expects to manipulate with the window manager.

A user can invoke a window manager to change the size, position, or state of any top-level window. By convention, a window manager can put managed windows into one of four user-visible states, and can change the state of any window upon user request. The states are:

Normal    The normal operating state of the window

Iconic    The window is unmapped, and represented by an icon. Depending on the window manager, the icon can be an application-provided Pixmap or window, or it can be an icon name string.

ClientIcon  The application wants its icon window to be visible. If it has no icon window, its regular top-level window should be visible.

Inactive   This is the state for a window that is seldom used. It is like the Iconic state, except that some window managers may represent the window on an Inactive Application Menu rather than as an icon.

Ignored    The window is to be ignored by the window manager. The application should not attempt to map an ignored window or its icon window.

Notice that neither the user nor the window manager knows about any window you create until you first map it. The user cannot see unmapped windows; that is why the window manager represents unmapped windows with icons or on an Inactive Application Menu.

None of this applies directly to subwindows of managed application windows (for most window managers). If your application has subwindows and the user iconifies your top-level managed windows, the subwindows automatically become unviewable.

Table 4-VIII summarizes the hints accepted by window managers for describing managed windows. You may choose to provide any or all of these hints from your application program. The more information you give the window manager, the more smoothly it will manipulate your windows.

The following sections discuss each of the types of window manager hint in detail. Many applications (for example, **helloworld.c** in Chapter 2) can take a shortcut by simply using the **XSetStandardProperties** call to set hints. **XSetStandardProperties** is described after the hints.

| **Hint Name** | *Xlib* **calls** | *Xlib* ¶ | **Description** |
|---|---|---|---|
| Window Name | **XSetStandardProperties** | 9.1.1 | The name of the window, |
| | **XStoreName** | 9.1.2 | including state (such |
| | **XFetchName** | 9.1.2 | as file name for an editor) |
| Icon Name | **XSetStandardProperties** | 9.1.1 | The name to display in the |
| | **XSetIconName** | 9.1.3 | window's icon, when the |
| | **XGetIconName** | 9.1.3 | window state is Iconic |
| Class | **XSetClassHint** | 9.1.8 | The application's class and |
| | **XGetClassHint** | 9.1.8 | its formal name |
| Command | **XSetStandardProperties** | 9.1.1 | The command line used to |
| | **XSetCommand** | 9.1.4 | run the application |
| Icon Pixmap | **XSetStandardProperties** | 9.1.1 | A Pixmap to display when |
| | **XSetWMHints** | 9.1.5 | the window state is Iconic |
| WM Hints | **XSetWMHints** | 9.1.5 | Miscellaneous hints to the |
| | **XGetWMHints** | 9.1.5 | window manager |
| Normal Size | **XSetStandardProperties** | 9.1.1 | Sizing hints for the window |
| | **XSetNormalHints** | 9.1.6 | when in its normal state |
| | **XGetNormalHints** | 9.1.6 | |

Table 4-VIII.  Hints to the window manager.

## Window Name

The Window Name is a standard null-terminated text string describing the window. Many window managers display the current Window Name in a prominent place, so your application can use it to show current state. In an editor, for example, you might use the name of the file being edited as the Window Name hint.

Use the **XStoreName** and **XFetchName** calls (*Xlib* ¶9.1.2) to set and get the Window Name hint. The calls have the form

```
Display* display;          /* pointer to Display structure */
Window window;             /* application window */
char * window_name;        /* null-terminated window name string */
char ** name_return;       /* returned window name string */
. . .
XStoreName ( display, window, window_name );
. . .
XFetchName ( display, window, &name_return );
. . .
XFree ( name_return );
```

**XStoreName** sets the Window Name hint for the specified *window*, and **XFetchName** retrieves its value. **XFetchName** returns a pointer to a Window Name string allocated by *Xlib*; you must use **XFree** to deallocate the string when you are finished using it.

## Icon Name

The Icon Name is a standard null-terminated text string. A window manager displays it as part of an icon when a window is in the Iconic state.

Use the **XSetIconName** and **XGetIconName** calls (*Xlib* ¶9.1.3) to set and get the Icon Name hint. The calls have the form

```
Display* display;          /* pointer to Display structure */
Window window;             /* application window */
char * icon_name;          /* null-terminated Icon Name string */
char ** name_return;       /* returned Icon Name string */
. . .
XStoreName ( display, window, icon_name );
. . .
XFetchName ( display, window, &name_return );
. . .
XFree ( name_return );
```

**XSetIconName** sets the Icon Name hint for the specified *window*, and **XGetIconName** retrieves its value. **XGetIconName** returns a pointer to an Icon

Name string allocated by *Xlib*; you must use **XFree** to deallocate the string when you are finished using it.

## Class

The class hint of an application consists of two null-terminated text strings. One is the formal name of the application, and the other is the class of the application (used when fetching the application's resources). To set and get the class hint, you must use the **XClassHint** structure defined (in **<X11/Xutil.h>**) as follows:

```
typedef struct {
    char *res_name;
    char *res_class;
} XClassHint;
```

The res_name field is a pointer to a null-terminated text string specifying the application's formal name. For example, **xedit**'s name is "xedit". The res_class field is a pointer to a null-terminated text string specifying the application's class. **xedit**'s class is "Editor". By convention, the name begins with a lower-case letter and the class with an upper-case letter. See Chapter 12 for further information on names and classes.

Use the **XSetClassHint** and **XGetClassHint** calls (*Xlib* ¶9.1.8) to set and get the Class hint. The calls have the form

```
Display* display;        /* pointer to Display structure */
Window window;           /* application window */
XClassHint hint;         /* class hint structure */
. . .
XSetClassHint ( display, window, &hint );
. . .
XGetClassHint ( display, window, &hint );
```

**XSetClassHint** sets the Class hint for the specified *window*, and **XGetClassHint** retrieves its values.

## Command

Use the Command hint to record the command line with which the user invoked your application. Some window managers show this information to the user in a status display. Other software may save this information and use it to rerun your application in a later workstation session.

Use the **XSetCommand** call (*Xlib* ¶9.1.5) to set the Command hint for a *window*. Specify the command line using the standard Unix main-procedure parameters *argv* and *argc*. The call has the form

```
Display* display;            /* pointer to Display structure */
Window window;               /* window for which to set hints*/
```

```
char **argv;                          /* Command line parameters */
int argc;
XSetCommand ( display, window, argv, argc );
```

## Icon Pixmap

The Icon Pixmap hint is optional; most window managers provide an icon for your window automatically if you do not supply one. If you do set an Icon Pixmap hint, you should create a Pixmap for the icon (see Chapter 8) and give the Pixmap's resource identifier to the window manager either with the **XSetWMHints** call or with the **XSetStandardProperties** call.

Your application can cooperate with the window manager by accepting a hint from it about what size your icon (Pixmap or window) should be. If you create your own icon, use the **XGetIconSizes** call to find out what the window manager's preferred icon sizes are.

**XGetIconSizes** returns an array of **XIconSize** structures. Each element of the array defines one or more icon sizes. **XIconSize** is defined (in **<X11/XUtil.h>** ) as follows:

```
typedef struct {
    int min_width, min_height;
    int max_width, max_height;
    int width_inc, height_inc;
} XIconSize;
```

The **XGetIconSizes** (*Xlib* ¶9.1.7) call retrieves the window manager's list of preferred icon sizes. The call has the form

```
Display* display;        /* pointer to Display structure */
Window window;           /* application window */
XIconSize * list;        /* returned icon size list pointer*/
int count;               /* returned length of icon size list */
Status status;           /* returned status */
. . .
status = XGetIconSizes ( display, window, &list, &count );
```

If the window manager has prepared a list of suggested icon sizes, **XGetIconSizes** returns a pointer to the *list*, the *count* of elements in the list, and a nonzero *status*. If the window manager has not suggested any icon sizes, **XGetIconSizes** returns a zero status.

The min_width and min_height fields in each **XIconSize** element of the returned *list* describe a minimum suggested width and height for an icon. Likewise, the max_width and max_height fields describe a maximum width and height, and the width_inc and height_inc describe an allowable increment between minimum and maximum height and width. Icon Pixmaps are bitmaps: they must have a depth of one.

For example, suppose **XGetIconSizes** returned a *count* of two, and a *list* of two **XIconSize** structures containing the following values:

| min_width | min_height | max_width | max_height | width_inc | height_inc |
|-----------|------------|-----------|------------|-----------|------------|
| 16        | 16         | 32        | 32         | 16        | 16         |
| 48        | 10         | 48        | 10         | 0         | 0          |

This pair of **XIconSize** items together specify five different allowable icon sizes. The first line specifies four: 16x16, 16x32, 32x16, and 32x32. The second specifies one: 48x10.

Your application, if it were to receive this *list*, should create an icon of one of the specified sizes.

## WM Hints

When you specify the WM Hints, you give a group of miscellaneous hints to the window manager, including:

- The initial application state (Normal, Iconic, ClientIcon, Inactive, or Ignored)
- The input focus model used by the application
- Optional Pixmaps to use as an icon and an icon mask
- An optional window to use as an icon
- The initial position of the icon
- Notification of actions upon windows (in some versions of X)

Use the **XWMHints** structure to specify the hints. The **XWMHints** structure, like the **XSetWindowAttributes** structure described earlier, uses a flags bitmask for specifying which fields of the structure are valid. Unlike **XSetWindowAttributes**, however, the flags bitmask is part of the structure it-

| Structure Definition | Mask Bit Names |
|---|---|
| typedef struct { | |
| long flags; | |
| **Bool** input; | InputHint |
| int initial_state; | StateHint |
| **Pixmap** icon_pixmap; | IconPixmapHint |
| **Window** icon_window; | IconWindowHint |
| int icon_x, icon_y; | IconPositionHint |
| **Pixmap** icon_mask; | IconMaskHint |
| **XID** window_group; | WindowGroupHint |
| unsigned int messages; | MessageHint |
| } **XWMHints**; | |

Table 4-IX. **XWMHints** structure and mask bits.

self.    The fields and bit mask names for the **XWMHints** structure are defined (in **<X11/Xutil.h>** ) as shown in Table 4-IX.

The fields in the **XWMHints** structure are defined as follows:

flags
:  The bitmask specifying which other fields contain valid information

input
:  Set this field to True if your application needs the window manager's help to acquire the input focus for your top-level window (see "Focus Models" in Chapter 10).  Otherwise, set it to False.

initial_state
:  This field can contain one of the symbolic values NormalState, ClientState, IconicState, InactiveState, or IgnoreState.  It tells the window manager into what state your application's window should be placed the first time you map the window.  Most applications start in Normal state.

icon_pixmap
:  If you create your own icon pixmap for your window (see the preceding section), put its X resource identifier into this field.

icon_window
:  If you create your own icon window, put its X resource identifier into this field.  You should use the the **XGetIconSizes** call discussed in the preceding section to determine how large to make your icon window.  If you define an icon window, the window manager maps it for you when it puts your application into the Iconic state.  Your application can draw into the icon window. An icon window should be a child of the root window, and should inherit its colormap and visual characteristic from the root.  The window manager (if it supports icon windows: not all do) maps and unmaps the icon window.

icon_x, icon_y
:  Use these fields to suggest an initial position (relative to the root window) for your application's icon.

icon_mask
:  If you create your own icon Pixmap for your window, you can also specify a mask through which to draw it.  Put the mask Pixmap's resource identifier here.

window_group
:  If your application has several top-level windows and you want the window manager to manipulate their state as if they were a unit, put the window identifier of the main application window—the group leader window—here.

messages
:  This field is a bitmask. (Note: not all versions of X have this field.) Your application should use it to solicit messages from the window manager.  These messages are delivered in the form of ClientMessage events; see near the end of this chapter. You may specify any combination of the following symbolic values (defined in **<X11/Xutil.h>**):

ConfigureDenied   Solicits notification when the window manager denies a request to change your window's geometry

WindowMoved   Solicits notification when a window manager moves, but does not resize, your window

FocusMessage   Solicits notification when the window manager expects your application to take the input focus using **XSetInputFocus** (see Chapter 10)

Use the **XSetWMHints** and **XGetWMHints** calls (*Xlib* ¶9.1.5) to set and get the window manager hints. These calls have the form

```
Display* display;          /* pointer to Display structure */
Window window;             /* application window */
XWMHints wmhint;           /* window manager hint structure */
. . .
XSetWMHints ( display, window, &wmhint );
. . .
XGetWMHints ( display, window, &wmhint );
```

To set the Window Manager hints for a specified *window*, you fill in an **XWMHints** structure and pass its address to **XSetWMHints**. To retrieve the *window*'s hints, you pass the address of a structure to **XGetWMHints**, and it fills in the structure for you.

**Example**: Hint that you want your application started in Iconic state

This code excerpt sets up an **XWMHints** structure to suggest an initial Iconic state. It also specifies the value False for the input hint.

```
#include   <X11/Xutil.h>
. . .
Display * display;
Window window;
XSetWMHints mywmhints;
. . .
mywmhints.initial_state = NormalState;
mywmhints.input = False;
mywmhints.flags = InputHint | StateHint;
XSetWMHints (display, window, &mywmhints );
```

# Normal  Size

You may use the Normal Size hint to tell the window manager the range of reasonable sizes for your window. When the user invokes the window manager to change your window's size, the window manager honors your size hint: it will not allow the user to specify arbitrary sizes, but only within the constraints given

| Structure   Declaration | Mask  Bit  Names | |
|---|---|---|
| typedef  struct  { | | |
|   long  flags; | | |
|   int  x,y; | PPosition | USPosition |
|   int  width,  height; | PSize | USSize |
|   int  min_width,  min_height; | PMinSize | |
|   int  max_width,  max_height; | PMaxSize | |
|   int  width_inc,  height_inc; | PResizeInc | |
|   struct  { | | |
|     int  x,y; | | |
|   }  min_aspect,  max_aspect; | PAspect | |
|   int  base_width,  base_height; | PBaseSize | |
| }  **XSizeHints**; | | |

Table 4-X. **XSizeHints** structure and mask bits.

by your hints.  You may specify any or all of the following constraints on window size:

- Initial window position
- Initial window size
- Minimum allowable window size
- Maximum allowable window size
- Width and height increments
- The range of allowable window aspect ratios

Use the **XSizeHints** structure to specify the size constraints.  The **XSizeHints** structure, like the **XWMHints** structure, has a flags bitmask in it for specifying which other fields of the structure are valid.  The fields and bit mask names for the **XSizeHints** structure are defined (in **<X11/XUtil.h>** ) as shown in Table 4-X.

The fields in the **XSizeHints** structure are defined as follows:

flags        The bitmask specifying which other fields contain valid information

x,y          The initial suggested position of the window (relative to the root window).  Notice that you may use either the PPosition or the USPosition bitmask bit with these fields.  Set the PPosition bit to inform the window manager that the suggested x,y position came from a program default.

        If the user specified the suggested position directly (on a command line, for example), specify the USPosition bit instead. Many window managers do not prompt the user for window position when they receive a size hint with the USPosition bit set, but rather use the hint position.

width, height    The initial suggested size of the window. You may use either the PSize or the USSize bitmask bit with these fields. Set the PSize bit to inform the window manager that the suggested width and height came from a program default. Set the USSize bit if the user specified the window size directly on a command line; the window manager may be able to bypass the window-size prompt.

min_width    The minimum useful window width.

min_height    The minimum useful window height.

max_width    The maximum useful window width.

max_height    The maximum useful window height.

width_inc    The window width increment. In an application which displays fixed-size characters, this should be the character width. For example, if base_width is 30, max_width is 60, and width_inc is 6, the allowable widths are 30, 36, 42, 48, 54, and 60.

height_inc    The window height increment, analagous to width_inc.

min_aspect    Specifies the minimum useful aspect ratio of the window. For example, if you specify a min_aspect.x value of 1 and a min_aspect.y value of 2, you are specifying that the window's width should be at least half the window's height. Notice that if you specify either min_aspect or max_aspect, you must specify both. They can be the same if you want your window always to have a specific aspect ratio.

max_aspect    Specifies the maximum aspect ratio of the window.

base_width    Specifies the beginning of the series of allowable widths for the window, in conjunction with width_inc. If base_width is not provided, min_width is used in its place.

base_height    The window base height, analagous to base_width.

Use **XSetNormalHints** and **XGetNormalHints** (*Xlib* ¶9.1.6) to set and get the Normal Size hints. These calls have the form

```
Display* display;          /* pointer to Display structure */
Window window;             /* application window */
XSizeHints normhint;       /* size hint structure */
. . .
XSetNormalHints ( display, window, &normhint );
. . .
XGetNormalHints ( display, window, &normhint );
```

To set the size hints for a specified *window*, you fill in an **XSizeHints** structure and pass its address to **XSetNormalHints**. To retrieve the *window*'s size hints, you pass the address of a structure to **XGetNormalHints** and it fills in the structure for you.

### Example: Specify minimum window sizes and aspect ratio limits

This code excerpt sets up an **XSizeHints** structure. It suggests a minimum normal size of 50x50 for a window, and constrains it so it is never more than twice as wide as it is high or vice versa.

```
#include   <X11/Xutil.h>
. . .
Display * display;
Window window;
XSetSizeHints  myhints;
. . .
mywmhints.min_width = 50;
mywmhints.min_height = 50;
mywmhints.min_aspect.x  = 1;
mywmhints.min_aspect.y  = 2;
mywmhints.max_aspect.x  = 2;
mywmhints.max_aspect.y  = 1;
mywmhints.flags = PMinSize | PAspect;
XSetNormalHints  ( display, window, &myhints );
```

## XSetStandardProperties

This *Xlib* call is a convenience function for applications wanting an easy way to specify a minimal set of window manager hints. With it, you may set the following hints:

- Window Name
- Icon Name
- Icon Pixmap
- Command
- Normal Size

**XSetStandardProperties** (*Xlib* ¶9.1.1) has the form

```
Display* display;          /* pointer to Display structure */
Window window;             /* window for which to set hints*/
char *window_name;         /* name of the window*/
char *icon_name;           /* name to display in window's icon*/
Pixmap icon_pixmap;        /* pixmap to be used for the icon*/
char **argv;               /* Command */
int argc;
```

```
XSizeHints  hints;                        /* Normal Size hints */
. . .
XSetStandardProperties ( display, window, window_name,
                                icon_name, icon_pixmap,
                                argv, argc, &hints );
```

An example of the use of **XSetStandardProperties** appears in Chapter 2 as part of **helloworld.c**.

# WINDOW SIZING STRATEGIES

Remember that it is up to the user, via the window manager, to control the configuration of your application's top-level windows. However, you may want your application to be able to change the size or position of its windows directly. If you do reconfigure a top-level window, you should, by convention, use the following two steps:

1) Use one of the *Xlib* calls to change the window configuration (**XMoveWindow**, **XResizeWindow**, **XMoveResizeWindow**, or **XConfigureWindow**).

2) Use **XSetNormalHints** to inform the window manager of the new configuration. If the user specified the new position or size directly, you should specify USPosition or USSize to let the window manager know that the new configuration came from the user. If your application program generated the new position or size, use PPosition or PSize instead.

Specify exactly the same parameters in both steps. If you move a window, the new position you specify should be relative to the root window. (If the window manager you are using reparents your top-level window, it should automatically compensate for that fact.)

Of course, there is no guarantee that the window manager will honor your request to reconfigure your window. The window manager may

- do exactly what you asked for,
- alter the size and position you asked for, or
- do nothing at all.

You can find out if the window manager denies your request. By setting the ConfigureDenied bit in a call to **XSetWMHints**, you solicit a message informing you of denial. The denial message comes in the form of a ClientMessage event (see near the end of this chapter).

You can also find out whether the window manager just moves your window without resizing it. By setting the WindowMoved bit in a call to **XSetWMHints**, you solicit a ClientMessage event telling you when the window manager moves your window. You may or may not receive a ConfigureNotify event when the window manager moves your window: if the window manager reparents your window with a decoration, your window will not move relative to the decoration window. Many applications do not care when their windows move, because all graphic output requests work relative to the window origin.

If the window manager changes your window's size (for any reason), you will receive a ConfigureNotify event for it (as long as you have solicited window notification events). If your application contains a hierarchy of subwindows, you must reconfigure them—possibly by either resizing or repositioning them—when the window manager changes the size of your top-level window.

Most of the time, your application will only reconfigure subwindows (below your top-level windows). One of the most interesting problems you face when you maintain a complex window hierarchy is what to do when the window manager changes the width and height of your top-level windows. You have a number of choices, of varying degrees of elegance and generality, open to you:

- Do nothing special. This works if all your subwindows are positioned relative to the upper left (northwest) corner of your main window. If the user makes your main window smaller, parts of your subwindows will, of course, be covered up. This approach is easy to implement, but it is probably not good enough for any but the simplest applications.

- Give the window manager a Normal Size hint with equal min_width and max_width values, and equal min_height and max_height values. This may prevent the window manager from allowing the user to change your top-level window's size. This is a crude approach, useful only for quick-and-dirty applications.

- If your subwindows are positioned relative to other corners or edges of your top-level window, you can set their win_gravity attributes (see "Attributes and Characteristics"), and otherwise use the do-nothing approach.

- You can solicit ConfigureNotify events (see the last section of this chapter) for your top-level window, and respond by reconfiguring and redrawing all your subwindows to fit inside the new top-level window boundaries.

    In other words, when you find out from the workstation that your top-level window has changed, use main force to fit all your subwindows to the new size. If you use this strategy, it is a good idea to set the win_gravity attribute of your subwindows to the UnmapGravity value. This way, you can resize them all before mapping them.

    Consider the example under the "Creating Windows" heading earlier in this chapter. If the top-level window were resized for you, you would resize the *message* and *drawing* windows to keep the same width as the top-level window.

This approach is probably good enough for most *Xlib* applications. It has the advantage that you can get fairly fast resizing without a lot of complex code.

• The most general approach to resizing is the one used by the X Toolkit and other human-interface packages. In this approach, each window in the hierarchy is responsible for resizing its own subwindows when its parent resizes it. This is elegant, because it allows applications to handle each window as an object that redraws itself at appropriate sizes on demand. However, this approach is difficult to program for good performance: as each level of the window hierarchy processes its ConfigureNotify events, it generates a flurry of new ConfigureNotify events for windows below it and, possibly, Expose events for windows above it. Often the events are redundant. If you want good performance with this strategy, your application has to understand how to interpret streams of events and extract the non-redundant information.

The best way to build an application with this resizing strategy is to use a toolkit and let it take care of window-size management for you.

## NOTIFICATION EVENTS

When you manipulate windows, the X workstation generates a variety of types of events to let your application (and other applications) know about the changes to the window hierarchy. The most important type of event resulting from window manipulations is the Expose event, which lets you know when your application must redraw window contents. Because the Expose event is related to graphical output, it is described in Chapter 5.

This section describes the following types of window notification events:

CirculateNotify   A window's position in the stacking order changed as a result of a window-circulation request

ConfigureNotify   A window was reconfigured: moved, resized, raised or lowered

CreateNotify   A subwindow was created

DestroyNotify   A window was destroyed

GravityNotify   A window's position changed due to gravity processing when its parent's size changed

MapNotify   A window was mapped

ReparentNotify   An **XReparentWindow** request was carried out

UnmapNotify   A window was unmapped

VisibilityNotify    A window's visibility (unobscured, partially obscured, or fully obscured) changed

ClientMessage    An application used **XSendEvent** (see "Putting Back and Sending Events" in Chapter 11) to send you a message. The window manager does this.

Many of these events are of interest to window managers. However, your application may also solicit them from your top-level windows, and use them to find out when the window manager (or some other application, including your own) changes the window hierarchy on the workstation.

The other type of event described in this section is the VisibilityNotify event. It lets you know when a window's visibility (unobscured, partially obscured, or fully obscured) changed.

Some window manipulations can cause the workstation to generate several types of events for your window. For each individual window, events come in a specific order: notification events come first, then VisibilityNotify events, then Expose events. However, if your application is receiving events from several different windows, the event order is only guaranteed for each window. You may, for example get Expose events for some windows before you get window notification events for others.

## Soliciting Window Notification Events

To solicit events of any type, use the **XSelectInput** call or set the *event_mask* attribute of the window. The **XSelectInput** call is described under the heading "Soliciting Events" in Chapter 3. Two *event_mask* bits are available for soliciting window-notification events: StructureNotifyMask and SubstructureNotifyMask.

If you specify StructureNotifyMask for a window, you are soliciting all the window notification events for that window. (It does not make sense to solicit CreateNotify events for a window; you would have to solicit the event before the window was created, which is impossible.)

If you specify SubstructureNotifyMask for a window, you are soliciting all the window notification events, including the CreateNotify event, for all that window's subwindows. Most window managers keep watch on top-level application events by soliciting events from the root window using SubstructureNotifyMask.

## Receiving and Processing Window Notification Events

Most applications use the **XNextEvent** call to retrieve events from the event queue. See "Accepting Events from the Event Queue" in Chapter 3 for a general discussion of event structures. The first field of all event structures is the event type (field name "type"). The union type **XEvent** defines the "type" field directly, so it can be used to look at the event before you know what type it is.  You should use the **XEvent** type to declare and allocate space for all event structures: it defines a structure that is guaranteed to be long enough for all event types.

Each type of window notification event has a distinct event structure.  Each event type's structure, and the fields in it, is described in the following sections.

The window notification event structures share most of the following fields:

| | |
|---|---|
| type | The event type |
| serial | Specifies the serial number of the last request processed |
| send_event | False unless this event was generated by some application issuing the **XSentEvent** request |
| display | Pointer to the display the event came from |
| event | The window from which the event was solicited |
| parent | The parent window of the window affected by the event |
| window | The window affected by the event.  This is the same as the *event* window if the event was solicited with StructureNotifyMask.  It is a child of the *event* window if the event was solicited with SubstructureNotifyMask |
| override_redirect | This Boolean field is True if the affected window's override_redirect attribute is True.  Window managers usually ignore window notification events with this value set to True. |

The sections to follow describe each event structure in detail.  Each event structure is summarized in a three-column display.  The left-hand column shows the event structure declaration, the middle column shows the name you would use to retrieve the field from an **XEvent** union named *ev*, and the right-hand column briefly describes the field.

**Example**: Declare an event structure, solicit events and get events

This example shows the use of **XSelectInput** to solicit window notification events from a specified window and all its subwindows.

It also shows how to declare an event structure and use **XNextEvent** to fill it in with events.  Notice that the **XEvent** is named *ev*; this is the name used in the middle column of the event structure displays.  Finally, it shows the skeleton of an event-handling main loop.

```
Display *display;      /* pointer to current Display structure */
Window window;         /* window you want button events from*/
```

```
XEvent ev;              /* event data structure */
int done;               /* flag to terminate main loop */
. . .
XSelectInput ( display, window,
    StructureNotifyMask | SubstructureNotifyMask );
. . .
done = 0;
while ( done = 0 ) {
 XNextEvent ( display, &ev );
 switch ( ev.type ) {
 case CirculateNotify:
   ...
   break;
 case ConfigureNotify:
   ...
   break;

  ....
 }
}
```

## CirculateNotify Events

| typedef struct { | | |
|---|---|---|
| int type; | ev.type | CirculateNotify |
| unsigned long serial | ev.xany.serial | Last request processed |
| **Bool** send_event; | ev.xany.send_event | From **XSendEvent**? |
| **Display** *display; | ev.xany.display | |
| **Window** event; | ev.xcirculate.event | Event window |
| **Window** window; | ev.xcirculate.window | Circulated window |
| int place; | ev.xcirculate.place | New window placement |
| } **XCirculateEvent**; | | |

A CirculateNotify event is generated whenever a window is actually restacked as the result of an **XCirculateSubwindows**, **XCirculateSubwindowsUp**, or **XCirculateSubwindowsDown** request.

The CirculateNotify event's data structure has the following specific field:

place               Has the value PlaceOnTop if the affected window moved to the top of the stacking order, and the value PlaceOnBottom if the affected window moved to the bottom of the stacking order

## ConfigureNotify Events

| typedef struct { | | |
|---|---|---|
| int type; | ev.type | ConfigureNotify |
| unsigned long serial | ev.xany.serial | Last request processed |
| **Bool** send_event; | ev.xany.send_event | From **XSendEvent**? |
| **Display** *display; | ev.xany.display | |
| **Window** event; | ev.xconfigure.event | Event window |
| **Window** window; | ev.xconfigure.window | Reconfigured window |
| int x; | ev.xconfigure.x | New window x position |
| int y; | ev.xconfigure.y | New window y position |
| int width; | ev.xconfigure.width | New window width |
| int height; | ev.xconfigure.height | New window height |
| int border_width; | ev.xconfigure.border_width | New border width |
| **Window** above; | ev.xconfigure.above | Sibling or None |
| **Bool** override_redirect; | ev.xconfigure.override_redirect | Prevent WM intervention |
| } **XConfigureEvent**; | | |

A ConfigureNotify event is generated whenever a window is actually reconfigured or restacked as the result of one of the following requests: **XConfigure-
Window**, **XRaiseWindow**, **XLowerWindow**, **XMoveWindow**, **XResizeWindow**, **XMoveResizeWindow**, or **XSetWindowBorderWidth**.

A ConfigureNotify event is also generated when a window's place in the stacking order is changed as a result of an **XMapRaised** request.

The ConfigureNotify event's data structure has the following specific fields:

x,y             The position of the window, relative to its parent, after the re-
                configuration

width, height   The size of the window after the reconfiguration

border_width    The border width of the window after the reconfiguration

above           The value None if the affected window is stacked at the bottom
                of the stacking order. Otherwise, the window identifier of the
                window immediately under the affected window after it is
                restacked.

> Be careful when interpreting the position of a top-level application
> window. Some window managers create other windows and use
> **XReparentWindow** to change top-level windows so they are not
> children of the root window. The window's x,y position, as re-
> ported in ConfigureNotify events, is relative to its parent. The
> parent may not be the root window.

## CreateNotify Events

| typedef struct { | | |
|---|---|---|
| int type; | ev.type | CreateNotify |
| unsigned long serial | ev.xany.serial | Last request |
| **Bool** send_event; | ev.xany.send_event | From **XSendEvent**? |
| **Display** *display; | ev.xany.display | |
| **Window** parent; | ev.xcreatewindow.parent | Parent |
| **Window** window; | ev.xcreatewindow.window | New window |
| int x; | ev.xcreatewindow.x | New x position |
| int y; | ev.xcreatewindow.y | New y position |
| int width; | ev.xcreatewindow.width | New window width |
| int height; | ev.xcreatewindow.height | New window height |
| int border_width; | ev.xcreatewindow.border_width | New border width |
| **Bool** override_redirect; | ev.xcreatewindow.override_redirect | No WM intervention |
| }**XCreateWindowEvent;** | | |

A CreateNotify event is generated whenever a window is created. CreateNotify events are delivered to applications soliciting events using SubstructureNotify-Mask on the parent window of the newly created window.

The CreateNotify event's data structure has the following specific fields:

x,y      The position of the new window, relative to its parent

width, height      The size of the new window

border_width      The border width of the new window

above      The value None if the affected window is stacked at the bottom of the stacking order. Otherwise, the window identifier of the window immediately above which the affected window is stacked.

## DestroyNotify Events

| typedef struct { | | |
|---|---|---|
| int type; | ev.type | DestroyNotify |
| unsigned long serial | ev.xany.serial | Last request processed |
| **Bool** send_event; | ev.xany.send_event | From **XSendEvent**? |
| **Display** *display; | ev.xany.display | |
| **Window** event; | ev.xdestroywindow.event | Event window |
| **Window** window; | ev.xdestroywindow.window | Destroyed window |
| } **XDestroyWindowEvent;** | | |

A DestroyNotify event is generated whenever a window is destroyed. If a hierarchy of windows is destroyed, DestroyNotify events are generated in bottom-up order: All a given window's inferiors are destroyed before the given window.

## GravityNotify Events

| typedef struct { | | |
|---|---|---|
| int type; | ev.type | GravityNotify |
| unsigned long serial | ev.xany.serial | Last request processed |
| **Bool** send_event; | ev.xany.send_event | From **XSendEvent**? |
| **Display** *display; | ev.xany.display | |
| **Window** event; | ev.xgravity.event | Event window |
| **Window** window; | ev.xgravity.window | Moved window |
| int x; | ev.xgravity.x | New x position |
| int y; | ev.xgravity.y | New y position |
| } **XGravityEvent**; | | |

A GravityNotify event is generated whenever a window position actually changes as a result of gravity processing. Gravity processing depends on the window's win_gravity attribute, and can take place when one of the following requests resizes the window's parent: **XConfigureWindow**, **XResizeWindow**, or **XMoveResizeWindow**.

The GravityNotify event's data structure has the following specific field:

x,y               The new position of the window, relative to its parent

## MapNotify Events

| typedef struct { | | |
|---|---|---|
| int type; | ev.type | MapNotify |
| unsigned long serial | ev.xany.serial | Last request processed |
| **Bool** send_event; | ev.xany.send_event | From **XSendEvent**? |
| **Display** *display; | ev.xany.display | |
| **Window** event; | ev.xmap.event | Event window |
| **Window** window; | ev.xmap.window | Newly mapped window |
| **Bool** override_redirect; | ev.xmap.override_redirect | Prevent WM intervention |
| }**XMapEvent**; | | |

A MapNotify event is generated whenever a window is actually mapped, as a result of an **XMapWindow**, **XMapRaised**, or **XMapSubwindows**.

## ReparentNotify Events

| typedef struct { | | |
|---|---|---|
| int type; | ev.type | ReparentNotify |
| unsigned long serial | ev.xany.serial | Last request processed |
| **Bool** send_event; | ev.xany.send_event | From **XSendEvent**? |
| **Display** *display; | ev.xany.display | |
| **Window** event; | ev.xparent.event | Event window |
| **Window** window; | ev.xparent.window | Reparented window |
| **Window** parent; | ev.xparent.parent | New parent window |
| int x; | ev.xparent.x | New x position |
| int y; | ev.xparent.y | New y position |
| **Bool** override_redirect; | ev.xparent.override_redirect | Prevent WM intervention |
| }**XReparentEvent**; | | |

A ReparentNotify event is generated whenever a window is actually reparented, as a result of an **XReparentWindow** request.

The ReparentNotify event's data structure has the following specific fields:

window        The window identifier of the reparented window

parent        The window identifier of the new parent window

x,y           The position of the new window, relative to its parent

## UnmapNotify Events

| typedef struct { | | |
|---|---|---|
| int type; | ev.type | UnmapNotify |
| unsigned long serial | ev.xany.serial | Last request processed |
| **Bool** send_event; | ev.xany.send_event | From **XSendEvent**? |
| **Display** *display; | ev.xany.display | |
| **Window** event; | ev.xunmap.event | Event window |
| **Window** window; | ev.xunmap.window | Moved window |
| **Bool** from_configure; | ev.xunmap.from_configure | If gravity processing |
| } **XUnmapEvent**; | | |

An UnmapNotify event is generated whenever a window is actually unmapped. A window can be unmapped as a result of an **XUnmapWindow** request or an **XUnmapSubwindows** request.

Gravity processing also causes a window to be unmapped if the window's win_gravity attribute has the value GravityUnmap. Gravity processing can take place when one of the following requests resizes the window's parent: **XConfigureWindow**, **XResizeWindow**, or **XMoveResizeWindow**.

If you receive an UnmapNotify event from a top-level application window (or icon window), you should treat the event as a notification from the window managerthat you do not need to do any further drawing to the window.

The UnmapNotify event's data structure has the following specific field:

from_configure   This Boolean field is True if the window was unmapped as a result of gravity processing on its parent. It is False otherwise.

## VisibilityNotify Events

Your application should solicit VisibilityNotify events if you want the workstation to inform you when a window's visibility (unobscured, partially obscured, or fully obscured) changes. VisibilityNotify events are caused when changes to the window hierarchy, such as stacking order change, alter the state of a window (see Figure 4-6).

To solicit VisibilityNotify events from a window, specify VisibilityChangeMask in a call to **XSelectInput**, or set it in the *event_mask* attribute of a window.

When an application's request causes several events, VisibilityNotify events come after any window notification events but before Expose events.

The event structure for the VisibilityNotify event type is defined as follows:

```
typedef struct {
  int type;                    ev.type                    VisibilityNotify
  unsigned long serial         ev.xany.serial             Last request processed
  Bool send_event;             ev.xany.send_event         From XSendEvent?
  Display *display;            ev.xany.display
  Window window;               ev.xvisibility.window      Affected window
  int state;                   ev.xvisibility.state       New window visibility
} XVisibilityEvent;
```

The VisibilityNotify event's data structure has the following fields:

type        The event type

serial      Specifies the serial number of the last request processed

send_event  False unless this event was generated by some application issuing the **XSentEvent** request

display     Pointer to the **Display** structure the event came from

window      The window for which the visibility has changed

state       This field has one of the following values (defined in the header file **<X11/X.h>**), describing the new state of the window:

VisibilityUnobscured | The window was formerly unviewable, fully obscured, or partly obscured, and now is completely visible

VisibilityPartiallyObscured | The window was formerly unviewable, fully obscured, or completely unobscured, and now is partially obscured by some other window

VisibilityFullyObscured | The window was formerly unviewable, partially obscured, or completely unobscured, and now is fully obscured by some other window

**Example**: Solicit VisibilityNotify events for a window

This example shows the use of **XSelectInput** to solicit VisibilityNotify events from a specified window.

```
Display *display;        /* pointer to current Display structure */
Window window;           /* window you want button events from*/
. . .
XSelectInput ( display, window, VisibilityChangeMask );
```

# ClientMessage Events

Applications use ClientMessage events to send arbitrary messages to one another. Your application does not have to solicit ClientMessage events explicitly; there is no way to prevent their delivery. To send a ClientMessage event, use the **XSendEvent** request described in "Putting Back and Sending Events" in Chapter 11.

The event structure for the ClientMessage event type allows applications to interpret the information in the event as either a series of bytes, short words, or long words. The event structure is defined as follows:

The ClientMessage event's data structure has the following fields:

type | The event type

serial | Specifies the serial number of the last request processed

send_event | True; this event can only be generated by some application issuing the **XSentEvent** request

display | Pointer to the **Display** structure the event came from

window | The window to which the event was sent

| typedef struct { | | |
|---|---|---|
| int  type; | ev.type | ClientMessage |
| unsigned long serial | ev.xany.serial | Last request processed |
| **Bool** send_event; | ev.xany.send_event | (always  True) |
| **Display**  *display; | ev.xany.display | |
| **Window**  window; | ev.xclient.window | Affected  window |
| **Atom**  message_type; | ev.xclient.message_type | X Atom for message type |
| int  format; | ev.xclient.format | Format:  8,16,  or 32 |
| union { | | |
|     char b [20]; | ev.xclient.data.b | Byte data (format = 8) |
|     short s [10]; | ev.xclient.data.s | Short data (format = 16) |
|     long l [5]; | ev.xclient.data.l | Long data (format = 32) |
| } data; | | |
| } **XVisibilityEvent**; | | |

message_type    By convention, this field contains an X atom (possibly one of the atoms defined in **<X11/Xatom.h>**; see Chapter 12) which identifies the kind of message.  In order for applications to send and receive messages, they must agree on the meanings of message_type values.

format    This field contains one of the values 8, 16 or 32.  It defines whether the remaining fields in the message should be interpreted as bytes, short words, or long words.

b    This array of twenty bytes is valid if the format field contains the value 8.  It contains arbitrary application-defined data.

s    This array of ten short words is valid if the format field contains the value 16.  It contains arbitrary application-defined data.

l    This array of five long words is valid if the format field contains the value 32.  It contains arbitrary application-defined data.

X's base window system places no specific interpretation on ClientMessage events, so applications sending them to one another must agree upon the message_type, format and content of the messages.

Applications need not use the b, s, or l fields if they do not need to transmit information in those fields.  However, an application creating and sending a ClientMessage event must set the format field to 8, 16, or 32.

By convention, window managers use ClientMessage events to inform other applications of certain actions on top-level windows.  In some versions of X, applications may solicit ClientMessages from the window manager by calling **XSetWMHints** (see the section entitled "WM Hints" earlier in this chapter).

By setting bits in the messages field of the **XWMHints** structure, applications can solicit three types of ClientMessage events. The three types of events can be distinguished by the values of their message_type fields. These values are type names, referred to by Atoms (see Chapter 12):

WM_CONFIGURE_DENIED  This message is sent by a window manager when it refuses to honor an application's request to reconfigure a top-level window. It is solicited by using ConfigureDenied in the **XWMHints** structure. The data fields are unused.

WM_WINDOW_MOVED  This message is sent by a window manager when it moves a window without resizing it, in response to a user request or an application's request. It is solicited by using WindowMoved in the **XWMHints** structure. The new x and y position of the window may be found in the data.s[0] and data.s[1] fields.

WM_TAKE_FOCUS  This message is sent by a window manager to tell an application to take the keyboard focus by calling **XSetInputFocus** (see Chapter 10). It is solicited by using FocusMessage in the **XWMHints** structure. The data.l[0] field contains a timestamp for use with the **XSetInputFocus** call.

# SUMMARY

*Windows* are rectangular screen areas. The X Window System uses windows to organize the screen for the purposes of both input and output operations. Any application can place output in a window and accept input from a window without regard to other windows on the workstation's screen.

Windows follow the *desktop metaphor*: they work like pieces of electronic "paper" stacked on an electronic "desktop." Windows have a nested or *hierarchical* organization. Each window (except a single *root window* on each workstation screen) has a *parent* window, and can only be seen through that parent. Any number of windows can share a single parent. Such windows are called *siblings*. These sibling windows can be *stacked* one on top of another in an arbitrary order. A window stacked over one of its siblings *obscures* the sibling.

Applications usually have a single *top-level* window, and several *descendant* windows nested hierarchically within the top-level window. Users manipulate the position and stacking of top-level windows using a *window manager application* designed for the purpose. Applications can have as many top-level windows as necessary.

A window's *geometry* is its width, height, border width, and x and y positions relative to its parent window. Each screen has a root window; the root window's upper left corner is considered to be its *origin* and has the coordinates (0,0). The origin—the (0,0) point—of all other windows is the upper left corner just inside the border.

When windows are first created, they are *unmapped*. No window is *viewable* by the user on the screen unless it *and all its ancestors* are mapped. A mapped window may still be *unviewable* because one or more of its ancestors is still unmapped. Even if a window is *viewable*, it may be *fully obscured* or *partially obscured* because other windows are stacked on top if it. It may also be *unobscured*. Programs may issue requests to draw things in windows regardless of whether they are unmapped, unviewable, viewable, or obscured.

A typical window's life cycle contains these major events:

- Creation via **XCreateSimpleWindow** or **XCreateWindow**.
- Solicitation of input events from that window, using **XSelectInput**.
- Mapping the window with **XMapWindow** or **XMapRaised**.
- Drawing to the window.
- Unmapping and remapping the window to hide and reveal it.
- Destroying the window.

The first time your application maps a top-level window, the window manager application may intervene and prompt the user to specify a size or position for it. Thereafter, it is a *managed* window, which the user may manipulate at will. This means that *a window's size and position may change unexpectedly*. Your application must be prepared for the window manager to change its windows.

A window's *configuration* is its geometry (width, height, border width, and position relative to its parent) and stacking order relative to its siblings. X provides a variety of calls allowing applications to move and resize a window, and do other things to manipulate its configuration.

Windows all have *characteristics*. Once a window is created, its characteristics cannot be changed. Many applications cause their windows automatically to inherit their characteristics from their parent windows. Characteristics include *class* (either InputOutput or InputOnly), *depth* (number of bits per pixel), and *visual* (defining how pixels are turned into colors on the screen; see Chapter 7).

Windows also have a large number of *attributes*. Unlike characteristics, attributes can be changed. A window's *appearance* attributes define the colors or patterns shown in its background and border. They also control the color map (see Chapter 7) used to display the window's contents, and the cursor to be shown in the window.

Another group of window attributes control how it processes and dispatches input events. This group of attributes includes the *event_mask* manipulated by the **XSelectInput** call when soliciting input events.

A window's *gravity* attributes govern what happens to the image in a window when the window's size changes, and what happens to a window when its parent's size changes.

Finally, each window has *backing store* attributes. By setting backing store attributes, you inform the workstation how the image in the window should be saved if the window is not visible. Many workstations do not provide backing store and thus ignore these attributes.

Your application may specify any or all of a window's characteristics and attributes when creating the window using the **XCreateWindow** call. Your application can change a window's attributes (but not its characteristics) using **XChangeWindowAttributes**. **XReparentWindow** allows you to change a window's parent.

X provides several calls allowing your application to give hints to a window manager. These *window manager hints* specify such things as the window's name, whether the window should be displayed normally or as an icon, and constraints upon the window's size. They allow your application to make suggestions to the window manager about how you want your windows managed.

One of the trickiest things about using the X Window System is the fact that the user (via the window manager) may alter the size, shape, and position of your windows at any time. Your application must accept the window sizing it is given by a window manager. X provides a variety of events which inform you of changes to your application's windows. Keeping track of these events is a good way of honoring window manager-induced changes to your windows.

# CHAPTER 5
# GRAPHICS

This chapter describes how your application generates drawings on the screen of your workstation. Fundamentally, your X workstation's screen is made up of small square discrete picture elements, or *pixels*. Taken together, the pixels form an array, or *raster*. All drawing operations ultimately reduce to illuminating the right pixels in the pixel array. Pixels are small, so the user's eye blends them together and receives the illusion of continuous drawing. This pixel raster method of drawing is often called *bitmapped graphics*. Figure 5-1 shows an enlarged pixel-oriented drawing. On screen, this drawing appears much more continuous than it does when enlarged.

The illusion of continuity is imperfect, however. Even when reduced to screen size, Figure 5-1's circle and diagonal line have visible discontinuities, or *jaggies*, along their edges. Such jaggies are inherent to bitmapped graphics technology. Of course, the smaller the individual pixels are, the less noticeable the jaggies. As workstation technology advances, the pixels become smaller. This means that on-screen graphics can become more and more detailed.

You don't, of course, have to draw pixel-by-pixel in X. The X Window System provides requests to allow you to draw objects such as points, lines, rectangles, and arcs. These objects are known as *graphic primitives*. When you issue object-drawing requests, X figures out which pixels should be illuminated. X provides a variety of two-dimensional graphic primitives, which your application can combine to generate the pictures you want on-screen.

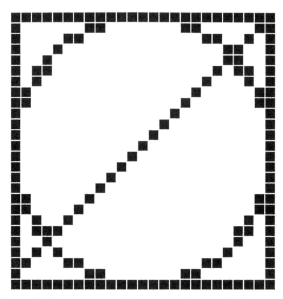

Figure 5-1.  Enlarged bitmap graphic of circle and diagonal line in square.

Primitives that display alphanumeric text are provided; those text requests are described in Chapter 6.  X also lets you specify pixel-rasters—*images*—directly if your application requires that generality; see Chapter 8 for information on how to display and manipulate images.

One thing is very important to keep in mind as you use graphic primitives: Once the workstation handles your request to draw an object (such as a line) the workstation has no memory of the fact that you drew a line, only that certain pixels are "lit."  Once your drawing is complete, the workstation's memory of what was drawn is contained entirely in the pixel raster.

Of course, before you can generate any output your application must establish a display connection (Chapter 3), then create and map a window to display the output (Chapter 4).  By virtue of the position of the window on the screen, the workstation knows where to display your pixel raster.  As you issue graphic primitive requests, the workstation illuminates the pixels you specify, and the user views them.

You can also create an invisible raster—a Pixmap—and put your drawing into it instead of into a window.  (See Chapter 8 for information about Pixmaps.)  When you issue a graphic primitive request you give the identifiers of two X resources:

- a Drawable, which can be either a window or a Pixmap, and is the destination raster;

- a **GC**, or *graphics context*, which specifies the rendering attributes to use when drawing.

Rendering attributes include such things as draw color, line width, and line style (solid, dashed, and so forth). As the workstation rasterizes graphic primitives sent to it by application programs, it interprets those primitives using the attribute values contained in the specified **GC**. Thus, your application must create at least one **GC** resource and load attribute values into it before you can issue graphic output requests. The **helloworld.c** example in Chapter 2 created and used a **GC**.

The use of rendering attributes from **GC** resources is the central concept in X graphics. Graphic primitives requested by your application are processed by a *graphics pipeline*—a series of operations that convert graphic primitives into pixels in a raster. The attribute values in **GC**s control the graphics pipeline.

The first section of this chapter lays the conceptual groundwork of **GC**s. It first discusses each stage of X's graphics pipeline. It then discusses the contents of the **GC** and how **GC**s are used to set up the pipeline. The pipeline discussion covers the default values in **GC** attributes; fortunately your application can often use the default settings for many attributes.

The second section covers the *Xlib* requests that create, alter, and delete **GC** resources. It also discusses how to set up **GC**s to carry out some basic capabilities of X graphics. (For simplicity, advanced capabilities such as patterning are deferred to the seventh section of this chapter.)

Only after **GC**s are established can we proceed to the drawing primitives. The third section of this chapter, "Drawing," discusses the *Xlib* requests that draw points, lines, rectangles, shapes, circles and arcs on the screen. In the third section, we specify exactly how you should set up the rendering attributes, and what primitives you should issue, to get the visual effects you desire.

As Chapter 4 discussed, various applications running on the workstation can change the window hierarchy by mapping, unmapping, creating, or restacking windows. Any of these changes is capable of damaging the raster contents of any of your application's windows. The fourth section of this chapter, "Expose Events," discusses *when* you should issue graphic primitive requests. It explains how to solicit, interpret, and respond to Expose events.

The fifth section of this chapter, "Clearing Windows," discusses how to clear all or part of a window.

The sixth section, "Copying Areas," describes how to copy the contents of all or part of a window to another raster in the same or a different window. Raster clearing and copying operations have some intricacies; what if your application attempts to copy a raster area from a window that is covered by another window? The sixth section discusses these intricacies.

The seventh section, "Advanced Drawing Techniques," describes some ways to use **GC** values to achieve special effects, such as screen-door patterns and stencilling, when drawing.

The eighth section, "Workstation Performance," explains how to exploit X to achieve the best possible drawing speed.

The last section, "Drawing Size," explains how to generate on-screen drawings of the size (in millimeters) you specify.

# THE GRAPHICS PIPELINE AND GCS

The rasterizationand drawing of X graphics occurs, conceptually, in a series or *pipeline* of operations, as shown in Figure 5-2. The rendering attribute values in **GC**s, as the preceding section pointed out, control various stages of the pipeline. Each stage of the pipeline is described in the following sections.

All X requests that generate graphical output (to any Drawable, either window or Pixmap) must specify the X resource identifier for a particular **GC**. The attribute values in the specified **GC** are used by the workstation as it interprets and rasterizes each graphic primitive.

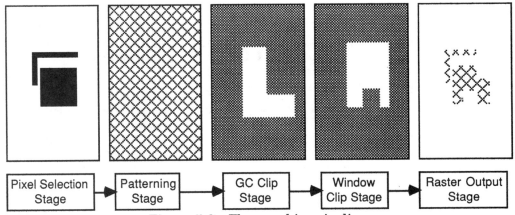

Figure 5-2.  The graphics pipeline.

It makes sense to think of each **GC** as being a *setup* for the graphics pipeline. During the initialization of your application program (or at any other time), you create as many of these pipeline setups as you need and preload attribute values into them. Then, during the execution of your program, you specify the appropriate pipeline setup (**GC**) as you request each graphic primitive.

Version 11 of the X Window System uses **GC**s this way in order to reduce network transmission overhead.  Version 10 X applications had to specify such things as line width and foreground pixel explicitly with every line-drawing request.  Experience proved that it was relatively uncommon for applications to change rendering attributes with every primitive.  Thus, rather than requiring the application to specify attributes-per-primitive redundantly and repeatedly, X11 requires applications to specify a **GC**-per-primitive.

Figure 5-2 shows an example of the operation of the pipeline on two lines and a rectangle.  At the Pixel Selection stage, the pixels to be drawn by the pipeline are shown in black. Next the Patterning stage applies (in this example) a cross-hatch pattern to them. They then pass through the two clipping (stencilling) stages. Finally, all the patterned pixels that survive clipping appear at the Raster Output stage and are displayed.

## Pixel Selection Stage

This first stage of the pipeline operates upon an incoming graphic primitive, such as a line, arc, or polygon. The Pixel Selection stage computes, mathematically, which pixels must be altered in the raster in order to display the shape of the primitive object. Most graphic primitives generate *foreground* pixels. For example, the foreground pixels for a filled rectangle constitute all the pixels inside the boundaries of the rectangle. Some operations also generate *background* pixels. For example, a line drawn using the LineDoubleDash style (see "Line Drawing Attributes" later in this chapter) contains background pixels where the dash pattern is off and foreground pixels where the pattern is on. Each generated foreground or background pixel is passed on to the next pipeline stage.

Most of the attribute values in **GC**s control how pixels are selected for particular types of graphic primitives. For example, lines can be drawn in many different ways. Line-drawing is controlled by the attributes line_width, line_style, cap_style, join_style, dash_offset, and dashes. The attributes that govern pixel selection are discussed along with the graphic primitives they control in the "Drawing" section of this chapter.

## Patterning Stage

This pipeline stage applies a pattern of pixel values (colors) to foreground and background pixels emanating from the previous stage. The Patterning stage of the pipeline uses the following attributes:

foreground  This attribute is often called the "draw color." It specifies the pixel value to use for foreground pixels. The **helloworld.c** example of Chapter 2 sets the foreground color to black. See Chapter 7 for a detailed discussion of pixel values.

background  This attribute specifies the pixel value to apply to background pixels. It is analogous to the foreground attribute.

stipple  This attribute is the X resource identifier of a Pixmap to use as a stipple pattern. It is used for hatch-patterning and screen-door patterning. See under the heading "Advanced Drawing Techniques" later in this chapter for further information on stipples and tiles.

tile  This attribute is the X resource identifier of a Pixmap to use as a tile pattern. This attribute is only used for tile-patterning.

fill_style          This attribute selects the fill style—the technique used for applying patterns—used for drawing. By default it has the value FillSolid. FillSolid applies a solid "draw color" to all the pixels of your primitive. Other fill styles, including hatching, tiling and screen-door-patterning, are also available. See "Advanced Drawing Techniques" in this chapter for a discussion of the other fill styles.

## GC Clipping Stage

Once colors are assigned to your graphic primitives, this pipeline stage (optionally) *clips* them—discards all pixels outside a region you specify. If you want to use clipping, you may specify the clip region in one of two ways:

- You may set the clip_maskattribute  to specify a clip mask or stencil.

- You may use the **XSetClipRectangles** request. This allows you to specify the clipping stencil in terms of a list of rectangular areas.

By default, no clip stencil is specified in this stage, and no clipping takes place. You need not change the default unless you wish to constrain drawing to part of your output window or Pixmap. See "Advanced Drawing Techniques."

## Window Clipping Stage

This pipeline stage discards all pixels which lie outside the boundaries of the window (or Pixmap) to which you are drawing. The only control you have over this pipeline stage is through the subwindow_mode attribute. With this attribute, you can control whether or not this pipeline stage will allow you to draw on pixels that belong to inferior windows. The subwindow_mode attribute can have one of the following values:

ClipByChildren    All pixels in inferior windows are clipped. This value is the default; ordinarily you do not wish your graphics operations to "print through" child windows.

IncludeInferiors  Graphic primitives are allowed to draw through subwindow boundaries.

This stage always discards pixels which would be drawn outside the boundaries of your window. It also discards pixels which would otherwise be drawn into other windows which are stacked on top of your windows.

## Raster Output Stage

This final stage of the graphics pipeline combines, bitwise, the generated pixel values for your graphic primitives (known as *source pixel values*) with the pixel values already present in the output raster (known as *destination pixel values*). Two GC attributes control the Raster Output stage:

function      This attribute specifies one of the sixteen possible Boolean functions of two input variables.

plane_mask      The operation of combining source with destination pixels is restricted to a subset of the bits in the pixel values by this mask. When a bit is 1 in the plane_mask, the corresponding bit position in destination pixels may be updated, and when a bit is zero, the corresponding bit position is protected. See the description of **XSetPlaneMask** under "Convenience Functions."

Using the specified function, X combines the pixel value already at a given position in a Drawable with the pixel value generated for that position by the graphics pipeline just described. This final combination of pixel values determines what is actually displayed. For a list of the available functions, see the description of **XSetFunction** under "Convenience Functions" later in this chapter.

For example, if the function is GXCopy, the new pixel value replaces the old one. If the function is GXor, the resulting pixel value is made by taking the logical OR of the new and old values.

# MANIPULATING GC RESOURCES

You must create at least one **GC** before your application can display graphic primitives on the workstation. You can create as many **GC**s as you like, because **GC**s, like other X resources, are not very expensive. If your application *uses* many different **GC**s in random order, some workstations may not perform well; see "Workstation Performance" in this chapter.

As Chapter 4 pointed out, some applications use many windows. You do not need to create separate **GC**s for each different Drawable your application uses. Once you create a **GC** to work with one Drawable, it will work with any other Drawable having the same depth and Visual type on the same screen.

Use the **XCreateGC** request to create and load initial values into **GC**s (see the "GC Creation" section). To load initial values into a **GC**, you can use either the **XGCValues** structure or convenience functions, both described in this chapter.

During the course of your application, you will probably want to change the attribute settings in at least some of your **GC**s. This is especially true on color workstations, where you will find yourself changing the foreground attribute. X provides a large number of convenience functions for changing **GC** contents. X also provides the **XChangeGC** request, which permits you to change any or all of the attributes in a GC at once.

If you want to copy attribute values from one **GC** to another, you can use the **XCopyGC** request. Finally, when you are finished using **GC**s, you destroy them with the **XFreeGC** request.

Note that X does not provide a way to inquire what attribute values are stored in a **GC**; your application program must keep track of all attribute settings.

For the sake of simplicity, this chapter separates the capabilities of the X graphics pipeline into "basic" and "advanced" categories. This section covers only the "basic" graphic capabilities—we defer discussion of such things as patterning to the "Advanced Drawing Techniques" section. Table 5-I is a summary of the X requests and convenience functions for manipulating **GC**s and their "basic" attributes. Table 5-I contains only those convenience functions that apply to all graphic primitives; convenience functions (such as **XSetLineWidth**) that apply only to certain primitives are described in the "Drawing" section of this chapter.

| Request/Function | Xlib ¶ | Description |
|---|---|---|
| **General-Purpose GC Manipulation Requests** | | |
| XCreateGC | 5.3 | Create and initialize a **GC** |
| XChangeGC | 5.3 | Change any or all attribute values |
| XCopyGC | 5.3 | Copy any attributes from **GC** to **GC** |
| XFreeGC | 5.3 | Destroy a **GC** |
| **Convenience Functions** | | |
| XSetForeground | 5.4.1 | Set foreground pixel value |
| XSetBackground | 5.4.1 | Set background pixel value |
| XSetFunction | 5.4.1 | Set function (see Table 5-III) |
| XSetPlaneMask | 5.4.1 | Set plane_mask |
| XSetState | 5.4.1 | Set foreground, background, plane_mask, function all together |

Table 5-I.  Basic **GC** Manipulation Requests and Convenience Functions.

## General-Purpose GC Manipulation Requests

This section describes the requests for creating, altering, copying and deleting **GC** resources.

### The GCValues structure and mask

The **XCreateGC**, **XChangeGC**, and **XCopyGC** requests all permit you to specify any combination of **GC** attribute values. In order to do this, you must declare a **XGCValues** structure and set the appropriate fields to the values you wish. Then, when you invoke the request, you must specify both the structure and a mask specifying which fields contain valid data.

The **XGCValues** structure is declared in the header file **<X11/Xlib.h>**, as shown in Table 5-II. The table shows both the structure declaration and the names of the mask bits used to declare which fields are valid.

## GC Creation

To create a new graphics context resource, use the **XCreateGC** request. **XCreateGC** (*Xlib* ¶5.3) has the form

    **Display** *display;*      /* *pointer to Display structure* */
    **Drawable** *drawable;*    /* *window or pixmap* */
    unsigned long *valuemask;* /* *mask bits* */
    **XGCValues** *values;*    /* *values structure* */
    **GC** *mygc;*        /* *created graphics context* */

    . . .
    *mygc* = **XCreateGC** ( *display, drawable, valuemask, &values* );

When you create a **GC**, you specify the Drawable you intend to use it with (because **GC**s are used with both windows and Pixmaps, you can specify either kind of Drawable resource). Once you have created a **GC**, you can use it with all other windows or Pixmaps on the same screen with the same depth (see Chapter 7;

| Structure Declaration | Mask Bit Name | Pipeline Stage |
|---|---|---|
| typedef struct { | | |
|    int function; | GCFunction | Raster Output |
|    unsigned long plane_mask; | GCPlaneMask | Raster Output |
|    unsigned long foreground; | GCForeground | Patterning |
|    unsigned long background; | GCBackground | Patterning |
|    int line_width; | GCLineWidth | Pixel Selection, Lines/Arcs |
|    int line_style; | GCLineStyle | Pixel Selection, Lines/Arcs |
|    int cap_style; | GCCapStyle | Pixel Selection, Lines/Arcs |
|    int join_style; | GCJoinStyle | Pixel Selection, Lines/Arcs |
|    int fill_style; | GCFillStyle | Patterning |
|    int fill_rule; | GCFillRule | Pixel Selection, Polygons |
|    int arc_mode; | GCArcMode | Pixel Selection, Filled Arcs |
|    **Pixmap** tile; | GCTile | Patterning |
|    **Pixmap** stipple; | GCStipple | Patterning |
|    int ts_x_origin; | GCTileStipXOrigin | Patterning |
|    int ts_y_origin; | GCTileStipYOrigin | Patterning |
|    **Font** font; | GCFont | Text (Chapter 6) |
|    int subwindow_mode; | GCSubwindowMode | Window Clipping |
|    Bool graphics_exposures; | GCGraphicsExposures | Window Clipping |
|    int clip_x_origin; | GCClipXOrigin | GC Clipping |
|    int clip_y_origin; | GCClipYOrigin | GC Clipping |
|    **Pixmap** clip_mask; | GCClipMask | GC Clipping |
|    int dash_offset; | GCDashOffset | Pixel Selection, Lines/Arcs |
|    char dashes; | GCDashList | Pixel Selection, Lines/Arcs |
| } **XGCValues**; | | |

Table 5-II. **XGCValues** structure and mask bits.

on most workstations, all windows have the same depth). Thus, your application does not need to create separate **GC**s for each window, but can share **GC**s among windows.

You also specify *values*, a **XGCValues** structure, and a *valuemask* indicating which values are set in *values*. As your **GC** is created, the attributes in it are set to the values you specify. Values you do not specify are set to the defaults. You may specify a zero *valuemask*; if you do, **XCreateGC** ignores the *values* parameter and sets all values in the newly created **GC** to the defaults.

**XCreateGC** is a function; its result is the resource identifier of the newly created **GC**. Your program must store this resource identifier for use with later drawing requests.

**Example**: Create a **GC** containing default values
_____

This is an example of the simplest possible **GC** creation. Neither *values* nor *valuemask* bits are specified.

```
Display *display;
Window window;        /* the window to draw to*/
GC mygc;              /* new gc resource */
  . . .
mygc = XCreateGC ( display, window, 0, 0 );
```

It is a good idea to create **GC**s this way, then change their attribute values using convenience functions such as **XSetForeground**. The use of convenience functions will probably make your application program easier to read and debug. Furthermore, *Xlib* has a cache for attribute values, so using convenience functions does not degrade performance.

**Example**: Create a **GC** suitable for rubber-band-line drawing
_____

In this example we create a **GC** while explicitly specifying foreground, plane_mask, and function attributes. By setting the foreground color to all ones, the plane mask to the bits that differ between the BlackPixel and WhitePixel values, and the function to GXxor (see Table 5-III), we create a **GC** that can be used for rubber-band-line drawing on a black-and-white screen. Note that when a primitive is drawn twice with this **GC**, it appears the first time it is drawn and disappears the second time.

```
Display *display;
Window window;                /* the window to draw to*/
GC mygc;                      /* created graphics context */
unsigned long valuemask;      /* mask bits */
XGCValues values;             /* values structure */
int screen;
  . . .
screen = DefaultScreen ( display );
valuemask = GCFunction | GCPlaneMask |
```

```
                        GCForeground | GCBackground;
       values.function = GXxor;
       values.plane_mask = BlackPixel ( display, screen ) ^
                             WhitePixel ( display, screen );
       values.foreground = 0xffffffff;
       mygc = XCreateGC ( display, window, valuemask, &values );
```

This example serves to illustrate how you would construct a *values* structure with a few attributes set in it, and how to use the *valuemask* parameter.

## GC Change

To change some or all of the parameter values stored in an existing **GC**, use the **XChangeGC** request (or the convenience functions described in the remainder of this chapter, if you prefer). **XChangeGC** (*Xlib* ¶5.3) has the form

```
Display *display;         /* pointer to Display structure */
GC mygc;                  /* gc to change */
unsigned long valuemask;  /* mask bits */
XGCValues values;         /* values structure */
   . . .
XChangeGC ( display, mygc, valuemask, &values );
```

When using the **XChangeGC** request, you must, of course, specify *mygc*, the resource identifier of the **GC** you wish to change. Note that you need not specify a window or Pixmap identifer; once you have created the **GC** you use its identifier.

You also specify *values*, a **XGCValues** structure, together with a *valuemask* indicating which values are set in *values*. For every bit set in the *valuemask*, this request changes the corresponding attribute to the specified value.

**Example**: Change a foreground attribute

```
Display *display;
GC mygc;                  /* graphics context to change*/
unsigned long valuemask;  /* mask bits */
XGCValues values;         /* values structure */
   . . .
valuemask = GCForeground;
values.foreground = WhitePixel ( display, DefaultScreen (display) );
XChangeGC ( display, mygc, valuemask, &values );
```

## GC Copying

The **XCopyGC** request copies attribute values from one **GC** to another. Both the source and the destination **GC**s must already exist; this request does not create a new **GC**. **XCopyGC** (*Xlib* ¶5.3) has the form

```
Display *display;        /* pointer to Display structure */
GC source;               /* source of copy operation*/
unsigned long valuemask; /* mask bits */
GC destination;          /* destination of copy operation*/
    . . .
XCopyGC ( display, source, valuemask, destination );
```

All the attribute values specified by the *valuemask* are copied from the *source* **GC** to the *destination* **GC**. Both **GC**s must already exist. The usage of the *valuemask* is the same as for **XCreateGC**.

## GC Deletion

When your application no longer needs **GC** resources, you can explicitly delete them via the **XFreeGC** request. Ordinarily, though, **GC**s are deleted automatically when your application terminates, so you probably do not need to delete them explicitly. The rules for **GC** lifetime are the same as for any other X resource (see Chapter 3). **XFreeGC** (*Xlib* ¶5.3) has the form

```
Display *display;        /* pointer to Display structure */
GC mygc;                 /* gc to delete /
    . . .
XFreeGC ( display, mygc );
```

This request destroys *mygc*. Your application must not refer to *mygc* in any subsequent requests, or you will receive a BadGC error event message.

## Convenience Functions

The convenience functions described in this section give your application control over the foreground and background "draw color" attributes used in the Patterning stage of the graphics pipeline. They also give you control over the function and plane_mask attributes which control the Raster Output stage.

All these convenience functions operate on previously created **GC** resources. As the first example under **XCreateGC** above pointed out, your application does not incur a performance penalty if you choose to create all your **GC**s with default values, then set their contents using convenience functions.

*Xlib* contains a cache for attribute values. As long as you refer to only one **GC** resource, this cache permits you to make several consecutive *Xlib* calls, including **XCreateGC**, **XChangeGC**, and **GC**-altering convenience functions, while only generating one single protocol request message to the X workstation server.

> Your application will not lose performance if you use **GC** convenience functions instead of an **XChangeGC** request. Don't be fooled by **XChangeGC**'s complex parameters into thinking it is any faster than several convenience functions. Convenience functions also make your code easier to read.

## XSetForeground

The **XSetForeground** function sets the *foreground* attribute in the **GC** you specify. **XSetForeground** (*Xlib* ¶5.4.1) has the form

```
Display *display;          /* pointer to Display structure */
GC mygc;                   /* gc */
unsigned long foreground;  /* foreground pixel value */
    . . .
XSetForeground ( display, mygc, foreground );
```

The *foreground* you specify is a pixel value, or "draw color."  For more information on pixel values and how they translate into colors, see Chapter 7.  The default *foreground* value in a newly created **GC** is 0, which is not much use because it does not give a predictable color.  See the example under "XSetBackground" for more information.

## XSetBackground

The **XSetBackground** function is analogous to **XSetForeground**, except that it sets the *background* attribute.  **XSetBackground** (*Xlib* ¶5.4.1) has the form

```
Display *display;          /* pointer to Display structure */
GC mygc;                   /* gc */
unsigned long background;  /* background pixel value */
    . . .
XSetBackground ( display, mygc, background );
```

If you create a **GC** without setting the background attribute, the default value is 1.

---

**Example**: Create a GC and set usable foreground and background
_____

This example shows how to create a **GC** for use with a window and set its *foreground* and *background* attributes to usable values.  In it, we use the BlackPixel and WhitePixel macros (see Chapter 7 for further information) to determine the correct pixel value settings for white and black.

```
Display *display;
Window mywindow;
GC mygc;
int screen;
    . . .
screen = DefaultScreen ( display );
mygc = XCreateGC ( display, mywindow, 0, 0 );
XSetForeground ( display, mygc, BlackPixel ( display, screen ) );
XSetBackground ( display, mygc, WhitePixel ( display, screen) );
```

## XSetFunction

**XSetFunction** selects the Boolean function used by the pipeline's Raster Output stage for combining pixels generated by graphic primitives with pixels already stored in the output raster. **XSetFunction** (*Xlib* ¶5.4.1) has the form

```
Display *display;       /* pointer to Display structure */
GC mygc;                /* gc */
int function;           /* function value */
    . . .
XSetFunction ( display, mygc, function );
```

This request sets the specified *function* into the specified **GC**. The *function* parameter must have one of the values specified in Table 5-III.

The default value for the function attribute is GXcopy, and the default *plane_mask* value is all ones. This useful combination of default values causes your source pixel values to simply overwrite the destination pixel values as you draw.

Your application may also use the function value GXxor. This Boolean function (exclusive-or) has a useful property: with it, a primitive drawn twice in the same place with the same foreground and plane_mask restores the original destination pixel values. Your application can, therefore, use GXxor to draw, then undraw, such things as rubber-band lines. The GXxor symbol appears very similar to GXor (inclusive-or); be careful not to confuse the two.

| Boolean Function | Xlib Symbol | Source 0 Dest 0 | Source 0 Dest 1 | Source 1 Dest 0 | Source 1 Dest 1 | Hexadecimal |
|---|---|---|---|---|---|---|
| Zero | GXclear | 0 | 0 | 0 | 0 | 0x0 |
| Source & Dest | GXand | 0 | 0 | 0 | 1 | 0x1 |
| Source & ~Dest | GXandReverse | 0 | 0 | 1 | 0 | 0x2 |
| Source | GXcopy | 0 | 0 | 1 | 1 | 0x3 |
| ~Source & Dest | GXandInverted | 0 | 1 | 0 | 0 | 0x4 |
| Dest | GXnoop | 0 | 1 | 0 | 1 | 0x5 |
| Source xor Dest | GXxor | 0 | 1 | 1 | 0 | 0x6 |
| Source | Dest | GXor | 0 | 1 | 1 | 1 | 0x7 |
| ~Source & ~Dest | GXnor | 1 | 0 | 0 | 0 | 0x8 |
| ~Source xor Dest | GXequiv | 1 | 0 | 0 | 1 | 0x9 |
| ~Dest | GXinvert | 1 | 0 | 1 | 0 | 0xa |
| Source | ~Dest | GXorReverse | 1 | 0 | 1 | 1 | 0xb |
| ~Source | GXcopyInverted | 1 | 1 | 0 | 0 | 0xc |
| ~Source | Dest | GXorInverted | 1 | 1 | 0 | 1 | 0xd |
| ~Source | ~Dest | GXnand | 1 | 1 | 1 | 0 | 0xe |
| One | GXset | 1 | 1 | 1 | 1 | 0xf |

Table 5-III.  Boolean functions.

## XSetPlaneMask

**XSetPlaneMask** sets the plane_mask used by the graphics pipeline's Raster Output stage. The plane_mask attribute is useful on color workstations in which the pixels in the output raster have multiple bits. When a bit in the plane_mask is zero, the corresponding bit in each output pixel is not changed. (The *plane_mask* attribute is most useful with the Private Color Cell color-allocation strategy described in Chapter 7.) **XSetPlaneMask** (*Xlib* ¶5.4.1) has the form

```
Display *display;          /* pointer to Display structure */
GC mygc;                   /* gc */
unsigned long plane_mask;  /* plane_mask value */
 . . .
XSetPlaneMask ( display, mygc, plane_mask );
```

This request sets the specified *plane_mask* into the specified **GC**. If you create a **GC** without setting the plane_mask attribute, the default value is all ones. This default value permits all bit positions in output pixels to be altered by drawing requests.

### Example: Create a **GC** suitable for rubber-band-line drawing

In this example we repeat the second example shown above under **XCreateGC**. However, this time we create a default **GC**, then use convenience functions to load the attribute values.

```
Display *display;
Window window;        /* the window to draw to*/
GC mygc;              /* created graphics context */
int screen;
unsigned long mask;   /* plane mask */
 . . .
screen = DefaultScreen ( display );
mask = BlackPixel ( display, screen ) ^ WhitePixel ( display, screen );
 . . .
mygc = XCreateGC     ( display, window, 0, 0 );
XSetForeground       ( display, mygc, 0xffffffff );
XSetBackground       ( display, mygc, 0 );
XSetFunction         ( display, mygc, GXxor );
XSetPlaneMask        ( display, mygc, mask );
```

## XSetState

**XSetState** combines the setting of foreground, background, function, and plane_mask into a single convenience function. It is useful in circumstances in which you wish to set all four attributes simultaneously. **XSetState** (*Xlib* ¶5.4.1) has the form

```
Display *display;          /* pointer to Display structure */
GC mygc;                   /* gc */
unsigned long foreground;  /* foreground value */
unsigned long background;  /* background value */
int function;              /* Boolean function */
unsigned long plane_mask;  /* plane_mask */

   . . .

XSetState ( display, mygc, foreground, background,
                          function, plane_mask );
```

# DRAWING

This section describes the Pixel Selection Stage of the X graphics pipeline. The Pixel Selection Stage converts your drawing primitives (lines, arcs, polygons) into the appropriate pixels.

Two kinds of X functions are described in this section: draw requests and attribute-setting requests. The draw requests operate the X graphics pipeline: in draw requests you specify the x,y coordinates of the graphic primitives you want to draw. The attribute-setting requests set up the pipeline so the primitives come out the way you want them (note that you could also use the **XChangeGC** request together with a **XGCValues** structure in place of some of the attribute-setting functions). Table 5-IV lists the requests and functions used in drawing. The table makes it clear that almost all graphic primitives can be requested in either a singular form (**XDrawArc**) or a plural form (**XDrawArcs**). Each request and function is described in detail in the sections to follow.

The first three parameters of all X drawing requests are always a display pointer, a Drawable (window or Pixmap) and a **GC**. The other parameters vary depending on the type of object being drawn. Graphic primitives are all one-way requests; *Xlib* puts several of them into a buffer and transmits them all at once to improve performance and reduce traffic on your display connection.

When you use a drawing request, you must specify the coordinates of the object. You always specify these coordinates in pixel units, as integers. There is no way (in unextended X) to specify a fractional pixel position. Coordinates are always relative to the origin of the Drawable you specify. The pixel in the upper left corner of the window or Pixmap has the coordinates (0,0); X increases to the right, and Y increases downwards.

Note that coordinates are simple integers which do not scale up or down. If your application makes a window bigger and redraws the window's contents using the same coordinate values, they will be the same size, and in the same position relative to the window's upper left corner.

Coordinates are signed integers: they may be either positive or negative. You may specify negative coordinates for things you want to draw. However, because

| Request/Function | Xlib ¶ | Description |
| --- | --- | --- |
| **Points** | | |
| **XDrawPoint** | 6.3.1 | Draw a single point |
| **XDrawPoints** | 6.3.1 | Draw multiple points |
| **Lines** | | |
| **XSetLineAttributes** | 5.4.2 | Set attributes such as line_width |
| **XSetDashes** | 5.4.2 | Select the dash pattern |
| **XDrawLine** | 6.3.2 | Draw a single line |
| **XDrawSegments** | 6.3.2 | Draw several disconnected lines |
| **XDrawLines** | 6.3.2 | Draw a connected series of lines |
| **Arc and Circle Outlines** | | |
| **XDrawArc** | 6.3.4 | Draw the outline of an arc (or circle) |
| **XDrawArcs** | 6.3.4 | Draw the outlines of several arcs |
| **Filled Arcs and Circles** | | |
| **XSetArcMode** | 5.4.7 | Set arc fill mode (chord or pie-slice) |
| **XFillArc** | 6.4.3 | Fill a single arc (or circle) |
| **XFillArcs** | 6.4.3 | Fill several arcs |
| **Rectangle Outlines** | | |
| **XDrawRectangle** | 6.3.3 | Draw the outline of a rectangle |
| **XDrawRectangles** | 6.3.3 | Draw the outlines of several rectangles |
| **Filled Rectangles** | | |
| **XFillRectangle** | 6.4.3 | Fill in the area of a rectangle |
| **XFillRectangles** | 6.4.3 | Fill in the areas of several rectangles |
| **Polygons** | | |
| **XSetFillRule** | 5.4.3 | Set the rule for pixel inclusion |
| **XFillPolygon** | 6.4.2 | Fill a polygon area |

Table 5-IV.   Drawing calls.

the origin of the Drawable always lies at (0,0), the negative part of the drawing always lies above the Drawable's top edge, or to the left of its left edge.

The measured size on the screen of the objects you draw depends on the size of the screen and the number of pixels across the screen. See "Drawing Size" at the end of this chapter for details.

## Points

The simplest graphic primitive is a single point. To the **XDrawPoint** request you specify an *x* and *y*, and the workstation draws one point—one pixel. To the

**XDrawPoints** request you specify a list of point coordinates, and the workstation draws them all, one after another.

The attributes in the specified **GC** control the drawing of the points. The points are drawn in the foreground pixel value, using the entire graphics pipeline *except* the Patterning stage (no stipple or tile pattern is ever used when drawing points).

**XDrawPoint** (*Xlib* ¶6.3.1) is very simple; it has the form

```
Display *display;        /* pointer to Display structure */
Drawable window;         /* window or pixmap */
GC gc;                   /* gc */
int x, y;                /* coordinates of point */
   . . .
XDrawPoint ( display, window, gc, x,y );
```

**XDrawPoints** is the form of **XDrawPoint** for drawing multiple points rapidly. It requires you to specify a list of points in an array of **XPoint** structures. The **XPoint** structure is defined (in **<X11/Xlib.h>**) as follows:

```
typedef struct {
    short x, y;
} XPoint;
```

**XDrawPoints** (*Xlib* ¶6.3.1) has the form

```
Display *display;        /* pointer to Display structure */
Drawable window;         /* window or pixmap */
GC gc;                   /* gc */
XPoint points [ ];       /* array of points */
int npoints;             /* number of points */
int mode;                /* CoordModeOrigin or CoordModePrevious */
   . . .
XDrawPoints ( display, window, gc, points, npoints, mode );
```

The result of this function is the drawing of all the points in *points*. *npoints* specifies how big the *points* array is.

The *mode* argument is useful when you want to define an **XPoint** array, then draw its contents in several places in a window. *mode* can have one of two symbolic values:

CoordModeOrigin     In this mode, you must specify all the x,y coordinates in *points* relative to the origin of the *window*.

CoordModePrevious   In this mode, you must specify the first x,y coordinate pair in the *points* array relative to the origin of *window*. Specify subsequent coordinate pairs relative to the preceding coordinate pair. This is often known as *relative mode* or *delta mode*.

**Example**: Draw a pattern of five dots in several places in a window.

This example illustrates the use of **XDrawPoints** in relative mode. We define and initialize a static **XPoints** array, specifying a pattern of five dots. The first entry in the **XPoints** array has the coordinates (0,0), and the others are defined as relative.

We then draw the pattern in several different places by altering the first **XPoints** entry and issuing the **XDrawPoints** request. Figure 5-3, which is annotated, shows the upper left corner of the window (including part of the window border) drawn by the following code:

```
#define FIGSIZE 5
XPoint figure [FIGSIZE] = {  {0,0}, {-2, -2}, {4,0}, {0,4}, {-4,0} };
Display *display;        /* pointer to Display structure */
Drawable window;        /* window or pixmap */
GC gc;                  /* gc */
. . .
figure[0].x = 10;   figure[0].y = 10;
XDrawPoints ( display, window, gc, figure, FIGSIZE, CoordModePrevious);
figure[0].x = 20;   figure[0].y = 10;
XDrawPoints ( display, window, gc, figure, FIGSIZE, CoordModePrevious);
figure[0].x = 10;   figure[0].y = 20;
XDrawPoints ( display, window, gc, figure, FIGSIZE, CoordModePrevious);
```

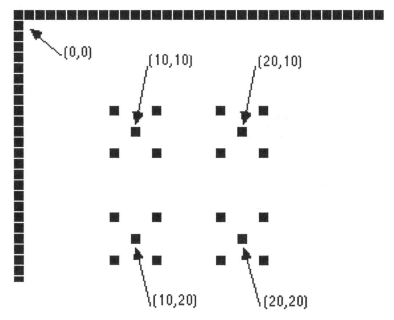

Figure 5-3. **XDrawPoints** example output, enlarged and annotated.

*figure*[0].x = 20;    *figure*[0].y = 20;
**XDrawPoints** ( *display, window, gc, figure,* FIGSIZE, CoordModePrevious);

The point of this example is to illustrate the initialization and use of
**XPoint** structures, and to show a use for CoordModePrevious.

## Lines

The X Window System allows you to draw straight lines specified by the coordinates of their endpoints. The attributes in the specified **GC** control the drawing
of lines. Lines are drawn using all stages of the graphics pipeline.

First we will describe line attributes. There are several line attributes which af-
ford you a large amount of control over how lines are drawn. Next, we will discuss the use of the **XDrawLine**, **XDrawLines**, and **XDrawSegments** requests.
A couple of examples conclude this section.

### Line-Drawing Attributes

The **XSetLineAttributes** convenience function allows you to set the values of
line-drawing attributes in a **GC**. **XSetLineAttributes** (*Xlib* ¶5.4.2) has the form

```
Display *display;        /* pointer to Display structure */
GC gc;                   /* gc */
unsigned int line_width; /* line width in pixels */
int line_style;          /* LineSolid, LineOnOffDash, LineDoubleDash */
int cap_style;           /* CapNotLast, CapButt, CapRound, CapProjecting */
int join_style;          /* JoinMiter, JoinRound, JoinBevel */
. . .
XSetLineAttributes ( display, gc, line_width, line_style,
                                  cap_style, join_style );
```

If you choose, you may use the **XCreateGC** or **XChangeGC** requests with an
**XGCValues** structure instead of this convenience function; see above.

*line_width* specifies the width of the line in pixels. The default value (in a newly
created **GC**) for *line_width* is zero. A zero value for *line_width* means the line
should be one pixel wide: as narrow as possible while still visible. When
*line_width* is zero, the workstation draws lines most rapidly. Usually you will
use a width of zero for slim lines. Lines with non-zero width are drawn precisely, as if they were polygons. If you require pixel-for-pixel reproducibility in
your application, and it runs on several vendors' workstations, you should set
*line_width* to one, not zero, when drawing slim lines. The *line_width* attribute
corresponds to the line_width field in the **XGCValues** structure.

The examples in Figure 5-5 were drawn in black with an exaggerated *line_width*
of 21 pixels. White zero-width lines were then drawn over the wide lines (in the
same coordinate positions). Note that the *line_width* is distributed equally on either side of the narrow line. Usually, you will find a smaller *line_width* to be
more useful.

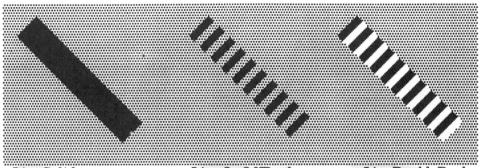

LineSolid                    LineOnOffDash              LineDoubleDash
Figure 5-4. *line_style* attribute settings.

Using the *line_style* attribute, you can select whether you want your lines solid or dashed. If you want them drawn with a dash pattern, you can select whether you want the space between the dashes to be transparent, or to be drawn in the background color. The *line_style* attribute corresponds to the line_style field in the **XGCValues** structure. *line_style* can have one of three values, illustrated in Figure 5-4.

LineSolid
: Lines are drawn solidly (not dashed) and efficiently with the foreground "draw color." LineSolid is the default.

LineOnOffDash
: Lines are drawn dashed (**XSetDashes**, described in the next section, lets you specify the dash pattern). Odd-numbered dash segments are drawn with the foreground pixel value, whereas even-numbered segments appear transparent.

LineDoubleDash
: Lines are also drawn dashed, but odd-numbered dash segments are drawn in the foreground color, and even-numbered dash segments in the background color. (Note: if hatch patterning or tile patterning is being used—see "Advanced Drawing Techniques" in this chapter—a *line_style* of LineDoubleDash is treated like LineSolid.)

Figure 5-5 illustrates *cap_style* and *join_style* combinations. *cap_style* controls the end-caps on lines (and unfilled arcs). End-caps appear at each end of lines drawn by **XDrawLine** and **XDrawSegments**. They also appear at the beginning and end of a series of lines drawn by **XDrawLines**.

The *cap_style* attribute corresponds to the cap_style field in the **XGCValues** structure. *cap_style* can have one of four values:

CapButt
: End-caps are squared off at endpoints perpendicular to the slope of the line.

Figure 5-5. *cap_style* and *join_style* combinations.

CapNotLast       Equivalent to CapButt for wide lines. When *line_width* is
                 zero or one, the last point of the line segment is not drawn.
                 A line segment drawn this way is often called a *continu-
                 able* line segment.

CapRound         End-caps are circles with diameter equal to the *line_width*.
                 This end-cap style is not meaningful unless the *line_width*
                 is 2 or greater.

CapProjecting    End-caps are, like CapButt, squared off. However, they
                 project half the line-width beyond the endpoints. This end-
                 cap style is not meaningful unless the *line_width* is 2 or
                 greater.

*join_style* controls how the intermediate points—corners—in a series of wide lines are drawn (with the **XDrawLines** request). *join_style* is only meaningful when the *line_width* is 2 or greater. The *join_style* attribute corresponds to the join_style field in the **XGCValues** structure. *join_style* can have one of three values:

JoinMiter   Outer edges of wide lines are extended. They meet at the same angle as would narrow lines.

JoinRound   Corners are rounded off, using a circle of diameter equal to *line_width* centered at the join point.

JoinBevel   Suppose the intersecting endpoints of the lines were both drawn as if they were endpoints, with CapButt end-caps. This would leave a small triangle. When the *join_style* is JoinBevel, this small triangle is filled.

## Dash Patterns

The **XSetDashes** function allows you to define arbitrary dash patterns. For example, if your application were drawing a map, you might use dots (short dashes) for drawing city limits, long dashes for county boundaries, and a dot-dash pattern for national borders. You would use **XSetDashes** to set up a **GC** for each of these patterns. **XSetDashes** (*Xlib* ¶5.4.2) has the form

```
Display *display;     /* pointer to Display structure */
GC gc;                /* gc */
int dash_offset;      /* starting point in the pattern */
char dash_list [ ];   /* array of characters defining the dash pattern */
int n;                /* length of dash_list */
. . .
     XSetDashes ( display, gc, dash_offset, dash_list, n );
```

The *dash_list* is an array of characters; *n* defines the length of *dash_list*. Each element in the *dash_list* array is the length (in pixels) of a segment of the pattern. Dashed lines are drawn (depending on the *line_style* setting; see above) as alternating segments, each of an element in the *dash_list*. Thus, the overall length of the dash pattern (in pixels) is the sum of all elements of the *dash_list*. When the pattern is used up, it repeats. For best results, define your *dash_list* arrays so they contain an even number of elements. Do not try to specify a zero-length *dash_list* element.

The *dash_offset* defines the phase of the pattern; that is, how many pixels into the *dash_list* you want to start using the pattern at the beginning of each new line. *dash_offset* is most often specified as zero. You may, however, find it useful to specify *dash_offset* as half of the first element in the *dash_list*; if two lines start at the same point, the patterns will match better.

When you draw dashed wide lines, you will probably want to increase the lengths of the dash pattern elements proportionally to the line width. Also, keep in mind that different makes and models of workstation vary in the details of how they use dash patterns, especially for drawing diagonal lines. Don't try to get pixel-for-pixel accuracy when drawing dashed lines.

**Example**: Three useful dash patterns

From left to right, these three objects are drawn with a dot (really a short dash) pattern, a long dash pattern, and a dot_dash pattern. The line_widths of the objects shown is 7. These patterns can be loaded into a **GC** as follows:

```
static char dot        [ ] = { 3,3 };
static char dash       [ ] = { 6,3 };
static char dot_dash   [ ] = { 9, 3, 3, 3 };
Display *display;      /* pointer to Display structure */
GC gc;                 /* gc to use */

. . .

XSetDashes ( display, gc, 0, dot, 2 );

. . .

XSetDashes ( display, gc, 0, dash, 2 );

. . .

XSetDashes ( display, gc, 0, dot_dash, 4 );
```

The dot pattern is 6 pixels long, and the dash pattern is 9 pixels long. The dot_dash pattern is a total of 18 pixels long, and consists of a long, then a short segment. Note that this example specifies *dash_offset* values of zero.

## Line-Drawing Requests

You may choose from among three different line-drawing requests, depending on what you want to draw.

**XDrawLine**          Draws a single line from one point to another.

**XDrawSegments**      The plural form of **XDrawLine**. It draws a *multiline*, or series of disconnected line segments.

**XDrawLines**         Draws a *polyline*, or connected series of lines.

## XDrawLine

In **XDrawLine**, each end of the line is styled according to the *cap_style* attribute. **XDrawLine** (*Xlib* ¶6.3.2) has the form

```
Display *display;      /* pointer to Display structure */
Drawable window;       /* window or pixmap */
GC gc;                 /* gc */
```

```
GC gc;                   /* gc */
int x1, y1;              /* coordinates of starting point */
int x2, y2;              /* coordinates of ending point */
    . . .
    XDrawLine ( display, window, gc, x1,y1, x2, y2 );
```

## XDrawSegments

**XDrawSegments** is more complicated, because it requires you to specify a list of line segment endpoints. You must specify these segments as an array of **XSegment** structures. The **XSegment** structure is defined (in **<X11/Xlib.h>**) as follows:

```
typedef struct {
    short x1, y1;
    short x2, y2;
} XSegment;
```

**XDrawSegments** draws a series of disconnected lines. Each end of each line is styled according to the *cap_style* attribute. If you draw dashed lines, the dash pattern starts over (at the *dash_offset*) for each new line. **XDrawSegments** (*Xlib* ¶6.3.2) has the form

```
Display *display;        /* pointer to Display structure */
Drawable window;         /* window or pixmap */
GC gc;                   /* gc */
XSegment segments [ ];   /* array of segments */
int nsegments;           /* number of segments */
    . . .
    XDrawSegments ( display, window, gc, segments, nsegments );
```

The result of this function is the drawing of all the line segments in *segments*. *nsegments* specifies how big the *segments* array is.

## XDrawLines

**XDrawLines** is easily the most powerful graphics primitive request in X. When you use **XDrawLines**, you specify an array of points (using an array of **XPoint** structures; see the description of the **XDrawPoints** request above). The workstation draws them connected together with lines, styled according to the current **GC** settings.

**XDrawLines** (*Xlib* ¶6.3.2) is similar to **XDrawPoints**; it has the form

```
Display *display;        /* pointer to Display structure */
Drawable window;         /* window or pixmap */
GC gc;                   /* gc */
XPoint points [ ];       /* array of points */
int npoints;             /* number of points */
int mode;                /* CoordModeOrigin or CoordModePrevious */
```

. . .
**XDrawLines** ( *display, window, gc, points, npoints, mode* );

*points* is an array of **XPoint** structures of length *npoints*. If the first and last point are identical, the workstation draws a closed polygon outline without any endpoints. Otherwise, the first and last points are styled according to the *cap_style* attribute. In either a closed or an open figure, the intermediate points are styled according to the *join_style* attribute. If you are drawing a dashed line, the dashing is continuous through all intermediate points, but restarts (at the *dash_offset*) at each endpoint.

If you want to draw a filled figure, use **XFillPolygon**.

If you specify a self-intersecting series of wide lines (using a *line_width* of one or greater), the workstation goes to a lot of trouble to avoid drawing any pixel more than once. When your **GC**'s *function* attribute has the value GXcopy, the number of times a pixel is drawn does not matter. However, with other *function* values (notably GXxor, which is used to draw and undraw rubber-band lines) pixels drawn twice would not look right. If your *line_width* is one or greater, this problem will not arise.

Most workstations draw lines faster when you specify a *line_width* of zero, however. When drawing zero-width self-intersecting lines, workstations do not atempt to avoid drawing pixels more than once. If you use a *function* value of GXxor to draw a self-intersecting line, for example, some pixels will appear to drop out because they were drawn more than once.

The *mode* argument can have the value CoordModeOrigin, in which case all the x,y coordinates are specified relative to the *window*'s origin. It also can have the value CoordModePrevious, which means that the first point is specified relative to *window*'s origin and the remaining points are specified in delta mode. See the description and example under **XDrawPoints** above for more information.

## Arcs, Circles, and Ellipses

X provides graphic requests that permit you to draw either unfilled or filled arcs. To draw a circle, you simply use the appropriate arc request and specify the angles appropriate to a full circle.

Generally, X's arcs allow you to draw either circular or elliptical arc segments. As Figure 5-6 shows, you define a rectangle, and X inscribes your arc about it. The following parameters define an arc:

x,y             The position of the upper left corner of the rectangle defining the arc. These values are signed sixteen-bit numbers.

width, height   The width and height of the arc's rectangle. These values are unsigned sixteen-bit numbers (they must be positive).

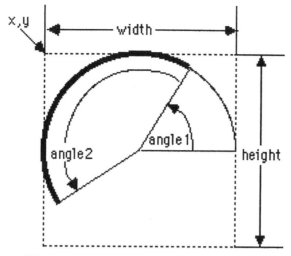

Figure 5-6.  The definition of an arc.

angle1            The starting angle (in sixty-fourths of degrees) of the arc
                  to be drawn.

angle2            The angle through which the arc is to be drawn
                  (beginning at angle1).  If you specify angle1 as 0 and
                  angle2 as 23040 (64 x 360), a full circle will be drawn.

When you specify an ellipse (that is, you specify unequal width and height) the
angles are applied as if you first drew a circular arc using the angles, then
scaled the circular arc in either the x or the y direction so it was elliptical.

> Take care that you do not exceed the sixteen bits of precision pro-
> vided by X when you compute x, y, width, and height.

## Unfilled Arcs

An unfilled arc is a form of line.  Arcs are drawn using the same pipeline
stages as lines:  the line-drawing attributes and the dash pattern are applied to
unfilled arcs.  As in wide lines, the line_width for wide arcs is distributed
equally on either side of the identical narrow arc.

You draw a single unfilled arc (or circle) with the **XDrawArc** request.
**XDrawArc** (*Xlib* ¶6.3.4) has the form.

```
Display *display;              /* pointer to Display structure */
Drawable window;               /* window or pixmap */
GC gc;                         /* gc */
int x, y;                      /* upper left of circumscribing rectangle*/
unsigned int width, height;    /* width, height of circumscribing rectangle*/
int angle1, angle1;            /* start and stop angles */
```

. . .

**XDrawArc** ( *display, window, gc, x, y, width, height, angle1, angle2* );

**XDrawArcs** is the plural form of **XDrawArc**. It permits you to specify a list of arcs. You must specify these arcs as an array of **XArc** structures. The **XArc** structure is defined (in **<X11/Xlib.h>**) as follows:

```
typedef struct {
    short x, y;
    unsigned short width, height;
    short angle1, angle2;
} XArc;
```

**XDrawArcs** (*Xlib* ¶6.3.4) has the form

| | |
|---|---|
| **Display** *\*display;* | /\*  pointer to Display structure \*/ |
| **Drawable** *window;* | /\* window or pixmap \*/ |
| **GC** *gc;* | /\* gc \*/ |
| **XArc** *arcs* [ ]; | /\* array of arcs \*/ |
| int *narcs;* | /\* number of arcs \*/ |

. . .

**XDrawArcs** ( *display, window, gc, arcs, narcs* );

This function draws all the arcs specified in the *arcs* array, which contains *narcs* elements.

If the beginning point of an arc in the *arcs* array is equal to the ending point of the previous arc, the *join_style* attribute is applied at that point just as if the arcs were two successive line segments in an **XDrawLines** request. Otherwise, the beginning and end of each arc has the *cap_style* attribute applied.

**Example**: Four arcs.

This example shows four unfilled arcs generated by X. On the left is a simple circle. Next is a full ellipse. Second from the right is a circular arc running from -45° to 45°. On the right is an an elliptical arc running from 135° to 225°. Notice that the circles are drawn by specifying 360° arcs starting at an angle of zero, whereas the partial circles start at the appropriate angle and, in this example, extend through 90°. The following code excerpt generated the four arcs:

**Display** *\*display;*
**Drawable** *window;*
**GC** *gc;*

. . .

**XDrawArc** ( *display, window, gc,*   20, 20, 40, 40,   0,    360\*64 );

```
XDrawArc ( display, window, gc,   70, 20, 60, 40,   0,     360*64 );
XDrawArc ( display, window, gc, 140,20, 40, 40, -45*64, 90*64 );
XDrawArc ( display, window, gc, 190,20, 60, 40, 135*64, 90*64 );
```

## Filled  Arcs

If you wish, you may draw filled arcs.  The Pixel Selection stage of the pipeline selects all the pixels inside the filled arc, and passes them on to the Patterning stage.  Line-drawing attributes (such as *line_width* and *cap_style*) are not applied to filled arcs.

Some graphics packages, such as GKS, are capable of filling and outlining a graphic primitive in a single operation.  X is not.  To fill a graphic primitive and draw an outline around it, you must use two drawing requests, one for the interior and another for the outline.

Filled arcs have an attribute-setting function of their own: **XSetArcMode**.  This attribute defines whether or not the arc should be drawn as a pie-slice. **XSetArcMode** (*Xlib* ¶5.4.7) has the form

```
Display *display;        /* pointer to Display structure */
GC gc;                   /* gc */
int arc_mode;            /* ArcChord or ArcPieSlice */
. . .
XSetArcMode ( display, gc, arc_mode );
```

Using the *arc_mode* attribute, you can select how you want arcs filled.  The *arc_mode* attribute corresponds to the arc_mode field in the **XGCValues** structure.  *arc_mode* can have one of two values:

ArcPieSlice Specifies that filled arcs are to be drawn as pie slices.  Arc-PieSlice is the default value.

ArcChord    Specifies that filled arcs are be closed off by drawing a line—a chord—from the starting point to the ending point.

You fill a single arc (or circle) with the **XFillArc** request.  **XFillArc** (*Xlib* ¶6.4.3) is analogous to **XDrawArc**; it has the form

```
Display *display;           /* pointer to Display structure */
Drawable window;            /* window or pixmap */
GC gc;                      /* gc */
int x, y;                   /* upper left of circumscribing rectangle*/
unsigned int width, height; /* width, height of circumscribing rectangle*/
int angle1, angle1;         /* start and stop angles */
. . .
XFillArc ( display, window, gc, x, y, width, height, angle1, angle2 );
```

**XFillArcs** is the plural form of **XFillArc**.  It permits you to specify a list of arcs.  You must specify these arcs as an array of **XArc** structures (see above). **XFillArcs** (*Xlib* ¶6.4.3) has the form

```
Display *display;        /* pointer to Display structure */
Drawable window;         /* window or pixmap */
GC gc;                   /* gc */
XArc arcs [ ];           /* array of arcs */
int narcs;               /* number of arcs */
    . . .
XFillArcs ( display, window, gc, arcs, narcs );
```

This function fills all the arcs specified in the *arcs* array, which contains *narcs* elements. If several of the arcs overlap, those pixels will be drawn several times.

**Example**: Three filled arcs.

This example shows three filled arcs. On the left is a full circle. The arcs in the middle and on the right run from -45° to 180° through an angle of 225°. The middle arc is filled with *arc_mode* ArcPieSlice, and the right arc is filled with *arc_mode* ArcChord. The following code excerpt generates these arcs:

```
Display *display;
Drawable window;
GC gc;
    . . .
XFillArc ( display, window, gc,    20, 20, 40, 40,  0,     360*64 );
XSetArcMode ( display, gc, ArcPieSlice );
XFillArc ( display, window, gc,    70,20, 40, 40, -45*64,225*64 );
XSetArcMode ( display, gc, ArcChord );
XFillArc ( display, window, gc,   120,20, 40, 40, -45*64,225*64 );
```

# Rectangles

X provides graphic requests that permit you to draw either unfilled or filled rectangles. All rectangles are defined by specifying the x,y coordinates of their upper left corner and a width and height.

> A rectangle's x or y position may be negative, which causes its upper left corner to be to be above or to the left of the window. However, the width and height of a rectangle must be positive.

## Unfilled Rectangles

Unfilled rectangles, like lines and unfilled arcs, are processed using the entire graphics pipeline. In particular, the line-drawing attributes and dash pattern are applied.  As in wide lines, the line_width for wide rectangles is distributed equally on either side of the identical narrow arc.  Drawing an unfilled rectangle is equivalent to using the **XDrawLines**request to draw a line around the outside of the rectangle.

You draw a single unfilled rectangle with the **XDrawRectangle** request. **XDrawRectangle** (*Xlib* ¶6.3.3) has the form

```
XDrawRectangle ( Display *, Drawable, GC, int, int,
                              unsigned int, unsigned int );
Display *display;              /* pointer to Display structure */
Drawable window;              /* window or pixmap */
GC gc;                        /* gc */
int x, y;                     /* upper left corner of rectangle*/
unsigned int width, height;   /* width and height of rectangle*/
    . . .
XDrawRectangle ( display, window, gc, x, y, width, height );
```

**XDrawRectangles** is the plural form of **XDrawRectangle**. It permits you to specify a list of rectangles. You must specify these rectangles as an array of **XRectangle** structures. The **XRectangle** structure is defined (in **<X11/Xlib.h>**) as follows:

```
typedef struct {
    short x, y;
    unsigned short width, height;
} XRectangle;
```

**XDrawRectangles** (*Xlib* ¶6.3.3) has the form

```
XDrawRectangles ( Display *, Drawable, GC, XRectangle *, int );
Display *display;              /* pointer to Display structure */
Drawable window;              /* window or pixmap */
GC gc;                        /* gc */
XRectangle rectangles [ ];    /* array of rectangles */
int nrectangles;              /* number of rectangles */
    . . .
XDrawRectangles ( display, window, gc, rectangles, nrectangles );
```

This function draws all the rectangles specified in the *rectangles* array, which contains *nrectangles* elements.

## Filled Rectangles

If you wish, you may draw filled rectangles. The Pixel Selection stage of the pipeline selects all the pixels inside the rectangular area, and passes them on to the Patterning stage. Line-drawing attributes (such as *line_width* and *cap_style*) are not applied to filled primitives.

Filled rectangles have a variety of uses:

- Setting all pixels in a window to a certain foreground value

- Clearing a Pixmap—an invisible raster area

- Inverting an area of a window (using the GXxor *function* setting described in the example accompanying the **XSetPlaneMask** call)

- Patterning an area of a window (using a patterning *fill_style*)

- Of course, drawing a rectangular object

Do not use filled rectangles to clear a window to its background. Rather, use the **XClearWindow** or **XClearArea** requests, described under the "Clearing Areas" heading later in this chapter.

You fill a single rectangle with the **XFillRectangle** request. **XFillRectangle** (*Xlib* ¶6.4.3) is analogous to **XDrawRectangle**; it has the form

```
Display *display;            /* pointer to Display structure */
Drawable window;             /* window or pixmap */
GC gc;                       /* gc */
int x, y;                    /* upper left of rectangle*/
unsigned int width, height;  /* width and height of rectangle*/
    . . .
XFillRectangle ( display, window, gc, x, y, width, height );
```

**XFillRectangles** is the plural form of **XFillRectangle**. It permits you to specify a list of rectangles. You must specify these rectangles as an array of **XRectangle** structures (see above). **XFillRectangles** (*Xlib* ¶6.4.3) has the form

```
Display *display;            /* pointer to Display structure */
Drawable window;             /* window or pixmap */
GC gc;                       /* gc */
XRectangle rectangles [ ];   /* array of rectangles */
int nrectangles;             /* number of rectangles */
    . . .
XFillRectangles ( display, window, gc, rectangles, nrectangles );
```

This function fills all the rectangles specified in the *rectangles* array, which contains *nrectangles* elements.

## Polygons

A polygon is an area defined by lines connecting a series of points, or *vertices*. The X Window System provides the **XFillPolygon** request to permit you to fill such an area. (To draw an outline around a polygon, use the **XDrawLines** request). Like other filled primitives, polygons are processed through the graphics pipeline. The Pixel Selection stage of the pipeline selects all the pixels inside the filled area, and passes them on to the Patterning stage. Line-drawing attributes (such as *line_width* and *cap_style*) are not applied to filled primitives.

## The Fill Rule

The Pixel Selection stage of the graphics pipeline must decide which pixels are inside the polygon and which pixels are outside. For a convex shape, such as a triangle or hexagon, this decision is unambiguous. However, if the outline of a polygon doubles back on itself, there is more than one way to make the pixel-inclusion decision. Consider the polygon with this outline:

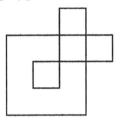

This polygon doubles back on itself: the long vertical edges cross the long horizontal edges. The question is, are the pixels under the area where the polygon crosses itself considered to be *inside* the polygon, or *outside* it? To allow your application to make the choice, X lets you specify one of two fill rules with the **XSetFillRule** convenience function.

One of the fill rules X provides is known as the even-odd rule. It selects the following filled area for our polygon:

How does X decide whether any given point—a *candidate point*—is inside the polygon? The even-odd rule uses a line drawn from the candidate point to some point already outside the polygon. Only if that line crosses the polygon boundary an odd number of times is the candidate point inside the polygon.

The other rule provided by X is the nonzero-winding-number rule. It selects exactly the same pixels as the even-odd rule on non-self-intersecting polygons. On our polygon, it selects these pixels:

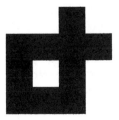

The nonzero-winding-number rule works as follows:  An automaton carrying out the rule stands at the candidate point, and rotates so as to point at every vertex on the polygon in order.  While pointing at all the vertices and back to the first vertex, the automaton spins around in place zero, one, two or more times.  The number of times the automaton spins around is the winding number for the candidate pixel.  The nonzero-winding-number rule, true to its name, selects all pixels with non-zero winding numbers.

The even-odd rule is used by standard packages such as GKS.  Your choice of fill rule depends on what meaning your application puts on self-intersecting polygons (if, indeed, you have any).

Use the **XSetFillRule** convenience function to choose the fill rule.  **XSetFill-Rule** (*Xlib* ¶5.4.3)has the form

```
Display *display;        /* pointer to Display structure */
GC gc;                   /* gc */
int fill_rule;           /* EvenOddRule or WindingRule */
 . . .
XSetFillRule ( display, gc, fill_rule );
```

The *fill_rule* attribute selects the fill rule to use; it corresponds to the fill_rule field in the **XGCValues** structure. *fill_rule* can have one of two values:

EvenOddRule   Selects the even-odd rule.  EvenOddRule is the default.

WindingRule   Selects the nonzero-winding-number rule.

## XFillPolygon

**XFIllPolygon** is the request that causes a filled polygon to be drawn.  When you use **XDrawLines**, you specify an array of vertices (using an array of **XPoint** structures; see the description of the **XDrawPoints** request above).

The last point in the **XPoint** array may or may not have the same position as the first point.  If not, the polygon is closed automatically by connecting the first and last points.  Note that it is a good idea to store your polygon vertices in **XPoint** arrays with the first and last points equal.  If you do, it will be easy for you to draw the polygon's outline using the **XDrawLines** request.

**XFillPolygon** (*Xlib* ¶6.4.2) has the form

```
Display *display;        /* pointer to Display structure */
Drawable window;         /* window or pixmap */
GC gc;                   /* gc */
XPoint points [ ];       /* array of points */
int npoints;             /* number of points */
int shape;               /* Complex, NonConvex, or Convex */
int mode;                /* CoordModeOrigin or CoordModePrevious */
 . . .
XFillPolygon ( display, window, gc, points, npoints, shape, mode );
```

*points* is an array of **XPoint** structures of length *npoints*. The *points* array defines the vertices of the polygon to draw.

The *shape* argument allows you to speed up the workstation by giving it a hint about how complicated a polygon you are specifying. *shape* can have one of three values:

Convex     Specify this *shape* value if you know that the polygon you are specifying is convex. A polygon is convex if and only if it is possible to draw a straight line from any point inside the polygon to any other point inside without crossing the polygon boundary. If you have convex polygons, you probably will know it because your application will have made them that way. Convex polygons are potentially the fastest to draw.

Note that triangles—three-sided polygons—are always convex. X workstations know this without the help of the *shape* hint; there is no need to program a special case for triangles.

NonConvex  Specify this *shape* value if you do not know your polygons are convex, but you do know their edges are not self-intersecting.

Complex    Specify this *shape* value if you do not know whether your polygons are self-intersecting. When you specify Complex, drawing the polygon potentially takes longer. However, the final picture will be correct. When in doubt about what the *shape* parameter should be, specify Complex.

> If your application had code in it to inspect all polygons and determine the ideal *shape* parameter for each one, it might take a long time. Don't inspect your polygons just so you can set the *shape* parameter; it's not worth the trouble.

The *mode* argument can have the value CoordModeOrigin, in which case all the x,y coordinates are specified relative to the *window*'s origin. It also can have the value CoordModePrevious, which means that the first point is specified relative to *window*'s origin and the remaining points are specified in delta mode. See the description and example under **XDrawPoints** above for more information.

# EXPOSE EVENTS

At any given time on an X Window System workstation, typically there are several windows belonging to several different applications. Sometimes the windows do not overlap one another at all. More typically, however, portions of some windows lie over portions of others. The windows can be regarded as overlapping sheets of paper stacked on the desktop of the root window. Some windows are on top of the stack; no part of these windows' surface area is covered by others. Other windows are either completely or partially covered, or obscured.

Windows can also be invisible for other reasons: they can be iconified; they can be unmapped. See Chapter 4.

By using a window manager application, the user can change the window stacking order and otherwise affect the visibility of windows. For example, most window managers provide a command called Raise, Pop, or Bring To Front, as well as other commands to control stacking order and window iconization. The window manager also lets the user move windows around on the screen. As far as the user is concerned, each window is represented by a complete rectangular sheet of paper. Moving the various sheets over and under one another simply exposes parts of each sheet to view, and conceals other parts. It appears to the user as if the graphics and text in each window are always there, and are simply made visible and invisible by stacking.

This elegant desktop metaphor is not trivial to present to the user. Most workstations have a single display surface and little or no additional image memory in which to retain graphical images from the obscured portions of windows. In the X Window System, *application programs are responsible for redrawing* windows or portions of windows that become exposed to view. The X workstation uses Expose events to notify your application when windows or parts of windows need redrawing.

## The Causes of Expose Events

Expose events can be generated as a result of requests from your application, the window manager, or other applications running on the workstation. A variety of requests cause Expose events:

**XMapWindow** and **XMapRaised** requests generate Expose events for the window being mapped and its mapped subwindows.

**XUnmapWindow** requests can generate Expose events for windows that become visible when the unmapped window goes away.

**XRaiseWindow**, **XLowerWindow**, and other requests that change the window stacking order can generate Expose events for any or all of the windows involved, and their subwindows (except the one that winds up at the bottom of the stacking order).

Requests that change the size of windows generate Expose events for parts of the resized window itself if it becomes larger in either dimension. They also can generate Expose events for subwindows, and for windows that may have been exposed by the operation.

Requests that change the position of windows generate Expose events for the moved window itself if part of it moves out from under other windows. Window-moving requests also can generate Expose events for subwindows and other windows that may have been exposed by the operation.

**XClearArea** requests (see under "Clearing Areas") can, if you wish, generate Expose events for the window area cleared.

Expose events tell your application *when* to draw. Your application should always be ready to process Expose events on any of its windows, by executing the graphics requests that draw the contents of the exposed window.

Many applications can have a simple, modular, and reliable design if they do all (or almost all) drawing in response to Expose events. You probably can design your application this way. This is true for two reasons:

- Your application can get Expose events for a newly created window, and you can draw the initial contents of the window in response. Simply solicit Expose events (with **XSelectInput**) on the window after you create it but before you first map it. When you issue the first **XMapWindow** request, you receive one or more Expose events, and you respond to them by drawing the window contents. This method was first presented in the **helloworld.c** example of Chapter 2. It is convenient because your application need not contain special-purpose code for first-time window drawing.

- You can use the **XClearArea** request (see "Clearing Areas" in this chapter) to force the workstation to send you Expose events for all or part of any window. When you wish to erase the graphical information in a window and draw something new, you can issue an **XClearArea** request. After the workstation has cleared the area, it sends the Expose event (or events); your application's Expose event handler responds by drawing the new window contents.

## Exposure of Parts of Windows

Almost all actions that cause window-exposure can expose just part of a window. Even after the exposure, the exposed window may still be partly covered by other windows. It is useful to think of the visible portion of the partly-covered window as being represented by several adjacent but non-overlapping rectangles. If such a partly-covered window is exposed, you receive a series of consecutive Expose events. Each event in the series describes one of the rectangles. The integer field "count" in the event's data structure is set to a positive number to let you know how many more Expose events are coming in the consecutive series. When the "count" field is set to zero, you know that the current event is the last Expose event of the series.

Figure 5-7 shows the Expose events generated when a window is unmapped. On the left is a configuration of three windows. When window C is unmapped (on the right) portions of windows A and B are exposed. The area exposed in window A is L-shaped, so a series of two Expose events is generated for window A. This series describes the areas E1 and E2. In window B, a single rectangular area (E3) is exposed, so a single Expose event—an Expose event series containing just one event—is generated for window B.

A series of Expose events tells your application what areas of a particular window must be redrawn. Each individual Expose event in the series describes a single rectangular area. If your application is capable of redrawing rectangular areas within windows, it should do so as it receives each Expose event: often only a small part of a window will require redrawing, and your application can save time.

However, it may prove simpler for you to redraw the entire window once at the end of each entire series of Expose events. In this case, you should ignore Expose events with nonzero "count" fields, and redraw the window when you receive Expose events with zero "count" fields.

A third strategy for redrawing window contents involves the **GC** Clipping stage of the graphics pipeline. See the example accompanying the description of the **XSetClipRectangles** request later in this chapter.

The workstation clears, to the background color or pattern, the rectangle described by each Expose event before it sends you the event. This means you can go ahead and draw on the area described by the Expose event assuming that all its pixels are set to the background. If you choose to wait for the zero "count" field and redraw the whole window, this partial clearing may present a problem: you will either have to clear the whole window again, or run the risk of redrawing some pixels (if the **GC** you use for drawing contains the default value for the function attribute, though, this should not be a problem).

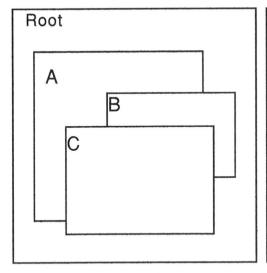

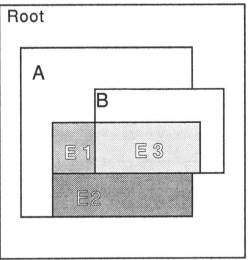

Beginning window configuration        Exposures when window C is unmapped

Figure 5-7.  Window exposure example.

The L-shaped region of window A in figure 5-7 is shown divided into two rectangles separated by a horizontal line. As of early 1988, all X Window System workstations divided partly obscured windows into rectangles for Expose event series using horizontal lines. However, there is nothing in X requiring a workstation to divide windows horizontally. The only guarantee is that every series of Expose events for a single window gives a series of non-overlapping rectangles. Therefore, you should avoid making your application depend upon any particular rectangle ordering in Expose events.

## Soliciting Expose Events

In order to receive Expose events, you must first solicit them with **XSelectInput**. See "Soliciting Events" in Chapter 3 for details. In the *event_mask* parameter, specify the bit mask named ExposureMask. (The bit names for the event selection mask are defined in the header file **<X11/X.h>**.)

Some workstations have backing store. Under some circumstances these workstations can restore the contents of exposed windows without intervention from your application. Only when they are unable to restore window contents automatically do such workstations generate Expose events. Your application's performance can be improved when the workstation has off-screen storage, because you will have to process fewer Expose events. However, you cannot (and should not) depend on off-screen storage to completely eliminate Expose events, so you still need to be able to process them. Vendor documentation gives information about the features of this off-screen storage, if the workstation has it.

> Even if your application runs on a workstation with backing store, design it to process Expose events.

## Receiving and Processing Expose Events

See "Accepting Events from the Event Queue" in Chapter 3 for a general discussion of event structures. The first field of all event structures is the event type (field name "type"). The union type **XEvent** defines the "type" field directly, so it can be used to look at the event before you know what type it is. You should use **XEvent** to declare and allocate space for all event structures: it defines a structure that is guaranteed to be long enough for all event types.

Expose events have the structure type **XExposeEvent**. The **XEvent** union defines the "xexpose" variant as an **XExposeEvent** structure.

Table 5-V shows the structure declaration and field names for the contents of the event structure for the Expose event, as defined in the header file **<X11/Xlib.h>.**

As with other events you may access the type field directly via the **XEvent** structure. Once you have determined that you have an Expose event, you may use the fields specific to the Expose event, which are defined as shown in Table 5-V.

| typedef struct { | | |
|---|---|---|
| int type; | ev.type | Expose |
| unsigned long serial | ev.xany.serial | Last request processed |
| **Bool** send_event; | ev.xany.send_event | From **XSendEvent**? |
| **Display** *display; | ev.xany.display | |
| **Window** window; | ev.xexpose.window | Exposed window |
| int x; | ev.xexpose.x | Rectangle origin x |
| int y; | ev.xexpose.y | Rectangle origin y |
| int width | ev.xexpose.width | Rectangle width |
| int height | ev.xexpose.height | Rectangle height |
| int count; | ev.xexpose.count | Remaining rectangles |
| } **XExposeEvent**; | | |

Table 5-V.  Expose event field names.

type        Identifies the event type.

serial      Specifies the serial number of the last request processed.

send_event  False unless this event was generated by some application issu-
            ing the **XSentEvent** request.

display     A pointer to the **Display** from which the event came.

window      Window id of the window needing redrawing.

x           X coordinate of the upper left corner of the rectangle needing re-
            drawing, relative to the origin of the window.

y           Y coordinate of the upper left corner of the rectangle needing re-
            drawing, relative to the origin of the window.

width       Width of the rectangle needing redrawing.

height      Height of the rectangle needing redrawing.

count       If this integer field contains the value zero, this event is the last
            of a series of Expose events generated by a single action.  If this
            integer field is non-zero, it specifies the minimum number of
            Expose events remaining in the present series.  There are at
            least this many more Expose events to process.

# CLEARING WINDOWS

In X, the operation of clearing an area of a window means resetting the pixels in
it to the window's background.  The window's background is an attribute of the
window;  it may (see Chapter 4) be one of the following:

  • A background_pixel value

- A background_pixmap tile pattern

- The special background_pixmap value None

If the background is a background_pixel value, clearing an area sets all the pixels in it to that value. If the background is a background_pixmap, clearing an area tiles it with the background pattern. If the background_pixmap attribute has the value None, the operation of clearing an area leaves the pixels in the area unchanged. The X requests **XClearWindow** and **XClearArea** carry out the appropriate area-clearing operation automatically.

When your application receives Expose events (see the preceding section), you can assume that each rectangular area described by the Expose events has been subjected to a clear operation. Note that other areas of the window (those not described by Expose events) are not cleared.

**XClearWindow** and **XClearArea** can only apply to a window. Clearing is, strictly speaking, a window operation rather than a graphic primitive operation, because it does not use a **GC**. Clearing does not use a *function* value other than GXcopy, either. Pixmaps (see Chapter 8) cannot be cleared, because they do not have background_pixel or background_pixmap attributes. To set the pixels in a Pixmap to a known value, use **XFillRectangle**.

## XClearWindow

The simplest way for your application to clear an entire window is by using the **XClearWindow** request. **XClearWindow** (*Xlib* ¶6.1) has the form

```
Display *display;    /* pointer to Display structure */
Window *window;      /* window to be cleared*/
 . . .
XClearWindow ( display, window );
```

The **XClearWindow** request is most useful for erasing the contents of a window prior to drawing a new picture in that window.

Because window areas are cleared prior to the delivery of Expose events, it is usually unnecessary to use the **XClearWindow** request while processing Expose events. There is, however, one combination of circumstances in which your Expose event processing should explicitly clear a window prior to redrawing it. If

- your application's Expose event strategy is to redraw the entire window at the end of each Expose series (when the "count" field is zero), and

- you draw using **GC**s with function attribute values other than GXcopy (see "**XSetFunction**" earlier in this chapter),

your windows may not redraw properly unless you clear them first.

## XClearArea

**XClearArea** allows you to clear an arbitrary rectangle within a window. **XClearArea** optionally allows you to expose the area you specify—to generate a series of Expose events describing the area. **XClearArea** (*Xlib* ¶6.4.3) has the form

```
Display *display;          /* pointer to Display structure */
Window window;             /*  window  */
int x, y;                  /* upper left of rectangle*/
unsigned int width, height; /* width and height of rectangle*/
Bool exposures;            /* True to generate Expose events */
. . .
XClearArea ( display, window, x, y, width, height, exposures );
```

The rectangle, in the *window*, cleared by this request has an upper left corner at (*x,y*) relative to the origin of *window*. The size of the rectangle is specified by *width* and *height*.

In this request, if you specify zero for either *width* or *height*, you are not specifying a rectangle of zero size. You may specify zero for *width;* if you do this it means that you want the cleared rectangle to extend all the way from *x* to the right edge of the window. Likewise, if you specify zero for *height,* it means that you want the rectangle to extend from *y* to the bottom edge.

This request's special meaning for zero *width* and *height* is convenient, because it allows you to clear all the way to the right edge or bottom edge of the window without first determining the size of the window.

A value of True for *exposures* causes the workstation to generate one or more Expose events describing the visible parts of the cleared window area. The workstation sends the Expose events to whatever applications have solicited them immediately after it performs the clear operation. Even if the background_pixmap attribute has the value None, Expose events are sent if you specify a True value for *exposures*.

**Example**: Clear and expose a whole window.

This example makes use of the special zero-valued *width* and *height* parameters to **XClearArea**. By specifying zero for *x, y, width*, and *height*, the entire window from point 0,0 to the right and bottom edges is cleared.

```
Display *display;          /* pointer to Display structure */
Window window;             /*  window  */
. . .
XClearArea ( display, window, 0, 0, 0, 0, True );
```

# COPYING AREAS

X provides two graphic primitives for copying rectangular areas of pixels from one place to another: **XCopyArea** and **XCopyPlane**. These primitives can copy raster images to and from any Drawable, either a window or a Pixmap. The **XCopyArea** and **XCopyPlane** requests both use the graphics pipeline, and require you to specify a **GC**. To both requests you must specify a source rectangle and a destination rectangle, and both requests combine the source and destination using the graphics pipeline's Raster Output stage.

The two most important uses for area-copying are

- Scrolling: moving images around inside windows. When scrolling, you primarily use the **XCopyArea** function to move a rectangle of pixels from one place to another within a window. For example, a terminal emulator application might move a full-width rectangle of pixels from the bottom of a window to the top.

- Displaying precomposed images in windows. To do this, you use ordinary drawing primitives to pre-draw raster images into Pixmaps (see Chapter 8). Then, when you wish to display these images, you copy them into windows. There are a great many ways to use this capability. For example, a computer-aided-drafting application might have a library of symbols. Such an application would compose the symbols just once, into Pixmaps, then use copy requests to replicate the symbols wherever needed in windows.

Although they work similarly, **XCopyArea** and **XCopyPlane** have entirely different purposes as far as your application is concerned. **XCopyArea** takes entire pixel values as its source, and uses them literally. Because of this, **XCopyArea** is usually used to copy whole rasters from place to place, as in scrolling. **XCopyPlane**, on the other hand, extracts a one-bit pixel value from each source pixel, then constructs a pattern using foreground and background pixel values. This extracted rectangle of one-bit pixel values is known as a *plane*. Thus, **XCopyPlane** can be used for a variety of purposes. It is especially useful for displaying precomposed images in windows. For further information on how pixel values and bit-planes within pixel values relate to the colors shown on a screen, see Chapter 7.

Windows can, of course, be covered by other windows in ways your application cannot predict. This fact complicates the area-copying requests: all or part of the raster in a source rectangle might be unavailable for copying because the corresponding area of a source window is stacked underneath some other window. The burden of supplying the missing pixels is on the X application. When source pixel values are unavailable for copying, your application receives Graphics-Expose events describing the incomplete destination rectangle. How you solicit and process the GraphicsExpose event type and the related event type NoExpose is discussed under the heading "GraphicsExpose and NoExpose Events" later in this chapter.

The source and destination Drawables must have the same root window. On a one-screen workstation, this is guaranteed to be true. However, on a multiple-screen workstation, you cannot use **XCopyArea** or **XCopyPlane** to transfer images from one screen's windows or Pixmaps to those on another screen. You can use the **XGetImage** and **XPutImage** requests (see Chapter 8) for transferring information between screens.

## XCopyArea

The **XCopyArea** request (often called pixel-BLT) combines the pixels from the source rectangle you specify with the pixels of a destination rectangle, according to the attributes of the **GC** you specify. **XCopyArea** uses the **GC** Clipping stage, Window Clipping stage, and Raster Output stage of the pipeline. That is, the source pixels are clipped by both the **GC** clip mask and the boundaries of the destination clip window, then the source pixel values are combined with the destination pixel values.

If your **GC** contains default values for the plane_mask and function attributes (all-ones and GXcopy, respectively), **XCopyArea** replaces the pixels in the destination rectangle with the pixels from the source rectangle.

**XCopyArea**  (*Xlib* ¶6.2) has the form

```
Display *display;          /* pointer to Display structure */
Drawable  src;             /* source window or pixmap */
Drawable  dest;            /* destination window or pixmap */
GC gc;                     /* gc */
int src_x,  src_y;         /* upper left corner of source rectangle*/
unsigned int width, height;  /* width and height of rectangle*/
int dest_x,  dest_y;       /* upper left corner of destination rectangle*/
   . . .
XCopyArea ( display, src, dest, gc, src_x, src_y,
                          width, height, dest_x, dest_y );
```

*src* specifies the source Drawable's X resource identifier. The source rectangle's upper left corner (relative to the origin of the *src* Drawable) is specified by *src_x* and *src_y*. Similarly, *dest*, *dest_x*, and *dest_y* specify the destination rectangle's Drawable and upper left corner. *width* and *height* specify the size of the rectangle to be copied. *gc* identifies the **GC** to use.

The *src* and *dest* Drawables must have the same depth—the same number of bits per pixel—as each other.

If you specify a rectangle *width* or *height* of zero, no pixels are copied. Zero *width* and *height* values do not have the same special meaning as they do for the **XClearArea** request.

It is possible for source pixel values to be unavailable for copying. Destination rectangle areas corresponding to unavailable source pixel values are cleared, as discussed under the heading "Clearing Areas" earlier in this chapter.   After clearing, these destination areas are subjected to GraphicsExpose processing (described under the heading "GraphicsExpose and NoExpose Events" later in this chapter).

## XCopyPlane

The **XCopyPlane** request (often called bit-BLT) copies a single bit-plane from the source rectangle to the destination rectangle.   When you use the **XCopy-Plane** request, you supply a *plane* mask containing exactly one nonzero bit.   The corresponding bit is extracted from the value of each source pixel.

The selected bits from the source pixels are used to construct a pattern colored with foreground and background:   if each source pixel's bit is non-zero, the Patterning stage of the graphics pipeline colors it with the foreground pixel value (from the specified **GC**).   If, on the other hand, the source pixel's bit is zero, the Patterning stage colors it with the background pixel value.

Finally, the **GC** Clipping stage, Window Clipping stage, and Raster Output stage of the pipeline combine the resulting pattern with the pixels of the destination rectangle, according to the attributes of the **GC** you specify.   The source pattern is clipped by both the **GC** clip mask and the boundaries of the destination clip window, then the source pattern values are combined with the destination pixel values.

Note that **XCopyPlane** and **XCopyArea** work the same way, except for the fact that **XCopyArea** uses source pixel values directly, and **XCopyPlane** constructs a source pattern using

- One selected bit from each source pixel value, and

- The foreground and background draw-color attributes in the **GC**.

**XCopyPlane**  (*Xlib* ¶6.2) has the form

```
Display *display;          /* pointer to Display structure */
Drawable  src;             /* source window or pixmap */
Drawable  dest;            /* destination window or pixmap */
GC gc;                     /* gc */
int src_x, src_y;          /* upper left corner of source rectangle*/
unsigned int width, height;  /* width and height of rectangle*/
int dest_x, dest_y;        /* upper left corner of destination rectangle*/
unsigned long plane;       /* plane-mask */      ← exactly 1 non-zero bit
   . . .
XCopyPlane ( display, src, dest, gc, src_x, src_y,
                        width, height, dest_x, dest_y, plane );
```

For **XCopyPlane**, you specify source and destination rectangles exactly as you do for **XCopyArea**.   See the preceding section for details.   **XCopyPlane** has one additional parameter: *plane*. You must select the bit-position you wish to extract from source pixels by specifying this bit mask with exactly one bit set.

Source pixel values may be unavailable to **XCopyPlane** just as they may be unavailable to **XCopyArea**. See the next section for details.

## GraphicsExpose and NoExpose events

Windows in X can, of course, be covered by other windows. Because of this fact, area-copying operations are complicated:   some or all of the pixel values in a source rectangle may be unavailable for copying because the corresponding area of a source window is stacked underneath some other window.

Furthermore, you may issue a copy request specifying a source rectangle which lies partially or completely outside the boundaries of the source Drawable. Pixels that lie outside the source Drawable, obviously, cannot be copied to the corresponding destination Drawable because their pixel values are unavailable.

In X, your application must bear the burden of supplying the unavailable pixels. When source pixel values are unavailable to a copy operation, they leave incomplete areas, or "holes," in the destination rectangle (exception: if the unavailable source pixels correspond to clipped areas in the destination, no holes are left). Your application receives GraphicsExpose events describing the holes. You respond to the GraphicsExpose events by issuing ordinary graphic primitive requests to fill in the holes in the destination rectangle. GraphicsExpose events come in series just like Expose events.

When the destination is in a Window, each hole is cleared to the window background immediately before the GraphicsExpose event is sent. When the destination is in a Pixmap, it is not possible to clear the holes because there is no background value, so the holes are left unchanged.

If a copy operation can be completed without leaving any holes in the destination rectangle, your application receives a single NoExpose event instead of a series of GraphicsExpose events. This NoExpose event type informs you that the copy operation is complete and it is safe to use the copy's destination. If your application issues a series of copy requests, you must make sure each copy operation completely finishes (including the filling of holes) before the next one starts. Because X is asynchronous, if you issue several copy requests without waiting for either GraphicsExpose or NoExpose events between them,  copy operations after the first will copy holes in the first copy's destination without waiting for the holes to be filled.

GraphicsExpose and NoExpose events are best explained with a series of examples. Figure 5-8 shows, on the left, a shaded source area at the bottom of the window. On the right, this shaded area has been copied (scrolled) to the top of its window. Because the window is not covered by any other window, the copy operation can finish normally and your application receives a NoExpose event.

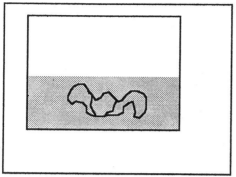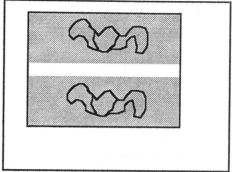

Figure 5-8.  Scrolling copy with all source pixels available.

Figure 5-9 shows the same situation, but with the source rectangle covered by another window.  When the shaded area is copied from the bottom to the top of the window, the copy operation leaves a hole in the destination rectangle (indicated by the diagonal hatch pattern in Figure 5-9).  The application receives a GraphicsExpose event describing the hole.  In response to the GraphicsExpose event, the application must redraw the missing part of the image.

Finally, Figure 5-10 shows the same situation a third time, but with both the source and destination rectangles covered.  Notwithstanding the unavailable source pixels for copying no holes are left in the destination, because the destination was clipped.  In this case, a NoExpose event is generated rather than a GraphicsExpose event, because the workstation can complete the copy operation without help from the application program.

This series of examples shows a copy operation from one rectangle to another within one window.  However, the same principles apply to copy operations between windows, and from windows to Pixmaps.

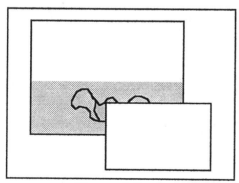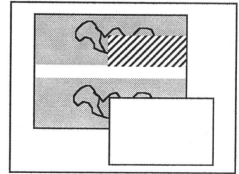

Figure 5-9.  Scrolling copy with unavailable pixels.

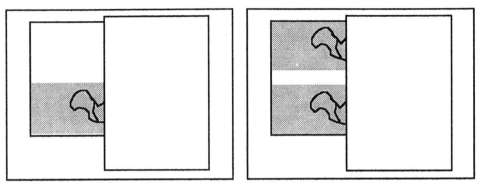

Figure 5-10.  Scrolling copy with unavailable pixels and clipped destination.

## Soliciting GraphicsExpose and NoExpose Events

In order to receive GraphicsExpose and NoExpose events you must, of course, solicit them ahead of time.  Unlike most other events, however, you solicit GraphicsExpose and NoExpose events by setting the **GC** attribute graphics_exposures to True (rather than by using **XSelectInput**).  When you use **XCopyArea** or **XCopyPlane**, if the graphics_exposures attribute is True in the **GC** you specify, you will receive either

- A series of GraphicsExpose events (possibly just one, possibly several), or

- A single NoExpose event.

If the graphics_exposures attribute is False, you will not receive either type of event.  The default value for graphics_exposures in newly created **GC**s is True.

Use the **XSetGraphicsExposures** convenience function to change the value of the graphics_exposures attribute.  **XSetGraphicsExposures** (*Xlib* ¶5.4.7) has the form

```
Display *display;          /* pointer to Display structure */
GC gc;                     /*  gc  */
Bool graphics_exposures;   /* True or False */
    . . .
XSetGraphicsExposures ( display, gc, graphics_exposures );
```

The *graphics_exposure* parameter corresponds to the graphics_exposures field in the **XGCValues** structure.  *graphics_exposure* can have either the value True (enabling GraphicsExpose and NoExpose event delivery) or the value False (disabling event delivery).

## Processing GraphicsExpose and NoExpose Events

GraphicsExpose events have the structure type **XGraphicsExposeEvent**, and NoExpose events have the structure type **XNoExposeEvent**. The **XEvent** union defines the "xgraphicsexpose" and "xnoexpose" variants appropriately.

Table 5-VI shows the type names and field names for the contents of the event structure for these events, as defined in the header file **<X11/Xlib.h>**.

Once you have determined, by examining the type field, that you have a GraphicsExpose or NoExpose event, you may use the fields specific to these event types, which are defined as follows:

type            Specifies the event type.

serial          Specifies the serial number of the last request processed.

send_event      False unless this event was generated by some application issuing the **XSentEvent** request.

display         Pointer to the **Display** from which the event came.

| typedef struct { | | |
|---|---|---|
| int type; | ev.type | GraphicsExpose |
| unsigned long serial | ev.xany.serial | Last request handled |
| **Bool** send_event; | ev.xany.send_event | From **XSendEvent**? |
| **Display** *display; | ev.xany.display | |
| **Drawable** drawable; | ev.xgraphicsexpose.drawable | Exposed drawable |
| int x; | ev.xgraphicsexpose.x | Rectangle origin x |
| int y; | ev.xgraphicsexpose.y | Rectangle origin y |
| int width | ev.xgraphicsexpose.width | Rectangle width |
| int height | ev.xgraphicsexpose.height | Rectangle height |
| int major_code | ex.xgraphicsexpose.major_code | Request code |
| int minor_code | ex.xgraphicsexpose.minor_code | Minor code |
| int count; | ev.xgraphicsexpose.count | Remaining rectangles |
| } **XGraphicsExposeEvent**; | | |
| typedef struct { | | |
| int type; | ev.type | NoExpose |
| unsigned long serial | ev.xany.serial | Last request handled |
| **Bool** send_event; | ev.xany.send_event | From **XSendEvent**? |
| **Display** *display; | ev.xany.display | |
| **Drawable** drawable; | ev.xnoexpose.drawable | Drawable |
| int major_code | ex.xnoexpose.major_code | Request code |
| int minor_code | ex.xnoexpose.minor_code | Minor code |
| } **XNoExposeEvent**; | | |

Table 5-VI.  GraphicsExpose and NoExpose event structures and field names.

drawable
: Resource identifier of the destination Drawable. This field is present in both GraphicsExpose and NoExpose events.

x
: X coordinate of the upper left corner of the rectangle that needs redrawing, relative to the origin of "drawable." It is not present in NoExpose events.

y
: Y coordinate of the upper left corner of the rectangle that need redrawing, relative to the origin of "drawable." It is not present in NoExpose events.

width
: Width of the rectangle that needs redrawing. It is not present in NoExpose events.

height
: Height of the rectangle that needs redrawing. It is not present in NoExpose events.

count
: If this integer field contains the value zero, this event is the last of a series of GraphicsExpose events generated by a single **XCopyArea** or **XCopyPlane** request. If this integer field is non-zero, it specifies the minimum number of GraphicsExpose events remaining in the present series. There are at least this many more GraphicsExpose events to process. This field is not present in NoExpose events.

major_code
: This field has (in unextended X) one of the following values:
  X_CopyArea     62
  X_CopyPlane    63
  It indicates the type of primitive the event results from. This field is available in both GraphicsExpose and NoExpose events. Note that the X_CopyArea and X_CopyPlane symbols are defined in the header file **<X11/Xproto.h>**.

minor_code
: Not used (in unextended X).

# ADVANCED DRAWING TECHNIQUES

This section describes several ways you can achieve special effects such as:

- Drawing with patterns (fill-styles) rather than solid colors
- Drawing "greyed-out" or screen-door-patterned images
- Clipping your drawing to arbitrary areas instead of just window boundaries
- Drawing into subwindows (rather than clipping at subwindow boundaries)

To get these effects, you must set **GC** attributes to control the Patterning stage, the **GC** Clipping stage, and the Window Clipping stage of X's graphics pipeline. Several convenience functions, listed in Table 5-VII, control these **GC** attributes.

| Call Name | Xlib ¶ | Description |
|---|---|---|
| **Fill Styles** | | |
| **XSetFillStyle** | 5.4.3 | Set fill_style (patterning method) |
| **XQueryBestStipple** | 5.4.4 | Determine the ideal stipple pattern size |
| **XQueryBestTile** | 5.4.4 | Determine the ideal tile pattern size |
| **XSetStipple** | 5.4.4 | Set the stipple pattern |
| **XSetTile** | 5.4.4 | Set the tile pattern |
| **XSetTSOrigin** | 5.4.4 | Set the stipple and tile pattern origin |
| **Clipping** | | |
| **XSetClipMask** | 5.4.6 | Set a clip_mask bitmap |
| **XSetClipRectangles** | 5.1.2 | Set the clip mask to a set of rectangles |
| **XSetClipOrigin** | 5.4.4 | Set the origin of the clip mask |
| **XSetSubwindowMode** | 5.4.7 | Control subwindow clipping |

Table 5-VII.  **GC** convenience functions for advanced drawing.

# Fill Style

Your application selects a fill style—a technique for coloring the pixels in your primitives—by using the *fill_style* attribute to control the Patterning stage of the pipeline.  You use the **XFillStyle** convenience function to select the *fill_style* you want.  The available fill stylesinclude:

- FillSolid.  This is the default fill_style.  It applies a solid pixel value or "draw color" to the pixels of your primitive.  It is commonly used with all sorts of primitives.  Some primitives, such as **XCopyPlane** requests and lines drawn with the *line_style* attribute set to LineDoubleDash (see Figure 5-4 ) generate both foreground and background pixels.  The FillSolid technique applies foreground color to foreground pixels and background color to background pixels.

- FillOpaqueStippled.  This fill_style is traditionally known as hatch patterning.  It applies a *stipple* pattern Pixmap (chosen using the **XSetStipple** convenience function) to your graphic primitive's pixels.  A stipple pattern is a raster containing pixels with values one and zero only.  The stipple pattern is repeated across the whole window, then applied to each pixel in your primitive.  The *foreground* pixel value is applied where the stipple-pattern's pixel value is one, and the *background* pixel value where the stipple-pattern's value is zero.

  It does not make sense to use the FillOpaqueStippled *fill_style* when you draw with a *line_style* of LineDoubleDash, because the **GC** only provides one *foreground* and one *background* pixel value attribute.  If you do attempt to draw using both LineDoubleDash and hatch patterning, the *line_style* is treated as if it had the value LineSolid.

That is, the *foreground* and *background* pixel values are applied to the stipple pattern, rather than to the alternate dashes in the line.

Use the hatch patterning technique when you wish to apply a cross-hatch or similar pattern to your graphic primitives. Use the *foreground* and *background* pixel values to select the foreground and background colors in your pattern. Figure 5-2 near the beginning of this chapter shows an example of hatch patterning.

- FillStippled. This fill_style is traditionally known as screen-door patterning. The FillStippled style makes use of the same stipple pattern Pixmap as FillOpaqueStippled (chosen via the **XSetStipple** convenience function), except that the stipple pattern is used as a mask. Pixels from your graphic primitive are not drawn unless the corresponding stipple-pattern pixel value is one. You can think of screen-door patterning as hatch-patterning where the hatch pattern has a transparent background.

  Use screen-door patterning to give a "dimmed" or translucent effect to your graphic primitives.

- FillTiled. This fill_style uses a *tile* pattern Pixmap (chosen via the **XSetTile** convenience function) to determine the pixel value to apply to each pixel in your primitive. A tile pattern is a rectangular raster of pixels, each with its own pixel value (color). The pattern is replicated, then applied to all the pixels selected by your primitive.

  Use tiling when you wish to color your primitives' pixels with a complex pattern (a pattern containing more than just a foreground and background).

  It does not make sense to use the FillTiled fill_style when you draw lines with a *line_style* of LineDoubleDash, because the pixel values used for drawing come from the tile pattern, not from the **GC** directly. If you do attempt to draw using both LineDoubleDash and tile patterning, the *line_style* is treated as if it were LineSolid.

With a couple of exceptions, all fill styles apply equally to all graphic primitives, regardless of whether they are outline primitives or area-filling primitives. The exceptions are points (described in the "Drawing" section earlier in this chapter) and image text (described in Chapter 6). Both points and image text are always drawn as if the fill_style were FillSolid.

The size of the stipple Pixmap or hatch Pixmap you specify can have a dramatic impact on the drawing speed of your workstation. The **XQueryBestStipple** and **XQueryBestTile** requests allow your application to determine the optimum size for stipple and tile Pixmaps on your workstation. If possible, you should use Pixmaps of the suggested sizes for stippling and tiling. If the Pixmaps you use are smaller or larger than the optimum, the workstation may be unable to exploit built-in pattern drawing hardware, and so will draw much more slowly.

The details of Pixmap creation are discussed in Chapter 8.

# XSetFillStyle

The **XSetFillStyle** convenience function sets the fill_style attribute in the **GC** you specify. It (*Xlib* ¶5.4.3) has the form

```
Display *display;       /* pointer to Display structure */
GC mygc;                /* gc */
int fill_style;         /* fill_style */
 . . .
XSetFillStyle ( display, mygc, fill_style );
```

This convenience function alters the fill_style in the specified graphics context. The allowable values (described in the preceding section, and defined in the header file **<X11/X.h>**) for fill_style are FillSolid, FillOpaqueStippled, FillStippled, and FillTiled. The fill_style attribute corresponds to the fill_style field in the **XGCValues** structure.

# XQueryBestStipple  and  XQueryBestTile

The **XQueryBestStipple** and **XQueryBestTile** requests allow you to find out the workstation's optimum sizes for tile and stipple Pixmaps. Before you create Pixmaps for tiles and stipples, it is wise to determine an optimum Pixmap size close to the size you actually want to use. (Chapter 8 covers the details of Pixmap creation.) The **XQueryBestStipple** and **XQueryBestTile** requests allow you to specify the pattern size your application wants to use. Upon return, they give you the optimum size closest to the size you wish to use. These requests (*Xlib* ¶5.4.4) have the form

```
Display *display;            /* pointer to Display structure */
Drawable which_screen;       /* any drawable on desired screen */
unsigned int width, height;  /* the size of your desired pattern*/
unsigned int width_return;   /* ideal pattern width*/
unsigned int height_return;  /* ideal pattern height*/
 . . .
XQueryBestStipple          ( display, which_screen, width, height,
                               &width_return, &height_return );

 . . .
XQueryBestTile             ( display, which_screen, width, height,
                               &width_return, &height_return );
```

To both of these requests, you specify the *width* and *height* of the pattern you want to use. The requests return the optimum pattern size closest to your desired size in *width_return* and *height_return*.

Stippling and tiling can work differently on different screens on a multiple-screen workstation, so you must tell the workstation the screen on which you intend to use the pattern. You do this by specifying, in *which_screen*, the window or Pixmap you intend to use for drawing with the pattern. In *which_screen*, you actually may specify the X resource identifier of any window or Pixmap on the screen you want to work with; the workstation only uses *which_screen* to identify a screen.

> Almost all workstations provide optimum stipple and tile pattern sizes of 8x8 and 16x16. If your application must run well on workstations from multiple vendors, these are good choices of pattern size.

## XSetStipple

The **XSetStipple** convenience function sets the *stipple* Pixmap attribute in the **GC** you specify. It (*Xlib* ¶5.4.3) has the form

```
Display *display;     /* pointer to Display structure */
GC mygc;              /* gc */
Pixmap stipple;       /* stipple pixmap */
. . .
XSetStipple ( display, mygc, stipple );
```

This convenience function sets the *stipple* Pixmap in the specified graphics context. *stipple* must be the X resource identifier of a Pixmap of depth one (a bitmap). The *stipple* attribute corresponds to the stipple field in the **XGCValues** structure. (For detailed information on how to create a Pixmap, see Chapter 8.)

If your workstation has more than one screen, remember that Pixmaps and **GC**s are both created in such a way that they belong to one of the screens—that is, they each have a particular root. It is an error to attempt to set a *stipple* Pixmap in a **GC** unless the Pixmap and the **GC** have the same root.

**Example**: Drawing with a stipple pattern

This filled circle and filled square are drawn on the left with a *fill_style* of FillSolid, and on the right with a *fill_style* of FillStippled (screen-door patterning), using a checkerboard pattern containing alternating 8x8 squares of ones and zeros. The following code excerpt shows how these figures were drawn. Note the use of the **XCreateBitmapFromData** function to create the *checker* Pixmap; Chapter 8 describes **XCreateBitmapFromData** in detail.

```
#define checker_width 16
#define checker_height 16
static char checker_bits [ ] = {
        0xff, 0x00, 0xff, 0x00, 0xff, 0x00, 0xff, 0x00,
        0xff, 0x00, 0xff, 0x00, 0xff, 0x00, 0xff, 0x00,
        0x00, 0xff, 0x00, 0xff, 0x00, 0xff, 0x00, 0xff,
        0x00, 0xff, 0x00, 0xff, 0x00, 0xff, 0x00, 0xff };
```

```
...
Display * display;
Window window;
GC gc;
Pixmap checker;
...
checker = XCreateBitmapFromData ( display, window, checker_bits,
                                      checker_width, checker_height);
XFillArc ( display, window, gc,  16, 16, 40, 40, 0, 360*64);
XFillRectangle ( display, window, gc, 64, 16, 40, 40 );
XSetStipple ( display, gc, checker);
XSetFillStyle (display, gc,  FillStippled);
XFillArc ( display, window, gc, 112, 16, 40, 40, 0, 360*64);
XFillRectangle ( dpy, window, gc, 160, 16, 40, 40 );
```

# XSetTile

The **XSetTile** convenience function is analogous to the **XSetStipple** function. **XSetTile** sets the *tile* Pixmap attribute in the **GC** you specify. It (*Xlib* ¶5.4.3) has the form

```
Display *display;       /* pointer to Display structure */
GC mygc;                /* gc */
Pixmap tile;            /* tile pixmap */
   . . .
XSetTile ( display, mygc, tile );
```

This convenience function sets the *tile* Pixmap in the specified graphics context. *tile* must be the X resource identifier of a Pixmap of the same depth as the *drawable* for which the **GC** was originally created. The *tile* parameter corresponds to the tile field in the **XGCValues** structure. (For detailed information on how to create a Pixmap, see Chapter 8.)

If your workstation has more than one screen, remember that it is an error to attempt to set a *tile* Pixmap in a **GC** unless the Pixmap and the **GC** have the same root.

# XSetTSOrigin

Stipple and tile patterns are anchored to the origin of the window or Pixmap into which you draw. By default, the origin (the upper left corner) of one repeat of the pattern corresponds to the origin of the output window or Pixmap. All the other repeats of the pattern are arranged relative to the anchored repeat, so the phase of the entire pattern is defined by the position of the anchored repeat. This is convenient; if you draw adjacent graphic objects using the same pattern, the pattern will appear to flow seamlessly from one object to the next.

If you want to change the phase of a pattern, use the **XSetTSOrigin** request. When you change the phase of the pattern, you cause some pixel (other than the

origin) of your output window or Pixmap to correspond to the origin of the pattern.
**XSetTSOrigin** (*Xlib* ¶5.4.3) has the form

```
Display *display;              /* pointer to Display structure */
GC mygc;                       /* gc */
int ts_x_origin, ts_y_origin; /* new pattern origin */
 . . .
XSetTSOrigin ( display, mygc, ts_x_origin, ts_y_origin );
```

In *ts_x_origin* and *ts_y_origin*, you specify the location in the output Drawable which you want to correspond to the origin of the tile or stipple pattern. You may specify either positive or negative numbers. Positive numbers cause the pattern to shift to the right (in x) or down (in y); negative numbers cause the pattern to shift to the left or up.

*ts_x_origin* corresponds to the ts_x_origin field in the **XGCValues** structure. Likewise, *ts_y_origin* corresponds to the ts_y_origin field.

X provides no way to set the tile origin and stipple origin separately. **XSetTS-Origin** changes the origin for both the tile and the stipple patterns.

**Example**: Changing a stipple pattern's origin

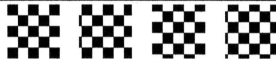

These four filled and stippled squares are drawn using the same pattern as in the example under the "XSetStipple" heading earlier in this chapter. The pattern is a checkerboard of alternating 8x8 squares. The only differences between the four rectangles are in the *ts_x_origin* and *ts_y_origin* settings used. The leftmost square is drawn using settings of zero (the default):

```
XSetTSOrigin ( display, gc, 0, 0 );
```

In the second-from-left square, the pattern is shifted to the right by two pixels:

```
XSetTSOrigin ( display, gc, 2, 0 );
```

In the second-from-right square, the pattern is shifted up by three pixels (note that the negative *ts_y_origin* value shifts the pattern up rather than down):

```
XSetTSOrigin ( display, gc, 0, -3 );
```

Finally, in the rightmost square, the pattern is shifted both in x and y— to the right by two pixels and up by three pixels:

```
XSetTSOrigin ( display, gc, 2, -3 );
```

## Clipping

This section describes the X requests your application can use to control the **GC** and Window Clipping stages of X's graphics pipeline. You only need use these requests if your application needs more control over clipping than is available in the default **GC** settings.

By default, all drawing requests are clipped to the boundaries of the destination window or destination Pixmap. Drawing requests to windows are also clipped so that they do not draw inside the boundaries of inferior windows nested inside the parent. Most of the time, this default clipping behavior is appropriate.

If your application requires drawing requests to be *stencilled*, or clipped to some subset of the destination window, you can use either the **XSetClipMask** or the **XSetClipRectangles** request to specify the subset.

If your application requires drawing requests to draw inside subwindows, you can use the **XSetSubwindowMode** function to allow this behavior.

## XSetClipMask

When you wish to stencil your output, or clip it to an arbitrary shape, you set up the **GC** Clipping stage of the graphics pipeline by specifying a *clip_mask* bitmap. The *clip_mask* bitmap restricts output: only pixels in which the *clip_mask* contains a value of one can be written. Pixels outside the boundaries of the *clip_mask* and pixels containing values of zero are clipped. Thus, the *clip_mask* serves as your stencil; you draw through it. Of course, you can use any drawing requests you wish to create the stencil pattern in the *clip_mask*.

The **XSetClipMask** convenience function sets the *clip_mask* Pixmap attribute in the **GC** you specify. It (*Xlib* ¶5.4.6) has the form

```
Display *display;      /* pointer to Display structure */
GC mygc;               /* gc */
Pixmap clip_mask;      /* clip_mask pixmap */
    . . .
XSetClipMask ( display, mygc, clip_mask );
```

For a Pixmap to be useful as a *clip_mask* it must be a bitmap—it must have a depth of one (See Chapter 8 for a discussion of Pixmaps). The *clip_mask* parameter corresponds to the clip_mask field in the **XGCValues** structure.

You may restore the **GC** Clipping stage of the pipeline to its default behavior—no clipping—by specifying the value None for the *clip_mask*.

If your workstation has more than one screen, remember that it is an error to attempt to set a *clip_mask* Pixmap in a **GC** unless the Pixmap and the **GC** have the same root.

## XSetClipOrigin

The *clip_mask* bitmap is, like the stipple and tile patterns, anchored to the origin of the window or Pixmap into which you draw. Unlike the stipple and tile patterns, however, the *clip_mask* is not repeated over the window. By default, the origin (the upper left corner) of *clip_mask* corresponds to the origin of the output window or Pixmap.

If you want to change the origin of the *clip_mask*, use the **XSetClipOrigin** request. When you change the *clip_mask* origin, you cause some pixel (other than the origin) of your output window or Pixmap to correspond to the origin of the *clip_mask*. **XSetClipOrigin** (*Xlib* ¶5.4.6) has the form

```
Display *display;              /* pointer to Display structure */
GC mygc;                       /* gc */
int clip_x_origin, clip_y_origin;  /* new pattern origin */
. . .
XSetClipOrigin ( display, mygc, clip_x_origin, clip_y_origin );
```

In *clip_x_origin* and *clip_y_origin*, you specify the location in the output Drawable which you want to correspond to the origin of the *clip_mask*. You may specify either positive or negative numbers. Positive numbers cause the clipped area to shift to the right (in x) or down (in y) within the output Drawable; negative numbers cause the pattern to shift to the left or up.

*clip_x_origin* corresponds to the clip_x_origin field in the **XGCValues** structure. Likewise, *clip_y_origin* corresponds to the clip_y_origin field.

## XSetClipRectangles

Specifying a bitmap of the size of your output Drawable is a very general and flexible way of specifying a stencil. However, many applications will find it easier and more economical to specify a clip stencil by means of a series of rectangles rather than a clip bitmap. If your application maintains its clip stencils in terms of a series of rectangles, use the **XSetClipRectangles** request in place of the **XSetClipMask** request. **XSetClipRectangles** (*Xlib* ¶5.4.6) has the form

```
Display *display;              /* pointer to Display structure */
GC gc;                         /* gc */
int clip_x_origin, clip_y_origin;  /* clip origin */
XRectangle rectangles [ ];     /* array of rectangles */
int n;                         /* number of rectangles */
int ordering;                  /* rectangle ordering */
. . .
XSetClipRectangles ( display, gc, clip_x_origin, clip_y_origin,
                     rectangles, n, ordering );
```

*rectangles* is an array of **XRectangle** structures of length *n*. When the workstation receives the **XSetClipRectangles** request, it sets the clipping stencil so it allows drawing within the union of the areas covered by the *rectangles*.

*clip_x_origin* and *clip_y_origin* specify the origin of the clipping stencil with respect to the output Drawable. See the preceding section for further information.

The *ordering* parameter allows you to speed up the workstation by letting it know if your list of rectangles is in a convenient order. You must specify one of the following values in the *ordering* parameter:

Unsorted    Specify this *ordering* value if you do not have any information about the order of your rectangles. If you are in doubt as to what *ordering* value to specify, you should specify Unsorted.

YSorted     Specify this *ordering* value if you know that the y origin of each rectangle in your list is greater than or equal to the y origins of all the preceding rectangles in the list.

YXSorted    Specify this *ordering* value if you know that your rectangles are YSorted, and you also know that rectangles with equal y origins have nondecreasing x origins.

YXBanded    Specify this *ordering* value if you know that your rectangles are YXSorted, and you also know that for every possible Y scan line in your output Drawable, all your rectangles including that scan line have identical y origins and y extents.

You might be tempted to sort your list of rectangles before sending it to the workstation, so that you can specify a more restrictive *ordering* parameter. Sorting the rectangles this way is usually not worth the trouble; simply specify Unsorted. The *ordering* parameter is provided for the use of those applications which compute lists of rectangles in a constrained order.

Once you have constructed a rectangle list and sent it to the workstation, the resulting *clip_mask* is functionally identical to one you might have set up using **XSetClipMask**. There is no way to retrieve the current clip rectangle list or the current *clip_mask* bitmap from any **GC**.

**Example**: Use **XSetClipRectangles** to process expose event series

The **XSetClipRectangles** request can be used to help redraw window contents in response to series of Expose or GraphicsExpose events. The idea is to accumulate the rectangles in the series, and use them in a **XSetClipRectangles** request immediately before redrawing the window. This technique is a good compromise between the very simple strategy of clearing and redrawing the entire window at the end of each series, and the complex strategy of redrawing the contents of individual exposed rectangles. If you use **XSetClipRectangles**, you need not clear the window before drawing, yet you need only draw the window's contents once.

The following code excerpt shows how you might process Expose events using **XSetClipRectangles**.

```
Display * display;
Window window;
GC gc;
. . .
/* Declare a static array to hold the list of rectangles */
#define MAXRECT 32
static XRectangle exp_rect [MAXRECT];
static exp_nrect = 0;
. . .
  /*  main event-reading loop  */
  while ( True ) {
   XNextEvent( display, &event );
    switch (event.type)   {
     /*  repaint window on expose events  */
    case Expose:
        /* make sure the static rectangle array is not overfull */
      if (exp_nrect < MAXRECT )
        { /* copy the current Expose rectangle into the array */
        exp_rect[exp_nrect].x           = event.xexpose.x;
        exp_rect[exp_nrect].y           = event.xexpose.y;
        exp_rect[exp_nrect].width       = event.xexpose.width;
        exp_rect[exp_nrect].height      = event.xexpose.height;
        }
      exp_nrect++;
      if (event.xexpose.count == 0)
        { /* last event of series */
        if (exp_nrect <= MAXRECT)
                /* if Expose series was short enough, send it to gc */
            XSetClipRectangles ( display, gc,
                  0,0, exp_rect, exp_nrect, Unsorted );
        else
          { /* otherwise clear the window and set the clip mask to None */
            XClearWindow ( display, window );
            XSetClipMask ( display, gc,  None );
          }
          /* call a routine to redraw the window contents */
        drawpix (display, window, gc);
          /* reset the rectangle count ready for next series */
        exp_nrect = 0;
        }
      break;
      . . .
    } /* switch  (event.type)  */
  }  /* while   (True) */
```

Note that the *ordering* parameter value is specified as Unsorted in this code excerpt. Although most X workstations provide Expose event rectangles in YXSorted order, X does not guarantee any particular order.

Note that this technique is easiest to use when your application draws using only one **GC**. If your application uses more than one **GC** during redrawing, you would have to send the clip rectangle list to all of them, by first using **XSetClipRectangles**, then using **XCopyGC** to copy the clip information from one **GC** to another. The following code excerpt copies clip information from *gc1* to *gc2*:

```
Display  *  display;
GC gc1, gc2;
...

XCopyGC ( display, gc1,
   (GCClipMask | GCClipXOrigin | GCClipYOrigin), gc2 );
```

## XSetSubwindowMode

By default, all graphics output to windows is clipped so that subwindows are not affected by drawing operations. You can use the **XSetSubwindowMode** convenience function to allow drawing within subwindows. The ability to draw within subwindows is especially useful for applications which must draw such things as selection rectangles or rubber-band lines into multiple windows. Note, however, that if your application enables drawing into subwindows, it is easy to corrupt those subwindows' contents by mistake.

**XSetSubwindowMode** (*Xlib* ¶5.4.7) has the form

```
Display *display;        /* pointer to Display structure */
GC gc;                   /* gc */
int subwindow_mode;      /* ClipByChildren, IncludeInferiors */
 . . .

XSetSubwindowMode ( display, gc, subwindow_mode );
```

You can specify one of two *subwindow_mode* values:

ClipByChildren    Graphic output is clipped so subwindows are unaffected.

IncludeInferiors   Graphic output draws into subwindows, ignoring subwindow boundaries.

The *subwindow_mode* parameter corresponds to the subwindow_mode field in the **XGCValues** structure.

# WORKSTATION PERFORMANCE

Drawing speed is important, especially when your application is highly interactive. The proper use of **GC**s can have a major effect on how fast your application draws. To help you design your application to work well with the X Window

System, this section discusses how *Xlib* and X workstation servers process **GC**s and the graphics requests that use **GC**s.

The X Window System's graphics pipeline provides several capabilities (wide-line drawing, stippling, and tiling, for example) which work slowly on most workstations.

Both *Xlib* and workstation servers use caching to optimize **GC** performance. When they chose the caching strategies, the designers of the X window system had particular usage patterns in mind. Your application will draw faster if you design it in the light of an understanding of these caching strategies.

Here are some rules of the road to use so your graphics applications run as fast as possible:

- Exploit the buffering of one-way X requests as much as possible. For example, you should obviously avoid using the **XFlush** and **XSync** functions (see Chapter 3) except immediately before some sort of delay. When you exploit buffering, you reduce network transmission overhead.

- Use the plural form (**XDrawArcs**, for example) of graphic primitive requests instead of the singular form (**XDrawArc**) whenever possible.

- Wherever possible, specify line_width attribute values of zero. When line_width is zero, the workstation server may use fast line-drawing hardware, even if that line-drawing hardware might not yield "perfect" results (especially if line segments cross, or if you are drawing styled—dashed—lines). In practice, line_width zero lines and arcs look just fine. Only if you require pixel-for-pixel accuracy in a portable (multi-vendor) application should you specify a line_width of one for your narrow lines and arcs.

- Avoid fill_styles other than FillSolid except where you need them. If you do specify stipple patterns or tile patterns, make them the size suggested by the **XQueryBestStipple** or **XQueryBestTile** functions.

- Avoid using a clip mask bitmap (set with **XSetClipMask**) unless you have no alternative.

- Avoid changing attribute values in **GC**s excessively or redundantly. Some applications, especially older graphics applications, issue calls to reset attribute values (such as foreground "draw color") immediately before drawing *every* primitive. If your X application did this, you would be issuing many extra—and redundant—X requests. Processing these requests takes time and slows down drawing.

- Exploit the fact that you can have multiple **GC**s stored in the server. For example, if you know your application will sometimes draw dotted lines and sometimes draw dashed lines, you should set up two **GC**s, one for the dotted lines and another for the dashed lines. In this case, using multiple **GC**s would be substantially faster than re-sending the line-style pattern each time you changed from dotted to dashed or vice versa (see the description of the **XSetDashes** request in the "Dash Patterns" section of this chapter).

- Exploit *Xlib*'s **GC** cache. *Xlib* accumulates your desired changes to multiple attribute values for a single **GC**. The **XChangeGC** request and all the **GC**-altering convenience functions operate directly on the **GC** cache. You may issue several such **GC**-changing functions in sequence. As long as you refer only to a single **GC** resource, *Xlib* accumulates all your requested changes in the cache. As soon as you use the **GC** you have been changing, or change some other **GC**, *Xlib* sends a change request to the workstation server.

  If you use it properly, this caching strategy can significantly reduce the number of **GC**-changing requests your application must send to the workstation. For example, there is a right way and a wrong way to change several attributes in two different **GC**s. The right way—which results in just two **GC**-changing requests—is to change all the attributes in one **GC**, then all the attributes in the next. The wrong way is to change the first attribute in both **GC**s, then the sec-ond attribute in both, and so forth.

- Exploit the workstation's **GC** cache. Internally, most workstations keep track of the current **GC**. If successive drawing requests use different **GC**s, the workstation must change the current **GC** before carrying out each request. Changing the current **GC** can be quite time-consuming, depending on the type of graphics drawing hard-ware in the workstation. To reduce this overhead inside your workstation you should design your application to issue consecutive drawing requests with the same **GC**, if possible.

  However, there is a tradeoff between reducing transmission time by using multiple **GC**s and exploiting the workstation server's **GC** cache. Consider the situation where you are drawing lines in any of a dozen different colors (foreground values). Should you create a dozen **GC**s, one for each different line-color, or should you use one **GC** and issue the **XSetForeground** function before drawing each line? The precise answer to this question depends on the relative speeds of network transmission and **GC** changing. In a tradeoff situation such as this, your best course of action is to do what makes your application program the simplest.

None of these points apply to the *correctness* of the pictures your application will draw, only to how fast they appear.

An application designed to exploit **GC**s and their caches will perform up to full potential. However, the X Window System has reasonably low overhead anyway, as long as you avoid worst-case behavior.

## DRAWING SIZE

Ordinarily, the exact size and scale of an on-screen drawing is not critical to your application, in the sense that the size and scale of a blueprint is critical to a machinist. It is difficult to take precise measurements from the face of a cathode-ray-tube (CRT) the way a machinist might take them from a blueprint with dividers. The CRT face is probably curved, and certainly covered with a thick glass shield. Furthermore, the electronics of most CRTs are not designed or calibrated to support such measurements. (There are exceptions, of course; some film recorders use extremely precise flat-face CRTs.)

> You should not encourage your application's users to believe the pictures you generate on-screen are drawn to any measurable scale.

Given that warning, there is a way for your application to draw to scale. You can determine the size of the screen (in millimeters) as well as the number of pixels on the screen of your workstation. Workstation screen sizes and resolutions vary from vendor to vendor and model to model; portable applications should not assume that all workstations have the same pixel size and resolution. Many workstations have a resolution of about 30 pixels per centimeter (75 pixels per inch). Others have a resolution of about 40 pixels per centimenter (100 pixels per inch).

The informational macros **DisplayHeight** and **DisplayHeightMM** return the height of a specified screen, in pixels and millimeters respectively. These informational macros, and their corresponding functions (*Xlib* ¶2.2.1) have the form

```
Display * display;       /* pointer to current display structure */
int screen;              /* screen number */
int pixels, mm;          /* screen sizes, pixels and millimeters */
. . .
pixels = XDisplayHeight ( display, screen ); /* callable function*/
pixels = DisplayHeight ( display, screen );   /* macro */
. . .
mm = XDisplayHeightMM ( display, screen ); /* callable function*/
mm = DisplayHeightMM ( display, screen );   /* macro */
```

Thus, you can use this information to scale your on-screen drawing. Of course, all graphic output primitives are specified in terms of pixels. If you want to scale your drawings in terms of millimeters, you must use display height information to determine how big the pixels are.

Most, if not all, X workstations have square pixels. Thus the factor by which you must multiply millimeters to obtain pixels is the same in both the X and Y dimensions.

**Example**: Draw a fifty-millimeter horizontal line

This example shows how to draw a horizontal line of a specified length. In the example, the horizontal line is drawn starting at pixel position (100,100) relative to the origin of the window.

```
Display *display;          /* pointer to current Display structure */
Window w;                  /* the window to draw to */
GC gc;                     /* the GC to draw with */
long pixels, mm, length;   /* variables for lengths */
. . .
pixels = DisplayHeight ( display, DefaultScreen ( display ));
mm = DisplayHeightMM ( display, DefaultScreen ( display ));
length = ( (50 * pixels ) + (mm /2) ) / mm ;
XDrawLine ( display, w, gc, 100, 100, 100+length, 100 );
```

Note that the formula shown for computing the integer *length* of the line rounds the length to the nearest number of pixels; that accounts for the (*mm* / 2) term in the numerator. Also note that sixteen bits of precision are not enough for this computation.

# SUMMARY

*Points, lines, rectangles, arcs,* and *shapes* are the geometric *graphic primitives* which you can draw with the X Window System. Your application issues requests describing these graphic primitives and the X workstation figures out which *pixels* to illuminate. When drawing, you always specify some *Drawable* (either a window or a Pixmap), and you always specify the position of your graphic primitive relative to the drawable's upper left corner.

You also must create a *graphics context* (**GC**) before drawing. The **GC** is an X Window System resource in which you store *rendering attributes* for use when drawing. Rendering attributes include such things as foreground and background pixel values (colors) and line widths. Successful use of X's graphic primitives depends on skillful exploitation of the capabilities of **GC**s.

X provides a rich graphics environment with many options. **GC**s contain 23 distinct attribute values (see Table 5-II) to manage these options. If X did not have **GC**s, it would be necessary to respecify many rendering attributes with every drawing request.

In order to provide a framework for understanding **GC**s, this chapter explains X's graphics in terms of a five-stage *graphics pipeline*. Each graphic primitive is processed through each of the pipeline stages in turn. Each **GC** attribute value relates to one of the pipeline stages. The stages are:

- Pixel Selection.  This stage determines where each primitive goes. It selects the pixels lying along a line or arc or inside a shape.

- Patterning.  This stage applies colors and patterns.

- **GC** Clip.  This stage *clips* primitives as specified in the **GC**.

- Window Clip.  This stage clips primitives to window boundaries.

- Raster Output.  This stage combines new graphics with whatever has already been drawn in the drawable.  This stage makes possible operations such as rubber-band lines.

Your application can, using **XCreateGC**, create as many **GC**s as necessary for drawing.  You must create at least one.  You can change attribute values in **GC**s either with the **XChangeGC** request or with one of the many convenience functions.

Once you have a **GC** set up, you may use it to draw:

- Points.  X allows you to illuminate single pixels.

- Lines.  X offers a wide variety of line styles, ranging from solid-colored narrow lines to wide dash-patterned polylines with high-quality joins between segments and end-caps.  **GC** attribute values control the various aspects of line style.

- Arcs and circles.  X provides both outlined and filled elliptical arcs. When specifying an arc, you give a rectangular bounding box and a pair of angles.  Unfilled arcs are drawn the same way as lines, using line styles, line widths, and dash patterns.  For filled arcs, a **GC** attribute controls the method used for selecting the pixels inside the arc.

- Rectangles.  X provides both outlined and filled rectangles.  Unfilled rectangles are drawn the same way as lines.

- Shapes.  X provides arbitrary filled shapes.  A **GC** attribute controls the algorithm used to fill each shape.

Successful use of X's graphic primitives depends also on knowing *when* to draw. Windows share screen space and are stacked on top of one another.  This stacking can change at any time, causing all or parts of windows to become *exposed*. Your application finds out about this via Expose events.  Your application can also use Expose events to find out when a newly mapped window first becomes available for drawing.

You should construct your application so it redraws its windows in response to Expose events.  Your application must keep track of everything in your windows, and be prepared to redraw any window at any time when asked to by Expose events.  You should solicit Expose events from each window using the **XSelect-Input** call before mapping each window.

X provides ways to *clear* windows, or set them to background values. You can clear an entire window or a rectangular portion of a window. You can optionally cause Expose events to be generated for the areas you clear.

You can copy rectangular areas. This capability is useful for scrolling, among other things. When copying, you may use either an *area-copy* (pixel-BLT) or a *plane-copy* (bit-BLT) operation. Because windows can be stacked on one another, the source pixels for copy operations may be obscured and unavailable. The workstation provides GraphicsExpose and NoExpose events to help you recover from this situation. Techniques for processing GraphicsExpose events are similar to those for processing Expose events. You solicit GraphicsExpose and NoExpose events using a **GC** attribute.

X provides four different patterning styles, controlled by **GC** attributes:

- Solid coloring. This style draws fastest. It applies solid color to the pixels of the primitive.

- Hatch patterning. In this style, you specify a *stipple bitmap*. The one and zero values in the stipple bitmap select foreground and background colors.

- Screen-door patterning. In this style you also specify a stipple bitmap. It differs from hatch-patterning in that one values specify foreground color, while zero values specify transparency. Screen-door patterning is useful for displaying grayed-out objects.

- Tile patterning. In this style, you specify a Pixmap, potentially containing many different pixel values or colors. This tile Pixmap is used as a pattern when drawing.

Along with the four patterning styles, you can use **GC** attributes to control the pattern's offset: you can shift the pattern origin arbitrarily. The pattern (stipple or hatch) is replicated over the entire window, and used to color the pixels selected by each primitive.

X also allows you to draw with a pattern of any size. However, most workstations have ideal pattern sizes which allow much better drawing performance than other sizes. X gives you the means to inquire the workstation's ideal pattern sizes.

X allows you to specify an arbitrary clipping region. When you set a clipping region in a **GC**, all primitives drawn through that **GC** are clipped, or confined to the region you specify. You may specify either a list of rectangles or an arbitrary bitmap to use as a clipping region.

With judicious use of **GC**s, applications can achieve high graphics performance. Simple drawings (narrow lines, solid colors, no clipping) are faster than complex graphics. Equally important to performance is the exploitation of the **GC** caches built into both *Xlib* and workstation. If you avoid switching between **GC**s too often, you can reduce both network transmission time and drawing time.

Different makes and models of workstations offer different scales (pixels per millimeter) on their screens. If you wish to draw to scale, you can do so by inquiring the size of the display in both pixels and millimeters. These values can be used to help you specify dimensioned drawings. However, keep in mind the difficulties of taking measurements from CRTs.

# CHAPTER 6
# TEXT

Displaying text is the most important output function of any computer system. Users certainly spend more time reading the text displayed by applications than they do on any other task related to computer use. Workstations allow your application to transcend the traditional limitations of text display terminals. No longer are all pages of text limited to a fixed number of characters of a fixed size. In the X Window System, text is a form of graphic output. This fact gives your application a wide range of options; you can tailor your textual output exactly to the needs of your user.

The most important factor governing the look of your application's text output is your choice of fonts. The first section of this chapter discusses what fonts are and how they work. Appendix D lists available fonts.

The second section describes a simple way of loading fonts into the workstation and making them available to your application for drawing character strings.

The third section describes, with examples, the X character-string drawing requests. These requests are graphic output primitives, just like the drawing requests of Chapter 5. If all you wish to do is display a few characters on the screen, you will understand how to do so after reading the first three sections of this chapter.

The fourth section of this chapter describes font structures and the *Xlib* calls that use them. Fonts contain a great deal of information. Your application can use font structures to retrieve that information in useful forms. For example, you may need to know how much space is taken up by a character string.

What fonts are available on the workstation? Where does the workstation get fonts? The fifth section of this chapter describes X requests that allow your application to search for fonts, and control where the workstation finds them.

The last section of this chapter describes X's capabilities for drawing strings of 16-bit characters. Such character strings are often used for Oriental character sets, such as Japanese Kanji.

Note that many existing text-only applications assume they are running on ordinary text display terminals. There is no need to reprogram these applications to run in windows on the X Window System; you can run them unchanged using a terminal emulator such as **xterm(1)**. If you are working with such an application, you should consult the terminal emulator documentation furnished by your workstation vendor.

# FONTS

A *font* describes the sizes and shapes of a collection of displayable text characters. X workstations ordinarily have several fonts available, stored in files accessible to the workstation's host cpu. The files containing fonts are not accessible directly to your application; the workstation loads font files and makes their contents available to you in response to X requests.

You can think of each font as an indexed list of character patterns. When you ask the workstation to draw a character string, it treats each character in the string as an index into the font. For example, the ASCII numeral "0" corresponds to the decimal value 48 (0x30 hexadecimal). When you request the drawing of a string containing a "0" digit, the workstation draws whatever character it finds at index position 48 in the font. Most fonts have a *replacement character*, which the workstation draws by default when your string specifies a character that is not present in the font.

Most fonts are used for drawing strings of ordinary text. Almost all such fonts contain the 96 displayable characters of the American Standard Code for Information Interchange (ASCII) character set, with a space character for the replacement character.

Some fonts contain arbitrary special-purpose collections of characters. The characters in these fonts do not necessarily conform to the standard ASCII character set. For example, the cursor font (see Appendix F and Chapter 9 under the heading "Creating, Changing, and Destroying Cursors") contains the shapes and sizes of some standard cursors.

*Xlib*'s text-drawing calls do not process control characters (newlines, tabs, and DELs, for example). X does not handle these control codes in any special way, so you should not attempt to draw strings containing them. Rather, X treats control characters exactly the same way as it treats all characters in strings—as indexes into the font. In fact, most of the public-domain fonts shipped by M.I.T. (with the second X Window System distribution in early 1988) used font indices

Figure 6-1. The character set in many X fonts.

1-31 (reserved in ASCII for control codes) to represent mathematical symbols. A typical character-code assignment for an X font is shown in Figure 6-1. Note that no symbols in this font are assigned to codes 0x00 (NULL), 0x09 (tab), 0x0a (newline), 0x0c (form feed), and 0x7f (DEL). This means that strings containing those codes will be drawn with replacement characters (blanks, usually) instead. If there is any special action to be taken for control characters, the application must be programmed to take it explicitly. For example, X terminal-emulator applications like **xterm** interpret ASCII control characters correctly.

In X, when you choose a font you are defining how you want character strings to look, as well as the character set to use. Your choice of font determines:

- The size of the characters

- The way characters are spaced: *fixed-pitch* fonts emulate typewriters or character-cell computer terminals by using the same amount of space for all characters, whereas *variable-pitch* fonts allow narrow characters (such as f, l, and i) to consume less on-screen space than wide characters (such as M and W).

This is a fixed-pitch font. ABCabc123

**This is a variable-pitch font. ABCabc123**

- The style of the characters

# Roman style

# **Bold Roman style**

# *Italic style*

# Gothic style

# **Bold gothic style**

# *Slant style*

Each separate font represents a single combination of size, spacing and style. For example, the X font named "vrb-25" contains 25-pixel-high variable-pitch roman bold characters. The X font named "9x15" contains a fixed-pitch terminal emulator font in which each character occupies a rectangle 15 pixels high and nine pixels wide. If your application displays both large text and small text, you must, therefore, use two different font files.

While using a font, your application may need information about the sizes of individual letters and the amount of space to leave between successive lines of text drawn with the font. Your application can request this information from the workstation in a *font structure*. Some font designers also make recommendations about such things as the amount of blank space to leave between sentences and positions of subscripts and superscripts. Part of the font structure contains, in the form of a *font property list*, whatever such recommendations the designer chose to make.

Each font has a *font name*. A font name is a text string identifying the font, such as "vrb-25" or "9x15". Your application only needs to use font names when loading fonts with the **XLoadFont** (see under the heading "Loading Fonts") or **XLoadQueryFont** requests (see under the heading "Loading Font Structures"). Once a font is loaded, your application refers to it by means of an X resource identifier. You can instruct the workstation to give you a list of the fonts available for loading. See under the heading "Searching for Fonts" later in this chapter.

The names of fonts available with the X Window System implementation shipped by M.I.T. in early 1988 are shown in Appendix D. If you are writing a portable application, you can assume that the fonts of Appendix D are available for your application to use. Workstation vendors or third parties may furnish other fonts; consult your supplier's documentation for further information.

# SIMPLE FONT SELECTION

This section describes the easiest way to load fonts and draw text from an X Window System application. If your application does not need the information in the font structure, you can use the methods of this section. However, if you must center your text or align several lines of text with each other, you should use the more sophisticated capabilities covered in later sections of this chapter.

| Request/Function | Xlib ¶ | Description |
|---|---|---|
| **XLoadFont** | 6.5.1 | Load a font; create a font resource id |
| **XSetFont** | 5.4.5 | Set the *font* attribute value in **GC** |
| **XUnloadFont** | 6.5.1 | Unload a font |

Table 6-I. *Xlib* calls for simple font selection.

Table 6-I summarizes the X calls you use to select fonts the simple way. X workstations draw text (just as they draw everying else) using the graphics pipeline discussed in Chapter 5. Before doing any drawing, you must create windows (or Pixmaps) and **GC**s. However, to draw text you must specify the font you want to use by doing two things:

- use the **XLoadFont** request to instruct the workstation to load the font you want, and create a **Font** resource identifier for it

- use the **XSetFont** convenience function to set the *font* attribute value in your **GC**.

Once you have loaded a font and set up the graphics pipeline, you may proceed to draw your text.

Note that **GC**s have a default font attribute setting (ordinarily the font named "8x13"). If your application can use the default font, you may skip the **XLoadFont** and **XSetFont** steps and just draw text. The **helloworld.c** example of Chapter 2 used the default font.

## Loading Fonts

Before your application can draw text with a font, you must tell the workstation to load the font by name. When you tell the workstation to load a font, the workstation creates an X resource identifier of type **Font**. Thereafter, you refer to the **Font** identifier when you want to refer to the font.

The **XLoadFont** request, given a font name, makes the workstation load a font. It does not, however, load the font's font structure; if you need the font structure use **XLoadQueryFont** instead. **XLoadFont** (*Xlib* ¶6.5.1) has the form

```
Display *display;        /* pointer to Display structure */
char name [ ];           /* font name */
Font font;               /* returned font resource identifier */
```

```
      . . .
      font = XLoadFont ( display, name );
```

This request creates an X resource identifier for the font referred to in *name*. *name* is an ordinary null-terminated text string. Most font names are encoded in ASCII, although X permits any character in the ISO Latin-1 character set (see Appendix C) to be used in a font name. Upper and lower case letters do not matter in the names of fonts. Also, do not include the ".snf" suffix on font names, even though most workstations load fonts from files with that suffix.

Avoid specifying the *name* of a nonexistent font. If an **XLoadFont** request fails because you specified a nonexistent font, the workstation generates an error event specifying a BadName error (see "Error Handling" in Chapter 3). Other parts of this chapter describe ways of finding out whether particular named fonts exist: see under the headings "Loading Font Structures" and "Searching for Fonts."

## Setting the Font Attribute in GCs

Before drawing text strings with a newly loaded font, use the **XSetFont** call to set the *font* attribute in an existing **GC**. **XSetFont** (*Xlib* ¶5.4.5) has the form

```
      Display *display;          /* pointer to Display structure */
      GC gc;                     /* gc */
      Font font;                 /* font resource identifier */
      . . .
      XSetFont ( display, gc, font );
```

Using the *font* parameter, you can select the font you want to use for subsequent text-drawing requests. The *font* parameter corresponds to the font field in the **XGCValues** structure (described under the "The **GCValues** Structure and Mask" heading in Chapter 5).

Newly created **GC**s have a default *font* attribute value; it depends on the make and model of the workstation, but on most workstations the default refers to the "8x13" font. If you do not set the font attribute explicitly, text-drawing requests use the default font.

If you have a multiple-screen workstation, you know that you must create and use most X resources (such as windows and **GC**s) specifically with reference to a single screen. Font resources are an exception; you may use any font with any **GC**, for drawing in any window or Pixmap on any screen.

## Unloading Fonts

When your application no longer needs the font resources you loaded with **XLoadFont**, you can explicitly release them with **XUnloadFont**. The workstation unloads your fonts automatically when your application terminates, so ordinarily you do not need to unload them explicitly. The rules for font lifetime are the same as for any other X resource (see Chapter 3). **XUnloadFont** (*Xlib* ¶6.5.1) has the form

**Display** *\*display;*                 /\* *pointer  to  Display  structure* \*/
**Font** *font;*                         /\* *font  to  unload* \*/
. . .
**XUnloadFont** (*display, font* );

This request releases resources for the font referred to by *font*. Your application must not refer to *font* in any subsequent requests. However, if, prior to calling **XUnloadFont**, you use **XSetFont** to set any **GC**'s font attribute value to *font*, you may continue to use that **GC** after you call **XUnloadFont**; the workstation does not actually destroy the font's resources until no references to it remain.

# DRAWING CHARACTER STRINGS

Once you have selected a font and other **GC** attributes, you can proceed to draw character strings. In the X Window System, you specify a single x,y position (relative to the origin of the drawable window or Pixmap) for every character string you want the workstation to draw. This character string *origin* lies at one end of the string (the left end for many languages), on the *baseline*. The base-line, as Figure 6-2 shows, lies immediately below the *ascenders*—the upright parts of capital letters and most lower-case letters. Some lower-case letters have *descenders*, which extend below the baseline.

The workstation draws each text string extending from the origin. For most languages, the text string extends to the right (although X allows fonts for draw-ing strings to the left). The first letter's origin is placed at the x,y position you specify, and each following letter is placed next to the preceding one. Most fonts, including the one enlarged in Figure 6-2 (it has the name "6x12"; see Appendix D), automatically put some space between letters to make strings readable.

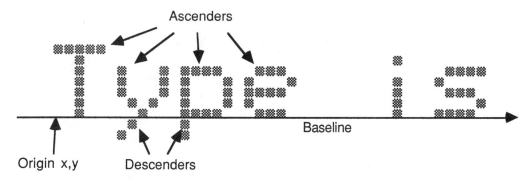

Figure 6-2.  Character string origin, baseline, ascenders, and descenders.

| Request/Function | Xlib ¶ | Description |
| --- | --- | --- |
| **XDrawString** | 6.6.2 | Draw a character string |
| **XDrawImageString** | 6.6.3 | Draw an opaque character string |
| **XDrawText** | 6.6.1 | Draw multiple text strings |

Table 6-I. *Xlib* calls for drawing character strings.

Each character string in X is drawn along just one horizontal baseline. If you want to draw several lines of text, you must draw several character strings at different positions. This approach differs from terminals which permit you to change the baseline by outputting control characters such as carriage-returns and newlines. Control characters (including tabs) are, as an earlier section of this chapter discussed, useless in X character strings. In most fonts, including the one shown in Figure 6-2, you can include space characters in a string. However, some special-purpose fonts do not even contain a space character.

The size of a character string as drawn (ignoring clipping) is completely determined by the letters in the string and the font you use to draw it. You cannot specify an explicit width and height for a character string, as you can for a rectangle or arc. You can determine in advance how much space a character string will take to draw; see under the heading "Font Structures" later in this chapter.

Your application can choose from among three X Window System requests for character-string drawing. These requests are summarized in Table 6-I. **XDrawString** and **XDrawImageString** both allow you to draw a single text string in two different ways. **XDrawText** is a plural form of **XDrawString**; with it you can draw several text strings with multiple fonts and spacings along a single baseline. The requests of this section allow you to specify text strings containing eight bits (one byte) per character. Corresponding X requests for drawing Oriental-language character strings containing 16 bits per character are available; see the section of this chapter entitled "16-Bit Character Strings."

## XDrawString

Use **XDrawString** to draw a single character string. **XDrawString** uses the entire graphics pipeline, including the Patterning stage, Clipping stages, and Raster Output stage (see Chapter 5). The shape of each character is represented within the font as a bitmap. The workstation draws the foreground pixels (the pixels with value one in the font bitmap) of each character with the *foreground* pixel value (if you use a *fill_style* of FillSolid) or the stipple or tile pattern (if you use a *fill_style* of FillOpaqueStippled, FillStippled or FillTiled). Background pixels (those with value zero in the font bitmap) are completely ignored by **XDrawString**.

This means that **XDrawString** is useful for drawing solid-colored or "dimmed" (screen-door patterned) text, as well as hatched or tiled text. **XDrawString** (*Xlib* ¶6.6.2) has the form

```
Display *display;              /* pointer to Display structure */
Drawable window;               /* window or pixmap */
GC gc;                         /* gc */
int x, y;                      /* character string origin*/
char string [ ];               /* character string */
int length;                    /* length of character string */
 . . .
```

**XDrawString** ( *display, window, gc, x, y, string, length* );

When you use this request, the workstation draws the *string* you specify starting at the *x,y* origin you specify. Use the *length* parameter to specify the number of characters in the *string*. Note that you must specify the *length* explicitly, even if you specify an ordinary null-terminated *string*.

**Example**: Drawing a character string

In the following code excerpt, we use the **XLoadFont**, **XSetFont**, and **XDrawString** requests to draw "Hello, World!" in large letters into a window with a checkerboard-stippled background. The text is drawn at the position $(x, y)$ in the specified *window*. That is, the lower left corner of the capital "H" is drawn at $(x,y)$, and the rest of the text string extends to the right. Note that "vrb-25" is a variable-pitch 25-point roman font; see Appendix D for other fonts.

```
Display *display;
Drawable window;
GC gc;
Font font;
int x, y;
 . . .
font = XLoadFont ( display, "vrb-25" );
 . . .
XSetFont ( display, gc, font );
 . . .
XDrawString ( display, window, gc, x, y,
              "Hello, World!", strlen("Hello, World!" ));
```

**Example**: Dimmed character strings

This example shows the effect of drawing text with a checkerboard stipplepattern and a *fill_style* of FillStippled. The resulting dimmed-text effect is useful in menus to show invalid selections (for example, a "Close File" selection might be invalid if no file were open). The word on the left is drawn with a fill_style of FillSolid, and the word on the right with a fill_style of FillStippled, using a checkerboard pattern containing alternating ones and zeros.

The following code excerpt shows how this example was drawn. Note the use of the **XCreateBitmapFromData** function to create the pattern Pixmap; Chapter 8 describes **XCreateBitmapFromData** in detail.

```
#define  pattern_width     8
#define  pattern_height    8
static char pattern_bits [ ] = {
      0x55, 0xaa, 0x55, 0xaa, 0x55, 0xaa, 0x55, 0xaa };
...
Display * display;
Window window;
GC gc;
Pixmap pattern;
...
pattern = XCreateBitmapFromData ( display, window, pattern_bits,
                              pattern_width, pattern_height );
font = XLoadFont ( display, "vr-25" );
XSetFont ( display, gc, font );
XDrawString ( display, window, gc, 10, 30,
                 "Bright", strlen ("Bright"));
XSetStipple ( display, gc, pattern );
XSetFillStyle ( display, gc, FillStippled );
XDrawString ( display, window, gc, 100, 30,
                 "Dimmed", strlen ("Dimmed"));
```

## XDrawImageString

Use **XDrawImageString** to draw a simple unpatterned character string. When carrying out an **XDrawImageString** request, the workstation ignores the *fill_style* attribute. Instead, it simply applies the *foreground* pixel value to each character's foreground pixels, and the *background* pixel value to each character's background pixels. Thus, **XDrawImageString** draws each character in a string as if its background were opaque. This fact distinguishes **XDrawImageString** from the other text-drawing requests, which treats character backgrounds as transparent. If the **GC**'s *background* attribute is the same as the window's background, the opaque background is not noticeable to the user unless character strings are drawn on top of other graphics.

**XDrawImageString** runs faster than **XDrawString** on some workstation models. It is especially suitable for use in applications like terminal emulators, which must draw large amounts of ordinary text very quickly. **XDrawImageString** (*Xlib* ¶6.6.3) has the form

```
Display *display;          /* pointer to Display structure */
Drawable window;           /* window or pixmap */
GC gc;                     /* gc */
int x, y;                  /* character string origin*/
char string [ ];           /* character string */
int length;                /* length of character string */
. . .
XDrawImageString ( display, window, gc, x, y, string, length );
```

The parameters of the **XDrawImageString** request are exactly the same as those of **XDrawString**.  See the preceding section.

**Example**:  Drawing an opaque-background character string

This example is the same as the first example under **XDrawString** above, except for the use of **XDrawImageString**.  The effect of the opaque-background text is illustrated by this example (compare the first example for **XDrawString** in the previous section).

```
Display *display;
Drawable window;
GC gc;
Font font;
int x, y;
. . .
font = XLoadFont ( display, "vrb-25" );
. . .
XSetFont ( display, gc, font );
. . .
XDrawImageString ( display, window, gc, x, y,
                   "Hello, World!", strlen("Hello, World!" ));
```

## XDrawText

**XDrawText** is the plural form of **XDrawString**.  (No plural form of **XDraw-ImageString** is available.)  **XDrawText** accepts an array of **XTextItem** structures.  Each item in the array specifies a single character string;  the workstation draws the specified character strings in order.  The **XTextItem** structure is defined (in **<X11/Xlib.h>**) as follows:

```
typedef struct {
    char *     chars;   /* pointer to character string */
```

```
    int        nchars;   /* number of characters in string */
    int        delta;    /* x delta, along baseline */
    Font       font;     /* resource id of font to use, or None */
} XTextItem;
```

The array of **XTextItem** structures allows you to draw several character strings along a common baseline. The fields in the **XTextItem** array have the following meanings:

chars      a pointer to the first character of the string to draw.

nchars      the number of characters in the string. Note that you must specify the number of characters in the string explicitly, even if it is an ordinary null-terminated string.

delta      an offset in pixels. It is applied *before* drawing the string. A positive number shifts the string's origin to the right, and a negative number shifts it to the left. If all the delta fields in an array of text items are zero, the strings are drawn adjacent to each other.

font      the X resource identifier of a font. If you specify the value None for the font, the workstation draws the string with the previous font from the **GC**. If you specify the resource identifier of a font, the workstation stores the specified font in the **GC**, then draws the string with it. Note that the **GC**'s font value may be changed during the execution of this drawing request.

The major use for the **XDrawText** request is drawing a single line of justified text. Each word in such a line of text would have its own **XTextItem** structure. The spaces between words would be specified in the delta fields. Additionally, some words could be drawn using different fonts, such as italics.

**XDrawText** (*Xlib* ¶6.6.1) has the form

```
Display *display;        /* pointer to Display structure */
Drawable window;         /* window or pixmap */
GC gc;                   /* gc */
int x, y;                /* character string origin*/
XTextItem items [ ];     /* array of text items*/
int nitems;              /* length of items array*/
    . . .
XDrawText ( display, window, gc, x, y, items, nitems );
```

*nitems* character strings, specified in the *items* array, are drawn in the *window* (or Pixmap) using the *gc*. Drawing begins at the *x, y* position you specify. Each successive character string begins at the x position where the previous one finished. For each string, its delta item is applied to the current x value before the string is drawn.

If a font field in one of the **XTextItem** structures contains an invalid value, the workstation will send your application a BadFont error event (see Chapter 3). If this happens, some, but not necessarily all, of the text items may have been drawn. Furthermore, after such an error, the new font attribute value in the **GC** is unpredictable. If your application attempts to recover from such errors, you should use **XSetFont** to set the **GC**'s font attribute to a known value.

# FONT STRUCTURES

Using **XLoadFont** to give your application access to font resources is fine as long as you want to draw each piece of text the simple way, by specifying the lower left corner of the first character of each string. However, many applications need to be able to compute how much space is occupied by each character string before they draw it. The font structure gives your application this ability; you need it if you wish, for example, to draw centered character strings or determine whether a window is large enough to hold an entire string.

This section describes the *Xlib* calls which allow your application to retrieve the font structure from the workstation as you load each font. This section also describes the *Xlib* service functions for using font structures. These service functions perform several useful operations for your application:

- computing the width of a text string drawn with the font
- computing the dimensions of a text string drawn with the font
- looking up properties of the font, such as the underline position.

You can also refer to font structure information directly, if *Xlib*'s service functions do not yield the information you need. The font structure is stored in a C-language structure with the data type **XFontStruct**. The contents of the font structure are discussed in detail in section 6.5.1 of *Xlib—C Language X Interface*. Table 6-II summarizes the X calls for creating, destroying, and using font structures.

## Loading Font Structures

The **XLoadQueryFont** request, given a font name, makes the workstation load a font and return the corresponding font structure. Use **XLoadQueryFont** in

| Request/Function | Xlib ¶ | Description |
| --- | --- | --- |
| **XLoadQueryFont** | 6.5.1 | Load a font and create a font structure |
| **XQueryFont** | 6.5.1 | Create a font structure for a loaded font |
| **XTextWidth** | 6.5.4 | Compute the width of a text string |
| **XTextExtent** | 6.5.5 | Compute the dimenions of a text string |
| **XGetFontProperty** | 6.5.1 | Find the value of a font property |
| **XFreeFont** | 6.5.1 | Destroy a font structure and unload the font |

Table 6-II. *Xlib* calls for font structure handling.

place of **XLoadFont** when your application requires the font structure. **XLoad-QueryFont** (*Xlib* ¶6.5.1) has the form

```
Display *display;            /* pointer to Display structure */
char name [ ];               /* font name */
XFontStruct *font_struct;    /* returned font structure pointer */
  . . .
font_struct = XLoadQueryFont ( display, name );
if ( font_struct  == 0 ) {  /* no such font */   }
```

This request loads the font referred to in *name*, and returns a pointer to the font structure corresponding to the font. *name* is an ordinary null-terminated text string. Most font names are encoded in ASCII. Upper and lower case letters do not matter in the names of fonts.

If an **XLoadQueryFont** request fails because you specified a non-existent font, it returns a null **XFontStruct** pointer. Unlike **XLoadFont**, however, it does not generate an error event. See under the heading "Searching for Fonts." **XLoadQueryFont**, like **XLoadFont**, creates an X resource identifier for the loaded font. The resource identifier is returned within the **XFontStruct** structure, in the "fid" field. See the next section for more information.

If a font is already loaded on the workstation and you know its resource identifier, you can use **XQueryFont** to retrieve the associated font structure. **XQueryFont** (*Xlib* ¶6.5.1) has the form

```
Display *display;            /* pointer to Display structure */
Font font;                   /* font resource id */
XFontStruct *font_struct;    /* returned font structure pointer */
  . . .
font_struct = XQueryFont ( display, font );
```

Given a *font* resource id, this request retrieves the font structure for the associated font.

## Font Structures and GC Font Attributes

The **XLoadQueryFont** request returns, in the "fid" field of the **XFontStruct** font structure, the resource identifier of the font. When you want to draw with a particular font, first use the **XSetFont** convenience function to set the *font* attribute value in a **GC**. See the description of **XSetFont** under the heading "Setting the Font Attribute in GCs" earlier in this chapter.

### Example

The following code excerpt demonstrates the use of the **XLoadQuery-Font** and **XSetFont** requests to load a font, then to set a **GC**'s font attribute from the fid field in the font structure.

```
Display *display;
GC gc;
XFontStruct *font_struct;
int x, y;
   . . .
font_struct  =  XLoadQueryFont ( display, "vrb-37" );
   . . .
XSetFont ( display, gc, font_struct->fid );
```

## Freeing Font Structures

**XFreeFont** releases both font resources in the workstation and the memory allocated in your application for the font structure by *Xlib*. The workstation unloads fonts automatically when your application terminates, so ordinarily you do not need to free them explicitly. The rules for font lifetime are the same as for any other X resource (see Chapter 3). **XFreeFont** (*Xlib* ¶6.5.1) has the form

```
Display *display;            /* pointer to Display structure */
XFontStruct *font_struct; /* pointer to font_struct to free */
   . . .
XFreeFont ( display, font_struct );
```

This request releases resources for the font described by the font structure pointed to by *font_struct*. Your application must not refer to the font structure, or to the font it described, in any subsequent requests. However, if, prior to calling **XFreeFont**, you use **XSetFont** to set any **GC**'s font attribute to *font_struct*->fid, you may continue to use that **GC** after you call **XFreeFont**; the workstation does not actually destroy the font's resources until all references to the font are gone.

## Computing Widths of Character Strings

The width of a character string is the sum of the widths of all the characters in the string. *Xlib* provides the utility function **XTextWidth** (*Xlib* ¶6.5.4) for you to use in computing character string widths. It has the form

```
XFontStruct *font_struct;  /* pointer to font structure */
char string [ ];            /* character string */
int length;                 /* number of characters in string */
int width;                  /* computed character string width*/
   . . .
width  =  XTextWidth ( font_struct, string, length );
```

Note that **XTextWidth** is different from most *Xlib* calls in that its first parameter is not a **Display** pointer. This utility function uses information from the *font_struct* you specify to compute the *width* (along the baseline, in pixels) of the *string* you specify. Use the *length* parameter to specify the number of characters in the *string*. Note that you must specify the *length* explicitly, even if you specify an ordinary null-terminated *string*. An example of the use of **XTextWidth** is presented under the "Font Properties" heading later in this chapter.

## Computing Dimensions of Character Strings

Often you need to know more than just the width of a character string. **XText-Extents** looks up or computes several useful characters-string dimensions:

- A hint about whether the font is usually used for drawing characters left-to-right (as in languages with Roman or Cyrillic alphabets) or right-to-left (as in Arabic or Hebrew).

- The font *ascent*: the height above the baseline of the tallest ascenders in the font.

- The font *descent*: the depth below the baseline of descenders in the font. The sum of the font ascent descent is the amount of vertical space occupied by a line of text drawn in the font.

- The overall size of the rectangle the character string covers, and the relationship of that rectangle to the character string's origin, in the form of an **XCharStruct** structure.

- The width of the character string, also as part of the **XCharStruct** structure.

**XTextExtents** returns all character-string specific dimensions by filling in an **XCharStruct** structure for you. The **XCharStruct** structure is defined as follows (in **<X11/Xlib.h>**):

```
typedef struct {
    short            lbearing;    /* origin to left edge of rectangle */
    short            rbearing;    /* origin to right edge of rectangle */
    short            width;       /* width of character string */
    short            ascent;      /* origin to top edge of rectangle */
    short            descent;     /* origin to bottom edge of rectangle */
    unsigned short   attributes;  /* flags (undefined) */
} XCharStruct;
```

The fields of the **XCharStruct** structure specify a character string's size. (Note that **XCharStruct** structures are also used within font structures to record the dimensions of individual characters; see *Xlib* ¶6.5.1.) The meanings of fields in **XCharStruct** structures are as follows:

lbearing   The left bearing—the distance in pixels from the origin to the left edge of the rectangle covered by the character string. If this number is negative, it means that the rectangle extends to the left of the origin. In other words, *add* the left bearing to the origin's x value to compute the left edge of the string's rectangle.

The left bearing is often zero. However, it can be either positive or negative depending on the font.

rbearing    The right bearing—the distance in pixels from the origin to the right edge of the rectangle covered by the character string. This number is usually positive, which means that the rectangle extends to the right of the origin. In other words, *add* the right bearing to the origin's x value to compute the right edge of the string's rectangle.

width    The character string's width (the same value that **XText-Width** returns). If this number is positive, it means that the character string runs to the right from the origin. In other words, *add* the width to the origin's x value to determine the origin of the next character string to compute the x position for the next string. A string's right bearing is often the same as its width. However, the right bearing can extend beyond the width, especially in italic fonts.

ascent    The distance in pixels from the origin to the top edge of the rectangle covered by the character string. This number is usually positive, which means that the rectangle extends above the origin. In other words, *subtract* the ascent from the origin's y value to compute the top of the string's rectangle. The ascent value for a specific character string may or may not be less than the ascent for an entire font.

descent    The distance in pixels from the origin to the bottom edge of the rectangle covered by the character string. This number is

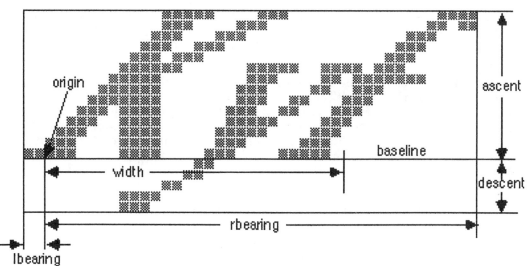

Figure 6-3.  Dimensions of "Kyf" in italics.

usually positive, which means that the rectangle extends below the origin. In other words, *add* the descent to the origin's y value to compute the bottom of the string's rectangle. The descent value for a specific character string may or may not be less than the descent for an entire font.

attributes    reserved for use in extensions to the X Window System and in fonts supplied by third-party vendors.

Figure 6-3 shows these character-string measurements. The font used in Figure 6-3 is contrived to illustrate the difference between string width and right bearing (it is not available on most X workstations). Notice that all the measurements shown are positive in the example except lbearing.

**XTextExtents** (*Xlib* ¶6.5.5) has the form

```
XFontStruct *font_struct;    /* pointer to font structure */
char string [ ];             /* character string */
int length;                  /* number of characters in string */
int direction_hint;          /* FontLeftToRight / FontRightToLeft */
int font_ascent;             /* font ascent */
int font_descent;            /* font descent */
XCharStruct  overall;        /* overall character string dimensions */
. . .
XTextExtents ( font_struct, string, length, &direction_hint,
                    &font_ascent, &font_descent, &overall );
```

Note that **XTextExtents** is different from most *Xlib* calls in that its first parameter is not a **Display** pointer. *Xlib* does not send any requests to the workstation when you use it. This utility func on uses information from the *font_struct* you specify to compute the dimensions of the *string* you specify. Use the *length* parameter to specify the number of characters in the *string*. Note that you must specify the *length* explicitly, even if you specify an ordinary null-terminated *string*.

**XTextExtents** returns the font's writing direction in *direction_hint*. A *direction_hint* value of FontLeftToRight indicates that the font is usually used for drawing Roman (or Cyrillic) characters, and that the width of a text string drawn in the font is likely to be positive. A *direction_hint* value of FontRightToLeft, on the other hand, indicates that the font is usually used for drawing Hebrew or Arabic characters, and that the width of a text string drawn in the font is likely to be negative. The direction hint depends only on the font, and not on the characters in *string*.

The font's overall ascent and descent are returned in *font_ascent* and *font_descent*. These values depend only on the font, and not on the *string*.

**XTextExtents** computes the dimensions of your text *string* and fills in the **XCharStruct** structure you specify in the *overall* parameter. You may use **XTextExtents** to retrieve just font-specific information (*direction_hint*, *font_ascent*, and *font_descent*).  Simply specify a *length* of zero.  You may also retrieve the **XCharStruct** dimensions for a single character, by specifying a one-character *string* and a *length* of one.

## Font Properties

Font properties are information about how to use a font.  They include the recommendations of the font designer about such such things as how much space to leave between words, and where to put underlines.  The X Window System defines several predefined font properties, detailed later in this section.  Font designers may also specify other font properties.  Many fonts do not have all the standard properties defined by X.

Your application may use the *Xlib* utility function **XGetFontProperty** to search a font structure for a font property, and retrieve it if it is defined.  Each font property has a predefined atom, the symbols for which are defined in **<X11/Xatom.h>**.  **XGetFontProperty** (*Xlib* ¶6.5.1) has the form

```
#include   <X11/Xatom.h>
  . . .
XFontStruct *font_struct;   /* pointer to font structure */
XAtom atom;                 /* atom specifying font property */
int exists;                 /* function value—nonzero if prop. exists */
unsigned long value;        /* returned property value */
  . . .
exists  =  XGetFontProperty ( font_struct, atom, &value );
```

Notice that **XGetFontProperty** is different from most *Xlib* calls in that its first argument is not a **Display** pointer.  Given a specified *atom* symbol (the standard font property *atom* symbols are discussed later in this section), **XGetFontProperty** searches the font structure.  If it finds the property associated with *atom*, it returns a function value of 1 (True), and returns the *value* of the property.

If the specified property is not defined for the font, **XGetFontProperty** returns a function value of zero (False).  Your application must allow for this case, because in many fonts some or all standard properties are not defined.

The standard font properties have the following meanings:

XA_MIN_SPACE             This property expresses the suggested minimum interword spacing in pixels.  Your application uses this property while justifying lines of text (so that they are aligned to both a left and a right margin) by moving words in the line closer together.  This value is always positive.

XA_NORM_SPACE            This property expresses the normal interword spacing in pixels.  If this property is not present, you should use the width of the space character. This value is always positive.

XA_MAX_SPACE

This property expresses the suggested maximum interword spacing in pixels. It is the maximum space that you can, in the opinion of the font's designer, leave between words while still allowing the user to read a line of text easily. Your application uses this property while justifying lines of text by moving words in the line farther apart. This value is always positive.

XA_END_SPACE

This property expresses the spacing in pixels to be left at the ends of sentences. This amount of space should be left in addition to the normal interword spacing. If this property is not present, you should use the interword spacing; that is, you should leave a total of two spaces between sentences. This value is always positive.

XA_SUPERSCRIPT_X

This property expresses the horizontal offset from the character origin where superscripts should begin, in pixels. This value may be positive or negative. If it is positive, superscripts should be offset to the right. In other words, add XA_SUPERSCRIPT_X's value to the character's x origin.

XA_SUPERSCRIPT_Y

This property expresses the vertical offset from the character origin where superscripts should begin, in pixels. This value may be positive or negative. If it is positive, superscripts should be offset *upwards*. In other words, subtract XA_SUPERSCRIPT_Y's value from the character's y origin.

XA_SUBSCRIPT_X

This property expresses the horizontal offset from the character origin where subscripts should begin, in pixels. This value may be positive or negative. If it is positive, subscripts should be offset to the right. In other words, add XA_SUBSCRIPT_X's value to the character's x origin.

XA_SUBSCRIPT_Y

This property expresses the vertical offset from the character origin where subscripts should begin, in pixels. This value may be positive or negative. If it is positive, subscripts should be offset *downwards*. In other words, add XA_SUBSCRIPT_Y's value to the character's y origin.

XA_UNDERLINE_POSITION

An underline is a rectangle (drawn using **XFillRectangle**; see Chapter 5) underneath text. This property expresses the vertical offset from the character origin to the top of an underline, in pixels. This value may be positive or negative. If it is positive, the underline should be offset downwards. In other words, add XA_UNDERLINE_POSITION's value to the character's y origin.

XA_UNDERLINE_THICKNESS

An underline rectangle should have the width of the character or character string (determined using **XTextWidth**) and the height in pixels specified by this property. This value is always positive.

XA_STRIKEOUT_ASCENT

The strikeout properties are used when you want to draw boxes around or diagonal lines through characters in the font. This property expresses the vertical offset from the baseline to the top of the strikeout box in pixels. This value is usually positive, indicating that the top of the box is above the baseline. In other words, subtract XA_STRIKEOUT_ASCENT's value from the baseline's y position.

XA_STRIKEOUT_DESCENT

This property expresses the vertical offset from the baseline to the bottom of the strikeout box in pixels. This value is usually positive, indicating that the bottom of the box is below the baseline. In other words, add XA_STRIKEOUT_DESCENT's value to the baseline's y position.

XA_ITALIC_ANGLE

This property expresses the angle of the dominant vertical staffs of characters in the font, in degrees scaled by 64, relative to the three-o'clock position from the character origin, with positive indicating counterclockwise motion (as in the **XDrawArc** functions). Roman (non-italic) fonts have an XA_ITALIC_ANGLE value of 5760, corresponding to a 90° angle. This value, although usually positive, may be negative.

| | |
|---|---|
| XA_X_HEIGHT | This property's value specifies the nominal height of lower-case letters (such $x$ or $n$) in pixels. This value, although usually positive, may be negative. |
| XA_QUAD_WIDTH | This property expresses the width of a printer's quad. A printer's quad ordinarily has a width equal to the nominal interline spacing. Often, XA_QUAD_WIDTH's value is called an *em* because it is equal to the width of an upper-case $M$. This value, although usually positive, may be negative. |
| XA_WEIGHT | This property expresses the weight or boldness of the font as a value between 0 and 1000. Normal fonts often have an XA_WEIGHT value of 500. |
| XA_POINT_SIZE | This property expresses the point size of the font, at the resolution for which it was created, in tenths of printer's points. There are 72.27 printer's points to the inch, although this number is usually rounded to 72 points per inch in the computer industry. This value is always positive. |
| XA_RESOLUTION | This property expresses the (positive) number of pixels per printer's point, in 1/100ths, at which this font was created. |
| XA_CAP_HEIGHT | This property expresses the vertical offset from the baseline to the top of the tallest capital letters, ignoring accents, in pixels. This value is usually positive, indicating that the tops of capital letters are above the baseline. In other words, subtract XA_CAP_HEIGHT's value from the baseline's y position. |

**Example**:  Draw underlined text

# Hello, World!

In the following code excerpt, we use font properties to draw an underline under some text. Note that we use the default value 3 for XA_UNDERLINE_POSITION if it is absent, and the default value 1 for XA_UNDERLINE_THICKNESS. We use **XTextWidth** to compute the character string's width.

```
#include   <X11/Xatom.h>
   . . .
static char text [ ] = "Hello, World!"
```

```
. . .
Display * display;
Drawable window;    /* window (or pixmap) for drawing */
GC gc;              /* gc for drawing */
int x,y;            /* text string position */
int pos;
int width;
unsigned int thick;
XFontStruct * font_struct;
. . .
if (! XGetFontProperty ( font_struct,
            XA_UNDERLINE_POSITION, &pos ) ) pos = 3;
if (! XGetFontProperty ( font_struct,
            XA_UNDERLINE_THICKNESS, &thick ) ) thick = 1;
width  = XTextWidth ( font_struct, text, strlen (text ) );
XSetFont ( display, gc, font_struct->fid );
XDrawString ( display, window, gc, x,y, text, strlen (text) );
XFillRectangle ( display, window, gc, x,y + pos, width, thick );
```

# SEARCHING FOR FONTS

What fonts are available on a workstation?  What are the names and characteristics of those fonts?  Where (in what font directory) are they stored? The X Window System provides requests for allowing applications to answer these questions while they are running.  Table 6-III summarizes the *Xlib* calls related to searching for fonts.

## Listing Available Fonts

You may use either **XListFonts** or **XListFontsWithInfo** to return a list of fonts matching a pattern string.  A pattern string may contain ordinarily alphabetic letters, numbers, and some special characters, such as -.  It may also

| Request/Function | Xlib ¶ | Description |
|---|---|---|
| XListFonts | 6.5.2 | Returns a list of names of available fonts |
| XFreeFontNames | 6.5.2 | Frees memory for a list of font names |
| XListFontsWithInfo | 6.5.1 | Returns font names and font structures |
| XFreeFontInfo | 6.5.1 | Frees memory for a list of font structures |
| XSetFontPath | 6.5.3 | Sets the workstation's font search path |
| XGetFontPath | 6.5.3 | Gets the workstation's font search path |
| XFreeFontPath | 6.5.3 | Frees memory for a font search path |

Table 6-III. *Xlib* calls for font searching.

contain **?** and **\*** characters. **?** characters in a pattern string match any single character in a font name, and **\*** characters match any sequence of zero or more names. Most font names are encoded in ASCII, although X permits any character in the ISO Latin-1 character set to be used in a font name. Upper and lower case letters do not matter in the names of fonts.

Groups of related fonts (such as bold and italic versions) have similar names, which allows you to exploit this pattern string capability. For example, the pattern string "vrb-\*" searches for variable-pitch roman bold fonts of all sizes. If your workstation has the fonts shown in Appendix D, this pattern string matches the following fonts:

vrb-25   vrb-31   vrb-37   vrb-30   vrb-35

## XListFonts

The **XListFonts** request returns a pointer to an array of character strings. This array contains the names of fonts which match the pattern string you specify. *Xlib* allocates memory for the array of names, and returns to you a pointer to the array. When you finish working with the array of names, you should use **XFreeFontNames** to tell *Xlib* to release the array's memory. **XListFonts** and **XFreeFontNames** (*Xlib* ¶6.5.2) have the form

```
Display *display;           /* pointer to Display structure */
char pattern [ ];           /* the pattern string */
int maxnames;               /* maximum number of font names to return*/
int count ;                 /* actual number of font names returned*/
char ** list;               /* pointer to the array of font names*/
. . .
list = XListFonts ( display, pattern, maxnames, &count );
. . .
XFreeFontNames ( list );
```

You specify the pattern string in the *pattern* parameter, and the maximum number of matching names you want returned in the *maxnames* parameter. **XListFonts** returns, as a function value, a pointer to an array of null-terminated character strings. It returns the size of the character string array in the *count* parameter. Each string in the array is the name of a font matching the pattern string. The font names in the array are not sorted in any particular order.

**XFreeFontNames** accepts, as its only parameter, a pointer previously returned by **XListFonts**. It frees the storage associated with that character string array.

## XListFontsWithInfo

**XListFontsWithInfo** is the request to use if you want an array of font structures along with the array of font names for the fonts matching your pattern string. This request is especially useful when you wish to examine properties for the fonts in the list. *Xlib* allocates memory for both arrays, and returns to you pointers to both arrays. When you finish working with the arrays, you should call **XFreeFontInfo** to tell *Xlib* to release their memory.   **XListFontsWith-Info** and **XFreeFontInfo** (*Xlib* ¶6.5.1) have the form

```
Display *display;            /* pointer to Display structure */
char pattern [ ];            /* the pattern string
int maxnames;               /* maximum number of font names to return*/
int count ;                 /* actual number of font names returned*/
char ** list;               /* pointer to the array of font name strins*/
XFontStruct  * info;        /* pointer to the array of font structures */
. . .
list = XListFontsWithInfo ( display, pattern, maxnames,
                                    &count, &info );

. . .
XFreeFontInfo (list, info, count );
```

You specify the pattern string and the maximum number of matching names as you do for **XListFonts** (see the preceding section).   **XListFontsWithInfo** returns, as a function value, a pointer to an array of font names in null-terminated character strings.   It also returns a pointer to an array of **XFontStruct** structures in the *info* parameter.   Both arrays contain the same number of elements; that number is returned in the *count* parameter.   Each string in the array is the name of a font matching the pattern string.

The font structures returned by **XListFontsWithInfo** are incomplete.   The fid fields in the array of **XFontStruct** structures contain zeros because calling **XListFontsWithInfo** does not load fonts.   Furthermore, **XListFontsWithInfo** does not return the per-character size information necessary for **XTextWidth** and **XTextExtents** to compute the dimensions of character strings.   Thus, you should only use the results of **XListFontsWithInfo** to decide whether or not you want to load the font, based on font properties and other font information.   The font names are not sorted in any particular order.   However, the *n*th name in the name array corresponds to the *n*th **XFontStruct** in the font structure array.

**XFreeFontInfo** accepts the *list*, *info*, and *count* parameters previously returned by **XListFontsWithInfo**.   It frees the storage associated with the font name and font structure arrays.

## The Workstation's Font Search Path

The **XGetFontPath** request returns a pointer to an array of character strings. This array contains the names of directories in which the workstation looks up font files in response to all requests which involve font names (**XLoadFont**, **XLoadQueryFont**, **XListFonts**, and **XListFontsWithInfo**). *Xlib* allocates memory for the array of directory names, and returns to you a pointer to the array.   When you finish working with the array, you should use **XFreeFontPath** to tell *Xlib* to release the array's memory.   **XGetFontPath** and **XFreeFontPath** (*Xlib* ¶6.5.3) have the form

```
Display *display;        /* pointer to Display structure */
int ndirs ;              /* number of directory names returned*/
char ** directories;     /* pointer to the array of directory names*/
 . . .
directories  = XGetFontPath ( display, &ndirs );
 . . .
XFreeFontPath ( directories );
```

**XGetFontPath** returns, as a function value, a pointer to an array of null-terminated character strings. It returns the size of the character string array in the *ndirs* parameter. Each string in the array is the name of a directory containing fonts. The exact form of the strings depends on the workstation CPU's operating system. On Unix-based workstations, the strings take the form of ordinary pathnames ending with "/". For example:

**/usr/x/fonts/**

If there is more than one directory name in the font search path, the workstation searches the directories in order whenever it looks up a font name.

**XFreeFontPath** accepts, as its only parameter, a pointer previously returned by **XGetFontPath**. It frees the storage associated with that character string array.

The **XSetFontPath** request allows an application program to change the workstation's font search path. A workstation has only one font search path, which it uses to process font requests from all application programs. If you change the font search path, the new search path persists, even after your application terminates, until the user's session on the workstation ends.

| **XSetFontPath** affects all applications running on the workstation. |
|---|

**XSetFontPath** (*Xlib* ¶6.5.3) has the form

```
Display *display;      /* pointer to Display structure */
char ** directories;   /* pointer to the array of directory names*/
int ndirs ;            /* the number of directory names in the array*/
 . . .
XSetFontPath ( display, directories, ndirs );
```

**XSetFontPath** accepts *directories*, a pointer to an array of character strings. It also accepts the number of directories in the array in the *ndirs* parameter. The exact form of the directory strings depends on the workstation CPU's operating system; consult your workstation vendor's documentation before using this request. If you specify an *ndirs* parameter of zero, the workstation's font search path is restored to its default value.

# 16-BIT CHARACTER STRINGS

The X Window System allows applications to draw character strings using very large character sets, such as the Japanese Kanji character set. Most western-language character sets (such as ASCII and ISO Latin-1) can be indexed with an ordinary eight-bit character—a number between zero and 255. However, Kanji and other oriental-language character sets contain several thousand distinct characters, and must be indexed with a 16-bit character. *Xlib* provides 16-bit versions of all calls for working with character strings. These 16-bit calls are summarized in Table 6-IV.

You must specify strings of 16-bit characters as arrays of **XChar2b** structures. The **XChar2b** structure is defined (in **<X11/Xlib.h>**) as follows:

```
typedef struct {
    unsigned char   byte1;    /* most significant half of character index */
    unsigned char   byte2;    /* least significant half of character index */
} XChar2b;
```

The meaning of each character code depends on the font you use (just as it does for 8-bit character strings). Oriental-language fonts are organized in one of two ways; consult your font supplier's documentation to find out how your font is organized.

- Row-column organization indexes each character according to its position in a large matrix of characters. Some row-column fonts have the 96 ASCII characters in row 0. If your font has row-column organization, put each character's row number in the byte1 field of the **XChar2b** structure, and put the column number in the byte2 field.

- Linear organization indexes characters with single 16-bit numbers in the range 0-65535. If your font is linearly organized, you must store the most significant eight bits of each character's index in the byte1 field, and the least significant eight bits in the byte2 field.

> For the sake of portability, avoid storing 16-bit character indices directly into **XChar2b** structures: Cpus from different vendors store the two bytes of a 16-bit number in different orders.

| Request/Function | Xlib ¶ | Description |
|---|---|---|
| **XDrawString16** | 6.6.2 | Draw a 16-bit string |
| **XDrawImageString16** | 6.6.3 | Draw a 16-bit opaque string |
| **XDrawText16** | 6.6.1 | Draw multiple 16-bit strings |
| **XTextWidth16** | 6.5.4 | Compute the width of a 16-bit string |
| **XTextExtents16** | 6.5.5 | Compute the dimensions of a 16-bit string |

Table 6-IV. *Xlib* calls supporting 16-bit character strings.

There is nothing stopping you from drawing 16-bit character strings with an eight-bit font or vice versa. If a given character is not present in the font, the workstation will simply draw the replacement character.

The following sections briefly discuss the 16-bit versions of X's character-string requests. For more information on any given request, see the discussion of the corresponding eight-bit request elsewhere in this chapter.

## Drawing 16-Bit Strings

## XDrawString16

**XDrawString16** (*Xlib* ¶6.6.2) is analogous to **XDrawString**. It has the form

```
Display *display;        /* pointer to Display structure */
Drawable window;         /* window or pixmap */
GC gc;                   /* gc */
int x, y;                /* character string origin*/
XChar2b string [ ];      /* character string */
int length;              /* number of characters in the string */
   . . .
XDrawString16 ( display, window, gc, x, y, string, length );
```

Use the *length* parameter to specify the number of characters (not the number of bytes) in the *string*.

## XDrawImageString16

**XDrawImageString16** is analogous to **XDrawImageString**. It (*Xlib* ¶6.6.3) has the form

```
Display *display;        /* pointer to Display structure */
Drawable window;         /* window or pixmap */
GC gc;                   /* gc */
int x, y;                /* character string origin*/
XChar2b string [ ];      /* character string */
int length;              /* number of characters in the string */
   . . .
XDrawImageString16 ( display, window, gc, x, y, string, length );
```

## XDrawText16

**XDrawText16** is analogous to **XDrawText**. **XDrawText16** accepts an array of **XTextItem16** structures. The **XTextItem16** structure, analogous to the **XText-Item** structure, is defined (in **<X11/Xlib.h>**) as follows:

```
typedef struct {
    XChar2b * chars;  /* pointer to character string */
    int       nchars; /* number of characters in string */
```

```
    int         delta;    /* x delta, along baseline */
    Font        font;     /* resource id of font to use, or None */
} XTextItem16;
```

**XDrawText16** (*Xlib* ¶6.6.1) has the form

```
Display *display;          /* pointer to Display structure */
Drawable window;           /* window or pixmap */
GC gc;                     /* gc */
int x, y;                  /* character string origin*/
XTextItem16 items [ ];     /* array of text items*/
int nitems;                /* length of items array*/
    . . .
XDrawText16 ( display, window, gc, x, y, items, nitems );
```

## Computing 16-Bit String Dimensions

### XTextWidth16

**XTextWidth16** (*Xlib* ¶6.5.4) is analogous to **XTextWidth**. It has the form

```
XFontStruct *font_struct;  /* pointer to font structure */
XChar2b string [ ];        /* character string */
int length;                /* number of characters */
int width;                 /* computed character string width*/
    . . .
width = XTextWidth16 ( font_struct, string, length );
```

Use the *length* parameter to specify the number of characters (not the number of bytes) in the *string*. See earlier in this chapter under the heading "Computing Widths of Character Strings" for further information.

### XTextExtents16

**XTextExtents16** (*Xlib* ¶6.5.4) is analogous to **XTextExtents**. It has the form

```
XFontStruct *font_struct;  /* pointer to font structure */
XChar2b string [ ];        /* character string */
int length;                /* number of characters in string */
int direction_hint;        /* FontLeftToRight / FontRightToLeft */
int font_ascent;           /* font ascent */
int font_descent;          /* font descent */
XCharStruct overall;       /* overall character string dimensions */
    . . .
XTextExtents16 ( font_struct, string, length,
                 &direction_hint, &font_ascent, &font_descent, &overall );
```

Use the *length* parameter to specify the number of characters (not the number of bytes) in the *string*.   See earlier in this chapter under the heading "Computing Extents of Character Strings" for further information.

# SUMMARY

Text is just another kind of graphic primitive, albeit an important one.  X allows application programs to use a variety of different *fonts* when drawing text.  In X, a font is a resource describing the shapes of characters.  By selecting a particular font, you choose character set (usually ASCII or Latin-1), size, spacing, and style.

To prepare to draw text, a simple X application need only use **XLoadFont** to load a font resource, and **XSetFont** to set that font resource as an attribute in a **GC** (see Chapter 5).  Once the **GC** has the font attribute set, the application can proceed to draw a character string by specifying the x,y position of the string's origin (usually the lower left corner) and the characters in the string.

As in other graphic primitive requests, you must specify a Drawable and a **GC** when drawing character strings.  **XDrawString** is the most common call for drawing character strings.  Depending on the attributes in the **GC** you specify with **XDrawString**, you can arrange to draw solid-colored or patterned (grayed) text.  **XDrawImageString** is suitable for drawing terminal-emulator characters.  It is faster (on many workstations) than **XDrawString**, but considerably less flexible.  Finally, word-processing programs can use **XDrawText** to draw a justified line of text containing several fonts.

Your application may need to be able to compute the size of character strings before drawing them.  To do this, you need *font structures* containing descriptive information about the fonts you use.  To retrieve a font structure, use **XLoad-QueryFont** in place of **XLoadFont**.  Once a font structure is available, you can use *Xlib* calls to compute a character string's width (**XTextWidth**) and overall extent (**XTextExtent**).  You can also retrieve font *properties*, such as interword spacing and the position and height of rectangles for underlining words.

**XListFonts** and **XListFontsWithInfo** are useful for searching for fonts. Other *Xlib* requests control where a workstation searches for font files.

X provides a full complement of requests supporting the 16-bit characters used for Oriental alphabets such as Kanji.  These requests include **XDrawString16**, **XDrawImageString16**, **XDrawText16**, **XTextWidth16**, and **XTextExtents16**.

# CHAPTER 7
# COLOR

Most vendors offer both black-and-white and color displays on different models of workstations as part of a compatible product family. The X Window System allows your application to exploit the color capabilities of each workstation or, if you prefer, treat all workstations as if they were simply black-and-white. Obviously, color is useful because your application can convey more information, more attractively, to the user in the same screen area. X has functions that allow your application to inquire the color capabilities of the workstation it is running on. Using these inquiry functions, you can write your application to adapt automatically to both color and monochrome workstations.

This chapter has two purposes. One is to describe the color model of the X Window System: that is, to explain conceptually how X displays color. The other is to explain how to use X for color applications. If your interest is in the X color model, you should read the chapter from beginning to end.

However, if you would rather start by getting your application up and running, go ahead and skip to the section entitled "Pixel Values and Color Cells." In that section we present three strategies, with examples, which your application can use for allocating shared color resources and displaying color pictures. You should plan, however, on coming back to the sections you skipped.

Color makes nice pictures. If your application *requires* color to run, however, owners of less expensive black-and-white workstations will be unable to use it. The section entitled "Monochrome and Gray Scale" presents some suggestions for making your application compatible with both color and black-and-white workstations.

The last section of the chapter, entitled "Color Map Manipulation," explains how to allocate private color resources.

# COLOR CONCEPTS

The X Window System allows you to describe color images. To describe these images, you need

- Planes and pixel values—ways of writing color images into workstation displays.

- Red, green, and blue (abbreviated *RGB*) primary values—for specifying what colors the screen should display.

- Visual classes—to describe the color capability of the workstation.

- Color maps—to translate between pixel values written in the frame buffer and visible colors on the screen.

The following sections describe these basic building blocks of the X Window System color model.

## Planes and Pixel Values

Many of the requests in preceding chapters, such as **XSetForeground**, accept *pixel* parameters. Up until this point, we have been assuming that all drawing was taking place on a black-and-white screen. We have been using the **Black-Pixel** and **WhitePixel** macros to retrieve valid pixel values for black and white, but we have been avoiding the question of what a pixel value means. Setting bits to the **BlackPixel** value (which is usually but not always zero) in display memory turns the corresponding screen area black. Likewise, setting bits to the **WhitePixel** value (usually but not always one) turns the screen area white.

On a black-and-white screen, each pixel is represented with a single binary digit. Single bit screens are said to have a display *depth* of one. On such screens, there is exactly enough room in each pixel value to store either **Black-Pixel** or **WhitePixel**; no other pixel values are possible.

In this chapter, we discuss how to use screens that have a depth of more than one. The pixels on such screens can have values other than zero or one—they are longer than one bit. For example, many color workstations have eight-bit pixel values, representable as a number in the range 0 - 255. Each pixel on such a screen is represented by eight bits. In general, pixel values are used for all drawing.

The number of bits per pixel is also referred to as the number of *planes* of display memory available on the workstation. A black-and-white screen has a single plane of display memory. Many color workstations have eight planes of display memory.  Each plane of display memory corresponds to a single bit in the pixel values for that display.

When you want to draw on the screen in a particular foreground color, your application must use the pixel value that corresponds to that color.  The workstation uses an X resource known as a *color map* to establish the relationship between pixel values and visible screen colors.  To draw with a particular color, your application takes the following steps:

- Find out the correct pixel value, using **BlackPixel**, **WhitePixel**, or one of the requests in this chapter

- Set that pixel value as a foreground (or background) attribute in a **GC**

- Issue drawing requests referring to that **GC**

The effect of these steps is to write values into pixels in the workstation's display memory.  Once the pixel values are in the display memory, the workstation uses those pixel values to look up colors in a color map to display on the screen.  Much of this chapter describes how color maps work and how your application can manipulate them to get the colors you want.

The important thing to keep in mind as you work with pixel values is that your application must obtain pixel values from X using one of the methods specified in this chapter.  You should not draw with any pixel values unless X gave them to you.

## Using Pixel Values

When drawing you use pixel values to choose colors. In this section, we summarize the X requests you may use to manipulate pixel values.  Of course, these requests assume that you already know what pixel values to use to get the colors you want;  how you determine what pixel values to use is the subject of the most of rest of this chapter.  Just for this section, we will assume that you already have valid pixel values in order to explain how to use them.  An understanding of the purposes of pixel values will help make the rest of the chapter clearer.

Pixel values are binary numbers.  This fact may tempt you to do arithmetic operations on pixel values.  For example, you might try to add one to a pixel value in order to display a slightly brighter color.  However, you cannot do this sort of thing unless you take explicit steps to set up X so you can.  Later sections of this chapter present three strategies for obtaining pixel values.  Two of these strategies ("Standard Shared Color Maps" and "Private Color Cells") set things up so pixel-value arithmetic is meaningful.

Table 7-I lists the X data structures and requests which allow you to use pixel values.  Drawing requests (such as **XDrawLine**) are not mentioned here;  they accept **GC** parameters which indirectly specify pixel values for drawing.

| Request/Function | Xlib ¶ | Description |
|---|---|---|
| **XSetWindowAttributes** | 3.2 | Structure describing window attributes, including background, border, and backing pixel values |
| **XCreateSimpleWindow** | 3.3 | Create a window; specify background |
| **XCreateWindow** | 3.3 | and border pixel values |
| **XChangeWindowAttributes** | 3.9 | Change window attributes |
| **XSetWindowBackground** | 3.9 | Set window background |
| **XSetWindowBorder** | 3.9 | Set window border |
| **XGCValues** | 5.3 | Structure describing graphic context (**GC**), including function, plane mask, foreground and background pixel values |
| **XCreateGC** | 5.3 | Create a new **GC** |
| **XChangeGC** | 5.3 | Alter a **GC** |
| **XSetState** | 5.4 | Change function, plane mask, foreground, and background in **GC** |
| **XSetFunction** | 5.4 | Change function in **GC** |
| **XSetPlaneMask** | 5.4 | Change plane mask in **GC** |
| **XSetForeground** | 5.4 | Change foreground pixel value |
| **XSetBackground** | 5.4 | Change background pixel value |

Table 7-I   Uses of Pixel Values in X.

As the table shows, pixel values are used for two different purposes: as window attributes, and in graphic contexts.

Each window has background and border patterns (Pixmaps). When you want the background or border (or both) to be solid colors rather than patterns, you specify the appropriate pixel values by filling in an **XSetWindowAttributes** data structure and calling either **XCreateWindow** or **XChangeWindowAttributes**. See Chapter 4 for further information.

Drawing operations use a source foreground pixel value, a source background pixel value, a plane mask, and a Boolean function. Each drawing operation generates *source pixels* in an appropriate pattern (in a straight line for **XDrawLine**; in the shape of a rectangle for **XFillRectangle**, for example). It then uses bitwise operations to combine these generated source pixels with the *destination pixels* (for which values are already stored in display memory). The new, combined, destination pixel values are computed as follows:

$$\text{dest} = \text{source } \mathbf{function} \text{ dest}$$

*source* and *dest* are source and destination pixel values. **function** is the Boolean function attribute.

Once each destination pixel value is computed, display memory is updated. The plane mask controls which bits of the pixel value are actually changed in the display memory. Many drawing operations work with all the bits in the plane mask set to one, which causes all the bits in each pixel to be changed when a new destination pixel is computed. However, you can set some of the bits of the plane mask to zero, in which case the corresponding bits in pixel values will not be changed when you draw into those pixels. Be careful with plane masks; they amount to a way of doing arithmetic on pixel values. You may find that unexpected pixel values get written and unexpected colors get displayed when you use plane masks.

## Red, Green, Blue

Video monitors supplied with color workstations display three primary colors, red, green, and blue, in combination. Three signals (often carried in three separate cables—look at the back of the monitor on your workstation) drive separate electron sources inside the picture tube. One of these electron sources lights the myriad of red dots or lines on the face of the tube, another lights the green, and the third lights the blue. The colored dots or lines on the face of the tube are small enough that a user's eye does not usually see them individually. Visually, they appear to mix; for example, a white or gray image on a color screen is made by combining red, green, and blue primaries in equal proportions.

Arbitrary combinations of three primary colors can be used to create a large number of distinct colors and shades. The set of all possible colors that a workstation screen can display is known as the screen's *gamut*. X Window System applications use **XColor** structures to specify red-green-blue values to requests that manipulate colors. The definition of **XColor**, available in the header file **<X11/Xlib.h>**, is:

```
typedef struct _XColor {
    unsigned long pixel;
    unsigned short red, green, blue;
    char flags;
    char pad;
} XColor;
```

In this structure, the "red," "green," and "blue" fields represent primary color components as 16-bit numbers, valued from 0 to 65535. The values represent scaled intensities: 65535 calls for full intensity in the primary color, 16384 for one-quarter intensity, and zero for no intensity. Most workstations do not make use of all 16 bits of this color primary specification; in fact, most ignore all but the most significant eight bits. However, this scaling of intensities allows X Window System applications to specify primary color component values in a way that is independent of the details of workstation hardware.

The "flag" bitmask contains a combination of the bits DoRed, DoGreen, and DoBlue (defined in the header file **<X11/X.h>**). Ordinarily, you set all three of these bits. If you clear any of these bits, certain color requests ignore the corresponding primary colors.

*Xlib* uses the "pixel" field to store the *pixel* value associated with the red-green-blue triplet in the structure.

**Example:** Define some colors
_____

This C code excerpt shows how you might define and fill in some **XColor** structures.

```
XColor cyan, white, gray, powder;

. . .

cyan.red = 0; cyan.green = 65535; cyan.blue = 65535;
cyan.flags = DoRed | DoGreen | DoBlue;

white.red = 65535; white.green = 65535; white.blue = 65535;
white.flags = DoRed | DoGreen | DoBlue;

gray.red = 8192; gray.green = 8192; gray.blue = 8192;
gray.flags = DoRed | DoGreen | DoBlue;

powder.red = 32768; powder.green = 32768; powder.blue = 65535;
powder.flags = DoRed | DoGreen | DoBlue;
```

When you decide what colors to use in your application, keep in mind that colors which contain large contributions from two or more of the primaries light the screen more brightly than colors involving just one primary. For example, the **XColor** ·structure named "powder" above contains a shade of blue which includes large contributions of red and green, as well as the brightest blue possible.

Also keep in mind a fact of the physiology of vision: the human eye is relatively insensitive to and unable to focus on images made primarily of pure blue light. This means that all users (not just color-blind ones) have difficulty distinguishing shades of blue, or blue against dark backgrounds. If you must display blue figures and letters against a dark background, use a light or pastel blue—a shade with substantial contributions of red and green, like the one in "powder" above.

## Visual Classes

Some workstation displays have one-bit pixels and a black-and-white display. Others have four-, eight-, or twelve-bit pixels. Each distinct pixel value serves as an index to a color map. In turn, the color map drives the display. Still others have 24-bit pixels, with eight bits each dedicated to representing the actual values of red, green, and blue. These different strategies for translating pixel values into colors on a screen are called _visual classes_ in the X Window System. Each visual class is especially suited to particular kinds of applications, by reason of both cost and capability.

A small but increasing number of general purpose workstations permit applications to select visual classes on a window-by-window basis. For example, a black-and-white electronic publishing application might share a workstation screen with a color eight-bit-pixel diagramming application and a 24-bit-pixel shaded mechanical design application.

The X Window System defines six visual classes.  Most workstations support just one of the six, but some allow you to use several visual classes at the same time.  The symbols for the visual classes (in the header file **<X11/X.h>**) are:

PseudoColor    In this visual class, each pixel value indexes a red-green-blue color map.  The contents of the color map may be changed dynamically.  Each pixel is treated as a single index into a single color map array.  Each entry in the color map contains a red-green-blue triplet.

DirectColor    In direct color, the pixel value is decomposed into separate bit fields for red, green, and blue.  The primary fields index the color map separately for each primary.  The color map is treated as three separate arrays containing red, green, and blue values.  The red field from the pixel indexes the red color map, the green field indexes the green color map, and the blue field indexes the blue color map.  Direct color requires more bits per pixel than pseudo-color, but allows more colors and shades to be displayed simultaneously.

GrayScale    GrayScale is like PseudoColor, except the video screen only displays black-and-white (or green, or amber).  A color map with red-green-blue primaries is available; just one of the primaries drives the video screen.  Red, green, and blue primaries should be set equal to each other in the color map, because the workstation vendor may use any primary color to drive the screen.  A few black-and-white displays have a visual class of GrayScale and a depth of one.

StaticColor    StaticColor is uncommon;  it is similar to PseudoColor, except that the contents of the color map are predefined and cannot be changed.

TrueColor    TrueColor is similar to DirectColor, except that the contents of a TrueColor color map are predefined to be a linear or near-linear ramp, and cannot be changed.  This visual class is commonly used in color workstations which lack color translation hardware.

StaticGray    StaticGray is similar to GrayScale, except that the contents of StaticGray color maps cannot be changed.  Most black-and-white displays have a visual class of StaticGray and a depth of one.

The combination of visual class and depth available on the workstation determines how many simultaneous colors the workstation can display, and how the pixel values for the workstation relate to colors.

## Color Maps

Color maps (sometimes known as color lookup tables) convert pixel values into colors on the screen. The exact structure of a color map, and of the pixel values which access it, depends on the visual class of the color map. Each window has a particular visual class, and a color map of that visual class, associated with it.

A color map is an array of color cells. Each color cell in a color map contains one combination of red, green, and blue primary color values, which specifies one color in the gamut of the workstation's screen. Your application uses an **XColor** structure to describe the contents of each color cell. Each window has a single associated color map, from which it uses as many color cells as it needs.

Color cells and color maps are the resources that the X Window System uses to tie together primary colors and pixel values. Color cells are often used dynamically: most workstations can load new red-green-blue primary values into color cells quite rapidly. On the other hand, color maps are relatively static: usually your application will share a color map with other applications running on the workstation. For this reason, almost all the X requests your application will use to manipulate colors are described in the  section later in this chapter entitled "Color Cell Manipulation."

When your application creates a window, you may specify any color map you wish. However, for best compatibility with other applications, you should use one of two standard ways of assigning  a color map when you create each window:

- Specify that the window share a color map with its parent window. As a result, all your windows inherit the root window's color map, and share it with other windows on the screen. This happens automatically when you use the **XCreateSimpleWindow** request (see Chapter 4).

- Specify that the window use one of the workstation's standard shared color maps. See the section entitled "Shared Color Maps" later in this chapter.

If your application uses either of these techniques, you need only concern yourself with color cells, and you may never have to create, manipulate, or delete a color map resource.

On the other hand, there may be circumstances in which your application will be unable to share color maps and will have to create private ones. For example, if you change the primary values in large numbers of color cells or if you need to use a visual class different from the root window's, you will have to create your own color map resources. In the X Window System, color maps are shareable resources which your application can create, destroy, and use. The section later in this chapter entitled "Color Map Manipulation" describes the requests that operate on color maps themselves, rather than the color cells within them.

Most workstations are capable of displaying, or *installing,* only one color map at a time. So, when several applications are running on a workstation, their windows will all display with correct colors only if they share a single color map. This fact means that you should avoid using private color maps if you can.

Some workstations have no color translation hardware at all. X supports these workstations with the StaticColor, TrueColor, and StaticGray visual classes. As far as an X application is concerned, these workstations do have color maps, but the color maps are preloaded with RGB values and cannot be changed.

## PseudoColor and StaticColor

Workstations are often described in marketing specifications as, for example, "displaying a palette of 256 colors at a time out of a gamut of 16,777,216 possible color combinations." This popular type of color display allows each pixel on the screen to be represented by a relatively small number of bits in the frame buffer (256 colors require eight bits, for example) while still allowing a rich gamut (256 distinct levels each for red, green, and blue primary colors yields 16,777,216 combinations). This strategy helps control the cost of the workstation by reducing the number of bits in the display memory. This visual class is called pseudo-color because the value stored into the pixel is interpreted as an index to a color cell rather than the actual color. The color cell contains the information which selects a single red-green-blue combination from the gamut based on the pixel value in the frame buffer.

Figure 7-1 shows a pixel value from an eight-plane display being used as an index into a cell in a color map. The red, green, and blue entries in the cell are used to generate output for display on the screen. Pseudo-color workstations have a much larger gamut than they can display in any single image.

Not all workstations have eight bits per pixel. Some low-cost workstations have four (allowing a palette of 16 colors at a time), and some have ten or twelve (all-

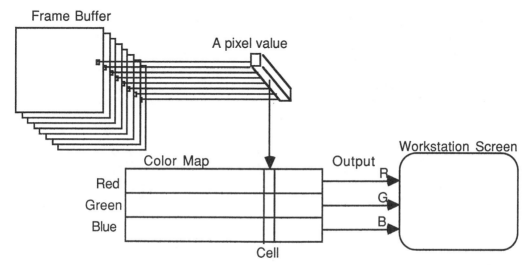

Figure 7-1. PseudoColor and StaticColor.

owing a palette of 1024 or 4096 simutaneous colors). Regardless of the actual number of colors in the palette, however, the principle remains the same: a pseudo-color pixel value is used as an index to a color cell within a color map. The color cell contains the actual red, green, and blue components of the color to display.

StaticColor color maps are similar to PseudoColor color maps, except that the cells in StaticColor color maps are permanently loaded with preset primary values. Because of this, private color cell allocation is not available in the StaticColor visual class. Note that the StaticColor visual class is rarely supported by general-purpose workstations.

## DirectColor and TrueColor

If your application displays smoothly shaded colored objects or full-color images, direct color yields a much more faithful rendering because it allows you to use more of the screen's gamut in a single image. In direct color, the display's frame buffer typically is three times deeper than in pseudo-color. Most direct-color display frame buffers use 24-bit pixels, and can display any combination of colors from their screen gamuts simultaneously.

In direct color, the pixel value is decomposed into separate fields which individually specify the red, green, and blue primary components of the color stored in that pixel, as the diagram shows. Each of these fields is a separate and distinct index to a cell in one of the color map's three channels (red, green, or blue).

In principle, the only difference between DirectColor and PseudoColor is the division of DirectColor pixel values into subfields which index the color map separately. Practically speaking, however, DirectColor workstations differ from PseudoColor workstations in another way: they have more planes. The extra planes permit them to represent more colors simultaneously. A PseudoColor workstation with 24 planes is theoretically possible, but the color map hardware for such a workstation would have to have over 16 million separate entries. The subfields in DirectColor permit the simultaneous display of many colors while still keeping the size of the color map within reason.

Workstation hardware which supports the DirectColor or TrueColor visual classes is more expensive, because of the cost of the extra planes of frame buffer memory. It is correspondingly less common than pseudo-color hardware; if possible, design your application to run on pseudo-color, but to take advantage of direct/true color if it is available.

True color is similar to direct color, except that the color map for true color cannot be changed, and private color cell allocation is not available. Each primary (red, green, blue) channel of the color map is loaded with a linear or near-linear function. On some workstations true color is implemented without using any color map hardware, although the X Window System provides your application with the illusion that it is using a color map resource of visual class TrueColor in these cases.

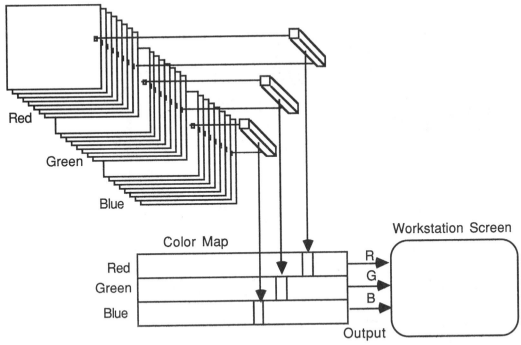

Figure 7-2.  DirectColor and TrueColor.

## GrayScale and StaticGray Color Maps

Some workstations provide multiple-plane frame buffers with a black-and-white video monitor.  These workstations are especially well suited to applications that display images in shades of gray, such as digitized black-and-white photographs or television images.  These workstations support either the GrayScale or the StaticGray visual class.  GrayScale "color" maps are set up so they function almost exactly like PseudoColor color maps:  red-green-blue primaries are available.  However, just one of the three primaries (green, ordinarily) drives the video screen.  The workstation vendor may use any primary color to drive the screen, however, so you should make sure that you set red, green, and blue equal to each other in **XColor** structures.  Notice that if an application displays a grayscale image correctly with a PseudoColor visual class, it will also work properly with a GrayScale visual class.

In GrayScale, the pixel value is treated as a single number, which indexes a single array in the color map, as the diagram shows.  Often the color map is loaded with a linear or near-linear ramp function.  However, it is possible to achieve special effects by manipulating color map entries.

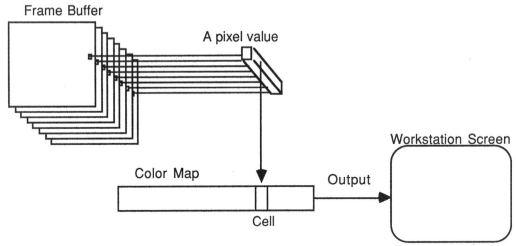

Figure 7-3.  GrayScale and StaticGray.

The StaticGray visual class is similar to the GrayScale visual class, except that the color map cannot be changed, and private color cells are not available.  The color map is permanently loaded with a linear or near-linear function.

# WORKSTATION CAPABILITIES

Workstations vary in their support for visual classes, and in the number of bits per pixel they provide.  Many color workstations support the PseudoColor visual class and provide eight bits per pixel.  Black-and-white workstations usually have one bit per pixel and support the  StaticGray visual class, although some support the GrayScale class.

However, X supports a wide variety of workstations.  To help you write your application so that it is compatible with as many kinds of workstation as possible, X provides functions that return information about the workstation's color support.

## Summary of Informational Functions

The X Window System provides a variety of informational functions, most in two forms: C language macros and callable functions.  These functions allow applications to determine the default visual class, depth, and other parameters for each screen on a workstation, so that applications can make intelligent decisions about how to use available color resources.  They also allow applications access to a list of visuals and depths that the screen is capable of displaying. Table 7-II presents a list of informational functions that relate to visual classes, depths, color maps, and pixel values.

| Macro | Function | Returns |
|---|---|---|
| DisplayCells | XDisplayCells | The screen's number of color map cells |
| DisplayPlanes | XDisplayPlanes | The screen's number of display planes |
| WhitePixel | XWhitePixel | Default pixel value for drawing white |
| BlackPixel | XBlackPixel | Default pixel value for drawing black |
| DefaultColormap | XDefaultColormap | The ID of the screen's default color map |
| DefaultVisual | XDefaultVisual | A pointer to the screen's default visual structure |
| DefaultDepth | XDefaultDepth | The depth of the screen's default root window |
| — | XMatchVisualInfo | Find matching visual information |

Table 7-II.  X Informational Functions related to visuals and color.

## Workstation and Screen Default Information

You may determine the total number of color cells on a screen with the **DisplayCells** macro or the **XDisplayCells** function (*Xlib* ¶2.2.1), which have the form

```
Display * display;      /* pointer to current display structure */
int screen;
int cells;
. . .
cells = XDisplayCells ( display, screen ); /* callable function */
cells = DisplayCells ( display, screen );  /* macro */
```

You may determine the total number of display planes on a screen with the **DisplayPlanes** macro or the **XDisplayPlanes** function (*Xlib* ¶2.2.1), which have the form

```
Display * display;      /* pointer to current display structure */
int screen;
int planes;
. . .
planes = XDisplayPlanes ( display, screen ); /* callable function */
planes = DisplayPlanes ( display, screen );  /* macro */
```

## Default Black and White Pixel Values

The **BlackPixel** and **WhitePixel** macros can be used for implementing monochrome applications.  They return pixel values for permanently allocated cells in the screen's default color map.  Ordinarily these cells are loaded with red-green-blue primary values which cause black-and-white displays.  However, most workstations allow the user to choose the colors displayed using **Black-Pixel** and **WhitePixel**:

— Some one-plane workstations can be set up (at workstation startup time; see your workstation vendor's documentation) to run in "reverse-video" mode. This causes **BlackPixel**'s returned pixel value to display white, and **WhitePixel**'s returned pixel value to display black.

— Some multi-plane workstations can be set up (at boot time) to run with arbitrary primary-color value settings for **BlackPixel** and **WhitePixel**.

**XBlackPixel** and **XWhitePixel** are functions corresponding to **BlackPixel** and **WhitePixel**. The functions and macros (*Xlib* ¶2.2.1) have the form

```
Display * display;        /* pointer to current display structure */
int screen;
unsigned long black, white;
. . .
black =  XBlackPixel ( display, screen ); /* callable function */
black =  BlackPixel ( display, screen );  /* macro */
white =  XWhitePixel ( display, screen ); /* callable function */
white =  WhitePixel ( display, screen );  /* macro */
```

## Default Color Map Information

You may determine the default color map for a screen with the **DefaultColormap** macro or the **XDefaultColormap** function (*Xlib* ¶2.2.1). Many applications will use this information whenever they access the color map (using requests described later in this chapter), so this may be the only informational function you have to use. The functions (*Xlib* ¶2.2.1 ) have the form

```
Display * display;        /* pointer to current display structure */
int screen;
Colormap cmap;
. . .
cmap =  XDefaultColormap (display, screen ); /* callable function */
cmap =  DefaultColormap (display, screen );  /* macro */
```

## Default Visual Information

Every screen has a default **Visual** structure, which contains information about its color capabilities. You can obtain a pointer to a screen's default **Visual** structure with the **DefaultVisual** macro or the **XDefaultVisual** function. A **Visual** structure is useful if you wish to find out details of a screen's color capability, and a **Visual** structure pointer is also required as input if you create a new color map. **Visual** structures are defined, in the header file **<X11/Xlib.h>**, as follows:

```
typedef struct _XVisual {
    VisualID visualid;
    int class;
    unsigned long red_mask, green_mask, blue_mask;
    int bits_per_rgb;
    int map_entries;
    ExtData * extension;
} Visual;
```

The "visualid" field contains the X resource identifier of the visual type described by the structure. The value in this field identifies the visual type to the workstation, so that the entire **Visual** structure does not have to be sent back and forth between the workstation and your application. The X Window System puts an appropriate value into the "visualid" field; your application should not change it.

The "class" field contains one of the visual classes PseudoColor, DirectColor, GrayScale, StaticColor, TrueColor, or StaticGray. From this field you can determine the visual class provided by this **Visual**.

The "red_mask," "green_mask," and "blue_mask" fields each contain one contiguous set of bits which describe which bits are in the red, green, and blue fields in a pixel value. "red_mask," "green_mask," and "blue_mask" are meaningless unless the "class" field is DirectColor or TrueColor.

The "bits_per_rgb" field specifies how many significant bits of precision are available in each color cell of the display hardware's color map to store red, green, and blue primary values. This field applies to all visual classes. For many workstations, this field has a value of eight, meaning that the display hardware uses the eight most significant bits of the 16-bit "red," "green," and "blue" fields in **XColor** structures. Note that this field is provided for your information only; you do not have to (and indeed, you should not) build your application to depend on particular values of "bits_per_rgb."

The "map_entries" field specifies how many color cells are available in a completely unused color map created with this **Visual** type.

The **DefaultVisual** macro and the **XDefaultVisual** function (*Xlib* ¶2.2.1 ) have the form

```
Display * display;      /* pointer to current display structure */
int screen;
Visual * vis;
. . .
vis = XDefaultVisual ( display, screen ); /* callable function */
vis = DefaultVisual ( display, screen );   /* macro   */
```

Both **XDefaultVisual** and **DefaultVisual** return, as their function values, pointers to a **Visual** structure. Your application may examine the **Visual** structure, but you should not alter it, nor should you release the memory it is in (that is, you should not use the **free** or **XFree** functions on it).

*COLOR VS. MONOCHROME CK.*

## Default Depth Information

The depth of a window is the number of planes, or the number of bits in pixel values for that window. You may determine the depth in the default root window for a specified screen with the **DefaultDepth** macro or the **XDefaultDepth** function (*Xlib* ¶2.2.1). The functions have the form

```
Display * display;       /* pointer to display structure */
int screen;
int depth;
. . .
depth =  XDefaultDepth ( display, screen );  /* callable function */
depth =  DefaultDepth ( display, screen );   /* macro */
```

**Example:**  What type of workstation is the application running on?

You should design your application to run on both one-plane black-and-white workstations and multiple-plane color workstations. This example explains how to tell them apart during the initialization of your application. First, you determine the default display depth; if the display depth is one, there is no point in having your application try to use more than one foreground and one background color. If the display depth is more than one, however, you may choose colors, and your choice will depend on the workstation's default visual class.

```
Display * display;       /* pointer to current display structure */
int screen;
int depth;
int class;
Visual * vis;

. . .

depth =  DefaultDepth ( display, screen );
vis =  DefaultVisual ( display, screen );
class =  vis.class;
if ( depth == 1) { /* One-plane monochrome */ }
else if ( class == PseudoColor ) { /* multi-plane color */ }
else if ( class == GrayScale ) { /* multi-plane monochrome */ }
else if ( class == DirectColor ) { /* direct color */ }
else if ( class == TrueColor ) { /* direct color, unchangeable color map*/ }
}
```

You should add StaticColor and StaticGray visual classes to this decision as well; although multiple-plane workstations with these visual classes are rare, you should write your application to run on all workstations.

## Selecting Visual Structures

Several vendors produce sophisticated and expensive workstations that are capable of selecting visual class and display depth on a window-by-window basis. Most workstations only offer a single visual class and depth, and portable applications can simply use the default visual type and depth. However, if your application is to run on a mutiple-visual-class workstation, and you want to use a visual class or depth other than the default, you can find it by using the Xlib application utility function **XMatchVisualInfo**.

To **XMatchVisualInfo**, you specify a screen, visual class, and display depth. If the workstation supports the combination you request, **XMatchVisualInfo** selects a visual structure for you and returns a description of it. You may use the selected visual structure in calls to **XCreateWindow** (see "Advanced Window Manipulation" in Chapter 4) and **XCreateColormap** (see "Color Map Manipulation" in this chapter).

The **XMatchVisualInfo** function returns a pointer to an **XVisualInfo** structure. **XVisualInfo** is defined in **<X11/Xutil.h>**. Most of its fields have the same meaning as the corresponding fields in the **Visual** structure described earlier.

```
typedef struct {
    Visual  *      visual;
    VisualID  *    visualid;
    int            screen;
    unsigned int   depth;
    int            class;
    unsigned long  red_mask, green_mask, blue_mask;
    int            colormap_size;
    int            bits_per_rgb;
} XVisualInfo;
```

**XMatchVisualInfo** (*Xlib* ¶10.8) has the form

```
Display * display;         /* pointer to display structure */
int screen;                /* screen number (from DefaultScreen)*/
int depth;                 /* desired depth */
int class;                 /* desired visual class */
XVisualInfo vinfo_ret;     /* returned visual info structure */
Visual * visual_to_use;    /* visual pointer to use */
Status result;             /* Boolean result */
    . . .
result = XMatchVisualInfo ( display, screen, depth, class, &vinfo_ret );
if ( result ) visual_to_use = vinfo_ret.visual;
```

To **XMatchVisualInfo**, you specify the *screen*, *depth*, and *class* (PseudoColor, DirectColor, TrueColor, GrayScale, StaticColor or StaticGray) for the kind of pixels you wish to use for drawing. **XMatchVisualInfo** searches for a matching **Visual**; if it finds one it returns a *result* of True and fills in *vinfo_ret* with information describing the found visual. If the workstation does not have the capability you are asking for, **XMatchVisualInfo** returns a *result* of False.

The *visual_to_use* fetched by the last line of the generic example is suitable for use with the **XCreateWindow** or **XCreateColormap** calls.

## PIXEL VALUES AND COLOR CELLS

The purpose of the X color-manipulation facilities is to let your application obtain pixel values which you can then use to draw the colors you want on the screen. This section describes the three important strategies you can use to get and work with pixel values. The strategies are:

- Shared color cells
- Standard color maps
- Private color cells

This section also describes a variety of service functions which you use in conjunction with all three strategies. The service functions provide ways of

- Translating named colors to RGB primary triplets
- Freeing color cells
- Querying color cell contents

By way of summary, Table 7-III lists the X requests and functions which allow you to obtain and manipulate pixel values and color cells. The table also shows the section of *Xlib—C Language X Interface* which describes each request. In the following sections, these requests and functions are described in the context of the color strategy for which they are useful.

| Request/Function | Xlib ¶ | Description |
|---|---|---|
| **DefaultColormap** | 2.2.1 | Determine the default color map |
| **XAllocColor** | 5.1.2 | Allocate a shared cell for a RGB triplet |
| **XAllocNamedColor** | 5.1.2 | Allocate a shared cell for a named color |
| **XGetStandardColormap** | 9.2.3 | Get information for standard color map |
| **XAllocColorCells** | 5.1.2 | Allocate private cells / planes |
| **XAllocColorPlanes** | 5.1.2 | Allocate private cells and plane groups |
| **XStoreColor** | 5.1.2 | Store one RGB triplet in one allocated cell |
| **XStoreNamedColor** | 5.1.2 | Store one named color in one allocated cell |
| **XStoreColors** | 5.1.2 | Store several RGB triplets in allocated cells |
| **XParseColor** | 10.4 | Convert a color specification string to RGB |
| **XLookupColor** | 5.1.2 | Look up RGB Values for a named color |
| **XFreeColor** | 5.1.2 | Free color cells |
| **XQueryColor** | 5.1.3 | Query the RGB contents of one cell |
| **XQueryColors** | 5.1.3 | Query the RGB contents of several cells |

Table 7-III.  X Color Cell Manipulation Requests

# STRATEGY: SHARED COLOR CELLS

The strategy of using shared color cells is the one most commonly used in X Window System applications. Standard X applications such as **xterm** and the various text editors use it to obtain pixel values for such things as window foreground, window background, and highlighting.

Using the shared color cell strategy has important advantages:

- The use of shared color cells is simple. Allocation of the cells is combined with the storing of their red-green-blue primary values.

- Sharing color cells conserves limited color resources. For example, many applications allocate pixel values to display black, white, and red. If they all use shared color cells to display these colors, each color only takes one cell in the color map. If they each allocate a separate cell, on the other hand, the color map will end up with multiple cells for black, red, and white.

- Applications using the shared-color-cell strategy need not know much about the specific visual class or depth of the workstation they are running on;  thus, applications using the shared-color-cell strategy are likely to be compatible with a wide variety of color workstations.

- Applications can specify the exact red-green-blue primary values for screen colors they want to use. As long as the color map is not full, the specified color is displayed.

Once allocated and stored, the primary values in shared color cells cannot be changed. This is a disadvantage of shared color cells: use private color cells if you want to change their primary values dynamically.

Using the shared color cell strategy also has a more subtle disadvantage:  you should not try to manipulate shared pixel values. When you allocate a shared color cell, the X request returns a pixel value that you can then use (for example, in a call to **XCreateGC**, **XSetState**, or **XSetForegroundColor** followed by graphic functions) to display that color. The disadvantage is that you must, if your application is to work properly, treat the pixel value as nothing more than a "magic number."

You should not make any assumptions about the numerical meaning of shared pixel values, or of any bits that may or may not be set in it. It does not make sense to change a shared pixel value by doing some sort of computation (such as addition or logical operations) on it unless you change it to another shared pixel value. For example, you might be tempted to add one to a shared pixel value to get the "next" color cell. This strategy might, by chance, work in one visual class, and have an entirely unexpected effect in another visual class. The standard color map and private color cell strategies (described in the next sections) provide an environment in which you can perform computations on pixel values.

You should also make no assumptions about the numerical or logical relationship between shared pixel values when you allocate several of them. For example, if you allocate two shared pixel values, one for foreground and the other for background, you should not assume that they are consecutive numbers, or that they differ by only one bit. If you want to allocate groups of color cells with defined relationships between their pixel values (for example, so you can draw using plane masks), use the private color cell strategy.

The shared color cell strategy is often used in combination with other strategies. As just one example, applications that display images may use shared color cells for such things as menus at the same time as they use the preallocated pixel values in a standard shared color map for displaying the image itself. Similarly, an application which displayed layers of graphical data would use shared color cells for text, and private color cells for graphics.

The **XAllocColor** and **XAllocNamedColor** requests support the shared color cell strategy. They both allow you to specify one color (by red-green-blue primary values or by name). They both return a single "magic number" pixel value that you can use to display the color you requested.

The **XAllocColor** and **XAllocNamedColor** requests search, starting with the color you specify, for the nearest color that the workstation can actually display. Therefore, these requests are suitable for use with all visual classes. Note that the **XAllocColor** and **XAllocNamedColor** requests function perfectly well with a TrueColor or DirectColor visual type.

If your application allows the user to specify colors by keying in text strings, you can use those text strings directly with **XAllocNamedColor**. However, you should, by convention, first use **XParseColor**, then **XAllocColor**. See **XParseColor** in the "Service Functions" section later in this chapter for more information.

When you no longer need shared colors, you can, if you wish, deallocate them using the **XFreeColors** request (described in the "Service Functions" section). All allocated colors are (usually—the ways of controlling the lifetime of color cell allocations are the same as for X resources) freed when your application terminates.

## XAllocColor

To the **XAllocColor** request, you specify primary color values in an **XColor** structure. **XAllocColor** finds or allocates a color cell, and returns to the "pixel" field in your **XColor** structure the index of the allocated color cell. The color cell is loaded with the color in the workstation's gamut that is the best possible approximation to your specified color. **XAllocColor** (*Xlib* ¶5.1.2) has the form

```
Display *display;      /* current display structure */
Colormap cmap;         /* resource id of color map */
XColor color;          /* RGB spec; contains pixel on return */
```

**Status** *result;*        */* result  -- zero if failure */*

. . .

*result* = **XAllocColor (**   *display, cmap, &color* **)**;

*cmap* is the resource identifier of the color map in which the allocation is to be made.  See the example below for more information.

*color* is the **XColor** structure.    Before calling **XAllocColor**, you should initialize the "red," "green", and "blue" fields in *color* to the desired primary values.  The DoRed, DoGreen, and DoBlue bits in the flag field are not used by this request.

Upon return, the "pixel" field in *color* contains the pixel value allocated for you. This same pixel value may also be used by other applications on the workstation that are sharing the color with you.

*result* is set to a nonzero value if the request succeeded, and a zero value if the request failed.    When **XAllocColor** fails, usually it is because no more unallocated color cells are left in the color map.

**Example:**  Use **XAllocColor** to obtain a color cell

This example fetches two color cells from the workstation's default color map, a bright yellow one and a dark gray one.   Then, assuming the application has already created the window *mywindow*, it makes *mywindow*'s background color gray.   Finally, it creates a graphic context which specifies the two allocated colors as foreground and background.   This code fragment shows how to specify the default *cmap*.

```
Display *display;    /* current display structure */
Colormap cmap;       /* resource id of color map */
Window mywindow;     /* window resource id */
XColor yellow;       /* RGB spec; contains pixel on return */
XColor gray;         /* RGB spec; contains pixel on return */
GC mygc;             /* graphic context resource id */
. . .
cmap = DefaultColormap ( display, DefaultScreen ( screen ));
yellow.red = 65535; yellow.green = 65535; yellow.blue = 0;
if ( XAllocColor ( display, cmap, &yellow  ) == 0)
    { . . . /* handle failure */ }
gray.red = 16384; gray.green = 16384; gray.blue = 16384;
if ( XAllocColor ( display, cmap, &gray  ) == 0)
    { . . . /* handle failure */ }
XSetWindowBackground ( display, mywindow, gray.pixel );
mygc = XCreateGC ( display, mywindow, 0, 0 );
XSetForeground ( display, mygc, yellow.pixel );
XSetBackground ( display, mygc, gray.pixel );
```

This example assumes that *mywindow* shares a color map with the root window on the screen. Note the use of the pixel values in calls to **XSet-Foreground** and **XSetBackground**.

# XAllocNamedColor

The **XAllocNamedColor** request is similar to **XAllocColor**, except that you specify the name of a color in a text string. **XAllocNamedColor** looks up the color in a predefined color-name data base (see the "Service Functions" section), finds or allocates a color cell, and returns two **XColor** structures. Upon return, one **XColor** structure informs you of the exact RGB components of the named color as defined in the data base. The other contains the workstation's best approximation of your specified color, and the index of the allocated color cell, in the "pixel" field. **XAllocNamedColor** (*Xlib* ¶5.1.2) has the form

```
Display *display;      /* current display structure */
Colormap cmap;         /* resource id of color map */
char * name;           /* text string specifying color name */
XColor exact;          /* exact RGB definition */
XColor color;          /* RGB spec; contains pixel value on return */
Status result;         /* result -- zero if failure */
. . .
result = XAllocNamedColor ( display, cmap, name , &exact, &color );
```

*cmap* is the resource identifier of the color map in which the allocation is to be made. See the examples for more information.

*name* is a null-terminated text string in which you specify the name of the color you want. Use ASCII encoding for the name; distinctions between upper and lower case make no difference. For more information about how a workstation translates color names into **XColor** structures, see under the heading "Looking Up RGB Values for a Named Color."

*exact* is the **XColor** structure in which the precise RGB primary values for your color are returned. The "red," "green," and "blue" fields in this structure are filled in on return, but the "pixel" field is not.

*color* is the **XColor** structure in which the color in the workstation's gamut that is its best approximation of the color in *exact* is returned. The "pixel" field in *color* returns the *pixel* value allocated for you. This pixel value may be shared with other applications on the workstation that request the same color. It remains allocated as long as any application is using it. The DoRed, DoGreen, and DoBlue bits in the flag field are not used by this request.

*result* is set to a nonzero value if the request succeeded, and a zero value if the request failed. When **XAllocNamedColor** fails, usually it is because no more color cells are available in the color map, or the color you specified is not available in the color data base.

**Example:**  Use **XAllocNamedColor**  to obtain a color cell
_____

This example fetches the pixel value for a color cell displaying orange from the workstation's default color map.

```
Display *display;      /* current display structure */
Colormap cmap;         /* resource id of color map */
char * name;           /* text string specifying color name */
XColor exact;          /* exact RGB definition */
XColor color;          /* RGB spec; contains pixel on return */
. . .
cmap = DefaultColormap ( display, DefaultScreen ( screen ));
if (XAllocNamedColor (display, cmap,
                    "orange", &exact, &color )== 0 )
       { . . .   /* failure */ }
```

If the **XAllocNamedColor** call succeeds, the pixel value for the allocated color cell is returned in _color.pixel._

# STRATEGY: STANDARD COLOR MAPS

Applications which display such things as smoothly shaded objects or digitized images require the ability to manipulate the red, green, and blue primary values in their images separately.  Typically these "true color" applications perform computations which determine the colors in their screen images in terms of the intensities of the red, green, and blue primaries.  For example, a three-dimensional drawing application might, for every point on the surface of a mechanical part, compute the intensity of red, green, and blue light reflected by the surface toward the viewer.  In order to display the mechanical part, the 3D application must compute a pixel value for each point on the surface once it knows the red, green, and blue components of the visible color of that point.

So they can perform arithmetic to convert RGB values to pixel values, such "true color" applications impose requirements on the organization of the color map they use.  A group of color cells must be loaded into the color map which cover a large range of colors— a large number of combinations of red, green, and blue intensities.  The group of color cells initialized this way must be as large as the visual class and depth of the color map will permit, so that displayed colors will be faithful to the computed red-green-blue values (the larger the number of color cells, the more intermediate shades can be displayed).

Obviously, workstations capable of using DirectColor or TrueColor visual classes are much better for this sort of thing than PseudoColor workstations.  However, if you choose the strategy of using shared standard color maps, your application can be compatible with a variety of workstations.

The X Window System (with the help of a window-manager application) provides several standard color maps.  These standard color maps contain color cells with preloaded red, green, and blue primary values.  Associated with each standard color map is a data structure, the **XStandardColormap** structure. It contains the information your application needs to compute a pixel value given a red-green-blue triplet. The sections entitled "The **XStandardColormap** structure" and "Getting a Standard Color Map" describe how to use and get these structures.

One of the standard color maps (named by the Atom XA_RGB_DEFAULT_MAP) actually refers to a subset of the "default" color map—the color map associated with the root window of the workstation's default screen. This is handy, because it means that a "true color" application can share a color map with other kinds of applications, and that it can use a combination of color strategies for its own purposes.

There is a disadvantage to using a standard shared color map, as compared with either of the other color strategies: Applications can not specify exact red-green-blue primary values for screen colors, but rather must take what they get when they compute pixel values from red-green-blue values. The computation rounds the original red-green-blue to the nearest available value in the color map. On an ordinary eight-plane PseudoColor workstation, this rounding is likely to be quite coarse.

Another disadvantage is that standard shared color maps are usually loaded by a window manager application. If no window manager is running on the workstation, or it has not loaded the shared color map you need, you must either load the standard color map yourself or choose some other color strategy. (See section 9.2.3 of *Xlib—C Language X Interface* for more information on loading standard color maps, but preferably obtain and run a window manager that loads the standard color maps.)

## The XStandardColormap structure

Each standard color map is described by an **XStandardColormap** structure. It is defined in **<X11/Xutil.h>** with the following fields:

```
typedef struct {
    Colormap colormap;
    unsigned long red_max;
    unsigned long red_mult;
    unsigned long green_max;
    unsigned long green_mult;
    unsigned long blue_max;
    unsigned long blue_mult;
    unsigned long base_pixel;
} XStandardColormap;
```

The "colormap" field contains the resource id of the X Window System **Colormap** resource described by this **XStandardColormap** structure. "colormap" is suitable for use whenever you must refer to the color map. For example, you can use it in the "colormap" field of an **XSetWindowAttributes** structure when creating a window (with **XCreateWindow**) or changing a window's attributes (with **XChangeWindowAttributes**).  See the example under "Getting a Standard Color Map."

The remaining fields describe how the color cells in the standard color map are set up.  "red_max," "green_max," and "blue_max" specify the maximum available value of each primary.  For example, if "red_max" has the value five, it means that the standard color map allows you to select the brightness of the red primary color using a number from zero (no red at all) to five (the brightest red available on the screen).

Suppose "red_max" and "green_max" had the value seven, and "blue_max" had the value three.  In this color map, there would be eight possible values of red, eight of green, and four of blue.  The total number of possible red-green-blue combinations in this color map would be the product 8 x 8 x 4, or 256.

The "base_pixel," "red_mult," "green_mult," and "blue_mult" fields specify the terms to be used to compute pixel values of given red-green-blue combinations. See the next section.

## Computing Pixel Values from RGB Values

The previous section described the fields of the **XStandardColormap** structure. This section describes how to use the values in those fields to convert red-green-blue primary color values to pixel values.  Both the cases of integer and floating-point primary color values are described.

Note that you do not have to use any X request to allocate or deallocate the pixel values in standard shared color maps; they are preallocated.

### Integer Primary Colors

If you are given $r$, $g$, and $b$ values in the ranges [0, red_max], [0, green_max], and [0, blue_max], you can compute the corresponding pixel value *pixel* using three multiplications and three additions, as follows:

```
XStandardColormap mystd;
unsigned long int r, g, b;
unsigned long int pixel;

. . .
pixel  =    mystd.base_pixel +
            ( r * mystd.red_mult ) +
            ( g * mystd.green_mult ) +
            ( b * mystd.blue_mult ) ;
```

Because the base_pixel field can be non-zero, it is possible for a standard color map to leave some color cells at the beginning of the color map for other purposes. This is the technique used by the "system default" color map so it can serve as both a standard shared color map and a source for allocated pixel values.

## Floating Point Primary Colors

Many computations of primary color intensities generate floating point values in the range [0.0, 1.0]. If you are given *red, green,* and *blue* values in this range you can compute the corresponding shared color map pixel value *pixel* as follows:

```
XStandardColormap mystd;
float red, green, blue;
unsigned long int pixel;
 . . .
pixel  =    mystd.base_pixel +
   ((unsigned long)( 0.5+( red * mystd.red_max )) * mystd.red_mult ) +
   ((unsigned long)( 0.5+( green * mystd.green_max )) * mystd.green_mult ) +
   ((unsigned long)( 0.5+( blue * mystd.blue_max )) * mystd.blue_mult ) ;
```

This method does not yield optimal performance on most workstations. Your application should organize pixel-value computations to be as fast as possible, particularly if you are computing a new pixel value for each point in your image.

## Available Standard Color Maps

A window manager application that provides standard color maps ordinarily provides several of them. The window manager makes them available to your application by creating X property data structures associated with the screen root window (for more information, see Chapter 9 of *Xlib—C Language X Interface*). However, complete familiarity with X properties is not necessary in order to use standard color maps, because the **XGetStandardColormap** function (described in the next section) hides most of the details for you.

When you want to get the **XStandardColormap** structure for a particular shared color map from the window manager (via the workststation), you refer to it by using a symbolic identifier such as XA_RGB_DEFAULT_MAP. These symbols (actually, they are "Predefined Atoms," as far as X's property facility is concerned, but we do not have to worry about those details here) are defined in the header file **<X11/Xatom.h>**.

Each of the standard color maps has a different purpose and is referred to by a different symbol. The available color maps are:

XA_RGB_DEFAULT_MAP    This standard shared color map is a subset of the root window's default color map. On an eight-plane PseudoColor display (which has a 256-entry color map) XA_RGB_DEFAULT_MAP typically is set up with "red_max," "green_max," and "blue_max" values of five (yielding a total of six shades, 0-5, of each primary color). This gives 216 colors uniformly distributed throughout red, green, and blue, and still leaves 40 entries available for allocation.

On workstations with other visual classes or depths XA_RGB_DEFAULT_MAP is set up to allow optimal sharing of the color map. You can trust XA_RGB_DEFAULT_MAP to give reasonable results in ordinary situations, regardless of the type or vendor of workstation.

XA_RGB_BEST_MAP    This standard shared color map is the one that should be used by image processing and 3D applications that have to use as many color cells as possible to achieve the desired results. "Best" means that the color cells are distributed so they provide as many perceptually distinct colors as possible. On eight-plane PseudoColor workstations, "red_max" and "green_max" are seven, and "blue_max" is three. On 24-plane DirectColor workstations, "red_max," "green_max," and "blue_max" are all 255. On other types of workstations, the vendor provides an appropriate XA_RGB_BEST_MAP.

XA_RGB_RED_MAP, XA_RGB_GREEN_MAP, XA_RGB_BLUE_MAP    These standard shared color maps provide optimal color cell allocation for displaying one of the three primary colors at a time. They are suitable for use in creating color separations, possibly for applications that drive a camera and expose each piece of film once for each primary color. These color maps work by ignoring two out of the three primary values. For example, XA_RGB_RED_MAP has "green_mult" and "blue_mult" fields of zero.

XA_RGB_GRAY_MAP    This standard shared color map provides an optimal color map for displaying gray-scale images. When computing pixel values based on XA_RGB_GRAY_MAP's **XStandardColormap** structure, you use only the "red_mult," "red_max," and "base_pixel" fields; the other fields do not contain usable values.

Some window manager applications may define other standard shared color maps; see the workstation vendor's documentation for details.

Note that on some DirectColor or TrueColor workstations some or all of the standard shared color map structures may actually make use of a single X **Colormap** resource. In this case the values of the **XStandardColormap** "colormap" fields will be set appropriately.

## Getting a Standard Color Map

The **XGetStandardColormap** function fills in an **XStandardColormap** structure for you, given the symbolic identifier (the "Predefined Atom") of the color map you want. **XGetStandardColormap** (*Xlib* ¶9.2.3) has the form

```
#include <X11/Xatom.h>

. . .

Display *display;              /* current display structure */
XStandardColormap stdcolor;    /* structure to fill in*/
Atom mapid;                    /* symoblic id of desired color map */
Status result;                 /* result -- zero if failure */

. . .

result = XGetStandardColormap (display,
                DefaultRootWindow (display ),
                &stdcolor, mapid  );
```

The first parameter is, as always, a pointer to the **Display** structure. The second parameter identifies a window. The specified window must be the screen root window.

*stdcolor* is the address of the **XStandardColormap** structure to be filled in.

*mapid* is the symbolic name of the desired standard shared color map.

*result* returns the value zero if the requested standard color map was not available, nonzero otherwise.

### Example: Set up a window to use XA_RGB_BEST_MAP

Assuming that the window *mywindow* has already been created, this code fragment retrieves the **XStandardColormap** structure for the XA_RGB_BEST_MAP and sets *mywindow*'s color map attribute to refer to it. It also sets *mywindow*'s background color to the white color computed from the information in the XA_RGB_BEST_MAP structure.

```
#include <X11/Xatom.h>
#include  <X11/X.h>
#include  <X11/Xlib.h>

. . .

Display *display;
Window mywindow;
XStandardColormap best_rgb;    /* structure to fill in*/
unsigned long whitepixel;      /* computed value for white */
XSetWindowAttributes  myattr;  /* attributes for mywindow */
unsigned long mymask;          /* attr. mask for mywindow */
Status result;                 /* result -- zero if failure */

. . .

result = XGetStandardColormap (display,
```

```
            RootWindow (display, DefaultScreen (display)),
            &best_rgb,  XA_RGB_BEST_MAP );
    mymask = CWColormap; myattr.colormap  =  best_rgb.colormap;
    whitepixel  =  best_rgb.base_pixel  +
                ( best_rgb.red_max * best_rgb.red_mult  ) +
                ( best_rgb.green_max * best_rgb.green_mult  ) +
                ( best_rgb.blue_max * best_rgb.blue_mult  );
    mymask |= CWBackPixel; myattr.background_pixel  =  whitepixel;
    XChangeWindowAttributes( display, mywindow, mymask, &myattr );
```

# STRATEGY: PRIVATE COLOR CELLS

The third color strategy available for applications to use involves allocating and using private read-write color cells.

The key advantage of using the private-color-cell strategy is that you can dynamically alter the primary color values stored in private color cells. A second advantage is that you can allocate private color cells in groups, whereas shared color cells are allocated one at a time. You use private color cell allocation when you want groups of pixel values that have a numerical relationship between them. For example, you can allocate two color cells that have pixel values that differ by only one bit (on DirectColor workstations, only three bits).

The major disadvantage to using private color cells is that there are not usually very many color cells available simultaneously. It is easy for applications that use private color cells to monopolize the color resources of the workstation. If your application makes extensive use of private color cells, you must allow for the possibility that the color map will fill up.

There are two ways to allocate groups of private color cells. **XAllocColorCells** works well in both PseudoColor and DirectColor visual types, and is suitable for pseudo-color applications, in which colors are symbolic. **XAllocColorPlanes** works best in the DirectColor visual type. You use it when you wish to construct pixel values from red, green, and blue subfields (see the section earlier in this chapter entitled "Direct Color and True Color" for an explanation of subfields).

Once you allocate private color cells, you must set their colors using **XStoreColor**, **XStoreNamedColor**, or **XStoreColors** requests before you use their pixel values (this means, of course, that private color cells are not much use in StaticColor, TrueColor, or StaticGray visual classes). You can alter color settings in private color cells as often as you wish. Changing color cells is faster than redrawing a complicated image with different pixel values, so you can use private color cells to generate interesting animation effects.

The section later in this chapter entitled "Using Private Color Cells" describes, by example, some ways to use private color cell allocation.

## XAllocColorCells

The **XAllocColorCells** request reserves groups of color cells for the private use of your application. This section covers the details of how to call **XAllocColorCells**.

**XAllocColorCells** (*Xlib* ¶9.2.3) has the form

```
        #define PLANES              8
        #define PIXELS              256
        . . .
        Display *display;              /* current display structure */
        Colormap cmap;                 /* resource id of color map */
        Bool contig;                   /* allocate contiguous planes if True*/
        unsigned long plane_masks [PLANES];/* array to return plane masks */
        unsigned int nplanes;          /* number of planes to allocate */
        unsigned long pixels [PIXELS]; /*  array for return of pixel values */
        unsigned int ncolors;          /* number of pixel values to allocate */
        Status result;                 /* result  -- zero if failure */

        . . .
        result = XAllocColorCells ( display, cmap,   contig,
                               plane_masks, nplanes, pixels, ncolors );
```

*cmap* is the resource identifier of the color map in which the allocation is to be made.

*contig* allows you to specify whether you want contiguous planes allocated (specify a value of True or 1) or whether your application can accept discontiguous planes (specify a value of False or 0). If you specify *nplanes* as zero, *contig* has no effect, but still must be specified. There is no way to specify that you want a numerically consecutive group of pixel values allocated and returned in *pixels*.

*plane_masks* is an array of 32-bit words in which **XAllocColorCells** returns the plane masks of the planes it allocates for you. The size of this array (PLANES) must be declared to be at least the value of *nplanes*. Upon return, each element in *plane_masks* is a longword with exactly one bit set (three bits if *cmap* refers to a DirectColor color map). No *plane_masks* value has any bits in common with any other, so each one identifies a distinct plane or bit-position in the pixel value.

A *contig* specification of True forces the bit positions of the set bits in *plane_mask* to be adjacent to one another.

*nplanes* is the parameter in which you specify how many planes you want to allocate. You may request allocation of zero or more planes.

*pixels* is an array of of 32-bit words in which **XAllocColorCells** returns pixel values. The size of this array (PIXELS) must be at least the value you specify for *ncolors*. If you request zero *nplanes* then *ncolors* color cells are allocated for you, and you access them via the values returned in the elements of the *pixels* array. When you set *nplanes* to a nonzero value, then a total of *ncolors* x $2^{nplanes}$ color cells are allocated for you. In this case, the values in *pixels* are the base pixel values. You may use all the pixel values generated by computing the logical OR of all possible combinations of *plane_masks* with the base pixel values. See the examples in the section entitled "Using Private Color Cells" for further information.

Remember that the primary color components in color cells are not automatically set when **XAllocColorCells** allocates them. You must use **XStore-Colors** or some other request to load red-green-blue values into your private color cells before you use the pixel values for drawing.

The loading of primary values into the allocated color cells works the same on PseudoColor and DirectColor visual types: in other words, **XAllocColorCells** simulates PseudoColor on DirectColor visual types.

*ncolors* is the parameter in which you specify how many base pixel values you want to allocate. You must request allocation of one or more base pixel values.

*result* is set to a nonzero value if the request succeeded, and a zero value if the request failed. Color cell allocation frequently fails; your application should be prepared to recover from it. When **XAllocColorCells** fails, usually it is because not enough color cells were available in the color map, or the available entries in the color map were fragmented in such a way that a request for planes could not be met. When **XAllocColorCells** fails, the X Window System makes no attempt to honor part of your request. If you wish, you can try to recover by repeating your allocation request, changing it in one or more of these ways:

- Change *contig* to FALSE if it was TRUE
- Reduce the value of *nplanes*
- Set *nplanes* to zero, and explicitly request *ncolors* •$2^{nplanes}$ colors
- Reduce the value of *ncolors*
- Use **XAllocColor** or **XAllocNamedColor**; try to share color cells

You can also recover from color cell allocation failure by allocating a new color map. See the section entitled "Color Map Manipulation" later in this chapter.

---

# XAllocColorPlanes

The **XAllocColorPlanes** request, like **XAllocColorCells**, reserves groups of color cells for the private use of your application. The difference is in the allocation of planes; **XAllocColorPlanes** allocates three sets of planes suitable for use as primary color subfields in DirectColor. Although the orientation of **XAllocColorPlanes** is toward DirectColor applications, it works on Pseudo-Color workststations (as long as the available planes are not used up). This section covers the details of how to call **XAllocColorPlanes**.

**XAllocColorPlanes** (*Xlib* ¶9.2.3) has the form

```
#define PIXELS              256
    . . .
```

| | |
|---|---|
| **Display** *\*display;* | /\* *current display structure* \*/ |
| **Colormap** *cmap;* | /\* *resource id of color map* \*/ |
| int *contig;* | /\* *allocate contiguous planes if True*\*/ |
| unsigned long *pixels* [PIXELS]; | /\* *array for return of pixel values* \*/ |
| unsigned int *ncolors;* | /\* *number of pixel values to allocate* \*/ |
| unsigned int *nred;* | /\* *number of red planes to allocate* \*/ |
| unsigned int *ngreen;* | /\* *number of green planes to allocate* \*/ |
| unsigned int *nblue;* | /\* *number of blue planes to allocate* \*/ |
| unsigned long *red_mask;* | /\* *returned red plane mask* \*/ |
| unsigned long *green_mask;* | /\* *... green plane mask* \*/ |
| unsigned long *blue_mask;* | /\* *... blue plane mask* \*/ |
| **Status** *result;* | /\* *result -- zero if failure* \*/ |

```
    . . .
result = XAllocColorPlanes ( display, cmap,  contig,
                    pixels, ncolors , nred, ngreen, nblue,
                    &red_mask, &green_mask, &blue_mask  );
```

*cmap* is the X resource identifier of the color map in which the allocation is to be made.

*contig* allows you to specify whether you require your red, green and blue subfields each to occupy contiguous bit positions in the pixel value (specify a value of True or 1—this is the usual specification) or whether your application can accept discontiguous subfields (specify a value of False or 0). See the description of *contig* under **XAllocColorCells** for other information.

*pixels* is an array of of 32-bit words in which **XAllocColorPlanes** returns pixel values. The size of this array (PIXELS) must be at least the value you specify for *ncolors*. A total of

$$ncolors \text{ x } 2^{(nred + ngreen + nblue)}$$

distinct pixel values are made available for your use by this request. The values in *pixels* are the base pixel values. You may use all the pixel values generated by computing the logical OR of all possible combinations of the bits set in *red_mask, green_mask,* and *blue_mask* with the base pixel values.

*red_masks, green_masks,* and *blue_masks* are 32-bit words in which **XAllocColorPlanes** returns the plane masks for the primary color subfields it allocates for you. No mask will have any bits in common with any other.

In keeping with its DirectColor purpose, **XAllocColorPlanes** treats the color map as three separate lookup tables. It allocates $ncolors \text{ x } 2^{(nred)}$ entries in the red lookup table, $ncolors \text{ x } 2^{(ngreen)}$ entries in the green table, and $ncolors \text{ x } 2^{(nblue)}$ entries in the blue table. Pixel values passed to **XStoreColor**, **XStoreColors**, or **XStoreNamedColor** are decomposed into separate subfields and the corresponding red, green, and blue lookup tables are updated. This is true regardless of whether the visual class is DirectColor or PseudoColor: in other words, **XAllocColorPlanes** simulates DirectColor on PseudoColor visual types.

This is handy because it allows you to load the color cells allocated with **XAllocColorPlanes** in many fewer calls than would otherwise be required. For example, when you set *nred, ngreen* and *nblue* to 8, you allocate over sixteen million distinct pixel values. It would be unreasonable to have to call **XStoreColor** sixteen million times; as it is you only need call **XStoreColor** 256 separate times.

*result* is set to a nonzero value if the request succeeded, and a zero value if the request failed. Color cell allocation frequently fails; your application should be prepared to recover from it. When **XAllocColorPlanes** fails, usually it is because not enough planes were available, probably because the workstation does not support the DirectColor visual class. See **XAllocColorCells** for a discussion of ways to recover from color-cell allocation failure.

All pixel values in the X Window System are, at their largest, 32-bit quantities. The *red_mask, green_mask,* and *blue_mask* items returned from the **XAllocColorPlanes** request tell you which of the 32 bits to use for the red, green, and blue subfields in a direct-color pixel value. Each mask consists of one contiguous set of bits. For example, a popular true-color representation scheme uses eight bits each of red, green, and blue. On display hardware which uses this scheme, the masks are (in hexadecimal) as follows:

> red_mask     0x00FF0000
> green_mask   0x0000FF00
> blue_mask    0x000000FF

Under this 8/8/8 color representation, the low-order eight bits in pixel values represent the blue field, the next the green, and the highest-order the red. The following code excerpt might be used to construct an 8/8/8 pixel value from three eight-bit color fields.

```
unsigned byte redval, greenval, blueval;
unsigned long pixelval;
. . .
pixelval = (redval << 16) | (greenval << 8) | (blueval);
```

Unfortunately, there is no guarantee that the masks returned from any particular **XAllocColorPlanes** call will use this 8/8/8 representation. To be portable, your application must assemble the color primary subfields according to the actual returned masks and pixel values.

## Storing Primary Color Values

The **XStoreColor**, **XStoreColors**, and **XStoreNamedColor** requests permit you to store primary color component values into your application's private color cells. You can change the primary color components of your private color cells as often as you wish, but you must set them at least once. When you change the primary values in a color cell, all the display pixels set to the corresponding pixel value change color on the screen. Previous chapters have discussed how you can create and change your display pixel-by-pixel by drawing graphics. Color-cell manipulation gives you another way to change your display.

Most workstation video hardware refreshes the screen 50, 60, or 72 times per second. Ordinarily, changes to color cells take effect right before a screen refresh. In some workstation hardware, there is a limit on the number of color cells that can be changed in a single screen refresh, so an operation that stores primary values into many color cells may take effect over several refresh periods. Thus, if you change a color cell's primary values very rapidly, there is no guarantee that you will actually see any but the last primary values on the screen.

## XStoreColor

**XStoreColor** is used for changing the primary components of a single private preallocated color cell. It (*Xlib* ¶9.2.3) has the form

```
Display *display;    /* current display structure */
Colormap cmap;       /* resource id of color map */
XColor color;        /* RGB / pixel spec*/
. . .
XStoreColor ( display, cmap, &color );
```

*cmap* is the X resource identifer of the color map in which you wish to store the new primary color values.

*color* is an **XColor** structure. Before calling **XStoreColor**, you should initialize the "red," "green", and "blue" fields in *color* to the desired primary components, and the "pixel" field to the pixel value for the color cell you wish to change. In addition, you must initialize the "flag" field in the **XColor** structure. Ordinarily you set all three flag bits: DoRed, DoGreen, and DoBlue. If you do not set DoRed, DoGreen, or DoBlue, the **XStoreColor** request does not update the corresponding primary color's value in the color cell, but leaves it at the previous setting.

## XStoreColors

**XStoreColors** is a plural form of **XStoreColor**. It is used for changing the primary components of several private preallocated color cells. It (*Xlib* ¶9.2.3) has the form

```
#define PIXELS   256
. . .
Display *display;        /* current display structure */
Colormap cmap;           /* resource id of color map */
XColor defs [PIXELS];    /* RGB / pixel spec array */
int ndefs;               /* number of elements in defs */
. . .
XStoreColors ( display, cmap, &defs, ndefs );
```

*cmap* is the X resource identifier of the color map in which you wish to store the new primary color values.

*defs* is an array of **XColor** structures (the maximum size of which is defined above as PIXELS) Before calling **XStoreColors**, you should initialize the fields in each element of the *defs* array, as described for the *color* parameter to the **XStoreColor** request. Do not forget to initialize the "flag" bit fields.

*ndefs* specifies the number of elements in *defs*. Note that if you use **XStore-Colors** to set primary component values for an entire group of color cells you allocated with **XAllocColorCells**, you must provide *ncolors* •$2^{nplanes}$ elements in *defs* (you can specify fewer, but then you will have to make multiple requests to fill in all the color cells in the group). You must enumerate each base color cell and each color cell derived by combining *plane_masks* entries with *pixels* entries. Take care not to attempt to store primary values into color cells that you have not allocated.

If you use **XStoreColors** to set primary component values for an entire group of color cells you allocated with **XAllocColorPlanes**, on the other hand, you need only provide *ncolors* •$2^n$ elements in *defs,* where *n* is the largest of *nred, ngreen,* and *nblue.* As the discussion of **XAllocColorPlanes** pointed out, the pixel values you provide in *defs* are decomposed into primary-color subfields and the three components of the color map are updated separately.

## XStoreNamedColor

The **XStoreNamedColor** request is similar to **XStoreColor**, except that you specify the name of a color in a text string. It is used for changing the primary components of one private preallocated color cell.

If your application allows the user to specify colors by keying in text strings, you can use those text strings directly with **XStoreNamedColor**. However, you should, by convention, first use **XParseColor**, then **XStoreColor**. See **X-ParseColor** in the "Service Functions" section for more information.

**XStoreNamedColor** (*Xlib* ¶9.2.3) has the form

```
Display *display;      /* current display structure */
Colormap cmap;         /* resource id of color map */
char * name;           /* the color name string */
unsigned long pixel;   /* pixel value of color map entry */
int flags;             /* DoRed, DoGreen, DoBlue bits */
. . .
XStoreNamedColor ( display, cmap, name, pixel, flags );
```

*cmap* is the resource id of the color map in which you wish to store the primary color values of the named color.

*name* is a null-terminated text string in which you specify the name of the color you want. Use ASCII encoding for the name; distinctions between upper and lower case make no difference. For information about how a workstation translates color names into **XColor** structures, see the section later in this chapter entitled "Color Name Translation."

*pixel* is the pixel value indexing the color cell you want to change.

*flags* has the same function as the "flag" field in the **XColor** structure. Ordinarily you set all three flag bits: DoRed, DoGreen, and DoBlue. If you do not set DoRed, DoGreen, or DoBlue, the **XStoreNamedColor** request does not update the corresponding primary color's value in the color cell, but leaves it at the previous setting.

## Using Private Color Cells

Because of the combination of pixel values and display planes inherent in the X Window System's color cell allocation capability, your application can use a variety of subtle and powerful techniques for creating and editing drawings on the screen. The purpose of this section is to discuss how to take advantage of X's private color cell capability. Several scenarios for color cell allocation are described.

### Several Colors, No Planes

The simplest way of using **XAllocColorCells** is to set *nplanes* to zero and *ncolors* to some small number. For example, if your application draws a map, it might use three colors: green for land, red for highways, and blue for water. In this case you would make the following call (obviously, you could call **XAlloc-Color** three times to obtain three shared colors in this case, but that would spoil the example):

```
Display *display;              /* current display structure */
Colormap cmap;                 /* resource id of color map */
unsigned long pixels [3];      /* array for return of pixel values */
Status result;                 /* result  -- zero if failure */
int flags = { DoRed | DoGreen | DoBlue };
. . .
cmap =  DefaultColormap ( display, DefaultScreen ( screen ));
result = XAllocColorCells (display, cmap,  FALSE, NULL, 0, pixels, 3 );
if ( result == 0  ) /* recover from errors here */  ;
XStoreNamedColor (  display, cmap, "Green",  pixels[0],  flags );
XStoreNamedColor (  display, cmap, "Red",    pixels[1],  flags );
XStoreNamedColor (  display, cmap, "Blue",   pixels[2],  flags );
```

What you get back in *pixels* is a list of three pixel values, corresponding to the three color cells allocated for you. The three **XStoreNamedColor** calls store color primary values in the color cells. You can proceed to store these pixel values into **GC**s (using, for example, **XSetForeground**) and use them to draw your map.

## One Color, One Plane

A second way to use **XAllocColorCells** is to set both *ncolors* and *nplanes* to one. This is a good way to run a one-plane black-and-white application on a pseudo-color workstation. In this case, you request one base pixel value and one plane from **XAllocColorCells**, as shown in the following code excerpts:

```
Display *display;              /* current display structure */
Colormap cmap;                 /* resource id of color map */
Window w;                      /* drawing window */
GContext gc;                   /* graphic context for drawing window */
unsigned long plane_mask ;     /* plane mask*/
unsigned long pixel;           /* pixel value */
Status result;                 /* result  -- zero if failure */
int flags = { DoRed | DoGreen | DoBlue };
. . .
/* ( create the window w and the graphic context gc ) */
. . .
cmap  =  DefaultColormap ( display, DefaultScreen ( screen ));
result  =  XAllocColorCells(display, cmap, FALSE,
                              &plane_mask,1 , &pixel, 1 );
if ( result == 0  ) /* recover from errors here */  ;
XStoreNamedColor ( display, cmap, "Green", pixel, flags );
XStoreNamedColor ( display, cmap, "Gray", pixel | plane_mask, flags );
. . .
XSetWindowBackground   ( display, w, pixel );
XSetPlanemask ( display, gc, plane_mask   );
XSetBackground   ( display, gc, pixel );
XSetForeground   ( display, gc, pixel | plane_mask );
. . .
XClearWindow   ( display, w );
```

This call to **XAllocColorCells** reserves two cells. The base color cell is indexed by the pixel value returned in *pixel*. The other color cell index is constructed by computing the logical OR of *pixel* and *plane_mask*. (Although the *pixels* and *plane_masks* parameters to **XAllocColorCells** are usually arrays, in this example we have taken a legitimate shortcut because both arrays have a length of one.) Once the color cells are allocated, the code fragment in the example stores colors into them.

The window background pixel value should be set to *pixel*. This allows window-clear operations (both explicit, as shown, and automatic, upon window exposure) to make sure that all the pixels in the window are set to the background value.

The plane mask in the **GC** the application will use for drawing should be set to *plane_mask*. This permits drawing operations to modify only the allocated plane—the plane that distinguishes foreground from background in this window. The background and foreground values in the **GC** should be set to *pixel* and *pixel*

| plane_mask. (Note that you could also set background to zero and foreground to all ones; because of the plane mask it makes no difference.) Once the foreground and background are set this way you can use **XSetFunction** to select any boolean drawing function. For example, you could draw highlight rectangles or rubber-band lines using the exclusive-or boolean function, and the boolean operations will be applied only to the *plane_mask* plane.

There is no way your application can predict what numerical *pixel* and *plane_mask* values will be returned from any given **XAllocColorCells** call. However, let's assume that it returned a *pixel* of 2 and a *plane_mask* of 4. These values would indicate that you have allocated color cells 2 and 6. As long as you set the planes you have not allocated to the values indicated in the base pixel value, you may set the plane you have allocated any way you please.

> Select a pair of sharply contrasting color combinations for applications that use one foreground color and one background color.

Notice that you can use **XChangeWindowAttributes** to set the backing-store window attributes *backing_pixel* and *backing_plane* (see Chapter 4 under the heading "Backing Store") to the *pixel* and *plane* values you get back from **XAllocColorCells** if your application works this way.

## One Color, Several Planes

A third way to use **XAllocColorCells** is to set *ncolors* to one and *nplanes* to some small number. This might be suitable, for example, in a window which displayed images. Suppose that the images were represented in gray scale with intensities stored as numbers in the range 0-63 (six bit planes). In this case, you would request a single base pixel value and six contiguous planes from **XAllocColorCells**, as shown in the following code excerpt:

```
Display *display;              /* current display structure */
Colormap cmap;                 /* resource id of color map */
unsigned long plane_masks [6]; /* array for return of plane masks */
unsigned long pixel;           /* returned pixel value */
Status result;                 /* result -- zero if failure */
XColor gray [64];              /* array of gray scales */
int shift;                     /* bit position of low-order plane */
unsigned int intensity;
int cell;
. . .
cmap = DefaultColormap ( display, DefaultScreen ( screen ));
result = XAllocColorCells ( display, cmap,
              True, plane_masks, 6, &pixel, 1 );
if ( result == 0  ) /* recover from errors here */  ;
for (  shift = 0;                   /*  compute bit position ...*/
         plane_mask[0] != (1 << shift);  /* ...of low-order plane  */
      shift++  );
for ( cell = 0; cell <= 64;  cell++ ) {  /* loop over all cells */
```

```
     intensity = cell  *  65536L / 64L;  /* compute scaled intensity */
       gray[cell].red = gray[cell].green = gray[cell].blue = intensity;
       gray[cell].pixel = (cell << shift )| pixel;  /* compute pixel value */
       gray[cell].flags = DoRed | DoGreen | DoBlue;  /* set flags */
       }
   XStoreColors ( display, cmap, gray, 64 );
```

The pixel value and plane masks that come back from this call to **XAllocColorCells** depend, obviously, on what cells were previously allocated. However, you are guaranteed (if the request does not fail) to be able to use 64 color cells, for which the corresponding pixel values can be generated from your input levels (which must be in the range 0-63) by a single shift and a single logical OR operation:

```
     pixelvalue  = ( level << shift )| pixel;
```

Note that this technique only works if you specify a *contig* value of True in your call to **XAllocColorCells**, because it depends on being able to shift all the bits in your input levels the same number of bit-positions.

Notice that you can use the backing-store window attributes *backing_pixel* and *backing_planes* (see Chapter 4 under the heading "Backing Store"). Using **XChangeWindowAttributes**, set the *backing_pixel* attribute to the *pixel* value you get back from **XAllocColorCells**. Set the *backing_planes* attribute to the logical OR of all the elements of your *plane_masks* array.

## Several Colors, Several Planes

For this last example, we add two overlay planes to the map-drawing application of the first example ("Several Colors, No Planes"). For purposes of the example, let us say that one overlay plane is used to draw filled polygons which define city boundaries. The second overlay plane is used for grid lines. Suppose we decide to use colors as follows:

| | |
|---|---|
| Land outside cities: | Green |
| Land inside cities: | Yellow |
| Highways outside cities: | Red |
| Highways inside cities: | Black |
| Water (everywhere): | Blue |
| Grid-lines (everywhere): | White |

Suppose that we first draw the base map (land, highways, and water) using the three base pixel values. Next, we draw the filled polygons representing the cities into the first overlay plane. Thereafter, we use the second overlay plane to draw grid lines. The advantage of this approach is that city boundaries and grid lines can be drawn and removed (by setting and clearing bits in the appropriate planes) without disrupting the base map.

The following code excerpt allocates the three colors and two planes, yielding a total of twelve allocated color cells. Note that contiguous planes are not required.

```
Display *display;              /* current display structure */
Colormap cmap;                 /* resource id of color map */
Window w;                      /* drawing window */
GContext gc;                   /* graphic context for drawing window */
unsigned long plane_masks [2]; /* plane masks*/
unsigned long pixels [3];      /* pixel values*/
Status result;                 /* result -- zero if failure */
int flags = { DoRed | DoGreen | DoBlue };
int i;
. . .
/* ( create the window  w and the graphic context gc ) */
. . .
cmap  =  DefaultColormap ( display, DefaultScreen ( screen ));
result  =  XAllocColorCells(display, cmap, False,
                              plane_masks, 2, pixels, 3  );
if ( result == 0  ) /* recover from errors here */  ;
```

We must store the appropriate colors into the allocated color cells. We want the base map to display in green, red, and blue.

land
highway
water

```
XStoreNamedColor ( display, cmap, "Green", pixels[0], flags );
XStoreNamedColor ( display, cmap, "Red", pixels[1], flags );
XStoreNamedColor ( display, cmap, "Blue", pixels[2], flags );
```

Next, we must set up the colors (yellow, black, and blue) which will be used inside city boundary polygons. Store these colors into the base pixels modified by the city-boundary plane:

```
XStoreNamedColor
          ( display, cmap, "Yellow",  pixels[0] | plane_mask[0], flags  );
XStoreNamedColor
          ( display, cmap, "Black",   pixels[1] | plane_mask[0], flags  );
XStoreNamedColor
          ( display, cmap, "Blue",    pixels[2] | plane_mask[0], flags  );
```

That takes care of six of our twelve allocated color cells. The other six are used only when the grid-line overlay plane has bits set in it. Regardless of what the base map or the city-boundary overlay shows, we want grid lines to be white. Therefore, we must set all six grid-line color cells to white, as follows:

```
for ( i  = 0; i < 3; i ++ ) {
    XStoreNamedColor ( display,  cmap,
            "White",  pixels[i] | plane_mask[1], flags  );
    XStoreNamedColor ( display,  cmap,
            "White",  pixels[i] | plane_mask[0] | plane_mask[1], flags  );
}
```

Now the application can proceed to draw the map using appropriate foreground colors and planemasks. Note that as you use more of them, overlay planes get progressively more costly in terms of the number of color cells you must initialize.

# SERVICE FUNCTIONS

This section describes X service functions which help your application deal with color. These functions are useful regardless of your choice of color strategy.

## Looking Up RGB Values for a Named Color

Each X Window System workstation contains a data base relating color names to primary component (red-green-blue) values. This color data base is used by the **XAllocNamedColor** and **XStoreNamedColor** requests (described earlier), as well as the **XLookupColor** request described in this section.

A list of the names in the color data base may be found in Appendix E. It is possible on some workstations to define your own color names and add them to the color data base. See your vendor's documentation for details.

If you use **XParseColor** (descibed in the next section) you may also specify a color numerically as a combination of primary colors. You do this with a text string of numbers beginning with a pound sign (#). Such a numeric text specification must have one of the following formats, depending on how precisely the primary colors are specified:

| | |
|---|---|
| #RGB | One hexadecimal digit (four bits) per primary |
| #RRGGBB | Two hexadecimal digits (eight bits) |
| #RRRGGGBBB | Three hexadecimal digits (twelve bits) |
| #RRRRGGGGBBBB | Four hexadecimal digits (16 bits) |

For example, yellow (a combination of bright red and bright green with no contribution from blue) might be specified by "#FFFF00."

By convention, when X users specify a color by entering in a text string (for example, in a command line), they may specify either the name of a color or one of these hexadecimal strings. If your application follows this convention, you should use **XParseColor** to interpret all such user-specified colors and turn them into **XColor** structures. If, on the other hand, your application needs only to translate named colors, you can use the **XLookupColor** request.

You may use **XAllocNamedColor** or **XStoreNamedColor** (described in preceding sections) directly. However, only **XParseColor** translates both named ("Yellow") and numeric ("#FFFF00") color strings. As far as users are concerned colors may be specified either way. Therefore, you should use **XParseColor** explicitly when processing color strings specified by users.

## XParseColor

Your application uses the **XParseColor** request to fill in an **XColor** structure based on any text-string color specification, either named ("Green") or numeric

("#00FF00").   When you call **XParseColor**, you specify the name of a color in a text string, and **XParseColor** returns an **XColor** structure containing the workstation's closest approximation to the color you specified.  **XParseColor** (*Xlib* ¶10.4) has the form

```
Display *display;    /* current display structure */
Colormap cmap;       /* resource id of color map */
char * name;         /* text string specifying color name */
XColor color;        /* approximate RGB spec*/
Status result;       /* result -- zero if color name unknown */
. . .
result = XParseColor ( display, cmap,  name, &color );
```

*cmap* is the resource identifer of the color map for which the named color should be looked up.  It is used in determining the screen for which the color should be looked up.

*name* is a null-terminated text string in which you specify the name of the color you want.  Use ASCII encoding for the name;  distinctions between upper and lower case make no difference.

*color* is the **XColor** structure in which the RGB primary values for your color are returned.  The "red," "green," and "blue" fields in this structure are filled in on return, but the "pixel" field is not.  The DoRed, DoGreen, and DoBlue flags in the "flags" field are all set.

*result* is set to a nonzero value if the request succeeded, and a zero value if the request failed.  When **XParseColor** fails, it is because the color you specified is not available in the color data base, or because the format of the hexadecimal color string was not correct.

## XLookupColor

The **XLookupColor** request looks up the values of the primary components of a named (but not a hexadecimal) color.  **XLookupColor** returns two **XColor** structures.  One informs you of the exact RGB components of the named color. The other contains the workstation's best approximation of your specified color. **XLookupColor** (*Xlib* ¶5.1.2) has the form

```
Display *display;    /* current display structure */
Colormap cmap;       /* resource id of color map */
char * name;         /* text string specifying color name */
XColor color;        /* approximate RGB spec*/
XColor exact;        /* exact RGB definition */
Status result;       /* result -- zero if color name unknown */
. . .
result = XLookupColor ( display, cmap,  name, &color, &exact );
```

*cmap* is the X resource identifier of the color map for which the named color should be looked up.  It is used in determining the hardware approximation returned in the *color* parameter.

*name* is a null-terminated text string in which you specify the name of the color you want.  Use ASCII encoding for the name;  distinctions between upper and lower case make no difference.

*exact* is the **XColor** structure in which the precise RGB primary values for your color are returned.  The "red," "green," and "blue" fields in this structure are filled in on return, but the "pixel" field is not.

*color* is the **XColor** structure in which the primaries for the workstation's best approximation of the color in *exact* are returned.  Again, the "red," "green," and "blue" fields in this structure are filled in on return, but the "pixel" field is not.

*result* is set to a nonzero value if the request succeeded, and a zero value if the request failed.  When **XLookupColor** fails, it is because the color you specified is not available in the color data base.

## Freeing Color Cells

When your application no longer needs allocated color cells, you use **XFree-Colors** to return them to the pool of unused color cells so other applications can allocate them.  Ordinarily you do not have to use **XFreeColors**, because terminating your application automatically frees all your allocated color cells.  You would use **XFreeColors** if your long-running application allocated a large number of color cells and used them for only a short time.

**XFreeColors** frees shared color cells allocated with **XAllocColor** or **XAlloc-NamedColor**.  If other applications are still using shared color cells when your application frees them, **XFreeColors** has no effect on those applications; they continue to have access to all their shared color cells.

**XFreeColors** also frees private color cells allocated with **XAllocColorCells** and **XAllocColorPlanes**.  You do not have to tell **XFreeColors** how the color cells you are freeing were originally allocated.

If your color strategy involves the use of pixel values in standard shared color maps, you should not call **XFreeColors** with those pixel values, because you did not allocate them in the first place.

**XFreeColors** (*Xlib* ¶5.1.2) has the form

```
#define PIXELS    256
    . . .
Display *display;              /* current display structure */
Colormap cmap;                 /* resource id of color map */
unsigned long pixels [PIXELS]; /* array for pixel values */
unsigned int npixels;          /* number of pixel values to allocate */
unsigned long plane_mask;      /* mask for planes to free */
    . . .
XFreeColors ( display, cmap, pixels, npixels, plane_mask );
```

*cmap* is the X resource identifer of the color map containing the pixels to be freed.

*pixels* is an array of of 32-bit words containing the pixel values corresponding to the color cells to be freed. Take care not to attempt to free pixel values that you have not allocated. Note that *pixels* is shown with a size of 256, which is enough for an 8-plane frame buffer. You may choose to allocate more or less space for *pixels*. *npixels* specifies the number of pixel values in *pixels*.

*plane_mask* specifies which planes you wish to free. It should be zero if you are freeing color cells allocated via **XAllocColor** or **XAllocNamedColor**. If it is nonzero, it must be the logical OR of one or more entries in the *plane_masks* array returned by **XAllocColorCells**. Take care not to attempt to free planes that you have not allocated.

## Query the RGB Contents of Color Cells

Use the **XQueryColor** and **XQueryColors** requests to obtain the primary color component values for specified colors cells. You may retrieve the primaries for any color cell, regardless of whether it is allocated by your application (for either shared or private use). However, the primary values stored in color cells not allocated by your application may change without notice, and may be invalid.

**XQueryColor** (*Xlib* ¶5.1.3) retrieves the primaries for a single color cell, and has the form

```
Display *display;     /* current display structure */
Colormap cmap;        /* resource id of color map */
XColor color;         /* RGB / pixel spec*/
. . .
XQueryColor ( display, cmap, &color );
```

*cmap* is the resource id of the color map from which you wish to retrieve values.

*color* is an **XColor** structure. Before calling **XQueryColor**, you should initialize the "pixel" field in *color* to the pixel value for the color cell you wish to retrieve. Upon return, the "red," "green," and "blue" fields in *color* are set to the primary components of the color cell.

**XQueryColors** (*Xlib* ¶5.1.3) is the plural form of **XQueryColor**. It is used for retrieving the primary components of several color cells. It has the form

```
#define PIXELS    256
. . .
Display *display;        /* current display structure */
Colormap cmap;           /* resource id of color map */
XColor colors [PIXELS];  /* RGB / pixel spec array */
int ncolors;             /* number of elements in  colors */
. . .
XQueryColors ( display, cmap, &colors,  ncolors );
```

*cmap* is the X resource identifier of the color map in which you wish to store the new primary color values.

*colors* is an array of **XColor** structures, the maximum size of which is defined above as PIXELS. Before calling **XQueryColors**, you should initialize the "pixel" fields in each element of the *colors* array just as you would for the *color* parameter to the **XQueryColor** request. Upon return, the "red," "green," and "blue" fields in *colors* are set to the primary components of the color cells. *ncolors* is used to specify the number of elements in *colors*.

# MONOCHROME AND GRAY SCALE

A display which supports the GrayScale or StaticGray visual classes is very likely to be less expensive, other things being equal, than a display which supports PseudoColor, because black-and-white video monitors are less costly than color. GrayScale has a second advantage: because black-and-white monitors only have one electron source (instead of three) illuminating the tube face, images they generate can be sharper and higher in contrast. Sharp high-contrast images are very important to the readability of text in editors, terminal emulators, and electronic publishing applications. (Some very high quality color monitors generate excellent high-contrast images, but they are expensive.)

## One-Plane Monochrome

When we began this chapter, the pixel values we knew how to work with were restricted to **BlackPixel** and **WhitePixel**. We then proceeded to develop the X Window System's color model in detail, and to understand how to use multi-bit pixels. Now we are coming full circle to revisit black-and-white, and to understand it in terms of the overall color model.

Most black-and-white workstation displays have only one plane in the frame buffer. The X Window System provides color maps containing just two color cells for these workstations. The visual class of a one-plane workstation is usually StaticGray, but some of them provide a two-entry changeable GrayScale color map instead. In either case, both cells in the default color map are permanently allocated and shareable, so the Private Color Cell strategy will not work on monochrome workstations (unless you create a totally private "color" map and the workstation boasts a GrayScale visual class rather than StaticGray). Both the Shared Color Cell and the Standard Color Map strategies work, if you allow for the fact that only two entries are available in any given color map.

If you know your application is running on a one-plane workstation (see the example in the earlier section entitled "Default Depth Information"), selecting pixel values from the default color map is straightforward: the pixel value returned by the **WhitePixel** macro displays white, and the pixel value returned by the **BlackPixel** macro displays black. The situation is more complicated, however, because your application should be designed to run compatibly on monochrome and color workstations.

**XAllocColor** and **XAllocNamedColor** requests can be used on one-plane workstations. One one-plane workstations, these requests return a pixel value of either 0 or 1, depending on whether the color you request is closer to black or white. Recall that **XAllocColor** and **XAllocNamedColor** both adjust the color you request so as to pick the nearest color the hardware is capable of displaying. In the one-plane case, either black or white is always the nearest color.

**Example:** Use **XAllocNamedColor** for black and white

This example fetches pixel values for black and white from the workstation's default color map.

```
Display *display;      /* current display structure */
Colormap cmap;         /* resource id of color map */
char * name;           /* text string specifying color name */
XColor exact;          /* exact RGB definition  (reused)*/
XColor black;          /* RGB spec;  contains pixel on return */
XColor white;          /* RGB spec;  contains pixel on return */
. . .
cmap =  DefaultColormap ( display, DefaultScreen ( screen ));
if (XAllocNamedColor ( display,  cmap,
                    "Black",&exact,&black   )== 0 )
    { . . .   /* failure */ }
if (XAllocNamedColor ( display,  cmap,
                    "White",&exact,&white   )== 0 )
    { . . .   /* failure */ }
```

Like **BlackPixel** and **WhitePixel**, this is a good, compatible technique to use in an application that uses just one color, because it works identically on one-plane and multi-plane workstations. Unlike **Black-Pixel** and **WhitePixel**, however, **XAllocNamedColor** returns true black and true white, even when the user has chosen reverse-video mode for the workstation, or chosen (on a color workstation) default colors other than black and white.

# Multiple-Plane Gray Scale

You may use all three color map strategies described in this chapter to manipulate GrayScale color maps. (Note that you should set red, green, and blue primary values equal to each other.) If you want a linear or near-linear relationship between pixel value and displayed gray level, it is your responsibility to initialize the color table appropriately, or to use a standard shared color map. The "One Color, Several Planes" example under "Using Private Color Cells" shows how to use private color cells in a way that is compatible with both color and gray scale workstations.

# COLOR MAP MANIPULATION

Color map manipulation is the creation, use, and deletion of entire color maps. The preceding sections have described several strategies for using color cells from color maps. When none of those strategies are sufficiently flexible for your application's needs, then you may need to resort to working with entire color maps.

Color maps are X resources. As with other X resources, they are potentially shareable by all applications running on the workstation. Color maps are referred to with a resource identifier; these resource identifiers are returned by the X requests **XCreateColormap** and **XCopyColormapAndFree**, the requests which create new color maps. Applications store color map resource ids in data items of the type **Colormap**. Table 7-IV summarizes X calls for color map manipulation.

Color maps are temporary. Color maps created by your application are destroyed when your application terminates. However, the lifetime of color maps follows the same rules as the lifetimes of other X resources, and there are ways to create resources that outlive the application that created them. No matter what their lifetime, color map resources are too volatile to use for permanent storage of a group of color cells.

Color maps belong to a particular screen. If your workstation has multiple screens, color maps can only be used for windows on the screen for which they were created.

There is, in principle, no such thing as a completely private color map. However, if you create a color map it is possible to keep it private by not telling other applications what its resource identifier is. It is also possible to prevent other applications from altering the contents of color map by allocating all the color cells in it at the time you create it. There is no need to create the default color map for each screen (nor is it possible to destroy the default color map); it always exists.

| Request/Function | Xlib ¶ | Description |
|---|---|---|
| **DefaultColormap** | 2.2.1 | Determine the default color map |
| **XCreateColormap** | 5.1.1 | Create a new color map resource |
| **XSetWindowColormap** | 5.1.1 | Set a window's color map attribute |
| **XCopyColormapAndFree** | 5.1.1 | Create a private copy of a color map |
| **XFreeColormap** | 5.1.1 | Destroy a color map resource |
| **XInstallColormap** | 7.3 | Install a color map into hardware |
| **XUninstallColormap** | 7.3 | Remove a color map from hardware |
| **XListInstalledColormaps** | 7.3 | Return a list of all installed color maps |

Table 7-IV.   X Color Map Manipulation Requests

## Creating Color Maps

The **XCreateColormap** request creates a color map resource and returns the new resource identifier. **XCreateColormap** (*Xlib* ¶5.1.1) has the form

> **Display** *\*display;*       /* *current display structure* */
> **Window** *w;*                 /* *window; identifies screen for color map* */
> **Visual** *vis;*               /* *pointer to visual structure for color map* */
> int *alloc;*                    /* *either* AllocNone *or* AllocAll */
> **Colormap** *result;*          /* *resource id of resulting color map* */
>
> . . .
>
> *result* = **XCreateColormap** ( *display, w, &vis, alloc* );

The color map is created for a particular screen;  by specifying the window $w$ you identify the screen $w$ is on.  Every color map is created with a particular visual type, identified by the **Visual** structure *vis* in the call.  See the example in the next section.

If you specify the constant value AllocAll for the *alloc* parameter, all the color cells in the color map are allocated for use by your application immediately after the color map is created.  (You may not specify an *alloc* value of AllocAll when the visual class is TrueColor, StaticGray, or StaticColor;  if you do an X error results.)

If the visual class of the color map is PseudoColor or GrayScale, all the color cells are allocated as if by a call to **XAllocColorCells** using an *ncolors* parameter from the "map_entries" field of the specified **Visual** structure (see the section entitled "Default Visual Information").  The allocated pixel values are in the range [0, map_entries-1].

If the visual class of the color map is DirectColor, all the color cells are allocated as if **XAllocColorPlanes** returned a single base pixel value of zero, and *red_mask, green_mask,* and *blue_mask* set to the values of the corresponding fields in the **Visual** structure.

If you specify the constant value AllocNone for the *alloc* parameter, none of the color cells is allocated.  The constants AllocAll and AllocNone are defined in the header file **<X11/X.h>**.

## Associating Color Maps with Windows

Once a color map has been created, you must associate it with one or more windows in order to use it.  A color map is an attribute of a window;  you can set window attributes when you create a window with **XCreateWindow** or you can use **XChangeWindowAttributes** to change window attributes (see the example in "Getting a Standard Color Map").

Or, you can use the **XSetWindowColormap** request to set the color map attribute for a specified window.  The **XSetWindowColormap** request (*Xlib* ¶5.1.1) has the form

```
Display  *display;       /* current  display  structure  */
Window  w;               /* window;  identifies  screen  for  color  map  */
Colormap  cmap;          /* resource  id  of  color  map  */
. . .
XSetWindowColormap  (    display, w, cmap  );
```

This request takes the color map whose resource identifier is *cmap* and makes it the current color map for the window *w*. Note, though, that you may also have to change the pixel value for the window's background color when you change the window's color map. This request generates a ColormapNotify event.

**Example:**  Create a new color map and make it current in a window

In this example, we create a color map and make it the current color map for a window *w* (assuming that *w* already exists). The purpose of this example is to show how to use informational macros to obtain the default **Visual** structure.

```
Display  *display;
Window  w;
Colormap  cmap;
. . .
cmap  = XCreateColormap  ( display, w,
            &DefaultVisual ( display, DefaultScreen (display)),
            AllocNone );
XSetWindowColormap  ( display, w, cmap  );
```

Note that none of the entries in the newly created color map are allocated, nor are there valid values in any of the color cells.

## Copying  Color  Maps

The **XCopyColormapAndFree** request is used to obtain a new color map when an attempt to allocate cells in another color map fails because the original color map is full. The request creates a new color map resource and returns the new resource id. The newly created color map is a copy of the specified color map.

- It has the same visual type and is created for the same screen as the specified color map.

- All the color cells which your application has already allocated from the original color map are copied, intact, to the new color map. All other entries in the newly created color map are left uninitialized.

- Your application's color cells in the original color map are freed.

This means that your application can use **XCopyColormapAndFree** to recover when all the cells or planes in a shared color map are used up. It gives your application a way of "moving out" of a shared color map into a private copy.

This can give both your application and others more color cells and planes to work with.

**XCopyColormapAndFree** (*Xlib* ¶5.1.1) has the form

```
Display *display;        /* current display structure */
Colormap cmap;           /* color map to copy*/
Colormap result;         /* resource id of resulting color map */
. . .
result = XCopyColormapAndFree ( display, cmap );
```

*cmap* identifies the original color map. *result* identifies the copy. All the characteristics of the copy come from the original.

## Freeing Color Maps

Use the **XFreeColormap** request to release a color map resource when you have finished using it. Note that color map resources, like other X resources, are ordinarily freed when the creating application terminates. An attempt to free a default color map is ignored and does nothing.

If the color map resource given to the **XFreeColormap** request is associated with a window, the color map attribute for that window is changed to None and the window receives a ColormapNotify event (see the last section of this chapter). Colors displayed by a window with a color map of None are unpredictable.

If the color map resource given to the **XFreeColormap** request has been installed on the screen the workstation uninstalls it automatically.

**XFreeColormap** (*Xlib* ¶5.1.1) has the form

```
Display *display;        /* current display structure */
Colormap cmap;           /* color map to copy*/
. . .
XFreeColormap ( display, cmap );
```

*cmap* identifies the color map to be freed.

## Installing and Uninstalling Color Maps

X color maps are virtual resources, analagous to virtual memory. Workstation display hardware has one or more physical color maps, analagous to physical, or working-set memory. Most workstation displays have a single color map. Therefore, when multiple X color maps are being used, an operation analagous to paging in virtual memory is required.

"Paging in" a color map to the display hardware is known as *installing* the color map. If a color map is uninstalled, its windows may display with false colors, because the pixel values in those windows are translated to screen colors using some other, possibly random, color map. When a color map is installed, its windows immediately display with true colors. (Do not confuse "false colors" and "true colors" with the visual classes PseudoColor and TrueColor; they are not the same thing.) This false-color display is the most important disadvantage of using multiple color maps. When a color map is paged in, or becomes installed, all the windows associated with it are sent a ColormapNotify event.

"Paging out" a color map is known as *uninstalling* it. All the windows associated with a color map are sent a ColormapNotify event when the color map is uninstalled.

The window manager application usually takes responsibility for installing and uninstalling color maps. The window manager usually installs the color map for a window at the same time as it assigns the keyboard focus to that window. Ordinary applications should accept the window manager's color map installation and uninstallation decisions.

Detailed descriptions of the X requests to support installation and uninstallation of color maps may be found in section 7.3 of *Xlib—C Language X Interface*.

By using the **XGetWindowAttributes** request (see "Advanced Window Manipulation" in Chapter 4) and looking at the "map_installed" field of the resulting **XWindowAttributes** field, you can determine whether the color map for a window is installed.

## Processing ColormapNotify Events

Your application can arrange to receive ColormapNotify events from the workstation. These events notify you of changes to the color maps in your windows. If you enable the delivery of ColormapNotify events for a certain window, you get an event each time

- The color map for that window is changed (using the **XSetWindowColormap** request, for example).

- The color map for that window becomes installed

- The color map for that window becomes uninstalled

Most applications will be able to ignore ColormapNotify events, and disable their delivery. However, if your application routinely uses a color map other than the default, you may want to take some special action (such as clearing your window) when your color map is not installed. It is a good idea to make it plain to the user when your application is displaying with "false" colors.

## Controlling Delivery of ColormapNotify Events

In order to receive ColormapNotify events (or any other kind of event) for a window, you must first express interest in them with **XSelectInput**. In the *event_mask* parameter, specify the bit mask named ColormapNotifyMask. (The bit names for the event selection mask are defined in the header file **<X11/X.h>**.)

## Receiving and Processing ColormapNotify Events

Once you have enabled event delivery, you read events from your application's queue using **XNextEvent** or one of the other queue-reading functions. The first field of all event structures is the event type (field name "type"). The union type **XEvent** defines the "type" field directly, so it can be used to look at the event so you can dispatch to appropriate code for the event type. You should use **XEvent** to declare and allocate space for all event structures: it defines a structure that is guaranteed to be long enough for all event types.

Expose events have the structure type **XColormapEvent**. The **XEvent** union defines the "xcolormap" variant to be an **XColormapEvent** structure. Table 7-V shows the type names and field names in the ColormapNotify event's structure, as defined in the header file **<X11/Xlib.h>**.

Once you know you have a ColormapNotify event, you may use the fields specific to the **XColormapEvent** structure, which are defined as follows:

| | |
|---|---|
| type | This field appears in all event structures. It is a sixteen-bit integer, and has the value ColormapNotify for these events. It is always the first integer in the event structure. |
| serial | The serial number of the last request processed. |
| send_event | False unless this event was generated by some application issuing the **XSentEvent** request. |
| display | A pointer to the **Display** structure for this event. |
| window | The identifier for the window affected by the colormap change. |
| colormap | The identifier for the color map that is the subject of this event. |
| new | True if this ColormapNotify event is the result of a request that changed the color map attribute for "window." In this case, the color map field has the new value of the color map attribute. |
| | False if this ColormapNotify event was caused by the color map becoming installed or uninstalled. |

```
typedef struct {
    int  type;                ev.type                ColormapNotify
    unsigned long serial;     ev.xany.serial         Last request processed
    Bool send_event;          ev.xany.send_event     From XSendEvent?
    Display * display;        ev.xany.display
    Window window;            ev.xcolormap.window    Affected window
    Colormap colormap;        ev.xcolormap.colormap  Color map identifier
    Bool new;                 ev.xcolormap.new       Color map changed?
    int  state;               ev.xcolormap.state     Color map installed?
} XColormapEvent;
```

Table 7-V  ColormapNotify event field names.

state          This field has either the value ColormapInstalled or the value
               ColormapUninstalled.  It specifies whether the color map was in-
               stalled or uninstalled at the time the event was sent.  This field is
               valid regardless of whether the "new" field is True or False.

# SUMMARY

In X, applications draw into windows and Pixmaps using using foreground and
background *pixel values*.  The relationship between pixel values used for drawing and the colors displayed on-screen is controlled by the *color cells* and *color
maps* described in this chapter.  Applications cannot make any assumptions
about the meanings of pixel values, even on black-and-white workstations.  For
example, it is incorrect to assume that a pixel value of zero means black and a
pixel value of one means white.

Instead of making assumptions about pixel values, applications must use X calls
to *generate* pixel values corresponding to desired colors.  For example, throughout
this book we have been using the informational macros BlackPixel and
WhitePixel to generate pixel values.

X supports both black-and-white and color displays, giving application developers
the challenge of making software that works properly for both.  When drawing,
pixel values are loaded into **GC**s in order to specify colors.  This chapter discusses what pixel values mean and how applications use X calls to obtain pixel
values representing desired colors.

Black-and-white workstations have one *plane*, or pixel values containing one bit.
Color workstations can have 4, 8, 10, 12, or 24 planes, although 4- and 8-plane
workstations are most common.  The numerical values in these planes serve as
indices into a *color map*.

On-screen colors are specified as linear combinations of red, green, and blue
*primary* colors.  Most workstations can display 256 shades in each primary
color, for a total *gamut* of over sixteen million possible *red-green-blue triplets* or
color combinations.  Each *color map cell* or entry in a color map contains a single red-green-blue triplet.  Color map cells are scarce, so X provides ways for applications to share them, or to allocate them as private resources if necessary.
The color maps from which color cells are allocated are virtual X resources.
Most applications share a single color map.  However, applications can create
and use private color maps.

Different workstation models support different *visual classes*: different strategies
for translating pixel values into red-green-blue triplets.  X offers six different
visual classes:

*PseudoColor* treats each pixel value as an index to a color map.

*DirectColor* treats each pixel value as three separate indices to the red, green,
and blue parts of the color map.

*GrayScale* is like PseudoColor, but provides only one primitive color (white) rather than three. It is used on displays designed to show shades of gray.

*StaticColor*, *TrueColor*, and *StaticGray* correspond to PseudoColor, DirectColor, and GrayScale, except that the primitive color values stored in the color maps cannot be changed. Black-and-white workstations are usually treated as StaticGray with a depth of one.

One of the most important things your application must do when initializing is determine the capabilities of the workstation it is running on. A variety of informational macros and functions allow you to find out the number of planes, the number of color map cells, the default color map, and the default visual class.

X supports three strategies for dealing with color: the *shared color cell* strategy, the *standard color map* strategy, or the *private color cell* strategy. In all of these strategies, you use *Xlib* facilities to *generate* pixel values: given a desired color, you ask *Xlib* to furnish an appropriate pixel value.

The shared color cell strategy is suitable for applications, such as terminal emulators and text editors, which use color symbolically. X generates pixel values which represent shared color cells when you use this strategy. Several applications which require the same shared color can conserve color resources by all using the same color cell.

The standard color map strategy is suitable for applications which interpolate between colors when generating, for example, shaded images. *Xlib* gives users of this strategy the information they need to generate pixel values directly from red-green-blue triplets directly.

The private color cell strategy requires you to allocate color cells, then to load red-green-blue triplets into them. The advantage of this strategy is that the red-green-blue triplet values can be changed at any time, causing instantaneous changes in the colors of displayed images. The disadvantage is that color cells run out quickly.

*Xlib* provides a variety of service functions for color. Included are functions to translate named colors ("Turquoise", for example) into red-green-blue triplets. Also included are functions to inquire the contents of color cells, and to free color cells.

Color cells are allocated from color maps. Applications should, if possible, avoid creating new color map resources: even though color maps are virtual resources, most workstations can only realize one color map at a time. If you require an entire color map, and you do not mind the fact that windows may "go technicolor" when more than one color map is used, you can create color maps and set them as attributes of windows. ColormapNotify events inform you when windows' color map attributes change, or when a window's virtual color map becomes physically installed or uninstalled in the workstation's display hardware.

# CHAPTER 8
# PIXMAPS, BITMAPS, AND IMAGES

This chapter describes how your application can use the X Window System to create, draw, and process rectangular areas of pixels, or *rasters*. X represents rasters in three distinct, but related, ways:

- *Pixmaps* are workstation-resident X resources to which you can issue all sorts of drawing requests.

- *Bitmaps* are two things:
  — Pixmaps with pixel-values limited to one bit (one and zero).
  — Text files of information for loading into bitmap-type Pixmaps.

- *Images* are data structures representing the contents of rectangular rasters in your application program.

*Xlib* provides a large variety of calls to manipulate pixmaps, bitmaps, and images, and to help you convert your application's rasters from one form to another.

This chapter has a section each for Pixmaps, bitmaps, and images. The section called "Pixmap Resources" describes Pixmaps, and how your application can create and destroy them. The most useful feature of Pixmaps is their ability to be operated upon by all kinds of drawing requests just as if they were windows. Thus, this chapter does not describe how to draw into Pixmaps; see Chapters 5, 6, and 7, and the last section ("Images") of this chapter for descriptions of drawing requests.

The "Bitmaps" section of this chapter describes how your application can read and write bitmap files, and load bitmap information into Pixmap resources on workstations. If you wish to create or use bitmaps for such things as cursor patterns (see Chapter 9) or stipple patterns (see Chapter 5), this is the section you should read.

The "Images" section of this chapter describes a collection of image-manipulation functions and an image data structure. *Xlib* provides these functions and this structure to make it easy for your application to compose pictures using rectangular arrays of pixels, then draw those pixels into windows or Pixmaps on your workstation.

# PIXMAP RESOURCES

A Pixmap, like a window, is a rectangular raster area on an X workstation into which applications can draw. Unlike a window, however, a Pixmap is never visible on-screen; a Pixmap's pixels are stored in memory in the workstation. Most applications make Pixmap contents visible by copying them to windows.

When your application creates a Pixmap, you must define these characteristics for it:

- Width and height. Every Pixmap has a positive width and height. Once a Pixmap is created, its width and height cannot be changed.

- Depth. This characteristic defines the number of planes (the number of bits per pixel) in the Pixmap. Whereas most application windows inherit their depth from their parent window, you must choose a Pixmap's depth based on what you want to use it for. Pixmaps should either have a depth of one (depth-one Pixmaps are called *bitmaps*) or the same depth as the window with which you will use it.

- Screen. On a multiple-screen workstation, you must decide with which screen each Pixmap is to be associated. The Pixmap's screen is important, because workstations cannot copy information between Pixmaps for one screen and windows for another, or vice versa. On a single-screen workstation, the problem does not arise.

Pixmaps are very simple. To understand what Pixmaps can and cannot do, it is instructive to compare them to windows.

- Pixmaps and windows use similar coordinate systems. The upper left corners of both Pixmaps and windows have the (x,y) coordinates (0,0). The sizes of both Pixmaps and windows are specified in pixels by width and height.

- Pixmaps, unlike windows, do not have background attributes. Because clearing a window (see "Clearing Windows" in Chapter 5) is defined as setting its pixels to the background, this means that you do not use the **XClearArea** request to clear a Pixmap. Instead, you use the **XFillRectangle** request to set all the pixels in a Pixmap to known values.

- Windows should be mapped to the screen (with **XMapWindow**, **XMapRaised**, or **XMapSubwindows**) after creation but before drawing. Pixmaps cannot be mapped to the screen. Once a Pixmap is created, you do not have to do anything else before you draw into it.

- Pixmaps do not have, nor do they need, borders. The purpose of borders is to set windows off visually one from another, and Pixmaps are not visible.

- Pixmaps are not arranged in a hierarchy the way windows are, and Pixmaps cannot be obscured by stacking. Therefore, applications do not receive Expose events for Pixmaps. It is possible for applications to receive GraphicsExpose and NoExpose events for Pixmaps, but only as the result of a copy request (**XCopyArea** or **XCopyPlane**) from an obscured window.

- When you draw to a Pixmap, the Window Clipping stage of X's graphics pipeline always clips your graphic primitives to the Pixmap's boundaries. However, because Pixmaps are not stacked, all the pixels inside the Pixmap are always available to be drawn, and are always available as source pixels for copy requests. You do not have to worry about Pixmaps being obscured.

- Pixmaps do not have a visual type, nor do they have a color map attribute. Pixel values in windows have colors assigned to them (for example, pixel values in windows with the DirectColor visual class have distinct red, green, and blue subfields; see Chapter 7). However, pixel values in Pixmaps have no color assigned to them at all until they are copied to some window.

- Pixmaps never appear directly on the screen. Therefore, they have no need for cursors, nor can direct input events ever originate from them (see Chapter 9). Of course, this also means that Pixmaps do not need a class—there can be no such thing as an InputOnly Pixmap.

The upshot of this is that only two types of events can originate from Pixmaps: GraphicsExpose and NoExpose. You solicit these event types by setting the graphics_exposure attribute in the **GC** you use for **XCopyArea** and **XCopyPlane** operations (see "Copying Areas" in Chapter 5).

Despite this difference in the way they handle events, Pixmaps are similar to other X resources in many ways. First of all, they are resident in the workstation, not your application. The fact that Pixmaps are workstation-resident can affect the application performance; remember that it takes about the same time to draw to a Pixmap as it does to draw to a window. If you wanted to draw a complex object (such as a symbol) multiple times, you might first compose it laboriously, using all the necessary graphic output requests, in a Pixmap. Once the object is drawn into the Pixmap, you then can copy it rapidly, using **XCopyArea** or **XCopyPlane** as many times as necessary to the appropriate places in windows.

Pixmaps are shareable between applications, like other X resources. Any application that knows the resource identifier of a Pixmap can operate on it. For example, you may create a Pixmap containing an icon for your application and use **XSetWMHints** (see Chapter 4) to tell a window manager the icon Pixmap's resource identifier.

The lifetime of Pixmaps follows the same rules as the lifetime of other resources; ordinarily the workstation destroys your application's Pixmaps when you close the display connection with which they were created. You can extend a Pixmap's lifetime; see under the heading "Controlling Resource Lifetime" in Chapter 3. However, Pixmap resources, like other resources, are not permanent. All Pixmaps (and all other resources) are destroyed when the user logs off the workstation. Your application must therefore create all the Pixmaps it needs at the beginning of every user session, if not more often.

| Request/Function | Xlib ¶ | Description |
|---|---|---|
| **XCreatePixmap** | 5.2 | Create a Pixmap resource |
| **XGetGeometry** | 4.1 | Determine the size of a Pixmap |
| **XFreePixmap** | 5.2 | Delete a Pixmap resource |

Table 8-I. *Xlib* calls for Pixmap handling.

You may create as many Pixmaps as your application needs, at any time. Table 8-I summarizes the *Xlib* requests for creating and maintaining Pixmaps. The only limit on the size and number of Pixmaps is virtual memory in the workstation. Some workstations use hidden display memory as a cache for Pixmaps. You may find that Pixmap operations slow down substantially if your Pixmaps are too large for your workstation's hidden display memory, even though the total size of Pixmaps on the workstation is not limited to what fits in hidden display memory. Consult your workstation vendor's documentation for details.

## Using Pixmaps

In Chapters 5 and 6 we have had many opportunities to refer to Pixmap resources. As we saw, X's graphic output requests (except **XClearArea** and **XClear-Window**) accept a Drawable parameter; they do not care whether you are drawing to a window or Pixmap. Thus, we have already discussed most of the X requests that operate on Pixmaps. In this chapter, we finally cover the creation and deletion of Pixmap resources.

Pixmaps are also useful for specifying window background and border patterns. The **XCreateWindow, XChangeWindowAttributes, XSetWindowBackgroundPixmap**, and **XSetWindowBorderPixmap** calls, described in

Chapter 4, all can be used to set the background_pixmap and border_pixmap window attributes.

Pixmaps are useful as tile patterns. The tile attribute in a **GC** specifies a tile pattern, as described in Chapter 5. The **XCreateGC**, **XChangeGC**, and **XSet-Fill** calls can all be used to set a **GC**'s tile attribute.

Bitmaps (depth-one Pixmaps) are useful as stipple patterns and clip masks. The **XCreateGC**, **XChangeGC**, **XSet Stipple**, and **XSetClipMask** calls can all be used to set a **GC**'s stipple and clip_mask attributes, analogously to the tile attribute. Bitmaps can be used to specify cursor shapes using the **XCreate-PixmapCursor** request. See Chapter 9.

On monochrome workstations, general Pixmaps and depth-one bitmaps are interchangeable, because both have depths of one. This presents you with a hazard if you are trying to develop portable applications: it is easy, but wrong, to use depth-one bitmaps for backgrounds, borders, and tiles. However, if you debug your application on a monochrome workstation you will not be able to tell the difference. Be careful to use bitmaps only where X allows them. See under the heading "Reading Bitmap Files" later in this chapter for a good way to create background, border, and tile Pixmaps.

## Pixmap Creation

**XCreatePixmap** is the call for creating new Pixmaps. The pixels in Pixmaps created this way are not initialized, so you should explicitly set them to known values with **XFillRectangle** or the equivalent. **XCreatePixmap** (*Xlib* ¶5.2) is a one-way request; it has the form

```
Display* display;        /* pointer to Display structure */
Drawable drawable;       /* specifies which screen the Pixmap is on*/
unsigned int width;      /* width of Pixmap*/
unsigned int height;     /* height of Pixmap*/
unsigned int depth;      /* depth (number of bits per pixel) of Pixmap*/
Pixmap pixmap;           /* created Pixmap's resource ID */
. . .
pixmap  = XCreatePixmap ( display, drawable, width, height, depth );
```

**XCreatePixmap** is very simple. As input, you specify the dimensions of the Pixmap (*width*, *height*, and *depth*).

In the *drawable* parameter, you must specify the X resource identifier of some previously existing Drawable (window or Pixmap). This parameter is used by multiple-screen workstations to determine which screen the new Pixmap will be created for; every Drawable is created for a particular screen. **XCreatePixmap** creates the new Pixmap for the same screen as the *drawable* you specify. It is important on multiple-screen workstations to specify the appropriate screen: the **XCopyArea** and **XCopyPlane** functions do not allow copying from one screen to another, even if source or destination pixels are in Pixmaps instead of windows. Note that the *drawable* must be specified even on single-screen workstations; simply specify the root window (or any other valid window).

As output, **XCreatePixmap** returns the resource identifier for the newly created Pixmap. A workstation's capacity for Pixmaps is not unlimited, so it is possible for an **XCreatePixmap** request to fail when the workstation attempts to carry it out. If the workstation does not have enough memory to hold your Pixmap, it does not create it. Rather, it sends you a BadAlloc error event message. Because **XCreatePixmap** is a one-way request, the error event message will arrive some time after you created the Pixmap.

If your application creates many Pixmaps (or very large Pixmaps) you probably should use a round-trip call immediately after each **XCreatePixmap** call, so you can avoid using each new Pixmap until you are sure you successfully created it. A good call to use is **XGetGeometry** (see the next section); you can attempt to retrieve the size of the newly created Pixmap. If the delivery of a BadAlloc error message event or a zero status return from **XGetGeometry** informs you that your **XCreatePixmap** request failed, you can try to recover by destroying some other Pixmap (preferably a large one) and trying the request again. Of course, to detect and recover from BadAlloc error event messages, you must write and establish an error event handler (see "Application-Defined Error Event Handling" in Chapter 3).

## Determining Pixmap Size

**XGetGeometry** (*Xlib* ¶4.1) is a round-trip request for finding out the width, height, and depth of any Drawable: any Pixmap or window. It has the form

```
Display *display;              /* pointer to Display structure */
Drawable drawable;             /* drawable for which to retrieve size*/
Window root;                   /* root window of drawable */
int x,y;                       /* origin of drawable */
unsigned int width, height;    /* size of drawable  */
unsigned int border_width;     /* border_width of drawable */
unsigned int depth;            /* depth of drawable */
Status status;                 /* status returned */
    . . .
status = XGetGeometry ( display, drawable,
                        &root, &x, &y, &width, &height,
                        &border_width, &depth );
```

This request retrieves the dimensions and root window of the Pixmap (or window) you specify in the *drawable* parameter. The returned *root* window identifier specifies the root window of the screen for which the drawable was created. *x* and *y* return the origin of the *drawable*; they both return values of zero if the *drawable* is a Pixmap. *width* and *height* return the size of the drawable. *border_width* returns the *drawable* window's border width, or zero if the *drawable* is a Pixmap. Finally, *depth* returns the depth of the Pixmap.

The *status* value of zero is returned by **XGetGeometry** if the operation succeeds. The only reason the operation can fail is if you specify an invalid *drawable* parameter, in which case a nonzero *status* value is returned.

## Pixmap Deletion

When your application no longer needs Pixmaps, you can explicitly delete them by using the **XFreePixmap** request. Ordinarily, though, the workstation deletes Pixmaps automatically when you close your application's display connection, so you probably do not need to delete them explicitly. The rules for Pixmap lifetime are the same as for any other X resource (see Chapter 3).

**XFreePixmap** (*Xlib* ¶5.2) is suitable for deleting Pixmaps created by **XCreate-Pixmap**, **XReadBitmapFile**, or **XCreateBitmapFromData**. It has the form

```
Display *display;        /* pointer to Display structure */
Pixmap pixmap;           /* pixmap to delete */
    . . .
XFreePixmap ( display, pixmap );
```

This request destroys the specified *pixmap*. If *pixmap* is being referred to by other X resources (for example, as the current tile or stipple attribute in a **GC**) at the time you issue the **XFreePixmap** request, *pixmap* is not destroyed until no references to it remain. In any case, your application must not refer to *pixmap* in any subsequent requests.

# BITMAPS

The term *bitmap* in the X Window System can refer to two different things:

- A *bitmap* resource is a Pixmap with depth one.

- A *bitmap file* is a text file containing ASCII information suitable for loading into a *bitmap* resource.

Bitmaps are useful for many things, including stipple patterns, clip masks, and cursor patterns. Bitmap files are formatted so they can be incorporated into C-language programs using the **#include** directive. *Xlib* provides functions, summarized in Table 8-II, to convert bitmap files to and from bitmap resources.

| Request/Function | Xlib ¶ | Description |
|---|---|---|
| **XReadBitmapFile** | 10.10 | Create a bitmap from a file |
| **XWriteBitmapFile** | 10.10 | Write a bitmap to a file |
| **XCreateBitmapFromData** | 10.10 | Create and load a bitmap from data |
| **XCreatePixmapFromBitmapData** | 10.10 | Create and load a pixmap from data |

Table 8-II. *Xlib* calls for bitmap handling.

In most Unix-based X implementations, a collection of bitmap files can be found in the directory **/usr/include/X11/bitmaps**.

> The Pixmaps you use for backgrounds, borders, and tile patterns must have the same depth as your windows. Avoid the direct use of bitmap calls to create Pixmaps for these uses; remember that monochrome one-plane workstations cannot tell bitmaps apart from general Pixmaps.

## Bitmap File Format

Figure 8-1 shows an example of a bitmap, named "arrow." The contents of the bitmap file describing this bitmap are as follows:

```
#define arrow_width 16
#define arrow_height 16
#define arrow_x_hot 12
#define arrow_y_hot 1
static char arrow_bits[ ] = {
    0x00, 0x00, 0x00, 0x10, 0x00, 0x18, 0x00, 0x1c,
    0x00, 0x1e, 0x00, 0x1f, 0x80, 0x1f, 0xc0, 0x1f,
    0xe0, 0x1f, 0x00, 0x1f, 0x00, 0x1b, 0x80, 0x11,
    0x80, 0x01, 0xc0, 0x00, 0xc0, 0x00, 0x00, 0x00};
```

*[handwritten annotations: 16 × 16 = 256 pixels; Really BYTES 32  Ea. BYTE = 8 pixels]*

Bitmap files can be written by the **bitmap(1)** utility program, or by the **XWriteBitmapFile** call. Notice that the contents of the bitmap file have the form of a C language declaration. Each bitmap file contains the following definitions:

width, height   The size of the bitmap in pixels. The width and height may be any number; they need not be multiples of eight.

x_hot, y_hot   The position of the bitmap's hotspot. (The arrow's tip is its

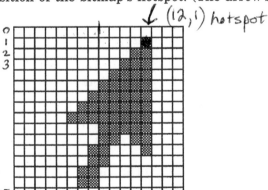

*[handwritten annotation: 0x10₁₆ = ; (12,1) hotspot]*

Figure 8-1. Example bitmap, enlarged to show individual pixels.

hotspot, in row 1 and column 12, counting from zero.) Many bitmaps do not have hotspots; in these bitmaps the x_hot and y_hot definitions are omitted.

bits

NOTE

An array of bytes initialized to contain the bits of the bitmap. The low-order bit of the array's first byte contains the leftmost pixel of the first row of the bitmap. The remaining bits of the first byte contain the next seven bits of the first row. Subsequent bytes go on to complete the first bitmap row, then complete the rest of the bitmap rows in order. Each new row begins with the low-order bit of a new byte.

Note that the symbols in the bitmap file are prefixed with the name of the bitmap: "arrow_width" and "arrow_height" in the example. These prefixes are provided for the convenience of C programs which incorporate bitmaps using **#include** directives.

## Reading Bitmap Files

Your application can use *Xlib*'s **XReadBitmapFile** utility to read a bitmap file and create a Pixmap. **XReadBitmapFile** (*Xlib* ¶10.10) has the form

```
Display *display;          /* pointer to Display structure */
Drawable drawable;         /* specifies which screen the Pixmap is on*/
char filename [ ];         /* file name */
unsigned int width;        /* width of bitmap*/
unsigned int height;       /* height of bitmap*/
Pixmap pixmap;             /* created Pixmap's resource ID */
int x_hot, y_hot;          /* bitmap's hotspot coordinates*/
int status;                /* returned status */
    . . .
status = XReadBitmapFile ( display, drawable, filename,
                           &width, &height,
                           &pixmap, &x_hot, &y_hot );
```

As input parameters, you specify a *drawable* and a *filename*. The *drawable* parameter specifies the Pixmap's screen exactly as it does in the **XCreatePixmap** request (see earlier in this chapter). The *filename* is a standard null-terminated string containing the path name of an existing bitmap file. The file must be accessible to the CPU running your application (but not necessarily accessible to the workstation CPU), and you must have permission to read it. The file must have either the standard X Version 11 bitmap file format or the format used by X Version 10.

**XReadBitmapFile** returns the *width* and *height* of the bitmap in the file to you. It also returns the X resource identifier of the *pixmap* it created, and the coordinates of the bitmap's hotspot in *x_hot* and *y_hot*. (If the bitmap file does not specify a hotspot, the value -1 is returned for *x_hot* and *y_hot*.)

Note that **XReadBitmapFile** ignores symbol prefixes (like "arrow_") showing the bitmap's name.

The *status* informs you of the success or failure of the operation. *status* has one of four values (defined in the header file **<X11/Xutil.h>**):

BitmapSuccess      The operation succeeded.

BitmapOpenFailed  The file cannot be read, because it does not exist, or because your application has insufficient permission.

BitmapFileInvalid  The file does not contain valid bitmap data.

BitmapNoMemory   The bitmap is too large for available memory.

---
**Example**: Create a window background from a bitmap file
---

The code excerpt of this example shows the steps necessary to create a window background Pixmap from a bitmap file.

Note that we must create two Pixmaps; one we create using **XReadBitmapFile**, and the other using **XCreatePixmap**. We then must draw pixel values into the second Pixmap using **XCopyPlane** and a **GC** resource created for the purpose. Only then can we use **XSetWindow-BackgroundPixmap**.

```
#include   <X11/Xutil.h>
. . .
Display * display;
Window window;      /* window to receive new background */
Window root;
Pixmap bitmap, backg;
GC gc;
int wx,wy;
unsigned int wwidth, wheight, wdepth, wborder;
unsigned int width, height;
int status;
. . .
XGetGeometry  ( display, window, &root, &wx, &wy,
                     &wwidth, &wheight, &wborder, &wdepth );
status = XReadBitmapFile ( display, root,
                     "/usr/include/X11/bitmaps/gray",
                     &width, &height, &bitmap, 0, 0 );
if (status != BitmapSuccess) { /* error ... */ }
backg = XCreatePixmap ( display, root, width, height, wdepth );
if (backg == None) { /* error ... */ }
gc = XCreateGC ( display, backg, 0, 0 );
```

```
if (gc == None) { /* error ... */ }
XSetForeground  ( display, gc,
                      BlackPixel (display, DefaultScreen(display)) );
XSetBackground  ( display, gc,
                      WhitePixel (display, DefaultScreen(display)) );
XSetGraphicsExposures ( display, gc, False );
XCopyPlane ( display, bitmap, backg, gc, 0, 0, width, height, 0, 0, 1 );
XFreePixmap ( display, bitmap );
XFreeGC ( display, gc );
XSetWindowBackgroundPixmap  ( display, window, backg );
```

## Writing Bitmap Files

Your application can write the contents of a bitmap resource to a bitmap file with *Xlib*'s **XWriteBitmapFile** call. **XWriteBitmapFile** (*Xlib* ¶10.10) has the form

```
Display *display;          /* pointer to Display structure */
char filename [ ];          /* file name */
Pixmap pixmap;              /* bitmap's Pixmap */
unsigned int width;         /* width of bitmap*/
unsigned int height;        /* height of bitmap*/
int x_hot, y_hot;           /* bitmap's hotspot coordinates*/
int status;                 /* returned status */

  . . .
status  = XWriteBitmapFile ( display, filename, pixmap, width, height,
                                 x_hot, y_hot );
```

In the *filename*, specify a standard null-terminated string containing the path name of the bitmap file you wish to create. The file will be created using the standard X Version 11 bitmap file format.

Use the *width* and *height* parameters to specify the size of the bitmap. If the bitmap has a hotspot, use the *x_hot* and *y_hot* parameters to specify its position, otherwise specify the value -1 for *x_hot* and *y_hot*.

Notice that **XWriteBitmapFile** uses the leaf name of your *filename* to write the bitmap's symbol prefix. For example, if you wrote a bitmap using the path name **/usr/staff/oj/myarrow**, the resulting bitmap's size would be defined by the symbols myarrow_width and myarrow_height.

The *status* informs you of the success or failure of the operation. *status* has one of three values (defined in the header file **<X11/Xutil.h>**):

BitmapSuccess        The operation succeeded.

BitmapOpenFailed   The file cannot be written, because the directory you
                   specified does not exist, or because your application has
                   insufficient permission.

BitmapNoMemory   The bitmap is too large for available memory.

## Creating Bitmap Resources from Data

You can incorporate bitmap data into your program in three ways:

- By using the **#include** directive of the C language to read a bitmap
  file written by **XWriteBitmapFile** or by the **bitmap(1X)** utility
  program

- By defining the size and contents of the bitmap as declarations directly in your program

- By computing the size and contents of the bitmap.

Your application can create a one-plane Pixmap and load it with your bitmap
data using *Xlib*'s **XCreateBitmapFromData** utility function.  **XCreateBitmapFromData** (*Xlib* ¶10.10) has the form

```
Display *display;          /* pointer to Display structure */
Drawable drawable;         /* specifies which screen the Pixmap is on*/
char data [ ];             /* character array containing bitmap data */
unsigned int width;        /* width of bitmap*/
unsigned int height;       /* height of bitmap*/
Pixmap pixmap;             /* created Pixmap's resource ID */
   . . .
pixmap = XCreateBitmapFromData ( display, drawable,
                                 data, width, height );
```

The *drawable* parameter specifies the Pixmap's screen exactly as it does in the
**XCreatePixmap** request (see earlier in this chapter).

The *width* and *height* parameters specify the size of the bitmap.   The *data*
parameter is a pointer to an array of bytes containing the bits.

**XCreateBitmapFromData** returns the X resource identifier of the *pixmap* it
created, or the value None (zero) if the workstation did not have enough memory
to create the bitmap.

Your application can create a multiple-plane Pixmap and load it with your
bitmap data using *Xlib*'s **XCreatePixmapFromBitmapData** utility function.
**XCreatePixmapFromBitmapData** (*Xlib* ¶10.10) has the form

```
Display *display;          /* pointer to Display structure */
Drawable drawable;         /* specifies which screen the Pixmap is on*/
char data [ ];             /* character array containing bitmap data */
unsigned int width;        /* width of bitmap*/
```

```
unsigned int height;          /* height of bitmap*/
unsigned long fg;             /* foreground pixel value */
unsigned long bg;             /* background pixel value */
unsigned int depth;           /* depth of created Pixmap */
Pixmap pixmap;                /* created Pixmap's resource ID */
  . . .
pixmap   = XCreatePixmapFromBitmapData ( display, drawable,
                                         data, width, height,
                                         fg, bg, depth );
```

**XCreatePixmapFromBitmapData** creates a Pixmap of the specified *depth*, and loads it with the bitmap data you specify. The *foreground* and *background* pixel values are written into the newly created Pixmap in positions corresponding to one and zero values in the bitmap *data* you specify.

The *drawable*, *data*, *width*, and *height* parameters have the same meanings as they do for **XCreateBitmapFromData**.

**XCreatePixmapFromBitmapData** returns the X resource identifier of the *pixmap* it created, or the value None (zero) if the workstation did not have enough memory to create the bitmap.

# IMAGES

*Xlib* provides support for image manipulation. Because the X display connection between the application and the workstation is a network link, images are hard to handle in the X environment. Images present *Xlib* with two major difficulties:

- Images typically contain large amounts of data. For example, a 512x512-pixel image with eight bits per pixel consumes a quarter-megabyte. *Xlib* takes a substantial amount of time (dozens of seconds) to convert such an image to protocol wire-format and transmit it over a display connection. Thus, it was necessary to design *Xlib* to minimize the frequency of such operations. Likewise, you should avoid designing your applications to need such operations frequently.

- The application's CPU and the workstation's CPU can be different makes and models. Different computer models often encode the bits within pixel values in different orders. *Xlib* must take this into account when transmitting images over a display connection.

To reduce the effect of these two problems on application programs, the designers of *Xlib* chose to represent images inside application programs using data structures known as **XImage** structures. *Xlib* provides utility functions for creating, deleting, and operating on pixel values in **XImage** structures. Your application can manipulate an image internally (by reading and writing pixel values) using these utility functions. *Xlib* also provides requests to transfer the pixels in **XImage** structures (or rectangular parts of **XImage** structures) back and forth between workstation and application.

Another nasty problem presents itself to programmers of image applications. As Chapter 7 discussed at length, pixel values in X represent color cells allocated from color maps. When you request color cells, X tells you the pixel values to use, rather than the other way around. If you allocate color cells from any color map that is being shared with other applications, it is unlikely that X will let you use the same pixel values each time you run your application. This means that you cannot directly use the pixel values from images you have previously stored. There are a couple of ways to get around this inconvenience:

- Create and use a private color map. If you do this, you can allocate all the color cells in the color map and initialize them in such a way that your stored pixel values will display with the colors you expect. This is fast and easy. However, most workstations display some windows in false colors when applications swap color maps in and out.

- Allocate color cells from a shared color map, using one of the color strategies discussed in Chapter 7. Translate your stored image's pixel values into the ones you got back from color cell allocation before you send the image to the workstation. This strategy is potentially quite slow and cumbersome, but if you use it your application's windows can coexist peacefully with others.

| Call | Xlib ¶ | Description |
|------|--------|-------------|
| **XCreateImage** | 10.9 | Create an empty **XImage** structure |
| **XSubImage** | 10.9 | Extract a rectangular subset from an image |
| **XPutPixel** | 10.9 | Store a pixel value into an image |
| **XGetPixel** | 10.9 | Retrieve a pixel value from an image |
| **XAddPixel** | 10.9 | Add a constant to all pixel values in an image |
| **XPutImage** | 6.7 | Draw an image into a window or Pixmap |
| **XGetImage** | 6.7 | Create an **XImage** with pixels from a drawable |
| **XGetSubImage** | 6.7 | Store drawable pixels into an existing **XImage** |
| **XDestroyImage** | 10.9 | Destroy an *Xlib*-created **XImage** structure |

Table 8-III. *Xlib* calls for image manipulation.

Note that X's graphic primitive requests (**XFillRectangle** and **XDrawText**, for example; see Chapters 5 and 6) do not operate on images in **XImage** structures. If you wish to compose an image by drawing it with graphic primitive requests, you must do so in a window or Pixmap on the workstation. When you finish drawing, you can retrieve your image in **XImage** form by using **XGetImage** or **XGetSubImage**.

All *Xlib*'s image manipulation functions make use of the **XImage** data structure. Many applications can simply use the image manipulation functions and do not need to examine the contents of the **XImage** structure. However, some applications need direct access to **XImage** structures. The section near the end of this chapter entitled "Image Data Structures" opens up the **XImage** structure to reveal its contents.

## Image Creation

**XCreateImage** is a utility function used for allocating memory for an **XImage** structure and initializing the structure. Your application should use this function when you want to create an image from scratch. (If you wish to create an **XImage** structure from pixels on a workstation, you should use **XGetImage** instead.)

**XCreateImage** is also useful when you already have stored the pixel values for an image in an array in your application, possibly by using a graphics software package other than *Xlib*. Once you create an **XImage** structure for such an image, you can use the **XPutImage** request (see under the heading "Sending Images to the Workstation" later in this chapter) to display the image on the workstation.

**XCreateImage** allocates memory for the **XImage** structure, but not the image itself. Your application must supply a pointer to the memory you want to use for storing the pixel values of the image; **XCreateImage** assumes that you allocate this memory somewhere else in your application. **XCreateImage** does not initialize your pixel-value memory, or alter it in any way.

**XCreateImage** (*Xlib* ¶10.9) has the form

| | |
|---|---|
| **Display** *`*display;`* | `/* pointer to Display structure */` |
| **Visual** * `visual;` | `/* pointer to `**Visual**` structure describing the image*/` |
| unsigned int `depth;` | `/* image depth*/` |
| int `format;` | `/* image format: XYBitmap, XYPixmap, or ZPixmap*/` |
| int `offset;` | `/* pixels to ignore at beginning of each scanline*/` |
| char * `data;` | `/* pointer to pixel-value data*/` |
| unsigned int `width;` | `/* image scan line width*/` |
| unsigned int `height;` | `/* number of image scan lines*/` |
| int `bitmap_pad;` | `/* alignment of scanline rows: 8, 16, or 32 */` |
| int `bytes_per_line;` | `/* the number of bytes between sucessive scanlines*/` |
| **XImage** * `image;` | `/* pointer to newly created `**XImage**` */` |

... 

    *image* = **XCreateImage** ( *display, visual, depth, format, offset, data,*
                              *width, height, bitmap_pad, bytes_per_line* );

**XCreateImage**, given parameters describing the size and format of the image, allocates and initializes an **XImage** structure. The function call returns a pointer to that structure. If **XCreateImage** fails (because no more memory is available or because you specified incorrect parameter values), it returns a null pointer.

If your image is designed for a DirectColor or TrueColor visual class, use the *visual* parameter to specify a pointer to a **Visual** structure (see Chapter 7 under the heading "Default Visual Information"). The **Visual** structure should be the one describing the window you will use on the workstation to display your image. Many workstations only supply one **Visual** structure; on such workstations you can use the *Xlib* macro **DefaultVisual** to supply a value for the *visual* parameter. See the example at the end of this section.

If your image is designed for any other visual class (PseudoColor, StaticColor, GrayScale, or StaticGray), you may, if you prefer, take a shortcut and specify a *visual* parameter value of None. However, for compatibility, it is best to always specify a usable **Visual** pointer.

The *depth* and *format* parameters together specify the number of planes (bits per pixel) in the image and the way the image is laid out in your application program's memory. The *format* parameter can have one of three symbolic values (defined in **<X11/X.h>**):

XYBitmap   The image is a bitmap; it must have a *depth* of one. The image is packed into memory one bit per pixel. If you use this *format*, subsequent **XPutImage** requests work like **XCopyPlane** (bit-BLT) requests. They apply foreground and background pixel values when drawing your image.

XYPixmap   The image may have any *depth* (one or greater). The *depth* must be the same as that of any drawable you will use on the workstation to display your image. The image is organized in memory as an array of individual bit planes, indexed from zero to the value of *depth*. The bits of each plane are packed into memory, one bit per pixel. The XYPixmap format is often known as a "plane-mode" image. If you use this *format*, subsequent **XPutImage** requests work like **XCopyArea** (pixel-BLT) requests. They do not apply foreground or background pixel values when drawing your image. Instead, **XPutImage** uses pixel values directly from your image.

ZPixmap   Like XYPixmap, the image may have any *depth*, as long as it is the same as that of the Drawable to be used. Unlike XYPixmap, however, a ZPixmap image is organized in memory as an array of pixel values. The ZPixmap format is often known as a "pixel-mode" image, and is most useful with 8-bit or 32-bit pixel values. If you use this *format*, subsequent **XPutImage** requests work like **XCopyArea** (pixel BLT) requests. They do not apply foreground or background pixel values when drawing your image. Instead, **XPutImage** uses pixel values directly from your image.

The *offset* specifies a number of pixels to ignore at the beginning of each scan-line. The *offset* is most useful for inserting padding into bitmaps or plane-mode images at the beginning of scanlines. Most images created by applications have *offset* values of zero.

In *data*, you specify a pointer to the image pixel-value memory. You may specify a value of None, and fill in the corresponding **XImage** field later if you prefer. For example, see the end of this section.

*width* and *height* specify the size of the image. The image has the number of scan lines you specify in *height*. Each scan line has the *width* you specify.

Although an image may have an arbitrary width, the first pixel value for each scan line always begins on a natural addressing boundary. In *bitmap_pad*, you specify which kind of natural boundary begins each scanline. A *bitmap_pad* value of 8 specifies that each scan line begins on a byte boundary. Likewise, *bitmap_pad* values of 16 and 32 specify that each scan line begins on a short or long integer boundary. *Xlib* pads the ends of scan lines to bring the beginning of the next scan line to the natural boundary you specify.

In *bytes_per_line*, you specify how many bytes lie between the starting pixels of consecutive scan lines. You may specify a value of zero for *bytes_per_line*, in which case **XCreateImage** assumes that your image's scan lines (padded according to *bitmap_pad*) are contiguous in memory.

When you are finished using an **XImage** structure created by **XCreateImage**, use **XFree** to deallocate the **XImage** structure.

### Example: Create an image

In this example, we create a 100x200-pixel image. We use the default depth and **Visual** structure to determine the *depth, format*, and image size. This code example uses **XCreateImage** to set up the **XImage** structure. It then uses the standard malloc function to allocate memory for the image.

```
Display *display;
Visual * visual;
unsigned int depth;
int screen;
int format;
unsigned int width;
unsigned int height;
int bitmap_pad;
XImage * image;
 . . .
width  = 100;  height  = 200;
screen  = DefaultScreen ( display );
depth  = DefaultDepth ( display, screen );
if ( depth == 1) {
    format = XYPixmap;        /* bitmap, but useful for pixel BLT */
    bitmap_pad  = 32;         /* long  alignment */
```

```
      }
      else { /* more than one deep */
          format = ZPixmap;        /* deep Pixmap, useful for pixel BLT */
          bitmap_pad = 8;
          if ( depth > 8 ) bitmap_pad = 32;
      }
      image  = XCreateImage ( display, DefaultVisual ( display, screen ),
                                  depth, format, 0, 0, width, height,
                                  bitmap_pad, 0 );
      if ( image == 0 ) { /* XImage structure allocation failure */
      image->data = malloc ( image->bytes_per_line * height );
      if ( image->data == 0 ) { /* image memory allocation failure */
```

In this example, we specify zero for the *bytes_per_line* parameter, and allow **XCreateImage** to compute the correct value. We then retrieve that value from the **XImage** structure and use it to compute the amount of memory to allocate for the image. We store the pointer to the allocated memory into the **XImage** structure. For details of the **XImage** structure, see "Image Data Structures" later in this chapter.

---

## Subimages

The **XSubImage** utility function copies a rectangular portion of an existing image into a new image, allocating and creating a new **XImage** structure in the process. This utility function (unlike **XCreateImage**) also allocates memory for the pixel values it copies. **XSubImage** (*Xlib* ¶10.9) requires the header file **<X11/Xutil.h>** and has the form

```
      #include   <X11/Xutil.h>
      . . .
      XImage * source;      /* pointer to source XImage */
      int x;                /* x-coordinate of subimage upper left corner */
      int y;                /* y-coordinate of subimage upper left corner */
      unsigned int width;   /* width of subimage */
      unsigned int height;  /* height of subimage */
      XImage * image;       /* pointer to newly created XImage */
      . . .
      image  = XSubImage ( source, x, y, width, height );
```

**XSubImage** differs from most *Xlib* functions in that its first parameter is not a **Display** pointer. You specify, in the *source* parameter, a pointer to a previously existing **XImage** structure. In *x, y, width*, and *height*, you specify the rectangle you wish to copy. *x* and *y* are the coordinates of the rectangle's upper left corner relative to the *source* image. As with Pixmaps and windows, an image's upper left corner has the coordinates (0,0).

**XSubImage** allocates and initializes a new **XImage** structure. It then allocates memory for the subimage and stores a pointer to that memory in the **XImage** structure. It copies the pixels from the *source* image to the newly created image. Finally, it returns a pointer to the new **XImage** structure.

**XSubImage** is not, strictly speaking, a single function. It is actually a macro providing transparent access to a bitmap-format-specific function in a dispatch table in the **XImage** structure (see under the heading "Image Data Structures"). The macro is defined in the **<X11/Xutil.h>** header file.

## Pixel Access

*Xlib* provides three ways for your application to operate on pixel values in an image: **XGetPixel, XPutPixel,** and **XAddPixel**. These calls all operate on pixel values one at a time. In particular, they work the same regardless of the image *format*: they work pixel-by-pixel even in XYPixmap-format images, where they have to assemble the pixel values from several planes.

**XGetPixel** retrieves a single pixel value from an image, and **XPutPixel** stores a single pixel value into an image. **XGetPixel** and **XPutPixel** (*Xlib* ¶10.9) require the header file **<X11/Xutil.h>** and have the form

```
#include   <X11/Xutil.h>
. . .
XImage * image;        /* pointer to XImage */
int x;                 /* x-coordinate of pixel */
int y;                 /* y-coordinate of pixel */
long pixel;            /* pixel value */
int status;            /* returned status*/
. . .
pixel = XGetPixel ( image, x, y );
. . .
status = XPutPixel ( image, x, y, pixel );
```

These calls differ from most *Xlib* calls in that their first parameters are not **Display** pointers. You specify, in the *image* parameter, a pointer to an **XImage** structure. In *x* and *y*, you specify the coordinates of the pixel to operate on. As with Pixmaps and windows, the upper left corner of images has the coordinates (0,0).

**XGetPixel** fetches a *pixel* value from the image, and **xPutPixel** stores a *pixel* value. **XPutPixel** returns a non-zero *status* when it succeeds, and a zero *status* if it fails (but in the first release of X version 11, **XPutPixel** always succeeds).

**XAddPixel** adds a constant value to every pixel value in an image. **XAdd-Pixel** might be useful, for example, to apply a base_pixel value from a standard colormap (see Chapter 7 under the heading "The XStandardColormap structure"). **XAddPixel** (*Xlib* ¶10.9) requires the header file **<X11/Xutil.h>** and has the form

```
#include   <X11/Xutil.h>
. . .
XImage * image;        /* pointer to XImage */
long value;            /* value by which to increment all pixels */
. . .
XAddPixel ( image, value );
```

This call differs from most *Xlib* calls in that its first parameter is not a **Display** pointer. You specify, in the *image* parameter, a pointer to an **XImage** structure. In the *value* parameter, you specify a number. **XAddPixel** adds the specified *value* to every pixel in the *image*.

**XGetPixel**, **XPutPixel**, and **XAddPixel** are not functions. They are actually macros like **XSubImage**.

## Sending Images to the Workstation

Once you have prepared an image in your application's memory, you can draw it (or any rectangular part of it) into a window or Pixmap on the workstation using the **XPutImage** request. **XPutImage** is a graphic primitive request. Like other graphic primitive requests, it uses a **GC** to set up the graphics pipeline as described in Chapter 5. The **GC** Clip, Window Clip, and Raster output stages of the pipeline are all applied to **XPutImage** requests.

The patterning stage's operation depends, however, on the format of the image This is why it is important to create the image with the correct format. If the image format is XYBitmap, the patterning stage works in the same way as it does for an **XCopyPlane** request: the foreground pixel value attribute from the **GC** is applied to all pixels with value one in the image, and the background pixel value attribute to all pixels with value zero in the image. In other words, XYBitmap-format images are drawn with a bit-BLT operation.

If the image format is either XYPixmap or ZPixmap, on the other hand, the patterning stage works in the same way as it does for an **XCopyArea** request. The foreground and background pixel value attributes from the **GC** are ignored, and the pixel values from the image are sent directly to the clipping and raster output stages of the pipeline. In other words, XYPixmap and ZPixmap-format images are drawn with a pixel-BLT operation. When you create XYPixmap and ZPixmap-format images, take care to assign them an appropriate depth.

The fill_style, stipple, and tile attributes are completely ignored: no tiling or stippling is possible with the **XPutImage** request. All drawing takes place as if the fill_style value were FillSolid.

**XPutImage** (*Xlib* ¶6.7) has the form

```
Display *display;        /* pointer to Display structure */
Drawable drawable;       /* destination for drawing*/
GC gc;                   /* GC for drawing */
XImage *image;           /* source image structure pointer*/
int src_x, src_y;        /* rectangle's upper left corner in source image */
int dst_x, dst_y;        /* rectangle's upper left corner in output */
unsigned int width;      /* width of image rectangle to display*/
unsigned int height;     /* height of image rectangle to display*/
   . . .
XPutImage ( display, drawable, gc, image,
                 src_x, src_y, dst_x, dst_y, width, height );
```

**XPutImage** draws a rectangular area of the *image* into the specified *drawable* using the attributes in the specified *gc*. The size of the rectangular area is defined by *width* and *height*. The upper left corner of the rectangle in the source *image* is defined by *src_x* and *src_y*, and in the destination *drawable* by *dst_x* and *dst_y*.

If the format of the source *image* is XYBitmap, its depth must be one. For other image formats, the depth of the source *image* must be the same as the depth of the destination *drawable*. This is why it is important to set the image depth correctly when creating the image.

If you only need to draw a very few pixels into a window or Pixmap, you can avoid the overhead of storing them into an image before sending them to the workstation: use **XDrawPoint** or **XDrawPoints**.

## Retrieving Images From the Workstation

Two requests, **XGetImage** and **XGetSubImage**, retrieve rectangular arrays of pixels from the workstation. Both requests make the pixels available to your application as images. **XGetImage** fetches pixels and creates a new **XImage** structure to describe them, whereas **XGetSubImage** updates a portion of an existing image with the pixel values it fetches.

## XGetImage

The **XGetImage** function is especially useful for retrieving information from the screen so it can be sent to a pixel-oriented hardcopy device. However, it can be used for many other purposes. It fetches a rectangular array of pixels, creating an **XImage** structure for them in the process. **XGetImage** (*Xlib* ¶6.7) has the form

```
Display *display;        /* pointer to Display structure */
Drawable drawable;       /* source drawable for pixels */
GC gc;                   /* GC for drawing */
int x, y;                /* rectangle's upper left corner in drawable */
unsigned int width;      /* width of rectangle to fetch*/
```

```
unsigned int height;          /* height of rectangle to fetch*/
unsigned long plane_mask;     /* mask specifying planes to fetch */
int format;                   /* XYPixmap or ZPixmap */
XImage image;                 /* newly created image structure */
   . . .
image = XGetImage ( display, drawable,
                    x, y, width, height, plane_mask, format );
```

**XGetImage** fetches a rectangle of pixels from the specified *drawable*. The rectangle has the specified *width* and *height*. In the source *drawable*, the rectangle's upper left corner is specified by *x* and *y* relative to the origin of the *drawable*.

If the source *drawable* is a Pixmap, then the specified rectangle must lie entirely within its boundaries, otherwise the **XGetImage** request will generate a Bad-Match error event.

If the source *drawable* is a window, the window must be mapped and the specified rectangle must lie completely within the boundaries of the *drawable* window. Furthermore, the specified rectangle must not be in a part of the *drawable* that cannot be seen because it is clipped by any of the *drawable*'s ancestor windows. If the *drawable*'s parent window is the root window, this means that the specified rectangle must be on-screen.

For best results, the *drawable* window should be first in the stacking order: stacked on top of all its sibling windows. Retrieved pixel values are unpredictable in parts of the rectangle obscured by non-inferior windows. If your workstation provides backing store, this may not matter, however.

Also, for best results, all inferior windows which lie within the specified rectangle should have the same depth (number of bits per pixel) as the source *drawable* window.

The rectangle you specify may include the *drawable*'s border, as long as the border's pixels meet the conditions just discussed.

**XGetImage** loads the retrieved pixels into memory inside your application program, and creates an **XImage** structure describing the pixels. The *format* parameter specifies the format that the image should have. You may select either XYPixmap or ZPixmap.

The *plane_mask* specifies which planes (bits) of the pixel values should be fetched. If you wish to fetch all bits of the pixel values, specify -1 for the *plane_mask* value.

If the *format* is XYPixmap, the depth of the resulting image is set equal to the number of planes actually fetched (in no case larger than the depth of the *drawable*). Planes from the image corresponding to zero bits in the *plane_mask* are completely omitted. For example, suppose the depth of your drawable is eight planes, and you specify a *plane_mask* value of FF35 hexadecimal ( 1111 1111 0011 0101 binary). First of all, **XGetImage** ignores all but the low-order eight bits (35) of the *plane_mask* because your drawable only has eight planes. Of those eight planes, only four (planes 0, 2, 4, and 5, corresponding to the nonzero bits in your *plane_mask*) are sent back to your application, and the resulting XYPixmap-format image has a depth of four.

On the other hand, if the *format* is ZPixmap, the depth of the resulting image is set equal to the depth of the *drawable*. The pixel values in the resulting image all contain zeros in bit-positions corresponding to the zeroes in the *plane_mask*. If you used a *format* of ZPixmap in the preceding paragraph's example, the image would have a depth of eight: exactly the depth of your *drawable*. However, bit positions 1, 3, 6, and 7 of all the pixel values in the image (corresponding to the zero bits of your *plane_mask*) would be zero.

## XGetSubImage

The **XGetSubImage** function updates an existing image in your application program with pixel values retrieved from the workstation. **XGetSubImage** (*Xlib* ¶6.7) has the form

```
Display *display;          /* pointer to Display structure */
Drawable drawable;         /* source drawable for pixels */
GC gc;                     /* GC for drawing */
int x, y;                  /* rectangle's upper left corner in drawable
*/
unsigned int width;        /* width of rectangle to fetch*/
unsigned int height;       /* height of rectangle to fetch*/
unsigned long plane_mask;  /* mask specifying planes to fetch */
int format;                /* XYPixmap or ZPixmap */
XImage image;              /* destination image structure */
int dst_x, dst_y;          /* rectangle's upper left corner in image */
    . . .
image = XGetSubImage ( display, drawable,
                  x, y, width, height , plane_mask, format ,
                  image, dst_x, dst_y );
```

**XGetSubImage**, like **XGetImage**, fetches a rectangle of pixels from the specified *drawable*. The rectangle has the specified *width* and *height*. In the source *drawable*, the rectangle's upper left corner is specified by $x$ and $y$ relative to the origin of the *drawable*.

The constraints upon the source rectangle are the same for **XGetSubImage** as they are for **XGetImage** (see the preceding section). The fields of the destination *image* structure are not altered in any way by this request, so the resulting depth (which depends on the *format* and *plane_mask* just as it does for **XGetImage**) must match the existing image's depth. If the fetched rectangle does not fit within the destination *image*, it is clipped.

As a convenience, **XGetSubImage** returns a pointer to an **XImage** structure—the same structure you specify in the *image* parameter.

## Image Deletion

**XDestroyImage** is a utility call for deallocating an image created entirely by *Xlib*. It deallocates both the pixel-value memory and the **XImage** structure itself. Thus, it is suitable for deallocating images created by **XSubImage** and **XGet-Image**.

However, **XImage** structures you created with **XCreateImage** should be deallocated with **XFree**. Pixel-value memory for these images should be deallocated with the same memory-allocation package you used to allocate it.

**XDestroyImage** (*Xlib* ¶10.9) has the form

```
XImage * image; /* pointer to XImage */
  . . .
XDestroyImage ( image );
```

The only parameter accepted by **XDestroyImage** is the *image* pointer. Note that **XDestroyImage** differs from most *Xlib* functions in that its first parameter is not a **Display** pointer.

**XDestroyImage** is not a function. It is actually a macro, like **XSubImage**.

## Image Data Structures

The image manipulation functions all use the **XImage** data structure. The contents of the **XImage** data structure is well-defined; if you wish, you can write image-manipulation code which refers to **XImage** structures directly.

The complexity of the **XImage** structure and the pixel-value data it describes comes from the fact that it contains fields specifying how the bits and bytes within an image's pixel values are ordered. Computers built by different vendors often differ in the order in which bits and bytes are stored within words. Because the X Window System allows workstation server software to run on a different kind of CPU from client application software, X is designed to deal with the need for swapping bytes. *Xlib* transmits almost all requests to the workstation in the format appropriate for the CPU running the application, and the workstation is responsible for changing the order where necessary.

Image requests (such as **XGetImage** and **XPutImage**) are exceptions to this rule: *Xlib* receives and transmits image data for you using the bit and byte ordering most convenient for the workstation. Image byte ordering depends on the type of workstation CPU. Image bit ordering depends not only on the type of CPU, but on the way the CPU's display hardware stores pixel values. On some display hardware, the least significant bit of each bitmap word is displayed leftmost; on other display hardware it is rightmost.

The problem is that the workstation's bit and byte ordering is not necessarily the one that is best for your application's CPU. The bit and byte ordering varies from workstation to workstation. Therefore, to be portable, your application must allow for the various possibilities. The values of fields in the **XImage** data structure describe the bit and byte ordering, and may vary depending on the type of CPU running your application, and the make and model of the workstation at the other end of the display connection. If you want your application to be able to read and write an image's pixel value data directly (without the help of **XGet-Pixel** and **XPutPixel**), you must use the fields in the **XImage** structure to access the pixel values.

The **XImage** structure is defined (in **<X11/Xlib.h>**) as follows:

```
typedef struct _XImage {
  int width, height;          /* size of image */
  int xoffset;                /* number of pixels offset in X direction */
  int format;                 /* Bitmap, XYPixmap, ZPixmap */
  char *data;                 /* pointer to image data */
  int byte_order;             /* data byte order, LSBFirst, MSBFirst */
  int bitmap_unit;            /* quant. of scanline 8, 16, 32 */
  int bitmap_bit_order;       /* LeastSignificant, MostSignificant */
  int bitmap_pad;             /* 8, 16, 32 */
  int depth;                  /* depth of image */
  int bytes_per_line;         /* accelerator to next line */
  int bits_per_pixel;         /* bits per pixel (ZFormat) */
  unsigned long red_mask;     /* bits in z arrangement */
  unsigned long green_mask;
  unsigned long blue_mask;
  char *obdata;               /* hook for object routines to hang on */
  struct funcs {              /* image manipulation routines */
    struct _XImage *(*create_image)();
    int (*destroy_image)();
    unsigned long (*get_pixel)();
    int (*put_pixel)();
    struct _XImage *(*sub_image)();
    int (*add_pixel)();
  } f;
} XImage;
```

After using an *Xlib* function to create an **XImage** structure, you can refer to and, if you are careful, alter fields in the structure. Some of the fields have symbolic values (such as LSBFirst); these symbols are defined in the header file **<X11/X.h>**. The fields have the following meanings:

width, height    These fields define the size of the image in pixels. An image is made of several *scan lines*, or rows of pixels. The number of pixels in each scan line is the width of the image, and the number of scan lines is the height.

xoffset    This field specifies how many pixels to ignore at the beginning of each scan line. It only applies to XYBitmap- and

XYPixmap-format images (it is zero in ZPixmap images). An image made by the **XGetImage** call may have a small positive xoffset. Each new scan line of an image begins in a new quantum (see bitmap_unit) of memory. The xoffset specifies by how many bits the left end of each scan line is padded. xoffset allows a workstation to send and receive a plane-mode image byte-for-byte without shifting all the bit positions, even when the scan lines of the image do not begin exactly on byte boundaries. The values of the bits within the pad at the beginning of each scan line are unpredictable. The width of each scan line (as specified in the width field) does not include the pad bits.

format
: This field may have one of the values XYBitmap, XYPixmap, or ZPixmap. The meanings of these values are described earlier in this chapter under the heading "Image Creation."

data
: This field is the pointer to the image's pixel-value data. When you use **XSubImage** or **XGetImage** to create an **XImage** data structure, *Xlib* allocates memory for the pixel values and fills in this field. When you allocate an **XImage** structure with **XCreateImage**, you must put the address of your pixel value data into the data field yourself.

byte_order
: This field may have one of the values LSBFirst (least-significant byte first), or MSBFirst (most-significant byte first). It specifies the order in which the bytes of each quantum (see bitmap_unit) are stored in image memory.

bitmap_unit
: This field may have one of the values 8, 16, or 32. It defines the number of bits in each quantum of scanline memory.

bitmap_bit_order
: This field may have one of the values LSBFirst or MSBFirst. It defines the graphical ordering of bits within each memory quantum (see bitmap_unit) of a bitmap. When the bitmap_bit_order is LSBFirst, the leftmost (on-screen) bit of each quantum is the least significant bit. When bitmap_bit_order is MSBFirst, the leftmost bit of each quantum is the most significant bit. This field does not apply to ZPixmap-format images.

bitmap_pad
: This field may have one of the values 8, 16, or 32. The end of each scanline in image memory is padded such that the next scanline begins on a byte boundary (when bitmap_pad is 8), short integer boundary (when bitmap_pad is 16), or long integer boundary (when bitmap_pad is 32).

depth
: This field specifies the depth (bits per pixel) of the image.

bytes_per_line

This field specifies the number of bytes between the starting pixels of consecutive scan lines. The value of this field takes into account the values of the xoffset and bitmap_pad fields. In all image formats, you may compute a pointer to the $n$th scan line as follows:

```
XImage * image;
char * ptr;
int n;

. . .

ptr = ( n * image->bytes_per_line ) +
            image->data;
```

bits_per_pixel

This field specifies the number of bits per pixel as stored for ZPixmap-format images. It can have one of the values 1, 4, 8, 16, 24, and 32. The pixel values are packed into memory in the order specified by bitmap_bit_order and byte_order. The bits_per_pixel field does not apply to XYBitmap- or XYPixmap-format images.

red_mask

This field, copied from the field of the same name in a **Visual** structure, specifies which bits of each pixel are used for the red subfield. This field is only meaningful for Direct-Color or TrueColor images.

green_mask

This field is the same as red_mask, except that it specifies the bits for the green subfield.

blue_mask

This field is the same as red_mask, except that it specifies the bits for the blue subfield.

struct funcs {...} f;

The **XImage** structure ends with a dispatch table containing the addresses of routines which actually implement **XCreateImage**, **XDestroyImage**, **XGetPixel**, **XPutPixel**, **XSubImage**, and **XAddPixel**. *Xlib* fills in this dispatch table with the appropriate functions when it creates each new **XImage** structure. The image-manipulation routine names are actually declared as macros (in **<X11/Xutil.h>**) which make their calls using this dispatch table.

The way an image's pixel values are laid out in memory depends on fields in the **XImage** structure. The three fundamental image formats are, of course, known as XYBitmap, XYPixmap, and ZPixmap. The following sections discuss the layout of each format.

## XYBitmap Image Format

XYBitmap-format images are one-plane bitmaps. A bitmap is made of scan-lines of packed bits, each one of which is a pixel value. The way the bits are packed in memory depends on the following **XImage** fields:

| | |
|---|---|
| format | The value XYBitmap. |
| data | Pointer to the beginning of scan-line zero (the first one). |
| width | The number of usable pixels (exclusive of pads) in each scan line. |
| height | The number of scan lines in the image. |
| bytes_per_line | The number of bytes between first pixels of consecutive scan lines. |
| bitmap_unit | One of the values 8, 16, or 32, specifying whether bits are packed into bytes, short integers, or long integer quanta. |
| bitmap_bit_order | Specifies (using values LSBFirst or MSBFirst) the graphical ordering of bits within each memory quantum. |
| byte_order | Specifies (using values LSBFirst or MSBFirst) the ordering of bytes within each quantum. |
| bitmap_pad | The padding at the end of scan lines, to round out the length of the scan line to an integral number of bytes, short integers, or long integers. |
| xoffset | The actual number of pixels of padding at the beginning of each scan line. |
| depth | The value 1 (bitmaps must be exactly one plane deep). |

### Example:  MakePixmapFromData

This example shows a routine to construct a deep Pixmap from bitmap-format data (see "Bitmap File Format" earlier in this chapter).  It works by initializing the fields of an **XImage** so they describe the bitmap data, then creating the Pixmap, then using **XPutImage** to load the Pixmap.  Note that the **XImage** structure is, in this example, a local variable; it is not allocated using **XCreateImage**.  A Pixmap created using this procedure is suitable for use as a background or border Pixmap, or tile pattern.

```
Pixmap MakePixmapFromData
        ( display, dr, data, w, h, d, fg, bg )
Display * display;    /* display pointer */
Drawable dr;          /* specifies root for pixmap */
char * data;          /* pointer to bitmap data */
unsigned int w,h;     /* width, height, of bitmap */
unsigned int d;       /* depth of Pixmap to create */
unsigned long fg, bg; /* foreground, background pixel values */
{
  XImage im;          /* Image structure */
  Pixmap p;           /* created Pixmap */
  GC gc;              /* GC for the XPutImage operation */
```

```
        /* set up XImage structure to match bitmap data */
    im.format = XYBitmap;
    im.width = w;
    im.height = h;
    im.xoffset = 0;
    im.byte_order = MSBFirst;
    im.bitmap_unit = 8;
    im.bitmap_bit_order = MSBFirst;
    im.bitmap_pad = 8;
    im.depth = 1;      /* it is a bitmap */
    im.bytes_per_line = (w+7) >> 3;
    im.data = data;
    p = XCreatePixmap ( display, dr, w, h, d );
    gc = XCreateGC ( display, p, 0, 0 );
    XSetForeground ( display, gc, fg );
    XSetBackground ( display, gc, bg );
    XPutImage ( display, p, gc, &im, 0,0,0,0,w,h );
    XFreeGC ( display, gc );
    return p;
}
```

## XYPixmap image format

XYPixmap-format images are organized as linear arrays of one-plane bitmaps. Except for the fact that they contain multiple bitmaps, XYPixmap-format images follow exactly the same rules for memory layout as XYBitmap-format images. All **XImage** fields in XYPixmap-format images have the same meanings as those for XYBitmap-format, with the following exceptions:

format               The value XYPixmap.
depth                The number of planes in the Pixmap.

The plane corresponding to the least significant bit of the pixel value comes *last*, *not first*, in the array of bitmaps. You may compute a pointer to the bitmap corresponding to the $n$th bit of the pixel value (where $n$ is zero for the least significant bit) as follows:

```
XImage * image;
char * bptr;
int n;
. . .
bptr = (( image->depth - (n + 1)) * image->bytes_per_line * image->height )
        + image->data;
```

## ZPixmap Image Format

ZPixmap-format images are rectangular arrays of pixel values. These pixel values may have any depth up to 32 bits per pixel. The way the pixel values are packed in memory depends on the following **XImage** fields:

format          The value ZPixmap.

data            Pointer to the first pixel of the first horizontal scan line.

width           The number of pixels in each scan line.

height          The number of scan lines in the image.

bytes_per_line  The number of bytes between consecutive scan lines.

depth           The actual number of bits per pixel used in the image.

bits_per_pixel  The number of bits per pixel *as stored* in the image. If this value is 1 or 4, pixel values are packed 8 to a byte or 2 to a byte respectively.

byte_order      Specifies (using values LSBFirst or MSBFirst) the ordering of bytes within each pixel value.

bitmap_pad      The padding at the end of scan lines, to round out their length to an integral number of bytes, short integers, or long integers.

# S U M M A R Y

Often applications must be able to draw *rasters*, or rectangular arrays of pixels. Some window **GC** attributes (backgrounds, borders, tile patterns, stipple patterns, and clip masks) also require you to specify rasters. The most common raster in the X window system is, of course, the window. However, X also provides Pixmaps. You can think of Pixmaps as stripped-down invisible windows: you can draw to them just as if they were windows, and then use them either as the source of copy operations or for attribute values in windows and **GC**s. You create Pixmap resources with the **XCreatePixmap** call. Ordinarily you create Pixmaps either with a depth of one (these are called *bitmaps*) or with the same depth as the windows you are using for display.

*Xlib* provides calls for handling *bitmap files*. Bitmap files are often used for storing such things as the shapes of cursors and stipple patterns. They are formatted in such a way that they can be **#include**d directly into C programs or read and written by *Xlib* routines.

You could conceivably draw an *image*, such as a digitized photograph, using repeated calls to **XSetForeground** and **XDrawPoint**. *Xlib* offers a better way, however. You can define and manipulate **XImage** structures in your application and use them to compose images locally. Once an image is composed, you may draw it all at once using **XPutImage**. X also allows you to retrieve the contents of windows and Pixmaps into **XImage** structures.

# CHAPTER 9
# THE MOUSE AND POINTER

Workstations that run the X Window System always have some sort of *pointing device,* ordinarily a mouse. However, any device (for example, a tablet or joystick) will work, as long as it responds to user action by delivering x and y coordinates and button-clicks to the workstation. Most workstations that support the X Window System come equipped with three-button mice, following a design originally based on Xerox's Smalltalk-80. In Smalltalk, the buttons were called Red, Yellow, and Blue to give some degree of independence from the physical mouse design. The Smalltalk-compatible buttons are arranged so that a user can push any combination of the three at the same time. Figure 9-1 shows an ordinary 3-button mouse.

Three-button mice are by no means universal, though. The Macintosh computer series manufactured by Apple Computer has a one-button mouse. Microsoft Corporation offers a two-button mouse. For a time, Digital Equipment Corporation sold VS100 workstations (for which early versions of the X Window System were developed) with a mouse that had a pair of rocker switches, each with two contact positions, for a total of four "buttons." X expresses no preference for any number of mouse buttons. X provides for up to five buttons, numbered 1-5.

Given the variety of mice, there are two reasonable strategies you can use to design a portable application. One alternative is to require a three-button mouse. Because most workstations furnish a three-button mouse, this is reasonable. The other strategy is to treat all mouse buttons identically, thus requiring a one-button mouse and supporting all mice with more buttons as if the buttons were wired together.

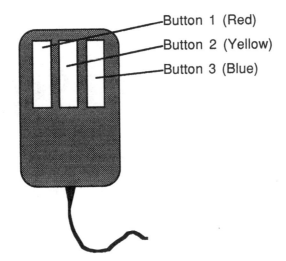

Figure 9-1. A three-button mouse.

A mouse uses an on-screen *tracking cursor*. The cursor is controlled by the X Window System. Unless your application intervenes, X makes the cursor respond to mouse motion automatically. The user controls the pointer position (that is, the position of the cursor on the screen) by moving the mouse. Application software can control several aspects of the on-screen cursor, such as size, shape, and color, on a per-window basis. An application can also affect pointer positioning, by controlling the sensitivity of the mouse, and by "warping" the pointer (moving it instantly).

## Mouse-Handling Strategies

If your application is to use the mouse effectively, you must make some decisions about how you will handle mouse input. You have several dimensions of choice open to you. You make these decisions based on what your application needs to do at the moment; you can switch strategies at any time.

- You may choose to ignore the mouse unless the user presses a mouse button. In this case, you should solicit ButtonPress events. See "Soliciting ButtonPress and ButtonRelease Events" later in this chaper.

- You may choose to respond when the user holds a mouse button and moves the mouse. This is often called "dragging" the mouse. In this case, you should solicit MotionNotify events when buttons are pressed ("Soliciting MotionNotify Events" in this chapter explains how). You may also wish to respond to the press and release of the buttons in this case.

- You may choose to respond when the user moves the cursor into or out of your window. See "Soliciting EnterNotify and LeaveNotify Events."

- You may choose to respond anytime the user moves the mouse.  If you use this strategy, you may have to respond to many events.  "Soliciting MotionNotify Events" explains.

- You may simply poll the mouse (ask the workstation where it is on the screen).  This strategy is fine for applications that use the mouse very little, but it does not perform well if used repeatedly.  See "Reading the Current Pointer Position."

- You may choose to ignore the mouse completely.

Your application can control the shape and color of the on-screen cursor.  This can be a very effective way of communicating with the user if you use it right, because the user's eyes are constantly on the cursor.  For example, you might display a text cursor in a text window, and an arrow cursor in a graphics-editor window.  See the "Cursors" section in this chapter.

# POINTER CONTROL

Your application can determine the position of the pointer at any time.  Futhermore, your software can control the pointer in two ways:

- by setting acceleration parameters that make the on-screen pointer more or less sensitive to rapid mouse motion.

- by causing the pointer to "warp," or move instantly to a specified screen position.

You can also confine the cursor to a specified window by means of a grab operation.  See Chapter 11 for details.

The feedback loop that coordinates pointer movement starts on the screen.  The user's eyes watch the cursor, and the user's hand moves the mouse.  The mouse senses motion and passes it back to the workstation.  The workstation applies acceleration parameters and the limiting window (if any) to the raw mouse position data, and displays the cursor on the screen at the current pointer position.

This eye/hand/mouse/cursor feedback loop (shown in Figure 9-2) is complex.  The more smoothly and unobtrusively the feedback loop works, the easier your application will be to use.  As an application developer, you only have direct control over the software components of the loop.  You can control the acceleration and threshold, the limiting window, and the cursor position, shape and size.  You do not have control over how the user moves the mouse, or how long it takes for the workstation to inform your application of mouse movements.

However, all the feedback loop components, particularly the human one, have to work adequately.  In other words, make things easy on your user.  Don't make the mouse jump around the screen in unpredictable ways.  Likewise, don't change the other parameters without a good reason; a good application gives the user the feeling that he or she is in control of the workstation, instead of the other

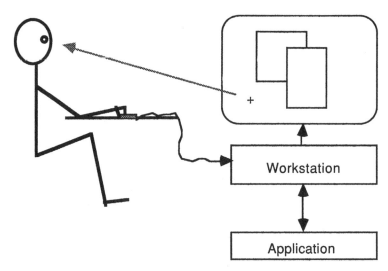

Figure 9-2. The feedback loop.

way around.  Lastly, build your application to be tolerant of the variation among human beings, if you can.   One workstation vendor failed to qualify for an important sale because the X Window System window manager it provided was configured to *require* the simultaneous use of two hands—one on the mouse and the other on the keyboard—to operate it!

## Reading the Current Pointer Position

Use **XQueryPointer** to read the current cursor position.  **XQueryPointer** is the simplest way of reading the mouse position.  As input to **XQueryPointer**, you specify a window resource identifier.  You get back a wealth of information about the pointer, including its position relative to the root window and the specified window, what subwindow it is in, and the current state of the buttons on the mouse.  The form of **XQueryPointer** (*Xlib*  ¶4.1) is

```
Display *display;          /* pointer to current Display structure */
Window win;                /* input window */
Window root;               /* returned   root window */
Window child;              /* returned child window */
int root_x,  root_y;       /* pointer relative to root */
int win_x,  win_y;         /* pointer relative to  win */
unsigned int keys_buttons; /* current mouse buttons */
. . .
XQueryPointer (display, win,  &root,  &child,  &root_x,
                       &root_y, &win_x, &win_y,  &keys_buttons );
```

The input (other than the *display* pointer provided in all requests) you specify to this request is *win,* a window id. **XQueryPointer** is an integer function which always returns a nonzero value (unless you have a multiple-screen workstation; see the next paragraph). In the *root* parameter **XQueryPointer** returns the window identifier of the screen root window.

If the pointer is within the boundaries of a mapped child window of *win,* the *child* parameter returns the id of that window. The *child* window is a first-generation descendant of its parent, but the pointer may actually be further down the hierarchy in a descendant window of *child.*

*root_x* and *root_y* return the pointer position relative to the origin of the *root* window. Likewise, *win_x* and *win_y* return the pointer position relative to the input window *win.*

On a multiple-screen workstation, the user can move the pointer from one screen to the other by manipulating the mouse. If your application is running on such a multiple-screen workstation, and the pointer is not on the same screen as the window you specified in the *win* parameter, **XQueryPointer** returns zero as a function result (otherwise it returns a nonzero result). In the *root* parameter **XQueryPointer** returns the window id of the screen root window for the screen the pointer is actually on.

The *keys_buttons* parameter is a mask with one bit in it for each mouse button and each keyboard modifier key (Shift, Control, Caps Lock, Meta, Hyper, and Super). If the button or key is being held by the user the corresponding bit is set. The bits have the symbolic names shown in Table 9-I and defined in the header file **<X11/X.h>**.

| Modifier Key or Button | Bitmask Symbol |
|---|---|
| Shift | ShiftMask |
| Caps Lock | CapsLockMask |
| Control | ControlMask |
| Meta or Compose (Modifier 1) | Mod1Mask |
| Modifiers 2-5 | Mod2Mask – Mod5Mask |
| Mouse Buttons 1-5 | Button1Mask – Button5Mask |

Table 9-I.  Modifier key bitmask symbols

**Example:**  How to determine where the pointer is

Suppose that your application wants to know what first-level window *cw* the pointer is currently in, if any, and the pointer's coordinates *xr, yr* relative to the root window window.

This problem is solved by specifying the root window as an input in a call to **XQueryPointer**.

```
Display  *display;     /*  pointer to current Display structure */
Window   curw;         /*  the window containing the pointer */
Window   rw,cw;        /*  the root and child windows */
```

```
int  xw, yw;              /* coordinate pair in window*/
int  xr, yr;              /* coordinate pair in the root window */
unsigned int keys buttons; /* button mask */
  . . .
XQueryPointer ( display, DefaultRootWindow ( display ),
                      &rw, &cw, &xr, &yr, &xw, &yw, &keys_buttons );
if (cw  != None ) {
   /* Pointer was in a child window */
   }
```

The usage of **XQueryPointer** shown in the example above is especially useful in X applications that make it their business to manipulate windows belonging to other applications, for example, in a window manager. The request is also useful for acknowledging a MotionNotify hint event (see "How to Process Pointer Motion Hints" below).

> Extensive use of **XQueryPointer** can degrade the performance of your workstation and application. Don't be deceived by the simplicity of **XQueryPointer**. It is ordinarily so slow that you won't have much success if you try to keep track of either mouse movement or button-clicks with it. Use event input instead.

If your application already has a coordinate pair and needs to transform it from one window's space to another, or determine which window it is in, use **XTranslateCoordinates**. This request has (*Xlib* ¶3.10) the form

```
Display *display;      /*  pointer to current Display structure */
Window sw;             /* source window */
Window dw;             /* destination window */
int src_x, src_y;      /* coordinate pair in  sw space */
int dest_x, dest_y;    /* coordinate pair in  dw space */
Window *child;         /* subwindow of destination window */
  . . .
XTranslateCoordinates ( display, sw, dw, src_x,src_y,
                       &dest_x,&dest_y, &child );
```

The *src_x, src_y* coordinate pair is translated from the *sw* frame of reference to the *dw* frame. If the point is contained in a mapped child of *dw,* the id of that *child* is returned as well. (A window is said to "contain" the pointer if the pointer is in a visible part of the window or a visible part of one of the window's inferiors.)

**XTranslateCoordinates** is as costly as **XQueryPointer**. However, it does yield consistent results even when more than one application is manipulating windows on the screen.

## Example: Determing what top-level window a point is in

Suppose your application already has the coordinates (relative to the root window) of a point in the variables *xpt* and *ypt,* and you want to determine the window id *wpt* of the window your point is in.

Use the screen root window as both source and destination in a call to **XTranslateCoordinates** to solve this problem.

```
Display  *display;        /* pointer to current Display structure */
Window  wpt;              /* the window containing the point */
int  xpt, ypt;           /* coordinate pair */
int  xjunk, yjunk;

. . .

XTranslateCoordinates ( display,
      DefaultRootWindow ( display ),
      DefaultRootWindow ( display ),
      xpt, ypt, &xjunk, &yjunk, &wpt );
```

Note that the returned x and y values are not of interest in this example, so we stored them into junk-variables. The resulting child window is returned in *wpt*.

# Controlling Pointer Motion Characteristics

You can control how the on-screen pointing device moves in response to mouse motion, using the Unix shell command **xset(1)** or the X requests **XChangePointerControl** and **XGetPointerControl**. The parameters you may set are

- Acceleration, specified by numerator and denominator. The acceleration is a mutiplier for movement. For example, specifying 3/2 means that the on-screen pointer moves one and one-half times as far as it would nominally for a particular mouse movement. Some workstations are not capable of handling all arbitrary acceleration fractions. These workstations will automatically use the nearest possible acceleration factor.

- Threshold, specified as an integer. The acceleration factor is only applied if a single mouse movement exceeds the threshold. For mouse movements less than the threshold, the nominal acceleration factor of 1/1 is used.

These parameters allow you to set up the pointer so it responds smoothly to small mouse movements, but leaps across the screen with a flick of the wrist. Pointer motion control settings take effect for a whole workstation, unlike cursor settings that are per-window.

One way to set acceleration and threshold is via the **xset(1)** Unix shell level command:

```
% xset -m  accel    threshold
```

*accel* is the desired acceleration and *threshold* is the threshold setting, specified as integers. (See your vendor's documentation if you are not using Unix or a compatible operating system.)

From within an application program, you may use **XChangePointerControl** and **XGetPointerControl** to set and query the current acceleration and threshold. They (*Xlib* ¶7.7.2) have the form

```
Display     *display;      /* pointer to current Display structure */
int         do_a;         /* non-zero to change acceleration */
int         do_t;         /* non-zero to change threshold */
int         acc_num;      /* numerator of acceleration term */
int         acc_denom;    /* denominator of acceleration term */
int         thresh;       /* threshold term */
    . . .
XChangePointerControl ( display, do_a, do_t, acc_num,
                        acc_denom, thresh );
    . . .
XGetPointerControl ( display,   &acc_num, &acc_denom, &thresh );
```

*do_a* and *do_t* can be set to zero if you want to leave either acceleration or threshold unchanged. If you set *acc_num*, *acc_denom* or *thresh* to −1 in a call to **XChangePointerControl**, X resets the values to the workstation defaults.

> Pointer acceleration and threshold are user-preference parameters. Many users include an **xset** command in their startup files, and expect their settings to persist for the whole session on the workstation. If your application changes these parameters, it should probably do so temporarily, and then only if it's really necessary (unless, of course, your application has the purpose of setting user preferences).

### Example:   Double the pointer acceleration

This example requires us to inquire, then modify, the acceleration parameter on the pointer.

```
Display *display;   /* pointer to current Display structure */
int acc_num;        /* numerator of acceleration term */
int acc_denom;      /* denominator of acceleration term */
int thresh;         /* threshold term */
    . . .
XGetPointerControl ( display, &acc_num, &acc_denom, &thresh );
acc_num = acc_num * 2;
XChangePointerControl ( display, True, False, acc_num,
                        acc_denom, thresh );
```

Some applications need an optional precision-mouse capability, in which the cursor moves very slowly in response to mouse manipulation. If you provide this capability, it will be easier for users to point exactly at points on the screen (at the cost of speed, of course). A good way to provide this capability without disrupting the user-preference settings is

(a)    When the user either moves the mouse into a window (which generates an EnterNotify event, see below) or presses a mouse button (ButtonPress event) respond by using **XGetPointerControl** to save the current acceleration and threshold. You then use **XChangePointerControl** to set a very small acceleration factor.

(b)    When the user moves the mouse back out of the window (LeaveNotify event) or releases the mouse button (ButtonRelease event) respond using **XChangePointerControl** to restore the acceleration and threshold settings you previously saved.

## Moving—Warping—the Pointer

Usually, the cursor moves on the screen only when the user manipulates the mouse. You may want your application to move the cursor without the help of the mouse. With the **XWarpPointer** request, your application can intervene in X's normal cursor tracking and move the pointer instantly. Each **XWarpPointer** request generates either a MotionNotify event or EnterNotify and LeaveNotify events, just as if the user had moved the pointer to the new position by manipulating the mouse very rapidly. **XWarpPointer** (*Xlib* ¶ 7.7.1) has the form

```
Display *display;              /* pointer to current Display structure */
Window srcwin, dstwin;         /* source and destination windows */
int src_x,  src_y;             /* position within source window */
unsigned int src_w, src_h;     /* width and height of source */
int dst_x,  dst_y;             /* destination x and y */
   . . .
XWarpPointer ( display, srcwin, dstwin, src_x, src_y, src_w, src_h,
                        dst_x, dst_y );
```

An **XWarpPointer** request can be either unconditional or conditional. A conditional **XWarpPointer** request is only carried out if the pointer's starting position is within a certain rectangle in a certain window.

To move the pointer unconditionally to the position (*dst_x, dst_y* ) relative to the window *dstwin*, you must specify None for *srcwin*, and zero values for *src_x*, *src_y*, *src_w*, and *src_h*. If you specify None for *dstwin*, the pointer moves relative to its current position: in this case *dst_x* and *dst_y* values are interpreted as the distance to move.

To move the pointer conditionally, the *src_x*, *src_y*, *src_w*, and *src_h* parameters let you specify a rectangle within the source window *srcwin*. If you specify something besides None for *srcwin*, it means that you want the pointer moved only on condition that (before it moves) it is in a visible (not covered by inferior windows) portion of the specified rectangle in *srcwin*.

*src_x* and *src_y* define the origin of the rectangle relative to *srcwin's* origin. *src_w* and *src_h* define the size of the rectangle. You may specify zero for *src_w;* if you do this it means that you want the rectangle to extend all the way from *src_x* to the right edge of the window. Likewise, if you specify zero for *src_h,* it means that you want the rectangle to extend from *src_y* to the bottom edge.

Moving the pointer within a window generates MotionNotify events. Moving the pointer from one window to another generates EnterNotify and LeaveNotify events. These events occur both when the pointer is moved by the user, and when the application intervenes and moves it by using **XWarpPointer.**

Warping the pointer might very well solve technical problems that Captain Kirk and Mr. Spock have as they operate the USS Enterprise. However, Dr. McCoy, with his renowned concern for the human beings under his care, would not approve of applications that use too much pointer warping. When the pointer jumps around the screen the user has trouble following it. A controversial use of **XWarpPointer** is in building applications that allow the user to move the cursor with arrow buttons on the keyboard as well as with the mouse. One thing is not controversial: the cursor is the user's to manipulate.

> If you must use **XWarpPointer**, be sure you give the user a sense of control over the cursor.

### Example:    Move the pointer unconditionally

Suppose you want to move the pointer to location (400,500) on the screen, regardless of what window that location is in. Do this:

**Display** *\*display;*

. . .

**XWarpPointer**       ( *display*, None,
                         DefaultRootWindow (*display*),
                         *0, 0, 0, 0, 400, 500* );

Note the use of the DefaultRootWindow informational macro to refer to the root window. Also note that the pointer will actually arrive in whatever window is located at (400,500). If the window of arrival has requested delivery of EnterNotify events (see the next section), it will get an EnterNotify event when you use **XWarpPointer.** Similarly, whatever window the pointer departs from may get a LeaveNotify event.

### Example:       Move the pointer up ten pixels

This example illustrates how to use conditional pointer movement. Suppose that you want to move the pointer up ten pixels from its current position in the root window. To do this, first use **XQueryPointer** to determine where the pointer is, then use **XWarpPointer** to move the pointer. Conditional movement is needed because it takes time for your application to receive the **XQueryPointer** results, compute the new position, and issue the **XWarpPointer** request. If the user moves the mouse during that short interval of time, the **XWarpPointer** request will move it back.  In the X Window System, you solve this problem with a conditional pointer movement:  if the user moves the pointer away from where your application thought it was, the workstation ignores your **XWarpPointer** request.  In this example, the source rectangle is an eight-by-eight region centered at the pointer position.

```
Display *display;
Window root;                    /* returned root window */
Window child;                   /* returned child window */
int root_x,  root_y;            /* pointer relative to root; new y pos*/
int new_x,  new_y;              /* new  x, y pos*/
int win_x,  win_y;              /* pointer relative to win */
unsigned int keys_buttons;      /* current mouse buttons */
. . .
XQueryPointer ( display,
                DefaultRootWindow (display),
                &root, &child, &root_x, &root_y,
                &win_x, &win_y, &keys_buttons );
new_x = root_x;
new_y = root_y - 10;            /* compute new y position, up ten */
if ( new_y < 0 ) new_y = 0;
root_x = root_x - 4;           /* compute x-origin of source rectangle */
if ( root_x < 0 ) root_x = 0;
root_y = root_y - 4;           /* compute y-origin of source rectangle */
if ( root_y < 0 ) root_y = 0;
XWarpPointer ( display, root, root, root_x, root_y, 8, 8, new_x, new_y );
```

# CURSORS

The cursor is the visible evidence of the pointer on the screen.  Each window has a particular *cursor* resource associated with it.  You may either explicitly specify a cursor for each of your applications or allow each of your windows to inherit its cursor from its parent window.  X defines a default cursor (a large "X"), and associates it with the root window.  Your application may use this default cursor simply by allowing all your windows to inherit the root window's cursor (the window created by **helloworld.c** in Chapter 2 inherited the root window's cursor).  If you prefer not to use the default cursor, you may define your own cursor resources and associate them with your windows.

A cursor has these characteristics:

- The color of the cursor foreground, specified as a red-green-blue triplet.  Cursor colors must be specified on all workstations including monochrome ones.

- The color of the cursor background, specified as a red-green-blue triplet.

- The cursor source. This must be a bitmap (also known as a Pixmap with a depth of one). The x and y size of the source bitmap may, in principle, be of arbitrary size. However, some workstations cannot completely display a cursor of a size larger than 16 x 16. When the cursor is displayed, "1" bits are shown in the cursor foreground color, and "0" bits in the cursor background color.

- Optionally, the cursor mask bitmap. If specified, the cursor mask bitmap must be identical in size to the cursor source bitmap. When the cursor is displayed, "0" bits in the mask let the underlying window show through, and "1" bits display either the cursor foreground or background color. If you omit the mask, all pixels of the cursor source are displayed in either the foreground or background color. In other words, the default mask is a solid rectangle the size of the source. You may specify the same bitmap for source and mask; this makes a cursor that contains no background color areas. This works nicely unless the user moves the cursor into an area of the screen of the same color as the cursor foreground, in which case the cursor will not be visible. Many cursor masks include the bits in the cursor source as well as all the bits around the perimeter of the cursor source.

- Cursor hotspot or active position, x and y, in pixels. This specifies one of the pixels in the cursor bitmap, assuming that the top left pixel is (0,0). The hotspot is the place the cursor points to. It is the pixel at the sharp end of the arrow, the center of the bullseye, the end of the finger, or whatever point is appropriate.

Whenever the pointer is in a particular window, that window's cursor, which it may have inherited from its parent, is displayed. (Exception: if a pointer grab is active, the cursor displayed is based on the parameters of the grab. See Chapter 11.) As the user moves the pointer from window to window, the shape of the cursor changes automatically.

## Creating, Changing, and Destroying Cursors

A cursor is a resource in the X Window System. You can create, change and destroy cursors at will. You may use the following requests to manipulate cursor resources:

**XCreateFontCursor** creates a cursor with a shape defined in a standard set of cursor shapes shipped with X. See Appendix F.

**XQueryBestCursor** lets you determine the cursor size that your workstation handles best.

**XCreatePixmapCursor** lets you create a cursor from arbitrary bitmaps.

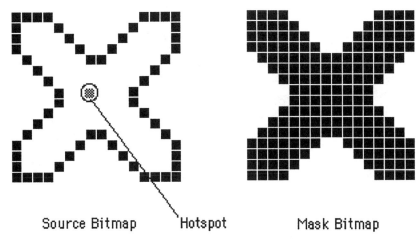

Source Bitmap      Hotspot      Mask Bitmap

Figure 9-3. The components of the default cursor.

**XGlyphCursor** creates a cursor based on characters in fonts.

**XRecolorCursor** lets you change the colors of a cursor.

**XFreeCursor** destroys a cursor resource when your application no longer needs it.

Before you declare that you want your window to display a certain cursor, you must create that cursor's resource. Do this once for each cursor shape you intend to use. As a result of creating each cursor, you get back its resource id (a data item of type **Cursor**). There are three ways to create a cursor resource:

1. Predefined standard cursor definitions are shipped with the X Window System in a standard font named "cursor". Your application can use them via definitions in the C header file **<X11/cursorfont.h>** and the **XCreateFontCursor** convenience function. The header file defines names for the shapes stored in the font (see Appendix F). This is the best way to create a cursor, because it is portable between applications and workstations. **XCreateFontCursor** takes (*Xlib* ¶6.8.1) the form

```
#include   <X11/cursorfont.h>
    . . .
Display *display;
Cursor curs; /* the cursor id, as created */
int shape;

    . . .
curs = XCreateFontCursor ( display, shape );
```

Cursors created with **XCreateFontCursor** initially have black for a foreground color and white for a background color. The colors are changeable via **XRecolorCursor** (see below).

2. You may use bitmaps (see Chapter 8 for information on creating bitmaps, or Pixmaps of depth one) for your cursor source and mask. To do this, use **XQueryBestCursor** (*Xlib* ¶6.8.2) to find out the ideal cursor size for your workstation, and **XCreatePixmapCursor** (*Xlib* ¶6.8.1) to create the cursor:

```
Display *display;
Drawable which_screen;        /* drawable on desired screen */
unsigned int width, height;   /* desired cursor size*/
unsigned int width_return;    /* ideal cursor width*/
unsigned int height_return;   /* ideal cursor height*/

 . . .
Pixmap csource, cmask;        /* source mask pixmaps */
XColor cfore, cback;          /* foreground , background */
int xhot, yhot;               /* hotspot position */
Cursor curs;                  /* resulting cursor value */

 . . .
XQueryBestCursor ( display, which_screen, width, height,
            &width_return, &height_return );

    . . .
curs = XCreatePixmapCursor ( display, csource, cmask,
            &cfore, &cback, xhot, yhot );
```

**XQueryBestCursor** returns the nearest cursor width and height (*width_return*, *height_return*) that your workstation can actually display on the screen identified by *which_screen*, given the height and width you want (*width, height*). You do not have to use this request, but if you try to create a cursor that is the wrong size for the workstation, the workstation may arbitrarily alter it (without informing you) so it is the right size. If you use a cursor of non-optimum size, you may also slow down the workstation. On many workstations, the optimum cursor size is 16x16 pixels. In *which_screen*, you should specify the X resource identifier of a window in which you intend to use the cursor.

The *cfore* and *cback* **XColor** structures are used to define the red, green, and blue values for the cursor foreground and background. The pixel-value fields in the **XColor** structures are ignored for the purposes of this request. See the sections entitled "Red, Green, Blue" and "Looking Up RGB Values for a Named Color" in Chapter 7 for information on **XColor** structures.

3. **XCreateGlyphCursor** works like **XCreatePixmapCursor**, except that it fetches the source and mask bitmaps from character bitmaps within fonts. To use fonts, first load them with **XLoadFont** or the equivalent (see Chapter 6), then use **XCreateGlyphCursor** (*Xlib* ¶6.8.1) as follows:

```
Display *display;        /* pointer to Display structure */
Font srcfont, mskfont;   /* fonts for foreground, background */
XColor cfore, cback;     /* colors */
int schar, mchar;        /* glyphs for foreground, background */
Cursor curs;

    . . .

curs = XCreateGlyphCursor( display, srcfont, mskfont,
                           schar, mchar, &cfore,&cback );
```

*srcfont* and *mskfont* may refer to the same font if you wish. *schar* and *mchar* refer to the characters to use for the source and mask, respectively. You may omit *mskfont* and *mchar* by specifying NULLs in those positions. If you specify a mask glyph, it must have the same size as the source glyph.

You only have to create each cursor resource once, so it usually makes sense to create all the cursors you need during initialization. Cursor creation can fail and return a *curs* value of None if the workstation's memory is used up.

You may change the colors of a cursor at any time after you create it using the **XRecolorCursor** request (*Xlib* ¶6.8.2). If a cursor is on the screen at the time you change its colors, you see the change as soon as the workstation carries out the **XRecolorCursor** request.

```
Display *display;        /* pointer to Display structure */
Cursor curs;             /* the cursor id */
XColor cfore, cback;     /* new foreground and background colors */

    . . .

XRecolorCursor ( display, curs, &cfore, &cback );
```

Once created, cursor resources stay around as long as your application is using X. (The lifetime of cursor resources is controlled in the same ways as the lifetimes of other resources.) If you prefer, however, you can destroy a cursor explicitly, using **XFreeCursor** (*Xlib* ¶6.8.2). Once a cursor is destroyed, you should not use its cursor id again or you will get an error.

```
Display *display;        /* pointer to current Display structure */
Cursor curs;             /* the cursor id */

    . . .

XFreeCursor ( display, curs );
```

Using **XFreeCursor** only eliminates the cursor resource. It does not have any destructive effect on fonts or bitmaps you may have used when you originally created the cursor.

## Displaying Cursors in Windows

Once you have created cursor resources, you may use the following requests to control what cursor is displayed in each window:

**XDefineCursor** selects a current cursor for a window.

**XUndefineCursor** removes the current cursor from a window.

Once you have created a cursor resource, you may select it as the current cursor for any window at any time. Each cursor resource may be used in as many windows as you wish at the same time. **XDefineCursor** (*Xlib* ¶6.8.3) sets the cursor that a window displays when the pointer is in it. **XUndefineCursor** removes the cursor definition from a window, causing it to use the cursor inherited from its parent. If you call **XUndefineCursor** on a root window, the default cursor (a large X) is restored to that window.

```
Display *display;       /* pointer to current Display structure */
Window w;               /* window id of window to get the cursor */
Cursor curs;            /* cursor to use */
  . . .
XDefineCursor ( display, w,  curs );
  . . .
XUndefineCursor ( display, w );
```

**XDefineCursor** is not an expensive operation. It is reasonable to change cursors as often as you like. For example, you might change to a different cursor every time you detect a mouse button press, and change back when the button is released.

If a child window inherits its cursor from a parent window, **XDefineCursor** and **XUndefineCursor** requests which operate on the parent window's cursor take effect in the child window at the same time.

If you use **XFreeCursor** while a cursor is still current for one or more windows, the cursor resource is not actually destroyed until all windows stop using it. However, once your application has freed a cursor resource, you should not refer to its resource id again in any future request.

# MOUSE EVENTS

There are five types of events that the X Window System uses to inform an application about mouse motion: ButtonPress, ButtonRelease, MotionNotify, EnterNotify, and LeaveNotify. As with all events, if your application wants them you must solicit their delivery. Ordinarily you use **XSelectInput** for that purpose (see the section entitled "Soliciting Events" in Chapter 3 for more information). Bits in the *event_mask* parameter relating to mouse events have the functions shown in Table 9-II. Detailed descriptions of the selection masks and events are found in the sections to follow.

## Soliciting ButtonPress and ButtonRelease Events

When you specify the ButtonPressMask bit in the *event_mask* parameter to **XSelectInput,** you will receive a ButtonPress event any time the user presses any mouse button when the pointer is in the window you specify. Keep in mind that it is possible for the user to press more than one mouse button at a time. If the user presses more than one button, you will receive more than one Button-Press event.

Similarly, when you specify the ButtonReleaseMask bit in the *event_mask* parameter to **XSelectInput**, you will receive a ButtonRelease event any time the user releases any mouse button.

Mouse events of all kinds are delivered in a special way while mouse buttons are pressed. With the generation of a ButtonPress event destined for your application, an active grab of the pointer automatically begins (see Chapter 11), and remains in effect until the user lets go of all the mouse buttons. This behavior is convenient if your application allows the user to "drag" objects by holding down a mouse button while moving the mouse; the grab ensures that your application will receive all the mouse events the user generates while holding mouse buttons, even if the user moves the mouse out of your window in the meantime.

Note that if you do not solicit ButtonRelease events, you will not receive the ButtonRelease event announcing the end of the active grab. However, as long as you solicit ButtonPress events, the active grab begins with the delivery of the

| Bit Mask Name | Event Selected | Circumstances of Event Delivery |
| --- | --- | --- |
| ButtonPressMask | ButtonPress | A press of any mouse button |
| ButtonReleaseMask | ButtonRelease | A release of any mouse button |
| OwnerGrabButtonMask | | If specified in conjunction with either of the above, allows normal delivery of mouse events while buttons are pressed |
| EnterWindowMask | EnterNotify | Whenever the pointer enters the window |
| LeaveWindowMask | LeaveNotify | Whenever the pointer leaves the window |
| PointerMotionHintMask | | If specified in conjunction with any of the below, requests motion hint events |
| PointerMotionMask | MotionNotify | Whenever the pointer moves |
| ButtonMotionMask | MotionNotify | When the pointer moves with any mouse button depressed |
| Button1MotionMask | MotionNotify | Whenever the pointer moves with button 1 depressed |
| Button2MotionMask | MotionNotify | Whenever the pointer moves with button 2 depressed |
| Button3MotionMask | MotionNotify | Whenever the pointer moves with button 3 depressed |
| Button4MotionMask | MotionNotify | Whenever the pointer moves with button 4 depressed (if button 4 exists) |
| Button5MotionMask | MotionNotify | Whenever the pointer moves with button 5 depressed (if button 5 exists) |

Table 9-II   Mouse event selection masks.

ButtonPress event; the user still must release the button before the grab terminates.

Ordinarily you should also specify the OwnerGrabButtonMask bit in the *event_mask* parameter whenever you solicit ButtonPress events. When you specify OwnerGrabButtonMask, all grabbed mouse events destined for your application are delivered normally. The effect of the grab is to "steal" all mouse events, but if you also specify OwnerGrabButtonMask, you will not steal mouse events from other windows in your own application.

If you do not specify the OwnerGrabButtonMask bit, the grab will steal all mouse events (yours as well as others) and send them to the same window as the original ButtonPress event. Furthermore, without OwnerGrabButtonMask, if you change your solicitation of mouse events for any of your application's windows (via **XSelectInput** or the equivalent) while one or more buttons are pressed, the new *event_mask* will not take effect until all buttons are released.

The fact that ButtonPress events cause grabs affords your application a great deal of control over the events you receive while the user is dragging the mouse. If you want to do things the easy way, simply specify OwnerGrabButtonMask. If you want to fully exploit the capabilities of the grab, see the section "Between ButtonPress and ButtonRelease" in Chapter 11.

Most direct input events may be solicited from a given window by more than one application at a time; the workstation sends these events to all applications wanting them. ButtonPress events, however, do not work this way. Only one application at a time can solicit ButtonPress events from any given window. If two applications try to solicit ButtonPress events, the workstation responds to the second **XSelectInput** with a BadValue error event message.

### Example: Solicit ButtonPress and ButtonRelease events

This example shows the use of **XSelectInput** to solicit ButtonPress and ButtonRelease events. It also specifies OwnerGrabButtonMask so that events occuring while buttons are pressed will be delivered normally.

```
Display *display;      /* pointer to current Display structure */
Window window;         /* window you want button events from*/
. . .
XSelectInput ( display, window,
      OwnerGrabButtonMask | ButtonPressMask | ButtonReleaseMask );
```

## Soliciting EnterNotify and LeaveNotify Events

When you specify the EnterWindowMask bit in the *event_mask* parameter to **XSelectInput,** you will receive an EnterNotify event any time the pointer moves into the window you specify. An EnterNotify event can be generated in the normal way by the user manipulating the mouse, and it can also be generated by an **XWarpPointer** request (see "Moving—Warping—the Pointer" earlier in this chapter). Special EnterNotify events are also generated when an active grab—including one triggered by a ButtonPress event—begins in the window (see the sections on pointer grabbing in Chapter 11).

If you select EnterWindowMask, and the pointer actually has moved into an inferior window (a child window, or a child of a child window, and so forth) to the window you specified, your window will receive an EnterNotify event with a "detail" field specifying that the notification involves an inferior window. See the section "EnterNotify and LeaveNotify Events—Specifics" below for more information.

Similarly, when you specify the LeaveWindowMask bit in the *event_mask* parameter to **XSelectInput,** you will receive a LeaveNotify event any time the pointer moves out of the window you specify, or when an active grab ends.

## Soliciting MotionNotify events

When you specify the PointerMotionMask bit in the *event_mask* parameter to **XSelectInput,** you will receive a MotionNotify event whenever the pointer moves from one place to another within the window you specify. A MotionNotify event can be generated in the normal way by the user manipulating the mouse, or by an **XWarpPointer** request.

If a particular mouse motion generates an EnterNotify or LeaveNotify event, it does not also generate a MotionNotify event.

When you specify the ButtonMotionMask bit in the *event_mask* parameter to **XSelectInput,** you will receive a MotionNotify event whenever the pointer moves with any mouse button depressed within the window you specify. Use the ButtonMotionMask bit when you want to receive events when the user holds down any mouse button, "dragging" the mouse.

Similarly, the bits Button1MotionMask-Button5MotionMask cause you to receive MotionNotify events when the pointer moves with the specified mouse button depressed. These bits can be used singly or in any combination when you want to receive events when the user drags the mouse with specific buttons pressed. For example, if you specify Button1MotionMask and Button3MotionMask, you will receive MotionNotify events when the user moves the mouse while holding either button 1 or button 3, or both.

You may solicit button motion events with or without also soliciting ButtonPress events. If you do not solicit ButtonPress events, no grab will activate (see "Soliciting ButtonPress and ButtonRelease events" above); nevertheless your application will still receive the solicited MotionNotify events as long as the user keeps the cursor in your window.

Each motion event represents an instantaneous hop of the pointer. If the user moves the pointer slowly and steadily in some sort of gesture, the X Window System reports the motion as a series of independent MotionNotify events. The series of MotionNotify events can potentially be very long, because some workstations detect and report as many as 60 mouse-motions per second.

Fortunately, there is a way to reduce the number of events your application must process: you may specify the PointerMotionHintMask bit in conjunction with the PointerMotionMask bit or any of the button motion bits. If you do this you will receive MotionNotify hint events instead of ordinary MotionNotify events. Hint events let you know that the pointer has moved, but do not give the details of the motion. For more information, see "How to Process Pointer Motion Hints," later in this chapter.

> Selecting MotionNotify events without also selecting the Motion-NotifyHintMask bit can generate large numbers of events. It is suitable for rubber-band line tracking and similar dynamic graphics applications. However, if your application has to process hundreds of events, performance can suffer.

The X Window System does not provide an explicit event to inform your application that the user has stopped moving the mouse. This is because X decomposes mouse gestures into primitive MotionNotify events.

## Receiving and Processing Mouse Events

Once your application uses **XSelectInput** to indicate that you want events delivered, your queue starts to receive them. Your application has to be ready to read them from the queue and process them. (For details about the various ways you can read and examine your queue, see the section in Chapter 3 entitled "Accepting Events from the Event Queue.") An event, as read from the queue, is a data structure. You pass a pointer to such a data structure to **XNextEvent** and the other queue handling functions; the contents of the data structure are filled in for you.

To interpret the event, your application has to decipher the contents of the event data structure. The first field in all event data structures is an integer which specifies the event type. The meaning of the rest of the data in the structure depends on the event type. Thus, the format of the structure, and the length, varies. Your application has to be ready to accept the data describing any event, which means that you have to supply the **XNextEvent** request with enough space for the largest possible event data structure. The header file **<X11/Xlib.h>** supplies a variety of C-language  structure and union type declarations which make it easy for you to handle this situation.

The first field of all event structures is the event type (field name "type"). The union type **XEvent** defines the type field directly, so it can be used to look at the event before you know what type it is.  You should use **XEvent** to declare and allocate space for all event structures: it defines a structure that is guaranteed to be long enough for all event types.

ButtonPress and ButtonRelease events have the same structure as each other. The structure type **XButtonEvent** is defined to let you access these events. If you prefer, the types **XButtonPressedEvent** and **XButtonReleasedEvent** are available as alternate names for **XButtonEvent**. The **XEvent** union defines the "xbutton" variant as an **XButtonEvent** structure.

MotionNotify events have the structure type **XMotionEvent**. The **XEvent** union defines the "xmotion" variant as an **XMotionEvent** structure.

EnterNotify and LeaveNotify events also have identical structures. Their structure type is **XCrossingEvent**, also available under the alternate names **XEnterWindowEvent** and **XLeaveWindowEvent**. The **XEvent** union defines the "xcrossing" variant as an **XCrossingEvent** structure.

Table 9-III shows the type names and field names for the contents of the event structures for all the pointer events, as defined in the header file **<X11/Xlib.h>.**

In the C language, such variant structures must be accessed via a union variant name. If, for example, you had a ButtonPress event in the XEvent structure named "current," you could retrieve the "window" field in the way shown in the following line of code:

```
w = current.xbutton.window; /* explicit union access via xbutton */
```

You must first determine the event type, then use the right variant structure. For example, it would be meaningless to try to access the "focus" field from a ButtonPress event, because **XButtonEvent** does not define that field.

The fields in pointer events are as follows:

type            Specifies the event type.

serial          Specifies the serial number of the last request processed.

send_event      False unless this event was generated by some application issuing the **XSentEvent** request.

display         The **Display** structure the event came from.

window          This field appears in all direct event structures. It is the window identifier of the event window.

root            This field appears in all pointer events (although not in all other events). On multi-screen workstations this field identifies which screen the pointer is actually on at the time of the event. It is the window id of the root window at the top of the window hierarchy containing the source window of the event. (The source window is the window the pointer is in at the time of the event. The source window is not necessarily the reported event window; see the section entitled "Events in Nested Windows" later in this chapter.) If your workstation has more than one screen, the source window may, during a grab, be on a different screen from the event window, in which case "root" is not the root window of "window."

| typedef struct { | | |
|---|---|---|
| int type; | ev.type | ButtonPress,ButtonRelease |
| unsigned long serial | ev.xany.serial | Last request processed |
| **Bool** send_event; | ev.xany.send_event | From **XSendEvent**? |
| **Display** *display; | ev.xany.display | |
| **Window** window; | ev.xbutton.window | Event window |
| **Window** root; | ev.xbutton.root | Root window |
| **Window** subwindow; | ev.xbutton.subwindow | Child window |
| **Time** time; | ev.xbutton.time | Event timestamp |
| int x | ev.xbutton.x | x position, event window |
| int y | ev.xbutton.y | y position, event window |
| int x_root | ev.xbutton.x_root | x position in root window |
| int y_root | ev.xbutton.y_root | y position in root window |
| unsigned int state; | ev.xbutton.state | Button and modifier state |
| int button; | ev.xbutton.button | Button number |
| **Bool** same_screen; | ev.xbutton.same_screen | False if inter-screen grab |
| } **XButtonEvent**; | | |
| typedef struct { | | |
| int type; | ev.type | MotionNotify |
| unsigned long serial | ev.xany.serial | Last request processed |
| **Bool** send_event; | ev.xany.send_event | From **XSendEvent**? |
| **Display** *display; | ev.xany.display | |
| **Window** window; | ev.xmotion.window | Event window |
| **Window** root; | ev.xmotion.root | Root window |
| **Window** subwindow; | ev.xmotion.subwindow | Child window |
| **Time** time; | ev.xmotion.time | Event timestamp |
| int x | ev.xmotion.x | x position, event window |
| int y | ev.xmotion.y | y position, event window |
| int x_root | ev.xmotion.x_root | x position, root window |
| int y_root | ev.xmotion.y_root | y position, root window |
| unsigned int state; | ev.xmotion.state | Button and modifier state |
| int is_hint; | ev.xmotion.is_hint | Nonzero on motion hints |
| **Bool** same_screen; | ev.xmotion.same_screen | False if inter-screen grab |
| } **XMotionEvent**; | | |

Table 9-III.  Pointer event structures and field names.

| typedef struct { | | |
|---|---|---|
| int type; | ev.type | EnterNotify, LeaveNotify |
| unsigned long serial | ev.xany.serial | Last request processed |
| **Bool** send_event; | ev.xany.send_event | From **XSendEvent**? |
| **Display** *display; | ev.xany.display | |
| **Window** window; | ev.xcrossing.window | Event window |
| **Window** root; | ev.xcrossing.root | Root window |
| **Window** subwindow; | ev.xcrossing.subwindow | Child window |
| **Time** time; | ev.xcrossing.time | Event timestamp |
| int x | ev.xcrossing.x | x position, event window |
| int y | ev.xcrossing.y | y position, event window |
| int x_root | ev.xcrossing.x_root | x position, root window |
| int y_root | ev.xcrossing.y_root | y position, root window |
| int mode; | ev.xcrossing.mode | Mode (normal, grab) |
| int detail; | ev.xcrossing.detail | Kind of crossing |
| **Bool** same_screen; | ev.xcrossing.same_screen | False if inter-screen grab |
| **Bool** focus; | ev.xcrossing.focus | KB focus on window |
| unsigned int state; | ev.xcrossing.state | Button and modifier state |
| } **XCrossingEvent**; | | |

Table 9-III continued.  Pointer event structures and field names.

subwindow

This field appears in all pointer events (although not in all other events). If the source window of the event (the window the pointer is in at the time of event) is an inferior of the event window (in the "window" field), then this field contains the window id of a first-level child window of "window." The child window can either be the source window of the event or an ancestor of the source window of the event. If the pointer is not in an inferior of "window," the "subwindow" field contains the special symbol None. The "subwindow" field always contains None unless an event took place in a subwindow but could not be delivered to that subwindow because of no outstanding solicitation for the event in the subwindow.

time

This field appears in all pointer events (although not in all other events). It is the X Window System timestamp at the time of the event. The timestamp value increases by one every millisecond, and is a 32-bit unsigned integer, in the range [0, 4,294,967,296). Timestamps are used as parameters to **XGrabPointer**, **XUngrabPointer**, **XGetMotionEvents**, **XGrabKeyboard**, and **XUngrabKeyboard**. You can also detect double-clicks and multiple-clicks by examining the timestamps on consecutive ButtonPress events.

> The timestamp value wraps around to zero approximately every 4.29 million seconds (just under 50 days). If your application makes use of the timestamp, you should anticipate this wraparound. If you don't, you may have an extremely irreproducible bug to track down.

x, y

These fields appear in all pointer events (although not in all other events). They are the coordinates of the pointer relative to the window specified in the "window" field. They are 16 bit numbers. On a workstation with more than one screen, they are zero if the source window for the event is on a different screen from the event window.

x_root, y_root

These fields appear in all pointer events (although not in all other events). They are the coordinates of the pointer relative to the root window (specified in the "root" field). They are 16 bit positive numbers.

state

This field appears in all pointer events (although not in all other events). It is a mask with one bit in it for each mouse button and each keyboard modifier key (such as Shift and Control). If the button or key was being held by the user *just before* the event, the corresponding bit is set in the state field. (Note that if an event reports a change in a mouse button or modifier key, the "state" field does not reflect the change, because it contains the state just before the event.) The bits have the same symbolic names as the bits in the *keys_buttons* parameter to the **XQuery-Pointer** request. See Table 9-I.

button

This field appears in ButtonPress and ButtonRelease events. It is the number (1-5) of the button that was pressed or released to generate the event.

is_hint

This field appears only in MotionNotify events. It has one of two values: NotifyHint or NotifyNormal (symbols defined in **<X11/X.h>**). NotifyHint indicates that you are receiving this event because you specified PointerMotionHintMask when you called **XSelectInput**. Once you get a MotionNotify event with an "is_hint" field value of NotifyHint, further delivery of MotionNotify hint events is (on most workstations) inhibited until you use either the **XQueryPointer** or **XGetMotionEvents** request. See the section later in this chapter entitled "How to Process Pointer Motion Hints". NotifyNormal indicates an ordinary motion event.

mode

This field appears in EnterNotify and LeaveNotify events. See the section entitled "EnterNotify and LeaveNotify Events—Specifics" for more information.

detail          This field appears in EnterNotify and LeaveNotify events. It allows the application to determine the relationship between the new and former pointer windows. See the section entitled "EnterNotify and LeaveNotify Events—Specifics" for more information.

same_screen     This field appears in all pointer-related events. In a single-screen workstation, this field is always true. It is false if the pointer (and the root window reported in the event) are not on the same screen as "window". "x" and "y" are zero if "same_screen" is false.

focus           This field appears in EnterNotify and LeaveNotify events. The value of this boolean field is true if the event window (the window identifier for which is in the "window" field) is the same as or an inferior of the input focus window (see the section entitled "Keyboard Focus", below). In other words, if "focus" is true in an EnterNotify event, X will be able to deliver forthcoming mouse and keyboard events via the same event window, if your application has selected them.

To receive and process events, you should use the following general sequence of operations:

1)  Declare space for event structures using the XEvent type.

2)  Read the event into the XEvent structure.

3)  Determine the type of the event; examine the type field.

4)  Once the event type is known, use the appropriate union variant to read the data fields.

The **helloworld** example in Chapter 2 shows a very simple main event loop.

## How to Process Pointer Motion Hints

The mouse can generate so many events that X and your application could be completely swamped if you tried to process all of them. The whole point of **XSelectInput** and all the different ways of soliciting mouse events is to allow you to set up X so that it only delivers the events you really want. If you select properly, your application will not have to work its way through a clogged event queue discarding redundant events. Sometimes you need to be able to control not only what events you receive, but the rate at which you receive them. This section presents a method you can use to control the rate of event delivery.

The need to limit the event-delivery rate is most important when you are processing mouse motion events. The trick is to make sure you receive exactly the information you need—no more and no less. For example, if your user is doing an operation such as selecting a menu item, all you care about is where the pointer is now, not the history of where it has been. On the other hand, there are times (for example when the user is digitizing a curve) when you care very much about the history of the pointer motion. X provides good ways of handling mouse motion with or without history, without making you process countless MotionNotify events. You can also eliminate redundant MotionNotify events with methods discussed under the "Event Compression" heading in Chapter 11.

When you use **XSelectInput** to express interest in MotionNotify events, you can specify PointerMotionHintMask together with some other mask if you want your MotionNotify events to serve as hints that the pointer has moved. For example, to receive hints that the user has moved the mouse with any button pressed, you specify

**XSelectInput** ( *display,window,* PointerMotionHintMask|ButtonMotionMask );

Thereafter, the is_hint field in the MotionNotify events arriving from *window* is set to the value NotifyHint (as opposed to NotifyNormal). When the is_hint field is set to NotifyHint, all the event tells you is that the user moved the pointer. Notice that the events also contain x and y fields, but they may not be up-to-date.

> Different makes and models of workstation use different methods to decide when, and how often, to send motion hint events. The only thing you can be sure of is that you will receive at least one new motion hint event each time the user moves the pointer, as long as you respond to each motion hint event.

If you do not care about the history of the pointer's motion, use **XQueryPointer** to determine the current pointer position whenever you get such a hint event.

**Example:** Find the current pointer position after a MotionNotify hint.

```
#include   <X11/Xlib.h>
Display *display;        /* pointer to current Display structure */
Window curw;            /* the window containing the pointer */
Window rw,cw;           /* the root and child windows */
int  xw, yw;            /* coordinate pair in window*/
int  xr, yr;            /* coordinate pair in the root window */
int  keys_buttons;      /* button mask */
XEvent current;         /* event to read */
. . .
XSelectInput ( display, curw,
    PointerMotionHintMask | ButtonMotionMask );
. . .
while (True) {
  XNextEvent ( display, &current );
  switch ( current.type ) {
  case MotionNotify:
    XQueryPointer ( display, current.xmotion.window,
          &rw, &cw, &xr, &yr, &xw, &yw, &keys_buttons );
```

*xmotion.is_hint*

```
        break;
    }
}
```

If you do care about the history of pointer motion, you can respond to hint events by using the **XGetMotionEvents** request. **XGetMotionEvents** would be useful if, for example, the user were digitizing a series of points. When you use **XGetMotionEvents**, you request a motion history buffer.

> Many workstations do not provide a motion history buffer. If the "motion_history" field of the **Display** structure contains the value zero, no motion history buffer is available, and the **XGetMotionEvents** request will not work.

A motion history buffer is an array of structures of the type **XTimeCoord**, defined (in **<X11/Xlib.h>**) as follows:

```
typedef struct _XTimeCoord {
    short x,y;          /* coordinate pair */
    Time time;                  /* X timestamp */
} XTimeCoord;
```

Each element of the motion history array corresponds to a single motion of the pointer. Each element contains the pointer's x and y coordinates (relative to the window you specify) and the time of the motion. If your request to **XSelectInput** had requested MotionNotify events without requesting pointer hints, each element of the motion history buffer would correspond to a single MotionNotify event. The beauty of **XGetMotionEvents** is that you can obtain a stream of motion events at once in a single easy-to-interpret array. **XGetMotionEvents** (*Xlib* ¶8.11) has the form

```
XTimeCoord * mptr;      /* pointer to the returned motion history */
Display * display;      /* pointer to current Display structure */
Window w;               /* window for which you want motion events */
Time start, stop;       /* Interval for which you want motion events */
int nevents;            /* the number of events in the array */
    . . .
if (display.motion_buffer  != 0) {
    mptr = XGetMotionEvents ( display, w, start, stop, &nevents );
    . . .
    XFree ( mptr );
}
```

**XGetMotionEvents** returns, as a function value, a pointer to an array of XTimeCoord structures. The number of structures in the array is returned in *nevents*. The elements in the array correspond to events that fall between the specified *start* and *stop* times (inclusive), and lie within the boundaries of the window *w* at its present position on the screen.

The trickiest part of using **XGetMotionEvents** is specifying the *start* and *stop* times correctly. *start* and *stop* must be valid X event timestamps. The *stop* time should probably come from the MotionNotify event you are processing by calling **XGetMotionEvents**. Alternatively, you may specify the symbol CurrentTime for the *stop* time. The *start* time can come from a previously received event, such as an EnterNotify or ButtonPress, that marked the beginning of the stream of motion events that your application is processing.

> Each time you call it, **XGetMotionEvents** allocates memory heap space for the array of **XTimeCoord** structures, then returns a pointer to the space it allocated. It is your responsibility to release the array space back to the memory heap, using the Xlib function **XFree**, when you have finished using it.

Once you have received a MotionNotify hint event, you must "take the hint" and use either **XQueryPointer** or **XGetMotionEvents**. Many workstations will stop sending MotionNotify hint events until you use one of these requests, or until the button state changes or the pointer moves into some other window.

The workstation satisfies **XGetMotionEvents** requests using an internal motion history buffer. The maximum number of **XTimeCoord** structures in the particular workstation's motion history buffer is available in the "motion_history" field of the **Display** structure returned by **XOpenDisplay**.

## EnterNotify and LeaveNotify Events—Specifics

If pointer motion causes the pointer to move into a different window, EnterNotify and LeaveNotify events are generated in place of MotionNotify. To receive EnterNotify events, your application must specify the EnterWindowMask bit in a call to **XSelectInput**. Likewise, to receive LeaveNotify events, your application must specify the LeaveWindowMask bit. Once your application has selected EnterNotify and LeaveNotify events, it can receive three categories of notifications, which you can tell apart by looking at the value of the "mode" field (in the XCrossingEvent structure or the xcrossing variant of the XEvent structure). The "mode" field has three possible values, NotifyNormal, NotifyGrab, and NotifyUngrab, defined in the header file **<X11/X.h>**.

NotifyNormal   The user or an **XWarpPointer** request moved the pointer across a window boundary.

NotifyGrab   This event reports pseudo-motion due to the start of a grab (Chapter 11).

NotifyUngrab   This event reports pseudo-motion at the end of a grab (Chapter 11).

The (x,y) position reported in both EnterNotify and LeaveNotify events is always the final position of the pointer, after the pointer motion. Therefore, in a LeaveNotify event, the reported (x,y) position is outside the window which has been left.

In a LeaveNotify event, if a child of the event window contained the starting position of the pointer, the "child" field contains the id of that child window; otherwise "child" is set to the value None. In an EnterNotify event, if a child of the event window contains the ending pointer position, the "child" field contains the id of that window, otherwise "child" is set to None. Remember that a child window is a first-level subwindow.

The "focus" field, a Boolean value, is set to True if the window receiving the event is the keyboard focus window or an inferior of the keyboard focus window. If your application's human interface cares whether the keyboard and pointer work with the same window, this field will prove useful. The section entitled "FocusIn and FocusOut Events—Specifics" in Chapter 10 contains an example showing how an application can tell that a window will receive keyboard events.

When a pointer grab activates (see Chapter 11), the first thing that happens is the automatic **XWarpPointer** operation into the *confine_to* window, if any. This automatic pointer motion generates EnterNotify and LeaveNotify events just as if the pointer had been moved manually by the user.

Next, EnterNotify and LeaveNotify events with mode NotifyGrab are generated as if the pointer were to suddenly warp from its current position in the window (or *confine_to* ) it started in, to the same position in the grab window. The pointer does not actually move when the events with NotifyGrab mode are generated.

When a pointer grab deactivates (see Chapter 11), EnterNotify and LeaveNotify events with mode NotifyUngrab are generated as if the pointer were to suddenly warp from its current position in the grab window to the same position in the window it is actually in at the time of the grab deactivation.

If your application is not concerned with grabs (most applications aren't) you should ignore EnterNotify and LeaveNotify events unless they have "mode" fields of NotifyNormal. If you do not check the "mode" field, you may perceive extra EnterNotify and LeaveNotify events as the result of grab operations from other applications.

The "detail" field lets your program determine where in the window hierarchy the pointer came from or where it is going. "detail" has one of five possible values, defined in the header file **<X11/X.h>**.

NotifyAncestor
: In a LeaveNotify event, this detail means that the pointer moved from this window to a direct ancestor (nearer the root) of this window. In an EnterNotify event, this detail means that the pointer moved into this window from a direct ancestor.

NotifyInferior
: In a LeaveNotify event, this detail means that the pointer moved from this window to an inferior (a child, or the child of a child, and so forth) of this window. In an EnterNotify event, this detail means that the pointer moved into this window from an inferior.

NotifyNonlinear        This detail, in both EnterNotify and LeaveNotify
                       events, means that the pointer moved between this
                       window and a sibling or "cousin" window.  Neither
                       window involved is the inferior of the other.

NotifyVirtual          This detail is only generated in windows the pointer
                       "passes through" in the hierarchy when the pointer is
                       moving from an ancestor to an inferior or vice versa.
                       This detail is received in windows for which the
                       pointer either started out in an inferior window and
                       moved to an ancestor or vice versa.

NotifyNonlinearVirtual This detail is only generated in windows the pointer
                       "passes through" in the hierarchy on the way to a sib-
                       ling or "cousin" window.

What actually happens is that every motion of the pointer in or out of a window
generates a series of events in all the windows it passes through as it works its
way through the hierarchy from where it started to where it ended up. (Note that
these events are discarded unless some application has enabled their delivery.)
The situation is best explained by a series of examples.  Figure 9-4 is a diagram
of a screen containing windows Root, A, B, C, D, and E.  The windows are arranged hierarchically such that A and E are children of the root window and B
is the child of A.  In turn, C and D are the children of B.  The figure also shows
the points 1-4.  For the purposes of the examples, suppose that delivery of EnterNotify and LeaveNotify events has been enabled for all the windows on the
screen including the root window.

**Example:**  Move from Point 1 to Point 2.

Window C receives LeaveNotify with detail NotifyNonlinear.

Window D receives EnterNotify with detail NotifyNonlinear.

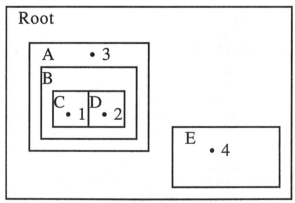

Figure 9-4.  Example window configuration.

**Example:** Move from Point 1 to Point 3.

Window C receives LeaveNotify with detail NotifyAncestor.

Window B receives LeaveNotify with detail NotifyVirtual.

Window A receives EnterNotify with detail NotifyInferior.

**Example:** Move from Point 3 to Point 1.

Window A receives LeaveNotify with detail NotifyInferior.

Window B receives EnterNotify with detail NotifyVirtual.

Window C receives EnterNotify with detail NotifyAncestor.

**Example:** Move from Point 2 to Point 4.

Window D receives LeaveNotify with detail NotifyNonlinear.

Window B receives LeaveNotify with detail NotifyNonlinearVirtual.

Window A receives LeaveNotify with detail NotifyNonlinearVirtual. Note that the root window does not receive any event; the pointer never actually stops being contained in the root window.

Window E receives EnterNotify with detail NotifyNonlinear.

**Example:** Activate a grab in window A.

In this example, assume that the pointer is at point 4, and that a grab activates in window A with a *confine_to* parameter specifying window B.

First, a warp to window B is carried out: Window E receives LeaveNotify with detail NotifyNonlinear, then Window A receives EnterNotify with detail NotifyNonlinearVirtual. Finally Window B receives EnterNotify with detail NotifyNonlinear.

Next, the grab is carried out. Window B receives LeaveNotify with mode NotifyGrab (signifying pseudo-motion at the start of a grab), and with detail NotifyAncestor. Then window A receives EnterNotify with mode NotifyGrab and with detail NotifyInferior.

> Hints for processing EnterNotify and LeaveNotify events:
> *Check the detail field*—if it is NotifyVirtual or NotifyNonlinear-Virtual, it wasn't this window that gained / lost focus!
> *Check the mode field*—ignore all events with modes other than NotifyNormal (unless you are working with pointer grabs).

# Events in Nested Windows

If your application's windows have no hierarchy—that is, they are all children of the workstation root window—it is straightforward to figure out which window's event selection to apply to each direct input event. It belongs to the window which the pointer is in. Things are not usually so simple, however. Most applications have one or more hierarchical levels of nested windows. Much of the power of the X Window System's input handling comes from the way events are delivered in nested windows. In the absence of grabs, device events are delivered as follows:

1. Every event originates in a *source window*–the window the pointer is actually in. Note that for a pointer to be in a window at all, the window must be mapped and at least part of it must be visible (not occluded by other windows). If a pointer is contained in several nested windows, the smallest one is considered the source window.

2. A search is made for the *event window*. This is defined as a window in which any X Window client application has expressed interest in the event by selecting it for delivery.

3. The search starts with the source window, and proceeds up the window hierarchy toward the root window.

4. The search terminates when an event window is found.

5. The search also terminates when either the root window is reached, or when a window that has listed the particular event type in its do-not-propagate mask is reached (see **XGetAttributes, XWindow,** and **XChangeWindowAttributes** ). This mask allows any window to shield its parent from particular events inside it.

6. The event is delivered to all applications that have solicited that particular event type in the event window. (Note that only one application at a time can solicit ButtonPress events from any given window).

Note that all these rules are applied according to the state of the event selection masks and the window hierarchy *before* the event is placed in any application's queue. Queue manipulation requests such as **XPutBackEvent** cannot cause an event to be delivered to a different client, or to a different event window in the same client. This bottom-up search behavior has useful implications for your application:

• Your application can create and map many subwindows without having to explicitly enable event delivery on them all. You can process subwindow events by default, by receiving them in a higher-level window. Alternatively, you can enable the delivery of some or all events to some or all of your subwindows.

• An application can, without interfering with others, set itself up as the default handler of all mouse events from the workstation. This is quite straightforward: all it has to do is solicit all mouse events from the root window. Any mouse events that are not selected by other clients lower in the hierarchy will be duly delivered to the default handler, as will any events that have their source in the root rectangle. This is a good way for window-manager applications to get their events.

## InputOnly Windows

All pointer input is delivered relative to some window on the screen. The X Window System provides a class of window called InputOnly. They are only useful for dividing the screen up for the purposes of input and window-property assignment; as far as graphics output goes, the X Window System acts as if they don't exist. Of course, any ordinary window (which has the class InputOutput) can also be used for controlling input. The *class* characteristic in the **XWindow** request (see Chapter 4) allows you to create an InputOnly window.

Windows in X are a cheap resource, and your application can create as many as you need. For example, in a two-dimensional graphic editor application you might create an InputOnly window of the same size as the bounding box of each object in a drawing. Hierarchically grouped objects, likewise, could be represented by nested windows. This approach might provide a convenient way of letting your user point to and select particular compound objects—each object's bounding box would be represented by its own window. There is no one best way to use windows to control input events; application developers will undoubtedly develop their own creative methods.

# SUMMARY

Workstations are interactive. Much of this interactivity comes from the fact that users can use a mouse to point to things on the screen with a tracking cursor. The mouse and cursor together are called the *pointer*. X provides a variety of ways for applications to receive input from the pointer and control cursor response. Your application can do the following:

- *Poll* the pointer position using **XQueryPointer**.
- Control the pointer's response with **XSetPointerControl**.
- Cause the pointer to jump using **XWarpPointer**.
- Create *cursors* (X resources) with arbitrary shapes and colors.
- Assign cursors as attributes of windows.
- Most importantly, solicit and receive *input events* from the pointer.

The pointer is always *in* some window, even if it is the root window. The position of the pointer with respect to the window hierarchy controls how pointer events are delivered. If the user moves the pointer into one of your application's windows and clicks a mouse button, your application will receive the ensuing pointer events (if you solicited them). It is possible to alter pointer event delivery with *pointer grabs*; see Chapter 11.

The way pointer events are solicited and the way they are processed are intertwined, and must be designed together if your application is to work properly. Pointer events, like other events, are solicited from windows. Pointer events fall into three groups:

- ButtonPress and ButtonRelease events let you know when the user presses and releases mouse buttons.

- MotionNotify events let you know when the user moves the pointer *within* a window.

- EnterNotify and LeaveNotify events let you know when the user moves the pointer *into* and *out of* a window.

The types of pointer events have a great deal in common: all their event structures contain the position of the cursor, the state of the mouse buttons and keyboard modifier keys, and the time of the event. Pointer motion events originate in the *source window* (the window with the pointer in it), and work their way up the event hierarchy toward the root window until they come to a window from which some application has solicited them.

You may solicit ButtonPress and ButtonRelease events together or separately. The workstation automatically grabs the pointer for your application when you receive a ButtonPress event. You will, unless you take special action (see Chapter 11), receive all subsequent pointer events as long as the user holds mouse buttons.

MotionNotify events come in two forms: ordinary motion events and motion hints. You can solicit continuous MotionNotify events. If you do so, you will receive an event any time the user moves the mouse when the cursor is inside your window. These events can be numerous: your application may become bogged down trying to process them.

You can also solicit MotionNotify events only when mouse buttons are pressed. This technique is useful for such human-interface operations as dragging objects. You will still receive large numbers of events this way, but only when mouse buttons are pressed.

Anytime you solict MotionNotify events, you may specify that you want to receive hints. MotionNotify hint events are much less numerous than ordinary MotionNotify events. However, if you solicit hints, you must respond to each hint by polling the pointer.

EnterNotify and LeaveNotify events announce when the pointer crosses window boundaries. From the bird's-eye point of view, when a pointer enters or leaves a window, the workstation generates a flurry of events to all the windows involved in the crossing. All a single application can see, however, is the worm's-eye view. Your application can examine the fields in each delivered EnterNotify and LeaveNotify event, and use them to keep track of where the pointer is in the window hierarchy relative to your window.

# CHAPTER 10
# THE KEYBOARD

Workstations that use the X Window System always have a typewriter keyboard. All of the popular keyboards have keys for each letter of the English alphabet, the ten numeric digits, a spacebar, a delete key, and a selection of "special" characters, such as !@#$%^&*(). All the keyboards also have modifier keys: Shift keys, a Caps Lock or Shift Lock key, and a Control key. This is all that is required of a keyboard to make it usable with the X Window System. Of course, many keyboards provide keys for letters, such as "üßéçÅñ", which are used in languages other than English. The X Window System allows your application to use all the alphanumeric keys on the keyboard. Most keyboards also have a variety of special function keys, such as arrows, page-up and page-down functions, a separate numeric keypad, meta-shift keys, and arbitrary function keys. The number and labelling of these keys vary widely between makes of keyboard.

Feedback mechanisms are built into most keyboards, including a bell or buzzer, a way of making keyclick sounds, and one or more small lightbulbs or light-emitting diodes (LEDs).

When your application interacts with the user, you may set things up so the keyboard works in a variety of ways, depending on what you need to do.

- The user may enter alphabetic and numeric text.

- In conjunction with mouse manipulation, the user can press modifier (Shift and Control, for example) keys, as described in Chapter 9.

- The user can use keyboard buttons instead of mouse buttons to signal mouse-position input.

- The user may use special function keys to control your application.

- You may use the keyboard bell and lights to alert the user.

The X Window System provides a low level single-keystroke-at-a-time interface between your application and the keyboard. Your application is responsible for defining how you want the keyboard to work when interacting with the user, and for making meaningful combinations (such as character strings) from the individual keystrokes.

Input event processing is the most important part of keyboard handling in X. Chapter 3 discusses the basics of input event processing.

This chapter explains how to use the X Window System's keyboard support capabilities. The first section, "Keyboard Events," covers what your application needs to do to accept and interpret keyboard events. The standard keyboard handling method is briefly explained in Chapter 2 and shown in the sample program **helloworld.c** in Appendix A.

The second section, "Keycodes, Keymaps, Keysyms, and Text," presents the details of how X decides what key is what. It explains the concepts behind the standard keyboard handling method presented in the first section.

The third section, "Keyboard Focus," describes how the X Window System decides which window receives keyboard events. Your application only receives keyboard events when one of your windows has the keyboard focus. The third section also describes what you can do to control the keyboard focus, and how you can tell, using events, when you gain or lose the keyboard focus.

The fourth section, "Controlling the Keyboard," explains how to ring the keyboard bell, light the keyboard LEDs and do such things as control the keyboard's auto-repeat capability. It also explains how to poll the keyboard to determine which keys are pressed at any given time.

Your application can temporarily "grab" the keyboard to reserve it for exclusive use. You can also "grab" particular keys. Most applications will not need to use these advanced techniques, but for those that do, they are described in Chapter 11.

# KEYBOARD EVENTS

Application programs receive raw low-level input from the keyboard via KeyPress and KeyRelease events. These events inform the application when a key is pressed or released. These events identify the key the user is pressing or releasing as well as the the current state of the Shift, Lock, and Control keys. Most applications that use keyboard input only use the KeyPress event.

> If you want your application to be portable, avoid depending on KeyRelease events.   Not all makes and models of keyboard generate KeyRelease events.

KeyPress and KeyRelease events are very similar to mouse ButtonPress and ButtonRelease events (see Chapter 9).   They are delivered via an event window, and the position of the pointer is reported in both types of events.   Thus, they can substitute for each other if you so choose.

Your application receives KeyPress and KeyRelease events depending on:

- Whether you have previously expressed interest in those events using **XSelectInput**.   See the section entitled "Controlling Delivery of Keyboard Events" below.

- Whether the keyboard focus is associated with your application's window.   Ordinarily a window-manager application controls the keyboard focus.   See the section entitled "Keyboard Focus" below.

- Whether your application has actively grabbed the keyboard.   You may activate a grab explictly via the **XGrabKeyboard** request or when the user triggers a passive grab via the **XGrabButton** request (see Chapter 11).

At first glance, it looks like setting your application up to receive keyboard events is complex.   Fortunately, what these conditions boil down to is that your application will receive KeyPress and KeyRelease events that are intended for it. Usually the only thing you have to do is use **XSelectInput** to control the delivery of keyboard events.   As far as most applications are concerned, focus and grabs are not important.

Besides KeyPress and KeyRelease, there is one other event type, MappingNotify, which you must handle if you want to process keyboard input correctly.   The workstation uses the MappingNotify event type to inform all applications when the configuration of the keyboard changes.   It is very simple to process MappingNotify events; see the description of **XRefreshKeyboardMapping** below.

## Controlling Delivery of Keyboard Events

As with all events, if your application wants KeyPress and KeyRelease you must solicit them ahead of time. Ordinarily you use the **XSelectInput** request for that purpose (see Chapter 3 for more information).   The bits in the *event_mask* parameter relating to keyboard events have the symbols KeyPressMask and KeyReleaseMask.

When you specify the KeyPressMask bit in the *event_mask* parameter to **XSelectInput,** you will receive a KeyPress event on every key downstroke.   Any time the user presses any key when the keyboard focus is in the window you specify, or grabbed by the window you specify (see Chapter 11), you receive the event.

Keep in mind that it is possible for the user to press and hold more than one key at a time. If the user presses more than one key at a time, you will receive more than one KeyPress event. Also keep in mind that you will receive KeyPress events when the user depresses Shift, Lock, Control, or other modifier keys.

When you specify the KeyReleaseMask bit in the *event_mask* parameter to **XSelectInput,** you will receive a KeyRelease event on each key upstroke—any time the user releases a key.

Note that the capability to detect and report upstrokes is not universal: some workstations cannot detect upstrokes on some or all of their keyboard keys. Avoid depending on KeyRelease events.

Also note that it is possible for your application to receive a KeyPress event and for some other application to receive the matching KeyRelease event, or vice versa. This is true even if you have selected both KeyPress and KeyRelease events, because the keyboard focus can change while the user is holding one or more keys.

A MappingNotify event is generated and delivered to all applications running on the workstation whenever the keyboard configuration (that is, the meanings of the keys) changes. MappingNotify events are special in that there is no need for you to request their delivery with **XSelectInput**. They are always delivered, regardless of any other event selection.

## Receiving and Processing Keyboard Events

Once your application has solicited keyboard events, your event queue will receive them as soon as the user starts pressing keys. Your application has to be ready to read them from the queue and process them. Use the **XNextEvent** call to read your event queue; see the section entitled "Reading the Event Queue" in Chapter 3.

Once you have received a keyboard event and read it from your queue, there are three kinds of things you can do with it:

- Use the keyboard event translation function **XLookupString** to determine what key was pressed.

- Directly inspect the information in the event data structure. You can do this, for example, to determine what window the event came from, or the mouse pointer's position when the key event occurred.

- With MappingNotify events, you always use the **XRefreshKeyboardMapping** function to keep the translation tables current.

Often your application wants to know both what key was pressed and where the mouse cursor was when the key was pressed. In this case you must both use a translation function and work directly with event data. The sample program **helloworld.c** in Appendix A gives an example.

## Keyboard Event Translation Function

There are several keyboard event translation functions.   The most useful is
**XLookupString**, which looks up the ASCII character string corresponding to a
KeyPress or KeyRelease event.   (Other key translation functions are described
below in the "Keycodes, Keymaps, Keysyms, and Text" section.)

Most keys correspond to single characters.   However, **XLookupString** returns
a string rather than a single character because some keys (such as function
keys, for example) generate multiple characters.   **XLookupString** is also
capable of handling multiple-key character composition sequences.
**XLookupString** (*Xlib* ¶10.1.1) has the form

```
XEvent event;           /* a KeyPress or KeyRelease event */
char buffer [20];       /* buffer for result string */
int bufsize = 20;       /* size of buffer */
KeySym key;             /* workstation-independent Key Symbol */
XComposeStatus cs;      /* state for multiple-key character composition*/
int count;              /* number of characters returned in buffer*/
  . . .
count = XLookupString ( &event, buffer, bufsize, &key, &cs );
buffer [ count ] = 0;
```

The primary input to **XLookupString** is the *event* data structure.   This data
structure must contain a KeyPress or KeyRelease event.   A secondary input is
the *cs* structure, which is used to keep track of multi-key sequences (for example,
a user might press Compose, then o, then A, to generate the Å character).   If you
prefer, you can specify zero in place of &*cs*, in which case **XLookupString** will
not attempt to translate multi-key sequences.

**XLookupString** returns the ASCII characters corresponding to the key in the
*buffer* you specify.   You should specify the length of *buffer* in the *bufsize* parameter; no more than this many characters are returned.   In the code excerpt above,
the size of the buffer was arbitrarily set to 20, but you should select a buffer size
appropriate to your application.   As a function result, **XLookupString** returns
the *count* of the characters it puts into *buffer*.   This *count* can be any number,
including zero.

> The character string returned in *buffer* is not terminated with a
> null character.   Thus, standard C functions such as **strcpy** and
> **strcmp** will not work on *buffer* directly, unless you first insert
> the null character.   The statement "*buffer* [ *count* ] = 0;" (above)
> inserts the null character.

A **Keysym** is a symbol which uniquely describes a keyboard key.   Every key
has a symbol, even if it translates to an ASCII *buffer* with a character *count* of
zero.   **XLookupString** returns the key's symbol in *key*.   If you prefer, you can
specify zero in place of &*key*, in which case **XLookupString** will not return a
Keysym.

## XRefreshKeyboardMapping

The **XRefreshKeyboardMapping** function updates the tables which the other translation functions use. We discuss it here because your application must use it to process MappingNotify events. **XRefreshKeyboardMapping** (*Xlib* ¶10.1.1) is very simple; it has the form

```
XEvent event;        /* a MappingNotify event */
   . . .
XRefreshKeyboardMapping ( &event );
```

The primary input to **XRefreshKeyboardMapping** is the *event* data structure containing the MappingNotify event.

## The Keyboard Event Data Structure

KeyPress and KeyRelease events share the same event data structure. The structure type **XKeyEvent** is defined to let you access these events. If you prefer, the types **XKeyPressedEvent** and **XKeyReleasedEvent** are available as alternate names for **XKeyEvent**. The **XEvent** union defines the "xkey" variant as an **XKeyEvent** structure.

Table 10-I shows the field names and data types for the **XKeyEvent** data structure, as defined in the header file **<X11/Xlib.h>**.

| | |
|---|---|
| type | Specifies the event type. |
| serial | Specifies the serial number of the last request processed. |
| send_event | False unless this event was generated by some application issuing the **XSentEvent** request. |
| display | The **Display** structure the event came from. |
| window | The window identifier of the event window. |
| root | This field is the window id of the root window at the top of the window hierarchy containing the source window of the event. The source window is the window the pointer is in at the time of the keyboard event. If your workstation has more than one screen, the source window may be on a different screen from the event window, in which case "root" is not the root window of "window." |
| subwindow | If the focus window is an inferior of the event window (in the "window" field), then this field contains the window id of a first-level child window of "window." The child window can either be the focus window or an ancestor of the focus window. If the pointer is not in an inferior of "window," the "subwindow" field contains the special symbol None. The "subwindow" field always contains None unless an event took place in a subwindow but could not be delivered to that |

| typedef struct { | | |
|---|---|---|
| int  type; | ev.type | KeyPress, KeyRelease |
| unsigned long serial | ev.xany.serial | Last request processed |
| **Bool** send_event; | ev.xany.send_event | From **XSendEvent**? |
| **Display** *display; | ev.xany.display | |
| **Window** window; | ev.xkey.window | Event window |
| **Window** root; | ev.xkey.root | Root window |
| **Window** subwindow; | ev.xkey.subwindow | Child window |
| **Time** time; | ev.xkey.time | Event timestamp |
| int x | ev.xkey.x | x position in event window |
| int y | ev.xkey.y | y position in event window |
| int  x_root | ev.xkey.x_root | x position in root window |
| int  y_root | ev.xkey.y_root | y position in root window |
| unsigned int state; | ev.xkey.state | Button and modifier state |
| int keycode; | ev.xkey.keycode | Keycode of key |
| **Bool** same_screen; | ev.xkey.same_screen | False if inter-screen grab |
| } **XKeyEvent**; | | |

Table 10-I.   Keyboard event type and field names.

                subwindow because of no outstanding **XSelectInput** for the event in the subwindow.

time        This field is the X Window System timestamp at the time of the event. The timestamp value increases by one every millisecond, and is a 32 bit unsigned integer, in the range [0, 4,294,967,296].   The "time" field is useful for measuring elapsed time between events.

x, y        These fields are the coordinates of the pointer relative to the window specified in the "window" field.   They are 16 bit positive numbers.   On a workstation with more than one screen, they are zero if the source window for the event is on a different screen from the event window.

x_root, y_root  These fields are the coordinates of the pointer relative to the root window (specified in the "root" field).   They are 16 bit positive numbers.

state      This field is a mask with one bit in it for each mouse button and each keyboard modifier key (such as Shift and Control) being held by the user *just before* the event.   The bits have the symbolic names shown in Table 9-I.

keycode   This field is the raw Keycode (see below) of the key that was pressed or released to generate the event.   Note that translation functions such as **XLookupString** use both the state and the keycode to determine what key was pressed.

# KEYCODES, KEYMAPS, KEYSYMS AND TEXT

The X Window System does not predefine the keys on the keyboard to be ASCII, or to have any other meaning in the conventional sense of character codes. Instead, X identifies each physical key on the workstation's keyboard by assigning it a small number, in the range 8-255. This small number depends on the make and model of workstation, and is called a *Keycode*. Whenever an X request or an X event refers to a single keyboard key, it uses a keycode.

In order to specify the state of all the keyboard keys at once, X uses a *Keymap* (sometimes called a *key_vector* in this book—an array of bytes with one bit per distinct Keycode. (In the Pascal programming language, a Keymap would be defined as a "SET OF Keycode.") Keymaps are used in KeymapNotify events (see the next section), and **XQueryKeymap** requests to specify the state (pushed or not) of all the keyboard keys simultaneously.

The correspondence between keyboard key and Keycode is completely dependent on the workstation. Some workstations assign Keycodes to keys based on the position of the key on the keyboard, and others use other strategies. This leads to a problem: if all applications had to process Keycodes directly, they would have trouble working on more than one type of keyboard. The X Window System solves this problem by providing *Keysyms*, or standard symbolic encodings, for the symbols engraved on keyboard keys. A representative selection of Keysyms follows:

| | |
|---|---|
| **XK_Return** | Return key |
| **XK_Delete** | Rubout or delete key |
| **XK_Compose** | Compose key, for introducing a multi-keystroke sequence |
| **XK_Up** | Up-arrow key |
| **XK_Down** | Down-arrow key |
| **XK_Help** | Help key |
| **XK_F1** | Function key 1 |
| **XK_Shift_L** | Shift modifier key on left side of keyboard |
| **XK_Shift_R** | Shift modifier key on right side of keyboard |
| **XK_Control_L** | Control modifier key on left side of keyboard |
| **XK_Control_R** | Control modifier key on right side of keyboard |
| **XK_space** | Space bar |
| **XK_0** | Zero-digit key, on main keyboard |
| **XK_KP_0** | Zero-digit key, on numeric keypad |
| **XK_a** | Lowercase A key (unshifted A key) |
| **XK_A** | Uppercase A key (unshifted A key) |
| **XK_ccedilla** | Lowercase ç (C with cedilla) |
| **XK_mu** | μ (Greek mu) key |

All keys, including the Shift, Lock and Control modifier keys, have at least one Keysym each. In principle, there is a Keysym for every symbol engraved on any key. Of course, every workstation does not have all the keys.

In addition, most keys correspond two at least two Keysyms—one with and one without the shift key pressed. "A" and "a," for example, are represented by distinct Keysyms, as the list above shows. X handles this shifting of keys by assigning an indexed list of Keysyms to each keycode. By convention, the Keysym in index zero corresponds to the unshifted key. Index one corresponds to the shifted key. It is possible to have more than two Keysyms in the list for a Keycode, but there is no convention assigning meaning to the additional Keysyms. Such additional Keysyms are provided to allow X to support keyboards with multiple shift keys in a general way.

X automatically manages the table which maps Keycodes to Keysyms as long as you make sure to call **XRefreshKeyboardMapping** each time you receive a MappingNotify event. Further details about the keyboard encoding tables are beyond the scope of this book. They can be found in Section 7.9 of *Xlib—C Language X Interface*. **xmodmap(1)** is a program with which users can change the mapping of Keycodes to Keysyms; whenever **xmodmap** is invoked, all applications running on the workstation receive MappingNotify events.

Keysym values are defined in the header file **<X11/keysym.h>**. Commonly used Keysyms are shown in Appendix C.

## Rationale

Your application translates raw Keycodes to meaningful text via a two-stage process (implemented in the **XLookupString** function described above):

> First, the Keysym is looked up in the list of Keysyms associated with the raw Keycode. The Keysym is chosen from the list based on the state of the Shift key and other modifier keys.

> Second, the Keysym is translated to a text string .

The designers of the X Window System had three specific goals in mind which made this two-stage translation scheme necessary. First, they wanted to be able to represent a Keycode in an eight-bit byte and an entire Keymap in a single X event record (each event record is limited in size to 248 data bits). Second, they wanted X to work compatibly with a wide variety of workstations and keyboards. Third, they wanted applications and users to have the freedom to define the meaning of each keyboard event, without insisting that certain keys have meanings as text.

The first goal was easy to meet: the keyboards being considered for X workstations all have fewer than 248 distinct keys. The second goal was much more troublesome: most workstation vendors have uniquely labelled keys on their keyboards, as well as several variant keyboards which support several different languages. Thus, the designers decided to make the raw Keycode numbers (which have values 8-255) completely workstation dependent. They introduced the Keysym, which is represented by a 29-bit number. There are enough distinct Keysym values available so that X can uniquely define:

- standard Keysyms, available on all workstations, for all "standard" keys (all the keys appearing on the ISO/ECMA standard multinational keyboard, and keys representing all the letters in the ASCII character set and the ISO character sets Latin 1, Latin 2, Latin 3, and Latin 4).

- vendor Keysyms, only available on workstations from particular vendors, for vendor-specific special keys (see your vendor's documentation).

> If you want your application to be portable, confine your use of keyboard keys to those with standard Keysyms. Avoid the use of vendor-specific Keysyms.

The Keycode-to-text translation facility in **XLookupString** meets the third design goal in two ways. First, an application program can use the Keysym directly while ignoring the text completely. Second, the **XRebindKeysym** function (see below) allows an application to define its own ASCII text translation for a particular Keysym.

## Key Translation Service Functions

The most important translation service functions, **XLookupString** and **XRefreshKeyboardMapping**, have already been explained under "Receiving and Processing Keyboard Events" above. A variety of other functions are listed in Table 10-II and described in the following subsections.

| Function | Purpose |
|---|---|
| **XLookupString** | Translate a keyboard event to its Keysym and ASCII |
| **XRefreshKeyboardMapping** | Maintain the Keycode-to-Keysym translation tables |
| **XRebindKeysym** | Define the ASCII text bound to a Keysym |
| **XKeysymToKeycode** | Translate a Keysym to its Keycode |
| **XStringToKeysym** | Translate the text of a Keysym name to the Keysym |
| **XKeysymToString** | Translate a Keysym to the text of its name |
| **XKeycodeToKeysym** | Look up a Keysym for the specified Keycode |
| **XLookupKeysym** | Look up a Keysym for the specified keyboard event |

Table 10-II.   Key translation service functions.

## XRebindKeysym

This function allows your application to assign an arbitrary ASCII text string to any Keysym you wish. In other words, **XRebindKeysym** provides a mechanism you can use to set up user-defined function keys. It alters the table which **XLookupString** uses to translate Keysyms to ASCII. The meaning of the Keysym is only altered within your application, not for all applications running on the workstation. **XRebindKeysym** (*Xlib* ¶10.1.1) has the form

```
Display * display;      /* pointer to current display structure */
KeySym reboundsym;      /* keysym to be rebound */
KeySym modlist [ ] ;    /* array of modifier Keysyms */
```

```
int modlength;            /* length of modlist array */
char newstring [ ] ;      /* string containing new ASCII for key */
int newlength;            /* length of newstring */
  . . .
```

**XRebindKeysym** ( *display, reboundsym, modlist, modlength,*
                         *newstring, newlength* );

This call associates the string *newstring,* for which the length is specified in *newlength,* with the Keysym *reboundsym,* but only when the modifier keys specified in *modlist* are all being pressed.

**Example:**  Bind "STOP" to Shift-F1, and "ABORT" to Control-Shift-F1

This example binds two strings to the same function key under different modifier key combinations.  Note that repeated calls (two for Shift, four for Control-Shift) to **XRebindKeysym** are required because some workstations treat the modifiers on the left and right sides of the keyboard differently.

```
#include <X11/keysym.h>
  . . .
Display * display;
KeySym modlist [2] ;    /* array of modifier Keysyms */
  . . .
modlist [1] = XK_Shift_R;    /* Do the right shift key */
XRebindKeysym ( display, XK_F1, modlist, 1, "STOP", 4 );
modlist [1] = XK_Shift_L; /* Do the left shift key */
XRebindKeysym ( display, XK_F1, modlist, 1, "STOP", 4 );

modlist [1] = XK_Shift_R;  modlist [2] = XK_Control_R; /* Do right mods */
XRebindKeysym ( display, XK_F1, modlist, 2, "ABORT", 5 );
modlist [1] = XK_Shift_L;  modlist [2] = XK_Control_R; /* Do L, R */
XRebindKeysym ( display, XK_F1, modlist, 2, "ABORT", 5 );
modlist [1] = XK_Shift_R;  modlist [2] = XK_Control_L; /* Do R, L */
XRebindKeysym ( display, XK_F1, modlist, 2, "ABORT", 5 );
modlist [1] = XK_Shift_L;  modlist [2] = XK_Control_L; /* Do left mods */
XRebindKeysym ( display, XK_F1, modlist, 2, "ABORT", 5 );
```

# XKeysymToKeycode

This function retrieves a workstation-dependent Keycode when you know the corresponding workstation-independent Keysym.  It is useful in setting up for X requests which require you to specify a Keycode directly. **XKeysymToKeycode** (*Xlib* ¶10.1.1) has the form

```
Display * display;        /* pointer to Display structure */
KeySym sym;               /* workstation-independent Key Symbol */
KeyCode code;             /* resulting Keycode */
```

```
   . . .
code  = XKeysymToKeycode ( display, sym );
```

The function returns the Keycode corresponding to the Keysym specified in *sym*. If no keycode contains *sym* in its translation table, then **XKeysymToKeycode** returns zero.

## XStringToKeysym

This function converts a null-terminated string containing the ASCII name of a Keysym (for example, the string "XK_F1" is the ASCII name for the Keysym of function key 1) to the Keysym code. This function is useful, for example, for reading disk files containing the names of Keysyms. **XStringToKeysym** (*Xlib* ¶10.1.1) has the form

```
KeySym sym;               /* workstation-independent Key Symbol */
char name  [ ] = {"XK_F1"};
   . . .
sym  = XStringToKeysym ( name );
```

Any null-terminated string may be specified in the *name* parameter. If the string is not the name of an existing Keysym, **XStringToKeysym** returns the special value NoSymbol.

## XKeysymToString

This function is the inverse of **XStringToKeysym**. It converts a Keysym to a null-terminated string containing the Keysym's ASCII name. **XKeysymToString** (*Xlib* ¶10.1.1) has the form

```
KeySym sym;               /* workstation-independent Key Symbol */
char * namepointer;;
   . . .
namepointer  = XKeysymToString ( sym );
```

The string returned as **XKeysymToString**'s function result may be displayed or written to a file with standard C functions such as **printf** and **strcpy**. However, you may not change the returned string in any way, and you must not deallocate it when you have finished using it. If the Keysym specified in *sym* is not defined, **XKeysymToString** returns a NULL pointer (*not* a character string with no characters in it).

## XKeycodeToKeysym

This function looks up one of the Keysyms in the internal translation table for the specified Keycode. **XKeycodeToKeysym** (*Xlib* ¶10.1.1) has the form

```
Display * display;        /* pointer to Display structure */
KeyCode code;             /* input Keycode */
int index                 /* index into Keysym list */
KeySym sym;               /* workstation-independent Key Symbol */
```

. . .
*sym* = **XKeycodeToKeysym** ( *display, code, index* );

Specify a Keycode in the *code* parameter. You also must specify the *index*, in the specified Keycode's translation table, of the Keysym you want returned. An *index* of zero refers to the unshifted (lower-case) key, and an *index* of one to the shifted key (note, though, that Keysyms for shifted (upper-case) alphabetic letters may not be available).

**XKeycodeToKeysm** returns, as a function result, the requested Keysym. If no Keysym was found for *code* at the specified *index*, the special value NoSymbol is returned instead.

## XLookupKeysym

**XLookupKeysym**, like **XLookupString**, accepts a KeyPress or KeyRelease event as input. It looks up one of the Keysyms in the translation table for the Keycode specified in the event. **XLookupKeysym** (*Xlib* ¶10.1.1) has the form

```
XEvent event;          /* a KeyPress or KeyRelease event */
int index              /* index into Keysym list */
KeySym sym;            /* workstation-independent Key Symbol */
. . .
sym = XLookupKeysym ( &event, index );
```

The primary input to **XLookupKeysym** is the *event* data structure. This data structure must contain a KeyPress or KeyRelease event. As in **XKeycodeTo-Keysym** above, you also specify the *index* of the Keysym you want returned.

**XLookupKeysym** returns, as a function result, the requested Keysym. If no Keysym was found for the Keycode in the event at the specified *index*, the special value NoSymbol is returned instead.

## Keysym Classification Macros

Keyboards are divided into sections, such as modifier (shift) keys, the numeric keypad, cursor-control keys, and various kinds of function keys. *Xlib* provides macros, shown in Table 10-III, which assist your application in classifying each Keysym according to which keyboard section it is on. Each of these macros returns the value True (1) if the Keysym is in the corresponding keyboard section, and False (0) if it is not. Note that a given Keysym can be in more than one of these classifications.

| Macro | Keyboard Section |
|-------|------------------|
| **IsModifierKey** ( *keysym* ) | Modifier (Shift, Lock, Control, Mod1...) key, on either right or left of keyboard |
| **IsKeypadKey** ( *keysym* ) | Numeric keypad key |
| **IsCursorKey** ( *keysym* ) | Alphanumeric cursor control (arrows, home, prior, next, begin, end) key |
| **IsPFKey** ( *keysym* ) | Programmed function key (PF1, PF2, PF3, PF4) |
| **IsFunctionKey** ( *keysym* ) | Function key (F1, F2...) |
| **IsMiscFunctionKey** ( *keysym* ) | Miscellaneous function (select, help, do...) key |

Table 10-III.  Keysym classification macros.

# KEYBOARD FOCUS

Most applications allow a window manager to take care of controlling the keyboard focus—of assigning the keyboard to a particular window.

However, your application can use the the **XSetInputFocus** and **XGetInputFocus** requests to change the keyboard focus window or find out what it is.  Also, your application can enable the delivery of FocusIn and FocusOut events, which inform you when your windows gain or lose the keyboard.

When the user is running several applications in several different windows, he has the idea that the keyboard "belongs" to one or another of them.  From the application's point of view, this "belonging" is the keyboard focus.

> Avoid "fighting" with the window manager over keyboard focus. Most well-behaved application programs will accept the window manager's focus assignments.

The keyboard is always focussed on some window, unless **XSetInputFocus** has been used to set the focus to None, in which case keyboard events are completely suppressed.  The window to which keyboard events are actually delivered is controlled by both the keyboard focus and the window the pointer is currently in. If the pointer is in the keyboard focus window or one of its inferiors, keyboard events are reported normally, by searching the window hierarchy.  However, if the pointer is not in the keyboard focus window or an inferior, the keyboard event is reported directly to the focus window.

If the keyboard is focussed on the root window, it behaves as if it were unfocussed:  all keyboard events are reported normally, because the pointer is always in the root window or an inferior.  Under these circumstances, the user can select which window he wants the keyboard to belong to simply by using the mouse to move the cursor into the window.  Some window managers provide this simple behavior; others require the user to click the mouse or otherwise change the focus actively.

When the focus changes, FocusOut events are generated for the window losing the focus and the hierarchy of windows between the losing window and the root window.  FocusIn events are generated for the window hierarchy gaining the focus (see the section entitled "Receiving and Processing Focus Events").   As usual, focus change events are only delivered if they were selected via a prior call to **XSelectInput.**

## XGetInputFocus

You may use the **XGetInputFocus** request to determine the current keyboard focus setting.   **XGetInputFocus** (*Xlib* ¶ 7.7.1) has the form

```
Display *display;        /* pointer to current display structure */
Window focus;            /* returned focus window*/
int revert_to;           /* returned revert_to instructions */
    . . .
XGetInputFocus ( display, &focus, &revert_to );
```

In the *focus* parameter is returned the current focus window, or the symbol None. In the *revert_to* parameter is returned one of the symbols RevertToParent, RevertToPointerRoot, or RevertToNone.   See below for explanations of these symbols.

## XSetInputFocus

Use the **XSetInputFocus** request if you want your application to alter the keyboard focus.   **XSetInputFocus** (*Xlib* ¶ 7.7.1) has the form:

```
Display *display;        /* pointer to current display structure */
Window focus;            /* window to which to set focus */
int revert_to;           /* what to do if focus becomes unviewable */
Time time;               /* time stamp of event triggering request */
    . . .
XSetInputFocus ( display, focus, revert_to, time );
```

*focus* specifies the window id of the window to which you want to set the keyboard focus.   For *focus,* you may specify one of three things:

The id of any window.   This window becomes the keyboard's focus window.

The symbol None instead of a window id.   None causes all keyboard events to be discarded until your application or some other application uses another **XSetInputFocus** request to set a focus window.

The symbol PointerRoot instead of a window id.   PointerRoot means that the root window should be used as the focus window.   (If your workstation has more than one screen, PointerRoot causes the focus window to be the root window of whichever screen the pointer is on at the time the user generates each keyboard event).

If the focus window becomes unviewable (because it was unmapped, destroyed, or completely occluded by other windows) X changes the input focus: another **XSet-InputFocus** operation (including delivery of FocusIn and FocusOut events) is carried out implicitly to set the focus to some other window. The *revert_to* parameter lets you control what window receives the focus in this case. You may specify one of three symbols for *revert_to* :

> RevertToParent causes the focus to revert to the *focus* window's parent, or closest viewable ancestor.

> RevertToPointerRoot causes the implicit **XSetInputFocus** to set the *focus* to PointerRoot.

> RevertToNone causes the implicit **XSetInputFocus** to set the *focus* to None.

The *revert_to* parameter is ignored if you call **XSetInputFocus** with a *focus* parameter of either PointerRoot or None. Note that the symbols Parent, PointerRoot, and None are defined in the header file **<X11/X.h>**.

> If you do set the keyboard focus, be sure you know what you are doing if you specify a *focus* of None or a *revert_to* of RevertToNone; a focus of None causes the keyboard to "go dead." When in doubt, use RevertToParent.

In the *time* parameter, specify the timestamp from the event (such as the ButtonPress or KeyPress event) that caused you to call **XSetInputFocus**.

## Focus Models

By convention, window managers support four different *input focus models*: four different ways of controlling how the workstation distributes keyboard events to applications:

1) No Input. This focus model is used by applications that do not expect any keyboard input.

2) Passive Input. Applications using this focus model expect keyboard input, but never use **XSetInputFocus**. They depend on the window manager to assign input focus to them. Many simple applications use this model. They work if the window manager sets the input focus to PointerRoot and the user moves the pointer into the window. They also work when the window manager explicitly sets focus to the application's top level window. See the example at the end of the "Focus Change Detail" section later in this chapter.

3) Locally Active Input. Applications using this focus model do use **XSetInputFocus**, but *only* to change the focus from one of its windows to another. In this model, the application waits (as it would if it were a Passive Input application) for the window manager to assign focus to one of its windows. Once the window manager assigns focus to any of its windows, the Locally Active Input applica-

tion is free to reassign focus to other windows.

4) Globally Active Input.   Applications using this focus model use **XSetInputFocus** to take the keyboard focus from other applications.   For example, suppose the application contained both a simulated button and a text field.   If the user activates a button (by pointing to it and clicking a mouse button), there is no point in assigning the focus to the application.   On the other hand, if the user points to the text field, the application should assume the user wants to type text, and should acquire the focus.

The window manager cannot implement Globally Active Input without application help, because it cannot tell which mouse-clicks in application windows should change the focus and which should not.

Your application should inform the window manager of the focus model you intend to use by using the **XSetWMHints** call immediately after you create your top-level window (see the "WM Hints" section of Chapter 4).

If your input focus model is Passive Input or Locally Active Input, set the "input" field in the **XWMHints** structure to True when you call **XSetWMHints**. If you do this, you are telling the window manager that you need its help to acquire the input focus.   If the window manager assigns focus at all (it doesn't have to: some window managers just leave the focus set to PointerRoot), it will assign it to your top-level window.   Thus, if your user is manipulating the pointer within your application's windows and subwindows, you can count on receiving keyboard events at any level of your window hierarchy you choose.   On the other hand, if the user moves the pointer outside your application's window hierarchy (without invoking the window manager to change focus), keyboard events will arrive via the window at the top of your window hierarchy.

## Soliciting FocusOut and FocusIn Events

When you specify the FocusChangeMask bit in the *event_mask* parameter to **XSelectInput,** you will receive a FocusOut event any time the keyboard focus is lost by the event window you specify, and a FocusIn event any time the keyboard focus is gained by the window you specify.   Focus changes are generated when some application uses the **XSetInputFocus** request .   The workstation also generates special FocusOut and FocusIn events when an active keyboard grab begins or ends (see Chapter 11).

You can find out when your application gains or loses the use of the keyboard via FocusIn and FocusOut events.   This is especially useful if your application uses the Passive Input or Locally Active Input focus models.   For example, you can cue the user by highlighting a window's border when it has the focus.   This way the user can tell which window is receiving information from the keyboard.

In X, FocusOut and FocusIn events are designed to allow your application to keep track of when a particular window gains or loses the focus, and why.   You can also keep track of whether a window's inferiors have gained or lost the focus. If you solicit LeaveNotify and EnterNotify events as well as FocusOut and FocusIn events, the workstation will send you enough information to allow your application reliably to determine whether it, or its inferiors, will receive keyboard events. See the section "Receiving and Processing Focus Events" later in this chapter for more information.

Unmapping a window or one of its ancestors can cause focus changes: the focus reverts to whatever was specified in the most recent *revert_to* parameter to the most recent **XSetInputFocus** call. For the purposes of event-generation, a focus reversion generates exactly the same events as any other focus change. FocusOut events caused by the unmapping of a window come after any UnmapNotify events (see Chapter 4) caused by the same operation. However, you cannot rely upon any particular ordering of FocusOut events relative to VisibilityNotify (Chapter 4), Expose (Chapter 5) or EnterNotify/LeaveNotify events (Chapter 9) caused by a particular window unmapping.

## FocusIn and FocusOut Events—Specifics

FocusIn and FocusOut events have identical structures. Their structure type is **XFocusChangeEvent**, also available under the alternate names **XFocusIn-Event** and **XFocusOutEvent**. The **XEvent** union defines the "xfocus" variant as an **XFocusEvent** structure.

As Table 10-IV shows, focus change events (defined in the header file **<X11/Xlib.h>**) have the following data fields:

type        Specifies the event type, FocusOut or FocusIn.

serial      Specifies the serial number of the last request processed.

send_event  False unless this event was generated by some application issuing the **XSentEvent** request.

display     The **Display** structure the event came from.

window      This field is the window identification of the event window.

| typedef struct { | | |
|---|---|---|
| int  type; | ev.type | FocusOut, FocusIn |
| unsigned long serial | ev.xany.serial | Last request processed |
| **Bool** send_event; | ev.xany.send_event | From **XSendEvent**? |
| **Display** *display; | ev.xany.display | |
| **Window** window; | ev.xfocus.window | Event window |
| int mode; | ev.xfocus.mode | Mode (Normal, Grab...) |
| int detail; | ev.xfocus.detail | Detail |
| } **XFocusChangeEvent**; | | |

Table 10-IV  FocusOut and FocusIn event types and field names.

KeymapNotify events have no "window" field.

mode   This field appears in FocusIn and FocusOut events.   It specifies the category of focus change notification (that is, whether or not the focus change is the result of a keyboard grab).   See below for more information, and see Chapter 11 for information on keyboard grabs.

detail   In this field is returned a value allowing the application to determine the relationship between the new and former focus windows.

## Focus Change Mode

Each FocusIn and FocusOut event structure has a mode member.   By looking at the mode member, your application can find out whether the event announces a normal keyboard-focus change, or a change due to a grab (see Chapter 11).   The mode field can have one of four symbolic values (defined in **<X11/X.h>**):

NotifyNormal   The focus changed while the keyboard was not grabbed.

NotifyGrab   This event reports a focus change due to the activation of a keyboard grab.

NotifyUngrab   This event reports a focus change due to the termination of a keyboard grab.

NotifyWhileGrabbed The focus changed while the keyboard was grabbed.

## Focus Change Detail

Whenever the input focus changes (as the result of an **XSetInputFocus** request issued by some application, or as the result of a grab), several windows potentially receive FocusOut events, and several others potentially receive FocusIn events.   The value in the detail field of each focus change event lets your program determine where in the window hierarchy, relative to the event window, the input focus came from or where it is going.

Applications use focus change events to keep track of which window, if any, they should expect to receive KeyPress and KeyRelease events from.   The most common use of focus change events is for highlighting the focus window.

When the focus changes, the workstation notifies all applications running on it by generating a series of FocusOut events, then a series of FocusIn events.   The workstation delivers each of these events to any application that has solicited it from its window by specifying FocusChangeMask in a call to **XSelectInput**.

The workstation generates FocusOut events starting with whatever window contains the pointer, and works its way up the window hierarchy towards the root. Four groups of windows can receive FocusOut events as the result of a focus change:

(1)   Pointer-containing inferiors of the window losing the focus (only if the pointer is in an inferior of the focus window)

(2)    The window losing the focus itself
(3)    Ancestors of the window losing  the focus
(4)    The root window (or windows) if the focus was PointerRoot or None.

Once the workstation has delivered all FocusOut events, it then works its way back down the window hierarchy delivering FocusIn events.  An analogous four groups of windows can receive FocusIn events:

(5)    The root window (or windows) if the new focus is PointerRoot or None
(6)    Ancestors of the window gaining the focus
(7)    The window gaining the focus itself
(8)    Pointer-containing inferiors of the window gaining the focus (only if the pointer is in an inferior of the focus window).

Notice that each focus change generates at most one FocusOut and at most one FocusIn event for each window, depending upon which window groups it is in relative to the windows losing and gaining the focus.  Notice also that a FocusChangeMask event-solicitation causes your application to receive FocusOut and FocusIn events for your window, regardless of which group your window is in.

If we look at the sequence of events when focus changes from the workstation's bird's-eye view, it looks as if the workstation generates a series of events to different windows.  However, application programs must take the worm's-eye view: you cannot necessarily tell what is happening to windows other than your own. The trick to interpreting FocusIn and FocusOut events is knowing how to use the detail field to figure out which window group your window is in with respect to each focus change.  Once you know what group your window is in, it will be straightforward to determine the significance of the event to your window.

In the rest of this section, we will discuss the eight window groups in bird's-eye-view order.  Remember, though, that your application can only see the worm's eye view.

Windows in group (1) are the first to receive FocusOut events when the focus changes.  If the pointer is in an inferior of the window losing the focus, that window receives a FocusOut event, as do all the windows in the hierarchy between the pointer window and the window actually losing the focus.  These windows, between the pointer window and the window losing focus, are the event windows for group (1) FocusOut events.  If the pointer is not in an inferior of the window losing the focus, group (1) has no windows in it.

Recall from earlier in this chapter that KeyPress and KeyRelease events are delivered normally to the window containing the pointer, as long as the pointer is in an inferior of the window presently holding the keyboard focus.  KeyPress and KeyRelease events propagate up the window hierarchy to parent windows: this means that the keyboard events can potentially be delivered to any ancestor of the pointer window.   These group (1) FocusOut events are delivered to those same windows.

From the worm's eye view, the significance of your window being in group (1) is that it should no longer expect keyboard events, even if the pointer is still contained in it. You can tell that an event window is in group (1) with respect to a focus change because the event's detail field will have one of the following two values (defined in **<X11/X.h>**:

| | |
|---|---|
| NotifyPointer | An ancestor of the event window has lost the focus. |
| NotifyPointerRoot | The focus was PointerRoot. |

Group (2) contains the window actually losing the focus. Group (2) always has exactly one window in it (unless the focus was PointerRoot or None). From the worm's point of view, if your window receives a group (2) FocusOut event, it means that the focus was set to your window, but has been changed to some other window. You should no longer expect to receive keyboard events from a window when it loses the focus. You can tell that an event window is in group (2) with respect to a focus change because the event's detail field will have one of three possible values:

| | |
|---|---|
| NotifyAncestor | The event window lost the focus to an ancestor window. |
| NotifyInferior | The event window lost the focus to an inferior window. |
| NotifyNonlinear | The event window lost the focus to an unrelated (neither ancestor nor inferior) window, or the new focus setting is PointerRoot or None. |

Group (3) windows are ancestors of the window losing the focus, up to but not including the common ancestor with the window gaining the focus.

From the worm's-eye view, when your application receives a group (3) FocusOut event, it means that some inferior of your event window has lost the focus. You can tell that an event window is in group (3) with respect to a focus change because the event's detail field will have one of two possible values:

| | |
|---|---|
| NotifyVirtual | An inferior of the event window lost the focus to an ancestor of the event window. |
| NotifyNonlinearVirtual | An inferior of the event window has lost the focus to an unrelated (neither ancestor nor inferior) window, or the new focus setting is PointerRoot or None. |

Only root windows can be in group (4). FocusOut events in group (4) are only generated if the focus was PointerRoot or None. On a multiple-screen workstation, group (4) events are generated for all screens' root windows if they are generated at all. The following two detail field values, when delivered as part of FocusOut events to root windows, identify group (4) events:

| | |
|---|---|
| NotifyPointerRoot | The focus was PointerRoot. |
| NotifyDetailNone | The focus was None. |

Group (5) is like group (4):  It only includes root windows.  FocusIn events in group (5) are only generated if the new focus setting is PointerRoot or None.  On a multiple-screen workstation, group (5) events are generated for all screens' root windows if they are generated at all.  The following two detail field values, when delivered as part of FocusIn events to root windows, identify group (5) events:

| | |
|---|---|
| NotifyPointerRoot | The new focus setting is PointerRoot. |
| NotifyDetailNone | The new focus setting is None. |

Group (6) windows are ancestors of the window gaining the focus, up to but not including the common ancestor with the window losing the focus.

From the worm's-eye view, when your application receives a group (6) FocusIn event, it means that some inferior of your event window has gained the focus.  You can tell that an event window is in group (6) with respect to a focus change because the event's detail field will have one of  two possible values:

| | |
|---|---|
| NotifyVirtual | An inferior of the event window gained the focus from an ancestor of the event window. |
| NotifyNonlinearVirtual | An inferior of the event window gained the focus from an unrelated (neither ancestor nor inferior) window, or the old focus setting was PointerRoot or None. |

Group (7) contains the window actually gaining the focus.  Group (7) always has exactly one window in it (unless the new focus setting is PointerRoot or None).  From the worm's point of view, if your window receives a group (7) FocusIn event, it means that the focus is now set to your window, meaning that your window can expect to receive all keyboard events except those going to your window's inferior windows.  You can tell that an event window is in group (7) with respect to a focus change because the event's detail field will have one of  three possible values:

| | |
|---|---|
| NotifyAncestor | The event window gained the focus from an ancestor window. |
| NotifyInferior | The event window gained the focus from an inferior window. |
| NotifyNonlinear | The event window gained the focus from an unrelated (neither ancestor nor inferior) window, or the old focus setting was PointerRoot or None. |

The focus change finishes by generating FocusIn events for group (8) windows.  Group (8) windows are in an analogous position to group (1) windows in the window hierarchy.

From the worm's eye view, the significance of your window being in group (8) is that it may expect keyboard events because the pointer is contained in it.  You can tell that an event window is in group (8) with respect to a focus change because the event's detail field will have one of the following two values:

NotifyPointer                An ancestor of the event window has gained the fo-
                             cus.

NotifyPointerRoot            The new focus setting is PointerRoot.

Recall from Chapter 9 that EnterNotify and LeaveNotify events also have a detail field with possible values NotifyAncestor, NotifyInferior, NotifyNonlinear,
NotifyVirtual, and NotifyNonlinearVirtual.   FocusIn and FocusOut events are
more complicated than EnterNotify and LeaveNotify because of the relationship
of focus to the pointer, and because focus can be set to PointerRoot or None.  However, notice that all four event types assign similar meanings to the five detail
values they use in common.

Focus change events are best explained by a series of examples.   Figure 10-1 is a
diagram of a screen containing windows Root, A, B, C, D, and E (the same example configuration as used in the section entitled "EnterNotify and LeaveNotify Events—Specifics" in Chapter 9).   For the purposes of the examples, suppose
that FocusIn and FocusOut events have been solicited for all windows including
the root window, and that the pointer is at point P in window C.

**Example:**  Focus starts in window D, changes to window C.

Window D receives FocusOut with detail NotifyNonlinear: group (2).

Window C receives FocusIn with detail NotifyNonlinear: group (7).

**Example:**  Focus starts in window B, changes to window E.

Window C receives FocusOut with detail NotifyPointer: group (1).

Window B receives FocusOut with detail NotifyNonlinear: group (2).

Window A receives FocusOut with detail NotifyNonlinearVirtual:   group
(3).

Window E receives FocusIn with detail NotifyNonlinear: group (7).

**Example:**  Focus starts in window E, changes to window A.

Window E receives FocusOut with detail NotifyNonlinear: group (2).

Window A receives FocusIn with detail NotifyNonlinear: group (7).

Windows B and C receive FocusIn with detail NotifyPointer: group (8).

**Example:**  Focus starts in window D, changes to window A.

Window D receives FocusOut with detail NotifyAncestor: group (2).

Window B receives FocusOut with detail NotifyVirtual: group (3).

Window A receives FocusIn with detail NotifyInferior: group (7).

Windows B and C receive FocusIn with detail NotifyPointer: group (8).

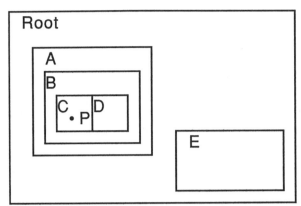

Figure 10-1.   Example window configuration.

**Example:**  Focus starts in window B, changes to PointerRoot.

Window C receives FocusOut with NotifyPointer: group (1).

Window B receives FocusOut with NotifyNonlinear: group (2).

Window A receives FocusOut with NotifyNonlinearVirtual: group (3).

The root window receives FocusIn with NotifyPointerRoot:  group (5).

Windows A, B, and C receive FocusIn detail NotifyPointerRoot: group (8).

**Example:**  Focus starts at PointerRoot, changes to window E.

Windows C, B, and A receive FocusOut with NotifyPointerRoot: group (1).

The root window receives FocusOut with NotifyPointerRoot:  group (4).

Window E receives FocusIn with NotifyNonlinear: group (7).

**Example:**  Highlighting a window border when focus is in the window

The important thing about focus is whether the keyboard is, as far as the user is concerned, focussed on your application's window or any of its subwindows.  This example explains how to use EnterNotify, Leave-Notify, FocusIn, and FocusOut events to keep track of the keyboard focus.

Your application cannot easily tell where the keyboard focus is unless you keep track of when you gain and lose the focus.  A window's gaining the focus is signalled by two things:  EnterNotify events with a True focus field (see Chapter 9) or FocusIn events in groups (7) or (8).  Conversely, a window's losing the focus is signalled by LeaveNotify events with a True focus field or FocusOut events in groups (1) or (2).  In this example, we use the Boolean variable *ptr_inside* to keep track of Enter-Notify events, and *focus_inside* to keep track of FocusIn events.

```
Display * mydisplay;
XEvent myevent;
```

```
Window mywindow;
long int hi_border, lo_border;     /* pixel values for border */
long int border;                    /* pixel values to draw into border */
Bool ptr_inside = False;            /* flag keepting track of pointer */
Bool focus_inside = False;          /* flag keepting track of focus */
 . . .
XSelectInput ( mydisplay, mywindow,
   FocusChangeMask | EnterWindowMask | LeaveWindowMask );
 . . .
while (True) {        /* main event loop */
 XNextEvent ( mydisplay, &myevent );
 switch ( myevent.type )
 {
   . . .
   case EnterNotify:
   case LeaveNotify:
    /* detect an Enter or Leave which carries implicit keyboard focus */
    if (  ( myevent.xcrossing.focus ) &&
          ( myevent.xcrossing.detail == NotifyAncestor ||
          ( myevent.xcrossing.detail == NotifyInferior ||
          ( myevent.xcrossing.detail == NotifyNonlinear ) ) ) {
     ptr_inside = (myevent.type == EnterNotify);
     if (ptr_inside || focus_inside) border = hi_border;
     else border = low_border;
     XSetWindowBorder ( mydisplay, mywindow, border );
     }
    break;
   case FocusIn:
   case FocusOut:
    /* detect an explicit FocusIn or FocusOut */
    if   ( myevent.xfocus.detail == NotifyAncestor ||
         ( myevent.xfocus.detail == NotifyInferior ||
         ( myevent.xfocus.detail == NotifyNonlinear )  {
     focus_inside = (myevent.type == FocusIn);
     if (ptr_inside || focus_inside) border = hi_border;
     else border = low_border;
     XSetWindowBorder ( mydisplay, mywindow, border );
     }
    break;
 }
}
```

This example only highlights the window when it, and none of its inferiors, owns the keyboard. If you prefer to highlight your application's window when it or any of its inferiors owns the keyboard, change the detail-checking to ignore only events with NotifyInferior details. The following code excerpt shows this:

```
case  EnterNotify:
case  LeaveNotify:
   if (   ( myevent..xcrossing.focus  )  &&
         ( myevent.xcrossing.detail  != NotifyInferior )  )  {

      . . .
      }
   break;
case FocusIn:
case FocusOut:
   if  ( myevent.xfocus.detail  != NotifyInferior)   {

      . . .
      }
   break;
```

## Soliciting KeymapNotify events

KeymapNotify events are described here because the workstation delivers them immediately after FocusIn (and EnterNotify) events if your application solicits them. When you specify the KeymapStateMask bit in the *event_mask* parameter to **XSelectInput** you will receive a KeymapNotify event immediately after each FocusIn or EnterNotify event (see Chapter 9). The information in the Keymap-Notify event record is a Keymap. You can use this Keymap to determine the state of all the keys on the keyboard at the time of the FocusIn or EnterNotify event.

Notice that your application only receives KeymapNotify events immediately after FocusIn or EnterNotify events are generated. However, if you selected KeymapNotify events without also selecting FocusIn and/or EnterNotify events, you will receive just the KeymapNotify events.

KeymapNotify events are useful if your application calls for the user to press and hold keyboard keys. They let you find out which keys start out pressed when your application's window gains the keyboard focus, or when the pointer enters your application's window.

## Receiving and Processing KeymapNotify Events

KeymapNotify events have the structure type **XKeymapEvent**. The **XEvent** union defines the "xkeymap" variant as an **XKeymapEvent** structure.

| typedef struct {<br> int type;<br> unsigned long serial;<br> **Bool** send_event;<br> **Display** *display;<br> **Window** window;<br> char key_vector[32];<br>} **XKeymapEvent**; | ev.type<br>ev.xany.serial<br>ev.xany.send_event<br>ev.xany.display<br><br>ev.xkeymap.window<br>ev.xkeymap.key_vector | KeymapNotify<br>Last request processed<br>From **XSendEvent**?<br><br>Event window<br>Key map |
|---|---|---|

Table 10-V  KeymapNotify event type and field names.

As Table 10-V shows, KeymapNotify events (defined in the header file **<X11/Xlib.h>**) have the following fields:

type   Specifies the event type.

serial   Specifies the serial number of the last request processed.

send_event  False unless this event was generated by some application issuing the **XSentEvent** request.

display  The **Display** structure the event came from.

window  This field is the window indentifier of the event window.

key_vector This field is an array of 32 8-bit bytes.  For information on how to interpret a key_vector, see the section entitled "Polling the Keyboard" below.

# CONTROLLING THE KEYBOARD

## Polling the Keyboard

You may determine the state (pressed or not pressed) of all the keys on the keyboard by using the **XQueryKeymap** request.  This request returns a Keymap or *key_vector*: a vector of 32 8-bit bytes.  Each bit in this vector corresponds to the Keycode of a particular key.  If the bit is set, the corresponding key is currently depressed by the user;  if the bit is zero, the corresponding key is not depressed. **XQueryKeymap** (*Xlib* ¶ 7.8) has the form

```
    Display        *display;        /* current display */
    char           key_vector[32];  /* Keymap vector */
    . . .
    XQueryKeymap ( display, key_vector );
```

Note that only the *last* 248 bits (31 bytes) of the *key_vector* are meaningful, because no Keycodes have values between 0 and 7.  In other words, the first byte of *key_vector* is unused.

This request (and the KeymapNotify event, which returns the same information) is most useful for applications which use both KeyPress and KeyRelease events. Using the *key_vector*, such applications can determine the current key state, and use that knowledge to figure out whether to expect a KeyPress or KeyRelease next from each key. Keep in mind that all direct input events already report the state of the keyboard modifier keys in the state field: you only need to use a *key_vector* (from either this **XQueryKeymap** request or from the KeymapNotify event) when you want the state of non-modifier keys.

**Example:** A function to determine whether a certain key is pressed

This function, named IsKeyPressed, accepts a Keysym as input. It converts the Keysym to a Keycode, then calls **XQueryKeymap**, and returns 1 if the specified key was pressed, or 0 otherwise. Remember that Keycodes are defined in the range 8-255.

```
int IsKeyPressed ( Display *display, KeySym sym )
{
char  key_vector[32];
KeyCode code;
int  keybit;
unsigned int byteindex;        /* keycode's byte */
unsigned int bitindex;         /* keycode's bit */
code = XKeysymToKeycode ( display, sym );
if (code == NoSymbol) return (0);
byteindex = (code / 8);
bitindex = code & 7;
XQueryKeymap    ( display, key_vector );
keybit = (  1 & (key_vector[ byteindex ] >> bitindex)  );
return  (keybit);
}
```

This example explains how you look up the bit for a particular Keycode in a *key_vector*. The first Keycode (8) is stored in the low-order bit of the second byte (byte index one) in the *key_vector*. Keycode 9 is in the next bit, and so forth up to Keycode 15. Keycode 16 is in the low order bit of byte index two, and so forth. Byte index zero is unused.

## Ringing the Keyboard Bell

Use the **XBell** request to sound the electronic bell or buzzer in the keyboard. **XBell** (*Xlib* ¶ 7.8) has the form

```
Display *display;       /* pointer to current display structure */
int percent;            /* loudness relative to base bell volume */
. . .
XBell ( display, percent );
```

You may control the loudness of the bell relative to the base bell volume (see **XSetKeyboardControl**). Specify *percent* as a number between -100 and 100. When the bell is sounded, the *percent* you specify is used to modify the base bell volume. A *percent* of -100 will prevent the bell from sounding, no matter what the base bell volume; a *percent* of zero will cause the bell to sound at the base volume, and a *percent* of 100 will cause the bell to sound at full volume.

The base bell volume is a user-preference setting. Ordinarily you should specify zero as the *percent* parameter to **XBell** so you honor the user's preference.

Use the keyboard bell sparingly. Good times to use it are when your application detects a typing error, or at the end of a lengthy noninteractive operation to get the user's attention.

> In some environments (hospitals, libraries, dormitories, for example) if users set the base bell volume to zero, it means they want quiet. Think twice before making your application sound the bell using a positive *percent*.

If your application needs an infallible way to get the user's attention, you can, during initialization, use **XGetKeyboardControl** (below) to determine the base bell volume. If the base bell volume is zero, your application can use a visual signal (such as a bright flashing area) rather than the bell.

## Keyboard Control Settings

The X Window System allows applications to control several details of keyboard operation, including:

- Key click volume
- Bell volume, tone, and duration
- LEDs: lamps on the keyboard
- Automatically repeating keyboard keys.

> Keyboard settings fall into the category of user-preference functions. Permanent settings of user-preference functions should be left to a user-preference-control application (such as **xset**; see the section in Chapter 8 entitled "Controlling Pointer Motion").

## Changing Keyboard Control Settings

Use the **XChangeKeyboardControl** request (*Xlib* ¶ 7.8) if you want to change keyboard control settings. It has the form

```
Display *display;         /* current display structure */
unsigned long value_mask; /* controls which settings get changed */
XKeyboardControl values; /* structure specifying settings */
. . .
XChangeKeyboardControl ( display, value_mask, &values );
```

*value_mask* is a bitmask containing one bit for each field in the *values* structure; see below.   If you set a bit in *value_mask*, it indicates that you have set the corresponding field in *values*.   *value_mask* lets you select which keyboard control settings you want to change in a single use of **XChangeKeyboardControl**.

*values* is a structure of type XKeyboardControl (defined in the header file **<X11/Xlib.h>**).   In the *values* parameter, you specify the following fields:

key_click_percent  Specify an integer in the range [-1, 100] inclusive.   This parameter sets the volume of the keyclick sound from off (0) to loud (100).   A value of -1 restores the default volume.   Specify KBKeyClickPercent in *value_mask* if you want to change keyclick volume.

bell_percent  Specify an integer in the range [-1, 100] inclusive.   This parameter sets the base bell volume from off (0) to loud (100).   A value of -1 restores the default volume.   Specify KBBellPercent in *value_mask* if you want to change base bell volume.

bell_pitch  Specify an integer. This parameter sets the pitch of the bell in Hz.   A value of -1 restores the default pitch.   Specify KBBellPitch in *value_mask* if you want to change bell pitch.

bell_duration  Specify an integer.   This parameter sets the duration of the bell tone in milliseconds.   A value of -1 restores the default duration.   Specify KBBellDuration in *value_mask* if you want to change bell duration.

led  Specify the number of a keyboard LED, in the range 1-32. If both this parameter and led_mode (below) are specified then the state of the specified LED is changed.   Specify both KBLed and KBLedMode in *value_mask* if you wish to turn a particular LED on or off.

led_mode  Specify 0 (off) or 1 (on).   If the led parameter (above) is not specified, all the LEDs on the keyboard are changed; otherwise the specified LED is changed.   Specify KBLedMode in *value_mask* if you want to turn all the LEDs on or off.   (Do not specify KBLed without also specifying KBLedMode; this generates a Match error event message).

key  Specify the Keycode of a key for which you want automatic repeat turned on or off.   If both this parameter and auto_repeat_mode (below) are specified then the auto-repeat mode of the specified key is changed.   Specify both KBKey and KBAutoRepeatMode in *value_mask* if you wish to turn auto-repeat on or off for a particular key. Note that many keyboards do not provide per-key control of automatic repeat. Settings that cannot be honored are ignored. To find out whether the workstation honored your request to set auto-repeat mode for a certain key, you should use **XGetKeyboardControl** as described below.

auto_repeat_mode  Specify 0 (off) or 1 (on). If the key parameter (above) is not specified, then auto-repeat mode is turned off or on for the entire keyboard, just as if **XAutoRepeatOff** or **XAutoRepeatOn** (below) were called. If the key parameter is specified, auto-repeat for that key is set according to auto_repeat_mode. Specify KBAutoRepeat-Mode in *value_mask* if you want to set auto-repeat for the entire keyboard. (Do not specify KBKey without also specifying KBAutoRepeatMode.)

Note that many keyboards do not let you set all of these parameters to any possible value. For example, keyboards that allow you to set the pitch of the bell tone to an arbitrary frequency are uncommon. If you specify parameters that cannot be honored in a **XChangeKeyboardControl** request, the workstation may either use the nearest value that it can honor or it may ignore the parameter entirely.

## Querying Keyboard Control Settings

Use the **XGetKeyboardControl** request if you want to determine the keyboard control settings and the keys that auto-repeat. **XGetKeyboardControl** (*Xlib* ¶7.8) has the form

```
Display *display;        /* current display structure */
XKeyboardState state;    /* structure returning settings */
. . .
XGetKeyboardControl ( display, &state );
```

*state* is a structure of type **XKeyboardState** (defined in the header file **<X11/Xlib.h>**. Upon return, the *state* parameter contains the following fields:

key_click_percent  The volume of the keyclick from off (0) to loud (100).

bell_percent  The base bell volume from off (0) to loud (100).

bell_pitch  The pitch of the bell sound in Hz.

bell_duration  The duration of the bell sound in milliseconds.

led_mask  A bitmask, with one bit per keyboard LED. The least significant bit of led_mask corresponds to LED number 1. Each nonzero bit in led_mask indicates a lit LED∏.

auto_repeats  This is a Keymap, identical in structure to the *key_vector* parameter returned by the **XQueryKeymap** request (see the section entitled "Polling the Keyboard" above). auto_repeats contains one bit for each Keycode; if a bit is set, it means that automatic repeat is enabled for the corresponding key.

## Controlling Auto-Repeat Mode

Use **XAutoRepeatOn** and **XAutoRepeatOff** (*Xlib* ¶ 7.8) to turn auto-repeat mode on and off for the entire keyboard at once. These convenience functions have the form

**Display** *\*display;*          */\* current display structure \*/*

. . .

**XAutoRepeatOff** ( *display* );

. . .

**XAutoRepeatOn** ( *display* );

You can determine which keys will auto-repeat by using the **XGetKeyboard-Control** request. However, there is no way you can determine whether auto-repeat mode is on or off for the entire keyboard. If you must temporarily turn off auto-repeat mode for the entire keyboard, turn it on when you are through.

Your application may need to change certain keyboard settings temporarily. For example, a spreadsheet program might carry out a recalculation when the user presses the space bar. In such a program, it would be a good idea to disable auto-repeat, to prevent a series of redundant recalculations if the user mistakenly leans on the space bar. Your application can do this safely:

- Respond to FocusIn events (see the example at the end of the section entitled "FocusIn and FocusOut Events—Specifics" above) by saving the keyboard control settings with **XGetKeyboardControl**, then setting them to whatever you require using **XChangeKeyboardControl** or **XAutoRepeatOff**.

- Respond to FocusOut events by restoring the saved keyboard control settings.

# SUMMARY

When the user types on the keyboard, X delivers events to application programs. The primary types of events you can solicit from keyboards are KeyPress and KeyRelease events. These events are low-level: for example, when the user types the upper case letter A, your application will receive up to four events (*up to four* because some keyboards do not deliver KeyRelease events correctly):

1. A KeyPress event for the Shift key.
2. A KeyPress event for the *A* key.
3. A KeyRelease event for the *A* key.
4. A KeyRelease event for the Shift key.

Keyboard events have a lot in common with pointer events: they all specify the pointer's position at the time of the event, a mask specifying the positions of the mouse buttons and modifier keys, and the time of the event. *Modifier keys* include the Shift, Caps Lock or Shift Lock, and Control keys. Some keyboards have Meta, Super, and Hyper shift keys: X supports these as well.

Your application may solicit either KeyPress and KeyRelease events, or you may solicit both event types together. Many keyboards do not generate KeyRelease events correctly: for portability you should avoid designing applications that depend on knowing when the user lets go of keys.

*Xlib* provides the **XLookupString** function to translate KeyPress events into ordinary ASCII character strings. As long as you scrupulously pass it all the KeyPress events you receive, **XLookupString** takes care of most of the complexity of the conversion process, including the recognition of upper- and lower-case characters.

The designers of X faced a difficult problem: X had to be workable with an enormous variety of keyboards, each with a different set of keys. To support all these keyboards in a compatible way, they designed a three-level translation process. At the first level, *Keycodes* are reported by the workstation to the application in keyboard events. Keycodes are small numbers: each distinct Keycode represents a particular key. However, keycodes are not portable, because each model of keyboard assigns them differently.

The second translation level represents keys as *Keysyms*. Keysyms are portable: each distinct key is represented by a distinct Keysym. For the purpose of assigning Keysyms, keys are distinguished by the legends engraved on them. Thus the up-arrow keys on various keyboards all have the Keysym "XK_Up," even though they appear in different places on the different keyboards.

Alphabetic and numeric keys actually have two Keysyms each: one for the lower-case (unshifted) version of the key and another for the upper-case version. **XLookupString**, as it translates Keycodes, looks up the appropriate Keysym from the two depending on whether a Shift key is pressed.

The third level of translation consists of character strings. **XLookupString** automates the entire translation process, although *Xlib* provides calls with which you can *rebind* certain Keysyms, or change the character strings they represent. *Xlib* also provides utility functions and macros to help you process and recognize various Keysyms.

Which window has the keyboard *focus*: which window receives keyboard events? Assigning pointer events to windows is straightforward, because the pointer is inherently in some window. With the keyboard, assigning the focus is quite a bit more complex to program. The focus can be, using **XSetInputFocus**, assigned to any subhierarchy in the window hierarchy.

Often the window manager application calls **XSetInputFocus** on behalf of applications. These applications are said to have a *passive model* of input focus—they take what they can get. This chapter shows code which such an application might use to highlight its border when it has the input focus to cue the user. Other applications may call **XSetInputFocus** explicitly, thereby *actively* assigning focus to themselves. Applications should use the **XSetWMHints** call (Chapter 4) to inform the window manager of their focus model.

Applications can solicit FocusIn and FocusOut events and use them to monitor when windows gain and lose the focus. These focus change events are similar in principle to EnterNotify and LeaveNotify events: the workstation generates a flurry of them, notifying each window involved, whenever the focus changes.

Applications can solicit KeymapNotify events. The workstation delivers one of these events immediately after each EnterNotify and FocusIn event. The KeymapNotify event contains an array of bits, with one bit corresponding to each possible Keycode. Each bit is set to one if the user is holding the corresponding key. You should use KeymapNotify events when you care whether the user is holding keys, because you will not always receive paired KeyPress and KeyRelease events, even if your keyboard is capable of generating them.

You can control the keyboard directly: you can poll it to determine the state of all the keys. You can also ring the bell (buzzer or beeper) on the keyboard, and light the keyboard's indicator lamps. Furthermore, some keyboards allow you to control the volume and pitch of the bell tone, the volume of the key-click sound, and the repeating action of certain keys.

# CHAPTER 11
# ADVANCED
# EVENT HANDLING

This chapter goes into depth on topics related to event handling. The most complex part of X is the way it controls and delivers events to application programs. For the most part, applications will work properly if they simply solicit events from windows with **XSelectInput**, read them with **XNextEvent**, and process them in the order delivered. Up until this point in this book, we have been assuming such simple event-processing was enough. In this chapter, we describe several variations on the basic way of handling events.

The first section of this chapter, "Polling the Queue," describes ways in which you can use *Xlib* to read events out of order from your event queue. The calls described in this section augment the very basic event-reading calls presented in Chapter 3, and give your application the flexibility of doing such things as processing events a window at a time.

This chapter's second section, "Event Compression," describes some techniques you can use to skip and ignore redundant events in your application's event queue. By saving wasted effort, for example in window redrawing, these techniques can improve your application's performance substantially.

"Multiple Display Connections," the third section, describes how to retrieve and process events when your application is connected to several workstations at a time.

You can use information from the fourth section, "Putting Back and Sending Events," to find out how to return an event to your own queue or send an event to some other application running on the workstation.

The remaining sections of the chapter discuss how you can *grab*, or temporarily arrange to steal all events from, either the pointer (the mouse) or the keyboard. The fifth section, "Grabbing the Pointer" describes how to do this to the pointer. As Chapter 9 pointed out, X makes sure you can receive a ButtonRelease event for every ButtonPress event if you want it. X does this by automatically grabbing the pointer. One of the things this section discusses is this automatic button grab feature.

Applications can grab individual combinations of mouse buttons and keyboard keys. For example, you might instruct your user to press the Control key on the keyboard and the middle mouse button to see an options menu. "Grabbing Mouse Buttons," the sixth section of this chapter, describes how to program this kind of human interface.

"Grabbing the Keyboard," the seventh section of this chapter, describes how you can ask X temporarily to direct all keyboard events to your application.

Applications can grab particular key combinations. In a text-editor application, for example, you might allow the user to save a file by pressing Control, Shift, and S. The eighth section, "Grabbing Individual Keys," tells how.

X's device-grab capability allows you to *freeze* a device, or cause it to stop generating events while you prepare to receive them. You can use this feature, described in "Synchronous Delivery of Grabbed Events," to give your application time to put up popup menus. You can also arrange to release a grab and replay a grabbed event as if the grab were not in effect.

Ordinarily, direct input events originate in a source window and work their way up the window hierarchy toward the root window until they find some window that has solicited them. However, the workstation searches the window hierarchy top-down, rather than bottom-up, when deciding how to deliver grabbed mouse buttons or keyboard keys. The last section of this chapter, "Passive Grab Activation," describes how your application can exploit this top-down search capability.

# POLLING THE QUEUE

Your application does not always have to read the oldest event in the queue first. If you prefer, you can look ahead or read selected events from the queue out of order. You can do this with or without blocking execution if the kind of event you wanted is not in the queue.

A variety of *Xlib* calls are available to choose events from your application's queue. Table 11-I summarizes these calls. You may use one of them to read any type of event from the queue, but you must also solicit delivery for that event type

| Request | Blocks? | Xlib ¶ | Description |
|---|---|---|---|
| **XPeekEvent** | yes | 8.8.1 | Copies oldest event in queue |
| **XCheckWindowEvent** | no | 8.8.3 | Gets events from a certain window |
| **XCheckTypedWindowEvent** | no | 8.8.3 | Gets a certain event type and window |
| **XCheckMaskEvent** | no | 8.8.3 | Gets certain event types |
| **XCheckTypedEvent** | no | 8.8.3 | Gets a certain event type |
| **XWindowEvent** | yes | 8.8.3 | Gets events from a certain window |
| **XMaskEvent** | yes | 8.8.3 | Gets certain event types |
| **XCheckIfEvent** | no | 8.8.2 | Gets event selected by a function |
| **XPeekIfEvent** | yes | 8.8.2 | Copies event selected by a function |
| **XIfEvent** | yes | 8.8.2 | Gets event selected by a function |

Table 11-I.   X event-choosing calls.

(with **XSelectInput**).  The *event_mask* parameters to these event-selection calls have no effect on the types of events that your application is soliciting.

These calls typically are used in modular applications, where you call a subroutine package to deal with events from certain windows, or with certain types of events.  They may also be used to skip over duplicate or redundant events in the queue.  See "Event Compression" later in this chapter.

> Your application may become confused about user input that involves multiple events if you read events out of order.  Even worse, you may block execution when events are waiting in the queue, which may make you think that you have "lost" events.  If you must use event-selection functions at all, use them with care.

## Looking Ahead in the Event Queue

If you want to look ahead at the next event in the queue, use **XPeekEvent**.  This call is analogous to **XNextEvent**, except that it gives back a *copy* of the event at the head of the queue *without removing it* from the queue.  It blocks execution if there is no event waiting to be read.  **XPeekEvent** (*Xlib* ¶8.8.1) has the form

```
Display *mydisplay;
XEvent myevent;
    . . .
XPeekEvent ( mydisplay, &myevent );
```

## Reading Events by Window and Event Type

The **XCheckWindowEvent** call accepts a window identifier and an event-selection mask, and tries to return the oldest event in the queue matching both the window and the mask.  If no such event is found, **XCheckWindowEvent** immediately returns a zero function value without blocking execution.  Note that you can use an all-ones *event_mask* to select all events if you want to read any event pertaining to a particular window. **XCheckWindowEvent** (*Xlib* ¶8.8.3) has the form

```
Display* display;
Window w;
long event_mask;
XEvent evt;
 . . .
if ( 0 != XCheckWindowEvent ( display, w, event_mask, &evt )) {
... process the event
}
```

The **XCheckTypedWindowEvent** call works just like **XCheckWindow-Event**, except that it chooses a single event type. In place of an *event_mask* (for example, ButtonReleaseMask), you specify a particular event type (for example, ButtonRelease). **XCheckTypedWindowEvent** (*Xlib* ¶8.8.3) has the form

```
Display* display;
Window w;
int event_type;
XEvent evt;
 . . .
if ( 0 != XCheckTypedWindowEvent ( display, w, event_type, &evt )) {
... process the event
}
```

**XCheckMaskEvent** works the same way, but accepts just an *event_mask*, and chooses the oldest event, from any window, matching the mask. **XCheck-MaskEvent** also returns a zero function value without blocking execution if no matching event is found. **XCheckMaskEvent** (*Xlib* ¶8.8.3) has the form

```
Display* display;
long event_mask;
XEvent evt;
 . . .
if ( 0 != XCheckMaskEvent ( display, event_mask, &evt )) {
    ... process the event
}
```

The **XCheckTypedEvent** call works just like **XCheckMaskEvent**, except that it chooses a single event type. In place of an *event_mask* you specify a particular event type. **XCheckTypedEvent** (*Xlib* ¶8.8.3) has the form

```
Display* display;
int event_type;
XEvent evt;
 . . .
if ( 0 != XCheckTypedEvent ( display, event_type, &evt )) {
```

```
      ... process the event
   }
```

**XCheckWindowEvent** and **XCheckMaskEvent** functions both have blocking forms as well. **XWindowEvent** returns the oldest event in the queue matching both the window and the *event_mask*, and blocks until a matching event is found. **XWindowEvent** (*Xlib* ¶8.8.3) has the form

```
   Display* display;
   Window w;
   long event_type;
   XEvent evt;
   . . .
   XWindowEvent ( display, w, event_mask, &evt );
```

**XMaskEvent** accepts just an *event_mask*, and returns the oldest event matching the mask. It too blocks until a matching event is found. **XMaskEvent** (*Xlib* ¶8.8.3) has the form

```
   Display* display;
   long event_mask;
   XEvent evt;
   . . .
   XMaskEvent ( display, mask, &evt );
```

## Choosing Events with a Boolean Function

If the ability to choose events from your application's queue by window and event mask or type is not flexible enough for you, use **XCheckIfEvent**, **XIfEvent**, or **XPeekIfEvent**. These event-reading calls require you to write a Boolean function to examine each event and return a Boolean value. If your function decides that an event matches, it should return a true result; otherwise it should return a false result. You can write as many of these functions as you wish, but you can only use one in each event-reading call. Your Boolean function should be written as in this example:

```
   Boolean myBoolean ( display, event, args )
   Display * display;
   XEvent * event;
   char * args;
     {
     ... /* decide based on args whether event is to be selected */
       return True;  /* if you want this event */
     ...
       return False;  /* if you do not want this event */
     }
```

The *event* parameter to your function is a pointer to the **XEvent** structure (within *Xlib* 's internal data structures) describing the event. The *args* parameter is passed on from your call to **XCheckIfEvent, XIfEvent,** or **XPeekIfEvent.** Your application may use the *args* parameter in any way you wish to pass on information to your Boolean function. Some applications use it as a value and others use it as a pointer to a data structure.

When you call the function **XCheckIfEvent,** you provide a pointer to the Boolean function you have written. As **XCheckIfEvent** works, it invokes your function for each event in the queue, oldest event first. Your Boolean function returns a true result whenever the event *Xlib* passes to it matches the selection criteria you are looking for. As soon as your function returns a true result for some event, **XCheckIfEvent** removes that event from the queue and returns it.

If **XCheckIfEvent** gets to the end of the event queue without getting any true result back from your Boolean function, it returns a zero function value, without blocking execution. **XCheckIfEvent** (*Xlib* ¶8.8.2) has the form

> **Display\*** *display;*
> **XEvent** *evt;*
> char *args [ ];*
>   *. . .*
> if ( 0 != **XCheckIfEvent** ( *display, &evt, myBoolean, &args* )) {
>   ... *process the event*
> }

**XIfEvent** (*Xlib* ¶8.8.2) is a form of **XCheckIfEvent** for blocking execution until it finds (using your Boolean function) a matching event. The function has the form

> **Display** *\*display;*
> **XEvent** *evt;*
> char *args [ ];*
>   *. . .*
> **XIfEvent** ( *display, &evt, myBoolean, &args* );
>   ... *process the event*

**XPeekIfEvent** (*Xlib* ¶8.8.2) is a form of **XIfEvent** which, like **XPeekEvent,** returns a *copy* of the matching event (if any) without removing it from the queue. It blocks execution until it finds (using your Boolean function) a matching event. The function has the form

> **Display\*** *display;*
> **XEvent** *evt;*
> char *args [ ];*
>   *. . .*
> **XPeekIfEvent** ( *display, &evt, myBoolean, &args* );
>   ... *process the event*

# EVENT COMPRESSION

By doing *event compression*, your application can significantly reduce the amount of event-processing work it has to do. You do event compression by writing application-specific code for ignoring redundant events. Event-compression code is application-specific because the kinds of event compression you can do depend, in often complex ways, on exactly how your application works. The *Xlib* calls described in the previous section are useful for many kinds of event compression.

The developers of most human-interface toolkits and user-interface management systems layered on X have used event-compression techniques within their code. If you use a toolkit or UIMS, your application's event-compression problems may be solved automatically.

Chapter 2's **helloworld.c** example shows a very simple and useful form of event compression. It compresses each series of Expose events to a single event simply by examining the count field in the event structure. **helloworld** only responds to Expose events when the count field is zero (indicating the end of each series). This works well for many simple applications. However, as Chapter 5 discussed, other applications may be unable to use this form of event compression, depending on the application's specific strategy for redrawing windows.

Recall, also, that the events in each Expose series are consecutive, which means that you run no risk of processing Expose events in the wrong order by ignoring some of them. Wrong-order event processing can be a significant complication for your application when you compress other kinds of events. This is yet another reason to use a toolkit or UIMS package.

To give the flavor of event compression, the two following sections discuss and give simple examples of the compression of MotionNotify events and Enter-Notify/ LeaveNotify event pairs. The event-compression techniques shown here only begin to scratch the surface of the possibilities.

## Compressing MotionNotify events

The ability to eliminate redundant MotionNotify events is very important, because it is easy for the user to generate lots of them. The best way of reducing your MotionNotify processing load is, of course, by using hint events (see "How to Process Motion Hints" in Chapter 9). However, you can also use event compression.

You can compress MotionNotify events as follows. Each time you receive a MotionNotify event, look ahead, using **XPeekEvent**, at the next event in the queue. If it also is a MotionNotify event for the same window, discard the first MotionNotify event and use the next one. Repeat this peek-ahead operation until the event you peek at is some other type of event, or comes from some other window.

You cannot just look ahead for MotionNotify events (using, for example, **XCheckTypedWindowEvent**), because you do not want to miss other intervening events.

**Example:**   Compress MotionNotify events from a window.

This example uses **XPeekEvent** to look ahead for consecutive Motion-Notify events for the same window. Note the use of **XEventsQueued** to prevent us from calling **XPeekEvent** when it would block execution.

```
Display * display;       /* pointer to current Display structure */
Window curw;             /*  the  window*/
XEvent current;          /*  event  to  read  */
XEvent ahead;            /*  event  to  peek  at  */
 . . .
XSelectInput( display, curw, PointerMotionMask );
 . . .
while (True) {
 XNextEvent ( display, &current );
 switch ( current.type ) {
 case MotionNotify:
   while ( XEventsQueued
               (current.xmotion.display, QueuedAfterReading) > 0) {
     XPeekEvent ( current.xmotion.display, &ahead );
     if (ahead.type != MotionNotify) break;
     if (ahead.xmotion.window != current.xmotion.window) break;
     XNextEvent ( current.xmotion.display, &current );
   }
   /* Process the compressed MotionNotify event */
   . . .
   break;
 } /* End switch ( current.type ) */
} /* End while (True)*/
```

# Compressing EnterNotify and LeaveNotify event pairs

Many applications and toolkits implement items on menus by putting each individual item into its own window. When the user points to such a menu-item window you may wish to highlight the window by, for example, changing the window's border_pixel value. You do this by soliciting EnterNotify and Leave-Notify events for each menu-item window, and responding to the events by changing the border color.

It is possible for the user to move the mouse into a window, and immediately out again. If you could detect this case, your application could ignore both the En-terNotify event and the matching LeaveNotify event, and thus save the effort of highlighting the window just to restore it to its normal state. This is the purpose of compressing EnterNotify and LeaveNotify events.

The technique for compressing EnterNotify and LeaveNotify events is similar to that shown in the previous section; upon receiving an EnterNotify event, you peek ahead for a corresponding LeaveNotify. The decision about whether a particular EnterNotify and LeaveNotify pair correspond to each other is made a little more complex by the mode and detail fields of their event structures.

This technique will not do you any good if you also solicit MotionNotify events from within window item menus or their ancestors. Obviously, you do want to solicit ButtonPress and ButtonRelease events, so you find out when the user actually selects the menu item.

**Example:** Compress EnterNotify and LeaveNotify events.

```
Display *display;      /* pointer to current Display structure */
Window itemw;          /* menu item window */
XEvent current;        /* event to read */
XEvent ahead;          /* event to peek at */
int good_enter;        /* non zero on detecting a good EnterNotify */
  . . .
XSelectInput ( display, itemw,
       EnterWindowMask | LeaveWindowMask | ButtonPressMask |
       ButtonReleaseMask | OwnerGrabButtonMask );
  . . .
while (True) {
 XNextEvent ( display, &current );
 switch ( current.type ) {
 case EnterNotify:
   good_enter = 1;
   if ( XEventsQueued
      (current.xcrossing.display, QueuedAfterReading)>0) {
     XPeekEvent ( current.xcrossing.display, &ahead );
     if  ( ahead.type == LeaveNotify &&
         ahead.xcrossing.window == current.xcrossing.window &&
         ahead.xcrossing.mode == current.xcrossing.mode &&
         ahead.xcrossing.detail == current.xcrossing.detail ) {
       /* matching LeaveNotify... read it and ignore them both */
       XNextEvent ( current.xcrossing.display, &current );
       good_enter = 0;
     }
   }
   if (good_enter) {
     /* Process the EnterNotify event if it was not ignored*/
       . . .
```

```
        }
        break;
    case LeaveNotify:
        /* Process any uncompressed LeaveNotify events*/
            . . .
        break;

    . . .
    } /* End switch ( current.type ) */
} /* End while (True)*/
```

# MULTIPLE DISPLAY CONNECTIONS

From a single X application program, you can use more than one display connection at a time. When you have more than one display connection at your disposal, your application can maintain windows on more than one workstation simultaneously.

For example, if your application's purpose is displaying volatile information such as a financial ticker tape, the current state of an industrial process, or the current situation in a multiplayer game or simulation, it may be a good idea for you to use the X Window System to draw the information in windows on several workstations. With this approach, a single application program (running in a single address space on a single cpu) is responsible for keeping track of the information in real time. Rather than redistributing the real-time information to several other programs running on other cpus, the single application program would use X's network transparency to draw directly on several different workstations. Obviously, the usefulness of multiple display connections is not limited to real-time information display; many other kinds of applications can exploit multiple connections as well.

It is not much harder to maintain multiple display connections than it is to maintain multiple independent windows using a single display connection. If your application is to use multiple independent windows, your event-handling code must be able to do such things as

- process Expose and GraphicsExpose events for each window separately
- take window-specific action upon receiving direct input events
- keep track of window geometry and attributes for each window separately

Doing these things is, of course, straightforward. The event structures returned to you by *Xlib* all contain a window identifier telling you which window is the subject of the event. Your program calls **XNextEvent** (or some other *Xlib* call for reading event structures from the queue), then uses the window identifier in each returned **XEvent** structure to decide what to do with each event. Your application receives and handles a single event stream, but one which refers to multiple windows.

When you use multiple display connections, there are only a few added complications:

1.  Windows, **GCs**, Pixmaps, and other X resource identifiers are only unique within a single workstation, and can only be used on that workstation. A window created on one workstation is quite likely to have the same numerical value for its window identifier as a window created on another workstation. On the other hand, you cannot draw on one workstation using a **GC** created on another. Thus, you must create and use separate X resources on each separate display connection.

2.  **XNextEvent** and the other *Xlib* calls for reading the event queue can read from only one display connection at a time. In a multiple-workstation application, your main loop must read events from several display connections.

3.  You must not use *Xlib* calls which block execution waiting for something to happen on any one display connection. If you do, events from other display connections may not get processed in a timely fashion.

4.  In your main loop, you must use the display pointer stored in each **XEvent** structure to determine which display to respond to, just as you would use the event's window.

The **helloworld.c** example of Chapter 2 is set up to use the window identifiers and display pointers from the event structures. For example, consider **helloworld.c**'s Expose-event processing code. It issues the **XDrawImageString** request to the display and window named within *myevent*.

```
case Expose:
if (myevent.xexpose.count == 0)
   XDrawImageString  (
       myevent.xexpose.display,  myevent.xexpose.window,  mygc,
       50,  50,  hello,  strlen(hello)   ) ;
break;
```

Of course, **helloworld.c** does not behave in a very interesting way. Its code assumes that it is supposed to draw "Hello, World!" in *any* window from which it receives an Expose event series. A real application would obviously draw different things in different windows. An application using multiple display connections would have to examine both display and window to determine exactly what to draw, and what **GC** to use in drawing it.

Every operating system has a limitation on the number of simultaneously open file-descriptors, and thus on the number of display connections your program can use at a time. Practically speaking, most applications should limit themselves to no more than about a dozen display connections. If you maintain more display connections, users may perceive degraded interactive performance.

*Xlib* is set up to make it fairly easy to read events from several display connections if your application is running on the Unix operating system. *Xlib* provides the **ConnectionNumber** macro to retrieve the Unix file descriptor for each display connection's socket. **ConnectionNumber** (*Xlib* ¶2.2.1) has the form

```
Display *display;      /* display structure pointer */
int fd;                /* returned file descriptor */
.. . .
fd = ConnectionNumber (  display );
```

You may, on Unix, use the **select(2)** system call to wait until there is something to read on a display connection's socket. Be careful, however, not to use the **select** system call to wait for new events until you have processed all the waiting events.

On operating systems other than Unix, consult your vendor's documentation for the equivalent to the **select** operation.

You can partially debug multiple-display-connection applications by establishing several display connections to a single workstation. Be careful with this debugging strategy, though: if you make errors like using a **GC** created for the wrong display connection, you will not catch them debugging this way.

### Example: Two-display event reading

This example shows the use of **ConnectionNumber**, **XEventsQueued**, **XFlush**, **select**, and **XNextEvent** for reading events from either one of two display connections. Note that we specify a ten-second timeout for **select**.

We use **XEventsQueued** to determine whether any events are waiting to be processed on each display connection. If there are, we read one with **XNextEvent** and proceed to the event-handling switch statement. If not, we use **XFlush** explicitly to send any queued output requests for that display connection.

If we determine that no events are waiting on either display connection, we **select** for read on both connection's file descriptors.

```
#include  <sys/time.h>
. . .
Display * dpy1;         /* one display connection */
Display * dpy2;         /* another display connection */
XEvent myevent;         /* event structure to fill in */
int done;               /* main loop termination flag */
int got_one;            /* event-wait loop termination flag */
int mask;               /* file-descriptor mask */
int readfds;            /* read-file-descriptor mask for select */
int wrfds;              /* write-file-descriptor mask—unused */
int exfds;              /* exception-file-descriptor mask—unused */
struct timeval timeout; /* timeout for select call */
int nfds;               /* number of file descriptors for select */
int nfound;             /* number of found file descriptors */
```

```
. . .
dpy1  =  XOpenDisplay  ("two:0");
dpy2  =  XOpenDisplay  ("three:0");
. . .
/* initialize variables for the select call *.
timeout.tv_sec = 10;      /* ten-second select timeout */
timeout.tv_usec = 0;
mask = (1<<ConnectionNumber(dpy1)) |
       (1<<ConnectionNumber(dpy2));
nfds = ConnectionNumber (dpy1);
if (nfds < ConnectionNumber (dpy2)
    nfds = ConnectionNumber (dpy2);
. . .
/*  main loop */
done = 0;
while ( ! done ) {
  got_one = 0;
  while ( ! got_one ) {
    /* Try the first display connection */
    if (XEventsQueued (dpy1, QueuedAfterReading) > 0) {
      XNextEvent ( dpy1, &myevent );
      got_one = 1;  continue;
    } else XFlush (dpy1);
    /* Try the second display connection */
    if (XEventsQueued (dpy2, QueuedAfterReading) > 0) {
      XNextEvent ( dpy2, &myevent );
      got_one = 1;  continue;
    } else XFlush (dpy2);
    /* background processing, if any, here*/
    . . .
    /* nothing on either display connection; do select */
    readfds = mask;      /* initialize read fd mask */
    wrfds = exfds = 0;
    nfound = select ( nfds, &readfds, &wrfds, &exfds, &timeout );
  } /* end while ( ! got_one ) */
  switch (myevent.type)  {
    /*  event-handling */
    . . .
  }
} /* end while ( ! done ) */
```

This example can easily be extended to allow a variable number of display connections, to allow the **select** call to wait for operations on other, non-X, file descriptors, or to allow operations involving timeouts.

This example also shows where to put background processing: immediately before the **select** call. Notice that you can control how often you perform background processing by changing the *timeout* parameter to **select**.

# PUTTING BACK AND SENDING EVENTS

If you read an event, then decide you want to process it later, you can put it back at the head of *Xlib*'s queue using **XPutBackEvent**. Events put back at the head of the queue are available to be read later, but only by your application. You may put back as many events as you wish. **XPutBackEvent** copies the contents of the **XEvent** structure you specify into its internal queue.

**XPutBackEvent** (*Xlib* ¶8.9) has the form

```
Display *display;
XEvent event;
   . . .
XPutBackEvent ( display, &event );
```

You can use the **XSendEvent** request to send events to other applications running on the workstation. These events are actually sent not to a specific application, but to the particular *window* you specify. **XSendEvent** (*Xlib* ¶8.10) has the form

```
Display *display;        /* pointer to Display structure */
Window window;           /* window to which to send the event */
Bool propagate;          /* True if event propagates up-hierarchy */
long event_mask; /* event mask to control event delivery*/
XEvent event;            /* event to send */
   . . .
XSendEvent ( display, window, propagate, event_mask, &event );
```

The first step to using **XSendEvent** is constructing a valid **XEvent** structure. You must use one of the existing X event types (or, if your workstation provides X extensions, one of the event types defined by a loaded extension). You must make sure all the fields of the event structure are set to valid values. Of course, if what you are doing is resending an event you received, you can use the event structure you received.

see p.
140-141

Applications often use the ClientMessage event type to send arbitrary messages to one another. The ClientMessage event type is described at the end of Chapter 4.

The second step is to decide which window you want to send the event to. You specify the destination window with the *window* parameter. You can specify one of three things in the *window* parameter:

The X resource identifier of a window. The workstation sends your event to the specified window.

The value PointerWindow.  The workstation sends your event to the window the pointer is in.

The value InputFocus.  The workstation sends your event the same way it sends KeyPress and KeyRelease events:  If the input focus is currently set to the window the pointer is in or any ancestor, your event is sent to the window the pointer is in.  If, on the other hand, the input focus is set to some other window, the event is delivered to the focus window.

The third step is to decide how the event should be delivered.  You specify this with the *event_mask* and *propagate* parameters.  You must specify an *event_mask* parameter containing some or all of the same bit masks an application might use in **XSelectInput**'s event mask (for example, KeyPressMask, ButtonPress-Mask, or PropertyChangeMask).  Whereas the type field of your **XEvent** structure defines the actual event type, the *event_mask* you specify is used to decide which applications have solicited your event.  Thus, for example, if you specified an event type of ButtonPress and an *event_mask* of KeyPressMask, the effect would be to deliver a ButtonPress event to each application that had solicited key presses.

If you specify a False *propagate* parameter, the workstation discards the event when no applications have a matching solicitation for it on the specified *window*.  If, on the other hand, *propagate* is True, the workstation propagates the event up the hierarchy toward the root window until the event's *event_mask* matches some solicitation, or until its *event_mask* matches a *do_not_propagate_mask*.

The event looks like a perfectly ordinary event to any application receiving it, with one exception:  The Boolean send_event field in the received event structure is set to True.  Most applications do not care whether the events they receive were generated automatically by the workstation, or by some other application with **XSendEvent**.  If the receiving application does care, however, it can examine the send_event field.

> It is clearly possible for one application running on a workstation to spoof another by sending it events.  Be careful with this capability.

# GRABBING THE POINTER

Up until this point we have discussed the use of **XSelectInput** to specify which pointer events we want, and what windows we want the events from.  In each call to **XSelectInput**, your application, of course, specifies a particular window.  Each pointer event can only be delivered to a window that contains the pointer.  Recall that a window contains the pointer if the pointer is inside the boundaries of the window or one of its inferior windows.

In many situations the ordinary window-containment method of delivering mouse events to windows will not work.  We have already come across one in connection with ButtonPressMask and ButtonReleaseMask: an application that solicits both press and release events should be able to expect to get a ButtonRelease event for every ButtonPress event. But what happens if the user moves the mouse out of the window (either on purpose or by mistake) while the button is still pressed? Without some way of working around the rule that pointer events are only reported to the pointer's window, applications would frequently lose ButtonRelease events that they were expecting.

The window-containment method also breaks down when implementing applications, such as window managers, requiring the user to point to windows (or things in windows) that belong to other clients.

Under some circumstances, you may wish to *freeze* the pointer's action until your application has time to prepare to receive it. For example, suppose you wanted to respond to a particular ButtonPress event by mapping a pop-up menu. The user would choose a menu item by dragging the cursor into the appropriate item (while holding the button down). When the menu window received a ButtonRelease event, you would unmap it and activate the selected option. The problem is that the user may *mouse-ahead* by pressing, then releasing, the button without giving you time to map the window.

To solve these problems, there is a way for an application to announce that it wants all mouse events delivered to it via a particular source window until further notice. You can explicitly establish such an *active pointer grab* using **XGrabPointer**. While an active pointer grab is in effect, further pointer events are only reported to the grabbing client. Furthermore, you may freeze the pointer or the keyboard while activating a grab, and unfreeze it whenever you are ready to continue accepting events (because you have mapped and drawn the necessary menu windows, for example).

Pointer grabs may confuse the user while they are in effect, because they put the pointer into a mode where it responds abnormally. During a grab you should make every effort to make it plain to the user that the pointer is working differently. **XGrabPointer** provides two ways you can help the user recognize that a grab is active:

1. You can *confine* the pointer, or set it up during the grab so the user cannot move it outside a certain window on the screen. You might confine the pointer to a window containing a popup menu, for example. This technique is subtle but effective. Because of your grab the user cannot even try to deliver a mouse click except where you (the grabbing application) want it delivered. If you confine the pointer to your window, the user will not realize that a grab is in effect unless he or she attempts to click on some other window, in which case the pointer will just not go there until after the grab.

2. You can change the shape of the cursor during the grab. If you are grabbing the screen root window, or asking the user to point at any arbitrary thing on the screen (possibly outside your application's window) during

the grab, changing the cursor shape is the only way of letting your user know that a grab is in effect.

Once you start an active pointer grab, it continues until you explicitly end it in one of the following ways:

- by issuing the **XUngrabPointer** request
- by making the source window or the confining window (if any) unviewable
- by closing your application's display connection (possibly by being interrupted or crashing)
- by using the **XAllowEvents** request to freeze and replay an event (see the section entitled "Synchronous Delivery of Grabbed Events" below)

If your application uses **XGrabPointer** indiscriminately, it can interfere with other applications on your workstation. Avoid letting the user put your application into a mode where the pointer is grabbed without making it easy and intuitive to get back out of that mode.

> If you must grab at all, do so for very limited periods of time. And, be careful to avoid bugs in your code which make it fail to end the grab.

## Starting a Pointer Grab

The **XGrabPointer** request is a round-trip request for establishing an active pointer grab. It returns a status value indicating its success or failure. **XGrabPointer** (*Xlib* ¶7.4) has the form

```
Display * display;          /* current display */
Window grab_window;         /* source window for grab */
Bool owner_events;          /* handle this application's events normally */
long event_mask;            /* events to report via source window */
int pointer_mode;           /* grab mode (async / sync ) for pointer */
int keyboard_mode;          /* grab mode for keyboard */
Window confine_to;          /* window to which to confine the cursor */
Cursor cursor;              /* cursor to display */
Time time;                  /* grab time */
int status;                 /* grab status */
  . . .
status = XGrabPointer ( display, grab_window,
              owner_events, event_mask,
              pointer_mode, keyboard_mode,
              confine_to, cursor, time   );
```

The *grab_window* parameter specifies the window you want used as the grab source window. It must be viewable when the grab begins or **XGrabPointer** fails.

If you specify *owner_events* as false, all pointer events are reported via the grab window. On the other hand, if you specify *owner_events* as true, pointer events that were already bound for your application are unaffected by the grab, and are reported normally. **XGrabPointer** makes the grab window "steal" all pointer events for you; *owner_events* makes it refrain from stealing your own events.

Use *event_mask* to select the pointer event types you want reported via the grab. A grab "steals" all pointer events, not just those in *event_mask*. It delivers the selected ones and discards the unselected ones (except your own events if *owner_events* is true). *event_mask* is a 32-bit mask. In it, each bit specifies a particular event type. The bits are the same as those used in calls to **XSelectInput**, and are summarized in Table 9-I.

*pointer_mode* controls the freezing of pointer events. Normally, you specify the value GrabModeAsync; this means that pointer event processing proceeds normally during the grab. If you specify the value GrabModeSync it means that your application will have to use the **XAllowEvents** request (see the section below entitled "Synchronous Delivery of Grabbed Events") to allow the delivery of pointer events (ButtonPress, ButtonRelease, EnterNotify, LeaveNotify, and MotionNotify) during the grab. At the beginning of a GrabModeSync grab, the pointer freezes: no pointer events are delivered until your application uses the **XAllowEvents** request to resume event delivery. The GrabModeAsync and GrabModeSync constants are defined in the header file **<X11/X.h>**.

*keyboard_mode* controls the freezing of keyboard events, once the pointer grab is triggered. Normally, you specify the value GrabModeAsync; this means that keyboard event processing proceeds normally during the pointer grab. If you specify the value GrabModeSync it means the keyboard will freeze when the pointer grab begins, and no keyboard events will be delivered *to any applications running on the workstation* until your application uses **XAllowEvents** to unfreeze the keyboard, or until the pointer grab otherwise ends.

If you want to force the pointer to stay within the bounds of a particular window during the duration of the grab, specify that window's identifier in *confine_to*. Otherwise, you may specify the value None. The *confine_to* window, if any, must be viewable or **XGrabPointer** fails. Ordinarily, it would be the same as the grab window, but it need have no relationship to *grab_window*. If, at the beginning of the grab, the cursor is not already inside *confine_to,* then it is automatically warped (see **XWarpPointer**) to the closest edge just before the grab takes effect. If the initial automatic warp generates any EnterNotify or LeaveNotify events for any applications, they are delivered normally, right before the grab. If the *confine_to* window is reconfigured while the grab is in effect, the pointer will, if necessary, be warped again (this time without generating EnterNotify or LeaveNotify events) so it remains confined. If the *confine_to* window stops being viewable, the workstation ends the grab with an automatic **XUngrabPointer**.

If you specify a *cursor* it will be displayed for the duration of the grab regardless of what window the pointer is in. If you specify the value None for *cursor,* the grab window's cursor will be displayed unless the pointer is in a subwindow of the grab window, in which case the normal cursor will be displayed (regardless of the value of *owner_events*).

The *time* parameter is used to make sure that grabs and ungrabs from different clients do not get confused because of communications delays. Most applications establish and release grabs when triggered by received events (such as Button-Press and ButtonRelease). They use the time stamp of the triggering event for the *time* parameter. Note that the *time* you specify does not establish the priority of your grab over some other client's; it only serves as a sort of postmark on your request, to determine whether it got delayed in transit from your application to the workstation.

The **XGrabPointer** request can fail; your application should be prepared for this. Success or failure is reported in the *status* value returned by **XGrab-Pointer**.

- The *status* value GrabSuccess indicates that the **XGrabPointer** request succeeded.

- Only one client can grab the pointer at a time. If some other client has already grabbed it, you will receive the AlreadyGrabbed error status. If, on the other hand, your application has already grabbed it, the new grab takes the place of the old.

- If you were in a close race with another client for the grab and lost, you may receive the GrabInvalidTime error status. If you do receive this status, it is very likely that two or more applications running on your workstation are in conflict: they are attempting to start a grab based on the same event. It is also possible that you made an error specifying the *time* parameter.

- If the pointer is frozen, by a grab coming from some other application with a *pointer_mode* of GrabModeSync, you will receive the GrabFrozen error status.

- The GrabNotViewable error status tells you that either your *grab_window* or *confine_to* window is unviewable.

## Modifying a Pointer Grab

Once you establish an active pointer grab, you can use the **XChangeActive-PointerGrab** request to change the cursor being displayed, or the events you wish to receive during the grab. Notice that you can also completely override your own active pointer grab by issuing a subsequent **XGrabPointer** request.

You may use **XChangeActivePointerGrab** to modify active pointer grabs established by any means: **XGrabPointer** requests, **XGrabButton** requests, and normal ButtonPress events.

**XChangeActivePointerGrab** (*Xlib* ¶7.4) has the form

```
Display * display;          /* current display */
long event_mask;            /* events to report via source window */
Cursor cursor;              /* cursor to display */
Time time;                  /* grab time */
    . . .
XChangeActivePointerGrab ( display, event_mask, cursor, time );
```

Use *event_mask* to select anew the pointer event types you want reported via the grab. The bits are the same as those used for soliciting mouse events in calls to **XSelectInput**.

The *cursor* you specify with be displayed for the remainder of the grab, regardless of what window the pointer is in. The *cursor* parameter is interpreted exactly as it is for the **XGrabPointer** request.

The *time* parameter is interpreted exactly as it is for the **XGrabPointer** request.

## Ending a Pointer Grab

The **XUngrabPointer** request ends an active pointer grab. It unfreezes and replays, if necessary, any frozen pointer or keyboard events. **XUngrabPointer** (*Xlib* ¶7.4) has the form

```
Display * display;          /* current display */
Time time;                  /* grab time */
int status;                 /* grab status */
    . . .
XUngrabPointer ( display, time );
```

You may use **XUngrabPointer** to end active pointer grabs established by any means: **XGrabPointer** requests, **XGrabButton** requests, and normal ButtonPress events. The only parameter is the *time* parameter. You cannot go wrong if you use the time from the most recent event you have received (usually the event inducing you to end the grab).

## Pointer Grabs and EnterNotify/LeaveNotify events

The workstation generates a series of EnterNotify and LeaveNotify events with mode NotifyGrab at the beginning and end of every pointer grab. See Chapter 9. Whenever an active pointer grab begins, the workstation generates EnterNotify and LeaveNotify events as if the pointer were warped using **XWarpPointer** (see Chapter 9).

If a *confine_to* window is defined, the workstation first warps the pointer to that window, and generates the expected series of EnterNotify and LeaveNotify events, with mode NotifyNormal. If no *confine_to* window is available, this step is skipped.

The workstation next generates a series of EnterNotify and LeaveNotify events with mode NotifyGrab. These events are delivered as if the pointer were warped into the grab window. However, this is a pseudo-warp: the pointer does not actually change position (although activating a grab may change the displayed cursor).

When an active pointer grab ends, the workstation reverses the sequence of pointer warps. It first undoes the pseudo-warp, delivering EnterNotify and LeaveNotify events with mode NotifyUngrab. Second, it warps the pointer from the *cnfine_to* window (if any) back to where it started.

## Between ButtonPress and ButtonRelease

One very common use for a grab, mouse dragging, is automated for you. The X Window System supports mouse drags explicitly: If you specify ButtonPressMask in a call to **XSelectInput**, then the workstation carries out **XGrabPointer** and **XUngrabPointer** requests for you automatically. This is a particularly safe, *spring-loaded*, kind of grab—all the user has to do to end it is release all the mouse buttons. It is doubly safe because it is automatic: you do not have to write or debug any application code to end the grab.

Specifically, when the workstation delivers a ButtonPress event to your application (in the absence of a pre-existing active pointer grab or passive button grab) it automatically starts an active grab for you in the window receiving the ButtonPress. The grab solves the problem of what to do if the user presses a mouse button and then drags the pointer out of your window: because of the grab, you still get the events.

You can do several things to control event delivery between ButtonPress and ButtonRelease events.

1. You can control the way events are delivered during the grab to your application when you call **XSelectInput**. If you specify OwnerGrabButtonMask at the same time as you solicit ButtonPress events with ButtonPressMask, the workstation starts the automatic pointer grab as if the *owner_events* parameter were True.

   In a grab started with a False *owner_events*, all pointer events are delivered directly to the grab window (the window that received the ButtonPress event). The workstation establishes the grab's *event_mask* from the grab window's *event_mask* when it starts the grab. This means that any calls you make to **XSelectInput** during the grab have no effect, and that the grab window gets all events, even if the user drags the mouse into another of your application's windows. This would be inconvenient if the user changed his mind while making a menu selection.

   On the other hand, all events for your application are delivered normally if the grab is started with a True *owner_events*. (Events that would have gone to other applications are still delivered to you via the grab window.)

Most applications should solicit ButtonPress events by specifying Owner-GrabButtonMask along with ButtonPressMask to get this behavior.

2.  You can explicitly terminate the automatic grab using **XUngrabPointer** while the mouse button is pressed. If you do this, some other window (possibly for some other application) may receive an unmatched ButtonRelease event.

3.  You can use **XChangeActivePointerGrab** during the automatic grab to force the display of a particular cursor, or to solicit different events by changing the *event_mask*.

4.  You can respond to the ButtonPress event, or to some subsequent event during the automatic grab, by completely overriding it with an explicit one by calling **XGrabPointer**. You would do this if, for example, you wanted to display a popup menu and confine the pointer to it.

While most applications will only control the grab using the first option, X gives you a great deal of flexibility in what you can do with ButtonPress events. X's layered human interface toolkit software manages grabs automatically and transparently. You can avoid this complexity by using a toolkit.

Unlike the pointer, X's keyboard is *not* automatically grabbed while keyboard keys are pressed. See "Grabbing Individual Keys" later in this chapter for more information.

# GRABBING MOUSE BUTTONS

"To display the main menu, hold both the Control and Shift Keys, and press the middle mouse button." This is an example of the instruction you give to the user when your application grabs individual mouse buttons. The X Window System calls this a *passive grab* to distinguish it from the active grab of the previous section.

When you set up a passive grab on the pointer, you are telling X to keep watch for a number of things to happen at the same time:

1.  a certain exact combination of keyboard modifier (Shift, Control, Meta, Shift-lock) keys are pressed (in the example, the Control and Shift keys),

2.  the pointer is contained in a certain window (that is, it is in the certain window or any of its inferior windows,

3.  a *confine_to* window (if one is specified) is viewable, and

4.  a certain mouse button is pressed.

When all these things happen at once, the passive grab automatically triggers a spring-loaded active grab. This works just as if you called **XGrabPointer** at precisely the moment the user pressed the mouse button. As long as the user keeps holding one or more mouse buttons, the active grab remains in effect. The active grab ends just as if you called **XUngrabPointer** at the instant the user lets go of all the mouse buttons. Notice that holding any mouse button, grabbed or not, keeps the active grab in effect once the grab is established. Notice also that the user may release the modifier keys without ending the grab.

Use the **XGrabButton** request (*Xlib* ¶7.4) to establish a passive grab. A passive grab, once established, can be activated any number of times, and remains in effect until your application explictly ends it. **XUngrabButton** is one way to end a passive grab; terminating your application's connection to X is the other. The requests have the form

```
Display *display;          /* current display */
int button;                /* specifies the mouse button */
int keys_buttons;          /* specifes the set of modifier keys /
Window grab_window;        /* source window for grab */
Bool owner_events;         /* handle this application's events normally */
long event_mask;           /* events to report via source window */
int pointer_mode;          /* grab mode (async / sync ) for pointer */
int keyboard_mode;         /* grab mode for keyboard */
Window confine_to;         /* window to which to confine the cursor */
Cursor cursor;             /* cursor to display */
 . . .
XGrabButton ( display, button, keys_buttons, grab_window, owner_events,
                event_mask, pointer_mode, keyboard_mode,
                confine_to, cursor );
 . . .
XUngrabButton ( display, button, modifiers, grab_window );
```

Use the *button* parameter to specify the mouse button you want to grab. You may specify any single button using the symbols Button1-Button5. The special symbol AnyButton lets you grab all the buttons at once.

Use the *keys_buttons* parameter to specify the combination of modifier keys you want. *keys_buttons* is a bitmask, with one bit for each key. Symbolic names for the bits (defined in **<X11/X.h>**, and the same as those used in the state field of direct input events) are shown in Table 9-I.

To trigger the grab, the user must press the exact modifier-key combination you specify in *keys_buttons*. For example, if you specify ShiftMask alone, and the user presses Control and Shift together, the active grab will not trigger. The special symbol AnyModifier lets you specify that you do not care what combination of keyboard modifier keys the user is pressing. It is equivalent to calling **XGrabButton** once for each possible combination of modifier keys.

*grab_window* serves a dual purpose. It is the window in which the pointer must be contained to satisfy the trigger conditions for an active grab. It also serves as the grab source window for event delivery from the active grab.

*pointer_mode* controls the delivery of pointer events once the active grab is triggered. Normally you specify the value GrabModeAsync; this means that pointer event processing proceeds normally during the active grab. If you specify the value GrabModeSync, it means that your application will have to use the **XAllowEvents** request (see the section below entitled "Synchronous Delivery of Grabbed Events") to allow the delivery of grabbed pointer events (ButtonPress, ButtonRelease, EnterNotify, LeaveNotify, and MotionNotify). The *pointer_mode* value GrabModeSync allows the delivery of exactly one pointer event to announce the triggering of the active grab. After the single pointer event is delivered, the pointer appears to freeze until your application uses the **XAllowEvents** request to resume event delivery. The GrabModeAsync and GrabModeSync constants are defined in the header file **<X11/X.h>**.

Note that in **XGrabButton**, GrabModeSync works differently than it does in **XGrabPointer** (in **XGrabPointer** it freezes the pointer immediately). When a button grab triggers, a single ButtonPress event is delivered *before* the pointer freezes and you must use the **XAllowEvents** request to resume event delivery. The delivered ButtonPress event signals the beginning of the active grab.

*keyboard_mode* controls the delivery of keyboard events, once the active grab is triggered. Normally, you specify the value GrabModeAsync; this means that keyboard event processing proceeds normally during the active pointer grab. If you specify the value GrabModeSync, it means the keyboard will freeze when the user triggers the active pointer grab, and no keyboard events will be delivered *to any applications running on the workstation* until your application uses **XAllowEvents** to restart event delivery, or until the active pointer grab ends.

All the other parameters are applied to the active grab at the time it is triggered. They have the same meanings as they do in the **XGrabPointer** and **XUngrabPointer** requests (described earlier in this chapter). Note that you may use the *confine_to* and *cursor* parameters, just as in the **XGrabPointer** requests, to cue the user that an active grab is in effect.

If you (or other applications) grab identical button and key combinations in different application windows, there is no conflict between the grabs. Only one of them triggers, depending on which window contains the pointer at the time the active grab triggers. If, on the other hand, there are identical passive grabs in a window and one of its inferior windows, the window closest to the root always takes precedence. For more information about event handling in nested windows, see the section entitled "Events in Nested Windows" near the end of Chapter 9.

The **XGrabButton** request can fail. Only one client can grab a particular combination of buttons in a particular window at a time. If some other client has already grabbed the combination you requested, you will, via the standard X error-reporting mechanism, receive the *AlreadyGrabbed* error event message. If, on the other hand, *your* application had previously grabbed the same combination, the new grab takes the place of the old.

(with **XChangeActivePointerGrab**), or completely supersede it (with **XGrab-Pointer**) while it is active. For example, you may want to create and map a menu window, then confine the pointer to it until the user makes a selection.

> Avoid using passive grabs in the root window. Grabs take precedence over ordinary event delivery; if you establish them in the root window, you deny all other windows on the workstation the ability to use the grabbed combinations of keys and buttons. This may wreck other applications' human interfaces.

**Example:** Grab on Control, Shift, and Middle Mouse Button

Suppose your application has a main window *mw*, which contains two separate drawing windows *dw1* and *dw2*. Suppose that you want the user to press Control, Shift, and the middle mouse button at the same time to display a main menu. Also, suppose that you want the user to be able to use Shift Lock for its ordinary purpose, not as a modifier key.

To solve this problem, you need to use a couple of tricks. One is to create drawing windows as subwindows of your application's main window, and do all your button-grabs on the main window. The only events you select on the main window will be those that you want to grab. This way, you will always know that main-window events are the result of grabs. You will also be able to detect when your grab is triggered, because you will receive an EnterNotify event with mode NotifyGrab. Likewise, when the user releases all the mouse buttons and the grab ends, you will receive a LeaveNotify event with mode NotifyUngrab.

The second trick is to call **XGrabButton** once with CapsLockMask, and once without. This will make your button-grab independent of the position of the CapsLock key.

```
/* declarations */
Window mw, dw1,dw2;
XEvent event;
Display *display;
int mask;

. . .
/* initialization:  setting event mask; establishing the grab */
mask =  ButtonPressMask | ButtonReleaseMask | OwnerGrabButtonMask |
        MotionNotifyMask | EnterNotifyMask | LeaveNotifyMask;
XGrabButton (  display, Button2, ControlMask|ShiftMask,
               mw, False, mask ,
               AsyncMode, AsyncMode, mw, None );
   XGrabButton (  display, Button2,
               ControlMask|ShiftMask|CapsLockMask,
               mw, False, mask ,
```

AsyncMode, AsyncMode, *mw,* None );

. . .

# GRABBING THE KEYBOARD

The keyboard is analogous to the pointer in the many situations for which ordinary methods—window-containment and input focus—of assigning keyboard events to windows will not work. To solve these problems, there is a way for an application to announce that it wants all keyboard events delivered directly to it via a particular source window until further notice. You can explicitly establish such an *active keyboard grab* using **XGrabKeyboard**. While an active grab is in effect, further keyboard events are only reported to the grabbing application. Your application must explicitly end an active grab

1. by issuing the **XUngrabKeyboard** request

2. by making the source window unviewable

3. by issuing the **XAllowEvents** request (see the section entitled "Synchronous Delivery of Grabbed Events" above)

4. by terminating your application's connection to the workstation

## Starting a Keyboard Grab

The **XGrabKeyboard** (*Xlib* ¶7.5) request is a round-trip request for starting an active keyboard grab. It returns a status value indicating its success or failure. It has the form

```
Display *display;              /* current display pointer*/
Window grab_window;            /* source window for grab */
Bool owner_events;             /* handle this application's events normally */
int pointer_mode;              /* grab mode (async / sync ) for pointer */
int keyboard_mode;             /* grab mode for keyboard */
Time time;                     /* grab time */
int status;                    /* grab request status*/
    . . .
status = XGrabKeyboard (    display, grab_window, owner_events,
                           pointer_mode, keyboard_mode, time );
    . . .
XUngrabKeyboard ( display, time );
```

The *grab_window* parameter specifies the window you want used as the grab source window. It must be viewable when the grab begins or **XGrabKeyboard** fails. The grab ends with an automatic **XUngrabKeyboard** if the grab window ceases to be viewable during the grab, or if this application terminates its connection.

If you specify *owner_events* as false, all KeyPress and KeyRelease events generated during the grab are reported via the grab source window. On the other hand, if you specify *owner_events* as true, keyboard events that were already bound for your application are unaffected by the grab, and are reported normally. **XGrabKeyboard** makes the grab window "steal" all keyboard events for you; *owner_events* makes it refrain from stealing your own events. Note that issuing an **XGrabKeyboard** request with true *owner_events* has almost exactly the same effect as saving the previous focus state, then changing the focus.

*pointer_mode* controls the delivery of pointer events once the keyboard grab has started. Normally, you specify the value GrabModeAsync; this means that pointer event processing proceeds normally during the grab. If you specify the value GrabModeSync it means that no pointer events (ButtonPress, Button-Release, EnterNotify, LeaveNotify, or MotionNotify) will be delivered to your application *or any other application running on the workstation* until your application uses **XAllowEvents** to resume event delivery or until the keyboard grab ends (see the section below entitled "Synchronous Delivery of Grabbed Events"). The GrabModeAsync and GrabModeSync constants are defined in the header file **<X11/X.h>**.

*keyboard_mode* controls the delivery of keyboard events, once the keyboard grab is triggered. Normally, you specify the value GrabModeAsync; this means that keyboard event processing proceeds during the keyboard grab. If you specify the value GrabModeSync it means the keyboard will freeze when the keyboard grab begins. No keyboard events will be delivered until your application uses **XAllowEvents** to restart event delivery, or until the keyboard grab ends.

The *time* parameter is used to make sure that grabs and ungrabs from different applications do not get confused because of communications delays. Your application probably establishes and releases grabs when it is triggered by received events (possibly KeyPress or EnterNotify). Use the time stamp of the triggering event for the *time* parameter. Note that the *time* you specify does not establish the priority of your grab over some other client's; it only serves as a sort of postmark on your request, to determine whether it got delayed in transit from your application to the workstation.

The **XGrabKeyboard** request can fail; your application should be prepared for this. Success or failure is reported in the *status* value returned by **XGrabKeyboard**.

- The *status* value GrabSuccess indicates that the **XGrabKeyboard** request succeeded.

- Only one client can grab the keyboard at a time. If some other client has already grabbed it, you will receive the AlreadyGrabbed error status. If, on the other hand, your application has already grabbed it, the new grab takes the place of the old.

- If you were in a close race with another client for the grab and lost, you may receive the GrabInvalidTime error status. If you do receive this status, it is very likely that two or more applications running on your workstation are in conflict: they are attempting to start a grab based on the same event. It is also possible that you made an error specifying the *time* parameter.

• If the keyboard is frozen, by a grab coming from some other application with a *keyboard_mode* of GrabModeSync, you will receive the GrabFrozen error status.

• The GrabNotViewable error status tells you that your *grab_window* is unviewable.

> If your application uses **XGrabKeyboard** indiscriminately, you will interfere with other applications running on the workstation.

## Ending a Keyboard Grab

The **XUngrabKeyboard** (*Xlib* ¶7.5) request terminates an active keyboard grab. It has the form

```
Display * display;              /* current display pointer*/
. . .
XUngrabKeyboard ( display, time );
```

You may use **XUngrabKeyboard** to end active keyboard grabs established either by **XGrabKeyboard** requests or **XGrabKey** requests. You cannot go wrong if you specify *time* using the time from the most recent event you have received (usually the event inducing you to end the grab).

## Keyboard Grabs and Focus Change Events

The workstation generates a series of FocusIn and FocusOut events with mode NotifyGrab at the beginning and end of every keyboard grab. See Chapter 10. Whenever an active keyboard grab begins, FocusIn and FocusOut events with mode NotifyGrab are generated as if the input focus were changed from the window in which the focus started to the grab window. When the active keyboard grab ends, FocusIn and FocusOut events are generated with mode NotifyUngrab as if the input focus were changed back to the keyboard focus window. Usually the keyboard focus window is the the window the focus was in before the grab.

However, if your application issues an **XSetInputFocus** request during the grab, the new focus window will receive the focus at the end of the grab.

**Example:** Focus starts in window E. Grab activates in window B.

Window E receives FocusOut, mode NotifyGrab, detail NotifyNonlinear.

Window A receives FocusIn, mode NotifyGrab, detail NotifyNonlinear-Virtual.

Window B receives FocusIn, mode NotifyGrab, detail NotifyNonlinear.

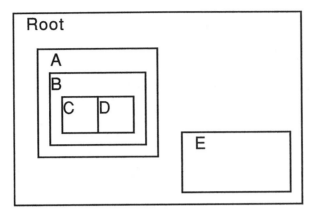

Figure 11-1.  Example Window Configuration.

**Example:**  Window B grab deactivates.  Focus moves back to Window E.

Window B receives FocusOut, mode NotifyUngrab, detail NotifyNonlinear.

Window A receives FocusOut, mode NotifyUngrab, detail NotifyNonlinearVirtual.

Window E receives FocusIn, mode NotifyUngrab, detail NotifyNonlinear.

# GRABBING INDIVIDUAL KEYS

"To print the screen, hold the Control key and press Function Key 5."  This is an example of the instruction you might give to the user when your application grabs individual keys.  The X Window System calls this a *passive keyboard grab*: it works very much like the passive pointer grabs described earlier in this chapter in "Grabbing Individual Mouse Buttons."

When you set up a passive grab on a key in a window, you are telling X to keep watch in the future for the following combination of circumstances:

- The user presses a specified combination of keyboard modifier (Shift, Lock, Control, Meta) keys.

- The user presses the grabbed key.

- The KeyPress event generated when the user pressed the grabbed key belongs to the specified window or one of its inferiors.  This can be assured if the input focus is on the specified window or one of its ancestors.

When these conditions are all met, the passive grab triggers an active keyboard grab.  Ordinarily, applications grab function keys and possibly control keys.

> **Grabbing a keyboard key prevents its use for the typing of text.**

When the right combination of keys is pressed, the passive grab automatically triggers an active grab. This works just as if you called **XGrabKeyboard** at precisely the moment the user pressed the grabbed keyboard key. The active grab ends just as if you called **XUngrabKeyboard** at the instant the user lets go of the grabbed key. The active grab continues as long as the user holds the grabbed key, regardless of what the user does with the modifier keys or other keys.

Use the **XGrabKey** request to establish a passive grab on a key. Once a passive key grab is established, it can be activated many times, and it stays established until your application explicitly ends it. **XUngrabKey** is one way to end a passive key grab; closing your application's display connection is the other. The requests (*Xlib* ¶7.5) have the form

```
Display * display;        /* Current Display pointer */
int keycode;              /* specifies the keycode */
int keys_buttons;         /* specifies the set of keyboard modifier keys /
Window grab_window;       /* source window for grab */
Bool owner_events;        /* handle this application's events normally */
int pointer_mode;         /* grab mode (async / sync ) for pointer */
int keyboard_mode;        /* grab mode for keyboard */
    . . .
XGrabKey ( display, keycode, modifiers, grab_window, owner_events,
            pointer_mode, keyboard_mode );

    . . .
XUngrabKey ( display, keycode, modifiers, grab_window );
```

Use the *keycode* parameter to specify the key you want to grab (or ungrab). You may specify any one key (a modifier key if you wish). You may also use the special symbol AnyKey to specify that you want passive grabs established on all non-modifier keys. Specifying a *keycode* of AnyKey is equivalent to calling **XGrabKey** once for every key on the keyboard.

Use the *keys_buttons* parameter to specify the combination of modifier keys you want. *keys_buttons* is a bitmask, with one bit for each key. Symbolic names (defined in **<X11/X.h>**) are shown in Table 11-II earlier in this chapter. The special symbol AnyModifier lets you specify that you do not care what combination of keyboard modifier keys the user is pressing. It is equivalent to calling **XGrabKey** once for each possible combination of modifier keys.

*grab_window* serves a dual purpose. It is the window via which the KeyPress event starting the grab would be delivered to satisfy the trigger conditions for an active grab. It also will serve as the grab source window for event delivery from the active grab.

*pointer_mode* controls the delivery of pointer events, once the active grab is triggered. Normally, you specify the value GrabModeAsync; this means that pointer event processing proceeds normally during the active pointer grab. If you spec-

ify the value GrabModeSync, it means the pointer will freeze when the user triggers the active keyboard grab, and no pointer events will be delivered *to any applications running on the workstation* until your application uses **XAllowEvents**
to restart event delivery, or until the active keyboard grab ends.

*keyboard_mode* controls the delivery of keyboard events once the active grab is
triggered. Normally you specify the value GrabModeAsync; this means that
keyboard event processing proceeds normally during the active grab. If you
specify the value GrabModeSync, it means that your application will have to use
the **XAllowEvents** request (see the section below entitled "Synchronous Delivery of Grabbed Events") to allow the delivery of grabbed keyboard events
(KeyPress and KeyRelease). The *keyboard_mode* of GrabModeSync allows the
delivery of exactly one KeyPress event to announce the triggering of the active
grab. After the single KeyPress event is delivered, the keyboard appears to
freeze until your application uses the **XAllowEvents** request to resume event
delivery. The GrabModeAsync and GrabModeSync constants are defined in the
header file **<X11/X.h>**.

If you (or other applications) grab identical key and modifier combinations in
different application windows, there is no conflict between the grabs. Only one
of them triggers, depending on which window the input focus (or pointer) is in.
If, on the other hand, there are two outstanding grabs in a window and one of its
inferior windows, the window closest to the root always takes precedence. This
window selection is in the reverse order from **XSelectInput**, which always
gives precedence to the window furthest away from the root.

The **XGrabKey** request can fail. Only one client can grab a particular combination of modifiers and keys in a particular window at a time. If some other
client has already grabbed the combination you requested, you will, via the X error-reporting mechanism, receive the *AlreadyGrabbed* error event. If, on the
other hand, your application had previously grabbed the same combination, the
new grab takes the place of the old.

A series of FocusIn and FocusOut events with mode NotifyGrab announce the
triggering of an active grab. See "Keyboard Grabs and Focus Change Events"
earlier in this chapter.

Avoid using passive key grabs in the screen root window. Grabs take precedence
over ordinary event delivery. If you establish them in the root window, you
deny all other windows on the workstation the ability to use the grabbed key and
modifier combination. This may wreck other applications' human interfaces.

# SYNCHRONOUS DELIVERY OF GRABBED EVENTS

Events delivered to your application as a result of an active grab can have their
rate of delivery controlled explicitly if you wish. The **XGrabPointer, XGrab-
Button, XGrabKeyboard**, and **XGrabKey** requests all allow your application

to specify both a *pointer_mode* and a *keyboard_mode*.   If you establish a grab by specifying the usual value of GrabModeAsync for both *pointer_mode* and *keyboard_mode,* event processing proceeds normally after the activation of the grab, and none of the material discussed in this section is relevant.   If you specify, on the other hand, the value GrabModeSync for either *pointer_mode* or *keyboard_mode,* then you must use **XAllowEvents** to synchronize further event delivery.

X provides synchronous delivery of grabbed events to meet the needs of applications which must put the user "on hold" while reorganizing the window hierarchy or altering the way events are delivered.   GrabModeSync settings for *pointer_mode* or *keyboard_mode* let an application start a safe period during which input from the user is suspended.   An application may wish to freeze the pointer and suspend pointer event delivery until it has had time to display a popup menu when an **XGrabButton** grab is activated.   If the **XGrabButton**'s *pointer_mode* value was GrabModeSync, the pointer freezes right after the event that triggers the active grab.   The same application also can suspend keyboard event delivery when the **XGrabButton** is activated, by specifying a *keyboard_mode* of GrabModeSync.   For example, if the popup menu had an option which caused keystrokes to be delivered to a newly created dialogue window, this would prove to be a good way to prevent stray keystroke events during the time it took to create the new window.

**XAllowEvents** can also allow an event to be frozen, then replayed after the grab ends.   This allows an application to process a grabbed event, then to allow the same event to be replayed, or delivered without being subjected to a grab, to whatever application would ordinarily have received it.   A replayed event is redelivered based on the state of the window hierarchy at the time of the replay, not at the time the event originally occurred.   This behavior is useful:  for example, it lets an application create a window, then redeliver a grabbed event to that window.

Window-manager applications and toolkits are major users of synchronized grabbed events.   However, synchronization may be useful to any application that uses pointer or keyboard grabs.

The pointer becomes frozen as the result of the following:

1.   An **XGrabPointer** request with a *pointer_mode* of GrabModeSync. This request immediately freezes the pointer, without establishing a replayable pointer event.   (The EnterNotify event with mode NotifyGrab that signals the grab activation is delivered normally.)

2.   An **XGrabKeyboard** request with a *pointer_mode* of GrabModeSync. This request immediately freezes the pointer, without establishing a replayable pointer event.

3.   The triggering of an active pointer grab established by an **XGrabButton** request with a *pointer_mode* of GrabModeSync. This request delivers the pointer event that triggered the active grab, then freezes the pointer.   The pointer event that triggered the active grab

is established as the replayable pointer event. (The EnterNotify event with mode NotifyGrab that signals the grab activation is delivered normally, before the replayable ButtonPress event.)

4.    The triggering of an active keyboard grab established by an **XGrabKey** request with a *pointer_mode* of GrabModeSync. This request immediately freezes the pointer, without establishing a replayable pointer event.

5.    An **XAllowEvents** request (see below) with an *event_mode* value of SyncPointer, followed by the delivery of a ButtonPress or ButtonRelease event. The ButtonPress or ButtonRelease event is established as the replayable pointer event.

Similarly, the keyboard becomes frozen as the result of the following:

1.    An **XGrabPointer** request with a *keyboard_mode* of GrabModeSync. This request immediately freezes the keyboard, without establishing a replayable keyboard event.

2.    An **XGrabKeyboard** request with a *keyboard_mode* of GrabModeSync. This request immediately freezes the keyboard, without establishing a replayable keyboard event.

3.    The triggering of an active pointer grab established by an **XGrabButton** request with a *keyboard_mode* of GrabModeSync. This request immediately freezes the keyboard, without establishing a replayable keyboard event.

4.    The triggering of an active keyboard grab established by an **XGrabKey** request with a *keyboard_mode* of GrabModeSync. This request delivers the keyboard event that triggered the active grab, then freezes the keyboard. The keyboard event that triggered the active grab is established as the replayable keyboard event.

5.    An **XAllowEvents** request (see below) with an *event_mode* value of SyncKeyboard, followed by the delivery of a KeyPress or KeyRelease event. The KeyPress or KeyRelease event is established as the replayable keyboard event.

Once the workstation has frozen a device on behalf of your application, you use the **XAllowEvents** request to *thaw* it. **XAllowEvents** (*Xlib* ¶7.5) has the form

```
Display *display;        /* current display */
int event_mode;          /* specifies what to thaw and how to thaw it */
Time time;          /* timestamp */
    . . .
XAllowEvents ( display, event_mode, time );
```

With a single **XAllowEvents** call, you can thaw either the pointer or the keyboard, but not both. The *event_mode* you specify determines which device is thawed, the permanency of the thaw, and whether the replayable event is replayed or discarded. If you try to thaw a device that was not frozen for your application, **XAllowEvents** has no effect. *event_mode* specifies the action to take. It must have one of the following values (defined as constants in the header file **<X11/X.h>**):

AsyncPointer      Thaw the pointer device, discard the replayable pointer event (if any), and proceed with normal processing of pointer events. This request works whether or not the pointer is grabbed by this application, so it is suitable for thawing any of the five types of pointer freezes. The thaw is permanent, until the next grab.

SyncPointer      Thaw the pointer device, discard the replayable pointer event (if any), and proceed with normal processing of pointer events until the next ButtonPress or ButtonRelease event is reported to this application. This request only works when the pointer is grabbed by this application, which is to say that it is only suitable for thawing pointer freeze types 1, 3, and 5 (see above). The thaw is temporary: when the ButtonPress or ButtonRelease event arrives, a pointer freeze of type 5 is established, unless the event also signals the end of the active pointer grab.

ReplayPointer      Replay the replayable pointer event. This request ends the active pointer grab. The replayed event is completely reprocessed, this time ignoring any passive grabs (established by prior **XGrabButton** requests) for which the *grab_window* lies in the window hierarchy between the window for the just-released grab and the root window. If no replayable pointer event has been established, this request has no effect and the active pointer grab does not end.

AsyncKeyboard      Thaw the keyboard device, discard the replayable keyboard event (if any), and proceed with normal processing of keyboard events. This request works whether or not the keyboard is grabbed by this application, so it is suitable for thawing any of the five types (see above) of keyboard freezes. The thaw is permanent (until the next grab).

SyncKeyboard      Thaw the keyboard device, discard the replayable keyboard event (if any), and proceed with normal processing of keyboard events until the next KeyPress or KeyRelease event is reported to this application. This request only works when the keyboard is grabbed by this application, which is to say that it is only suitable for thawing keyboard freeze types 2, 4, and 5 (see above). The thaw is temporary: when the KeyPress or KeyRelease event arrives, a keyboard freeze of type 5 is established, unless the event also signals the end of the active keyboard grab.

ReplayKeyboard      Replay the replayable keyboard event. This request ends the active keyboard grab. The replayed event is completely reprocessed, this time ignoring any passive grabs (established by prior **XGrabKey** requests) for which the *grab_window* lies in the window hierarchy between the window for the just-released grab and the root window. If no replayable keyboard event has been established, this request has no effect and the keyboard grab does not end.

Thus, you may permanently dismiss a pointer freeze with an *event_mode* of AsyncPointer. Similarly, you may dismiss a keyboard freeze with an *event_mode* of AsyncKeyboard. Using *event_mode* values of SyncPointer or SyncKeyboard, you may temporarily end pointer or keyboard freezes. Lastly, you may end a freeze, end the grab, and replay the event when *event_mode* is ReplayPointer or ReplayKeyboard.

There is one more complication: The pointer or the keyboard may be twice-frozen (on behalf of two separate grabs), either in the same application or in separate applications. If a device is twice-frozen on behalf of your application, you only need thaw it once, with a single call to **XAllowEvents**. On the other hand, if two different applications both have a device frozen, it stays frozen until they both thaw it.

# PASSIVE GRAB ACTIVATION

Ordinary ungrabbed events are delivered bottom-up. Some parts of a human interface, such as the display of system menus, require a top-down approach to the search for an event window. This top-down capability is provided by passive grabs.

Every passive grab of the pointer device is established in a *grab_window*. Grabs of the same mouse-buttons and modifier keys can be made, as long as they are made in different windows. When an event might be the trigger for a passive grab, the search for the passive grab is made starting with the root window, and working down the hierarchy level by level. For a pointer grab to be activated,

1. The current state of the buttons and keys must match the grabbed state, and the *confine_to* window, if any, must be viewable.

2. The pointer must be in the *grab_window* or in one of its inferiors.

The implication of starting the search at the root window is that passive grabs near the root window override (and prevent the activation of) those farther down the hierarchy.

# SUMMARY

X applications can use the techniques described this chapter to achieve greater control over input events, and to add to the options they have for human interface design. Handling events properly can significantly add to the performance of your application, and give your users the feeling that it "snaps."

Ordinarily, applications read the event queue in order, using **XNextEvent**. It is also possible to read the queue out of order: *Xlib* provides a variety of calls which you can use to choose events from the queue according to their event type or window, or other criteria.

X workstations often deliver redundant events. For example, you may receive long streams of MotionNotify events or paired EnterNotify/LeaveNotify events. If you use techniques described in this chapter to compress such redundant events you can significantly improve your application's performance.

Your application can connect to several workstations at once. If you wish to do this, you must use an event-processing loop containing a **select** call like the one described in this chapter. You must also take care to distinguish resources for different workstations: window and other resource identifiers are only valid on the single workstation for which they were created.

You can return events to your own event queue (with **XPutBackEvent**) or send events to other applications (with **XSendEvent**). These capabilities increase the flexibility of your event-handling and allows suites of application programs to communicate with one another.

Applications can establish an *active grab* on the pointer or keyboard, thereby arranging to steal all events from the device until further notice. Applications can also establish *passive grabs* on particular combinations of mouse buttons and/or keyboard keys. Passive grabs convert to active grabs when the user presses the grabbed button and key combination. An automatic active grab begins whenever an application receives a ButtonPress event.

When setting up a grab, you can arrange for the input devices to be *frozen* if you wish. One good use for this is to give yourself time to display a pull-down menu or otherwise prepare to handle a series of events. Once a device is frozen, you can arrange to *thaw* it temporarily (allowing just one event), thaw it permanently (dismissing the grab), or *replay* a frozen event as if no grab were in effect. Finally, you can confine the pointer to a specific window during a grab. Confining the pointer is useful for asking Yes/No questions of the user.

Unlike ordinary pointer events which originate in subwindows and work their way up the window hierarchy toward the root, passive grabs of buttons and keys work their way from the root down.

# CHAPTER 12
# COMMUNICATING
# BETWEEN
# APPLICATIONS

Most users run several applications at a time on an X workstation. In X, the base window system is designed in such a way that each application can work as if it were the only application running on the workstation. For example, the workstation automatically clips graphical output to window boundaries.

Application programs do not exist in a vacuum on workstations, however. Individual applications must be able to communicate with one another, and pass information back and forth. In previous chapters, we have seen *Xlib* calls for passing information between applications:

- Window manager interaction calls such as **XStoreName**, **XGet-Name**, and **XSetStandardProperties** (Chapter 4).

- The color map sharing call, **XGetStandardColormap** (Chapter 7).

These calls are special cases of X's general mechanisms for information sharing. This chapter explains how applications, even applications from different vendors, can share arbitrary information.

Text-based applications (such as **xterm**) have a cut-and-paste capability. For example, a user can select text (using the left mouse button) in one **xterm** window and paste it (using the middle mouse button) into another. The first section of this chapter explains how you can build this character-string cut-and-paste capability into your application. By using X's cut buffers, your application can copy characters to and paste characters from **xterm** and other text-based applications.

Your application can also store arbitrary data, or *properties*, in the workstation for use by other applications. X's property capability is described in the second section of this chapter.

Finally, X provides *selections*. Selections are a way for applications to exchange arbitrary information (such as formatted text, bitmaps, or graphics). The potential of selections is enormous: they promise to allow cut-and-paste between text editors, text formatters, bitmap editors, graphics editors, and other application programs. The final section of this chapter is an introduction to the use of selections.

# CUT BUFFERS

X provides buffers for moving data from application to application. These buffers are usually used for cut-and-paste operations. For example, **xterm(1)** supports a cut-and-paste capability. The **xterm** user can highlight an arbitrary range of text by dragging the mouse over the text with the left button pressed. **xterm** highlights the text range by reversing the foreground and background colors. When the user selects a useful range of text and releases the button, **xterm** copies the selected text into a cut buffer. Later on, the **xterm** user can retrieve—paste—that copied text by pressing the middle mouse button.

What makes cut-and-paste especially useful is the fact that the user can cut or copy from one application's window and paste into another's. To make this possible, *Xlib* provides a series of utility calls (summarized in Table 12-I) for manipulating cut buffers. The cut buffers themselves are stored in the workstation where all running applications can use them. *Xlib*'s cut-buffer calls make use of X's property mechanism to accomplish this; see the "Properties" section later in this chapter. Regardless of the number of applications running on a workstation, or the number of screens it has, each workstation provides exactly one set of cut buffers.

Eight separate cut buffers are provided in X. Each of these is stored as a simple "bag of bytes." The workstation makes no attempt to give them any meaning. When applications use cut-buffers, they have to agree about the type and format of the information in them. If you program your application to use cut buffers, it is a good idea to make it robust enough to deal gracefully with unexpected cut buffer contents or sizes.

| Request/Function | Xlib ¶ | Description |
|---|---|---|
| **XStoreBytes** | 10.7 | Store data in cut buffer 0 |
| **XStoreBuffer** | 10.7 | Store data in a numbered cut buffer |
| **XFetchBytes** | 10.7 | Retrieve data from cut buffer 0 |
| **XFetchBuffer** | 10.7 | Retrieve data from a numbered cut buffer |
| **XRotateBuffers** | 10.7 | Interchange data among the cut buffers |

Table 12-I. *Xlib* calls for cut-buffer manipulation.

Notice that the contents of cut buffers are not necessarily in the form of null-terminated text strings. When you store information into cut buffers, you specify both a pointer to the bytes and the number of bytes you want stored.

The cut buffers provided by *Xlib* are numbered zero through seven. Each cut buffer is stored as a property of the root window for screen zero (see "Properties" later in this chapter). The properties have the predefined atoms XA_CUT_BUFFER0 – XA_CUT_BUFFER7. The *Xlib* cut buffer calls automatically read and write those properties; you may use cut buffer calls without concerning yourself with window properties.

**xterm** only uses cut buffer zero. The format **xterm** uses is a simple stream of ordinary ASCII (or Latin-1) characters, with lines separated by newline characters. If you program your application to use this data format you will be able to cut and paste between your application and **xterm**.

Cut buffers are the simple X mechanism for cut and paste between applications. X also provides a more flexible and general *selection* mechanism which makes it possible for applications to exchange structured data. The selection mechanism is described under "Selections" later in this chapter.

## Storing Data In Cut Buffers

Use the **XStoreBytes** (*Xlib* ¶10.7) call to store a stream of bytes into cut buffer zero. It has the form

```
Display* display;            /* pointer to Display structure */
char bytes [ ];              /* pointer to byte string to store */
int nbytes;                  /* length of byte string to store */
   . . .
XStoreBytes ( display, bytes, nbytes );
```

To **XStoreBytes**, you pass *bytes*, a pointer to the information you want stored, and *nbytes*, the length of the information. **xterm** uses **XStoreBytes**.

Use the **XStoreBuffer** (*Xlib* ¶10.7) call to store a stream of bytes into the cut buffer you specify. It has the form

```
Display* display;              /* pointer to Display structure */
char bytes [ ];                /* pointer to byte string to store */
int nbytes;                    /* length of byte string to store */
int buffer;                    /* buffer in which to store */
. . .
XStoreBuffer ( display, bytes, nbytes, buffer );
```

To **XStoreBuffer**, you pass *bytes*, a pointer to the information you want stored, and *nbytes*, the length of the information. You also must specify the *buffer* number in which you want your information stored. *buffer* must be a number between zero and seven.

You may clear any cut buffer by storing a zero-length string into it. To do this, specify an *nbytes* value of zero.

## Retrieving Data From Cut Buffers

Use the **XFetchBytes** (*Xlib* ¶10.7) call to retrieve a stream of bytes from cut buffer zero. It has the form

```
Display* display;              /* pointer to Display structure */
int nbytes_return;             /* length of returned byte string */
char * bytes_return;           /* pointer to returned byte string */
. . .
bytes_return = XFetchBytes ( display, &nbytes_return );
. . .
if ( bytes_return ) XFree ( bytes_return );
```

**XFetchBytes** retrieves the contents of cut buffer zero from the workstation. *Xlib* allocates storage for the data and passes you a pointer to the data in *bytes_return*. It also returns the length of the byte string in *nbytes_return*.

If you fetch information from a cut buffer into which nothing has been stored, you will receive an *nbytes_return* value of zero and a null *bytes_return* pointer.

Use **XFree** to release the returned storage when your application has finished using it.

Use the **XFetchBuffer** (*Xlib* ¶10.7) call to retrieve a stream of bytes from a specified cut buffer. It has the form

```
Display* display;              /* pointer to Display structure */
int nbytes_return;             /* length of returned byte string */
int buffer;                    /* buffer from which to retrieve */
char * bytes_return;           /* pointer to returned byte string */
. . .
bytes_return = XFetchBuffer ( display, &nbytes_return, buffer );
```

. . .
if ( *bytes_return* ) **XFree** ( *bytes_return* );

**XFetchBuffer** retrieves the contents of the cut *buffer* you specify from the workstation. *Xlib* allocates storage for the data and passes you a pointer to the data in *bytes_return*. It also returns the length of the byte string in *nbytes_return*. *buffer* specifies which cut buffer to retrieve; it must be a number between zero and seven.

## Interchanging Data among Cut Buffers

If you use all eight cut buffers, you can treat them as a ring of connected buffers. For example, you might store the eight most recent cut strings in the eight cut buffers. The **XRotateBuffers** call allows you to rotate the ring, interchanging the data stored in all eight buffers. For example, if you store data into buffer 0, then rotate the ring one position, you will then be able to retrieve the value from buffer 1. Likewise, data previously stored into buffer 1 can, after the rotation, be retrieved from buffer 2. Buffer 7's data is moved into buffer 0.

Use the **XRotateBuffers** (*Xlib* ¶10.7) call to rotate the cut buffer ring. It has the form

> **Display\*** *display;*              /* *pointer to Display structure* */
> int *rotate;*                          /* *number of positions to rotate buffers* */
>   . . .
> **XRotateBuffers** ( *display, rotate* );

**XRotateBuffer** rotates the contents of the eight cut buffers the number of places you specify in *rotate*. You may specify any number in *rotate*. If you specify zero, nothing happens. If you specify a positive number, the data values stored in the buffers move down the specified number of places (that is, buffer 0's value is moved to buffer *n* when you specify a *rotate* value of *n*). Likewise, if you specify a negative number, the data moves up the specified number of places (buffer *n*'s value is moved to buffer 0 when you specify a *rotate* value of –n).

Before you attempt to use **XRotateBuffers**, you must store something—a zero-length string will do—into all eight buffers.

# PROPERTIES

In X, applications which must share information with one another use *properties*, a general mechanism provided by X's base window system. Each window on a workstation can have any number of properties stored with it. Each property is an arbitrary collection of data. X's base window system provides general-purpose ways for application programs to store and retrieve properties of windows.

The usefulness of properties for inter-application communication comes from the following:

1) Your application can create any property for any window, and/or store data into any property for any window.

2) Your application can retrieve the data in any property for any window, even if that data was stored by some other application.

3) Your application can solicit PropertyNotify events to find out when other applications alter any of a given window's properties.

In other words, applications communicate by *hanging properties on windows*, as if the properties were tags. Any application can come along and write information on any property, or can read any property. Notice that the window system does not show the properties to the user, but merely stores them so applications can share them.

Each property has a name. A property name is an arbitrary character string. (Property name strings are, like font name strings, defined in the Latin-1 character set. See Appendix C.) The workstation keeps each window's properties separate from those of all other windows. For example, you might hang a property named "WM_HINTS" on each top-level window in your application: the workstation will store different data in each window's property. However, you cannot hang two different properties of the same name on a single window.

Each property also has a data type. For example, a property's type can be an integer, a character string, a window resource identifier, an x,y point, or a rectangle. When an application creates a property, it must specify the data type of the property. Other applications can, upon reading the property, find out its type.

Before communicating via properties, applications must agree about the name and type of the property they will use to pass information. Applications must also agree about the window on which the property will be hung. For example, some properties are hung on root windows, and other are hung on top-level application windows. Given this agreement, applications can use the *Xlib* calls described later in this chapter to create, write, read, and delete properties.

The hint-passing and information-sharing calls in *Xlib* (**XStoreName**, for example) use properties. X's base window system provides a predefined set of property names for these purposes, and *Xlib* specifically manipulates those predefined *standard properties*. If you wish, you can use general-purpose property-manipulation calls with standard properties. For example, your application could, if you wanted it to, use **XGetWindowProperty** (described later in this chapter) in place of **XGetName** to read Window Name hints from other applications' windows. Alternatively, if you are developing a suite of application programs you can define your own properties. This allows you to extend X's application communication capability for your own needs.

Any property can be hung on any window. For example, there is nothing stopping you from using **XSetName** to give a subwindow a name. However, without agreement among applications to read Window Name hints from subwindows, setting the property is useless. Properties of the same name, but containing different data, can be hung from different windows. For example, each top-level window can have its own property defining its own Window Name hint.

| Request/Function | Xlib ¶ | Description |
|---|---|---|
| **XInternAtom** | 4.2 | Return an Atom corresponding to a name |
| **XGetAtomName** | 4.2 | Return the name corresponding to an atom |
| **XChangeProperty** | 4.3 | Change a property, creating it if necessary |
| **XGetWindowProperty** | 4.3 | Retrieve a property |
| **XRotateWindowProperties** | 4.3 | Interchange data for a list of properties |
| **XListProperties** | 4.3 | Determine which properties a window has |
| **XDeleteProperty** | 4.3 | Delete a property |

Table 12-II. *Xlib* calls for property manipulation.

## The Life Cycle of Properties

When your application uses a property, the first thing you must do is use **XInternAtom** to translate the character strings for the property name and type into Atoms. Atoms, described in the next section, are 32-bit unique identifiers representing names.

Once you have Atoms for the property's name and type, you can proceed to hang the property on any window. You do this by storing data into the property with **XChangeProperty**. If the property does not already exist for the window, **XChangeProperty** automatically creates it.

You can read the data from a property by using **XGetWindowProperty**. Many applications assume that other applications have already hung properties on windows, and just use **XGetWindowProperty** to read them.

You can find out what properties are hung on any given window by using **XListProperties**.

You can *rotate* the data in a list of a particular window's properties—circularly permute them—by using **XRotateWindowProperties**. This property-manipulation call supports capabilities like that in **XRotateBuffers** (see "Cut Buffers" earlier in this chapter).

You can find out when any properties hung on a particular window are changed. To do this, you must solicit PropertyNotify events from the window.

The workstation deletes all properties hung on a window at the same time that it deletes the window. You can also use **XGetWindowProperty** to delete a property explicitly at the same time as you read its data, or **XDeleteProperty** to delete a property without reading it. As long as you do not delete a property explicitly or delete its window, the property survives the termination of the application that created it. For example, if your application hung a property on the root window, that property would survive the termination of your application. The data for your property can be read and written by other applications and by subsequent runs of your application. (Recall that the workstation ordinarily destroys your windows when your application terminates. This, of course, means that properties hung on your application's windows will be deleted as well.)

Properties only last as long as a user's session on the workstation. When the last application's display connection terminates, the workstation deletes all properties on all windows.

You may use the **xprop(1)** shell command in Unix or compatible systems to display properties' data values.

## Atoms and Property Names

Properties have names defined by variable-length character strings. In property names, upper-case and lower-case make a difference (for example, "Color" and "color" define different properties). Property types are also defined by character strings, which means that applications can use standard types or define their own.

Names which are private to an organization should begin with a single underscore character, to ensure that they will not be the same as commonly-used X names. Similarly, names which are private to a single user or application program should begin with two underscore characters.

It is inconvenient and wasteful to specify property names and types by transmitting entire character strings over the display connection between application and workstation. For that reason, X provides *Atoms* to use in place of character-string names. Atoms are 32-bit unique identifiers. When your application knows the name of a property, you use the **XInternAtom** call to look up the Atom corresponding to that name. Conversely, **XGetAtomName** returns a name as a character string, given an Atom.

Atoms are unique. If two applications look up an Atom for the same name, they receive the same unique identifier. However, this uniqueness only extends to applications running on *one workstation* for *one user session*. If your application uses several display connections simultaneously to several different workstations, you must take care not to confuse the Atoms for the different connections. Similarly, your application must not attempt to store Atom values in files and reuse them for a subsequent user session.

X defines certain atoms for predefined properties and data types. If you want to use one of these predefined atoms, use the insert file **<X11/Xatom.h>**. There is no need to use **XInternAtom** to look up Atom values for predefined Atoms. See Appendix G for a list of predefined Atoms.

## Converting a Name to an Atom

**XInternAtom** (*Xlib* ¶4.3) returns a unique Atom when you give it a name string. It is a round-trip request, and has the form

**Display\*** *display;*          /* *pointer to Display structure* */
char *atom_name* [ ];          /* *the name of the atom* */
**Bool** *only_if_exists;*          /* False *if this is possibly first use*/
**Atom** *atom;*          /* *returned atom* */
. . .

*atom* = **XInternAtom** ( *display, atom_name, only_if_exists* );

Use the *atom_name* string to specify a name in the form of a Latin-1 (ASCII) null-terminated character string. **XInternAtom** associates a 32-bit unique identifier with your *atom_name* and returns its value in *atom*, the function result.

During each user session, the workstation keeps an internal list of all names and Atoms, for all applications. The *atom_name* you specify may already exist in the internal list, if some application has already used it during the current user session. In this case, **XInternAtom** returns its *atom* value.

If you specify a new *atom_name*, however, the workstation uses the *only_if_exists* parameter to decide what to do. If you specify True for *only_if_exists* along with a new *atom_name*, the workstation returns an *atom* value of None. However, if you specify False, the workstation makes a new entry in its internal list, creates a new *atom* value for the new name, and returns that *atom* value to you. Most applications should specify False for *only_if_exists*.

The workstation destroys its internal list of names and atoms at the end of each user session (when the last application closes its display connection).

You may use **XInternAtom** to look up a predefined Atom if you wish. Remember, though, that the predefined Atoms are defined in the header file **<X11/Xatom.h>**; you may be able to save a round-trip **XInternAtom** request if you take advantage of this fact. If you do use **XInternAtom** to retrieve a predefined Atom, omit the leading "XA_" from the name when specifying the name string. For example, if you look up the string "INTEGER" you will receive the XA_INTEGER atom.

## Converting an Atom to a Name

If you have an Atom (previously obtained via **XInternAtom**), and want to know the character-string name associated with it, use **XGetAtomName** (*Xlib* ¶4.2). It is a round-trip request, and has the form

**Display\*** *display;*          /* *pointer to Display structure* */
**Atom** *atom;*          /* *Atom to look up*/
char \**atom_name* ;          /* *returned name of the atom* */

```
. . .
atom_name = XGetAtomName ( display, atom );
. . .
XFree ( atom_name );
```

Given a valid *atom*, **XGetAtomName** returns a pointer to its *atom_name* string. If you specify an invalid *atom*, **XGetAtomName** generates the BadAtom error event message. If you provide an error-handler (see Chapter 3) you may allow your application to continue after the error by returning from the error handler. If you do this, **XGetAtomName** returns a null string pointer for *atom_name*.

**XGetAtomName** automatically allocates storage within *Xlib* for the *atom_name* string. When your application is through with the string, you must explicitly free the string's storage with **XFree**.

You may retrieve the name of one of the predefined Atoms. However, the retrieved name string does not include the leading "XA_" characters in the symbolic name of the atom. For example, if you use **XGetAtomName** to look up the name for the XA_INTEGER atom, the retrieved string is "INTEGER", not "XA_INTEGER".

## Property Data Format and Type

Two things define how each property is stored:

- *format* defines whether the property is stored as a series of 8-bit bytes, 16-bit short words, or 32-bit long words.

- *type* defines the meaning of the property's values.

When you store data into a property, you must specify both the format and the type of the data. When you retrieve data from a property, the workstation returns the data's format and type.

Each property has a particular format. Possible values for a format parameter are 8, 16, and 32, meaing that the data is a series of 8-bit bytes, 16-bit short words, or 32-bit long words respectively. In general, it is not possible to mix data items of different lengths in a single property and still guarantee workstation interoperability in a network containing workstations from several vendors.

Each property has a particular data type. Every data type has a name, which you specify using an Atom. Most applications will be able to use the  predefined type Atoms. However, you may, if you wish, specify your own application-defined type name, and use **XInternAtom** to retrieve an Atom value for it.

The predefined data type Atoms have the following meanings:

XA_ARC                    This data type is an array of six 16-bit integers, defined
                          as in the **XArc** structure (see Chapter 5).

XA_ATOM                This data type is a 32-bit word.  It is an Atom.

XA_BITMAP              This data type is a 32-bit word.  It is the X resource
                       identifier of a bitmap (one-plane Pixmap).

XA_CARDINAL            Properties of this type contain arbitrarily-sized arrays
                       of unsigned integers.  The size of the integers is deter-
                       mined by the property's format.

XA_COLORMAP            This data type is a 32-bit word.  It is the X resource
                       identifier of a color map.

XA_CURSOR              This data type is a 32-bit word.  It is the X resource
                       identifier of a cursor.

 XA_DRAWABLE           This data type is a 32-bit word.  It is the X resource
                       identifier of a drawable:  a window or Pixmap.

XA_FONT                This data type is a 32-bit word.  It is the X resource
                       identifier of a loaded font.

XA_INTEGER             Properties of this type contain arbitrarily-sized arrays
                       of signed integers.  The size of the integers is deter-
                       mined by the property's format.

XA_PIXMAP              This data type is a 32-bit word.  It is the X resource
                       identifier of a Pixmap.

XA_RECTANGLE           This data type is an array of **XRectangle** structures
                       (see Chapter 5).

XA_RGB_COLOR_MAP       This data type is an **XStandardColormap** structure
                       (see Chapter 7).

XA_STRING              This data type is a string of characters.

XA_VISUALID            This data type is a 32-bit word.  It is a Visual ID (see the
                       **Visual** data structure in "Default Visual Information"
                       in Chapter 7).

XA_WINDOW              This data type is a 32-bit word.  It is the X resource
                       identifier of a window.

XA_WM_HINTS            This data type is an **XWMHints** structure (see Chapter
                       4).  The **XSetWMHints** call creates a property of this
                       type.

XA_WM_SIZE_HINTS       This data type is an **XSizeHints** structure (see Chapter
                       4).  The **XSetNormalHints** call creates a property of
                       this type.

## Creating and Storing Data Into Properties

**XChangeProperty** stores data into a property hung on a window. If the specified property does not already exist, **XChangeProperty** automatically creates it for you. **XChangeProperty** (*Xlib* ¶4.3) is a one-way request, and has the form

```
Display* display;              /* pointer to Display structure */
Window window;                 /* window on which to hang property*/
Atom property;                 /* atom for property name */
Atom type;                     /* atom for type name */
int format;                    /* data format:  8, 16, or 32 */
int mode;                      /* operation (replace, prepend, append)*/
unsigned char * data;          /* new property data*/
int nelements;                 /* size of data*/
   . . .
XChangeProperty ( display, window, property, type,
                    format, mode, data, nelements );
```

**XChangeProperty** loads data into the *property* you specify hung on the *window* you specify. In the *data* parameter, you pass a pointer to an array containing the number of elements in *nelements*. If you specify a *format* value of 8, the *data* parameter must point to an array of 8-bit bytes. Likewise, if you specify a *format* of 16, *data* must point to an array of 16-bit short words, and if you specify a *format* of 32, *data* must point to an array of 32-bit long words. Notice that *nelements* is the number of items, not necessarily bytes, in the *data* array.

In the *mode* parameter, you specify how you want the workstation to combine any previously stored data for the property with the new data. The *mode* parameter can have one of the following three values (defined in **<X11/X.h>**):

PropModeReplace    Any data previously stored for the property is discarded, as is the previously stored *format* and *type*.

PropModePrepend    The *data* specified in this call to **XChangeProperty** is prepended to any existing property data, then stored in the property. The *format* and *type* specified in this call must match those previously stored, or the workstation sends a BadMatch error event message and does not alter the property value.

PropModeAppend     The *data* specified in this call to **XChangeProperty** is appended to any existing property data, then stored in the property. The *format* and *type* specified in this call must match those previously stored, or the workstation sends a BadMatch error event message and does not alter the property value.

**XChangeProperty** automatically creates the *property* and hangs it on the *window* if the property does not already exist. When **XChangeProperty** creates a new property, it always works as if the mode were PropModeReplace:  the property takes on the *format* and *value* you specify.  Notice that because **XChange-Property** is a one-way request, it does not tell you whether it created a new property or altered an existing one.

**XChangeProperty** generates a PropertyNotify event for the specified window.

## Retrieving Data From Properties

**XGetWindowProperty**  retrieves data from a property hung on a window. This round-trip request allows you to do several things with a property:

- You can determine whether a property exists.

- You can determine the *format*, *type*, and length of data stored in a property.

- You can retrieve all the data stored in a property, if you know how long it is.

- You can retrieve some of the data stored in a property.  This permits you to retrieve property data in segments, if the property's data is very long.

- You can simultaneously retrieve data from a property and delete the property from its window.

**XGetWindowProperty** (*Xlib* ¶4.3) has the form

```
Display* display;              /* pointer to Display structure */
Window window;                 /* window on which property is hung */
Atom property;                 /* atom for property name */
long long_offset;              /* start of data segment to retrieve */
long long_length;              /* length of data segment to retrieve */
Bool delete;                   /* delete property after reading?*/
Atom req_type;                 /* property type to retrieve */
Atom actual_type_return;       /* property type actually retrieved */
int actual_format_return;      /* property format actually retrieved */
unsigned long nitems_return;   /* number of items actually returned */
unsigned long bytes_after_return;  /* bytes remaining after this segment */
unsigned char * prop_return;   /* pointer to retrieved property data*/
  . . .
XGetWindowProperty ( display, window, property, long_offset, long_length,
                     delete, req_type, &actual_type_return,
                     &actual_format_return, &nitems_return,
                     &bytes_after_return, &prop_return );
```

. . .
    **XFree** ( *prop_return* );

When you call **XGetWindowProperty**, you specify the following parameters:

*window* and *property* specify which property to retrieve from which window. The *window* must exist and the *property* Atom must be valid, or the workstation will send you an error event message. The *window* does not necessarily have to have the specified *property* hanging from it, however.

*long_offset* and *long_length* allow you to specify which segment of the property's data you wish to retrieve. If your property's data is fairly short ( 32768 bytes or less) you can retrieve the whole property at once by specifying a zero value for *long_offset* and a *long_length* value of 8192. If your property is longer, you will receive a non-zero *bytes_after_return* value. You should retrieve long properties in segments, using multiple calls to **XGetWindowProperty**. Specify the number of 32-bit long words in each segment using *long_length*, and each segments's offset (in 32-bit long words) from the beginning of the property in *long_offset*. (The 32768-byte limit is not hard-and-fast; it is merely a rule of thumb to use for deciding whether you should read the property in segments.)

*delete* allows you to delete the property as it returns the property's value to you. If you specify a *delete* parameter of True and retrieve the entire property, **XGetWindowProperty** deletes the property immediately after it sends its data to you (before any other application can have a chance to retrieve or change the property). However, if you are reading the property in segments and specifying True for *delete*, **XGetWindowProperty** will not delete the property unless you read the last segment: unless the returned *bytes_after_return* value is zero. When **XGetWindowProperty** actually deletes a property, it generates a PropertyNotify event for the window.

*req_type* allows you to specify the Atom for the type of the property. In the *req_type* parameter, you may specify either an actual type Atom or the special value AnyPropertyType.

Depending on whether the *property* you specify exists on the *window* you specify, and whether the *req_type* you specify matches the actual type of the property, **XGetWindowProperty** returns the actual property type and format. If your *req_type* matches the property's actual type, **XGetWindowProperty** also returns the property's data.

If you are not sure of the existence and type of a property, you should call **XGetWindowProperty** with a *long_offset* value of zero and a *long_length* value of 8192. The form of the returned parameters to such a call tells you the property's circumstances as follows:

- If the *actual_format_return* parameter, upon return, contains a value of zero, you know that the specified *property* does not exist for the specified *window*.

- If the *nitems_return* parameter, upon return, contains a zero value and the *actual_format_return* value contains a nonzero value, your specified *req_type* did not match the actual property type. In this case, **XGetWindowProperty** does not attempt to return the property's data. It does use the *actual_type_return* parameter to tell you the property's actual type and the *bytes_after_return* parameter to tell you the actual length.

- If the *nitems_return* value is nonzero, the type Atom you specified in *req_type* matched the property's actual type (the special value AnyPropertyType matches all actual types; the actual property type is always returned in *actual_type_return*). In this case, property data is returned.

When everything matches and **XGetWindowProperty** actually returns property data, *Xlib* allocates a buffer for the data and returns a pointer to that buffer in the *prop_return* parameter. You should interpret the buffer pointed to by *prop_return* as an array of bytes, short integers, or long integers, depending on whether the *actual_format_return* parameter contains the value 8, 16, or 32 respectively. *nitems_return* tells you the number of items (of the size specified in *actual_format_return*) in the buffer.

If you actually receive property data and the *bytes_after_return* parameter is still nonzero, you did not retrieve all the property data. In this case, you should read the data in segments.

Do not forget to use **XFree** to release the buffer's storage when you have finished using the buffer.

**Example**: Determine a property's existence, type, format, and length

The Boolean function shown in this example uses **XGetWindow-Properties** to query the workstation about a particular property for a particular window. If the property does not exist for the window the function returns a False value. If the property does exist, the function returns a True value, and the property's type Atom, format, and overall length in bytes. Notice that we use the predefined atom XA_INTEGER for the req_type parameter. We could have chosen any predefined atom type.

```
#include   <X11/Xatom.h>
Bool PropertyTypeFormatLength ( display, window, property,
                                        type, format, length )

    Display * display;
    Window window;
    Atom property;
    Atom * type;
    int * format;
```

```
        long * length;
    {

        int ret_status;
        Atom ret_atom;
        int ret_format, ret_len, ret_after;
        char * ret_prop;

        XGetWindowProperty ( display, window, property,
            0, 8192, False, XA_INTEGER
            &ret_atom, &ret_format, &ret_len, &ret_after, &ret_prop );

        if ( ret_format == 0 ) {     /* nonexistent property */
            *type = None;
            *format = 0;
            *length = 0;
            return False;
        }
        *type = ret_atom;            /* property exists */
        *format = ret_format;
        *length = ret_after;
        if ( ret_len == 0 ) return True;
        /* property type matched...compute total length in bytes */
        *length += ret_len * ( ret_format >> 3 );
        XFree ( ret_prop );          /* do not want the actual data */
        return True;
    }
```

## Interchanging Property Data

Many applications use X's property capability to implement a ring of related properties (for example, the cut-buffers described earlier). A ring of such properties might be used, for example, to save the ten most recent commands to an interactive program.

You may implement a property ring of any size. In order to implement a property ring, you must first give each of the properties in the ring a distinct name and Atom. Next, you must hang all the properties in the ring on your window, even if you do not yet have real data to store in them.

Once your property ring is created, you can *rotate* or circularly interchange the values of the individual properties using the **XRotateWindowProperties** call. **XRotateWindowProperties** (*Xlib* ¶4.3) is a one-way call. It has the form

```
Display* display;              /* pointer to Display structure */
Window window;                 /* window for property ring */
Atom properties [ ];           /* array listing properties in ring */
int num_prop;                  /* number of properties in array */
int npositions;                /* number of positions to rotate */
. . .
XRotateWindowProperties ( display, window, properties,
                          num_prop, npositions );
```

When you call **XRotateWindowProperties**, you specify an array of Atoms listing the ring of *properties*. The size of the property-ring is *num_prop*. You can rotate the ring any number of positions, specified by *npositions*.

**Example**: Rotating a ring containing three properties

Suppose we want to define a ring of three properties for a window, named "RING_TOP", "RING_1", and "RING_2". We would first have to retrieve Atoms for each of the property names into an array. We also retrieve an Atom to use for the property type.

```
Display* display;         /* pointer to Display structure */
Window window;            /* window on which property ring is hung */
Atom properties [3];      /* Atoms for property ring */
Atom type;                /* Atom for data type */
. . .
properties [0] =    XInternAtom ( display, "RING_TOP", False );
properties [1] =    XInternAtom ( display, "RING_1", False );
properties [2] =    XInternAtom ( display, "RING_2", False );
type =              XInternAtom ( display, "RING_TYPE", False );
```

Once we have the atoms, we must hang all the properties on the window, putting initialization data in the properties.

```
XChangeProperties ( display, window, properties [0], type, 8,
                    PropModeReplace, "TOP", strlen("TOP") );
XChangeProperties ( display, window, properties [1], type, 8,
                    PropModeReplace, "ONE", strlen("ONE") );
XChangeProperties ( display, window, properties [2], type, 8,
                    PropModeReplace, "TWO", strlen("TWO") );
```

Now that the properties are all created, we can use **XRotateWindow-Properties** to exchange the values of the properties. For example, suppose we rotate using an *npositions* parameter of 1:

```
XRotateWindowProperties ( display, window, properties, 3, 1 );
```

In this case, the data in the last property moves to the top property, and all the other property data moves down one position. The top property (named "RING_TOP") takes on the value "TWO". The property named "RING_1" takes on the value "TOP", and the property named "RING_2" takes on the value "ONE".

Suppose we rotate using an *npositions* parameter of –1:

**XRotateWindowProperties** ( *display*, *window*, *properties*, 3, –1 );

In this case, the data in the top property moves to the last property, and all the other property data items move up one position. The top property (named "RING_TOP") takes on the value "ONE". The property named "RING_1" takes on the value "TWO", and the property named "RING_2" takes on the value "TOP".

Notice that, in this ring of three properties, a rotation of 2 positions down (an *nproperties* value of 2) is equivalent to a rotation of 1 position up (an *nproperties* value of –1). Notice also that a rotation of 3 positions does nothing and a rotation of 4 positions is equivalent to a rotation of 1 position.

The *nproperties* parameter can take any integer value, not just 1 or –1. The number of positions rotated is *npositions* modulo *num_prop*. It is perfectly valid to specify an *nproperties* parameter of zero: nothing happens.

The *window* and all the *properties* must exist, or the workstation will send you an error event message.

When **XRotateWindowProperty** actually changes properties it generates a PropertyNotify event for each property involved.

## Listing Properties for a Window

You can use **XListProperties** to find out what properties are hanging from a window. **XListProperties** (*Xlib* ¶4.3) has the form

```
Display* display;          /* pointer to Display structure */
Window window;             /*  window  */
int num_prop_return;       /* number of properties on window */
Atom * properties          /* array listing properties on window */
    . . .
properties = XListProperties ( display, window, &num_prop_return );
    . . .
XFree ( properties );
```

As its function result, **XListProperties** returns a pointer to an array of Atoms. Each Atom in the array corresponds to a property hanging from the *window* you specify. Upon return from the call, *num_prop_return* contains the number of Atoms in the array.

**XListProperties** automatically allocates storage within *Xlib* for the *properties* array. When your application is through with the array, you must explicitly free the array's storage with **XFree**.

## Deleting Properties

You can use **XDeleteProperty** to delete a property from a window explicitly. If your application hangs properties from root windows, you should delete those properties when you longer need them: properties can outlive your application.

On the other hand, if you only create properties on your own windows, you may be able to take advantage of the fact that automatic window-destruction when your application terminates will also delete the properties you created.

**XDeleteProperty** (*Xlib* ¶4.3) has the form

> **Display\*** *display;*      /\* pointer to Display structure \*/
> **Window** *window;*      /\* window \*/
> **Atom** *property;*      /\* property to delete \*/
>   . . .
> XDeleteProperty ( *display, window, property* );

**XDeleteProperty** deletes the specified *property* from the specified *window*, and generates a PropertyNotify event announcing the deletion.

If you attempt to delete a nonexistent *property*, no harm is done: **XDeleteProperty** does nothing, and generates no event, in this case.

Notice that using **XDeleteProperty** has no effect on the Atom value for the *property*. You may continue to use the Atom value to create properties for other windows. You may also recreate the property (using **XChangeWindowProperty**) for the same *window* at a later time.

## PropertyNotify Events

Your application should solicit PropertyNotify events if you want the workstation to inform you about changes to any property hung on a window. PropertyNotify events are generated whenever a property's contents are altered via **XChangeProperty**. PropertyNotify events are also generated whenever **XDeleteProperty** or **XGetWindowProperty** are used to delete a property.

The **XRotateProperties** request generates PropertyNotify events for all the properties involved, unless no property rotation takes place because of an *npositions* parameter of zero (or zero modulo *num_prop*).

Notice that your application can force the generation of a PropertyNotify event on a particular property without changing the property. To do this, call **XChangeProperty** with zero-length data and a *mode* of PropModeAppend.

To solicit PropertyNotify events from a window, specify PropertyChangeMask in a call to **XSelectInput**, or set it in the *event_mask* attribute of a window. Multiple applications can solicit PropertyNotify events from any given window. When multiple applications solicit PropertyNotify events the workstation sends the events to all applications soliciting them (this is, of course, true for most event types).

The event structure for the PropertyNotify event type is defined as follows:

| typedef struct { | | |
|---|---|---|
| int  type; | ev.type | PropertyNotify |
| unsigned long serial | ev.xany.serial | Last request processed |
| **Bool** send_event; | ev.xany.send_event | From **XSendEvent**? |
| **Display** *display; | ev.xany.display | |
| **Window** window; | ev.xproperty.window | Window for property |
| **Atom** atom; | ev.xproperty.atom | Atom for property name |
| **Time** time; | ev.xproperty.time | Time when the property changed |
| int  state; | ev.xproperty.state | PropertyNewValue/PropertyDeleted |
| } **XPropertyEvent**; | | |

The PropertyNotify event's data structure has the following fields:

type
: The event type.

serial
: Specifies the serial number of the last request processed.

send_event
: False unless this event was generated by some application issuing the **XSentEvent** request.

display
: Pointer to the **Display** structure the event came from.

window
: The window for which a property has changed.

atom
: The Atom for the name of the property that was changed.

time
: The X Window System timestamp at the time the property changed.

state
: This field has one of the following values (defined in the header file **<X11/X.h>**), describing what happened to the property; whether it received a new value or was deleted:

PropertyNewValue
: The property received a new value, due to an **XChangeProperty** request or an **XRotateProperties** request.

PropertyDeleted
: The property was deleted, either via **XDeleteProperty** or via **XGetWindowProperty** with a True *delete* parameter.

**Example**:  Solicit PropertyNotify events for a window

This example shows the use of **XSelectInput** to solicit PropertyNotify events from a specified window.

```
Display *display;        /* pointer to current Display structure */
Window window;           /* window you want button events from*/
. . .
XSelectInput ( display, window, PropertyChangeMask );
```

## Using Properties to Pass Information

X's property-manipulation capabilities are designed to avoid many of the pitfalls encountered when programming several asynchronous applications to share a common data base.  The workstation serializes all requests to read, write, rotate, and delete properties, ensuring that one request finishes completely before the next begins.

There are three common ways to use properties for a shared data base:

- as a repository for *state* information.

- as a *queue* for passing a stream of information from one process to another.

- as a *history*: a fixed number of records of recent events.

Applications can use X's property-manipulation requests to implement any of these.  To pass information (in any of these ways) the interested applications must agree on the name, type, and format of the property (or properties) to use, as well as which window to use.

Using X properties to share state information is straightforward.  A single property is chosen to be the repository of the state.  Any application can announce a change in the state by changing the property via **XChangeProperty** with a *mode* of PropModeReplace.  Other interested applications can interrogate the state at any time by using **XGetWindowProperty** to read the property's data. Applications can solicit PropertyNotify events in order to find out when to interrogate the state: when the property is changed.

An X property can also be used as a queue for passing information from a *producer* application to a *consumer* application.  A queue contains a stream of information, whereas a state contains only a present value.  A queueing mechanism must be designed to ensure that the consumer receives all the information generated by the producer.  This makes it different from a state-sharing mechanism, in which consumers of the state information only care about the current state.

When an X property is used as a queue, by convention the producer stores data into the property using **XChangeProperty** with a *mode* of PropModeAppend. The consumer uses **XGetWindowProperty** simultaneously to read and delete the entire property. This ensures that the consumer neither misses any information nor receives any information twice.

The **XRotateWindowProperties** call allows applications to use several properties as a *history ring*. In such a history ring, a producer application records information about each event by doing two things:

1) storing (via **XChangeProperty** with a *mode* of PropModeReplace) into the top property ("RING_TOP" in the example under "Interchanging Window Properties").

2) Rotating the values downward (using **XRotateProperties** with an *npositions* parameter of 1).

Any application which wants to know the most recent history item can read the ring property one from the top ("RING_1" in the example). Similarly, the second most recent history item is available in the ring property two from the top ("RING_2") and so forth. By convention, applications should *not* read the top property ("RING_TOP") because it may be in the process of being changed by the producer: at any given time it may contain either the oldest or the newest event.

# SELECTIONS

A *selection* is an advanced form of cut buffer. Cut buffers, as described earlier in this chapter, are very simple, but they have two important limitations:

- Cut buffer data is stored in the workstation, not the application. This means that every cut operation and every paste operation results in an X protocol request. The vast majority of cut-and-paste operations take place within a single application, so using the workstation to store the data consumes network bandwidth.

- Cut buffer data must be stored using a single common data type and format regardless of whether it contains text, graphics, or anything else. Because the cut buffers contain streams of bytes, and because **xterm** stores unadorned streams of text into cut buffers, the usefulness of cut buffers for transferring images, graphics, paragraph-formatting information (anything except text) is limited.

X provides a *selection mechanism* to overcome these limitations of cut buffers. It is helpful to think of a *selection* as a token that is passed from application to application. One application at a time "holds the token" or *owns* the selection. The owner of a selection is responsible for:

- maintaining the selection's data value (whatever was cut or copied) internally using any convenient data type and format.  No other application sees the data as it is stored internally.

- translating the selection's data value upon request from some other application to whatever data type and format (within reason) the other application asks for, and storing the translated data into a property on the workstation.

When an application carries out a cut or copy operation (any operation that would result in writing data to the cut buffer) it "takes the token" by asserting its ownership of the selection.  It then stores the cut-buffer data value internally, and *does not send it* to the workstation.

Usually a paste operation comes shortly after a cut operation, and in the same application.  As long as your application still owns the selection, you can paste the easy way:  internally, without having to fetch data values from the workstation.

If one application cuts and a different one pastes, however, the selection's data values must be transferred between applications via the workstation.  If your application attempts to paste a selection when you are not the selection's owner, you must do it the hard way:

- First you must ask the owner to convert the selection to the data type and format you want and store it in a property.

- Next you must then wait for a SelectionNotify event letting you know that the selection's owner has stored it (or did not know how to convert it to the data type you requested).

- Next you must retrieve the selection's value from the property.

- Only then can you complete the paste operation.

X provides a request (**XSetSelectionOwner**) for allowing applications to assert or relinquish ownership of a selection.  X also provides a request (**XGetSelectionOwner**) for finding out who owns a selection.  Most importantly, X provides a way for one application to ask another to convert a selection's data to a specified data type and store it in a property (the **XConvertSelection** request).

By asserting ownership of a selection, an application solicits two types of events. SelectionClear events inform an application that it has lost ownership of a selection, when some other application takes it.  If your application asserts ownership of a selection, you must keep track of whether you lose ownership:  you need to know whether to paste the easy way (if you still own the selection) or the hard way (if you do not).

SelectionRequest events inform the owner of a selection that another application wishes to carry out a paste operation, and needs to know the selection's data value.  The receiver of a SelectionRequest event must (for details, see the description of the SelectionRequest event later in this chapter) do the following:

- Convert the selection to the data type requested.

- Store the selection's data into a property.

- Use **XSendEvent** (see Chapter 11) to send a SelectionNotify event announcing the availability of the selection to the requestor.

The receiver of a SelectionRequest event does not lose ownership of the selection.

Each selection has only one owner at a time, or possibly no owners.  How many distinct selections are available?  As many as necessary.  Selections, like properties, have names and associated Atoms.  Predefined in X (and available in the header file **<X11/Xatom.h>**) are atoms for two commonly used selections:

XA_PRIMARY          This selection corresponds to the "main" cut buffer. Most applications use this selection to cut and paste.

XA_SECONDARY        This selection is used by applications which must pass pairs of cut buffers back and forth.

You may define your own nonstandard selection names and use **XInternAtom** (see earlier in this chapter) to retrieve Atom values for them if you wish.  Non-standard selections are useful only for passing information back and forth between individual applications in a large suite of cooperating programs.

| Avoid nonstandard selection names if possible. |

The point of the selection mechanism is to allow all kinds of applications to share information.  If you use nonstandard selection names, your application's data will not be accessible to other applications via cut-and-paste.

Keep in mind that further developments in the X Window System are likely to define other standard selection names, and are likely to refine the conventions for use of the selection mechanism.

| Request/Event | Xlib ¶ | Description |
|---|---|---|
| **XSetSelectionOwner** | 4.4 | Assert or relinquish ownership of a selection |
| **XGetSelectionOwner** | 4.4 | Determine ownership of a selection |
| **XConvertSelection** | 4.4 | Ask a selection's owner to store the data |
| SelectionClear event | 8.4.9.3 | Notification of loss of selection ownership |
| SelectionRequest event | 8.4.9.4 | Notification of request to store data |
| SelectionNotify event | 8.4.9.5 | Notification of availability of data |

Table 12-III.  *Xlib* calls and events relating to selections.

## Asserting Selection Ownership

When your user asks your application to carry out a cut or copy operation (any operation which results in writing data into a cut buffer) you should assert ownership of the selection by using the **XSetSelectionOwner** call. **XSetSelectionOwner** (*Xlib* ¶4.4) is a one-way request.  It has the form

```
Display* display;        /* pointer to Display structure */
Atom selection;          /* atom for selection name */
Window owner;            /* new owning window, or None */
Time time;               /* time of selection change */
   . . .
XSetSelectionOwner ( display, selection, owner, time  );
```

When calling **XSetSelectionOwner**, you must specify in *selection* the Atom for the name of the selection you wish to take.

In *owner*, you should specify one of your application's top-level windows.  It does not matter which window; as long as you specify any of one of your windows, your application will gain ownership of the *selection* you specify.

Use the *time* parameter to specify the current time.  Users activate cut and copy operations using direct input events such as ButtonRelease or KeyPress.  Direct input events have "time" fields in their event structures.  Use these event timestamps to specify the *time* parameter.  If some other application has already asserted ownership with a later *time* than yours, you will not gain ownership.

Once you assert selection ownership, you can carry out the cut or copy operation.  The details of how to do this depend on your application.  However, you do not send the cut or copied data to the workstation, but rather keep it in your application.

If you assert selection ownership when you already have it, nothing happens and no harm is done.  If you specify the value None in place of a window in the *owner* parameter, thereafter the selection has no owner.

Use the **XGetSelectionOwner** request to find out what window has been assigned ownership of the selection.  This request allows you to verify that your application has actually gained ownership of the selection.  **XGetSelectionOwner** (*Xlib* ¶4.4) is a round-trip request.  It has the form

```
Display* display;        /* pointer to Display structure */
Atom selection;          /* atom for selection name */
Window owner;            /* new owning window, or None */
   . . .
owner = XGetSelectionOwner ( display, selection  );
```

The *owner* returned by **XGetSelectionOwner** is the window specified in the most recent call (by any application) to **XSetSelectionOwner**. If the selection has no owner, the returned *owner* has the value None.

## Losing Selection Ownership

Once your application owns a selection, you can lose it in any one of four ways:

- Another application can assert ownership of the selection.

- You can voluntarily relinquish your ownership of a selection by calling **XSetSelectionOwner** and specifying an *owner* value of None.

- You (or some other application) can destroy the *owner* window you used when asserting ownership. If this happens, it results in the selection having no owner.

- You can close your display connection when your application exits, or when you call **XCloseDisplay**.

When you lose selection ownership, the workstation sends you a SelectionClear event (unless, of course, you lose ownership by closing your display connection). You do not need to use **XSelectInput** to solicit SelectionClear events; when you assert ownership of a selection you automatically solicit them.

The event structure for the SelectionClear event type is defined as follows:

| | | |
|---|---|---|
| typedef struct { | | |
| int type; | ev.type | SelectionClear |
| unsigned long serial | ev.xany.serial | Last request processed |
| **Bool** send_event; | ev.xany.send_event | From **XSendEvent**? |
| **Display** *display; | ev.xany.display | |
| **Window** window; | ev.xselectionclear.window | Window losing ownership |
| **Atom** selection; | ev.xselectionclear.selection | Selection name's atom |
| **Time** time; | ev.xselectionclear.time | Selection loss timestamp |
| } **XSelectionClearEvent**; | | |

The SelectionClear event's data structure has the following fields:

| | |
|---|---|
| type | The event type. |
| serial | Specifies the serial number of the last request processed. |
| send_event | False unless this event was generated by some application issuing the **XSendEvent** request. |
| display | Pointer to the **Display** structure the event came from. |
| window | The window losing ownership of the selection. |

selection          The Atom for the name of the selection for which ownership
                   was lost.

time               The X Window System timestamp at the time ownership
                   changed.

When you receive the SelectionClear event, it means that you no longer own the
selection, so you do not have to maintain a value for the selection internally.
Notice that the SelectionClear event does not tell you who does own the selection,
but only that you no longer own it.

You also receive a SelectionClear event if you use the **XSetSelectionOwner**
request to change the *owner* window from one of your windows to another.
Therefore, you should either keep watch for this case, or always assign your selections to a particular window (for example, your application's top-level window).

**Example**: Assert and track ownership of the primary selection

This example shows how to take ownership of the primary (cut-and-
paste) selection.  It assumes you have a valid display pointer named
*mydisplay* and your application does a cut or copy when responding to a
ButtonRelease event.  Notice that this example does not show how to
store the cut or copied data, but only how to assert selection ownership.

It is conceivable that some other application could slip in and snatch
property ownership away from you before you have a chance to do the cut
or copy operation.  This example shows how to use **XGetSelectionOwner** to find out if this happens, and save yourself the trouble of storing
the data.

This example also shows how to use SelectionClear events to keep track
of whether your application has lost selection ownership.  It takes into
account the fact that you receive a SelectionClear event when you lose
ownership, and also when you change the *owner* window for a selection.

```
#include  <X11/Xatom.h>
Display* mydisplay;
XEvent myevent;
Window ownerwindow;  /* window owning selection, or None */
. . .
while (True) { /* application main loop */
  . . .
  XNextEvent ( mydisplay, &myevent );
  . . .
  switch ( myevent.type ) {
    . . .
    case ButtonRelease:
```

```
      . . .
      ownerwindow _ myevent.xbutton.window;
      XSetSelectionOwner ( mydisplay, XA_PRIMARY,
                           ownerwindow,  myevent.xbutton.time );
      if ( ownerwindow == XGetSelectionOwner
                          ( mydisplay, XA_PRIMARY ) ) {
        /* ownership assertion success:  store data to be cut or copied */
        . . .
      } else {
        /* ownership assertion failure: clear ownerwindow */
        ownerwindow = None;
      }
      break;
    case SelectionClear:
      /* make sure we did not change the owner window ourselves */
      if ( ( myevent.xselectionclear.window == ownerwindow ) &&
         ( myevent.xselection.selection == XA_PRIMARY )              ) {
        /* lost primary selection ownership to some other application */
        ownerwindow = None;
        /* remove data previously cut or copied */
        . . .
      }
      break;
    . . .
  }
}
```

## Requesting Selection Data

From the bird's-eye view, a request by one application for data in a selection
owned by a second application results in a flurry of X requests and events:

1) When an application requests data from a selection, it sends an
   **XConvertSelection** request to the workstation. = server

2) The workstation forwards the **XConvertSelection** request to the
   selection's owner in the form of a SelectionRequest event.

3) The selection's owner responds to the SelectionRequest event by
   storing the selection into a property via the **XChangeProperty** request (using the requestor-specified data type).

4) If the selection's owner wants to be notified when the requestor accepts the data, the owner solicits PropertyNotify events from the

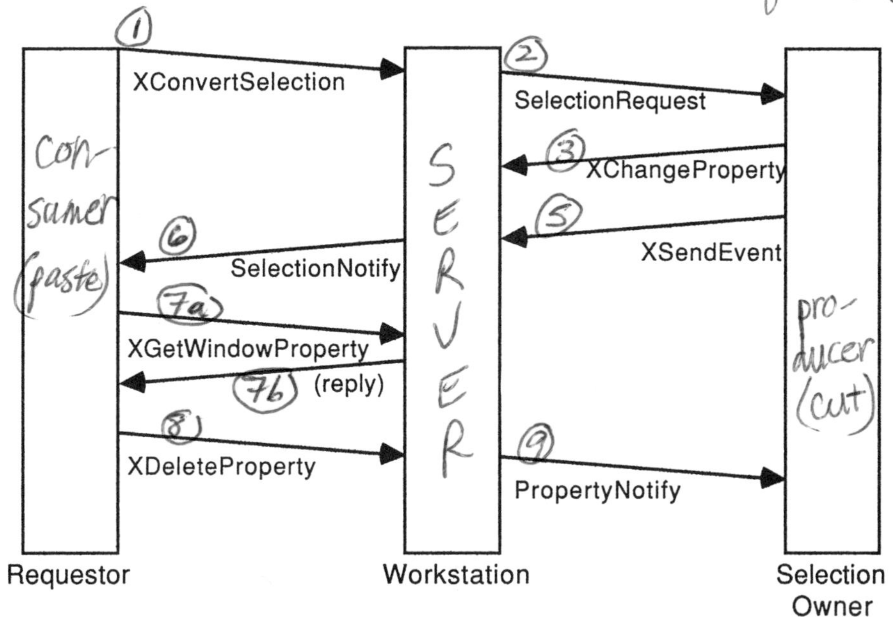

OPTIONAL : ④   Req  Property Notify  → Owner

Figure 12-1.  Bird's-eye view of the activity initiated by **XConvertSelection**.

requestor's window using **XSelectInput** with PropertyChange-
Mask (this step is optional).

5) The selection's owner then uses **XSendEvent** to send a Selection-
Notify event back to the requestor.  The SelectionNotify event tells
the requestor where (which window and which property) to find the
selection's data.

6) The workstation receives the **XSendEvent** request from the owner
and forwards the SelectionNotify event to the requestor.

7) The requestor responds to the SelectionNotify event by using the
**XGetWindowProperty** round-trip request to retrieve the selection's data.

8) The requestor, when it has retrieved and processed the data, deletes
the property using the **XDeleteProperty** request.  By convention, it
refrains from deleting the property until it has completely processed
the data.

9) The workstation sends a PropertyNotify event announcing the
deletion of the property to the selection's owner (if the owner carried
out step 4 above).

No individual application can see this bird's-eye view, however.  Each application is either a selection requestor or a selection owner, and each has only a

worm's-eye view of the overall process. This section describes the process from the worm's-eye view of the selection requestor. See the next section for the selection owner's view. Most applications will have to be able to play both roles: if the user will cut from an application, it plays the owner role. If the user will paste into an application, it plays the requestor role.

When your (requestor) application receives a paste command from your user, you should treat it as a request from the user to retrieve and use the data value associated with a selection. Ordinarily, you insert the retrieved data into whatever document or drawing the user is manipulating. The exact meaning of *paste* depends on the application.

If your application took ownership of the selection during a previous cut or copy operation, and still has ownership, none of this process applies. All you have to do is retrieve the data you saved away during the cut operation.

However, if some other application owns the selection, the user is attempting to cut and paste between applications, and you must use the **XConvertSelection** request to ask the selection's owner to make data available to you.

The selection's owner will, if it knows how, convert the selection to the data type you specify. For example, a text editor might request character strings (XA_STRING), and a bitmap editor might request bitmaps (XA_BITMAP). If the owner cannot convert the selection to the exact format you want, it does not convert it at all.

**XConvertSelection** (*Xlib* ¶4.4) is a one-way request. It has the form

```
Display* display;        /* pointer to Display structure */
Atom selection;          /* atom for selection name */
Atom target;             /* atom for name of desired data type*/
Atom property;           /* atom for name of desired property */
Window requestor;        /* window on which to hang property */
Time timestamp;          /* timestamp of request */
    . . .
XConvertSelection ( display, selection, target,
                    property, requestor, timestamp  );
```

When you issue an **XConvertSelection** request, you specify several things:

- The Atom for the name of the *selection* you want. Ordinarily this is XA_PRIMARY, although you can specify XA_SECONDARY or some other Atom.

- The Atom for the *target* data type to which you want the selection converted. See "Property Data Format and Type" earlier in this chapter for a list of predefined Atoms for standard data types. If you want a character string, for example, you specify the XA_STRING data type atom for *target*.

- The Atom for the *property* in which you want the selection owner to store the selection's data. You may choose any property Atom you wish for this purpose. It is wise, however, to use **XInternAtom** to retrieve an Atom that is not used for any other purpose, to avoid confusion.

- The X resource identifier for the *requestor*: the window on which you want the selection owner to hang the *property* it creates.

- The *timestamp* for your **XConvertSelection** request.

Once you have issued your **XConvertSelection** request, the selection's owner has some work to do before you can retrieve the data you requested (see the next section for what the selection's owner must do). When the owner finishes, it sends you a SelectionNotify event. You do not have to use **XSelectInput** to solicit SelectionNotify events; a call to **XConvertSelection** is sufficient.

The event structure for the SelectionNotify event type is defined as follows:

```
typedef struct {
    int  type;                ev.type                    SelectionNotify
    unsigned long serial      ev.xany.serial             Last request
    Bool send_event;          ev.xany.send_event         From XSendEvent?
    Display *display;         ev.xany.display
    Window  requestor;        ev.xselection.requestor    Requesting window
    Atom  selection;          ev.xselection.selection    Selection
    Atom  target;             ev.xselection.target       Data type used
    Atom  property;           ev.xselection.property     Property used
    Time  time;               ev.xselection.time         Timestamp
}XSelectionEvent;
```

The SelectionNotify event's data structure has the following fields:

type        The event type.

serial      Specifies the serial number of the last request processed.

send_event  Usually True. This event type is usually generated when the selection owner issues an **XSendEvent** request.

display     Pointer to the **Display** structure the event came from.

requestor   The requestor window from the **XConvertSelection** call.

selection   The Atom for the name of the requested selection. The property containing the selection's data value is hung on this window.

target      The Atom for the name of the data type to which the selection was converted. This is ordinarily the same as the data type you requested via **XConvertSelection**.

property    The Atom for the name of the property on which the converted data was stored, or None. This is ordinarily the same as the property requested via **XConvertSelection**. If the selection had no owner, or if the owner could not convert the selection to the data type you requested, this field contains the value None.

time        The X Window System timestamp at the time the selection was stored.

When your application pastes a selection you must first issue an **XConvert-Selection** request, then later you must respond to the SelectionNotify event. Between the time you issue **XConvertSelection** and the time you receive the event, the selection's owner stores it for you. If the selection has no owner, you will not wait forever; the workstation sends the SelectionNotify event itself specifying a property of None. Requesting an ownerless selection is the result of a user's attempt to paste without cutting first.

You cannot necessarily trust the owner of the selection. It may terminate (due to bugs) while it is storing the selection. In this case, your application will never receive the SelectionNotify event. If you do not want other applications' bugs to affect your application, you must program your application modelessly, so that it does not get stuck waiting for SelectionNotify events. For example, you might set up your application to permit the user to repeat the paste operation if it does not work the first time. If the owning application has terminated, the second attempt at **XConvertSelection** will result in an immediate SelectionNotify event from the workstation.

When you receive a SelectionNotify event, use **XGetWindowProperty** (see earlier in this chapter) to retrieve the selection's data. The event structure contains the *requestor* window identifier, the Atom naming the *property* to retrieve, and the *target* data type with which the property is stored.

To prevent workstation memory from being wasted by old copies of stored selection properties, the application requesting a selection should delete the selection's property after it finishes retrieving the selection. Use an explicit **XDeleteProperty** call after your application's paste operation is complete.

### Example: Requesting selections and honoring SelectionNotify events

This code excerpt shows how a very simple application program might use the **XConvertSelection** request to ask a selection's owner to deliver the selection's data value for pasting.

The middle mouse button (button 2) triggers the paste operation by causing the **XConvertSelection** request to be issued. Notice, however, that the paste operation works in two phases: it cannot be completed until the SelectionNotify event arrives.

In this example, we assume that the selection's data value is received into the character string pointed to by *dispdata*. In a real application, the code for pasting (as shown in this example) and the code for honoring selection requests (as shown in the example of the next section) would be combined in a single main loop.

```
Display * mydisplay;          /* display pointer */
XEvent myevent;               /* event structure for reading events */
Window mywindow;              /* application window */
Atom myproperty;              /* property to use */
char * dispdata;              /* pointer to selection's data value */
. . .
myproperty = XInternAtom ( mydisplay, "MyProperty", False );
while ( True ) {              /* main application loop */
 XNextEvent ( mydisplay, &myevent );
 switch (myevent.type)   {
 . . .

 /*   process mouse-button presses   */
 case ButtonPress:
   . . .
   /* mouse button 2  means paste */
   if (myevent.xbutton.button == 2) {
     if ( /* we own the selection locally . . . */ ) {
       /* do a local paste operation */
       . . .
     }
     else {
       /* we don't own the selection...we have to get it */
       XConvertSelection ( mydisplay,
         XA_PRIMARY,              /* primary selection */
         XA_STRING,               /* target data type */
         myproperty,              /* property to use */
         mywindow,                /* selector window */
         myevent.xbutton.time );  /* selection timestamp */
     }
   } /* end if (...button == 2) */
   break;

 /* a SelectionNotify event came through...fetch the pasted data */
 case SelectionNotify:
   /* ensure that it is for the primary selection */
   if ( myevent.xselection.selection == XA_PRIMARY ) {

     /* now we can get the selection's value */
     Atom ret_type;
     int ret_format, ret_len, ret_after;
```

```
        char * ret_prop;

        /* fetch the returned property's value */
        XGetWindowProperty ( mydisplay,
            myevent.xselection.requestor,
            myevent.xselection.property,
            0, 8192, False,
            myevent.xselection.target,
            &ret_type, &ret_format, &ret_len,
            &ret_after, &ret_prop);
        if (ret_len > 0) {
            /* if we actually received anything, stash it away */
            ret_prop[ret_len-1] = 0;
            dispdata = (char *) malloc (ret_len);
            strcpy (dispdata, ret_prop);

            /* finish the paste operation...application-dependent */
            . . .

            /* clean up the property */
            XFree (ret_prop);
            XDeleteProperty ( mydisplay,
                myevent.xselection.requestor,
                myevent.xselection.property );
        } /* end if ( ret_len > 0 ) */
    }
    break;

    . . .
} /* switch (myevent.type) */
} /* while (done == 0) */
```

## Honoring Requests for Selections

This section describes the cut-and-paste process from the worm's-eye view of the the selection owner. As described earlier, your application gets to be the owner of a selection by asserting ownership using the **XSetSelectionOwner** request. By asserting ownership, your application automatically solicits SelectionRequest events. You do not have to use **XSelectInput** to solicit these events.

When you are the selection owner, you play a vital role in the cut-and-paste process. The beginning of this process is announced to you by the delivery of a SelectionRequest event. The event structure for the SelectionRequest event type is defined as follows:

| typedef struct { | | |
|---|---|---|
| int type; | ev.type | SelectionRequest |
| unsigned long serial | ev.xany.serial | Last request |
| **Bool** send_event; | ev.xany.send_event | From **XSendEvent**? |
| **Display** *display; | ev.xany.display | |
| **Window** owner; | ev.xselectionrequest.owner | Owning window |
| **Window** requestor; | ev.xselectionrequest.requestor | Requesting window |
| **Atom** selection; | ev.xselectionrequest.selection | Selection |
| **Atom** target; | ev.xselectionrequest.target | Data type wanted |
| **Atom** property; | ev.xselectionrequest.property | Property to use |
| **Time** time; | ev.xselectionrequest.time | Timestamp |
| }**XSelectionRequestEvent**; | | |

The SelectionRequest event's data structure has the following fields:

type
: The event type.

serial
: Specifies the serial number of the last request processed.

send_event
: False unless this event was generated by some application issuing the **XSendEvent** request.

display
: Pointer to the **Display** structure the event came from.

owner
: The window owning the selection.

requestor
: The window requesting the selection's data value. You should respond by hanging a property on this window.

selection
: The Atom for the name of the selection being requested.

target
: The Atom for the name of the data type being requested.

property
: The Atom for the name of the property on which the translated data should be stored.

time
: The X Window System timestamp at the time the selection's data value was requested.

Upon receiving a SelectionRequest event, you should examine the target data type wanted by the requestor. If your application contains code to translate your internal cut-buffer to the requested data type, you should do so. If the requested data type is an X resource (such as a bitmap, Pixmap, cursor or color map) you should create the resource and initialize it.

Next, you should use **XChangeProperty** to store the data into a property. Specifically, you should hang the property on the requestor window. The requestor passes you a valid property Atom in the SelectionRequest event, and you should use that property.

Next, you should (optionally) solicit PropertyNotify events from the requestor window, using **XSelectInput** specifying PropertyChangeMask. If you have created any X resources while translating your cut-buffer to the requestor's target data type, you need to know when you can delete them. You will receive a PropertyNotify event from the requestor's window letting you know when the requestor has read and deleted the property you created.

Next, fill in the fields of a SelectionNotify event (see the preceding section) and send it back to the requestor using **XSendEvent**. The requestor will proceed to read the selection's data. Before you send the event, fill in the fields of the event's data structure as follows:

type
: The value SelectionNotify.

requestor
: The requestor window from the SelectionRequest event structure.

selection
: The Atom for the name of the requested selection, from the SelectionRequest event structure.

target
: The Atom for the data type to which you actually converted the selection.

property
: The Atom for the name of the property on which you actually stored the selection's data. If you could not store the selection's data, specify None.

time
: The X Window System timestamp from the SelectionRequest event structure.

Finally, when a PropertyNotify event arrives announcing the deletion of the property, you can delete any resources you may have created in response to the original SelectionRequest event. You may also wish to cancel your solicitation of PropertyNotify events from the requestor window by calling **XSelectInput** without specifying PropertyChangeMask.

You might not be able to convert your internal cut-buffer to the requested target data type. For example, the requestor may request a format which you do not understand, or possibly your internal cut-buffer contains, at the moment of the SelectionRequest event, application-specific data which is impossible to convert to a standard data type for export. If this happens, you *must still send* the SelectionNotify event. Put the value None in the event's property field before you send it.

**Example**: Responding to SelectionRequest events.

This code excerpt shows how a very simple selection-owning application might respond to a SelectionRequest event. In this example, we assume that the selection's data value is stored in the character string pointed to by *seldata*. We also assume that the application only knows how to honor a request for a text string (the XA_STRING data type Atom).

Real applications would obviously be able to translate selections to a variety of requested data types.

For simplicity, this example does not show the optional use of Property-Notify events to find out when the requestor actually receives the selection's value.

```
Display * mydisplay;        /* display pointer */
XEvent myevent;             /* event structure for reading events */
Window mywindow;            /* application window */
char * seldata;             /* pointer to selection's data value */
. . .
while ( True ) {            /* main application loop */
 XNextEvent ( mydisplay, &myevent );
 switch (myevent.type)  {

 . . .
 /* a SelectionRequest event came through:  store the selection */
 case SelectionRequest:
   {

     /* create a SelectionNotify event structure for sending */
     XEvent ev;
     ev.type                  = SelectionNotify;
     ev.xselection.requestor  = myevent.xselectionrequest.requestor;
     ev.xselection.selection  = myevent.xselectionrequest.selection;
     ev.xselection.target     = myevent.xselectionrequest.target;
     ev.xselection.time       = myevent.xselectionrequest.time;
     ev.xselection.property   = myevent.xselectionrequest.property

     /* check for correct selection, and ability to translate the type */
     /* for simplicity, we only return the XA_STRING type */
     if  (  ( myevent.xselectionrequest.selection == XA_PRIMARY ) &&
            ( myevent.xselectionrequest.target   == XA_STRING )         )

       /* store the selection's data value into the property */
       XChangeProperty (mydisplay,
         ev.xselection.requestor,    /* window identifier */
         ev.xselection.property,     /* property Atom */
         ev.xselection.target,       /* data type Atom */
         8 ,                         /* byte format */
         PropModeReplace,            /* property replace mode */
         seldata,                    /* selection's data */
         strlen ( seldata ) + 1);    /* selection's length */
     }
     else {
```

```
        /* wrong selection or wrong target data type */
        ev.xselection.property  = None;
    }

    /* send the SelectionNotify event to the requestor */
    XSendEvent ( mydisplay, ev.xselection.requestor,False, 0, &ev );
    }
    break;

    . . .
  }  /* switch  (myevent.type) */
}  /* while  (done == 0) */
```

# SUMMARY

Most of the components of X go to a great deal of trouble to ensure that applications can operate independently of one another. However, *cooperation* between applications is one of the most important capabilities of workstation software. X provides explicit ways for applications to share state information with each other, as long as they are connected to the same workstation.

The notion of *cut-and-paste* is at the heart of the cooperation between applications running on a workstation: users expect to be able to *cut* or *copy* information selected from one application's window and *paste* it into another's. X provides a ring of eight global cut-buffers. These cut-buffers are especially useful for simple text-based applications, because they do not have any particular data structure. Any application can store and retrieve character strings from cut-buffers. Additionally, applications can treat the cut-buffers as a circular list and *rotate* the values stored in them. Two things make the cut-buffer facility convenient: its simplicity, and the fact that the **xterm(1)** terminal emulator uses it.

Unstructured streams of bytes are too limited for most information-sharing applications, however. To get around these limitations, X provides ways for applications to hang *properties* with arbitrary names and data types on windows. Once an application creates a property on a window and stores information into it, that information is available to any other application that wishes to retrieve it. Applications can find out when any of a window's properties are created, changed, or deleted by soliciting PropertyNotify events.

Properties and data types have names: arbitrary text strings. However, X requires these names to be converted to unique identifiers known as Atoms. Many predefined Atoms are available within X, and applications can use the **XInternAtom** call to retrieve new Atoms for application-defined names.

The predefined Atoms identify commonly used X properties and data types. Properties named by predefined Atoms are widely used for such things as window-manager hints and standard color maps. In fact, *Xlib* calls such as **XSet-**

**StandardProperties** and **XGetStandardColormap** are implemented using properties. Window managers solicit PropertyNotify events from top-level application windows, so whenever an application calls **XSetStandardProperties** or the like, the window manager is informed and can retrieve the data.

If applications are to communicate using properties, they must agree on:

- The Atom (or name) of the property.

- The data type Atom (or name) of the property.

- The format of the property (bytes, short integers, or long integers).

One application can use **XChangeProperty** to store property data, and another can retrieve the data with **XGetWindowProperty**.

X provides a flexible set of ways for reading and writing properties. It is easy to implement both state storage and queues using X's properties.

Cut-buffers and properties do not provide quite enough capability to allow arbitrary cut-and-paste (as opposed to cut-and-paste of character strings). The problems are two:

- Most cut-and-paste takes place within a single application. It is unreasonable to waste communication bandwidth by transmitting everything that is cut to the workstation.

- Multiple applications may have different formats for representing the same data. For example, one application may represent an object in a Pixmap, and another in text formatted like a bitmap file.

X's *selection* capability addresses these problems. When a user performs a cut or copy operation, the application doing the cut claims *ownership* of the selection. As long as the user cuts and pastes within that application, it retains ownership of the selection. However, when the user performs a paste operation in another application, it sends a *conversion request* to the selection's owner. The owner responds by converting the selected data to the requested data type and storing it into a property.

This appendix presents complete source for the trivial example **helloworld.c**. No additional source code is required, except for the header files **<X11/Xlib.h>**, **<X11/X.h>**, and **<X11/Xutil.h>**.

The only object library required is **libX11.a**, which on most Unix and compatible systems has the full pathname **/usr/lib/libX11.a**.

```
/*   X include files   */
#include  <X11/Xlib.h>
#include  <X11/Xutil.h>
/*    declarations    */
char hello[ ]   = {"Hello, World."};
char hi[ ]      = {"Hi!"};
main(argc,argv)
    int  argc;
    char  **argv;
{
```

```
/*  declarations  */
Display *mydisplay;
Window  mywindow;
GC mygc;
XEvent myevent;
KeySym mykey;
XSizeHints myhint;
int myscreen;
unsigned long myforeground, mybackground;
int i;
char  text[10];
int done;

/*   initialization   */
mydisplay = XOpenDisplay("");
myscreen = DefaultScreen (mydisplay);

/*   default pixel values   */
mybackground = WhitePixel (mydisplay, myscreen);
myforeground = BlackPixel (mydisplay, myscreen);

/*   default program-specified window position and size   */
myhint.x = 200;   myhint.y = 300;
myhint.width=350,  myhint.height=250;
myhint.flags = PPosition | PSize;

/*   window creation   */
mywindow = XCreateSimpleWindow (mydisplay,
  DefaultRootWindow (mydisplay),
  myhint.x, myhint.y, myhint.width, myhint.height,
  5, myforeground, mybackground);
XSetStandardProperties (mydisplay, mywindow, hello, hello,
  None, argv, argc, &myhint);

/*   GC creation and initialization   */
mygc = XCreateGC (mydisplay, mywindow, 0, 0);
XSetBackground (mydisplay, mygc, mybackground);
XSetForeground (mydisplay, mygc, myforeground);

/*   input event selection   */
XSelectInput (mydisplay, mywindow,
  ButtonPressMask | KeyPressMask | ExposureMask );

/*   window mapping   */
XMapRaised (mydisplay, mywindow);
```

```
/*   main event-reading loop   */
done = 0;
while ( done == 0 )
{
  /*   read the next event   */
  XNextEvent ( mydisplay, &myevent );
  switch (myevent.type)
  {
  /*   repaint window on expose events   */
  case Expose:
    if (myevent.xexpose.count == 0)
    XDrawImageString (
      myevent.xexpose.display, myevent.xexpose.window, mygc,
      50, 50,
      hello, strlen (hello)   );
    break;

  /*   process keyboard mapping changes   */
  case MappingNotify:
    XRefreshKeyboardMapping ( &myevent );
    break;

  /*   process mouse-button presses   */
  case ButtonPress:
    XDrawImageString (
      myevent.xbutton.display, myevent.xbutton.window, mygc,
      myevent.xbutton.x, myevent.xbutton.y,
      hi, strlen (hi)   );
    break;

  /*   process keyboard input   */
  case KeyPress:
    i = XLookupString ( &myevent, text, 10, &mykey, 0 );
    if (i == 1 && text[0] == 'q') done = 1;
    break;

  } /*   switch (myevent.type) */
} /* while (done == 0) */

/*   termination   */
XFreeGC (mydisplay, mygc);
XDestroyWindow (mydisplay, mywindow);
XCloseDisplay (mydisplay);
exit (0);
}
```

# APPENDIX B
# X PROTOCOL
# REQUEST CODES

This appendix shows the numbers and names of the major X request codes. The primary use of this information is in deciphering messages printed by *Xlib*'s default error event handler. The request code names are defined in the header file **<X11/Xproto.h>**. Note that a particular request code can be generated either by an *Xlib* request call or a convenience function.

| | | | |
|---|---|---|---|
| X_CreateWindow | 1 | X_GetAtomName | 17 |
| X_ChangeWindowAttributes | 2 | X_ChangeProperty | 18 |
| X_GetWindowAttributes | 3 | X_DeleteProperty | 19 |
| X_DestroyWindow | 4 | X_GetProperty | 20 |
| X_DestroySubwindows | 5 | X_ListProperties | 21 |
| X_ChangeSaveSet | 6 | X_SetSelectionOwner | 22 |
| X_ReparentWindow | 7 | X_GetSelectionOwner | 23 |
| X_MapWindow | 8 | X_ConvertSelection | 24 |
| X_MapSubwindows | 9 | X_SendEvent | 25 |
| X_UnmapWindow | 10 | X_GrabPointer | 26 |
| X_UnmapSubwindows | 11 | X_UngrabPointer | 27 |
| X_ConfigureWindow | 12 | X_GrabButton | 28 |
| X_CirculateWindow | 13 | X_UngrabButton | 29 |
| X_GetGeometry | 14 | X_ChangeActivePointerGrab | 30 |
| X_QueryTree | 15 | X_GrabKeyboard | 31 |
| X_InternAtom | 16 | X_UngrabKeyboard | 32 |

| | | | |
|---|---|---|---|
| X_GrabKey | 33 | X_InstallColormap | 81 |
| X_UngrabKey | 34 | X_UninstallColormap | 82 |
| X_AllowEvents | 35 | X_ListInstalledColormaps | 83 |
| X_GrabServer | 36 | X_AllocColor | 84 |
| X_UngrabServer | 37 | X_AllocNamedColor | 85 |
| X_QueryPointer | 38 | X_AllocColorCells | 86 |
| X_GetMotionEvents | 39 | X_AllocColorPlanes | 87 |
| X_TranslateCoords | 40 | X_FreeColors | 88 |
| X_WarpPointer | 41 | X_StoreColors | 89 |
| X_SetInputFocus | 42 | X_StoreNamedColor | 90 |
| X_GetInputFocus | 43 | X_QueryColors | 91 |
| X_QueryKeymap | 44 | X_LookupColor | 92 |
| X_OpenFont | 45 | X_CreateCursor | 93 |
| X_CloseFont | 46 | X_CreateGlyphCursor | 94 |
| X_QueryFont | 47 | X_FreeCursor | 95 |
| X_QueryTextExtents | 48 | X_RecolorCursor | 96 |
| X_ListFonts | 49 | X_QueryBestSize | 97 |
| X_ListFontsWithInfo | 50 | X_QueryExtension | 98 |
| X_SetFontPath | 51 | X_ListExtensions | 99 |
| X_GetFontPath | 52 | X_ChangeKeyboardMapping | 100 |
| X_CreatePixmap | 53 | X_GetKeyboardMapping | 101 |
| X_FreePixmap | 54 | X_ChangeKeyboardControl | 102 |
| X_CreateGC | 55 | X_GetKeyboardControl | 103 |
| X_ChangeGC | 56 | X_Bell | 104 |
| X_CopyGC | 57 | X_ChangePointerControl | 105 |
| X_SetDashes | 58 | X_GetPointerControl | 106 |
| X_SetClipRectangles | 59 | X_SetScreenSaver | 107 |
| X_FreeGC | 60 | X_GetScreenSaver | 108 |
| X_ClearArea | 61 | X_ChangeHosts | 109 |
| X_CopyArea | 62 | X_ListHosts | 110 |
| X_CopyPlane | 63 | X_SetAccessControl | 111 |
| X_PolyPoint | 64 | X_SetCloseDownMode | 112 |
| X_PolyLine | 65 | X_KillClient | 113 |
| X_PolySegment | 66 | X_RotateProperties | 114 |
| X_PolyRectangle | 67 | X_ForceScreenSaver | 115 |
| X_PolyArc | 68 | X_SetPointerMapping | 116 |
| X_FillPoly | 69 | X_GetPointerMapping | 117 |
| X_PolyFillRectangle | 70 | X_SetModifierMapping | 118 |
| X_PolyFillArc | 71 | X_GetModifierMapping | 119 |
| X_PutImage | 72 | X_NoOperation | 127 |
| X_GetImage | 73 | | |
| X_PolyText8 | 74 | | |
| X_PolyText16 | 75 | | |
| X_ImageText8 | 76 | | |
| X_ImageText16 | 77 | | |
| X_CreateColormap | 78 | | |
| X_FreeColormap | 79 | | |
| X_CopyColormapAndFree | 80 | | |

# APPENDIX C
# LATIN-1 AND
# STANDARD KEYSYMS

No book about programming for computer displays would be complete without the obligatory appendix showing the ASCII character set. This appendix goes further: it shows the standard Keysyms for the ISO Draft International Standard 8859/1 character set, commonly known as Latin-1. Latin-1 is the character set used in X for such things as font and property names. The first half of the Latin-1 character set is the same as the ASCII character set.

This appendix also shows the names of standard Keysyms for miscellaneous standard keyboard function keys. As Chapter 10 explains, each Keysym is intended to match the engraving on a particular key. Not all keyboards have all Keysyms.

The header file **<X11/keysym.h>** contains definitions for all the miscellaneous Keysyms and for a large variety of character Keysyms.

| | | | | | | | | |
|---|---|---|---|---|---|---|---|---|
| 32 | 0x20 | | XK_space | | 81 | 0x51 | Q | XK_Q |
| 33 | 0x21 | ! | XK_exclam | | 82 | 0x52 | R | XK_R |
| 34 | 0x22 | " | XK_quotedbl | | 83 | 0x53 | S | XK_S |
| 35 | 0x23 | # | XK_numbersign | | 84 | 0x54 | T | XK_T |
| 36 | 0x24 | $ | XK_dollar | | 85 | 0x55 | U | XK_U |
| 37 | 0x25 | % | XK_percent | | 86 | 0x56 | V | XK_V |
| 38 | 0x26 | & | XK_ampersand | | 87 | 0x57 | W | XK_W |
| 39 | 0x27 | ' | XK_quoteright | | 88 | 0x58 | X | XK_X |
| 40 | 0x28 | ( | XK_parenleft | | 89 | 0x59 | Y | XK_Y |
| 41 | 0x29 | ) | XK_parenright | | 90 | 0x5a | Z | XK_Z |
| 42 | 0x2a | * | XK_asterisk | | 91 | 0x5b | [ | XK_bracketleft |
| 43 | 0x2b | + | XK_plus | | 92 | 0x5c | \ | XK_backslash |
| 44 | 0x2c | , | XK_comma | | 93 | 0x5d | ] | XK_bracketright |
| 45 | 0x2d | − | XK_minus | | 94 | 0x5e | ^ | XK_asciicircum |
| 46 | 0x2e | . | XK_period | | 95 | 0x5f | _ | XK_underscore |
| 47 | 0x2f | / | XK_slash | | 96 | 0x60 | ` | XK_quoteleft |
| 48 | 0x30 | 0 | XK_0 | | 97 | 0x61 | a | XK_a |
| 49 | 0x31 | 1 | XK_1 | | 98 | 0x62 | b | XK_b |
| 50 | 0x32 | 2 | XK_2 | | 99 | 0x63 | c | XK_c |
| 51 | 0x33 | 3 | XK_3 | | 100 | 0x64 | c | XK_d |
| 52 | 0x34 | 4 | XK_4 | | 101 | 0x65 | e | XK_e |
| 53 | 0x35 | 5 | XK_5 | | 102 | 0x66 | f | XK_f |
| 54 | 0x36 | 6 | XK_6 | | 103 | 0x67 | g | XK_g |
| 55 | 0x37 | 7 | XK_7 | | 104 | 0x68 | h | XK_h |
| 56 | 0x38 | 8 | XK_8 | | 105 | 0x69 | i | XK_i |
| 57 | 0x39 | 9 | XK_9 | | 106 | 0x6a | j | XK_j |
| 58 | 0x3a | : | XK_colon | | 107 | 0x6b | k | XK_k |
| 59 | 0x3b | ; | XK_semicolon | | 108 | 0x6c | l | XK_l |
| 60 | 0x3c | < | XK_less | | 109 | 0x6d | m | XK_m |
| 61 | 0x3d | = | XK_equal | | 110 | 0x6e | n | XK_n |
| 62 | 0x3e | > | XK_greater | | 111 | 0x6f | o | XK_o |
| 63 | 0x3f | ? | XK_question | | 112 | 0x70 | p | XK_p |
| 64 | 0x40 | @ | XK_at | | 113 | 0x71 | q | XK_q |
| 65 | 0x41 | A | XK_A | | 114 | 0x72 | r | XK_r |
| 66 | 0x42 | B | XK_B | | 115 | 0x73 | s | XK_s |
| 67 | 0x43 | C | XK_C | | 116 | 0x74 | t | XK_t |
| 68 | 0x44 | D | XK_D | | 117 | 0x75 | u | XK_u |
| 69 | 0x45 | E | XK_E | | 118 | 0x76 | v | XK_v |
| 70 | 0x46 | F | XK_F | | 119 | 0x77 | w | XK_w |
| 71 | 0x47 | G | XK_G | | 120 | 0x78 | x | XK_x |
| 72 | 0x48 | H | XK_H | | 121 | 0x79 | y | XK_y |
| 73 | 0x49 | I | XK_I | | 122 | 0x7a | z | XK_z |
| 74 | 0x4a | J | XK_J | | 123 | 0x7b | { | XK_braceleft |
| 75 | 0x4b | K | XK_K | | 124 | 0x7c | | | XK_bar |
| 76 | 0x4c | L | XK_L | | 125 | 0x7d | } | XK_braceright |
| 77 | 0x4d | M | XK_M | | 126 | 0x7e | ~ | XK_asciitilde |
| 78 | 0x4e | N | XK_N | | | | | |
| 79 | 0x4f | O | XK_O | | | | | |
| 80 | 0x50 | P | XK_P | | | | | |

| 160 | 0xa0 |   | XK_nobreakspace | 208 | 0xd0 | Đ | XK_Eth |
|-----|------|---|-----------------|-----|------|---|--------|
| 161 | 0xa1 | ¡ | XK_exclamdown | 209 | 0xd1 | Ñ | XK_Ntilde |
| 162 | 0xa2 | ¢ | XK_cent | 210 | 0xd2 | Ò | XK_Ograve |
| 163 | 0xa3 | £ | XK_sterling | 211 | 0xd3 | Ó | XK_Oacute |
| 164 | 0xa4 | ¤ | XK_currency | 212 | 0xd4 | Ô | XK_Ocircumflex |
| 165 | 0xa5 | ¥ | XK_yen | 213 | 0xd5 | Õ | XK_Otilde |
| 166 | 0xa6 | ¦ | XK_brokenbar | 214 | 0xd6 | Ö | XK_Odiaeresis |
| 167 | 0xa7 | § | XK_section | 215 | 0xd7 | × | XK_multiply |
| 168 | 0xa8 | ¨ | XK_diaeresis | 216 | 0xd8 | Ø | XK_Ooblique |
| 169 | 0xa9 | © | XK_copyright | 217 | 0xd9 | Ù | XK_Ugrave |
| 170 | 0xaa | ª | XK_ordfeminine | 218 | 0xda | Ú | XK_Uacute |
| 171 | 0xab | « | XK_guillemotleft | 219 | 0xdb | Û | XK_Ucircumflex |
| 172 | 0xac | ¬ | XK_notsign | 220 | 0xdc | Ü | XK_Udiaeresis |
| 173 | 0xad | - | XK_hyphen | 221 | 0xdd | Ý | XK_Yacute |
| 174 | 0xae | ® | XK_registered | 222 | 0xde | Þ | XK_Thorn |
| 175 | 0xaf | ¯ | XK_macron | 223 | 0xdf | ß | XK_ssharp |
| 176 | 0xb0 | ° | XK_degree | 224 | 0xe0 | à | XK_agrave |
| 177 | 0xb1 | ± | XK_plusminus | 225 | 0xe1 | á | XK_aacute |
| 178 | 0xb2 | 2 | XK_twosuperior | 226 | 0xe2 | â | XK_acircumflex |
| 179 | 0xb3 | 3 | XK_threesuperior | 227 | 0xe3 | ã | XK_atilde |
| 180 | 0xb4 | ´ | XK_acute | 228 | 0xe4 | ä | XK_adiaeresis |
| 181 | 0xb5 | µ | XK_mu | 229 | 0xe5 | å | XK_aring |
| 182 | 0xb6 | ¶ | XK_paragraph | 230 | 0xe6 | æ | XK_ae |
| 183 | 0xb7 | · | XK_periodcentered | 231 | 0xe7 | ç | XK_ccedilla |
| 184 | 0xb8 | ¸ | XK_cedilla | 232 | 0xe8 | è | XK_egrave |
| 185 | 0xb9 | 1 | XK_onesuperior | 233 | 0xe9 | é | XK_eacute |
| 186 | 0xba | º | XK_ordmasculine | 234 | 0xea | ê | XK_ecircumflex |
| 187 | 0xbb | » | XK_guillemotright | 235 | 0xeb | ë | XK_ediaeresis |
| 188 | 0xbc | 1/4 | XK_onequarter | 236 | 0xec | ì | XK_igrave |
| 189 | 0xbd | 1/2 | XK_onehalf | 237 | 0xed | í | XK_iacute |
| 190 | 0xbe | 3/4 | XK_threequarters | 238 | 0xee | î | XK_icircumflex |
| 191 | 0xbf | ¿ | XK_questiondown | 239 | 0xef | ï | XK_idiaeresis |
| 192 | 0xc0 | À | XK_Agrave | 240 | 0xf0 | ð | XK_eth |
| 193 | 0xc1 | Á | XK_Aacute | 241 | 0xf1 | ñ | XK_ntilde |
| 194 | 0xc2 | Â | XK_Acircumflex | 242 | 0xf2 | ò | XK_ograve |
| 195 | 0xc3 | Ã | XK_Atilde | 243 | 0xd3 | ó | XK_oacute |
| 196 | 0xc4 | Ä | XK_Adiaeresis | 244 | 0xd4 | ô | XK_ocircumflex |
| 197 | 0xc5 | Å | XK_Aring | 245 | 0xd5 | õ | XK_otilde |
| 198 | 0xc6 | Æ | XK_AE | 246 | 0xd6 | ö | XK_odiaeresis |
| 199 | 0xc7 | Ç | XK_Ccedilla | 247 | 0xf7 | ÷ | XK_division |
| 200 | 0xc8 | È | XK_Egrave | 248 | 0xf8 | ø | XK_oslash |
| 201 | 0xc9 | É | XK_Eacute | 249 | 0xf9 | ù | XK_ugrave |
| 202 | 0xca | Ê | XK_Ecircumflex | 250 | 0xfa | ú | XK_uacute |
| 203 | 0xcb | Ë | XK_Ediaeresis | 251 | 0xfb | û | XK_ucircumflex |
| 204 | 0xcc | Ì | XK_Igrave | 252 | 0xfc | ü | XK_udiaeresis |
| 205 | 0xcd | Í | XK_Iacute | 253 | 0xfd | ý | XK_yacute |
| 206 | 0xce | Î | XK_Icircumflex | 254 | 0xfe | þ | XK_thorn |
| 207 | 0xcf | Ï | XK_Idiaeresis | 255 | 0xff | ÿ | XK_ydiaeresis |

# MISCELLANEOUS KEYSYMS

## TTY functions

XK_BackSpace
XK_Tab
XK_Linefeed
XK_Clear
XK_Return
XK_Pause
XK_Escape
XK_Delete

## International, multi-key character composition

XK_Multi_key
XK_Kanji

## Cursor control and motion

XK_Home
XK_Left
XK_Up
XK_Right
XK_Down
XK_Prior
XK_Next
XK_End
XK_Begin

## Misc. Function Keys

XK_Select
XK_Print
XK_Execute
XK_Insert
XK_Undo
XK_Redo
XK_Menu
XK_Find
XK_Cancel
XK_Help
XK_Break
XK_Mode_switch
XK_script_switch
XK_Num_Lock

## Keypad Keys

XK_KP_Space
XK_KP_Tab
XK_KP_Enter
XK_KP_F1
XK_KP_F2
XK_KP_F3
XK_KP_F4
XK_KP_Equal
XK_KP_Multiply
XK_KP_Add
XK_KP_Separator
XK_KP_Subtract
XK_KP_Decimal
XK_KP_Divide

XK_KP_0
XK_KP_1
XK_KP_2
XK_KP_3
XK_KP_4
XK_KP_5
XK_KP_6
XK_KP_7
XK_KP_8
XK_KP_9

## Auxiliary Functions

Notice that F11-F20 are also called L1-L10 for keyboards having a block of function keys on the left side. Similarly, F21-F35 are also called R1-R15 for keyboards having a block of function keys on the right side.

XK_F1
XK_F2
XK_F3
XK_F4
XK_F5
XK_F6
XK_F7
XK_F8
XK_F9
XK_F10

| | |
|---|---|
| XK_F11 | XK_L1 |
| XK_F12 | XK_L2 |
| XK_F13 | XK_L3 |
| XK_F14 | XK_L4 |
| XK_F15 | XK_L5 |
| XK_F16 | XK_L6 |
| XK_F17 | XK_L7 |
| XK_F18 | XK_L8 |
| XK_F19 | XK_L9 |
| XK_F20 | XK_L10 |

| | |
|---|---|
| XK_F21 | XK_R1 |
| XK_F22 | XK_R2 |
| XK_F23 | XK_R3 |
| XK_F24 | XK_R4 |
| XK_F25 | XK_R5 |
| XK_F26 | XK_R6 |
| XK_F27 | XK_R7 |
| XK_F28 | XK_R8 |
| XK_F29 | XK_R9 |
| XK_F30 | XK_R10 |
| XK_F31 | XK_R11 |
| XK_F32 | XK_R12 |
| XK_R13 | XK_F33 |
| XK_F34 | XK_R14 |
| XK_F35 | XK_R15 |

## Modifiers

Distinct Keysyms for keys on left- and right-hand sides of the keyboard are available.

| | |
|---|---|
| XK_Shift_L | XK_Shift_R |
| XK_Control_L | XK_Control_R |
| XK_Caps_Lock | |
| XK_Shift_Lock | |
| XK_Meta_L | XK_Meta_R |
| XK_Alt_L | XK_Alt_R |
| XK_Super_L | XK_Super_R |
| XK_Hyper_L | XK_Hyper_R |

# APPENDIX D
# FONTS

This appendix shows the fonts available on the first X sample implementation shipped by M.I.T. in late 1987. The fonts shipped by M.I.T. are all public-domain. Most of them contain the ASCII character set; those marked [UC] contain only upper-case letters.

## FONTS FOR ROMAN-ALPHABET TEXT

| | |
|---|---|
| 6x10 | ABCDabcd0123 Type is to read! |
| 6x12 | ABCDabcd0123 Type is to read! |
| 6x13 | ABCDabcd0123 Type is to read! |
| 8x13 | ABCDabcd0123 Type is to read! |
| 8x13bold | **ABCDabcd0123 Type is to read!** |
| 9x15 | ABCDabcd0123 Type is to read! |
| fixed | ABCDabcd0123 Type is to read! |
| micro | ABCDabcd0123 Type is to read! |
| serif10 | ABCDabcd0123 Type is to read! |
| serifb10 | **ABCDabcd0123 Type is to read!** |

| | |
|---|---|
| serifi10 | *ABCDabcd0123 Type is to read!* |
| sans12 | ABCDabcd0123 Type is to read! |
| sansb12 | **ABCDabcd0123 Type is to read!** |
| sansi12 | *ABCDabcd0123 Type is to read!* |
| serif12 | ABCDabcd0123 Type is to read! |
| serifb12 | **ABCDabcd0123 Type is to read!** |
| serifi12 | *ABCDabcd0123 Type is to read!* |
| sub | ABCDabcd01 23 Type is to read! |
| subsub | ABCDabcd01 23 Type is to read! |
| sup | ABCDabcd01 23 Type is to read! |
| supsup | ABCDabcd01 23 Type is to read! |
| variable | ABCDabcd0123 Type is to read! |
| vtbold | **ABCDabcd0123 Type is to read!** |
| vtsingle | ABCDabcd0123 Type is to read! |
| fg-13 | ABCDabcd0123 Type is to read! |
| fgb-13 | **ABCDabcd0123 Type is to read!** |
| vg-13 | ABCDabcd0123 Type is to read! |
| fg-16 | ABCDabcd0123 Type is to read! |
| fg-18 | ABCDabcd0123 Type is to read! |
| fcor-20 | ABCDabcd01 23 Type is |
| fg-20 | ABCDabcd0123 Type is to read! |
| fgi-20 | *ABCDabcd0123 Type is to read!* |
| vg-20 | ABCDabcd01 23 Type is to read! |

| | |
|---|---|
| vgi-20 | *ABCDabcd0123 Type is to read* |
| vr-20 | ABCDabcd0123 Type is to read! |
| fg-22 | ABCDabcd0123 Type is to |
| fgs-22 | ABCDabcd0123 Type is to |
| fg-25 | ABCDabcd0123 Type is |
| fg1-25 | ABCDabcd0123 Type is to |
| fgb-25 | ABCDabcd0123 Type is |
| fgb1-25 | ABCDabcd0123 Type is |
| fgi1-25 | *ABCDabcd0123 Type is* |
| fqxb-25 | **ABCDabcd0123** |
| fr-25 | ABCDabcd0123 Type is |
| fr1-25 | ABCDabcd0123 Type is |
| fr2-25 | ABCDabcd0123 Type is |
| fr3-25 | ABCDabcd0123 Type is |
| fri1-25 | *ABCDabcd0123 Type is* |
| ipa-s25 | ABCDabcd0123 Type is |
| met25 | ABCDabcd0123 Type is |

vctl-25    ABCDabcd0123 Type is to

vg-25    ABCDabcd0123 Type is to

vgb-25    **ABCDabcd0123 Type is to**

vgbc-25    **ABCDabcd0123 Type is to**

vgh-25    ABCDabcd0123 Type is to

vgi-25    *ABCDabcd0123 Type is to*

vmic-25    **ABCDabcd0123 Type is**

vr-25    ABCDabcd0123 Type is to

vrb-25    **ABCDabcd0123 Type is to**

vri-25    *ABCDabcd0123 Type is to*

vr-27    ABCDabcd0123 Type is to

xif-s25    ABCDabcd0123 Type is

fg-30    ABCDabcd0123 Type

fgb1-30    ABCDabcd0123 Type is

swd-s30    ABCDabcd0123

vr-30    ABCDabcd0123 Type is to

vrb-30   ABCDabcd0123 Type is

vri-30   *ABCDabcd0123 Type is to*

vg-31   *ABCDabcd01 23 Type is*

vgb-31   **ABCDabcd01 23 Type**

vgi-31   *ABCDabcd01 23 Type is*

vgvb-31   **ABCDabcd01 23 Type**

vr-31   ABCDabcd0123 Type is to

vrb-31   ABCDabcd0123 Type is

vri-31   *ABCDabcd0123 Type is to*

frb-32   ABCDabcd Type is

fr-33   ABCDabcd0123

fri-33   *ABCDabcd0123*

vrb-35   ABCDabcd0123 Type

vbee-36   ABCDabcd0123

vply-36    **ABCDabcd0123 Type is to read!**

vrb-37    **ABCDabcd0123**

vxms-37    ABCDabcd0123

fg-40    ABCDabcd01 23

vg-40    ABCDabcd01 23

vgl-40    ABCDabcdØ1 23

vr-40    ABCDabcd01 23

vri-40    *ABCDabcd01 23*

vshd-40 [UC]    ABCD0123

vxms-43    ABCDabcd01

vsgn-57 [UC]    ABCDØ1

ABC

vsg-114 [UC]

# SPECIAL- PURPOSE FONTS

| | |
|---|---|
| apl-s25 | ∝⊥∩⌊$ABCD0123$ |
| arrow3 | ⟨BREAK⟩⟨CLEAR⟩⟨CALL⟩⟨ESC⟩ |
| chp-s25 | |
| chs-s50 | |
| cyr-s25 | АБДабд |
| cyr-s30 | АБДабд |
| cyr-s38 | АВСДавсд0123 |
| dancer | |
| ger-s35 | $\mathfrak{ABCD}abcd$ |
| grk-s25 | $ABX\Delta\alpha\beta\chi\delta$ |
| grk-s30 | $ABX\Delta\alpha\beta\chi\delta$ |
| hbr-s25 | אבגדבֶָ |

hbr-s40  שׁדסבא

krivo  لل مم بﺑ\*لﻬ ﺔ

lat-s30  ĀBČDābčd0123

oldera  ظخ طشلع تيبلًتپب 1

plunk  ∀∈ℂ▽✿∼©∂○□△◇⊥

rot-s16  ⋌⊡⊓⊔ω σ∩ ᴎ⊘⊦ᴎω

sym-s25  ∝ℂil√⊕ ⊂∈

stempl  ■ ▮ ▶▪ ▪

sym-s53  ⌐⌐L⅂√|

# APPENDIX E
# COLOR NAMES

This appendix lists the names of colors available for use with **XAllocNamed-Color**, **XStoreNamedColor**, **XStoreNamedColors**, **XLookupColor**, and **XParseColor** (see Chapter 7).

| | | | | | | | |
|---:|---:|---:|---|---:|---:|---:|---|
| 112 | 219 | 147 | aquamarine | 47 | 47 | 79 | MidnightBlue |
| 112 | 219 | 147 | Aquamarine | 35 | 35 | 142 | navy blue |
| 50 | 204 | 153 | medium aquamarine | 35 | 35 | 142 | NavyBlue |
| 50 | 204 | 153 | MediumAquamarine | 35 | 35 | 142 | navy |
| 0 | 0 | 0 | black | 35 | 35 | 142 | Navy |
| 0 | 0 | 0 | Black | 50 | 153 | 204 | sky blue |
| 0 | 0 | 255 | blue | 50 | 153 | 204 | SkyBlue |
| 0 | 0 | 255 | Blue | 0 | 127 | 255 | slate blue |
| 95 | 159 | 159 | cadet blue | 0 | 127 | 255 | SlateBlue |
| 95 | 159 | 159 | CadetBlue | 35 | 107 | 142 | steel blue |
| 66 | 66 | 111 | cornflower blue | 35 | 107 | 142 | SteelBlue |
| 66 | 66 | 111 | CornflowerBlue | 255 | 127 | 0 | coral |
| 107 | 35 | 142 | dark slate blue | 255 | 127 | 0 | Coral |
| 107 | 35 | 142 | DarkSlateBlue | 0 | 255 | 255 | cyan |
| 191 | 216 | 216 | light blue | 0 | 255 | 255 | Cyan |
| 191 | 216 | 216 | LightBlue | 142 | 35 | 35 | firebrick |
| 143 | 143 | 188 | light steel blue | 142 | 35 | 35 | Firebrick |
| 143 | 143 | 188 | LightSteelBlue | 165 | 42 | 42 | brown |
| 50 | 50 | 204 | medium blue | 165 | 42 | 42 | Brown |
| 50 | 50 | 204 | MediumBlue | 204 | 127 | 50 | gold |
| 127 | 0 | 255 | medium slate blue | 204 | 127 | 50 | Gold |
| 127 | 0 | 255 | MediumSlateBlue | 219 | 219 | 112 | goldenrod |
| 47 | 47 | 79 | midnight blue | 219 | 219 | 112 | Goldenrod |

| | | | |
|---|---|---|---|
| 234 | 234 | 173 | medium goldenrod |
| 234 | 234 | 173 | MediumGoldenrod |
| 0 | 255 | 0 | green |
| 0 | 255 | 0 | Green |
| 47 | 79 | 47 | dark green |
| 47 | 79 | 47 | DarkGreen |
| 79 | 79 | 47 | dark olive green |
| 79 | 79 | 47 | DarkOliveGreen |
| 35 | 142 | 35 | forest green |
| 35 | 142 | 35 | ForestGreen |
| 50 | 204 | 50 | lime green |
| 50 | 204 | 50 | LimeGreen |
| 107 | 142 | 35 | medium forest green |
| 107 | 142 | 35 | MediumForestGreen |
| 66 | 111 | 66 | medium sea green |
| 66 | 111 | 66 | MediumSeaGreen |
| 127 | 255 | 0 | medium spring green |
| 127 | 255 | 0 | MediumSpringGreen |
| 143 | 188 | 143 | pale green |
| 143 | 188 | 143 | PaleGreen |
| 35 | 142 | 107 | sea green |
| 35 | 142 | 107 | SeaGreen |
| 0 | 255 | 127 | spring green |
| 0 | 255 | 127 | SpringGreen |
| 153 | 204 | 50 | yellow green |
| 153 | 204 | 50 | YellowGreen |
| 47 | 79 | 79 | dark slate grey |
| 47 | 79 | 79 | DarkSlateGrey |
| 47 | 79 | 79 | dark slate gray |
| 47 | 79 | 79 | DarkSlateGray |
| 84 | 84 | 84 | dim grey |
| 84 | 84 | 84 | DimGrey |
| 84 | 84 | 84 | dim gray |
| 84 | 84 | 84 | DimGray |
| 168 | 168 | 168 | light grey |
| 168 | 168 | 168 | LightGrey |
| 168 | 168 | 168 | light gray |
| 168 | 168 | 168 | LightGray |
| 192 | 192 | 192 | gray |
| 192 | 192 | 192 | grey |
| 192 | 192 | 192 | Gray |
| 192 | 192 | 192 | Grey |
| 159 | 159 | 95 | khaki |
| 159 | 159 | 95 | Khaki |
| 255 | 0 | 255 | magenta |
| 255 | 0 | 255 | Magenta |
| 142 | 35 | 107 | maroon |
| 142 | 35 | 107 | Maroon |
| 204 | 50 | 50 | orange |
| 204 | 50 | 50 | Orange |
| 219 | 112 | 219 | orchid |
| 219 | 112 | 219 | Orchid |
| 153 | 50 | 204 | dark orchid |
| 153 | 50 | 204 | DarkOrchid |
| 147 | 112 | 219 | medium orchid |
| 147 | 112 | 219 | MediumOrchid |
| 188 | 143 | 143 | pink |
| 188 | 143 | 143 | Pink |
| 234 | 173 | 234 | plum |
| 234 | 173 | 234 | Plum |
| 255 | 0 | 0 | red |
| 255 | 0 | 0 | Red |
| 79 | 47 | 47 | indian red |
| 79 | 47 | 47 | IndianRed |
| 219 | 112 | 147 | medium violet red |
| 219 | 112 | 147 | MediumVioletRed |
| 255 | 0 | 127 | orange red |
| 255 | 0 | 127 | OrangeRed |
| 204 | 50 | 153 | violet red |
| 204 | 50 | 153 | VioletRed |
| 111 | 66 | 66 | salmon |
| 111 | 66 | 66 | Salmon |
| 142 | 107 | 35 | sienna |
| 142 | 107 | 35 | Sienna |
| 219 | 147 | 112 | tan |
| 219 | 147 | 112 | Tan |
| 216 | 191 | 216 | thistle |
| 216 | 191 | 216 | Thistle |
| 173 | 234 | 234 | turquoise |
| 173 | 234 | 234 | Turquoise |
| 112 | 147 | 219 | dark turquoise |
| 112 | 147 | 219 | DarkTurquoise |
| 112 | 219 | 219 | medium turquoise |
| 112 | 219 | 219 | MediumTurquoise |
| 79 | 47 | 79 | violet |
| 79 | 47 | 79 | Violet |
| 159 | 95 | 159 | blue violet |
| 159 | 95 | 159 | BlueViolet |
| 216 | 216 | 191 | wheat |
| 216 | 216 | 191 | Wheat |
| 252 | 252 | 252 | white |
| 252 | 252 | 252 | White |
| 255 | 255 | 0 | yellow |
| 255 | 255 | 0 | Yellow |
| 147 | 219 | 112 | green yellow |
| 147 | 219 | 112 | GreenYellow |

# APPENDIX F
# STANDARD CURSOR
# SHAPES AND SYMBOLS

This appendix shows the collection of standard cursor shapes along with their symbolic names. The header file **<X11/cursorfont.h>** defines the names, and the **cursor** font defines the shapes. The **XCreateFontCursor** request (see Chapter 9) may be used to create cursor resources with these shapes.

XC_X_cursor

XC_arrow

XC_based_arrow_down

XC_based_arrow_up

XC_boat

XC_bogosity

XC_bottom_left_corner

XC_bottom_right_corner

XC_bottom_side

XC_bottom_tee

XC_box_spiral

XC_center_ptr

XC_circle

XC_clock

XC_coffee_mug

XC_cross

XC_cross_reverse

XC_crosshair

XC_diamond_cross

XC_dot

XC_dotbox

XC_double_arrow

XC_draft_large

XC_draft_small

XC_draped_box

XC_exchange

XC_fleur

XC_gobbler

XC_gumby

XC_hand1

XC_hand2

XC_heart

XC_icon

XC_iron_cross

XC_left_ptr

XC_left_side

XC_left_tee

XC_leftbutton

XC_ll_angle

XC_lr_angle

XC_man

XC_middlebutton

XC_mouse

XC_pencil

XC_pirate

XC_plus

XC_question_arrow

XC_right_ptr

XC_right_side

XC_right_tee

XC_rightbutton

XC_rtl_logo

| | | | |
|---|---|---|---|
| ⛵ | XC_sailboat | ☿ | XC_trek |
| ⇓ | XC_sb_down_arrow | ⌐ | XC_ul_angle |
| ⟷ | XC_sb_h_double_arrow | ☂ | XC_umbrella |
| ⟸ | XC_sb_left_arrow | ¬ | XC_ur_angle |
| ⟹ | XC_sb_right_arrow | ⌚ | XC_watch |
| ⇑ | XC_sb_up_arrow | I | XC_xterm |
| ⇕ | XC_sb_v_double_arrow | | |
| ◫ | XC_shuttle | | |
| ⌐⊔ | XC_sizing | | |
| ✳ | XC_spider | | |
| ᕯ | XC_spraycan | | |
| ☆ | XC_star | | |
| ◉ | XC_target | | |
| ＋ | XC_tcross | | |
| ↖ | XC_top_left_arrow | | |
| ⌈⌐ | XC_top_left_corner | | |
| ↗ | XC_top_right_corner | | |
| ↑ | XC_top_side | | |
| ⊤ | XC_top_tee | | |

# APPENDIX G
# PREDEFINED ATOMS

This appendix shows the names of all the standard predefined Atoms. In general, Atoms represent arbitrary Latin-1 names.

Atoms are used in X for naming the following kinds of things:

- Window manager hint properties (Chapter 4).
- ClientMessage event types (Chapter 4).
- Font properties (Chapter 6).
- Standard shared color maps (Chapter 7).
- Cut-buffers (Chapter 12).
- General-purpose properties (Chapter 12).
- Property data types (Chapter 12).
- Selections (Chapter 12).

Individual application or suites of applications can define their own property names, and use **XInternAtom** (see Chapter 12) to create unique Atoms for those names. If possible, applications should use predefined atoms rather than creating new ones with **XInternAtom**. Doing this both improves performance (**XInternAtom** is a round-trip request) and increases the likelihood that applications will be able to share properties, data types, and selections. You can interactively examine the names and contents of properties with the **xprop(1)** utility function.

The predefined Atoms are defined in the header file **<X11/Xatom.h>** as small integers. The symbols for the Atoms are prefixed with "XA_". However, the text of the name corresponding to the each Atom has no prefix. The following line defines the Atom named WM_CLASS:

```
# define XA_WM_CLASS  ((Atom) 67)
```

## Window Manager Hints
XA_WM_CLASS
XA_WM_COMMAND
XA_WM_CLIENT_MACHINE
XA_WM_HINTS
XA_WM_ICON_NAME
XA_WM_ICON_SIZE
XA_WM_NAME
XA_WM_NORMAL_HINTS
XA_WM_TRANSIENT_FOR
XA_WM_ZOOM_HINTS

## Font Properties
XA_MIN_SPACE
XA_NORM_SPACE
XA_MAX_SPACE
XA_END_SPACE
XA_SUPERSCRIPT_X
XA_SUPERSCRIPT_Y
XA_SUBSCRIPT_X
XA_SUBSCRIPT_Y
XA_UNDERLINE_POSITION
XA_UNDERLINE_THICKNESS
XA_STRIKEOUT_ASCENT
XA_STRIKEOUT_DESCENT
XA_ITALIC_ANGLE
XA_X_HEIGHT
XA_QUAD_WIDTH
XA_WEIGHT
XA_POINT_SIZE
XA_RESOLUTION
XA_COPYRIGHT
XA_NOTICE
XA_FONT_NAME
XA_FAMILY_NAME
XA_FULL_NAME
XA_CAP_HEIGHT

## Resource Data Base
XA_RESOURCE_MANAGER

## Standard Color Maps
XA_RGB_BEST_MAP
XA_RGB_BLUE_MAP
XA_RGB_DEFAULT_MAP
XA_RGB_GRAY_MAP
XA_RGB_GREEN_MAP
XA_RGB_RED_MAP

## Cut Buffers
XA_CUT_BUFFER0
XA_CUT_BUFFER1
XA_CUT_BUFFER2
XA_CUT_BUFFER3
XA_CUT_BUFFER4
XA_CUT_BUFFER5
XA_CUT_BUFFER6
XA_CUT_BUFFER7

## Data Types
XA_ARC
XA_ATOM
XA_BITMAP
XA_CARDINAL
XA_COLORMAP
XA_CURSOR
XA_DRAWABLE
XA_FONT
XA_INTEGER
XA_PIXMAP
XA_POINT
XA_RECTANGLE
XA_RGB_COLOR_MAP
XA_STRING
XA_VISUALID
XA_WINDOW
XA_WM_HINTS
XA_WM_SIZE_HINTS

## Selections
XA_PRIMARY
XA_SECONDARY

# INDEX

_Xdebug, 56

**A**cceleration, 333
Accepting events, 396
Acquiring input focus, 124, 142, 376
Active Grabs, (See Keyboard Grabs;
    Pointer Grabs)
Animation with color cells, 271
Application, 15, 21
Application termination, 25, 39
Arabic, 228
arc_mode--GC attribute,173
  converting to/from names, 439
  data types, 440
  life-cycle, 437
  predefined, 438
  property type, 441
  selection names, 454
  uniqueness, 438
Arcs (See Drawing, arcs)
Atoms (See also Properties), 438
Automatic-flush action, 55

**B**ack-door interfaces, 2
Background, 21
background--GC attribute, 149

Background processing, 54, 408
Bevelling, 166
Bit Gravity, 104, 112
Bit-BLT (See Drawing, rectangles,
    copying), 189, 312, 316
Bit-ordering, 320
Bitmap files, 303
  format, 304
  reading, 305
  writing, 307
bitmap(1), 66, 304
Bitmaps, 297, 303
  clip mask, 201, 206, 301
  copying, 189, 191
  creating from data, 308
  cursor, 338, 340
  hazards, 304
  icon, 122
  images, 323
  property type, 441
  stipple, 301
black, 22, 287
BlackPixel, 21, 44, 256
BLT (See Drawing, rectangles,
    copying), 188, 189, 312, 316
Boolean functions, 151
event-selection, 399

_Backing Store 107-8, 109-112_

Boolean functions (cont'd)
  table, 158
Border (See Windows, border)
Boxes (See Drawing, rectangles)
Buffer, request, 55
Buffering, 29, 54ff., 206
  disabling, 56
  flushing, 54, 56, 407
  synchronizing, 56
Button Grabs (See Pointer Grabs)
ButtonPress events, 343, 415
ButtonRelease events, 343
Byte-ordering, 6, 320

Cap_style--GC attribute, 165
Characters
  justifying, 232
  size, 215, 227, 228, 230, 234
  spacing, 215
  style, 216
  subscripts, 232
  superscripts, 232
  underlined 233, 234
Character set, 215
Character strings, 24, 362
  multiple, 223
Checkerboard, 198, 200
Children, 68
Choosing events with a boolean
      function, 399
Chord, 173
Circles (See Drawing, arcs)
CirculateNotify event, 134, 93
Class
  applications, 121
  windows, 98, 110
Clearing windows, 184
Client (See Application), 27
ClientMessage event, 129, 140, 408
clip_mask--GC attribute, 150, 201, 301
clip_x_origin--GC attribute, 202
clip_y_origin--GC attribute, 202
Clipping, 150, 182, 201, 205
Closing the Display Connection, 38
Colons, 36
Color cells, 250, 272

allocating, 262, 273
  failure, 273
dynamic, 271
freeing, 285
private, 271
  using, 278
retrieving, 286
sharing, 261
total available, 255
Color lookup tables (See Color maps)
Color maps, 40, 244, 250, 251, 252, 289
  copying, 291
  creating, 289
  default, 256
  freeing, 292
  installing, 292
  property type, 441
  standard, 265, 268
    getting, 270
  virtual resources, 292
  window attribute, 101, 250, 290
ColormapNotify events, 291, 292, 294
Colors, 40, 44, 149, 157, 195, 207, 247,
      251
  black and white, 44, 287
  capabilities, 244
  concepts, 244
  defining, 248
  drawing with (See Drawing, color)
  false, 292
  naming, 264, 283
  palette, 251
  primary, 247
  storing, 276, 277
  strategies, 260
    private color cells, 271
    shared color cells, 261
    standard color maps, 265
  translation hardware, 251
  workstation capabilities, 258
Command line arguments
  display name, 34
  geometry, 86
Communicating between applications,
      7, 431ff.
Compressing events, 401

Computation, background, 56
ConfigureNotify event, 93, 94, 95, 106, 135
Confining the pointer to a window, 410, 414
ConnectionNumber, 406, 407
Control key (See Modifier keys)
Convenience functions, 32
Convex polygons (See Drawing, polygons)
Copying
  areas, 188, 191
  bitmaps, 189, 191
  color maps, 291
  GCs, 156
  images, 314
  Pixmaps, 188, 189, 191
  planes, 189, 191, 316
  rectangles, 188, 189, 191
  screen-to-screen (not possible), 302
  windows, 188, 189, 191
CreateNotify event, 136
Creating
  bitmaps, 308
  color maps, 289
  cursors, 339
  fonts (See Fonts, loading)
  GCs, 153, 154
  images, 311
  Pixmaps, 308
  properties (See Properties, storing)
  windows, 76, 109, 118, 119
Crosshatch patterns, 195
Cursors, 40, 102, 214, 301, 328, 329, 337
  changing colors, 341
  creating, 339
  destroying, 341
  font, 339
  Pixmaps, 338, 340
  property type, 441
  windows, 342
Cut buffers, 432
  retrieving data, 434
  rotating data, 435
  storing data, 433
  xterm(1), 433

Cut-and-paste (See Cut-buffers; Selections)
Cyrillic, 228

Dashed lines, 167
Data Structures (See Structures)
Debugging
  Multi-workstation applications, 406
  Setting _XDebug, 56
Declarations, 20, 32
DECnet, 36
Decorating window managers, 117
DefaultColormap, 256
DefaultDepth, 258
DefaultRootWindow, 44
DefaultScreen, 21, 43
DefaultVisual, 257
Delay, 29, 31
Delivering mouse events to windows, 409
Depth (See Pixel values, depth), 249
Desktop metaphor, 65, 66, 180
Destroying resources, 42
DestroyNotify event, 136
Device coordinate origin, 72
Dimmed text, 222
Direct input events, 48
DirectColor visual class, 249, 252, 274, 312
Display connection, 21, 27, 29, 37, 405
  closing for other applications, 42
  multiple, 38, 404
DISPLAY environment variable, 21, 34, 37
Display name, 21, 34, 36, 37, 43, 45
Display number, 34
Display structure, 37, 43
DisplayCells, 255
DisplayHeight, 208
DisplayHeightMM, 208
DisplayPlanes, 255
DisplayString, 45
Dotted lines, 167
Dragging the pointer, 328

Drawables (See also Pixmaps;
    Windows), 146, 300
  property type, 441
Drawing, 6,160
  16-bit characters, 240
  absolute mode, 162
  arcs, 170, 171
    filled, 173
    property type, 440
  attribute copying, 156
  attributes, 147, 148, 156
  background, 157, 160
  characters, 219, 221
    dimmed, 222
    multiple strings, 223
    opaque, 222
    solid-colored, 220
    underlined, 234
  circles (See Drawing, arcs)
  clipping, 150, 201
  color, 157, 160, 244, 245, 246
  coordinates, 160
  delta mode, 162
  ellipses (See Drawing, arcs)
  event processing, 180, 191
  fill pattern origin, 200
  fill style, 195, 197, 198, 199, 206
  foreground, 157, 160
  function, 158, 160, 280
  GC creation, 153, 154
  images, 312, 316
  lines, 164, 168
    bevelling, 166
    cap style, 165
    length, 209
    mitering, 166
    style, 165, 167
    width, 164, 206
  patterning, 149
  performance, 206
  plane mask, 159, 160
  planes, 281
  points, 162
  polygons, 170
    fill rule, 177
    filled, 178

    self-intersecting, 177
    preparing for, 148
    rectangles, 175
      clearing, 186
      clipping with, 202
      copying, 188, 189, 191
      filled, 175
      hazards, 174
      images, 316
      property type, 441
    relative mode, 162
    segment,s 169
    size, 208
    smooth-shading, 252, 265
    state setting, 160
    summary, 161

ECMA, 370
Editing session, 66
Ellipses (See Drawing, arcs)
EnterNotify events, 336, 345, 354, 384,
    402, 414
Enterprise, U.S.S., 336
Errors
  codes, 57
  events, 31
    handling, 58, 59, 302
  I/O, 61
Even-odd rule, 177
event_mask, 50, 102, 132, 343, 397, 409,
    412
  retrieving, 113
  table of bits, 52
Events, 7, 46, 66
  accepting, 396
  ButtonPress, 343, 415
    structure, 348
  ButtonRelease, 343
    structure, 348
  CirculateNotify, 93
    structure, 134
  ClientMessage, 129, 408
    structure, 140
  ColormapNotify, 291, 292
    structure, 294
  compressing, 352, 401

Events (cont'd)
  ConfigureNotify, 93, 94, 95, 106
    hazards, 135
    structure, 135
  CreateNotify
    structure, 136
  Delivery, 51, 358
  DestroyNotify
    structure, 136
  EnterNotify, 336, 345, 354, 384, 402,
    414
    structure, 349
  Expose, 23, 25, 105, 180, 185, 203
    forcing, 186
    hazards, 107
    structure, 184
  FocusIn, 374, 375, 377, 384, 422, 425
    structure, 378
  FocusOut, 374, 375, 377, 384, 422, 425
    structure, 378
  GraphicsExpose, 299
    structure, 193
  GravityNotify, 106
    structure, 137
  KeymapNotify, 386
    structure, 387
  KeyPress, 24, 362, 364, 366
    structure, 367
  KeyRelease, 362, 364, 366
    hazards, 363
    structure, 367
  LeaveNotify, 336, 345, 354, 384, 402,
    414
    structure, 349
  limiting rates, 352
  looking ahead, 396
  MapNotify
    structure, 137
  MappingNotify, 23, 364, 366
  MotionNotify, 336, 345, 401
    hazards, 346
    hint acknowledgement, 354
    hints, 346, 350, 351
  mouse, 342
  NoExpose, 299
    structure, 193

propagating, 103, 409
PropertyNotify, 443, 444, 448
  structure, 450
putting back, 408
queue, 46
reading, 53, 396
ReparentNotify, 116
  structure, 138
selecting for (See Events, soliciting)
SelectionClear
  structure, 456
SelectionNotify, 462
  structure, 461
SelectionRequest
  structure, 465
sending, 408
soliciting, 50, 52, 133
  retrieving event_mask, 113
stray, preventing, 426
top-down delivery, 429
types, 47
UnmapNotify, 107
  structure, 138
unsolicited, 47
VisibilityNotify
  structure, 139
waiting in queue, 53
windows, in, 47, 102, 113
exit, 56
Expose event, 23, 25, 105, 185

Feedback loop, 329
Files
  bitmap, 303
    format, 304
    reading, 305
    writing, 307
  header, 20, 32
  include (See Bitmap files; Header
    files)
fill_rule--GC attribute, 178
fill_style--GC attribute, 150, 197
Fill styles, 195
Flushing the request buffer, 53
Focus models, 124, 376

FocusIn and FocusOut events, 374, 375, 377, 378, 384, 422, 425
font--GC attribute, 218
Fonts (See also Characters), 40, 214, 217
  ascenders, 228
  character set, 215
  creating (See Fonts, loading)
  cursor, 339
  descenders, 228
  directories, 238
  GC attribute setting, 218
  groups, 236
  loading, 217, 226
  names, 218, 236
  properties, 231
  property type, 441
  search path, 237
  searching, 236, 237
  sixteen-bit, 239
  unloading, 219, 227
foreground--GC attribute, 21, 149
Freezing keyboard and pointer, 412, 418, 421, 425, 426
Function keys, 361
function--GC attribute, 151

Gamut, 247, 251
GC, 20, 22, 39, 146, 148, 151, 152
  background, 157, 160
  cacheing, 206
  cap_style, 165
  changing, 155
  clip rectangles, 202
  clipping, 182, 201
  clip_mask, 201
  copying, 156
  creating, 153, 154
  dash pattern, 167
  deleting, 156
  fill_rule, 177
  fill_style, 197, 206
  foreground, 157, 160
  function, 158, 160
  graphics_exposures, 192
  inquiring (not possible), 152

join_style, 166
line attributes, 164
line_style, 165
line_width, 164, 206
plane_mask, 159, 160
state-setting, 160
stipple, tile origin, 200
stipple, 198
structure, 153
subwindow_mode, 205
tile, 199
Geometry specification, 87
Gothic, 216
Grabs
  keyboard (See Keyboard Grabs)
  pointer (See Pointer Grabs)
Graphic Context (See GC)
Graphic primitives, 145
graphics_exposures--GC attribute, 192
Graphics pipeline (See Pipeline), 147
GraphicsExpose events, 299
Gravity, 103
GravityNotify event, 106, 137
GrayScale, 249, 253, 287, 312

Handling
  error events, 58
  Expose events, 181
  I/O errors, 61
Hatch Patterns, 195
Hazards, 15
Header files, 20, 32
Hebrew, 228
Hidden display memory (See Pixmaps), 40, 300
Hierarchies of windows, 66
History information, 452
Hotspots, 305, 306, 338

I/O error handler, 61
Icons, 118, 120, 122, 123, 124, 125, 300
Images (See also XImage structure), 297, 309, 315
  bitmaps, 312, 323
  color maps for, 310

Images (cont'd)
  copying, 314
  creating, 311
  deleting, 320
  depth, 317
  drawing, 316
  format
    XYBitmap (See also XCopyPlane),
       316, 327
    XYPixmap (See also XCopyArea),
       316, 329
    ZPixmap (See also XCopyArea),
       316, 329
  pixel mode, 312, 319, 326
  plane mode, 312, 319, 325
  retrieving, 317, 319
  size, 313
  subimages, 314
Include files (See Header files and
       Bitmap files)
Information sharing, 7, 431
Informational macros, 33, 43
init(8), 36
Input, 7
ISO, 370
Italic, 216

Jaggies, 145
Japanese language, 239
join_style--GC attribute, 167

Kanji (See Drawing, 16-bit
       characters; Fonts, 16-bit)
Key grabs (See Keyboard Grabs)
key_vector (See Keymap)
Keyboard, 18, 24, 361
  auto repeat, 391-392
  bell, 388, 390
  events, 24, 362-364, 366-367
    processing, 364
    soliciting, 363
  focus, 351, 355, 363, 374
    hazards, 374
    tracking, 384
  focus reversion, 376

  hazards, 376
  key click, 390
  key state, 387
  lights, 390
  polling a key, 388
  translating events to strings, 365
Keyboard grabs
  active, 420
  ending, 420, 422
  events, 422
  failure, 421, 425
  freezing, 421, 425, 426
  hazards, 425
  passive, 423
  replaying frozen events, 429
  starting, 420
  triggering, 423, 425
Keyboard mapping changes, 23
Keycode, 367, 368, 369, 388
Keymap, 368, 369, 387
KeymapNotify events, 386, 387
KeyPress events, 24, 362, 364, 366, 367
KeyRelease events, 362, 364, 366, 367
Keysym, 24, 365, 368
  classification macros, 373
  hazards, 370

LeaveNotify events, 336, 345, 354, 384,
       402, 414
Line-length formula, 209
Lines (See Drawing, lines)
line_style--GC attribute, 165
line_width--GC attribute, 164
Loading and using a font, 226
Looking ahead in the event queue, 396

Macros (See also Informational
       macros), 43
Main loop, 19, 23
Manager, window (See Window
       manager)
MapNotify event, 137, 80, 81
MappingNotify events, 23, 364
Measuring character strings, 230
Mechanism, not policy, 3

Millimeters, 208
Mitering, 166
Model independence, 5
Modifier keys, 331, 350, 361, 368, 416,
    417, 423
    symbols for, 331
Monochrome (See Colors, black and
    white)
    one-plane workstations, 304
Motion history buffer, 353
    hazards, 353
MotionNotify events, 336, 345, 401
Mouse (see also Pointer), 327
    dragging, 344
Mouse-ahead, 410
Multi-key sequences, 365
Multilines (See Drawing, segments)
Multiple display connections, 38, 404
Multiple workstations, 34
Multiple-screen workstations, 34, 331,
    351

**N**aming Properties (See also Atoms),
    436
Nesting windows, 68
Network, 29, 34
    circuit, 21, 27, 37
    DECnet, 36
    delay, 29
    TCP/IP, 36
    transparency, 4
    trouble, 38, 61
    UDS, 36

**O**ne-way request, 30
Opaque-background text, 223
Optimizing, 206
Organizing information visually, 66
Output buffering, 55
OwnerGrabButtonMask, 344

**P**assive Grabs (See Keyboard Grabs;
    Pointer Grabs)
Pasting
    via cut-buffers, 434

    via selections, 458, 462
Patterns, 195
Performance, 206
Permission failure, 38
Pie slice, 173
Pipeline, 147ff.
    diagram ,148
    GC clipping stage, 149, 201ff.
    patterning stage, 149, 157, 194ff., 316
    pixel selection stage, 149, 160ff.
    raster output stage, 151, 158, 159
    window clipping stage, 149, 205
Pixel values, 21, 44, 244, 247
    black and white, 44, 244, 256, 287
    computing from RGB, 267, 268
    depth, 244
        default, 258
    numerical relationships, 271
Pixel-BLT, 188, 312, 316
Pixels, 145, 146, 187, 208, 315, 317
Pixmaps, 40, 297, 301, 308
    background, 304
    border, 304
    clearing, 176, 299
    clip_mask bitmap, 201, 206
    copying, 187, 188, 189, 191
    creating from data, 308
    creation, 301
    cursor, 338, 340
    deleting, 303
    depth, 298
    hazards, 301
    icon bitmap, 122
    lifetime, 300
    property type, 441
    size, 298, 302
    stipple bitmap, 195, 197, 198, 200, 206,
        301
    tile, 196, 199, 200, 206
    window background, 112
    window border, 112
Plane copying, 189, 191
plane_mask--GC attribute, 151
Planes, 244, 245, 255
    contiguous, 272, 274

Pointer grabs, 414-415
  activation, 355
  active, 410
  automatic, 343
  changing, 416
  ending, 411, 416
  events, 414
  failure, 413, 418
  freezing, 412, 418, 426
  modifying, 413
  passive, 416, 417
  replaying frozen events, 428
  starting, 411
  top-down activation, 429
  triggering, 415, 416, 418
Pointer, 328
  acceleration, 333
  controlling, 329, 333
  dragging, 328
  moving, 335, 336
    conditionally, 335, 337
  polling, 330
  precision control, 335
Pointing device, 327
Points (See Drawing, points)
Polygons (See Drawing, polygons
Polylines (See Drawing, lines)
Primitives (See Graphic Primitives
      and Drawing)
Privileged software, 2
Processing, background, 54, 408
Program structure, 26
Programmer (You), 8
Prompts to the user, 26
Properties
  creating (See Properties, storing)
  data type (See also Atoms), 436, 440
    predefined, 440
  deleting, 438, 443, 449
  format, 440
  general description, 436
  life-cycle, 437
  names (See also Atoms), 436, 438
  querying
    contents, 443
    data type, 443

  example, 445
  existence, 443
  format, 443
  list, 448
  retrieving data, 443
    segmented, 443
  rotating, 446
  storing, 442
  using, 237
    history information, 446, 452
    queue information, 442, 452
    state information, 442
  windows, 437
PropertyNotify events, 443, 444, 448,
      450, 466
Protocol, 11
  specification, 29
ProtocolRevision, 45
ProtocolVersion, 45
PseudoColor visual class, 249, 251,
      273, 312
Putting back events, 408

**Q**Length macro (See XEventsQueued)
Queue (See Events, queue)
Queuing between applications, 452

**R**aster, 145, 151, 187
Reading events, 396
Rectangles (See Drawing, rectangles)
Release number, 45
ReparentNotify event, 116, 138
Request buffer, 55
Requests, 32
Resources (See also Cursors; Fonts;
      GCs; Pixmaps; Windows), 39,
      405
  identifiers, 20, 41
  lifetime, 41
  retained, 42, 43
Revision numbers, 45
RGB (Red, Green, Blue), 244, 247
Ringing the bell, 388
Roman, 216, 228
Root window, 39, 44, 68, 77, 302, 374

Round-trip request, 30
Rubber-band lines, 154, 159, 280
Running applications, 37

Scaled drawings, 208
Screen, 66, 78, 114, 116, 199, 298, 301
  layout, 66
  number, 34, 43
Screen-door patterns, 195
Scrolling, 187, 191
select(2), 406
Selecting for events (See Events,
        soliciting; XSelectInput)
SelectionClear events, 456
SelectionNotify event, 461, 462, 466
SelectionRequest event, 465, 466
Selections, 452
  conversion
    requesting, 460
    retrieving data, 462
    storing data, 464
  names (See also Atoms), 454
  ownership
    asserting, 455
    losing, 456
    responsibilities, 452, 464
    retrieving, 455
  paste operation, 458
  requesting conversion, 458
  using, 453
Sending events, 408
Server (See Workstation), 27
ServerVendor, 45
Shapes (See Drawing, polygons)
Shift keys (See Modifier keys)
Simultaneous display connections, 38,
        404
Sixteen-bit character strings, 239
sleep, 56
Soliciting events (See XSelectInput
        and Events, soliciting)
Squares (See Drawing, rectangles)
Stacking, 68
Standard color maps, 265, 268, 270
  property type, 441
State data, 451

StaticColor visual class, 249, 252, 312
StaticGray visual class, 249, 253, 287,
        312
Stipple Patterns, 195
stipple--GC attribute, 149, 198, 301
strcmp, 365
strcpy, 365
Structures
  Display, 37, 43
  events
    ButtonPress, 348
    ButtonRelease, 348
    CirculateNotify, 134
    ClientMessage, 140
    ColormapNotify, 294
    ConfigureNotify, 135
    CreateNotify, 136
    DestroyNotify, 136
    EnterNotify, 349
    Expose, 184
    FocusIn, 378
    FocusOut, 378
    GraphicsExpose, 193
    GravityNotify, 137
    KeymapNotify, 387
    KeyPress, 367
    KeyRelease, 367
    LeaveNotify, 349
    MapNotify, 137
    NoExpose, 193
    PropertyNotify, 450
    ReparentNotify, 138
    SelectionClear, 456
    SelectionNotify, 461
    SelectionRequest, 465
    UnmapNotify, 138
    VisibilityNotify, 139
  GC, 153
  Visual, 256, 257
  XArc, 172, 173
  XButtonEvent, 347
  XChar2b, 239
  XCharStruct, 228
  XClassHint, 121
  XColor, 247
  XCrossingEvent, 347

Structures (cont'd)
  XErrorEvent, 60
  XEvent, 400, 408
  XGCValues, 153
  XIconSize, 122
  XImage, 321
  XMotionEvent, 347
  XPoint, 162
  XRectangle, 175
  XSegment, 169
  XSetWindowAttributes, 110
  XStandardColormap, 266
  XTextItem, 223
  XTimeCoord, 353
  XVisualInfo, 259
  XWindowAttributes, 113, 114
  XWindowChanges, 94
  XWMHints, 123
Subroutine package, 32
subwindow_mode--GC attribute, 150, 205
Subwindows
  clipping with, 205
  destroying, 84
  mapping, 81
  unmapping, 83
    automatically (See Windows, win_gravity)
Synchronous delivery of grabbed events, 426
Synchronous mode, 56
System trouble, 38, 61

TCP/IP, 36
Temporarily retained resources, 42, 43
Terminal emulator, 66
Terminating, application, 25, 39
Text (See Characters; Drawing characters)
tile--GC attribute, 150, 199
Tiles, 195, 301
Time stamp, 353, 367
  hazards, 350
Top-level windows, 71, 118
Transient windows, 71, 118

Translucency, 196
Triangles (See Drawing, polygons)
Trouble, system or network, 38, 61
TrueColor visual class, 249, 252, 312
ts_x_origin--GC attribute, 200
ts_y_origin--GC attribute, 200

UDS, 36
Underlining, 233, 234
Unfilled rectangles, 174
Unique identifiers (See Atoms)
Unix-domain socke,ts, 36
UnmapNotify event 107, 138
User, 8
Using the keyboard, 361
uwm(1), 80

Vendor, 45
Vendor independence, 5
VendorRelease, 45
vi(1), 66
VisibilityNotify event, 139
Visual classes, 248
  default, 257
  DirectColor, 252, 274
  GrayScale, 253, 287
  multiple, 259
  PseudoColor, 251, 273
  StaticColor, 252
  StaticGray, 253, 287
  TrueColor, 252
Visual structure, 256, 257
Visuals, 98
  property type, 441
  selecting, 259
  structure, 256, 257

Wait, 56
Warping the pointer (see Pointer, moving)
White, 22, 287
WhitePixel, 21, 44, 256
Winding number, 177

Window manager hints, 116, 119
  Class, 121
  Command line, 121, 128
  Icon Name, 120, 128
  Icon Pixmap, 124, 128
  Icon sizes, 122
  Icon window, 124
  Initial icon position, 124
  Initial state, 124
  Input focus model, 124, 376
  messages, 124
  Name, 120, 128
  Normal size, 126, 128, 129
  property type, 441
  Standard properties, 128
  Window group, 124
Window manager, 10, 66, 73, 74, 78,
    80, 116, 132, 139, 180, 300, 377,
    410
Windows, 6, 20, 39, 65, 115, 299
  aspect ratio, 126
  attributes, 99, 110
    getting, 113
  background, 82, 99, 112, 184, 300
    hazards, 304
  backing store, 107, 183, 281
  bit_gravity, 104, 112
  border, 75, 82, 101, 112, 300
    border_width, 71, 90
    hazards, 304
  characteristics, 97, 110
  circulating, 92
  class, 98, 110
  clearing, 182, 184
  clipping, 150, 201, 205
  color maps, 101, 250, 290
  configuration, 142
  configuring, 94
  copying, 187, 188, 189, 191
  creating, 76, 109, 118, 119
  cursors, 338, 342
  damage, 180, 191
  depth, 88, 98
  descendant, 150
  destroying, 75, 84
  events in, 47, 102, 113

  focus setting, 124, 142, 376
  geometry, 71, 85, 88, 110
  gravity, 105, 138
  hierarchy, 70, 114
  iconic state, 120, 123, 125
  icons, 124, 180
  InputOnly, 98, 111, 359
  mapping, 73, 80, 81, 180
  nesting, 68
  origin, 71
  parent, 77, 110, 115
  position, 71, 89, 90, 126, 129, 142
    hazards, 88
  property type, 441
  raising, 80, 93
  root, 77, 115
  size, 71, 90, 104, 105, 126, 129, 130, 180
  stacking, 85, 92, 93, 180
  state, 124
    iconic, 118
    ignored, 118
    inactive, 118
  translating coordinates between, 332
  unmapping, 75, 83
  visibility, 73
  win_gravity, 105
wm(1), 80
Workstation, 15, 21

**X** Client (See Application)
X Error (See Error event), 57
X Protocol, 11
X Server (See Workstation)
XAddPixel, 315
XAllocColor, 262
XAllocColorCells, 272
XAllocColorPlanes, 273
XAllocNamedColor, 264
XAllowEvents, 412, 427
XArc structure, 172, 173
XBlackPixel, 44, 256
XButtonEvent structure, 347
XChangeActivePointerGrab, 413, 416
XChangeGC, 155
XChangePointerControl, 334
  hazards, 334

XChangeProperty, 442
XChangeWindowAttributes, 102, 111
XChar2b structure, 239
XCharStruct structure, 228
XCheckIfEvent, 400
XCheckMaskEvent, 398
XCheckTypedEvent, 398
XCheckTypedWindowEvent, 398
XCheckWindowEvent, 398
XCirculateSubwindows, 92
XCirculateSubwindowsDown, 92
XCirculateSubwindowsUp, 92
XClassHint structure, 121
XClearArea, 186
XClearWindow, 185
xclock(1), 66
XCloseDisplay, 24, 38
XColor structure, 247
XConfigureWindow, 94, 96
XConvertSelection, 460
XCopyArea, 188, 194, 312, 316
XCopyColormapAndFree, 291
XCopyGC, 156
XCopyPlane, 189, 194, 195, 312, 316
XCreateBitmapFromData, 198, 222, 308
XCreateColormap, 289
XCreateFontCursor, 339
XCreateGC, 22, 153
XCreateGlyphCursor, 340
XCreateImage, 311
XCreatePixmap, 301
XCreatePixmapCursor, 340
XCreatePixmapFromBitmapData, 308
XCreateSimpleWindow, 22, 77
XCreateWindow, 109
XCrossingEvent structure, 347
Xdebug, 56
XDefaultColormap, 256
XDefaultDepth, 258
XDefaultRootWindow, 44
XDefaultScreen, 43
XDefaultVisual, 257
XDefineCursor, 342
XDeleteProperty, 449
XDestroyImage, 320
XDestroySubwindows, 84

XDestroyWindow, 24, 84
XDisplayCells, 255
XDisplayName, 61
XDisplayPlanes, 255
XDisplayString, 45
XDrawArc, 171, 173
XDrawArcs, 172
XDrawImageString16, 240
XDrawImageString, 23, 222, 223
XDrawLines, 169
XDrawPoint, 162, 317
XDrawPoints, 162, 317
XDrawRectangle, 175
XDrawRectangles, 175
XDrawSegments, 169
XDrawString16, 240
XDrawString, 220
XDrawText16, 240
XDrawText, 223
XErrorEvent structure, 60
XEvent structure, 400, 408
XEventsQueued, 53, 54, 402, 403, 407
XFetchBuffer, 434
XFetchBytes, 434
XFetchName, 120
XFillArcs, 173
XFillRectangle, 176
XFillRectangles, 176
XFlush, 54, 56, 407
XFree, 115, 320
XFreeColormap, 292
XFreeColors, 285
XFreeCursor, 341
XFreeFont, 227
XFreeFontNames, 236
XFreeGC, 24, 156
XFreePixmap, 303
XGCValues structure, 153
XGeometry, 86
XGetAtomName, 439
XGetClassHint, 121
XGetErrorText, 59
XGetFontPath, 237
XGetFontProperty, 231
XGetGeometry, 88, 96, 302
XGetIconName, 120

XGetIconSizes, 122
XGetImage, 317
XGetInputFocus, 375
XGetMotionEvents, 353
XGetNormalHints, 127
XGetPixel, 315
XGetPointerControl, 334
XGetSelectionOwner, 455
XGetStandardColormap, 270
XGetSubImage, 317, 319
XGetWindowAttributes, 113
XGetWindowProperty, 443
XGetWMHints, 125
XGrabButton, 426
XGrabKey, 424, 427
XGrabKeyboard, 420, 424, 426
XGrabPointer, 410, 411, 416
xhost(1), 38
XIconSize structure, 122
XImage structure, 321
XInternAtom, 439
XKeycodeToKeysym, 372
XKeysymToKeycode, 371
XKeysymToString, 372
XKillClient, 42
XListFonts, 236
XListFontsWithInfo, 236
XListProperties, 448
XLoadFont, 217
XLoadQueryFont, 225, 226
XLookupColor, 284
XLookupKeysym, 373
XLookupString, 24, 365, 369
    hazards, 365
XLowerWindow, 93
XMapRaised, 22, 80
XMapSubwindows, 81
XMaskEvent, 399
XMatchVisualInfo, 259
xmodmap, 369
XMotionEvent structure, 347
XMoveResizeWindow, 90
XMoveWindow, 89
XNextEvent, 23, 53, 55, 364, 402, 403,
    405, 407
XOpenDisplay, 21, 37, 407

XParseColor, 284
XPeekEvent, 397, 400, 402, 403
XPeekIfEvent, 400
XPending (See XEventsQueued)
XPoint structure, 162
xprop(1), 438
XProtocolRevision, 45
XProtocolVersion, 45
XPutBackEvent, 408
XPutImage, 316
XPutPixel 315
XQueryBestCursor 340
XQueryBestStipple 197
XQueryBestTile 197
XQueryColor 286
XQueryColors 286
XQueryKeymap 368, 387
XQueryPointer 330, 331
    hazards 332
XQueryTree 114
XRaiseWindow 93
XReadBitmapFile 305
XRebindKeysym 370
XRecolorCursor 341
XRectangle structure 175
XRefreshKeyboardMapping 23, 369
XReparentWindow 115
XResizeWindow 90
XRestackWindows 93
XRootWindow 44
XRotateBuffers 435
XRotateWindowProperties 446
XSegment structure 169
XSelectInput 22, 50, 97, 102, 403
XSendEvent 408
XServerVendor 45
xset(1) 333
XSetArcMode 173
XSetBackground 22, 157
XSetClassHint 121
XSetClipMask 201
XSetCloseDownMode 41
XSetCommand 121
XSetDashes 167
XSetErrorHandler 60
XSetFillRule 178

XSetFillStyle, 197
XSetFont, 218, 223
XSetFontPath, 238
XSetFcreground, 22, 157
XSetGraphicsExposures, 192
XSetIconName, 120
XSetInputFocus, 375, 422
XSetLineAttributes, 164
XSetNormalHints, 127
XSetPlaneMask, 159
XSetSelectionOwner, 455
XSetStandardProperties, 22
XSetState, 160
XSetStipple, 198
XSetTile, 199
XSetWindowAttributes structure, 110
XSetWindowBackground, 82
XSetWindowBackgroundPixmap, 112
XSetWindowBorderPixmap, 112
XSetWindowBorderWidth, 90
XSetWindowColormap, 290
XSetWMHints, 125, 300
XStandardColormap structure, 266
XStoreBuffer, 433
XStoreBytes, 433
XStoreColor, 276
XStoreColors, 276
XStoreName, 120
XStoreNamedColor, 277
XStringToKeysym, 372
XSubImage, 314
xswa (See XSetWindowAttributes
        structure)
XSync, 56

XSynchronize, 56
xterm(1), 8, 66, 70, 214
    cut-buffers, 433
XTextExtents16, 241
XTextExtents, 228
XTextItem structure, 223
XTextWidth16, 241
XTextWidth, 227, 234
XTimeCoord structure, 353
XTranslateCoordinates, 332
XUndefineCursor, 342
XUngrabKey, 424
XUngrabKeyboard, 422, 424
XUngrabPointer, 414, 416
XUnmapSubwindows, 83
XUnmapWindow, 83
XVendorRelease, 45
XVisualInfo structure, 259
XWarpPointer, 335, 414
    hazards, 336
XWhitePixel, 44, 256
XWindowAttributes structure, 113, 114
XWindowChanges structure, 94
XWindowEvent, 399
XWMHints structure, 123
XWriteBitmapFile, 307
XYBitmap (See also XCopyPlane), 316,
        327
XYPixmap (See also XCopyArea), 316,
        329

ZPixmap (See also XCopyArea), 316,
        329